# QuickPass™

## More Than a Textbook

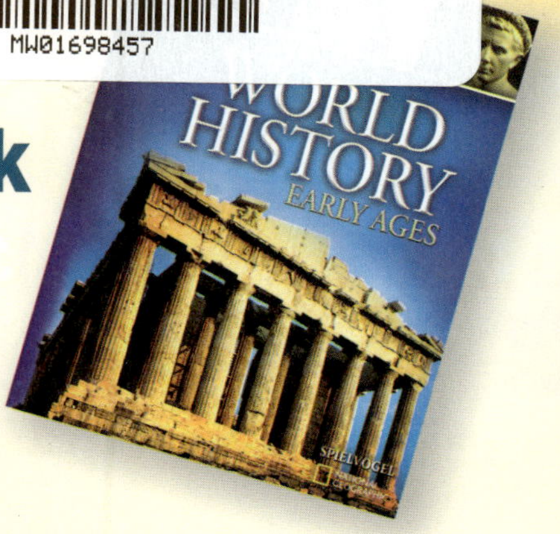


### Find it faster.

Visit History ONLINE at glencoe.com and enter a QuickPass™ chapter code to go directly to the chapter resources you need.

**GWHEA7447c1**

Enter this code with the appropriate chapter number.

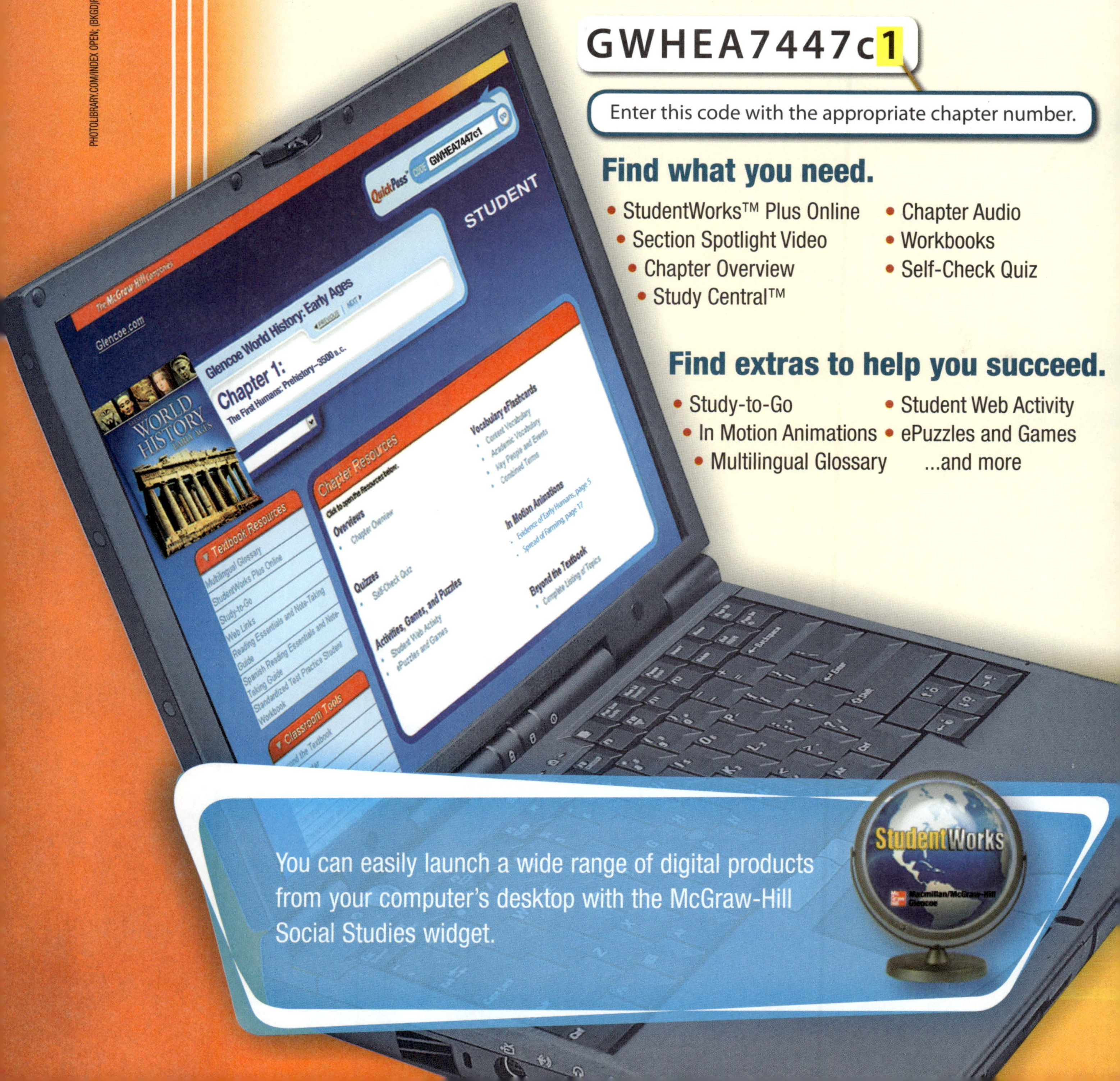


### Find what you need.

- StudentWorks™ Plus Online
- Section Spotlight Video
- Chapter Overview
- Study Central™
- Chapter Audio
- Workbooks
- Self-Check Quiz

### Find extras to help you succeed.

- Study-to-Go
- In Motion Animations
- Multilingual Glossary
- Student Web Activity
- ePuzzles and Games
- ...and more

You can easily launch a wide range of digital products from your computer's desktop with the McGraw-Hill Social Studies widget.

StudentWorks

Macmillan/McGraw-Hill Glencoe

PHOTOLIBRARY.COM/INDEX OPEN, (BKGD)RYAN MCVAY/GETTY IMAGES

MW01698457

★★ Make history ★★

# COME ALIVE

with GLENCOE'S

# TECHNOLOGY TOOLS

Review lesson content, take notes, and build vocabulary at Study Central!

Learn key vocabulary with eFlashcards!

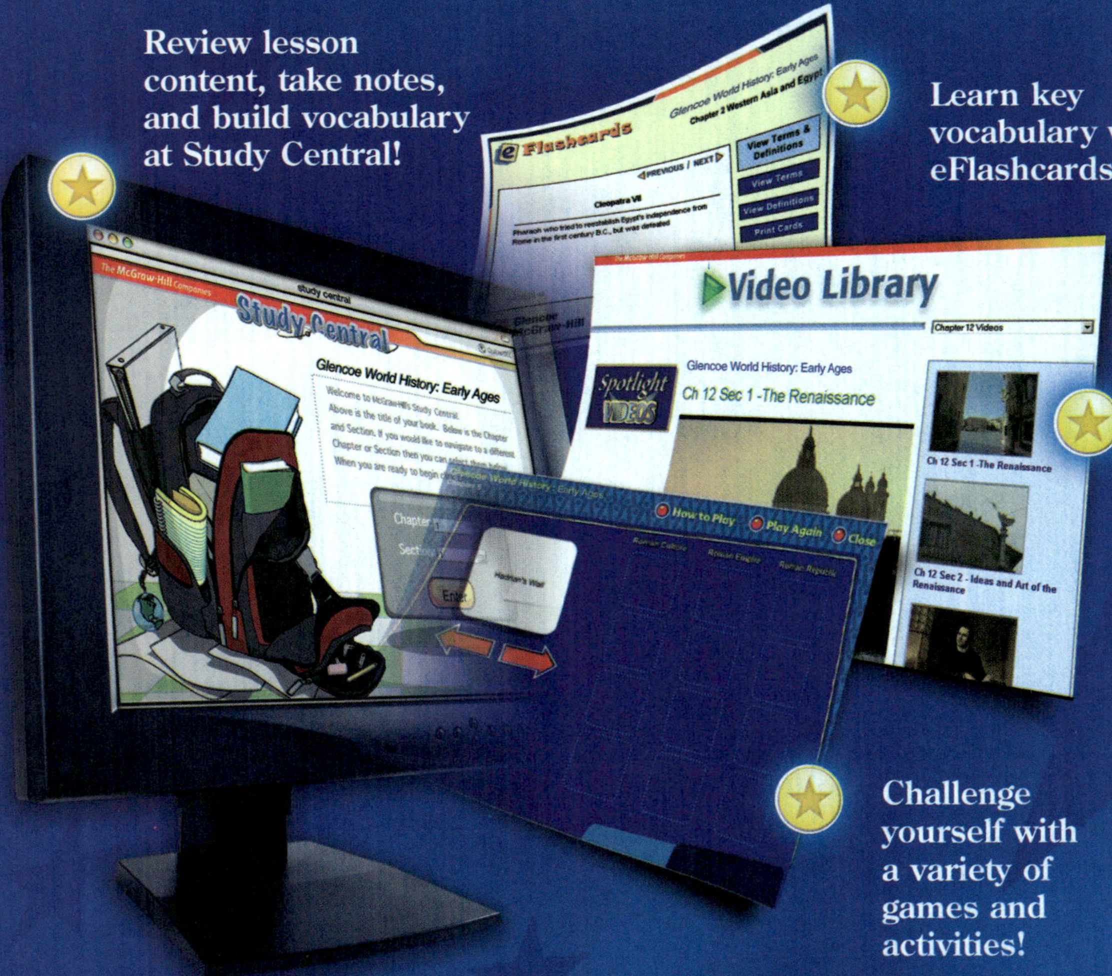


Bring the sights and sounds of history alive with Spotlight Videos!

Challenge yourself with a variety of games and activities!

**Find maps in motion, interactive graphic organizers, and more on StudentWorks™ *Plus* or online at glencoe.com.**

GLENCOE

# WORLD HISTORY

## EARLY AGES

JACKSON J. SPIELVOGEL, PH.D.

NATIONAL GEOGRAPHIC

McGraw Hill Glencoe

## About the Cover

Main image: Parthenon on the Acropolis in Greece
Top images (left to right): painting of Genghis Khan; bust of Nefertiti; terra-cotta warrior from Xi'an, China; painting of Isabella I; bust of Augustus.

The McGraw-Hill Companies

Glencoe



Send all inquiries to:
Glencoe/McGraw-Hill
8787 Orion Place
Columbus, OH 43240-4027

ISBN: 978-0-07-892744-7
MHID: 0-07-892744-7

Printed in the United States of America.

4 5 6 7 8 9 RJE 14 13 12 11 10

# AUTHORS

## JACKSON J. SPIELVOGEL

**Jackson J. Spielvogel** is associate professor emeritus of history at The Pennsylvania State University. He received his Ph.D. from The Ohio State University, where he specialized in Reformation history under Harold J. Grimm. His articles and reviews have appeared in such journals as *Moreana, Journal of General Education, Archiv für Reformationsgeschichte,* and *American Historical Review.* He has also contributed chapters or articles to *The Social History of the Reformation, The Holy Roman Empire: A Dictionary Handbook, Simon Wiesenthal Center Annual of Holocaust Studies,* and *Utopian Studies.* His book *Hitler and Nazi Germany* was published in 1987 (fifth edition, 2005). His book *Western Civilization* was published in 1991 (seventh edition, 2009). He is the co-author (with William Duiker) of *World History,* published in 1994 (fifth edition, 2007). Professor Spielvogel has won five major university-wide teaching awards, and in 2000, he became the first winner of the Schreyer Institute's Student Choice Award for innovative and inspiring teaching.

NATIONAL GEOGRAPHIC

The National Geographic Society, founded in 1888 for the increase and diffusion of geographic knowledge, is the world's largest nonprofit scientific and educational organization. Since its earliest days, the Society has used sophisticated communication technologies, from color photography to holography, to convey geographic knowledge to a worldwide membership. The School Publishing Division supports the Society's mission by developing innovative educational programs—ranging from traditional print materials to multimedia programs including CD-ROMs, videos, and software.

## CONTRIBUTING AUTHOR

**Dinah Zike,** M.Ed., is an award-winning author, educator, and inventor known for designing three-dimensional hands-on manipulatives and graphic organizers known as Foldables™. Foldables are used nationally and internationally by teachers, parents, and educational publishing companies. Dinah has developed over 150 supplemental educational books and materials. She is the author of *The Big Book of Books and Activities,* which was awarded Learning Magazine's Teachers' Choice Award. In 2004 Dinah was honored with the CESI Science Advocacy Award. Dinah received her M.Ed. from Texas A&M, College Station, Texas.

# CONSULTANTS & REVIEWERS

### Academic Consultants

**Jeremy Baskes, Ph.D.**
Associate Professor
Department of History
Ohio Wesleyan University
Delaware, Ohio

**David Berger, Ph.D.**
Dean
Bernard Revel Graduate School of Jewish Studies
Yeshiva University
New York, New York

**Michael C. Brose, Ph.D.**
Associate Professor
Department of History
University of Wyoming
Laramie, Wyoming

**Amy Benjamin**
Differentiated Instruction Consultant
Hendrick Hudson High School
Montrose, New York

**Stephen F. Dale, Ph.D.**
Professor, Department of History
The Ohio State University
Columbus, Ohio

**Steven Gish, Ph.D.**
Distinguished Research Professor
Department of History
Auburn University Montgomery
Montgomery, Alabama

**Richard Golden, Ph.D.**
Professor of History and Director, Jewish Studies Program
University of North Texas
Denton, Texas

**Lyman Johnson, Ph.D.**
Professor
Department of History
The University of North Carolina at Charlotte
Charlotte, North Carolina

**Lisa Lindsay, Ph.D.**
Associate Professor
Department of History
The University of North Carolina at Chapel Hill
Chapel Hill, North Carolina

**Farid Mahdavi, Ph.D.**
Lecturer
Department of History
San Diego State University
San Diego, California

**Guy Welbon, Ph.D.**
Emeritus Associate Professor
Department of South Asia Studies
University of Pennsylvania
Philadelphia, Pennsylvania

### Teacher Reviewers

**Eric A. Byar**
Lincoln-Way East High School
Frankfort, Illinois

**Maggie Favretti**
Scarsdale High School
Scarsdale, New York

**Scott K. Grunder**
Walnut Hills High School
Cincinnati, Ohio

**Carl Hansen**
Hilton High School
Hilton, New York

**Roberta Heath**
Capital High School
Charleston, West Virginia

**Thomas J. Lawson**
McCluer High School
Florissant, Missouri

**Laura Delmore Lay**
James River High School
Midlothian, Virginia

**Rosanne Lichatin**
West Morris Central High School
Chester, New Jersey

**Lisa L. McBride, NBCT**
Owasso Mid-High School
Owasso, Oklahoma

**Donald V. Morabito**
Great Valley High School
Malvern, Pennsylvania

**Donald Perreault**
Valley Regional High School
Deep River, Connecticut

**Kevin Bryan Richins**
Lynden High School
Lynden, Washington

**Christina M. Smith**
Algonquin Regional High School
Northborough, Massachusetts

**Belinda Spencer**
Northwestern High School
Detroit, Michigan

**Kathleen H. Stokes**
Cherokee High School
Marlton, New Jersey

**Denise Tanner**
Friendswood High School
Friendswood, Texas

# CONTENTS

Phaestos Disc, Minoan writing (see page 18)

Frankish king Charles Martel at the Battle of Tours (see page 195)

# Contents

▲ Wu Zhao, empress of China for half a century (see page 268)

# FEATURES

## ANALYZING PRIMARY SOURCES



## PEOPLE *in* HISTORY

The Consistory, a special court for enforcing moral discipline, oversaw the moral life and doctrinal purity of Genevans. It could punish those who deviated from the church's teachings and moral principles. Citizens in Geneva were punished for such "crimes" as dancing, singing obscene songs, drunkenness, swearing, and playing cards.

Calvin's success in Geneva made the city a powerful center of Protestantism. John Knox, the Calvinist reformer of Scotland, called Geneva "the most perfect school of Christ on earth." Missionaries trained in Geneva were sent to all parts of Europe. Calvinism became established in France, the Netherlands, Scotland, and central and eastern Europe. By the mid-sixteenth century, Calvinism had replaced Lutheranism as the most important and dynamic form of Protestantism. Calvin's Geneva stood as the fortress of the Protestant Reformation.

✓Reading Check **Explaining** How did the Consistory enforce moral discipline in Geneva?

### Reformation in England

MAIN IDEA For political, not religious, reasons, Henry VIII established the Church of England.

HISTORY & YOU As a child, how did you react when someone told you no? Read about how Henry VIII reacted after the pope said no.

The English Reformation was rooted in politics, not religion. **King Henry VIII** wanted to divorce his first wife, Catherine of Aragon, with whom he had a daughter, Mary, but no son. Since he needed a male heir, Henry wanted to marry Anne Boleyn. Impatient with the pope's unwillingness to **annul** (declare invalid) his marriage to Catherine, Henry turned to England's own church courts.

#### The Break from Rome

As the archbishop of Canterbury, head of the highest church court in England, Thomas Cranmer ruled in May 1533 that the king's marriage to Catherine was "null and

PEOPLE *in* HISTORY

**Henry VIII**
1491–1547 King of England

Historians have found it ironic that Henry VIII, who led the break between England and the Roman Catholic Church, was proclaimed "Defender of the Faith" by the head of the church he left. However, that is how Pope Leo X praised him after Henry's attack on Martin Luther in 1521. In *Assertio Septem Sacramentorum* (Declaration of the Seven Sacraments), Henry upheld Church doctrines that Luther and his followers were trying to discredit. To this day, all British coins carry the initials F.D. after the reigning monarch's name. They refer to the Latin words *Fidei Defensor*, or "Defender of the Faith," a hereditary title for all British monarchs since Henry VIII. **Who was Henry VIII attacking in his book?**

**Thomas More**
1478–1535 British Author and Theologian

*A Man for All Seasons*—that was the title of a twentieth-century movie about Thomas More. He was a trusted adviser to Henry VIII and the author of the book *Utopia*, which means a perfectly harmonious society. Published in 1516, the book is a work of fiction about an ideal state. More describes how goods are produced and shared equally among the Utopians. *Utopia* became a model for Utopian Socialists, who in the 1800s attempted to set up communities based on the socialistic principles described in the book. More was later beheaded under orders from Henry VIII for not supporting England's break with the Church of Rome. In 1935, More was made a saint. **For what group did More's book become an inspiration?**

## CONNECTING TO THE UNITED STATES



## NATIONAL GEOGRAPHIC GEOGRAPHY & HISTORY

## SCIENCE, TECHNOLOGY, & SOCIETY



## TIME LINE



## *HISTORY & ARTS* PRIMARY SOURCE

PRIMARY SOURCE *HISTORY & ARTS*

*Kinship with Ancestors in African Societies*

Many peoples placed mother-and-child figures in shrines near graves.

Spirits of ancestors were believed to participate in family life and were honored at festivals.

Masks were worn during initiation and funerary rites and linked the living to their ancestors.

DOCUMENT-BASED QUESTIONS

Art was a fundamental part of African life. Headdresses and masks were worn by dancers as part of ceremonies. Paintings decorated homes and sculptures marked graves. Much of the wood and leather artwork did not survive in the sub-Saharan climate.

1. **Drawing Conclusions** Why would it be difficult to find many examples of ancient African art?
2. **Making Inferences** Why is African art stylized and abstract, not realistic?

**Family and Lineage**

Few Africans, of course, ever had an audience with their kings. Most people lived in small villages in the countryside. Their sense of identity was determined by their membership in an extended family and a lineage group.

At the basic level was the extended family, made up of parents, children, grandparents, and other family dependents. They lived in small, round dwellings made of packed mud, with a thatch roof of plant material such as straw. These extended family units were in turn combined into larger communities known as **lineage groups**.

Lineage groups served as the basic building blocks of African society. All members of a lineage group could claim to be descended from a real or legendary common ancestor. As in China, the elders—the leading members of the lineage group—had much power over the others in the group. A lineage group provided mutual support for all its members. Members of extended families and lineage groups were expected to take care of one another.

**The Role of Women**

Women were usually subordinate to men in Africa, as they were in most early societies around the world. In some cases, they were valued for the work they could do or for their role in having children and thus increasing the size of the lineage group. Women often worked in the fields while the men of the village tended the cattle or hunted. In some communities, women were merchants.

There were some key differences between the role of women in Africa and elsewhere.

CHAPTER 7 Early African Civilizations 251

## TURNING POINT



## TIME NOTEBOOK



## Social History



## INFOGRAPHICS

# Primary Source Quotes

## Unit 1
### *The First Civilizations and Empires*



## Unit 2
### *New Patterns of Civilization*

## PRIMARY SOURCES & LITERATURE LIBRARY

**Aztec drawing of a sacrifice ritual (see page 387)**

# CHARTS & GRAPHS

## UNIT 1



## UNIT 2



## MINI ALMANAC



**COMPARING TWO ANCIENT CULTURES**
3000 B.C.–A.D. 500

| INDIA | CHINA |
|---|---|
| **Geographic and Environmental Features** | |
| Himalaya<br>Indus River<br>Deccan Plateau<br>Monsoons | Himalaya<br>Gobi<br>Huang He<br>Chang Jiang |
| **Early Civilizations, Empires, Dynasties** | |
| Indus Valley Civilization<br>Mauryan Empire<br>Kushān Empire<br>Empire of Guptas | Shang Dynasty<br>Zhou Dynasty<br>Qin Dynasty<br>Han Dynasty |
| **Religions and Philosophies** | |
| Hinduism<br>Buddhism | Confucianism<br>Daoism<br>Legalism |
| **Famous People** | |
| Mauryan king Aśoka<br>Buddha | Confucius<br>Qin Shihuangdi |
| **Social and Political Structures** | |
| Caste System<br>*Varnas* | Mandate of Heaven<br>Dynastic Cycles<br>The Rule of Merit |
| **Economy and Trade** | |
| Cotton cloth<br>Ivory<br>Jewelry<br>Stamp seals<br>Pepper | Silk cloth<br>Spices<br>Teas<br>Porcelain |
| **Inventions and Accomplishments** | |
| Indus Valley script<br>The Vedas in Sanskrit<br>Algebra and zero | Silk<br>Silk Road<br>Great Wall<br>Paper |

# MAPS

NATIONAL GEOGRAPHIC

## REFERENCE ATLAS



## UNIT 1



## UNIT 2



Maps In Motion — See *StudentWorks™ Plus* or glencoe.com.

Maps labeled with the In Motion icon have been specially enhanced on the StudentWorks™ Plus DVD and on glencoe.com. These In Motion maps allow you to interact with layers of displayed data and to listen to audio components.

Entries in **blue** indicate In Motion maps.

# UNDERSTANDING THE BIG IDEAS

*World history is the story of the human community—how people lived on a daily basis, how they shared ideas, how they ruled and were ruled, and how they fought. As you read, you will see a number of "big ideas" or broad themes behind world history events. These big ideas are described below.*

## ▶ Order and Security

**Throughout history, people and governments have tried to resolve conflicts and establish order and security.**

People have sought ways to protect themselves from danger and uncertainty. To provide for their security, people have created communities, nations, and organizations. To help provide order, people have created laws and economic systems.

## ▶ Ideas, Beliefs, and Values

**Ideas, beliefs, and values have resulted in distinct societies and political systems.**

Throughout history, people have sought to find a deeper meaning to human life. Religion, cultural values, and codes of ethics have always influenced social customs, laws, and forms of government.

## ▶ Physical Geography

**Physical geography influences the development of culture and trade.**

People and societies have been affected by the physical world in which they exist. In turn, human activities have had a profound impact on the world.

## ▶ Self-Determination

**The quest for national self-determination is universal.**

Free will is the cornerstone of humanity. People unite as a nation because they believe that independence is essential to freedom—and that freedom is essential to leading a full life.

### ▶ Struggle for Rights
**Throughout history, people have struggled for rights.**

The struggle for rights has been reflected in struggles for the vote, for economic freedom, for personal liberties, and for national independence. There are few nations in the world whose history has not been marked by a struggle for rights among its people.

### ▶ New Technologies
**New technologies bring changes that can be both positive and negative for societies.**

For thousands of years, people have made scientific discoveries and technological innovations that have changed the world. New discoveries can bring benefits, or pose new dangers, to the world.

### ▶ Devastation of War
**War causes immeasurable devastation.**

Wars have always meant destruction and disruption to some level. In the modern period, wars usually have brought greater devastation than in earlier epochs. Genocide and ethnic cleansing have also characterized the wars of the twentieth century. Recovering from such losses is costly, and the desire for revenge or triumph can color the attitudes of an entire generation.

### ▶ Competition Among Countries
**Countries compete for natural resources and strategic advantages over other countries.**

Competition among nations has led to the development of stable economies in some cases, but also to the depletion of economies in others. Strong economies tend to mean stronger governments, and this provides a sense of safety for citizens.

### ▶ Human Rights
**A totalitarian system violates human rights in pursuit of power.**

By definition, the totalitarian state smothers the individuality of its citizens. This system seeks to control political, economic, social, intellectual, and cultural areas of life and does so through propaganda and through force.

#### Using the BIG IDEAS

You will find BIG IDEAS listed at the beginning of each section in the text. Use these clues to help you preview the material you are about to read. You can also use the BIG IDEAS to compare and contrast how different peoples and societies dealt with similar issues.

# SCAVENGER HUNT

*Glencoe World History: Early Ages* contains a wealth of information. The trick is to know where to look to access all the information in the book. If you run through this scavenger hunt exercise with your teachers or parents, you will see how the textbook is organized, and how to get the most out of your reading and study time. Let's get started!

1. How many chapters and how many units are in the book?

2. What time period does Unit 1 cover?

3. On what pages is the time line for Chapter 3?

4. In what two places can you find the Content Vocabulary for Section 2 of Chapter 6?

5. Where can you find a map on climate zones and geography in Africa?

6. How are the Academic Vocabulary words for Section 3 of Chapter 12 indicated in the narrative?

7. The Web site has six activities for each chapter. The first previews the chapter. The second has activities. The third has quizzes. What do the others do?

8. Where do you look if you want to quickly find all the maps in the book?

9. Most sections of a chapter include primary sources from the time in the narrative. Where else can you find extended primary sources in the textbook?

10. Where can you learn the definition of a physical map, a political map, and a thematic map?

# Reference Atlas

NATIONAL GEOGRAPHIC



## ATLAS KEY

## SYMBOL KEY

- Canal
- Claimed boundary
- International boundary
- Depression
- Elevation
- National capital
- Towns
- Below sea level
- Dry salt lake
- Lake
- Rivers
- Lava
- Sand
- Swamp

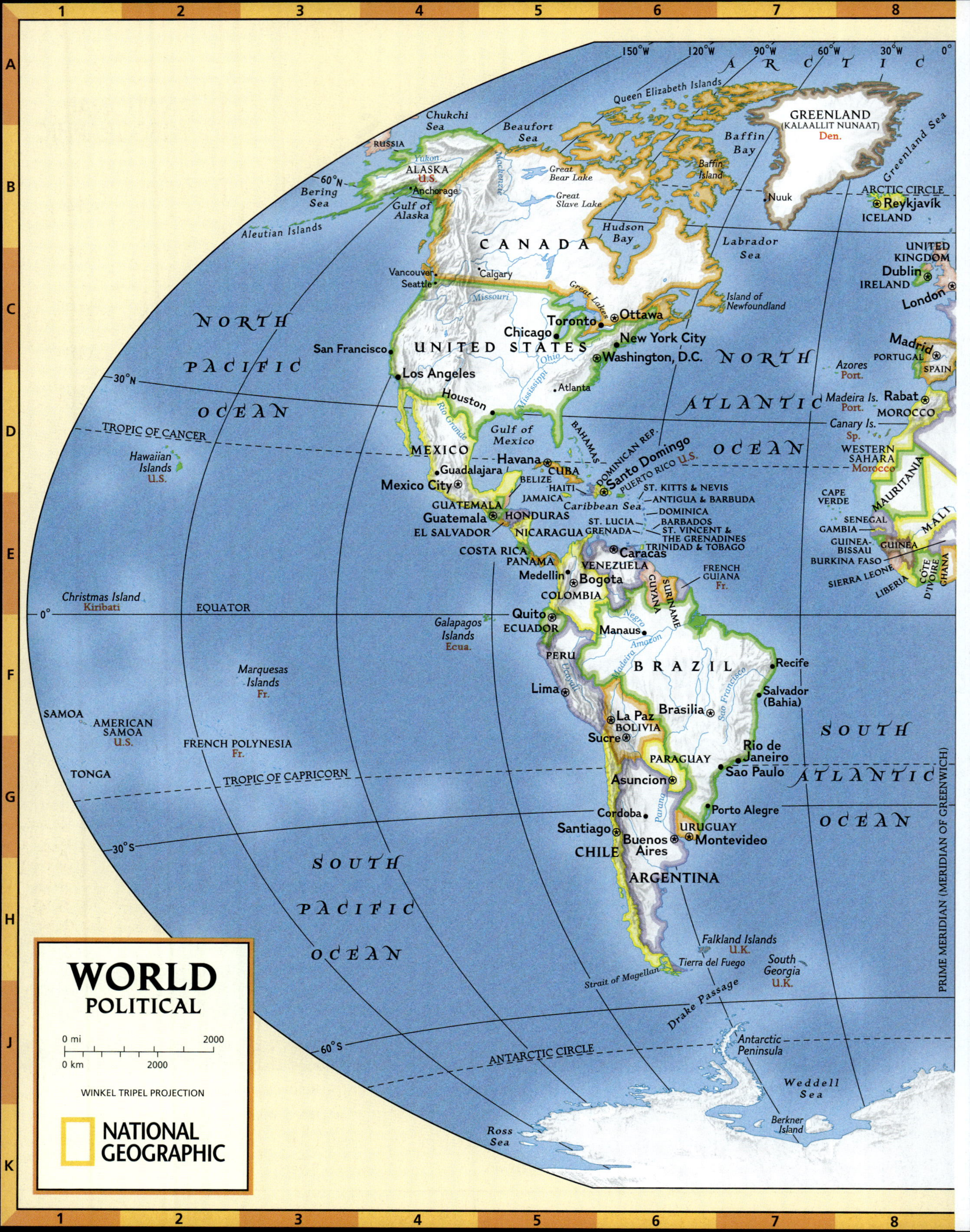
WORLD
POLITICAL
0 mi 2000
0 km 2000
WINKEL TRIPEL PROJECTION
NATIONAL GEOGRAPHIC
A R C T I C
150°W
120°W
90°W
60°W
30°W
0°
Queen Elizabeth Islands
GREENLAND
(KALAALLIT NUNAAT)
Den.
Greenland Sea
Baffin Bay
Baffin Island
Nuuk
ARCTIC CIRCLE
Reykjavík
ICELAND
Chukchi Sea
Beaufort Sea
RUSSIA
Yukon
ALASKA
U.S.
60°N
Bering Sea
Anchorage
Gulf of Alaska
Aleutian Islands
Mackenzie
Great Bear Lake
Great Slave Lake
Hudson Bay
Labrador Sea
CANADA
Calgary
Vancouver
Seattle
UNITED KINGDOM
Dublin
IRELAND
London
Missouri
Great Lakes
Ottawa
Toronto
Island of Newfoundland
NORTH PACIFIC OCEAN
Chicago
New York City
UNITED STATES
San Francisco
Washington, D.C.
Ohio
Los Angeles
NORTH ATLANTIC OCEAN
Madrid
PORTUGAL
SPAIN
Azores
Port.
30°N
Mississippi
Atlanta
Houston
Rio Grande
Madeira Is.
Port.
Rabat
MOROCCO
Canary Is.
Sp.
Gulf of Mexico
BAHAMAS
TROPIC OF CANCER
MEXICO
DOMINICAN REP.
Santo Domingo
PUERTO RICO U.S.
WESTERN SAHARA
Morocco
Hawaiian Islands
U.S.
Havana
CUBA
Guadalajara
BELIZE
HAITI
ST. KITTS & NEVIS
ANTIGUA & BARBUDA
MAURITANIA
Mexico City
JAMAICA
Caribbean Sea
DOMINICA
CAPE VERDE
GUATEMALA
Guatemala
HONDURAS
EL SALVADOR
NICARAGUA
ST. LUCIA
GRENADA
BARBADOS
ST. VINCENT & THE GRENADINES
TRINIDAD & TOBAGO
SENEGAL
GAMBIA
MALI
GUINEA-BISSAU
GUINEA
BURKINA FASO
COSTA RICA
PANAMA
Caracas
VENEZUELA
FRENCH GUIANA
Fr.
SIERRA LEONE
LIBERIA
CÔTE D'IVOIRE
GHANA
Medellín
Bogota
COLOMBIA
GUYANA
SURINAME
Christmas Island
Kiribati
EQUATOR
0°
Quito
ECUADOR
Galapagos Islands
Ecua.
Negro
Manaus
Amazon
PERU
Madeira
BRAZIL
Recife
Marquesas Islands
Fr.
Ucayali
São Francisco
Salvador (Bahia)
Lima
Brasilia
SAMOA
AMERICAN SAMOA
U.S.
La Paz
BOLIVIA
Sucre
SOUTH ATLANTIC OCEAN
FRENCH POLYNESIA
Fr.
Rio de Janeiro
PARAGUAY
Sao Paulo
TONGA
TROPIC OF CAPRICORN
Asuncion
Parana
Porto Alegre
Cordoba
Santiago
URUGUAY
Montevideo
30°S
Buenos Aires
CHILE
SOUTH PACIFIC OCEAN
ARGENTINA
PRIME MERIDIAN (MERIDIAN OF GREENWICH)
Falkland Islands
U.K.
Tierra del Fuego
South Georgia
U.K.
Strait of Magellan
Drake Passage
60°S
Antarctic Peninsula
ANTARCTIC CIRCLE
Weddell Sea
Ross Sea
Berkner Island

## ABBREVIATIONS

| | |
|---|---|
| AUST. | AUSTRIA |
| B.&H. | BOSNIA & HERZEGOVINA |
| BELG. | BELGIUM |
| CROAT. | CROATIA |
| CZECH REP. | CZECH REPUBLIC |
| DEM. REP. OF THE CONGO | DEMOCRATIC REPUBLIC OF THE CONGO |
| EQ. GUINEA | EQUATORIAL GUINEA |
| EST. | ESTONIA |
| HUNG. | HUNGARY |
| KOS. | KOSOVO |
| LITH. | LITHUANIA |
| MACED. | MACEDONIA |
| MOLD. | MOLDOVA |
| NETH. | NETHERLANDS |
| SERB. | SERBIA |
| MONT. | MONTENEGRO |
| SLOV. | SLOVENIA |
| SWITZ. | SWITZERLAND |
| U.A.E. | UNITED ARAB EMIRATES |

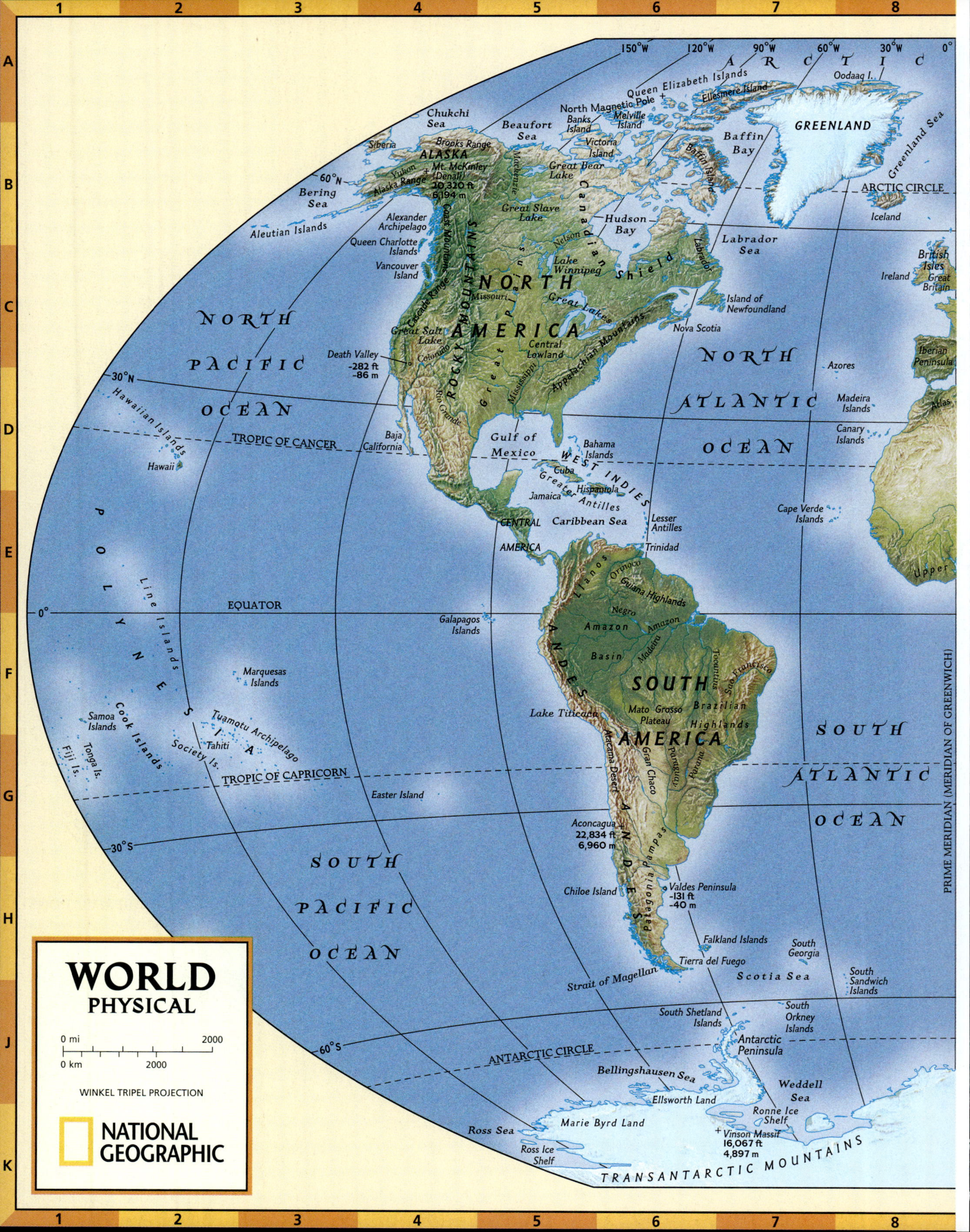

WORLD
PHYSICAL
0 mi
2000
0 km
2000
WINKEL TRIPEL PROJECTION
NATIONAL GEOGRAPHIC
1 2 3 4 5 6 7 8
A B C D E F G H J K
150°W
120°W
90°W
60°W
30°W
0°
60°N
30°N
0°
30°S
60°S
ARCTIC
Oodaaq I.
Queen Elizabeth Islands
Ellesmere Island
North Magnetic Pole
Banks Island
Melville Island
Victoria Island
Chukchi Sea
Beaufort Sea
Baffin Bay
Baffin Island
GREENLAND
Greenland Sea
ARCTIC CIRCLE
Iceland
Siberia
Brooks Range
ALASKA
Yukon
Mt. McKinley (Denali) 20,320 ft 6,194 m
Alaska Range
Bering Sea
Aleutian Islands
Mackenzie
Great Bear Lake
Great Slave Lake
Canadian Shield
Hudson Bay
Labrador
Labrador Sea
Alexander Archipelago
Queen Charlotte Islands
Vancouver Island
Coast Mountains
Nelson
Lake Winnipeg
British Isles
Ireland
Great Britain
NORTH AMERICA
Cascade Range
ROCKY MOUNTAINS
Missouri
Great Plains
Great Lakes
Island of Newfoundland
Nova Scotia
Great Salt Lake
Colorado
Central Lowland
Appalachian Mountains
Mississippi
Death Valley -282 ft -86 m
NORTH PACIFIC OCEAN
NORTH ATLANTIC OCEAN
Iberian Peninsula
Azores
Madeira Islands
Atlas
Canary Islands
Rio Grande
Hawaiian Islands
Hawaii
TROPIC OF CANCER
Baja California
Gulf of Mexico
Bahama Islands
WEST INDIES
Cuba
Hispaniola
Greater Antilles
Jamaica
Caribbean Sea
CENTRAL AMERICA
Lesser Antilles
Trinidad
Cape Verde Islands
POLYNESIA
Line Islands
EQUATOR
Llanos
Orinoco
Guiana Highlands
Negro
Amazon
Amazon Basin
Madeira
Galapagos Islands
ANDES
Tocantins
São Francisco
SOUTH AMERICA
Brazilian Highlands
Mato Grosso Plateau
Marquesas Islands
Lake Titicaca
Atacama Desert
Gran Chaco
Paraguay
Paraná
Samoa Islands
Cook Islands
Tuamotu Archipelago
Tahiti
Society Is.
Tonga Is.
Fiji Is.
TROPIC OF CAPRICORN
Easter Island
SOUTH ATLANTIC OCEAN
Upper
PRIME MERIDIAN (MERIDIAN OF GREENWICH)
Aconcagua 22,834 ft 6,960 m
Pampas
SOUTH PACIFIC OCEAN
Valdes Peninsula -131 ft -40 m
Chiloe Island
Patagonia
Falkland Islands
South Georgia
Tierra del Fuego
Strait of Magellan
Scotia Sea
South Sandwich Islands
South Shetland Islands
South Orkney Islands
Antarctic Peninsula
ANTARCTIC CIRCLE
Bellingshausen Sea
Weddell Sea
Ellsworth Land
Ronne Ice Shelf
Marie Byrd Land
Ross Sea
Vinson Massif 16,067 ft 4,897 m
Ross Ice Shelf
TRANSANTARCTIC MOUNTAINS

9
10
11
12
13
14
15
16
A
B
C
D
E
F
G
H
J
K
30°E
60°E
90°E
120°E
150°E
O C E A N
Svalbard
Barents Sea
Novaya Zemlya
Kara Sea
Laptev Sea
East Siberian Sea
Norwegian Sea
Scandinavia
Lena
Central Siberian Plateau
S I B E R I A
Yenisey
Ural Mountains
Ob
West Siberian Plain
Irtysh
Angara
60°N
Bering Sea
Kamchatka Peninsula
Sea of Okhotsk
Aleutian Is.
North Sea
Baltic Sea
Northern European Plain
E U R O P E
Volga
Alps
Danube
Elbrus 18,510 ft 5,642 m
The Steppes
Aral Sea
A S I A
Altay Mountains
Lake Baikal
Amur
Kuril Islands
Hokkaido
GOBI
Tian Shan
Corsica
Sardinia
Black Sea
Caucasus Mts.
Caspian Sea
Taklimakan Desert
Kunlun Shan
Huang He (Yellow R.)
North China Plain
Sea of Japan (East Sea)
Korea
Japan
Honshu
NORTH
Mediterranean Sea
Sicily
Mountains
Cyprus
Zagros Mountains
Indus
HIMALAYA
Plateau of Tibet
Brahmaputra
Chang Jiang (Yangtze R.)
Yellow Sea
East China Sea
Nampo Shoto
30°N
PACIFIC
Dead Sea -1,349 ft -411 m
Mt. Everest 29,028 ft 8,848 m
Ganges
Ryukyu Islands
S A H A R A
Libyan Desert
Nile
Red Sea
ARABIAN PENINSULA
INDIA
Salween
Taiwan
Philippine Sea
OCEAN
S A H E L
Blue Nile
Arabian Sea
Deccan Plateau
Bay of Bengal
Mekong
Hainan
Luzon
Indochina Peninsula
South China Sea
Philippine Islands
Mariana Islands
Niger
A F R I C A
Gulf of Aden
Ethiopian Highlands
Somali Peninsula
Andaman Islands
Andaman Sea
Sri Lanka
Nicobar Is.
M I C R O N E S I A
Marshall Islands
Guinea
White Nile
Malay Peninsula
Gulf of Guinea
Congo
Maldive Islands
EQUATOR
Sumatra
Borneo
Moluccas
M E L A N E S I A
Gilbert Islands
Lake Victoria
Congo Basin
Kilimanjaro 19,340 ft 5,895 m
Seychelles
Indonesia
Celebes
Greater Sunda Islands
New Guinea
Bismarck Archipelago
Lower Guinea
Lake Tanganyika
Java
Solomon Islands
Arafura Sea
Madagascar
Zambezi
Mascarene Islands
INDIAN
Coral Sea
Vanuatu
Fiji Islands
Namib Desert
Kalahari Desert
Drakensberg
Great Sandy Desert
AUSTRALIA
Great Dividing Range
New Caledonia
OCEAN
Lake Eyre -52 ft, -16 m
Great Victoria Desert
SOUTH PACIFIC OCEAN
Darling
Murray
Tasman Sea
Mt. Kosciuszko 7,310 ft 2,228 m
North Island
Tasmania
NEW ZEALAND
Kerguelen Islands
South Island
The Atlantic, Indian, and Pacific Oceans merge around Antarctica. Some define this as an ocean, calling it the Antarctic Ocean, Austral Ocean, or Southern Ocean. While most accept four oceans (including the Arctic Ocean), there is little international agreement on the name and extent of a fifth ocean.
Auckland Islands
South Magnetic Pole
60°S
Queen Maud Land
A N T A R C T I C A
Transantarctic Mountains
Victoria Land
Ross Sea
Ross Ice Shelf

NORTH AMERICA
POLITICAL
0 mi 1000
0 km 1000
AZIMUTHAL EQUIDISTANT PROJECTION
NATIONAL GEOGRAPHIC
1. BAJA CALIFORNIA
2. BAJA CALIFORNIA SUR
3. SONORA
4. CHIHUAHUA
5. SINALOA
6. DURANGO
7. COAHUILA
8. NUEVO LEON
9. ZACATECAS
10. TAMAULIPAS
11. NAYARIT
12. AGUASCALIENTES
13. SAN LUIS POTOSI
14. JALISCO
15. GUANAJUATO
16. QUERETARO
17. HIDALGO
18. COLIMA
19. MICHOACAN
20. MEXICO
21. DISTRITO FEDERAL
22. TLAXCALA
23. MORELOS
24. PUEBLA
25. VERACRUZ
26. GUERRERO
27. OAXACA
28. TABASCO
29. CHIAPAS
30. CAMPECHE
31. QUINTANA ROO
32. YUCATAN
ASIA
ARCTIC OCEAN
EUROPE
GREENLAND (KALAALLIT NUNAAT) Den.
Greenland Sea
Chukchi Sea
Bering Sea
Bering Strait
Point Barrow
Beaufort Sea
North Magnetic Pole
Queen Elizabeth Islands
Ellesmere Island
Parry Islands
Banks Island
Victoria Island
Boothia Peninsula
Baffin Bay
Qeqertarsuaq
Baffin Island
Davis Strait
ARCTIC CIRCLE
Nuuk (Godthab)
ALASKA U.S.
Yukon
Gulf of Alaska
YUKON TERRITORY
Mackenzie
Great Bear Lake
NUNAVUT
NORTHWEST TERRITORIES
Great Slave Lake
Southampton Island
Labrador Sea
CANADA
Hudson Bay
BRITISH COLUMBIA
ROCKY MOUNTAINS
Athabasca
ALBERTA
SASKATCHEWAN
Churchill
MANITOBA
Severn
Lake Winnipeg
ONTARIO
QUEBEC
NEWFOUNDLAND AND LABRADOR
Vancouver Island
PACIFIC OCEAN
Gulf of St. Lawrence
St.-Pierre & Miquelon Fr.
P.E.I.
N.B.
NOVA SCOTIA
WASHINGTON
Missouri
OREGON
MONTANA
NORTH DAKOTA
MINN.
Lake Superior
Ottawa
ME.
IDAHO
WYOMING
SOUTH DAKOTA
WIS.
MICHIGAN
Lake Huron
VT.
N.H.
MASS.
R.I.
CONN.
L. Ontario
NEW YORK
Great Salt Lake
NEVADA
Lake Michigan
L. Erie
PA.
N.J.
NEBRASKA
IOWA
UTAH
ILL.
IND.
OHIO
DEL.
MD.
CALIFORNIA
COLORADO
KANSAS
W.VA.
VA.
Washington, D.C.
ATLANTIC OCEAN
UNITED STATES
MISSOURI
KENTUCKY
Arkansas
TENNESSEE
N.C.
Bermuda Islands U.K.
ARIZONA
OKLAHOMA
Mississippi
ARK.
S.C.
NEW MEXICO
MISS.
ALA.
GEORGIA
TEXAS
Rio Grande
LA.
FLORIDA
Guadalupe I. Mex.
TROPIC OF CANCER
MEXICO
Gulf of Mexico
BAHAMAS
Nassau
Havana
CUBA
Santo Domingo
DOMINICAN REPUBLIC
HAITI
Port-au-Prince
PUERTO RICO U.S.
ANTIGUA AND BARBUDA
ST. KITTS AND NEVIS
BARBADOS
DOMINICA
ST. LUCIA
ST. VINCENT AND THE GRENADINES
GRENADA
TRINIDAD AND TOBAGO
Cayman Is. U.K.
JAMAICA
Kingston
Mexico City
BELIZE
Belmopan
Caribbean Sea
HONDURAS
Tegucigalpa
GUATEMALA
Guatemala
San Salvador
EL SALVADOR
NICARAGUA
Managua
COSTA RICA
San Jose
Panama Canal
Panama
PANAMA
Cocos I. C.R.
SOUTH AMERICA
EQUATOR

NORTH AMERICA
PHYSICAL
0 mi 1000
0 km 1000
AZIMUTHAL EQUIDISTANT PROJECTION
NATIONAL GEOGRAPHIC
ASIA
ARCTIC OCEAN
EUROPE
GREENLAND
Gunnbjorn 12,139 ft 3,700 m
Nuuk (Godthab)
Cape Farewell
ARCTIC CIRCLE
Greenland Sea
Oodaaq Island
Lincoln Sea
Queen Elizabeth Islands
Ellesmere Island
North Magnetic Pole
Hayes Peninsula
Baffin Bay
Davis Strait
Labrador Sea
Baffin Island
Chukchi Sea
Bering Sea
Point Barrow
Seward Peninsula
St. Lawrence Island
Nunivak Island
Brooks Range
North Slope
Beaufort Sea
Yukon
ALASKA
Mt. McKinley (Denali) 20,320 ft 6,194 m
Kuskokwim
Alaska Range
Bristol Bay
Aleutian Range
Kenai Peninsula
Kodiak I.
Gulf of Alaska
19,551 ft 5,959 m Mt. Logan
Yukon Plateau
Mackenzie Mts.
Mackenzie
Banks Island
Melville Island
Devon I.
Somerset I.
Prince of Wales I.
Victoria Island
Boothia Peninsula
Melville Peninsula
Foxe Basin
Great Bear Lake
Southampton Island
Hudson Strait
Ungava Bay
Great Slave Lake
Slave
CANADA
Hudson Bay
Belcher Islands
James Bay
LABRADOR
Island of Newfoundland
Avalon Peninsula
Alexander Archipelago
Queen Charlotte Islands
Coast Mountains
ROCKY MOUNTAINS
Peace
Lake Athabasca
Athabasca
Churchill
Nelson
CANADIAN SHIELD
Fraser Plateau
Columbia Mts.
Saskatchewan
Lake Winnipeg
GREAT PLAINS
Laurentian Mountains
St. Lawrence
Gaspé Pen.
Gulf of St. Lawrence
Cape Breton Island
Prince Edward Island
Nova Scotia
Bay of Fundy
Gulf of Maine
Cape Cod
Long Island
Vancouver Island
Olympic Peninsula
PACIFIC OCEAN
Cascade Range
Columbia Plateau
Snake
Missouri
Lake Superior
Ottawa
Lake Michigan
L. Michigan
Lake Huron
L. Ontario
L. Erie
APPALACHIAN MOUNTAINS
Cape Mendocino
Coast Ranges
Sierra Nevada
Great Basin
Great Salt Lake
Mt. Whitney 14,494 ft 4,418 m
Colorado
Colorado Plateau
Death Valley -282 ft -86 m
Grand Canyon
High Plains
Platte
CENTRAL LOWLAND
Ohio
Washington
Chesapeake Bay
Cape Hatteras
ATLANTIC OCEAN
Bermuda Islands
UNITED STATES
Arkansas
Ozark Plateau
Mississippi
Red
COASTAL PLAIN
Channel Islands
Sonoran Desert
Baja California
Gulf of California
Rio Grande
Florida
TROPIC OF CANCER
MEXICO
Sierra Madre Occidental
Sierra Madre Oriental
Gulf of Mexico
Florida Keys
BAHAMAS
Havana
CUBA
WEST INDIES
Virgin Islands
Puerto Rico
Hispaniola
HAITI
DOMINICAN REPUBLIC
Guadeloupe
Martinique
Greater Antilles
Lesser Antilles
Orizaba 18,855 ft 5,747 m
Mexico City
Yucatan Peninsula
Cozumel Island
Cayman Islands
JAMAICA
Kingston
Caribbean Sea
Trinidad
Isthmus of Tehuantepec
Gulf of Tehuantepec
BELIZE
Belmopan
HONDURAS
Tegucigalpa
GUATEMALA
Guatemala
San Salvador
EL SALVADOR
NICARAGUA
Managua
Lake Nicaragua
COSTA RICA
San José
Isthmus of Panama
Panama
PANAMA
CENTRAL AMERICA
SOUTH AMERICA
EQUATOR
100°W
90°W
80°W
70°W
1 2 3 4 5 6 7
A B C D E F G H J K

SOUTH AMERICA
POLITICAL
0 mi 800
0 km 800
AZIMUTHAL EQUIDISTANT PROJECTION
NATIONAL GEOGRAPHIC
Caribbean Sea
ATLANTIC OCEAN
PACIFIC OCEAN
EQUATOR
TROPIC OF CAPRICORN
VENEZUELA
COLOMBIA
GUYANA
SURINAME
FRENCH GUIANA
Fr.
ECUADOR
PERU
BOLIVIA
BRAZIL
PARAGUAY
URUGUAY
CHILE
ARGENTINA
AMAZON BASIN
ANDES
Boundary claimed by Suriname
Barranquilla
Cartagena
Santa Marta
Maracaibo
Lake Maracaibo
Barquisimeto
Caracas
Valencia
Orinoco
Ciudad Guayana
Georgetown
Paramaribo
Cayenne
Bucaramanga
San Cristobal
Medellin
Bogota
Cali
Malpelo I.
Col.
Boa Vista
Esmeraldas
Quito
Guayaquil
Marajo Island
Belem
Negro
Amazon
Manaus
Santarem
Amazon (Solimoes)
Madeira
Tapajos
Xingu
Iquitos
Maranon
Fortaleza
Teresina
Natal
Campina Grande
Recife
Purus
Ucayali
Rio Branco
Porto Velho
Tocantins
Teles Pires
Sao Francisco
Callao
Lima
Machu Picchu
Cuzco
Ayacucho
Lake Titicaca
Trinidad
La Paz
Salvador (Bahia)
Brasilia
Goiania
Arequipa
Arica
Oruro
Santa Cruz
Sucre
Uberandia
Uberaba
Belo Horizonte
Iquique
Campo Grande
Paraguay
Tarija
Campinas
Nova Iguacu
Rio de Janeiro
Londrina
Sao Paulo
Santos
Antofagasta
Salta
Asuncion
Curitiba
San Felix I.
San Ambrosio I.
Chil.
San Miguel de Tucuman
Parana
Uruguay
Uruguaiana
Porto Alegre
Santa Maria
La Serena
Coquimbo
Cordoba
Valparaiso
Mendoza
Rosario
Santiago
Buenos Aires
Montevideo
Juan Fernandez Is.
Chil.
La Plata
Rio de la Plata
Concepcion
Mar del Plata
Bahia Blanca
Negro
Puerto Montt
Comodoro Rivadavia
Falkland Islands (Islas Malvinas)
Stanley
Administered by United Kingdom
(Claimed by Arg.)
Rio Gallegos
Strait of Magellan
Punta Arenas
TIERRA DEL FUEGO
Ushuaia
Cape Horn
South Georgia I.
U.K.
N
80°W
60°W
50°W
40°W
10°N
0°
10°S
20°S
30°S
40°S
50°S
100°W
90°W
70°W
30°W
20°W

SOUTH AMERICA
PHYSICAL
AZIMUTHAL EQUIDISTANT PROJECTION
0 mi 800
0 km 800
NATIONAL GEOGRAPHIC
Caribbean Sea
ATLANTIC OCEAN
PACIFIC OCEAN
Caracas
Lake Maracaibo
Orinoco
VENEZUELA
LLANOS
Angel Falls
Total drop 3,212 ft 979 m
GUYANA
Georgetown
SURINAME
Paramaribo
Cayenne
FRENCH GUIANA
GUIANA HIGHLANDS
Boundary claimed by Suriname
Bogota
COLOMBIA
Malpelo I.
Quito
ECUADOR
EQUATOR
Negro
Amazon
Marajo Island
AMAZON BASIN
Selvas
Madeira
Tapajos
Xingu
Purus
Ucayali
Teles Pires
Tocantins
BRAZIL
Sao Francisco
ANDES
PERU
Lima
Machu Picchu
Lake Titicaca
BOLIVIA
La Paz
MATO GROSSO PLATEAU
BRAZILIAN HIGHLANDS
Brasilia
Altiplano
Sucre
Salar de Uyuni
Paraguay
PARAGUAY
GRAN CHACO
Asuncion
Iguazu Falls
TROPIC OF CAPRICORN
San Felix I.
San Ambrosio I.
Parana
Uruguay
Aconcagua 22,834 ft 6,960 m
Santiago
CHILE
ARGENTINA
PAMPAS
Juan Fernandez Is.
Buenos Aires
URUGUAY
Montevideo
Rio de la Plata
Negro
PATAGONIA
-131 ft -40 m
Valdes Peninsula
Chiloe Island
Gulf of San Jorge
Taitao Peninsula
Wellington I.
Falkland Islands (Islas Malvinas)
Stanley
Strait of Magellan
Tierra del Fuego
Cape Horn
South Georgia I.
N
10°N
0°
10°S
20°S
30°S
40°S
50°S
100°W
90°W
80°W
70°W
60°W
50°W
40°W
30°W
20°W

EUROPE
POLITICAL
0 mi 400
0 km 400
AZIMUTHAL EQUIDISTANT PROJECTION
NATIONAL GEOGRAPHIC
ATLANTIC OCEAN
ICELAND
Reykjavík
Akureyri
Faeroe Islands
Den.
Torshavn
Shetland Islands
Lerwick
Orkney Islands
Rockall
U.K.
Isle of Lewis
Inverness
Aberdeen
UNITED KINGDOM
SCOTLAND
Glasgow
Edinburgh
NORTHERN IRELAND
Belfast
IRELAND
Dublin
Cork
Irish Sea
Liverpool
Manchester
WALES
Birmingham
ENGLAND
Cardiff
London
Southampton
Celtic Sea
Land's End
English Channel
North Sea
Norwegian Sea
ARCTIC CIRCLE
PRIME MERIDIAN (MERIDIAN OF GREENWICH)
NORWAY
Tromso
Trondheim
Alesund
Bergen
Stavanger
Oslo
SWEDEN
Are
Sundsvall
Uppsala
Stockholm
Goteborg
Gotland
Malmo
Gulf of
Skagerrak
DENMARK
Arhus
Copenhagen
Baltic
Kiel
Hamburg
Gdansk
Bydgoszcz
POLAND
Lodz
Wroclaw
Oder
GERMANY
Berlin
Bonn
Frankfurt
Rhine
Munich
NETH.
Amsterdam
The Hague
BELGIUM
Brussels
LUX.
CZECH REP.
Prague
Bratislava
SLOVAKIA
Vienna
AUSTRIA
LIECH.
Zurich
Bern
SWITZERLAND
ALPS
Geneva
FRANCE
Paris
Le Havre
Brest
Rennes
Nantes
La Rochelle
Limoges
Bordeaux
Lyon
Strasbourg
Toulouse
Marseille
Nice
MONACO
Bay of Biscay
Donostia-San Sebastian
Pyrenees
ANDORRA
SPAIN
La Coruña
Vigo
Bilbao
Valladolid
Madrid
Zaragoza
Barcelona
Valencia
Cordoba
Seville
Murcia
Cartagena
Malaga
Cadiz
GIBRALTAR
U.K.
Strait of Gibraltar
PORTUGAL
Porto
Coimbra
Lisbon
Cape St. Vincent
Palma
Balearic Islands
Sp.
Mediterranean
AFRICA
Corsica
Fr.
Sardinia
It.
Cagliari
Tyrrhenian Sea
ITALY
Milan
Turin
Genoa
Venice
SAN MARINO
VATICAN CITY
Rome
Naples
Palermo
Sicily
Messina
Catania
Valletta
MALTA
Ionian Sea
Adriatic Sea
SLOVENIA
Ljubljana
Zagreb
CROATIA
HUNGARY
Budapest
BOSNIA & HERZEGOVINA
Sarajevo
MONTENEGRO
Podgorica
Tiranë
ALBANIA
60°N
50°N
40°N
30°N
70°N
40°W
30°W
20°W
10°W
0°
10°E
1
2
3
4
5
6
7
8
A
B
C
D
E
F
G
H
J
K

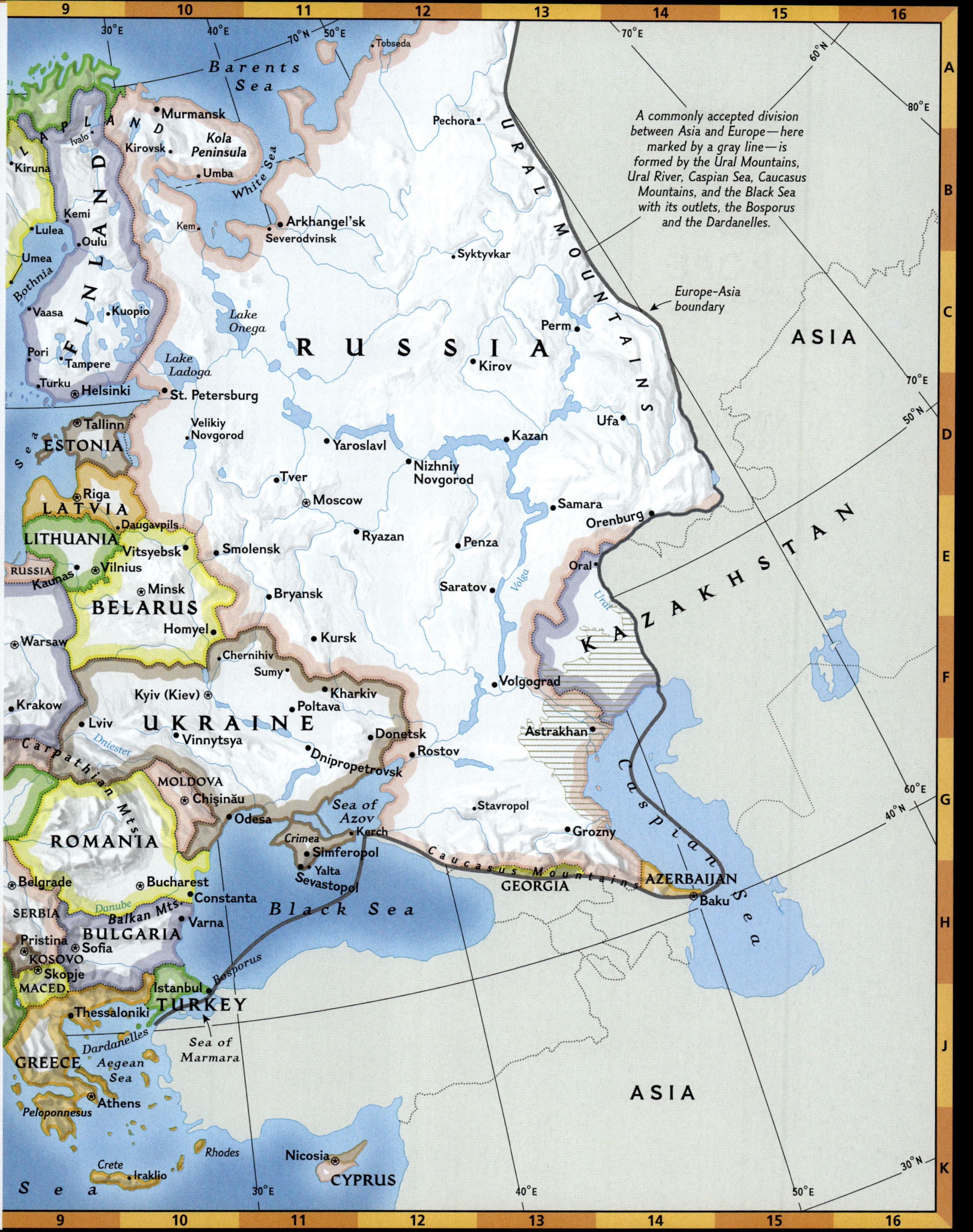
A commonly accepted division between Asia and Europe—here marked by a gray line—is formed by the Ural Mountains, Ural River, Caspian Sea, Caucasus Mountains, and the Black Sea with its outlets, the Bosporus and the Dardanelles.
Europe-Asia boundary
RUSSIA
ASIA
KAZAKHSTAN
URAL MOUNTAINS
Barents Sea
White Sea
Kola Peninsula
LAPLAND
FINLAND
Bothnia
ESTONIA
LATVIA
LITHUANIA
RUSSIA
BELARUS
UKRAINE
MOLDOVA
ROMANIA
SERBIA
KOSOVO
MACED.
BULGARIA
GREECE
TURKEY
GEORGIA
AZERBAIJAN
CYPRUS
Lake Onega
Lake Ladoga
Carpathian Mts.
Balkan Mts.
Caucasus Mountains
Black Sea
Sea of Azov
Caspian Sea
Aegean Sea
Sea of Marmara
Bosporus
Dardanelles
Crimea
Peloponnesus
Crete
Rhodes
Volga
Ural
Dniester
Danube
Murmansk
Kirovsk
Umba
Kem
Arkhangel'sk
Severodvinsk
Tobseda
Pechora
Syktyvkar
Ivalo
Kiruna
Kemi
Lulea
Oulu
Umea
Vaasa
Kuopio
Pori
Tampere
Turku
Helsinki
St. Petersburg
Tallinn
Velikiy Novgorod
Riga
Daugavpils
Vitsyebsk
Vilnius
Kaunas
Minsk
Homyel
Warsaw
Krakow
Lviv
Smolensk
Tver
Moscow
Yaroslavl
Nizhniy Novgorod
Kirov
Perm
Kazan
Ufa
Samara
Orenburg
Oral
Ryazan
Penza
Saratov
Bryansk
Kursk
Chernihiv
Sumy
Kharkiv
Kyiv (Kiev)
Poltava
Vinnytsya
Donetsk
Dnipropetrovsk
Rostov
Volgograd
Astrakhan
Stavropol
Grozny
Baku
Chişinău
Odesa
Kerch
Simferopol
Yalta
Sevastopol
Belgrade
Bucharest
Constanta
Varna
Pristina
Sofia
Skopje
Istanbul
Thessaloniki
Athens
Iraklio
Nicosia
30°E
40°E
50°E
70°E
80°E
70°N
60°N
50°N
40°N
30°N
Sea

EUROPE
PHYSICAL
0 mi 400
0 km 400
AZIMUTHEL EQUIDISTANT PROJECTION
NATIONAL GEOGRAPHIC
ATLANTIC OCEAN
Reykjavik
ICELAND
ARCTIC CIRCLE
PRIME MERIDIAN (MERIDIAN OF GREENWICH)
Norwegian Sea
Faeroe Islands
Shetland Islands
Orkney Islands
Outer Hebrides
Highlands
British Isles
Edinburgh
Belfast
UNITED KINGDOM
IRELAND
Dublin
Irish Sea
Great Britain
Cardiff
London
North Sea
SCANDINAVIA
NORWAY
SWEDEN
Gulf of
Oslo
Stockholm
Jutland
DENMARK
Copenhagen
Zealand
Baltic
Amsterdam
NETH.
Berlin
POLAND
Oder
English Channel
BELGIUM
Brussels
Rhine
GERMANY
LUX.
Seine
Paris
Brittany
Elbe
Prague
CZECH REP.
Loire
Danube
Bratislava
SLOVAKIA
FRANCE
Vienna
LIECH.
Bay of Biscay
Mont Blanc
15,771 ft
4,807 m
Bern
SWITZ.
AUSTRIA
Budapest
HUNGARY
ALPS
Massif Central
Rhone
SLOVENIA
Drava
Ljubljana
Zagreb
CROATIA
Sava
Po
Cantabrian Mountains
Pyrenees
MONACO
Riviera
SAN MARINO
Adriatic Sea
BOSNIA &
Sarajevo
HERZEGOVINA
Douro
IBERIAN PENINSULA
PORTUGAL
Lisbon
Tagus
Madrid
SPAIN
Ebro
ANDORRA
Corsica
Apennines
ITALY
VATICAN CITY
Rome
MONTENEGRO
Tiranë
ALBANIA
Sardinia
Tyrrhenian Sea
Balearic Islands
GIBRALTAR
Strait of Gibraltar
Baetic Mountains
Mediterranean
Ionian Sea
Sicily
Etna
10,902 ft
3,323 m
Valletta
MALTA
AFRICA

Barents Sea
North Cape
Kola Peninsula
White Sea
Pechora
URAL MOUNTAINS
Europe-Asia boundary
ASIA
FINLAND
Bothnia
Lake Region
Lake Onega
Lake Ladoga
Northern Dvina
RUSSIA
EUROPEAN PLAIN
Helsinki
Gulf of Finland
Tallinn
ESTONIA
Riga
LATVIA
LITHUANIA
Vilnius
RUSSIA
Minsk
BELARUS
Warsaw
Moscow
Oka
Volga
Kama
Ural
CENTRAL RUSSIAN UPLAND
Dnieper
Don
KAZAKHSTAN
Caspian Depression
Kyiv (Kiev)
UKRAINE
Vistula
Carpathian Mountains
Dniester
MOLDOVA
Chişinău
ROMANIA
Tisza
Sea of Azov
Crimea
Elbrus 18,510 ft 5,642 m
Caucasus Mountains
Caspian Sea
GEORGIA
AZERBAIJAN
Baku
Belgrade
Bucharest
Danube
BALKAN PENINSULA
SERBIA
BULGARIA
Balkan Mountains
Sofia
KOSOVO
Skopje
MACED.
Black Sea
Bosporus
TURKEY
Sea of Marmara
Dardanelles
GREECE
Aegean Sea
Athens
Peloponnesus
ASIA
Crete
Rhodes
Nicosia
CYPRUS
Sea
30°E
40°E
50°E
60°E
70°E
80°E
70°N
60°N
50°N
40°N
30°N

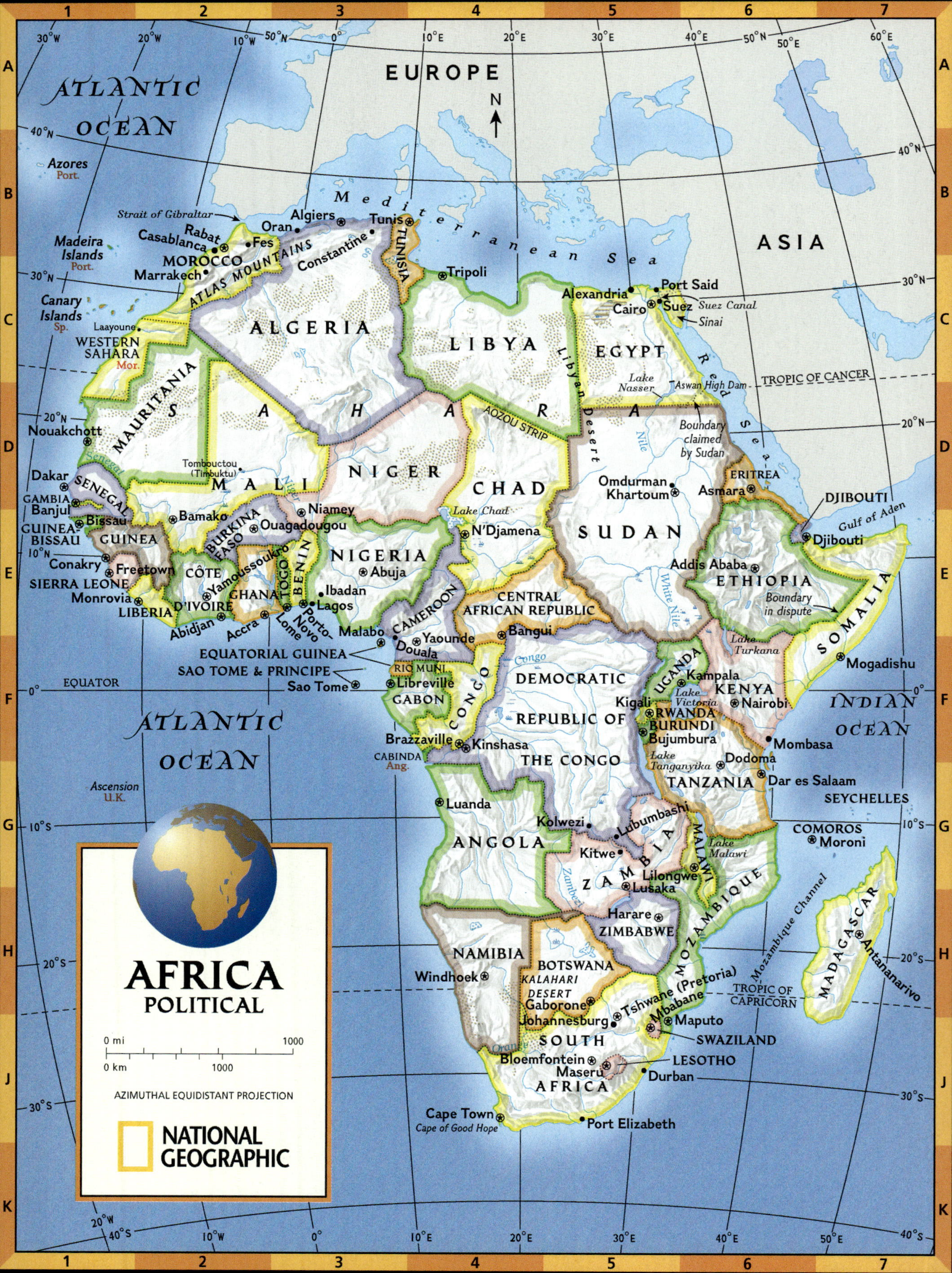

EUROPE
ASIA
ATLANTIC OCEAN
INDIAN OCEAN
Mediterranean Sea
Red Sea
Gulf of Aden
Mozambique Channel
AFRICA
POLITICAL
0 mi 1000
0 km 1000
AZIMUTHAL EQUIDISTANT PROJECTION
NATIONAL GEOGRAPHIC
Azores Port.
Madeira Islands Port.
Canary Islands Sp.
Strait of Gibraltar
Rabat
Casablanca
Fes
MOROCCO
Marrakech
ATLAS MOUNTAINS
Oran
Algiers
Constantine
Tunis
TUNISIA
Tripoli
ALGERIA
LIBYA
EGYPT
Alexandria
Cairo
Port Said
Suez
Suez Canal
Sinai
Lake Nasser
Aswan High Dam
TROPIC OF CANCER
Libyan Desert
SAHARA
AOZOU STRIP
Boundary claimed by Sudan
Laayoune
WESTERN SAHARA Mor.
MAURITANIA
Nouakchott
Senegal
Dakar
SENEGAL
GAMBIA
Banjul
GUINEA-BISSAU
Bissau
GUINEA
Conakry
Freetown
SIERRA LEONE
Monrovia
LIBERIA
CÔTE D'IVOIRE
Yamoussoukro
Abidjan
GHANA
Accra
TOGO
Lome
BENIN
Porto-Novo
Tombouctou (Timbuktu)
MALI
Niger
Bamako
BURKINA FASO
Ouagadougou
Niamey
NIGER
NIGERIA
Abuja
Ibadan
Lagos
CHAD
Lake Chad
N'Djamena
SUDAN
Nile
White Nile
Omdurman
Khartoum
ERITREA
Asmara
DJIBOUTI
Djibouti
ETHIOPIA
Addis Ababa
Boundary in dispute
SOMALIA
Mogadishu
CENTRAL AFRICAN REPUBLIC
Bangui
CAMEROON
Yaounde
Douala
Malabo
EQUATORIAL GUINEA
SAO TOME & PRINCIPE
Sao Tome
RIO MUNI
Libreville
GABON
CONGO
Congo
Brazzaville
Kinshasa
CABINDA Ang.
DEMOCRATIC REPUBLIC OF THE CONGO
UGANDA
Kampala
Lake Turkana
KENYA
Nairobi
Mombasa
Lake Victoria
Kigali
RWANDA
BURUNDI
Bujumbura
Lake Tanganyika
Dodoma
TANZANIA
Dar es Salaam
SEYCHELLES
COMOROS
Moroni
EQUATOR
Ascension U.K.
Luanda
ANGOLA
Kolwezi
Lubumbashi
Kitwe
ZAMBIA
Lusaka
Zambezi
Lilongwe
MALAWI
Lake Malawi
Harare
ZIMBABWE
MOZAMBIQUE
MADAGASCAR
Antananarivo
NAMIBIA
Windhoek
BOTSWANA
KALAHARI DESERT
Gaborone
Johannesburg
Tshwane (Pretoria)
Mbabane
Maputo
SWAZILAND
TROPIC OF CAPRICORN
Orange
SOUTH AFRICA
Bloemfontein
Maseru
LESOTHO
Durban
Cape Town
Cape of Good Hope
Port Elizabeth

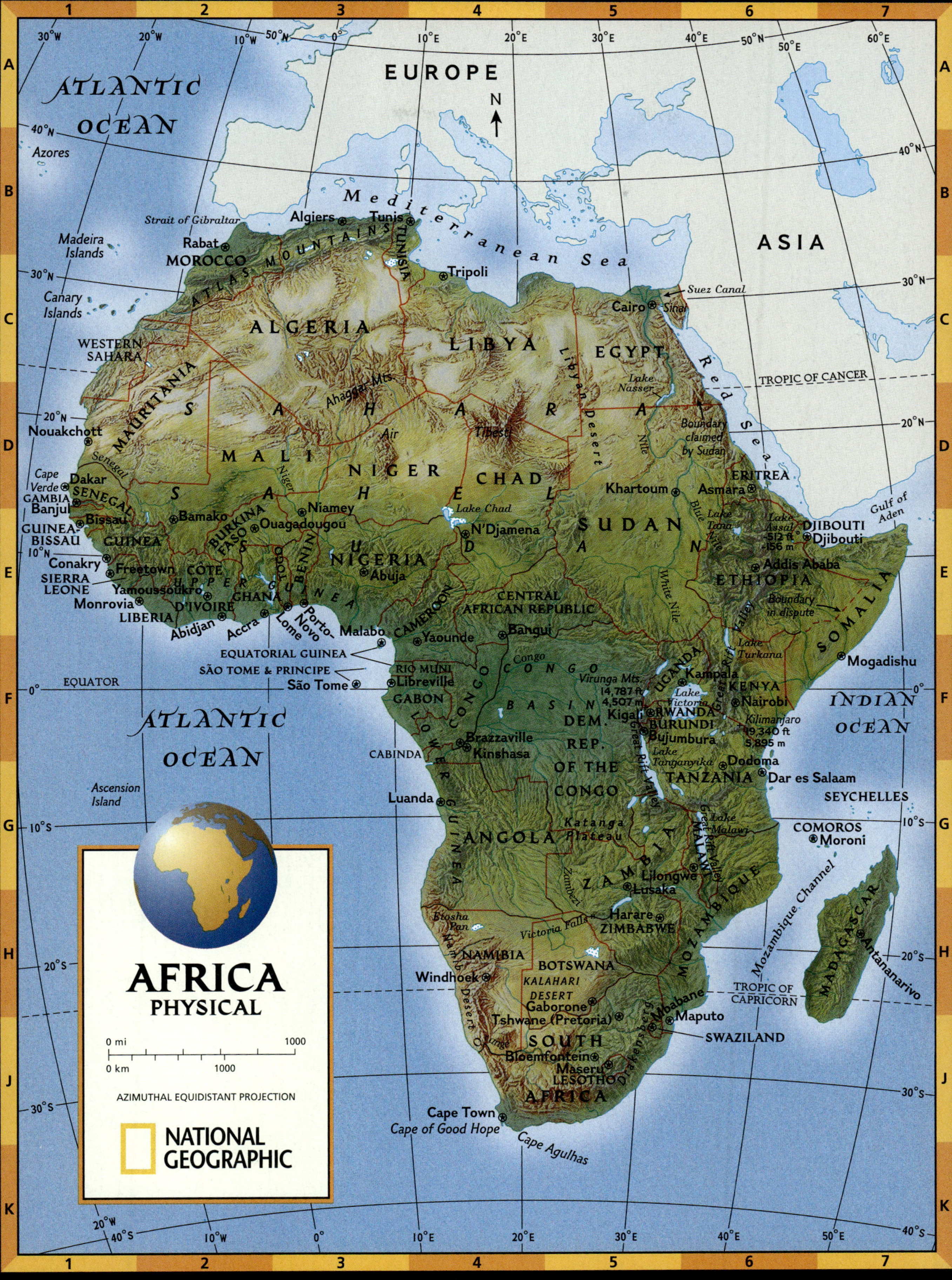

EUROPE
ASIA
ATLANTIC OCEAN
ATLANTIC OCEAN
INDIAN OCEAN
Mediterranean Sea
Red Sea
Gulf of Aden
Mozambique Channel
Azores
Madeira Islands
Canary Islands
Strait of Gibraltar
ATLAS MOUNTAINS
Ahaggar Mts.
Tibesti
Air
SAHARA
SAHEL
Libyan Desert
GUINEA
Suez Canal
Sinai
TROPIC OF CANCER
TROPIC OF CAPRICORN
EQUATOR
Algiers
Tunis
TUNISIA
Tripoli
Rabat
MOROCCO
ALGERIA
LIBYA
EGYPT
Cairo
Lake Nasser
Nile
Boundary claimed by Sudan
WESTERN SAHARA
MAURITANIA
Nouakchott
MALI
NIGER
CHAD
SUDAN
Khartoum
ERITREA
Asmara
DJIBOUTI
Djibouti
Lake Assal -512 ft -156 m
Lake Tana
Blue Nile
White Nile
Addis Ababa
ETHIOPIA
Boundary in dispute
SOMALIA
Mogadishu
Cape Verde
Dakar
SENEGAL
Senegal
GAMBIA
Banjul
GUINEA-BISSAU
Bissau
GUINEA
Conakry
SIERRA LEONE
Freetown
LIBERIA
Monrovia
Bamako
BURKINA FASO
Ouagadougou
Niamey
Niger
COTE D'IVOIRE
Yamoussoukro
Abidjan
GHANA
Accra
TOGO
Lome
BENIN
Porto-Novo
NIGERIA
Abuja
Lake Chad
N'Djamena
CAMEROON
Yaounde
Malabo
CENTRAL AFRICAN REPUBLIC
Bangui
EQUATORIAL GUINEA
SÃO TOME & PRINCIPE
São Tome
RIO MUNI
Libreville
GABON
CONGO
CONGO BASIN
Congo
Brazzaville
Kinshasa
CABINDA
LOWER GUINEA
DEM. REP. OF THE CONGO
Virunga Mts. 14,787 ft 4,507 m
UGANDA
Kampala
Lake Victoria
Lake Turkana
KENYA
Nairobi
Kilimanjaro 19,340 ft 5,895 m
RWANDA
Kigali
BURUNDI
Bujumbura
Great Rift Valley
Lake Tanganyika
Dodoma
TANZANIA
Dar es Salaam
SEYCHELLES
COMOROS
Moroni
Luanda
ANGOLA
Katanga Plateau
Lake Malawi
MALAWI
Lilongwe
ZAMBIA
Lusaka
Zambezi
Harare
ZIMBABWE
Victoria Falls
MOZAMBIQUE
MADAGASCAR
Antananarivo
Etosha Pan
NAMIBIA
Namib Desert
Windhoek
BOTSWANA
KALAHARI DESERT
Gaborone
Tshwane (Pretoria)
Mbabane
Maputo
SWAZILAND
SOUTH AFRICA
Bloemfontein
Maseru
LESOTHO
Drakensberg
Orange
Cape Town
Cape of Good Hope
Cape Agulhas
Ascension Island
AFRICA
PHYSICAL
0 mi 1000
0 km 1000
AZIMUTHAL EQUIDISTANT PROJECTION
NATIONAL GEOGRAPHIC

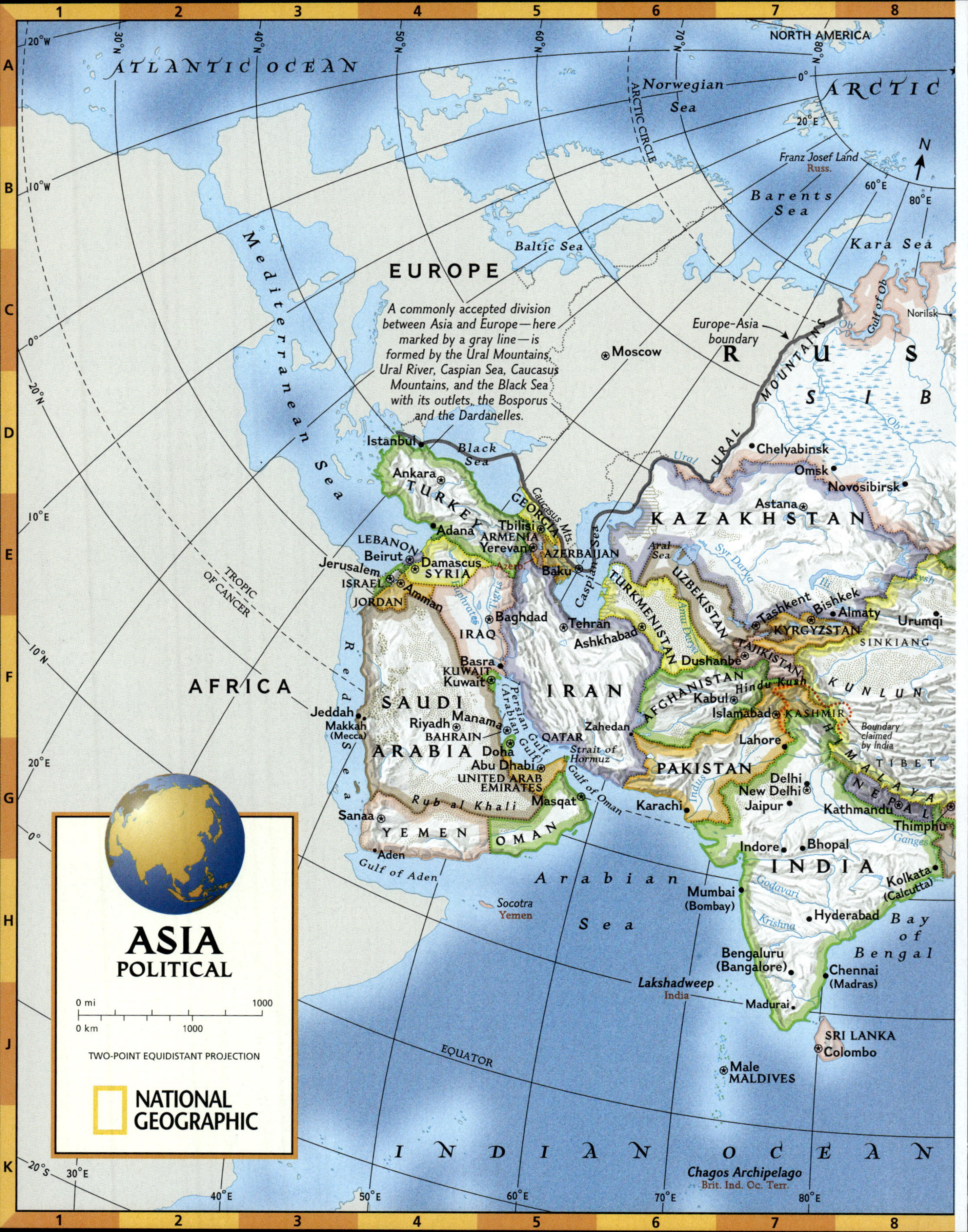

ASIA
POLITICAL
0 mi 1000
0 km 1000
TWO-POINT EQUIDISTANT PROJECTION
NATIONAL GEOGRAPHIC
A commonly accepted division between Asia and Europe—here marked by a gray line—is formed by the Ural Mountains, Ural River, Caspian Sea, Caucasus Mountains, and the Black Sea with its outlets, the Bosporus and the Dardanelles.
Europe-Asia boundary
ATLANTIC OCEAN
NORTH AMERICA
Norwegian Sea
ARCTIC
ARCTIC CIRCLE
Franz Josef Land
Russ.
Barents Sea
Kara Sea
Baltic Sea
EUROPE
Mediterranean Sea
Moscow
RUSSIA
SIBERIA
URAL MOUNTAINS
Gulf of Ob
Norilsk
Chelyabinsk
Omsk
Novosibirsk
Astana
KAZAKHSTAN
Istanbul
Black Sea
Ankara
TURKEY
GEORGIA
Tbilisi
Caucasus Mts.
ARMENIA
Yerevan
AZERBAIJAN
Baku
Caspian Sea
Aral Sea
Syr Darya
UZBEKISTAN
TURKMENISTAN
Ashkhabad
Tashkent
Bishkek
Almaty
KYRGYZSTAN
TAJIKISTAN
Dushanbe
Urumqi
SINKIANG
KUNLUN
Adana
LEBANON
Beirut
Damascus
SYRIA
Jerusalem
ISRAEL
Amman
JORDAN
Euphrates
Tigris
Baghdad
IRAQ
Tehran
IRAN
Basra
KUWAIT
Kuwait
TROPIC OF CANCER
AFRICA
Red Sea
Jeddah
Makkah (Mecca)
SAUDI ARABIA
Riyadh
Manama
BAHRAIN
Persian (Arabian) Gulf
QATAR
Doha
Abu Dhabi
UNITED ARAB EMIRATES
Strait of Hormuz
Zahedan
AFGHANISTAN
Kabul
Hindu Kush
Islamabad
KASHMIR
Boundary claimed by India
Lahore
PAKISTAN
Indus
TIBET
HIMALAYA
NEPAL
Kathmandu
Thimphu
Rub al Khali
Masqat
OMAN
Gulf of Oman
Karachi
Delhi
New Delhi
Jaipur
Sanaa
YEMEN
Aden
Gulf of Aden
Socotra
Yemen
Arabian Sea
Indore
Bhopal
INDIA
Ganges
Kolkata (Calcutta)
Mumbai (Bombay)
Godavari
Hyderabad
Krishna
Bay of Bengal
Bengaluru (Bangalore)
Chennai (Madras)
Lakshadweep
India
Madurai
SRI LANKA
Colombo
Male
MALDIVES
EQUATOR
INDIAN OCEAN
Chagos Archipelago
Brit. Ind. Oc. Terr.

NORTH AMERICA
Bering Strait
Chukchi Sea
North Pole
OCEAN
Wrangel I.
Gulf of Anadyr
Anadyr
East Siberian Sea
Bering Sea
North Land
New Siberian Islands
Laptev Sea
Commander Is.
Kamchatka Peninsula
Kolyma Range
Cherskiy Range
Verkhoyanski Mountains
Magadan
Sea of Okhotsk
Lena
Aldan
Yakutsk
S I A
E R I A
Sakhalin
Kuril Islands
Yenisey
Lake Baikal
Amur
Hokkaido
Sapporo
Irkutsk
MANCHURIA
Vladivostok
Sea of Japan (East Sea)
JAPAN
Tokyo
Ulaanbaatar
Herlen
MONGOLIA
ALTAY MTS.
GOBI
Changchun
Shenyang
NORTH KOREA
P'yŏngyang
Seoul
SOUTH KOREA
Honshu
Kyoto
Osaka
Hiroshima
Kyushu
Beijing
Qingdao
Yellow Sea
Shijiazhuang
Marcus I. Jap.
TROPIC OF CANCER
Bonin Is. Jap.
Volcano Is. Jap.
Huang He (Yellow R.)
Xuzhou
Lanzhou
Xian
East China Sea
Shanghai
Nanjing
CHINA
SHAN
Ryukyu Islands
Okinawa
Chang Jiang (Yangtze R.)
Nanchang
Chengdu
Fuzhou
Taipei
Parece Vela Jap.
Changsha
TAIWAN
The People's Republic of China claims Taiwan as its 23rd province.
Boundary claimed by China
BHUTAN
BANGLADESH
Dhaka
Guiyang
Kunming
Guangzhou
Hong Kong
Macau
Irrawaddy
PACIFIC OCEAN
Philippine Sea
Luzon
Quezon City
Manila
Samar
PHILIPPINES
Leyte
MYANMAR (BURMA)
Nay Pyi Taw
Hanoi
Haiphong
Hainan
South China Sea
LAOS
Vientiane
Da Nang
Mindoro
Panay
Negros
THAILAND
Bangkok
CAMBODIA
VIETNAM
Phnom Penh
Ho Chi Minh City
Palawan
Mindanao
EQUATOR
Andaman Islands India
Andaman Sea
Gulf of Thailand
Bandar Seri Begawan
BRUNEI
SABAH
SARAWAK
MALAYSIA
Halmahera
Morotai
Biak
Jayapura
New Guinea
Moluccas
Nicobar Islands India
Kuala Lumpur
Medan
SINGAPORE
Borneo
Celebes
Buru
Ceram
Aru Is.
Kepi
Merauke
Dolak
INDONESIA
Tanimbar Is.
Sumatra
Jambi
GREATER SUNDA ISLANDS
Mentawai Islands
Java Sea
Jakarta
Java
Dili
EAST TIMOR (TIMOR-LESTE)
Kupang
Timor Sea
AUSTRALIA
80°N
70°N
60°N
50°N
40°N
30°N
20°N
10°N
0°
10°S
20°S
180°
160°E
100°E
120°E
110°E
130°E
140°E
150°E
170°E
160°W
170°W
9
10
11
12
13
14
15
16
A
B
C
D
E
F
G
H
J
K

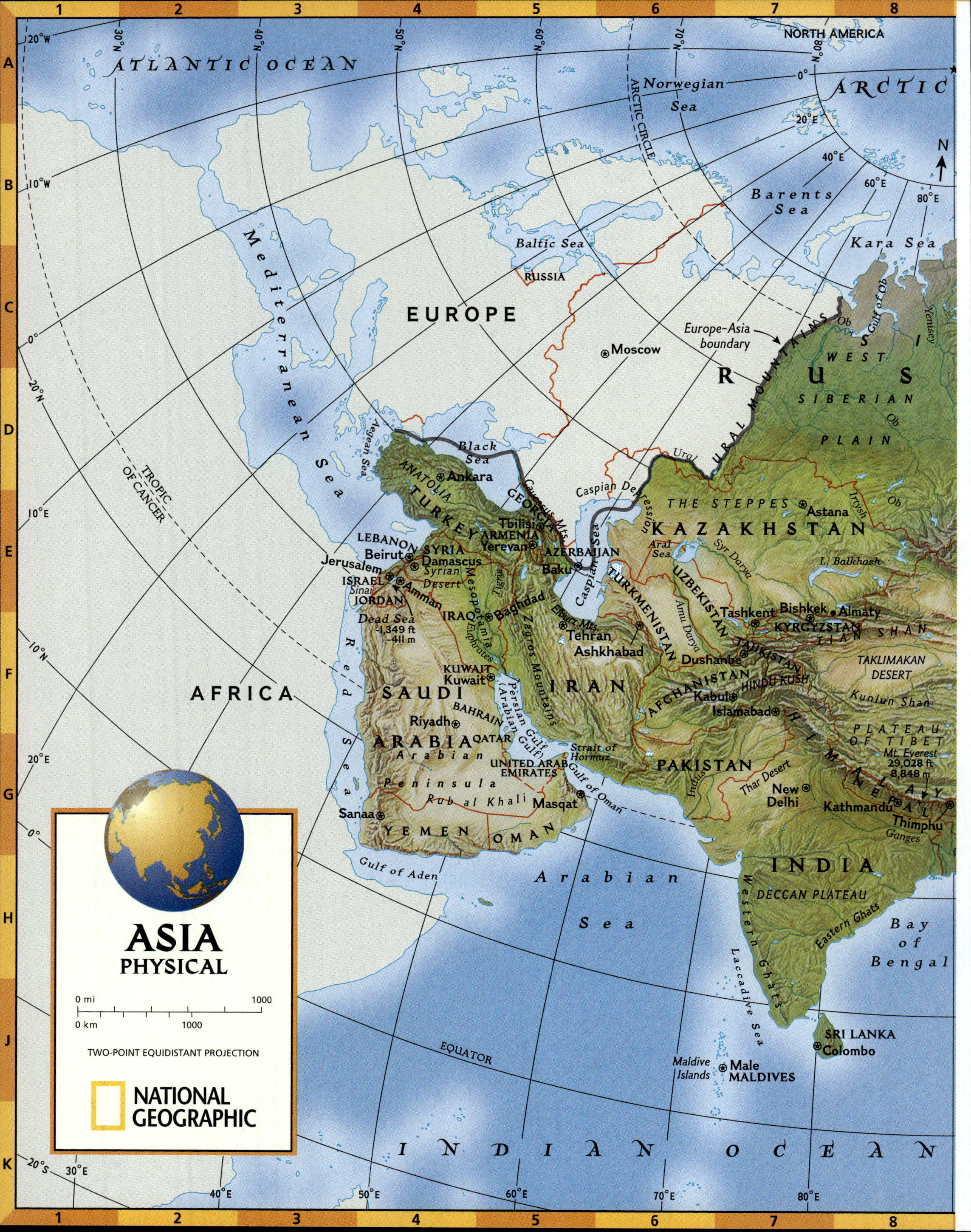
ASIA
PHYSICAL
0 mi 1000
0 km 1000
TWO-POINT EQUIDISTANT PROJECTION
NATIONAL GEOGRAPHIC
ATLANTIC OCEAN
NORTH AMERICA
ARCTIC
Norwegian Sea
ARCTIC CIRCLE
Barents Sea
Kara Sea
Baltic Sea
RUSSIA
EUROPE
Moscow
Europe-Asia boundary
Mediterranean Sea
TROPIC OF CANCER
EQUATOR
URAL MOUNTAINS
RUSSIA
WEST SIBERIAN PLAIN
Ob
Gulf of Ob
Yenisey
Irtysh
Ural
Black Sea
Aegean Sea
ANATOLIA
Ankara
TURKEY
GEORGIA
Caucasus Mts.
Tbilisi
ARMENIA
Yerevan
AZERBAIJAN
Baku
Caspian Sea
Caspian Depression
THE STEPPES
Astana
KAZAKHSTAN
Aral Sea
Syr Darya
L. Balkhash
UZBEKISTAN
Amu Darya
TURKMENISTAN
Ashkhabad
Tashkent
Bishkek
Almaty
KYRGYZSTAN
TIAN SHAN
TAJIKISTAN
Dushanbe
TAKLIMAKAN DESERT
Kunlun Shan
HINDU KUSH
AFGHANISTAN
Kabul
Islamabad
PLATEAU OF TIBET
Mt. Everest 29,028 ft 8,848 m
HIMALAYA
NEPAL
Kathmandu
Thimphu
Ganges
LEBANON
Beirut
SYRIA
Damascus
Syrian Desert
Jerusalem
ISRAEL
Sinai
JORDAN
Amman
Dead Sea -1,349 ft -411 m
IRAQ
Baghdad
Mesopotamia
Tigris
Euphrates
Zagros Mountains
Elburz Mts.
Tehran
IRAN
KUWAIT
Kuwait
SAUDI ARABIA
BAHRAIN
QATAR
Riyadh
Persian Gulf (Arabian Gulf)
Strait of Hormuz
UNITED ARAB EMIRATES
Gulf of Oman
Arabian Peninsula
Rub al Khali
Masqat
OMAN
Sanaa
YEMEN
Gulf of Aden
Red Sea
AFRICA
PAKISTAN
Indus
Thar Desert
New Delhi
INDIA
DECCAN PLATEAU
Western Ghats
Eastern Ghats
Bay of Bengal
Arabian Sea
Laccadive Sea
SRI LANKA
Colombo
Maldive Islands
Male
MALDIVES
INDIAN OCEAN

NORTH AMERICA
Bering Strait
North Pole
Chukchi Sea
Chukchi Peninsula
OCEAN
Wrangel Island
Gulf of Anadyr
East Siberian Sea
Bering Sea
North Land
New Siberian Islands
Aleutian Islands
Laptev Sea
Kolyma
Kolyma Range
Commander Islands
Taymyr Peninsula
Cherskiy Range
Kamchatka Peninsula
Verkhoyanski Mountains
Lena
Aldan
CENTRAL SIBERIAN PLATEAU
SIBERIA
ASIA
Sea of Okhotsk
Sakhalin
Kuril Islands
Angara
Amur
Sikhote Alin Range
Lake Baikal
Yablonovyy Range
Greater Khingan Range
Manchurian Plain
Hokkaido
Yenisey
Sea of Japan (East Sea)
JAPAN
Tokyo
Ulaanbaatar
MONGOLIA
ALTAY MOUNTAINS
GOBI
NORTH KOREA
Honshu
P'yŏngyang
Seoul
SOUTH KOREA
Beijing
North China Plain
Shikoku
Kyushu
Nampo Shoto
TROPIC OF CANCER
PACIFIC OCEAN
Yellow Sea
Huang He (Yellow R.)
Qaidam Basin
East China Sea
Ryukyu Islands
CHINA
Mekong
Yangtze
Salween
Sichuan Basin
Chang Jiang (Yangtze R.)
Gongga Shan 24,790 ft 7,556 m
Mariana Islands
Taipei
TAIWAN
Philippine Sea
BHUTAN
Brahmaputra
BANGLADESH
Dhaka
MYANMAR (BURMA)
Hanoi
Luzon
PHILIPPINE ISLANDS
Caroline Islands
South China Sea
Hainan
Nay Pyi Taw
Vientiane
LAOS
Manila
PHILIPPINES
THAILAND
Mekong
EQUATOR
Bangkok
CAMBODIA
VIETNAM
Andaman Islands
Phnom Penh
Sulu Sea
Mindanao
Bandar Seri Begawan
BRUNEI
Celebes Sea
Gulf of Thailand
Andaman Sea
Malay Peninsula
Nicobar Islands
MALAYSIA
Moluccas
New Guinea
Kuala Lumpur
SINGAPORE
Borneo
Celebes
INDONESIA
Sumatra
Arafura Sea
GREATER SUNDA ISLANDS
EAST TIMOR (TIMOR-LESTE)
Dili
Timor Sea
Mentawai Islands
Java Sea
AUSTRALIA
Jakarta
Java
80°N
70°N
60°N
50°N
40°N
30°N
20°N
10°N
0°
10°S
20°S
180°
160°E
120°E
100°E
160°W
170°W
170°E
150°E
140°E
130°E
110°E
9
10
11
12
13
14
15
16
A
B
C
D
E
F
G
H
J
K

RUSSIA
Lake Baikal
Yablonovyy Range
Ulaanbaatar
MONGOLIA
ALTAY MOUNTAINS
GOBI
Greater Khingan Range
Manchurian Plain
Amur
Sikhote-Alin Range
Sakhalin
KAMCHATKA PENINSULA
Sea of Okhotsk
Bering Sea
ALEUTIAN ISLANDS
KURIL ISLANDS
Hokkaido
Beijing
P'yŏngyang
NORTH KOREA
Seoul
SOUTH KOREA
Sea of Japan (East Sea)
Honshu
JAPAN
Tokyo
Yellow Sea
Kyushu
Shikoku
NAMPO SHOTO
Huang He (Yellow)
CHINA
Chang Jiang (Yangtze)
Mekong
INDIA
East China Sea
RYUKYU ISLANDS
Taipei
TAIWAN
NORTH PACIFIC
Hawaiian
MYANMAR (BURMA)
Nay Pyi Taw
Hanoi
LAOS
VIETNAM
Vientiane
THAILAND
Bangkok
CAMBODIA
Phnom Penh
Hainan
Luzon
South China Sea
PHILIPPINE ISLANDS
Manila
PHILIPPINES
Andaman Sea
Sulu Sea
Bandar Seri Begawan
BRUNEI
Mindanao
Celebes Sea
Kuala Lumpur
MALAYSIA
SINGAPORE
Borneo
Sumatra
INDONESIA
GREATER SUNDA ISLANDS
Celebes
MOLUCCAS
Jakarta
Java Sea
Java
LESSER SUNDA ISLANDS
Dili
EAST TIMOR (TIMOR-LESTE)
Arafura Sea
NEW GUINEA
PAPUA NEW GUINEA
Port Moresby
MARIANA ISLANDS
NORTHERN MARIANA ISLANDS
U.S.
MICRONESIA
Philippine Sea
GUAM
U.S.
PALAU
Melekeok
CAROLINE ISLANDS
FEDERATED STATES OF MICRONESIA
Palikir
Ralik Chain
Ratak Chain
MARSHALL ISLANDS
Majuro
POLYNESIA
Tarawa (Bairiki)
Gilbert Islands
Yaren
NAURU
KIRIBATI
Phoenix Is.
MELANESIA
Solomon Is.
SOLOMON ISLANDS
Honiara
Santa Cruz Islands
TUVALU
Funafuti
Tokelau
N.Z.
WALLIS AND FUTUNA IS.
Fr.
AMERICAN SAMOA
U.S.
SAMOA
Apia
CORAL SEA ISLANDS TERRITORY
Austral.
VANUATU
Port-Vila
NEW CALEDONIA
Fr.
Suva
FIJI ISLANDS
TONGA
Niue
N.Z.
Nuku'alofa
Coral Sea
TROPIC OF CAPRICORN
AUSTRALIA
Darling
Great Australian Bight
Canberra
Norfolk Island
Austral.
Lord Howe Island
Austral.
Kermadec Islands
N.Z.
Tasman Sea
NEW ZEALAND
Wellington
Tasmania
Chatham Island
N.Z.
INDIAN OCEAN
105°E
120°E
135°E
150°E
165°E
180°
1
2
3
4
5
6
7
8
A
B
C
D
E
F
G
H
J
K

PACIFIC RIM
PHYSICAL/POLITICAL
0 mi 1500
0 km 1500
MILLER CYLINDRICAL PROJECTION
NATIONAL GEOGRAPHIC
Gulf of Alaska
Kodiak I.
Alexander Archipelago
Queen Charlotte Islands
Vancouver Island
Coast Mountains
ROCKY MOUNTAINS
Cascade Range
GREAT PLAINS
CANADA
CANADIAN SHIELD
Hudson Bay
Ottawa
Great Lakes
Missouri
CENTRAL LOWLAND
APPALACHIAN MTS.
Washington, D.C.
UNITED STATES
Mississippi
COASTAL PLAIN
ATLANTIC OCEAN
Baja California
Gulf of California
Sierra Madre Occidental
Sierra Madre Oriental
MEXICO
Gulf of Mexico
Mexico City
Nassau
BAHAMAS
Havana
CUBA
JAMAICA
HAITI
DOMINICAN REPUBLIC
Santo Domingo
BELIZE
HONDURAS
Tegucigalpa
GUATEMALA
Guatemala
San Salvador
EL SALVADOR
NICARAGUA
Managua
San Jose
COSTA RICA
Panama
PANAMA
Caribbean Sea
Caracas
LLANOS
VENEZ.
Bogota
COLOMBIA
Quito
ECUADOR
AMAZON BASIN
BRAZIL
PERU
Lima
ANDES
BOLIVIA
La Paz
CHILE
Santiago
ARGENTINA
PATAGONIA
Chiloe Island
Galapagos Islands
Ecua.
TROPIC OF CANCER
EQUATOR
IC OCEAN
Hawaiian Islands
HAWAII
U.S.
Kiritimati
Line Islands
POLYNESIA
Marquesas Is.
Tuamotu Archipelago
Society Is.
COOK ISLANDS
N.Z.
FRENCH POLYNESIA
Fr.
Austral Is.
Pitcairn Island U.K.
SOUTH PACIFIC OCEAN
45°N
30°N
15°N
0°
15°S
30°S
45°S
165°W
150°W
135°W
120°W
105°W
90°W
75°W
9 10 11 12 13 14 15 16
A B C D E F G H J K

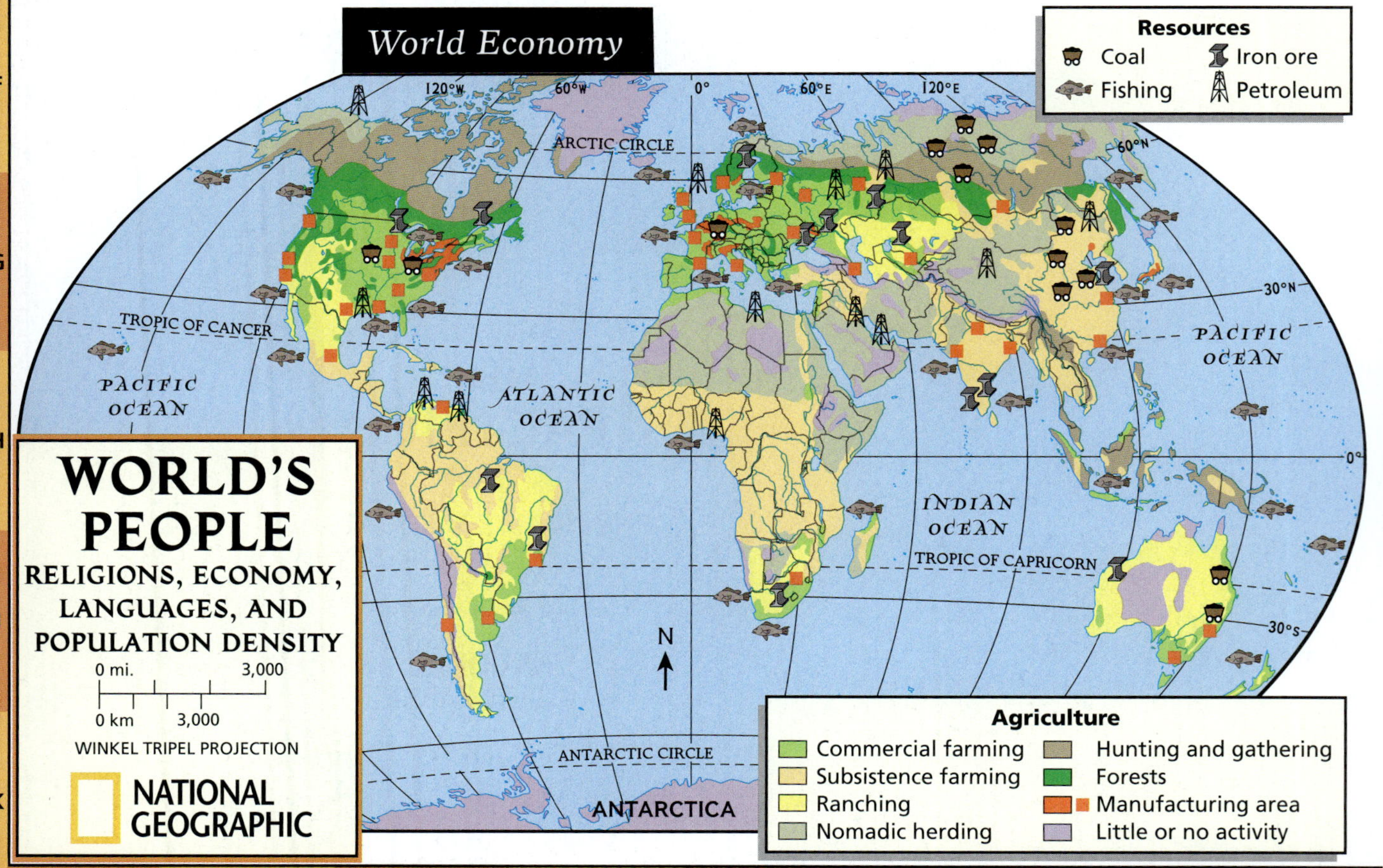


# WORLD'S PEOPLE

**RELIGIONS, ECONOMY, LANGUAGES, AND POPULATION DENSITY**

0 mi. 3,000
0 km 3,000

WINKEL TRIPEL PROJECTION

NATIONAL GEOGRAPHIC

# World Language Families

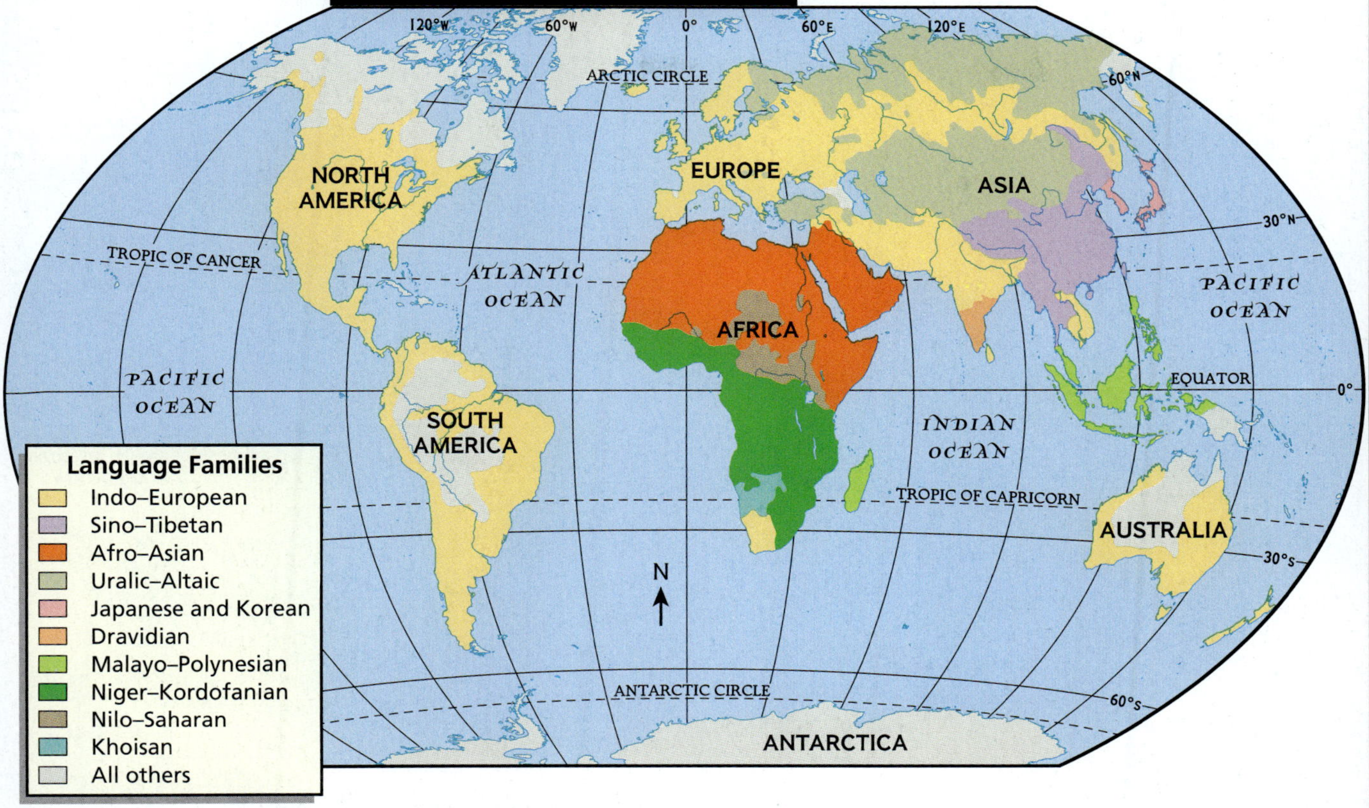


# World Population Density

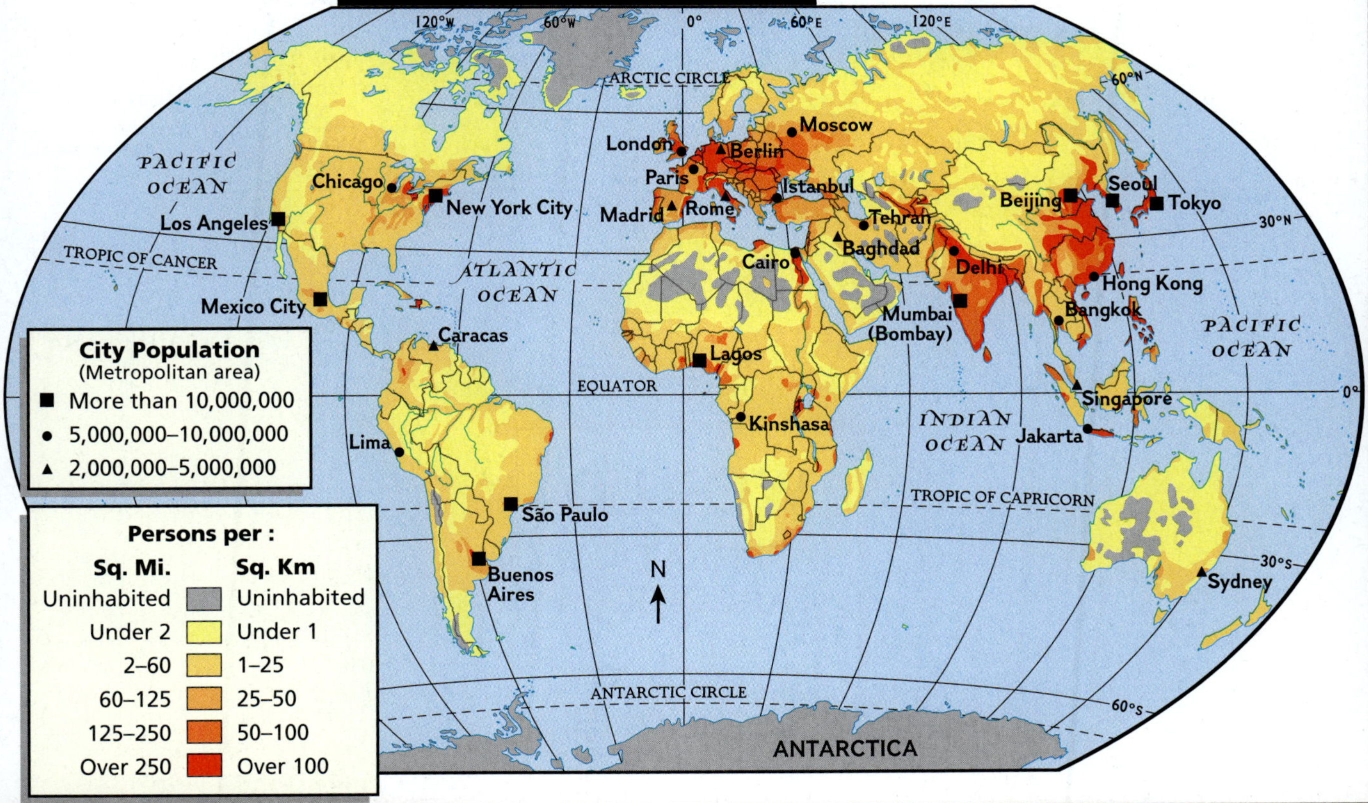

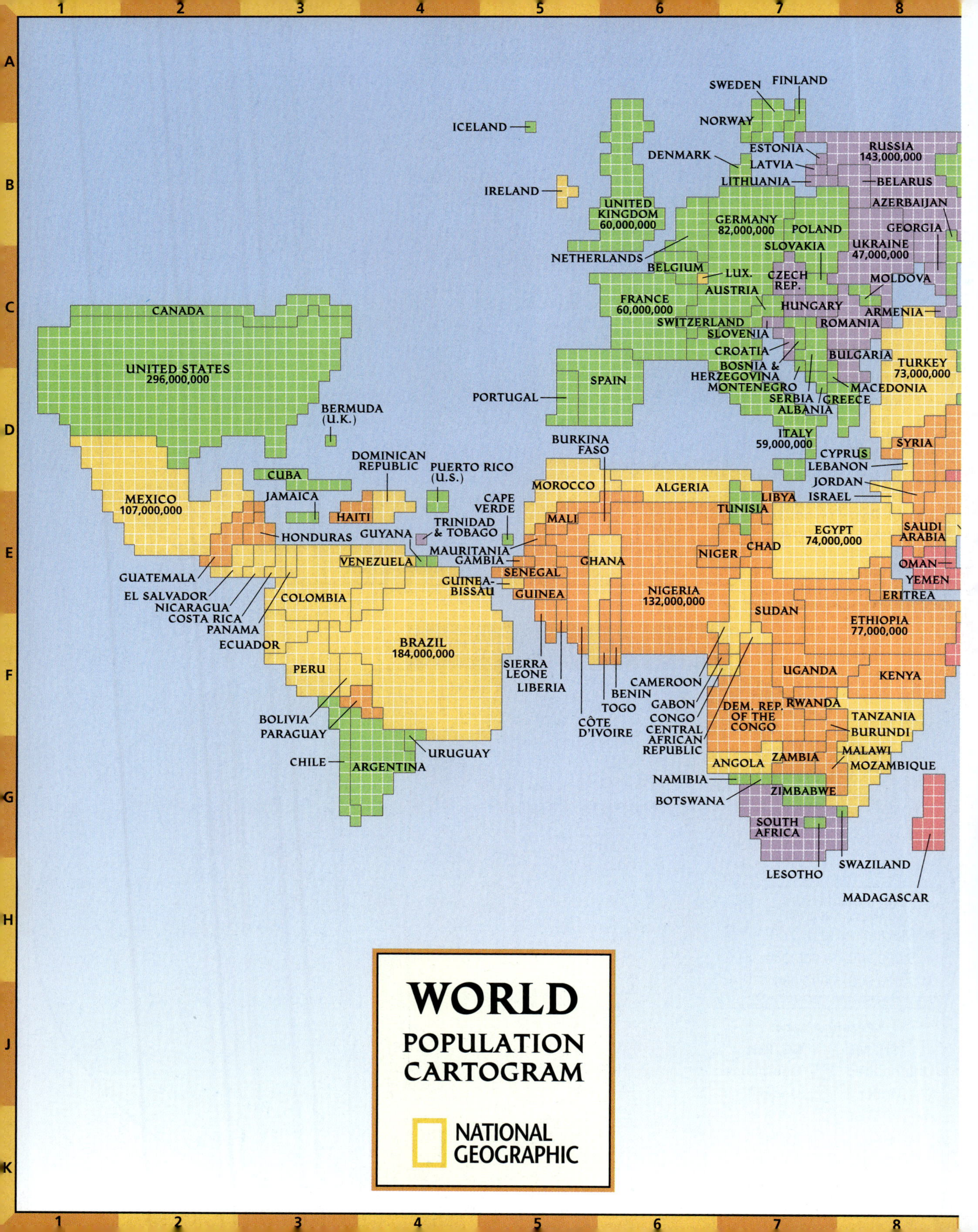
WORLD
POPULATION
CARTOGRAM
NATIONAL GEOGRAPHIC
CANADA
UNITED STATES
296,000,000
MEXICO
107,000,000
BERMUDA (U.K.)
CUBA
JAMAICA
HAITI
DOMINICAN REPUBLIC
PUERTO RICO (U.S.)
HONDURAS
GUATEMALA
EL SALVADOR
NICARAGUA
COSTA RICA
PANAMA
ECUADOR
GUYANA
TRINIDAD & TOBAGO
VENEZUELA
COLOMBIA
BRAZIL
184,000,000
PERU
BOLIVIA
PARAGUAY
CHILE
ARGENTINA
URUGUAY
ICELAND
IRELAND
UNITED KINGDOM
60,000,000
SWEDEN
FINLAND
NORWAY
DENMARK
ESTONIA
LATVIA
LITHUANIA
RUSSIA
143,000,000
BELARUS
AZERBAIJAN
GEORGIA
GERMANY
82,000,000
POLAND
SLOVAKIA
UKRAINE
47,000,000
NETHERLANDS
BELGIUM
LUX.
CZECH REP.
MOLDOVA
AUSTRIA
HUNGARY
FRANCE
60,000,000
ARMENIA
SWITZERLAND
ROMANIA
SLOVENIA
CROATIA
BULGARIA
BOSNIA & HERZEGOVINA
MONTENEGRO
MACEDONIA
TURKEY
73,000,000
SPAIN
PORTUGAL
SERBIA
ALBANIA
GREECE
ITALY
59,000,000
CYPRUS
SYRIA
LEBANON
JORDAN
ISRAEL
SAUDI ARABIA
OMAN
YEMEN
ERITREA
CAPE VERDE
MOROCCO
BURKINA FASO
ALGERIA
LIBYA
TUNISIA
MALI
MAURITANIA
GAMBIA
SENEGAL
GUINEA-BISSAU
GUINEA
GHANA
NIGER
CHAD
EGYPT
74,000,000
NIGERIA
132,000,000
SUDAN
ETHIOPIA
77,000,000
SIERRA LEONE
LIBERIA
CÔTE D'IVOIRE
TOGO
BENIN
CAMEROON
GABON
CONGO
CENTRAL AFRICAN REPUBLIC
DEM. REP. OF THE CONGO
UGANDA
KENYA
RWANDA
TANZANIA
BURUNDI
MALAWI
ANGOLA
ZAMBIA
MOZAMBIQUE
NAMIBIA
ZIMBABWE
BOTSWANA
SOUTH AFRICA
LESOTHO
SWAZILAND
MADAGASCAR

9
10
11
12
13
14
15
16
A
B
C
D
E
F
G
H
J
K
MONGOLIA
NORTH KOREA
SOUTH KOREA
KAZAKHSTAN
KYRGYZSTAN
UZBEKISTAN
TAJIKISTAN
TURKMENISTAN
CHINA 1,304,000,000
JAPAN 128,000,000
AFGHANISTAN
IRAN 70,000,000
NEPAL
PAKISTAN 162,000,000
IRAQ
KUWAIT
BAHRAIN
QATAR
U.A.E.
TAIWAN
VIETNAM 83,000,000
MYANMAR (BURMA)
BANGLADESH 144,000,000
LAOS
THAILAND 66,000,000
INDIA 1,104,000,000
SOMALIA
CAMBODIA
PHILIPPINES 85,000,000
MALAYSIA
SINGAPORE
PAPUA NEW GUINEA
I N D O N E S I A 222,000,000
SOLOMON ISLANDS
FIJI ISLANDS
SRI LANKA
EAST TIMOR (TIMOR-LESTE)
AUSTRALIA
NEW ZEALAND
POPULATION GROWTH RATE (excluding effects of migration)
3% and above
2-2.9%
1-1.9%
0-.9%
Population loss
Each square represents one million people.
CIA, The World Factbook, 2006; Population Reference Bureau, 2005 World Population Data Sheet, 2006.
Not all countries shown

# GEOGRAPHIC DICTIONARY

**As you read about the world's geography, you will encounter the terms listed below. Many of the terms are pictured in the diagram.**

**absolute location** exact location of a place on the Earth described by global coordinates

**basin** area of land drained by a given river and its branches; area of land surrounded by lands of higher elevations

**bay** part of a large body of water that extends into a shoreline, generally smaller than a gulf

**canyon** deep and narrow valley with steep walls

**cape** point of land that extends into a river, lake, or ocean

**channel** wide strait or waterway between two landmasses that lie close to each other; deep part of a river or other waterway

**cliff** steep, high wall of rock, Earth, or ice

**continent** one of the seven large landmasses on the Earth

**delta** flat, low-lying land built up from soil carried downstream by a river and deposited at its mouth

**divide** stretch of high land that separates river systems

**downstream** direction in which a river or stream flows from its source to its mouth

**elevation** height of land above sea level

**Equator** imaginary line that runs around the Earth halfway between the North and South Poles; used as the starting point to measure degrees of north and south latitude

**glacier** large, thick body of slowly moving ice

**gulf** part of a large body of water that extends into a shoreline, generally larger and more deeply indented than a bay

**harbor** a sheltered place along a shoreline where ships can anchor safely

**highland** elevated land area such as a hill, mountain, or plateau

**hill** elevated land with sloping sides and rounded summit; generally smaller than a mountain

**island** land area, smaller than a continent, completely surrounded by water

**isthmus** narrow stretch of land connecting two larger land areas

**lake** a sizable inland body of water

**latitude** distance north or south of the Equator, measured in degrees

**longitude** distance east or west of the Prime Meridian, measured in degrees

**lowland** land, usually level, at a low elevation

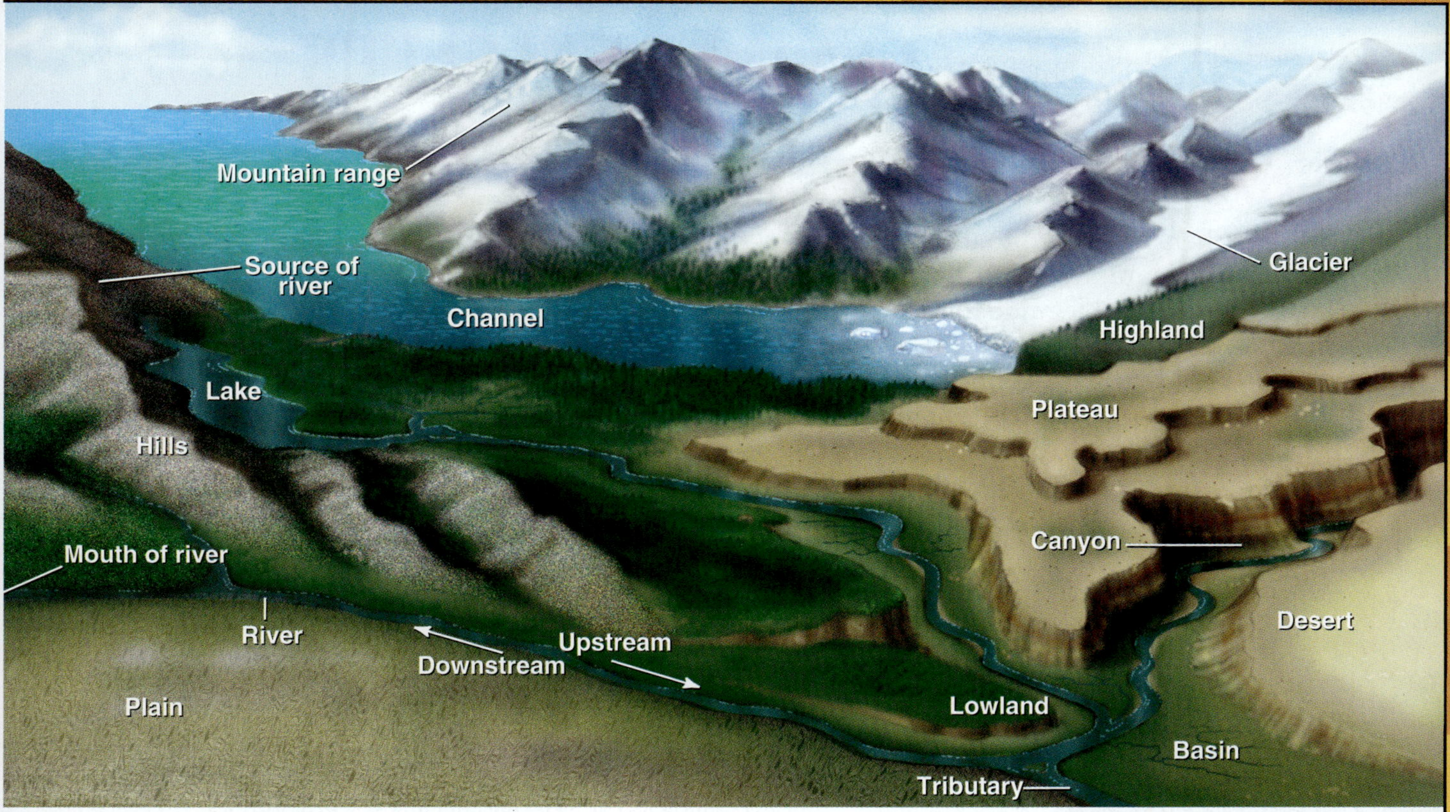


**map** drawing of the Earth shown on a flat surface

**meridian** one of many lines on the global grid running from the North Pole to the South Pole; used to measure degrees of longitude

**mesa** broad, flat-topped landform with steep sides; smaller than a plateau

**mountain** land with steep sides that rises sharply (1,000 feet or more) from surrounding land; generally larger and more rugged than a hill

**mountain peak** pointed top of a mountain

**mountain range** a series of connected mountains

**mouth** (of a river) place where a stream or river flows into a larger body of water

**ocean** one of the four major bodies of salt water that surround the continents

**ocean current** stream of either cold or warm water that moves in a definite direction through an ocean

**parallel** one of many lines on the global grid that circles the Earth north or south of the Equator; used to measure degrees of latitude

**peninsula** body of land jutting into a lake or ocean, surrounded on three sides by water

**physical feature** characteristic of a place occurring naturally, such as a landform, body of water, climate pattern, or resource

**plain** area of level land, usually at low elevation and often covered with grasses

**plateau** area of flat or rolling land at a high elevation, about 300 to 3,000 feet (90 to 900 m) high

**Prime Meridian** line of the global grid running from the North Pole to the South Pole at Greenwich, England; starting point for measuring degrees of east and west longitude

**relief** changes in elevation over a given area of land

**river** large natural stream of water that runs through the land

**sea** large body of water completely or partly surrounded by land

**seacoast** land lying next to a sea or an ocean

**sound** broad inland body of water, often between a coastline and one or more islands off the coast

**source** (of a river) place where a river or stream begins, often in highlands

**strait** narrow stretch of water joining two larger bodies of water

**tributary** small river or stream that flows into a large river or stream; a branch of the river

**upstream** direction opposite the flow of a river; toward the source of a river or stream

**valley** area of low land usually between hills or mountains

**volcano** mountain or hill created as liquid rock and ash erupt from inside the Earth

# ESSENTIAL ELEMENTS

## How Do I Study Geography?

Geographers have tried to understand the best way to teach and learn about geography, so they created the *Five Themes of Geography.* The themes acted as a guide for teaching the basic ideas about geography to students. However, many thought that the Five Themes were too broad. In 1994, geographers created 18 national geography standards. These standards were more detailed about what should be taught and learned. The Six Essential Elements act as a bridge connecting the Five Themes with the standards.

## 5 Themes of Geography

### 1 Location

Location describes where something is. Absolute location describes a place's exact position on the Earth's surface. Relative location expresses where a place is in relation to another place.

### 2 Place

Place describes the physical and human characteristics that make a location unique.

### 3 Regions

Regions are areas that share common characteristics.

### 4 Movement

Movement explains how and why people and things move and are connected.

### 5 Human-Environment Interaction

Human-Environment Interaction describes the relationship between people and their environment.

# 6 Essential Elements

# 18 Geography Standards

## I. The World in Spatial Terms

Geographers look to see where a place is located. Location acts as a starting point to answer "Where Is It?" The location of a place helps you orient yourself as to where you are.

1 How to use maps and other tools
2 How to use mental maps to organize information
3 How to analyze the spatial organization of people, places, and environments

## II. Places and Regions

**Place** describes physical characteristics such as landforms, climate, and plant or animal life. It might also describe human characteristics, including language and way of life. Places can also be organized into regions. **Regions** are places united by one or more characteristics.

4 The physical and human characteristics of places
5 How people create regions to interpret Earth's complexity
6 How culture and experience influence people's perceptions of places and regions

## III. Physical Systems

Geographers study how physical systems, such as hurricanes, volcanoes, and glaciers, shape the surface of the Earth. They also look at how plants and animals depend upon one another and their surroundings for their survival.

## IV. Human Systems

People shape the world in which they live. They settle in certain places but not in others. An ongoing theme in geography is the movement of people, ideas, and goods.

## V. Environment and Society

How does the relationship between people and their natural surroundings influence the way people live? Geographers study how people use the environment and how their actions affect the environment.

7 The physical processes that shape Earth's surface
8 The distribution of ecosystems on Earth's surface
9 The characteristics, distribution, and migration of human populations
10 The complexity of Earth's cultural mosaics
11 The patterns and networks of economic interdependence
12 The patterns of human settlement
13 The forces of cooperation and conflict
14 How human actions modify the physical environment
15 How physical systems affect human systems
16 The meaning, use, and distribution of resources

## VI. The Uses of Geography

Knowledge of geography helps us understand the relationships among people, places, and environments over time. Applying geographic skills helps you understand the past and prepare for the future.

17 How to apply geography to interpret the past
18 How to apply geography to interpret the present and plan for the future

NATIONAL GEOGRAPHIC

# GEOGRAPHY SKILLS HANDBOOK

## CONTENTS



**Throughout this text, you will discover how geography has shaped the course of events in world history. Landforms, waterways, climate, and natural resources all have helped or hindered human activities. Usually people have learned either to adapt to their environments or to transform it to meet their needs. The resources in this Geography Skills Handbook will help you get the most out of your textbook—and provide you with skills you will use for the rest of your life.**

*Geographers use a wide array of tools to collect and analyze information to help them understand the Earth. The study of geography is more than knowing a lot of facts about places. Rather, it has more to do with asking questions about the Earth, pursuing their answers, and solving problems. Thus, one of the most important geographic tools is inside your head: the ability to think geographically.*

# Globes and Maps

A **globe** is a scale model of the Earth. Because Earth is round, a globe presents the most accurate depiction of geographic information such as area, distance, and direction. However, globes show little close-up detail. A printed **map** is a symbolic representation of all or part of the planet. Unlike globes, maps can show small areas in great detail.

## From 3-D to 2-D

Think about the surface of the Earth as the peel of an orange. To flatten the peel, you have to cut it like the globe shown here. To create maps that are not interrupted, mapmakers, or **cartographers**, use mathematical formulas to transfer information from the three-dimensional globe to the two-dimensional map. However, when the curves of a globe become straight lines on a map, distortion of size, shape, distance, or area occurs.

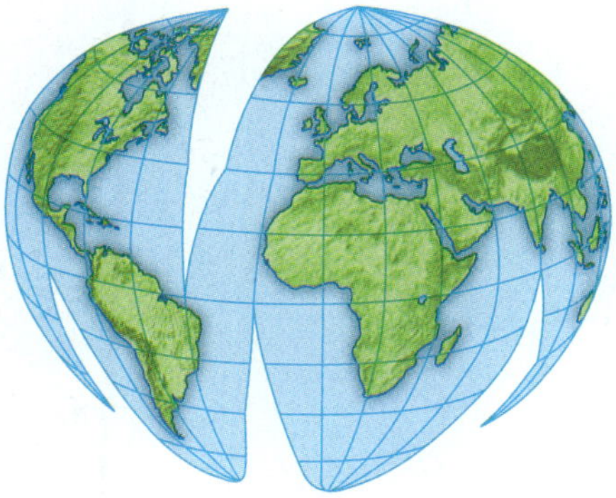

## Great Circle Routes

A straight line of true direction—one that runs directly from west to east, for example—is not always the shortest distance between two points. This is due to the curvature of the Earth. To find the shortest distance, stretch a piece of string around a globe from one point to the other. The string will form part of a *great circle*, an imaginary line that follows the curve of the Earth. Ship captains and airline pilots use these **great circle routes** to reduce travel time and conserve fuel.

The idea of a great circle route is an important difference between globes and maps. A round globe accurately shows a great circle route, as indicated on the top right map. However, the flat map below it shows the great circle distance (dotted line) between Tokyo and Los Angeles to be far longer than the true direction distance (solid line). In fact, the great circle distance is 315 miles (506 km) shorter.

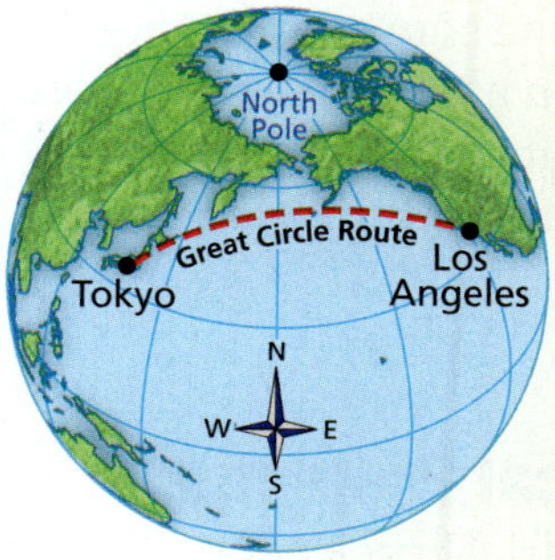

### PRACTICING THE SKILL

1. **Explain** the significance of: globe, map, cartographer, great circle route.
2. **Describe** the problems that arise when the curves of a globe become straight lines on a map.
3. **Use** a Venn diagram like the one below to identify the similarities and differences between globes and maps.

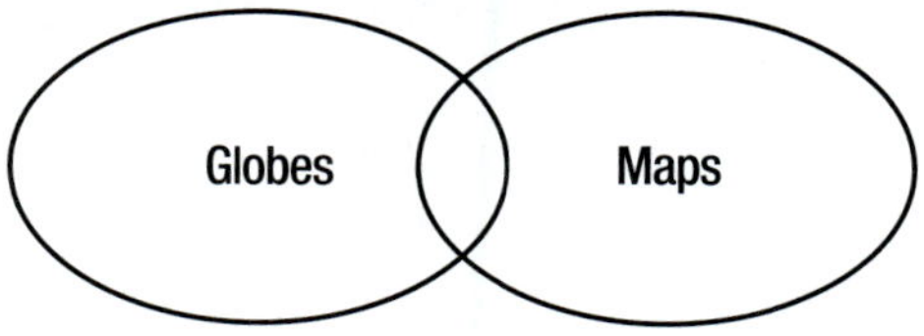

# Projections

To create maps, cartographers project the round Earth onto a flat surface—making a **map projection**. Distance, shape, direction, or size may be distorted by a projection. As a result, the purpose of the map usually dictates which projection is used. There are many kinds of map projections, some with general names and some named for the cartographers who developed them. Three basic categories of map projections are shown here: **planar**, **cylindrical**, and **conic**.

## Planar Projection

A planar projection shows the Earth centered in such a way that a straight line coming from the center to any other point represents the shortest distance. Also known as an azimuthal projection, it is most accurate at its center. As a result, it is often used for maps of the Poles.

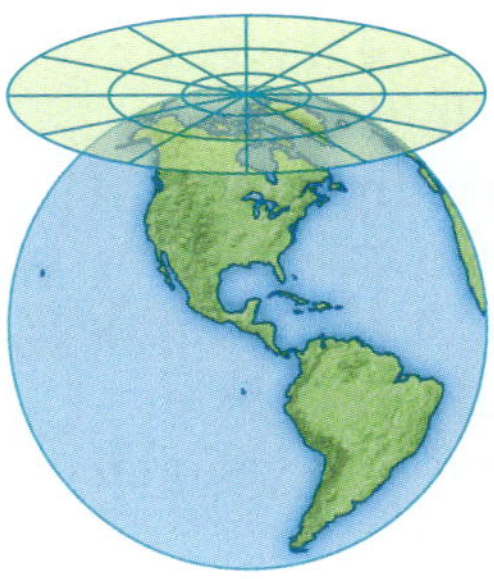

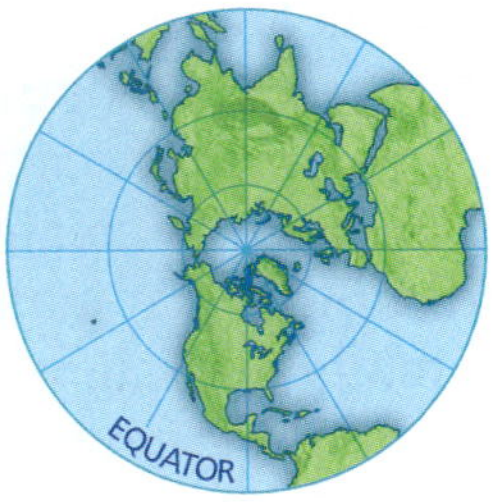


## Cylindrical Projection

A cylindrical projection is based on the projection of the globe onto a cylinder. This projection is most accurate near the Equator, but shapes and distances are distorted near the Poles.

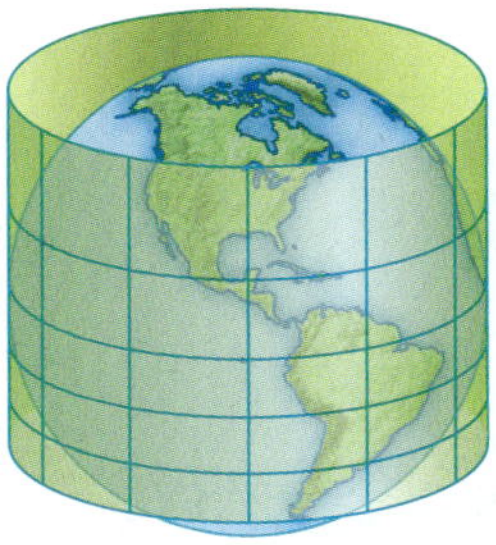

## Conic Projection

A conic projection comes from placing a cone over part of a globe. Conic projections are best suited for showing limited east-west areas that are not too far from the Equator. For these uses, a conic projection can indicate distances and directions fairly accurately.

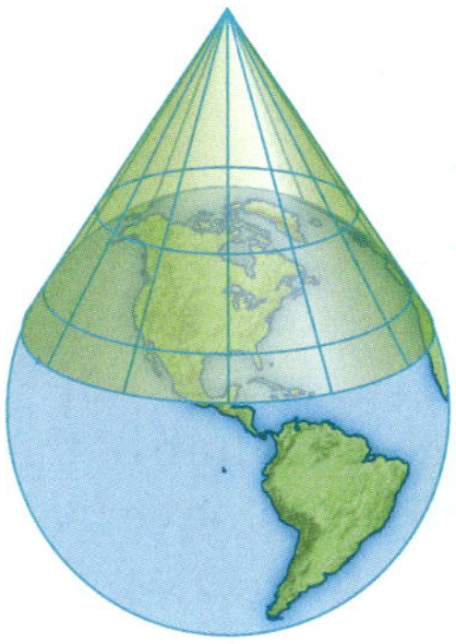

## Common Map Projections

Each type of map projection has advantages and some degree of inaccuracy. Four of the most common projections are shown here.

### Winkel Tripel Projection

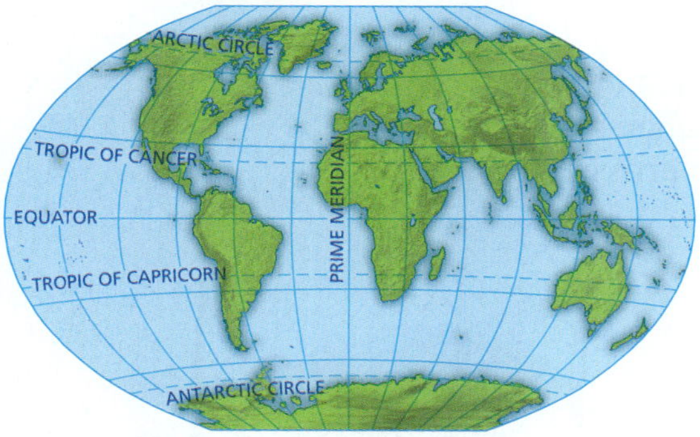


Most general reference world maps are the Winkel Tripel projection. It provides a good balance between the size and shape of land areas as they are shown on the map. Even the polar areas are depicted with little distortion of size and shape.

### Robinson Projection

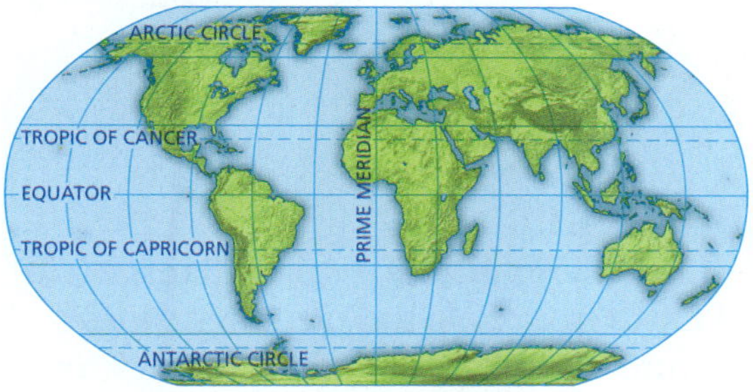


The Robinson projection has minor distortions. The sizes and shapes near the eastern and western edges of the map are accurate, and outlines of the continents appear much as they do on the globe. However, the polar areas are flattened.

### Goode's Interrupted Equal-Area Projection

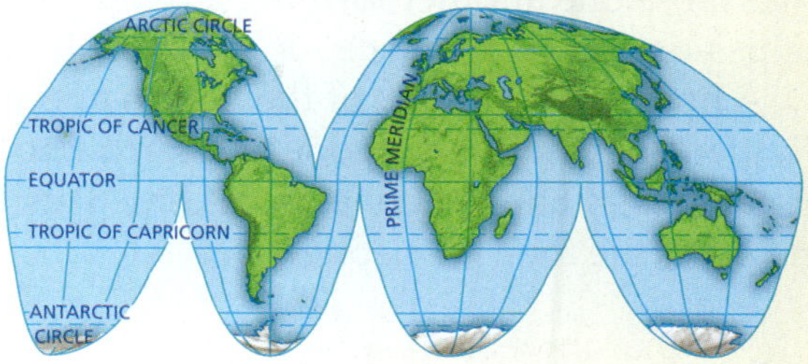


An **interrupted projection** looks something like a globe that has been cut apart and laid flat. Goode's Interrupted Equal-Area projection shows the true size and shape of Earth's landmasses, but distances are generally distorted.

### Mercator Projection

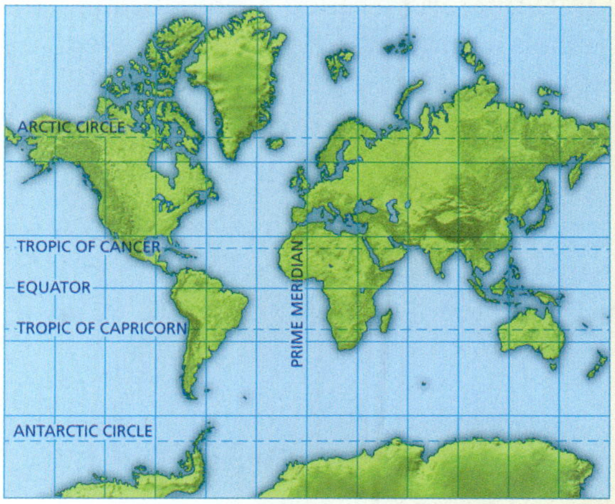


The Mercator projection increasingly distorts size and distance as it moves away from the Equator. However, Mercator projections do accurately show true directions and the shapes of landmasses, making these maps useful for sea travel.

### PRACTICING THE SKILL

1. **Explain** the significance of: map projection, planar, cylindrical, conic, interrupted projection.
2. **How** does a cartographer determine which map projection to use?
3. **How** is Goode's Interrupted Equal-Area projection different from the Mercator projection?
4. **Which** of the four common projections described above is the best one to use when showing the entire world? Why?
5. **Use** a Venn diagram like the one below to identify the similarities and differences between the Winkel Tripel and Mercator projections.

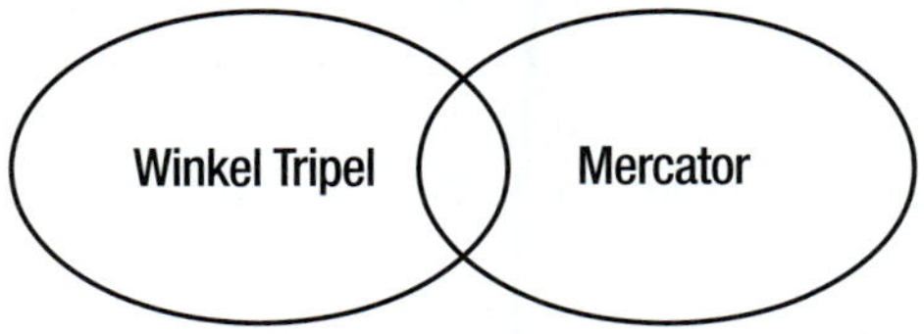

# Determining Location

Geography is often said to begin with the question: *Where?* The basic tool for answering the question is **location.** Lines on globes and maps provide information that can help you locate places. These lines cross one another forming a pattern called a **grid system,** which helps you find exact places on the Earth's surface.

A **hemisphere** is one of the halves into which the Earth is divided. Geographers divide the Earth into hemispheres to help them classify and describe places on Earth. Most places are located in two of the four hemispheres.

## Latitude

Lines of **latitude,** or parallels, circle the Earth parallel to the Equator and measure the distance north or south of the Equator in degrees. The Equator is measured at 0° latitude, while the Poles lie at latitudes 90°N (north) and 90°S (south). Parallels north of the Equator are called north latitude. Parallels south of the Equator are called south latitude.

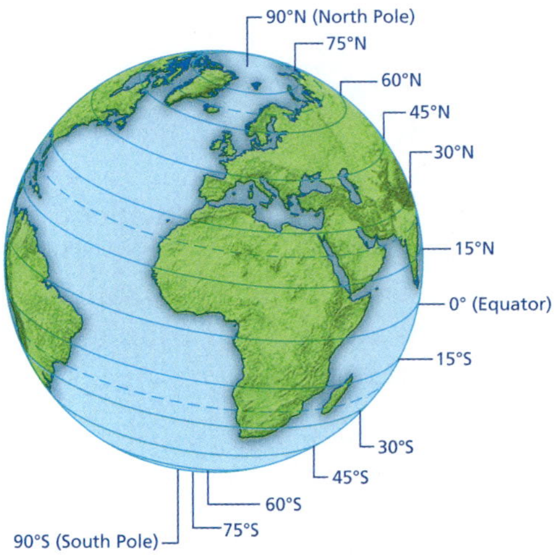


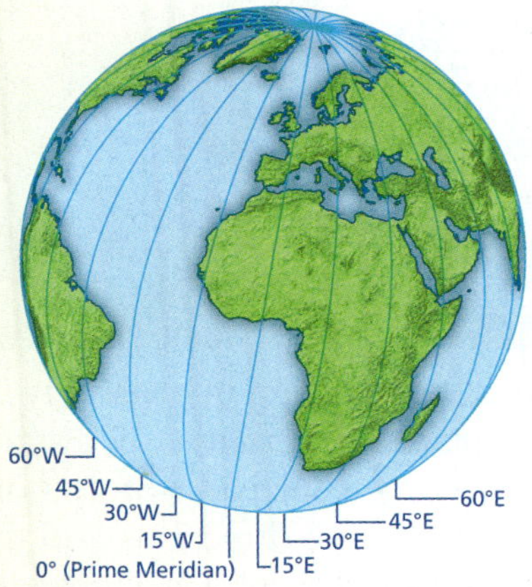


## Longitude

Lines of **longitude,** or meridians, circle the Earth from Pole to Pole. These lines measure distance east or west of the **Prime Meridian** at 0° longitude. Meridians east of the Prime Meridian are known as east longitude. Meridians west of the Prime Meridian are known as west longitude. The 180° meridian on the opposite side of the Earth is called the International Date Line.

## The Global Grid

Every place has a global address, or **absolute location.** You can identify the absolute location of a place by naming the latitude and longitude lines that cross exactly at that place. For example, Tokyo, Japan, is located at 36°N latitude and 140°E longitude. For more precise readings, each degree is further divided into 60 units called minutes.

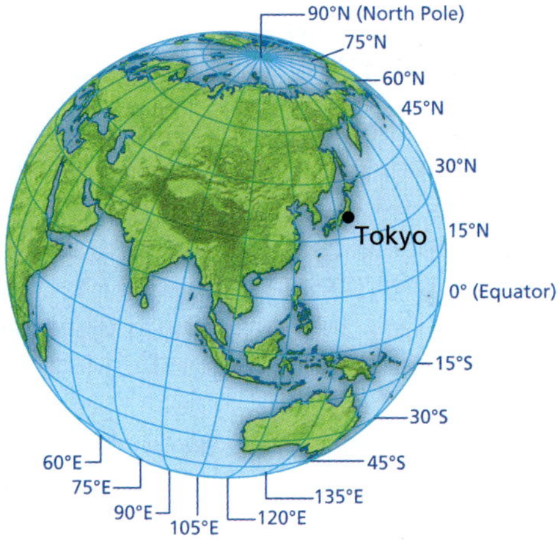

## Northern and Southern Hemispheres

The diagram below shows that the Equator divides the Earth into the Northern and Southern Hemispheres. Everything north of the Equator is in the **Northern Hemisphere**. Everything south of the Equator is in the **Southern Hemisphere**.

**Northern Hemisphere**

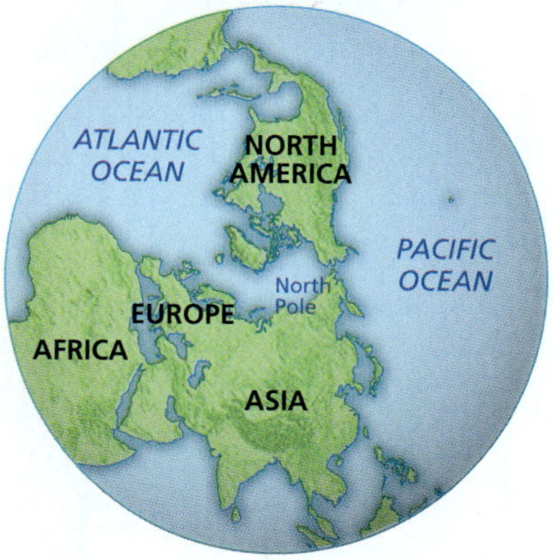


**Southern Hemisphere**

## Eastern and Western Hemispheres

The Prime Meridian and the International Date Line divide the Earth into the Eastern and Western Hemispheres. Everything east of the Prime Meridian for 180° is in the **Eastern Hemisphere**. Everything west of the Prime Meridian for 180° is in the **Western Hemisphere**.

**Eastern Hemisphere**

**Western Hemisphere**

### PRACTICING THE SKILL

1. **Explain** the significance of: location, grid system, hemisphere, Northern Hemisphere, Southern Hemisphere, Eastern Hemisphere, Western Hemisphere, latitude, longitude, Prime Meridian, absolute location.
2. **Why** do all maps label the Equator 0° latitude and the Prime Meridian 0° longitude?
3. **Which** lines of latitude and longitude divide the Earth into hemispheres?
4. **Using** the Reference Atlas maps, fill in a chart by writing the latitude and longitude of three world cities. Have a partner try to identify the cities listed in your chart.
5. **Use** a chart like the one below to identify the continents in each hemisphere. Some may be in more than one hemisphere.

| Hemisphere | Continents |
|---|---|
| Northern | |
| Southern | |
| Eastern | |
| Western | |

# Reading a Map

In addition to latitude and longitude, maps feature other important tools to help you interpret the information they contain. Learning to use these map tools will help you read the symbolic language of maps more easily.

### Key
The **key** lists and explains the symbols, colors, and lines used on the map. The key is sometimes called a legend.

### Title
The title tells you what kind of information the map is showing.

### Scale Bar
The **scale bar** shows the relationship between map measurements and actual distances on the Earth. By laying a ruler along the scale bar, you can calculate how many miles or kilometers are represented per inch or centimeter. The map projection used to create the map is often listed near the scale bar.

### Compass Rose
The **compass rose** indicates directions. The four **cardinal directions**—north, south, east, and west—are usually indicated with arrows or the points of a star. The **intermediate directions**—northeast, northwest, southeast, and southwest—may also be shown.

### Cities
Cities are represented by a dot. Sometimes the relative sizes of cities are shown using dots of different sizes.

### Capitals
National capitals are often represented by a star within a circle.

### Boundary Lines
On political maps of large areas, boundary lines highlight the borders between different countries or states.

## Using Scale

All maps are drawn to a certain scale. **Scale** is a consistent, proportional relationship between the measurements shown on the map and the measurement of the Earth's surface.

**Small-Scale Maps** A small-scale map, like this political map of France, can show a large area but little detail. Note that the scale bar on this map indicates that about 1 inch is equal to 200 miles.

**Large-Scale Maps** A large-scale map, like this map of Paris, can show a small area with a great amount of detail. Study the scale bar. Note that the map measurements correspond to much smaller distances than on the map of France.

## Absolute and Relative Location

As you learned on page GH6, absolute location is the exact point where a line of latitude crosses a line of longitude. Another way to indicate location is by **relative location**, or the location of one place in relation to another. To find relative location, find a reference point—a location you already know—on a map. Then look in the appropriate direction for the new location. For example, locate Paris (your reference point) on the map of France above. The relative location of Lyon can be described as southeast of Paris.

**PRACTICING THE SKILL**

1. **Explain** the significance of: key, compass rose, cardinal directions, intermediate directions, scale bar, scale, relative location.
2. **Describe** the elements of a map that help you interpret the information displayed on the map.
3. **How** does the scale bar help you determine distances on the Earth's surface?
4. **Describe** the relative location of your school in two different ways.
5. **Use** a Venn diagram to identify the similarities and differences of small-scale maps and large-scale maps.

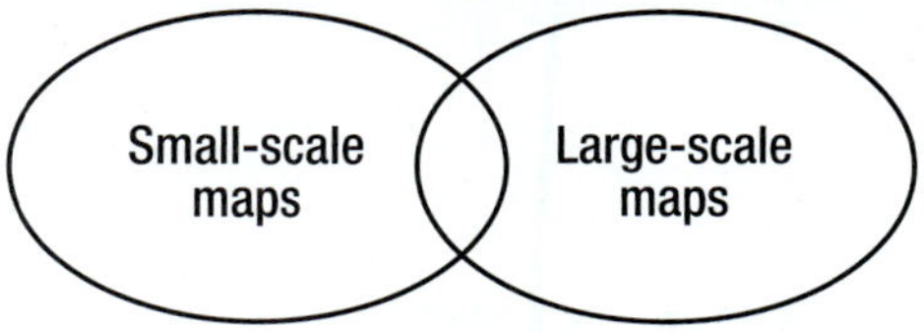

# Physical and Political Maps

Physical and political are the two main types of maps in this book. A **physical map** shows the location and the topography, or shape of the Earth's physical features. A study of an area's physical features often helps explain its historical development. A **political map** shows the boundaries and locations of political units such as countries, states, and cities. Nonsubject area is usually shown in a different color to set it apart from the main area of the map. This nonsubject area gives you a context for the region you are studying.

## Physical Maps

Physical maps use shading and texture to show general relief—the differences in elevation, or height, of landforms. Landforms are physical features such as plains, mountains, plateaus, and valleys. Physical maps show rivers, streams, lakes, and other water features.

## Political Maps

Many features on a political map are human-made, or determined by humans rather than by nature. Some human-made features are boundaries, capital cities, and roads. Political maps may also show physical features such as mountains and rivers.

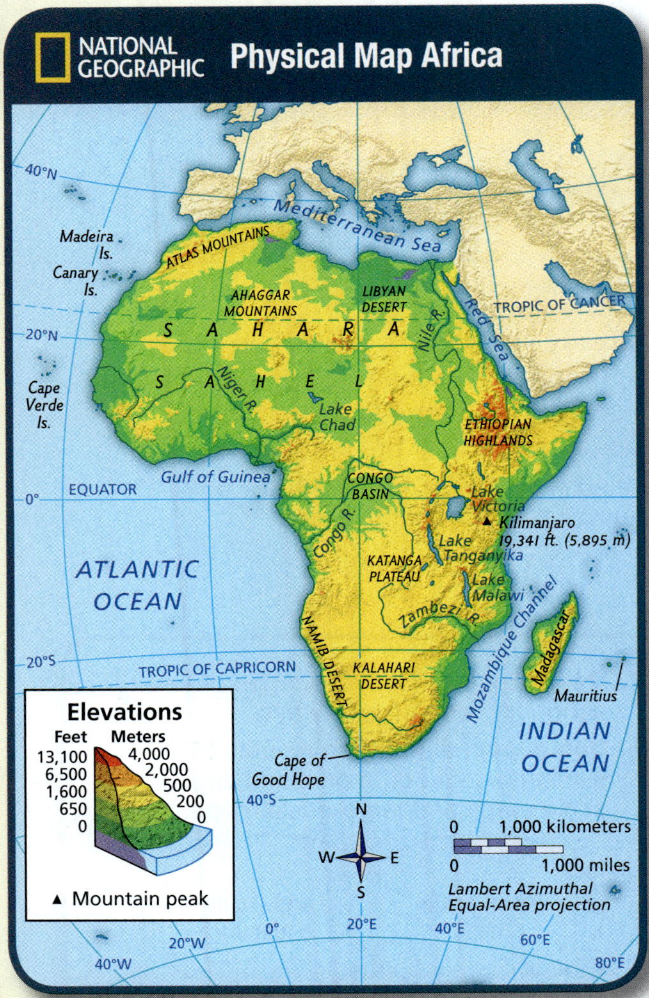

# Thematic Maps

Maps that emphasize a particular kind of information or a single idea are called **thematic maps**. This textbook includes thematic maps that show ancient civilizations, migrations, natural resources, war, and trade and exploration.

## Qualitative Maps

Maps that use colors, symbols, lines, or dots to show information related to a specific idea are called **qualitative maps**.

## Flow-Line Maps

Maps that use arrows to show the movement of people, ideas, or physical systems are called **flow-line maps**.

NATIONAL GEOGRAPHIC **Qualitative Map**

NATIONAL GEOGRAPHIC **Flow-Line Map**

**PRACTICING THE SKILL**

1. **Explain** the significance of: physical map, political map, thematic map, qualitative map, flow-line map.
2. **Complete** a Venn diagram like the one to the right to compare physical and political maps.

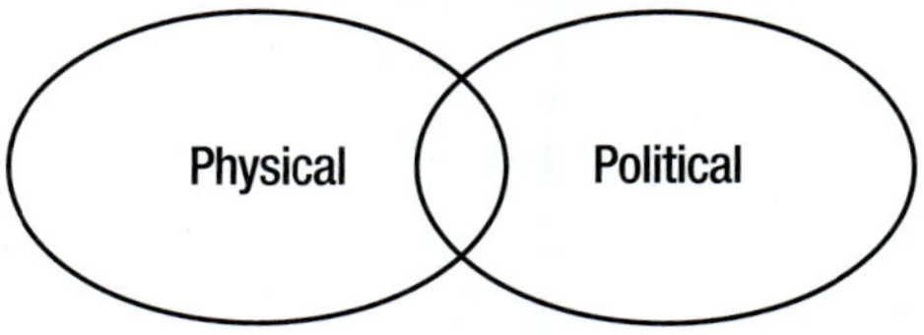

# Understanding Earth's Physical Systems

Earth is composed of four **physical systems**. The atmosphere, hydrosphere, and lithosphere form the biosphere, the part of the Earth where life exists. A change in one physical system can affect one or more of the other physical systems. Interactions of Earth's physical systems account for changes to our world, from earthquakes to erosion to the greenhouse effect.

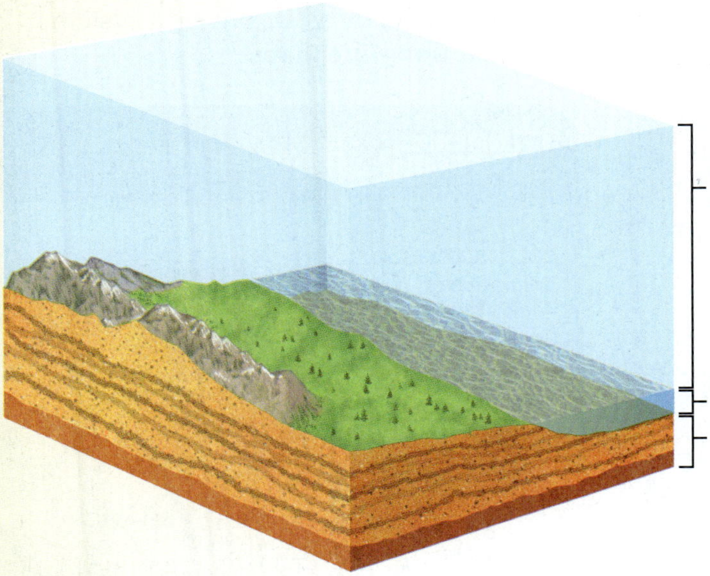

**Biosphere** People, animals, and plants live in the biosphere—water, land, and air. Life outside the biosphere, such as on a space station, can exist only with mechanical life-support systems.

**Atmosphere** The layer of gases (78 percent nitrogen, 21 percent oxygen, and 1 percent other) which extends 348 miles (560 km) above Earth's surface makes up the atmosphere.

**Hydrosphere** Water in the form of oceans, rivers, and glaciers accounts for 70 percent of Earth's surface and is called the hydrosphere.

**Lithosphere** The lithosphere is the 30 percent of Earth's surface that is land, including continents and islands.

## Earth's Physical Systems

| | Some Interactions | Example |
|---|---|---|
| **Atmosphere:** | | |
| **Monsoons** | Seasonal winds blow warm, moist ocean air across land, causing rainfall; dry winter winds blow across land to sea. | Monsoons water crops and generate electricity. In 2007 more than 2,000 people in India, Pakistan, and Bangladesh died from monsoonal flooding. |
| **Rain Shadow Effect** | Winds push moist air up a mountain side; air cools, releasing precipitation; dry air descends on the opposite side of mountain. | Death Valley, in California and Nevada, is a large desert surrounded by mountains. It is one of the hottest places on Earth: 134° F recorded in 1913. |
| **Hydrosphere:** | | |
| **Ocean Currents** | Earth's rotation, water temperature, and wind cause ocean currents: the flow of cold or warm water in a specific direction. | The Gulf Stream—a warm-water current flowing from the Gulf of Mexico to the North Atlantic—warms the coast of Europe. |
| **Water Cycle** | Surface water evaporates, as the air rises it cools, water vapor condenses, forming clouds, and precipitation follows. | In 1996 over two days, about 70" of "lake effect" snow fell on Cleveland, Ohio. Warm moist air from Lake Erie met cold drier air, causing the snowfall. |
| **Lithosphere:** | | |
| **Earthquakes** | Violent movements of tectonic plates cause land or ocean floor to drop or rise, causing tsunamis—tidal waves. | In 1755 the Lisbon Earthquake flattened buildings; a 50-foot tsunami and fires destroyed the rest of the Portuguese capital, killing about 50,000. |
| **Volcanoes** | Eruptions of molten lava, accompanied by ash and gas, can form new islands or blow up mountains and kill surrounding life forms. | In A.D. 79 Mount Vesuvius erupted, burying the cities of Pompeii and Herculaneum in Italy. Vesuvius has erupted 50 times since then. |

# Ecosystems and Biodiversity

An **ecosystem** is a community of plants and animals that depend upon one another, and their surroundings, for survival. There are many different ecosystems on Earth. Plants, animals, and micro-organisms interact within an ecosystem. **Biodiversity** is the variation of life forms within an ecosystem.

**Rain Forests** are one type of ecosystem. Nowhere is biodiversity more apparent than in tropical rain forests, which harbor at least half of all animal and plant species on Earth. Although the world's largest remaining tropical rain forests are in Brazil, there are temperate rain forests from North America to Australia, as seen in the photograph.

**Desert** climates occur in just under one-third of the Earth's total land area. The natural vegetation of a desert ecosystem consists of scrub and cactus, plants that tolerate low and unreliable precipitation, low humidity, and wide temperature ranges. This arid landscape is in Arizona.

**Biodiversity at Risk** As human communities expand, they threaten natural ecosystems. Because the Earth's land, air, and water are interrelated, what affects one part of the system affects all the other parts—including humans and other living things. The photograph shows deforestation, in this case clear-cutting of the Brazilian rain forest.

## PRACTICING THE SKILL

1. **Explain** the significance of: physical systems, ecosystem, biodiversity.
2. **Complete** a table like the one to the right to list some of the types of interactions in the physical systems.

| | Interactions |
|---|---|
| Atmosphere | |
| Hydrosphere | |
| Lithosphere | |

UNIT 1

# The First Civilizations and Empires

## Prehistory–A.D. 500

### ▶ Why It Matters

For hundreds of thousands of years, human beings survived by hunting, fishing, and gathering food and supplies in an often hostile environment. In the space of a few thousand years, human beings began to master the art of growing food crops. As more food was produced, the population grew, and people began to live in cities, form governments, and develop writing and art. Historians call this process the beginning of civilization.

*The "Maiden Porch" of the Erechtheum, overlooking the city of Athens, Greece, is an example of Greek architecture from the fifth century B.C.*

# CHAPTER 1

# The First Humans

## Prehistory–3500 B.C.

**Section 1** Early Humans

**Section 2** The Neolithic Revolution

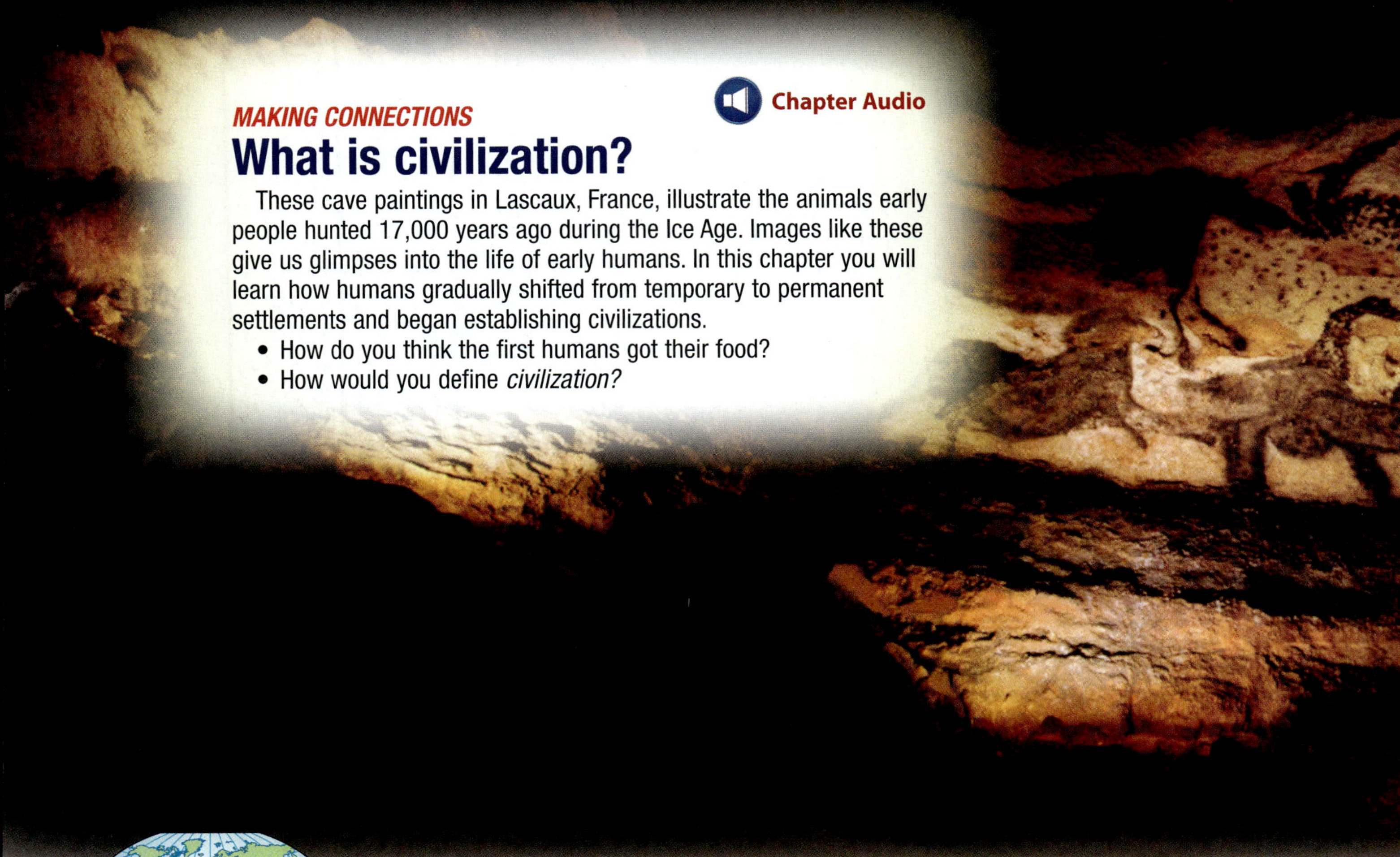

*MAKING CONNECTIONS*

Chapter Audio

## What is civilization?

These cave paintings in Lascaux, France, illustrate the animals early people hunted 17,000 years ago during the Ice Age. Images like these give us glimpses into the life of early humans. In this chapter you will learn how humans gradually shifted from temporary to permanent settlements and began establishing civilizations.

- How do you think the first humans got their food?
- How would you define *civilization?*

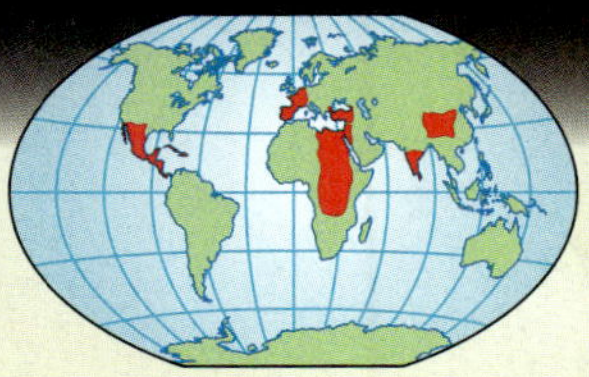

THE WORLD ▶

**c. 3,000,000 B.C.** Australopithecines flourish in Africa

**c. 1,500,000 B.C.** *Homo erectus* appears

3,500,000 B.C. — 2,000,000 B.C. — 200,000 B.C.

**c. 2,500,000 B.C.** Paleolithic humans carve with stone tools

**c. 250,000 B.C.** *Homo sapiens* species develops

**c. 100,000 B.C.**
Neanderthals living in Germany

**c. 8000 B.C.**
Systematic agriculture develops

**150,000 B.C.** — **10,000 B.C.** — **3500 B.C.**

**c. 8000 B.C.**
Neolithic humans practice burial rituals

**3000 B.C.**
Bronze Age begins

**FOLDABLES™ Study Organizer**

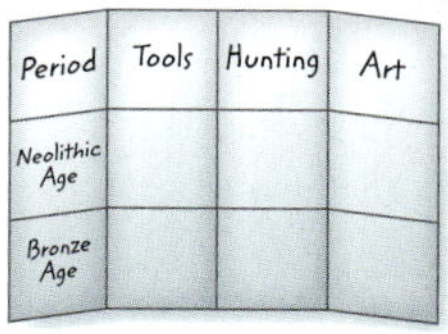


**Describing** Create a Three-Tab Book to record aspects of tools, hunting, and art that occurred during the Neolithic Age and the Bronze Age. Conduct additional research to add facts, illustrations, or maps to your Foldable.

**History ONLINE** Visit glencoe.com and enter *QuickPass*™ code GWHEA7447c1 for Chapter 1 resources.

SECTION 1

Section Audio    Spotlight Video

# Early Humans

### GUIDE TO READING

**The BIG Idea**

**Physical Geography** Human life developed in different stages over millions of years and by 10,000 B.C., *Homo sapiens sapiens* had spread throughout the world.

**Content Vocabulary**

- prehistory *(p. 4)*
- archaeology *(p. 4)*
- artifact *(p. 4)*
- anthropology *(p. 4)*
- fossil *(p. 4)*
- hominid *(p. 6)*
- *Australopithecus (p. 7)*
- *Homo sapiens sapiens (p. 7)*
- "out-of-Africa" theory *(p. 7)*

**Academic Vocabulary**

- theory *(p. 4)*
- survive *(p. 8)*

**People and Places**

- Olduvai Gorge *(p. 6)*
- Paleolithic Age *(p. 8)*

**Reading Strategy**

**Summarizing Information** As you read, create a chart like the one below showing the effects of three tools on the lifestyle of early humankind.

| Tool | Effect |
|---|---|
| | |
| | |
| | |

*Where did early humans live? How did they live, and what happened to them? To answer these questions, scientists study the evidence left by prehistoric people. Although researchers have new and better ways of studying the past, there is much we still do not know.*

## Before History

**MAIN IDEA** Scientists use fossils and artifacts as clues to how early humans lived.

***HISTORY & YOU*** What would people in the future think of American culture based on what we leave behind?

Historians rely mostly on documents, or written records, to create their pictures of the past. However, no written records exist for the prehistory of humankind. In fact, **prehistory** means the time before writing was developed. The story of prehistoric humans depends on archaeological and, more recently, biological evidence. Archaeologists and anthropologists use this information to create **theories** about our early past.

### Archaeology and Anthropology

**Archaeology** is the study of past societies through analysis of what people left behind. Archaeologists dig up and examine **artifacts**—objects made by humans. Artifacts may be tools, weapons, art, and even buildings made by early humans.

**Anthropology** is the study of human life and culture. Culture includes what people wear, how they organize their society, and what they value. Anthropologists use artifacts and human **fossils** to create a picture of people's everyday lives. Fossils are rocklike remains of biological organisms—a leaf imprint or a skeleton.

Archaeologists and anthropologists have developed scientific methods to carry out their work. They excavate, or dig up land, at sites around the globe to uncover fossil remains of early humans, ancient cities, burial grounds, and other objects. The examination and analysis of these remains give archaeologists a better understanding of ancient societies. By examining artifacts such as pottery, tools, and weapons, for example, these scientists learn about the social and military structures of a society. By analyzing bones, skins, and plant seeds, they are able to piece together the diet and activities of early people. One of the most important and difficult jobs of both archaeologists and anthropologists is dating their finds.

**Geography SKILLS**

1. **Location** On which continent was *Homo habilis* discovered?
2. **Place** Why would caves help preserve paintings?

**Maps In MOtion** See *StudentWorks™ Plus* or glencoe.com.

## Dating Artifacts and Fossils

Dating human fossils and artifacts helps scientists understand when and where the first humans lived.

One method used to determine age is radiocarbon dating. All living things absorb a small amount of radioactive carbon, or C-14, from the atmosphere. After a living thing dies, it slowly loses C-14. By measuring the amount left in an object, a scientist can figure its age. This method is accurate for objects no more than about 50,000 years old.

For objects dating back to 200,000 years ago, scientists can make relatively precise measurements using thermoluminescence. This measures the light given off by electrons trapped in the soil surrounding fossils and artifacts.

Microscopic and biological analyses of organic remains—such as blood, hairs, and plant tissues left on tools and weapons—give scientists still more information. Such analyses have shown that blood molecules may survive millions of years. This recent scientific discovery is especially useful in telling us more about humans, their use of tools, and the animals they killed. Ancient deoxyribonucleic acid (DNA) is providing new information on human evolution. The analysis of plant remains on stone tools yields evidence on the history of farming. All of these techniques give us insight into the lives of early peoples.

**✓Reading Check** **Describing** How do archaeologists and anthropologists determine the ages of fossils and artifacts?

## Early Development

**MAIN IDEA** Using remains and technology, scientists identify important stages in human development.

***HISTORY & YOU*** How did humans change? Read about the early stages of human development.

In recent decades, modern science has produced a clearer picture of how early humans developed. Pieces of the puzzle are still missing, however. When a new skull or skeleton is unearthed, scientists may find that they have to revise their ideas about prehistoric human life.

### Hominids to *Homo Sapiens*

What is a **hominid**? A hominid was a humanlike creature that walked upright. The earliest hominids lived in Africa four million years ago. They existed for millions of years, slowly changing over time.

Louis and Mary Leakey spent most of their lives searching for clues about early human life. They made a dramatic discovery of a skeleton at **Olduvai Gorge** in East Africa. According to their son:

**PRIMARY SOURCE**

"My father was ill that morning, so my mother set out alone . . . but found very little until just before noon, when she noticed a scrap of enormously thick bone protruding from beneath the surface. She instantly realized that it was part of a hominid skull—and that two teeth were embedded in the rock just above it. Elated, she drove back to camp to tell my father Louis. As he remembered it, she rushed in crying, 'I've got him! I've got him! I've got him!'"

—Richard Leakey, *TIME*, July 17, 1959

Leakey's discovery of a hominid in 1959 was the oldest at that time—about 1.8 million years old.

## PEOPLE *in* HISTORY

**Louis Leakey**
1903–1972

**Mary Leakey**
1913–1996 Paleoanthropologists

Paleoanthropologists study early human society. For three generations, beginning with the husband and wife team of Louis and Mary, the Leakeys have searched for early human remains in Africa.

Born in Kenya, Louis discovered some stone tools and an interest in prehistory. In the 1930's, Louis and Mary began looking for evidence of early humans at Olduvai Gorge. Mary is credited with discovering *Proconsul africanus* in 1948, *Australopithecus boisei* in 1959, *Homo habilis* in 1960, and an 89-foot-long trail of early human footprints called the "Laetoli footprints" in 1979. **What do the Leakeys' finds illustrate about where early human life began?**

**Richard Leakey**
1942–present

**Louise Leakey**
1972–present

**Meave Leakey**
1942–present Paleoanthropologists

Richard, a son of Louis and Mary, found his first fossil at age six. Meave, a zoologist, joined Richard's expedition in 1969. Richard and Meave focused their search at Koobi Fora, near Lake Turkana in Kenya. Over a thirty-year period, this Leakey team made 200 significant fossil finds.

Meave and Louise Leakey were named National Geographic Society's explorers-in-residence in 2002. The Leakey mother and daughter paleontologists found a 3.5-million-year-old skull near Turkana. **Why were the Leakeys' fossil finds significant?**

For decades, scientists assumed these earliest of upright creatures must also have used tools. In 1974, Donald Johanson challenged this theory when his team found a new skeleton in Ethiopia. Johanson nicknamed the female skeleton "Lucy" and suggested that she was the common ancestor for several types of early human life. Scientists called this type of hominid ***Australopithecus*** (aw•STRAY•loh•PIH•thuh•kuhs), or "southern ape." It flourished in eastern and southern Africa.

In a 1991 interview, Johanson explained why "Lucy" changed the ideas of many scientists about hominids that walked upright:

**PRIMARY SOURCE**

"People felt that there were a number of evolutionary changes, which all went together. That our ancestors stood up to free their hands so that they could make and use stone tools. In order to make and use stone tools, they had to have large brains . . . Here comes Lucy, about 3.5 million years old . . . very small brain, . . . and we have never found any stone tool, stone artifacts, associated with her species. Yet she is walking upright. So it appears that . . . walking on two legs, precedes by perhaps as much as a million and a half years, the manufacture of stone tools and the expansion of the brain."

—Donald Johanson, 1991 interview

From 2.5 to 1.6 million years ago, a more advanced hominid developed with a somewhat larger brain. This hominid was named *Homo habilis*, meaning "handy human." *Homo habilis* may have used stone tools. The earliest remains of this hominid were discovered near Olduvai Gorge. Another hominid, *Homo erectus*, "upright human," existed from 1.8 million to 100,000 years ago. Although other hominids walked on two legs, *Homo erectus* had arms and legs in modern human proportion. Remains in Asia show that *Homo erectus* was probably the first hominid to leave Africa.

Around 200,000 years ago, *Homo sapiens* emerged. *Homo sapiens*, "wise human," showed rapid brain growth and mastered fire. Two kinds of early humans descended from *Homo sapiens:* Neanderthals and *Homo sapiens sapiens*. In the Neanderthal, a valley in Germany, the earliest remains of Neanderthals, or Neandertals, were found. They probably lived between 100,000 B.C. and 30,000 B.C. Other Neanderthal remains have been found in Europe and Turkey. Besides using many kinds of stone tools, European Neanderthals made their clothes from animal skins. Neanderthals seem to be the first early people to bury their dead. According to some scholars, burying the dead indicates a belief in an afterlife.

## *Homo Sapiens Sapiens*

The second group descended from *Homo sapiens* is ***Homo sapiens sapiens***, meaning "wise, wise human." These are the first to have an anatomy similar to people today. Physical evidence suggests that *Homo sapiens sapiens* appeared in Africa between 150,000 and 200,000 years ago. They probably spread out of Africa to other parts of the world about 100,000 years ago, replacing populations of earlier hominids in Europe and Asia. This is referred to as the **"out-of-Africa" theory** (or replacement theory).

Another theory, the multiregional model, states that the development from earlier hominids to anatomically modern humans occurred in different locations in Africa, Asia, and Europe. The timing and reasons for early human migrations are still debated among scholars.

By 30,000 B.C., *Homo sapiens sapiens* had replaced the Neanderthals. The Neanderthals died out, possibly as a result of conflicts with *Homo sapiens sapiens*. The spread of these first modern humans was a slow process. Over many thousands of years, *Homo sapiens sapiens* spread over the globe as they searched for food and new hunting grounds. In a whole generation, they may have moved only two to three miles. Over hundreds of thousands of years, this was enough to populate the world. Today, all humans, whether they are Europeans, Australian Aborigines (A•buh•RIHJ•NEES), or Africans, belong to the same subgroup of human beings.

✓ **Reading Check** **Summarizing** Identify and describe all the important stages in early human development.

## The Paleolithic Age

**MAIN IDEA** Early humans used fire, made tools, and adapted to survive.

**HISTORY & YOU** Could you live in the wild with only tools you made? Read how early humans managed to survive.

One of the basic distinguishing features of the human species is the ability to make tools. The term **Paleolithic Age** is used to designate the early period of human history (approximately 2,500,000 B.C. to 10,000 B.C.) in which humans used simple stone tools. Paleolithic is Greek for "old stone," and the Paleolithic Age is sometimes called the Old Stone Age.

### Hunting and Gathering

For hundreds of thousands of years, humans relied on hunting and gathering for their daily food. Paleolithic peoples had a close relationship with their environment. They came to know what animals to hunt and what plants to eat. They gathered wild nuts, berries, fruits, wild grains, and green plants. Around the world, they hunted and ate various animals, including buffalo, horses, bison, and reindeer. In coastal areas, fish and shellfish provided a rich source of food.

### The Paleolithic Way of Life

Early humans were able to sustain themselves through the use of stone tools. To make such tools, early people used very hard stones, such as flint. They used one stone to chip away parts of another, creating an edge. Hand axes of various kinds—pointed tools with one or more cutting edges—were the most common. Hand axes eventually were set in wooden handles, making them easier to use. By attaching wooden poles to spear points and hardening the tips in fire, humans created spears to kill large animals.

Over the years, Paleolithic hunters developed better tools. The invention of the spear, and later the bow and arrow, made hunting much easier. Harpoons and fishhooks made of bone increased the catch of fish.

Early humans used sharp-edged tools to cut up plants, dig up roots, and cut branches to build simple shelters. Scraping tools were used to clean animal hides for clothing and shelter. By the end of the Paleolithic period, there is evidence of such refined tools as bone needles. These needles could be used for making nets and baskets and even sewing hides together for clothing.

Because Paleolithic people were hunters and gatherers, they had to follow animal migrations and vegetation cycles. Paleolithic humans were nomads—people who move from place to place to **survive.** Archaeologists and anthropologists think these nomads probably lived in small groups of twenty or thirty. Hunting depended on careful observation of animal behavior patterns and demanded group cooperation for success.

### The Roles of Men and Women

The main job of Paleolithic peoples was finding enough to eat. Both men and women were responsible for finding the food needed for survival. Paleolithic parents passed on their practices, skills, and tools to their children to ensure the survival of later generations.

Since women bore and raised children, they probably stayed closer to camp. They played an important role in acquiring food by gathering berries, nuts, roots, and grains. Women taught the children which foods were edible. They trapped small animals and kept the camp safe.

In the constant search for food, men had to travel far from camp to hunt herds of large animals. What the women caught and gathered had to feed the group if there was no game. Because both men and women were responsible for finding and acquiring the food needed to sustain life, many scientists believe there was equality between them. It is likely that both men and women made decisions that affected the activities of the Paleolithic group.

### Adapting to Survive

Groups of Paleolithic people, especially those groups who lived in cold climates, found shelter in natural caves. Over a period of time, people created new types of shelter as well. Perhaps most common was a simple structure made of wood poles or sticks covered with animal hides. In places where wood was scarce, they might use the large bones of mammoths to build frames that were then covered by animal hides. The systematic use of fire made it possible to provide a source of both light and heat within both the caves and the handmade structures in which they lived.

## Use of Fire

Another important result from the migration of early hominids was the use of fire. As early hominids moved from the tropics into colder regions, they needed to adjust to new climate conditions. In response, *Homo erectus* first learned to make fires. Archaeologists have discovered the piled remains of ashes in caves that prove that Paleolithic people used fire systematically as long ago as 500,000 years.

# SCIENCE, TECHNOLOGY, & SOCIETY

## Digging Through the Past: Calendars and Periodization

***Societies developed calendars to measure time and to record significant events. Historians describe the past by dividing time into periods based on events or themes.***

When early humans recorded the days between full moons, they produced the first calendars. As religions and cultures developed, so did calendar systems. Today many people use two calendars—one religious and one secular. For example, individuals may use the Orthodox, Jewish, or Muslim calendars for holy days, but most countries adopted the Gregorian calendar for civil affairs. On the Gregorian calendar, the era after the birth of Jesus is labeled A.D., Latin for *anno domini*, "in the year of our Lord." The years before Jesus' birth are referred to as B.C. for "before Christ." Alternatively, some label those eras B.C.E. "Before the Common Era" and C.E. "Common Era."

Scientists divide the past into time periods to help categorize information. Different fields of study use different types of "periodization." Historians and archaeologists often describe the past based on tool-making technology. The Stone Age (Paleolithic, Mesolithic, and Neolithic), Bronze Age, Copper Age (Chalcolithic), and Iron Age give chronology, or time order, to human development. For example, the building of Stonehenge spanned the Neolithic and Bronze Ages.

**CRITICAL THINKING SKILLS**

1. **Drawing Conclusions** Why would most countries adopt the same calendar?
2. **Interpreting** Use the table of contents to identify other time periods historians use to describe the past.

◂ **Cleaning a skull found at an Inca cemetery near Lima, Peru**

## HISTORY & ARTS — PRIMARY SOURCE

# Chauvet Cave

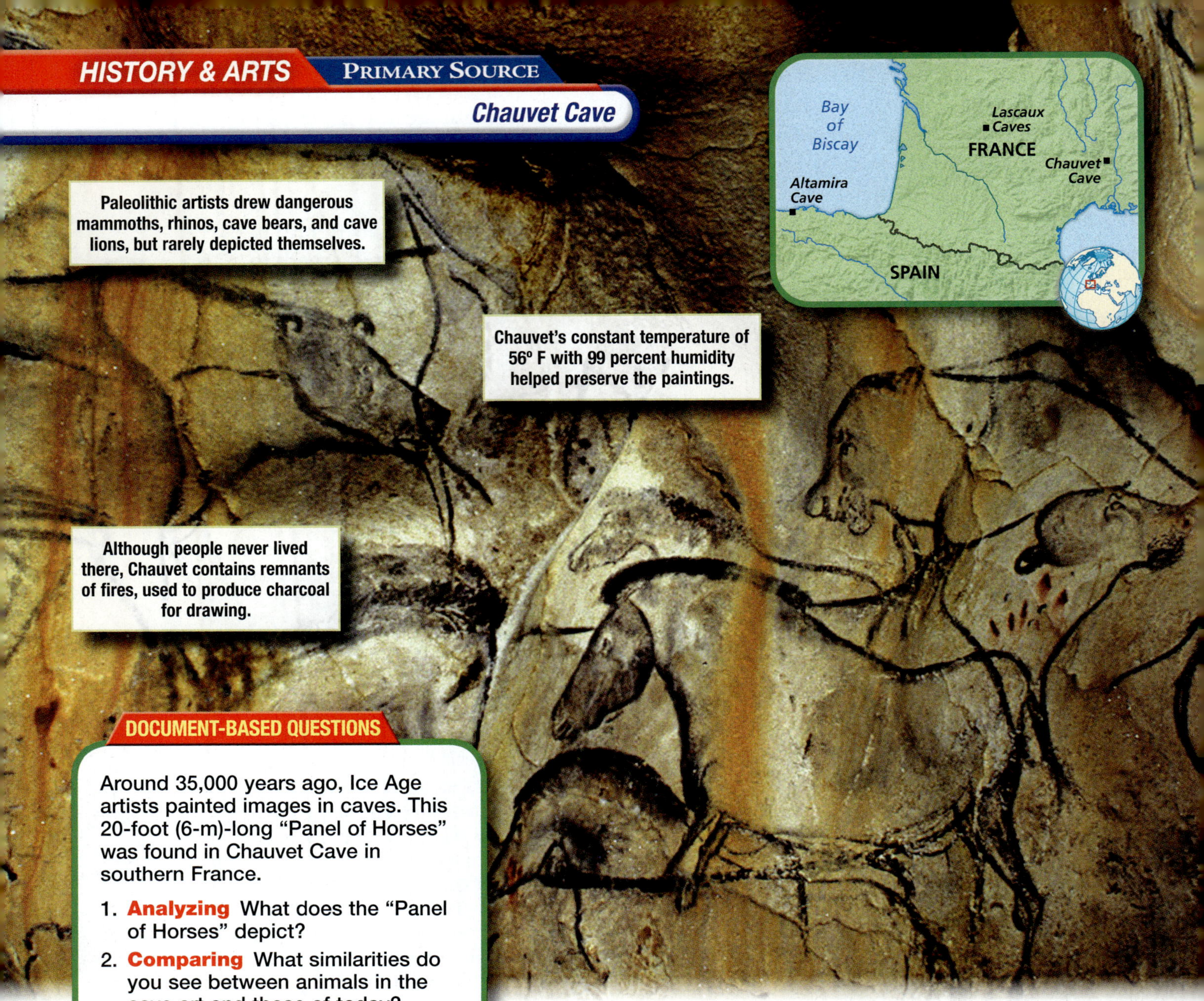


Paleolithic artists drew dangerous mammoths, rhinos, cave bears, and cave lions, but rarely depicted themselves.

Chauvet's constant temperature of 56° F with 99 percent humidity helped preserve the paintings.

Although people never lived there, Chauvet contains remnants of fires, used to produce charcoal for drawing.

### DOCUMENT-BASED QUESTIONS

Around 35,000 years ago, Ice Age artists painted images in caves. This 20-foot (6-m)-long "Panel of Horses" was found in Chauvet Cave in southern France.

1. **Analyzing** What does the "Panel of Horses" depict?
2. **Comparing** What similarities do you see between animals in the cave art and those of today?

At a *Homo erectus* site in northern China, remnants of hearths, ashes, charcoal, and charred bones have been dated to 400,000 years ago.

Fire not only gave warmth, but kept wild animals away from the campsite. Armed with spears, hunters used fire to flush out wild pigs for the kill. People gathered around the fire to trade stories and to cook. Cooked food tasted better, lasted longer, and was easier to chew and digest (in the case of some plants, such as wild grains), so it seems likely that nutrition improved.

Scholars believe that the discovery of a means for starting fires occurred independently throughout the world, in different places at different times. Archaeologists lack concrete evidence on how early peoples started fires. They have been able to examine the methods used by traditional peoples. On that basis, archaeologists deduce that the earliest humans used friction to start fires.

Eventually, some Paleolithic peoples developed sturdy, drill-like wooden devices to start fires. Other early humans discovered that a certain stone, iron pyrites, gave off a spark when struck against a rock and that spark could ignite dry grass or leaves.

## The Ice Ages

Having fire to create a source of heat was especially important when Ice Age conditions descended on the Paleolithic world. The most recent Ice Age began about 100,000 B.C. and ended about 8000 B.C. During this time, sheets of thick ice covered large parts of Europe, Asia, and North America. As sea levels went down, people migrated across land bridges that had not existed before.

Ice Age conditions posed a serious threat to human life, and the ability to adapt was crucial to human survival. The use of fire, for example, reminds us that early humans sometimes adapted not by changing themselves to better fit their environment but by changing the environment.

## Creating Art

The importance of art to human life is basic. Art existed even in prehistory among the hunters and gatherers of the Paleolithic Age. In 1940, a bad storm near Lascaux (la•SKOH) in southern France uprooted a large tree, revealing a cave. French children playing nearby soon found the cave and the paintings inside. Many of these paintings had deteriorated, but scientists used special tools to determine what is being depicted, such as horses, bulls, and stags.

Another famous discovery was made in Spain in 1879 when a little girl wandered into a cave on her grandfather's farm near Altamira. Like many other caves covered with Paleolithic art, the cave near Altamira shows evidence that the paintings may have been created over a span of time, not all at once. Scientists can date the art based on pigments from the paintings.

In 1994, Jean-Marie Chauvet and his friends discovered paintings in southern France. Carbon dating showed works at Chauvet Cave were nearly twice as old as those at Lascaux and Altamira, but the drawings were more advanced. Scholars had assumed the opposite—that the earliest art would be crude and gradually would become more detailed.

Using stone lamps filled with animal fat to light the caves, early artists painted with fingers and twigs and even blew paint through hollow reeds. They mixed mineral ores with animal fat to make red, yellow, and black paint. A variety of realistically painted animals cover the caves. Few humans appear in these paintings, and when they do appear, they are drawn as sticklike figures. This has led some scholars to think the work was done for a magical or religious ritual to bring success in hunting. Others believe the paintings were made simply to please the eye. Recent discoveries of art by early humans show that prehistoric art existed in other areas of the world.

✓Reading Check **Identifying** What are two important innovations of Paleolithic peoples?

## SECTION 1 REVIEW

### Vocabulary

1. **Explain** the significance of: prehistory, archaeology, artifact, anthropology, fossil, hominid, Olduvai Gorge, *Australopithecus*, *Homo sapiens sapiens*, "out-of-Africa" theory, Paleolithic Age.

### Main Ideas

2. **Discuss** what kinds of materials archaeologists use to study prehistory.
3. **Explain** what the caves of Lascaux suggest about early human society.
4. **Create** a diagram like the one shown below to compare and contrast *Australopithecus* and Neanderthal.

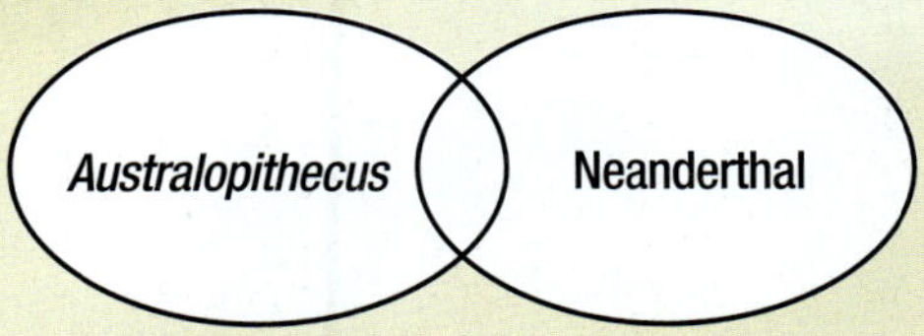


### Critical Thinking

5. **The BIG Idea** **Explaining** Explain the difference between the "out-of-Africa" and multiregional theories.
6. **Comparing** Discuss the difference between the roles of Paleolithic men and women.
7. **Analyzing Visuals** Examine the cave paintings shown on page 10. What do they tell you about human/animal interactions during the Paleolithic Age?

### Writing About History

8. **Descriptive Writing** Imagine you are part of an archaeological team at a recently discovered site, keeping a daily journal. Describe the conditions of the site, the sorts of artifacts you are finding, and what you hope to find based on the evidence so far. Read magazine articles or books in a library or on the Web to help you with this project.

**History ONLINE**

For help with the concepts in this section of *Glencoe World History*, go to glencoe.com and click Study Central™.

# Early Housing

What a house looks like has much to do with where it is located, when it was built, and what materials were available. Zhoukoudianzhen Cave, in China, shows evidence of use from around 700,000 to around 200,000 years ago. Pincevent, in modern-day France, shows how early humans lived in northern Europe at the end of the Ice Age, around 13,000 years ago. And Çatalhüyük, in modern-day Turkey, was an early farming village from 6700 B.C. to 5700 B.C.

## Zhoukoudianzhen Cave

These *Homo erectus* used wood, bamboo, and stone tools to scrape, chop, and cut.

## Pincevent Site

## Temporary Settlements

Before around 8000 B.C. early humans were nomads who lived in temporary settlements. They moved every season, migrating with the animals they hunted. Early humans used caves for shelter. If they lived in a place without rock outcroppings, they made their homes out of available materials. Tents made of animal bones or wood were covered with animal hides or turf.

## ÇATALHÜYÜK

## PERMANENT SETTLEMENTS

After 8000 B.C., people began settling in one place, planting crops, and raising livestock. The first farming settlements developed in river valleys where the soil was fertile. As the population grew, more cropland was needed to feed the villagers. After years of growing crops, the soil became depleted, decreasing the amount of food produced. Unless the soil was replenished, such as through silt left by flooding, villages would be abandoned.

### ANALYZING VISUALS

1. **Comparing** Why are there similarities between the homes despite the differences in era and location?
2. **Making Connections** What impact did farming villages have on the environment?

SECTION 2

Section Audio    Spotlight Video

# The Neolithic Revolution

## GUIDE TO READING

### The BIG Idea

**Ideas, Beliefs, and Values**

Systematic agriculture brought huge economic, political, and social changes for early humans.

### Content Vocabulary

- systematic agriculture *(p. 14)*
- domestication *(p. 14)*
- artisan *(p. 16)*
- culture *(p. 18)*
- civilization *(p. 18)*
- monarch *(p. 18)*
- priest *(p. 19)*

### Academic Vocabulary

- revolution *(p. 14)*
- role *(p. 16)*

### People and Places

- Neolithic Revolution *(p. 14)*
- Mesoamericans *(p. 15)*
- Çatalhüyük *(p. 16)*
- Bronze Age *(p. 16)*
- Iron Age *(p. 16)*

### Reading Strategy

**Comparing and Contrasting** As you read, create a chart like the one below listing the six major characteristics of a civilization.

| Civilization | |
|---|---|
| 1. | 4. |
| 2. | 5. |
| 3. | 6. |

*The development of systematic agriculture and civilization was a dramatic change, or revolution, during the Neolithic Age. The transition of humans from nomadic hunters to farmers and herders is part of the Neolithic Revolution. This revolution led to the development of traditional economies based on agriculture with limited trade.*

## The Neolithic Revolution

**MAIN IDEA** Civilization developed from the agricultural revolution of the Neolithic Age.

**HISTORY & YOU** How did early American pioneers meet their basic needs? Read how the Neolithic farmers affected human progress.

The end of the last Ice Age, around 8000 B.C., was followed by what is called the **Neolithic Revolution**—that is, the **revolution** that occurred in the Neolithic Age, the period of human history from 8000 B.C. to 4000 B.C. The word *Neolithic* is Greek for "new stone." The name *New Stone Age,* however, is somewhat misleading. The real change in the Neolithic Revolution was the shift from the hunting of animals and the gathering of food to the keeping of animals and the growing of food on a regular basis—what we call **systematic agriculture**.

Early humans had to move from place to place, following the herds and finding plants. During the Neolithic Age, humans began planting crops, providing a regular food source. **Domestication** of animals, adapting them for human use, added a reliable source of meat, milk, and wool. Animals could also be used to do work. Growing crops and taming food-producing animals caused an agricultural revolution. Because there was enough food, humans had more control over their lives. It also meant they could give up their nomadic ways of life and begin to live in settled communities. Some historians believe this revolution was the single most important development in human history.

This shift to food producing from hunting and gathering was not as sudden as was once believed. During the Mesolithic Age ("Middle Stone Age," about 10,000 B.C. to 7000 B.C.) there was a gradual shift from the old food-gathering and hunting economy to a food-producing one. There was also a gradual taming of animals. Moreover, throughout the Neolithic period, hunting and gathering remained a way of life for many people around the world.

# Connecting to the United States

## Today's Agricultural Revolution

The Neolithic Agricultural Revolution made the first cities possible. In the United States and other developed countries, the agricultural revolution continues. American farmers produce more food than ever before to support most Americans, who live in cities or suburbs. Cities continue to spread as farmland shrinks. Until now, most Americans have never raised their own food or faced food shortages.

- Productivity means high crop yields produced on less land by fewer people.
- High productivity creates surpluses, which may be stored or traded.
- The United States exports billions of dollars worth of agricultural products annually.

*Large crops are harvested more quickly due to modern machinery.* ▼

**U.S. Agricultural Productivity**

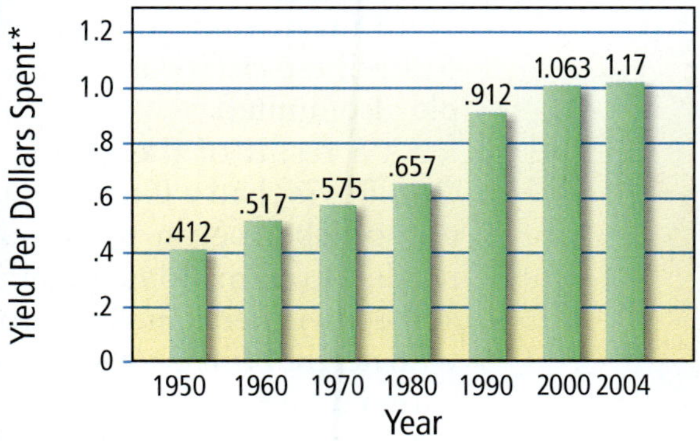


**Source:** *USDA Economic Research Service*

* Dollars spent on land, labor, and investment

**Connecting to Today**

1. **Examining** Which period shows the largest increase in productivity?
2. **Drawing Conclusions** What is the impact of urbanization on farming?

## The Growing of Crops

Between 8000 B.C. and 5000 B.C., systematic agriculture developed in various parts of the world. In Southwest Asia, people began growing wheat and barley and domesticating pigs, cows, goats, and sheep by 8000 B.C. From there, farming spread into Southeastern Europe. By 4000 B.C., farming was well established in central Europe and the coastal regions of the Mediterranean Sea.

By 6000 B.C., the cultivation of wheat and barley had spread into the Nile Valley of Egypt. These crops soon spread up the Nile to other areas of Africa—Sudan and Ethiopia. In central Africa, a separate farming system emerged. There, people grew root crops called tubers, such as yams, and tree crops, such as bananas. Farming wheat and barley also moved eastward into India between 7000 B.C. and 5000 B.C.

By 5000 B.C., farmers in Southeast Asia were growing rice. From there, rice farming spread into southern China. By 6000 B.C., farming millet and domesticating dogs and pigs seem to have been established in northern China. In the Western Hemisphere, **Mesoamericans**—inhabitants of present-day Mexico and Central America—grew beans, squash, and maize. They also domesticated dogs and fowl in this period between 7000 B.C. and 5000 B.C.

## Neolithic Farming Villages

Growing crops on a regular basis gave rise to more permanent settlements called Neolithic farming villages. These villages appeared in Europe, India, Egypt, China, and Mesoamerica. The oldest and biggest villages, however, were located in Southwest Asia. Jericho, near the Dead Sea, was in existence by 8000 B.C.

**Çatalhüyük** (chah•TAHL•hoo•YOOK) in modern Turkey was an even larger community covering 32 acres. Between 6700 B.C. and 5700 B.C., the city probably had about 6,000 inhabitants. Their simple mud brick houses were built so close together that there were few streets. People walked on the roofs and entered their homes through holes in the rooftops.

Archaeologists have found a dozen products that were grown outside the city walls, including fruits, nuts, and three kinds of wheat. Domesticated animals provided meat, milk, and hides. Scenes on the walls of the city's ruins show that the people also hunted.

As a result of the steady food supply, Çatalhüyük had a food surplus. Specialization of labor began when not all villagers needed to farm. Some became **artisans**, or skilled workers, making goods to trade with neighboring people. These goods were bartered, or exchanged, not sold. This was the beginning of a traditional economy based on agriculture and limited trade.

Besides homes, Çatalhüyük had special buildings that were shrines containing figures of gods and goddesses. Statues of women giving birth or nursing a child have also been found there. Both the shrines and the statues point to the growing **role** of religion in the lives of Neolithic peoples.

## Neolithic Revolution—Effects

The Neolithic agricultural revolution caused dramatic changes that affected how people would live to the present day. Once people began settling in villages or towns, they saw the need to build walls for protection and storehouses for goods. Storing surplus products encouraged trade. Trading encouraged more people to learn crafts. This led to the division of labor.

As artisans became more skilled, they made more refined tools. Flint blades were used to make sickles and hoes for farming. Eventually, many of the food plants still in use today began to be cultivated. Some plants, such as flax and cotton, were used to make yarn and cloth.

The change to systematic agriculture also had consequences for how men and women related to one another. Men became more active in farming and herding animals, jobs that took them away from the settlement. Instead of the whole family moving as in earlier times, women remained behind. They cared for children, wove cloth for clothes, and did other tasks that kept them in one place. As men took on more and more responsibility for obtaining food and protecting the settlement, they began to play a more dominant role in society.

## The End of the Neolithic Age

Between 4000 B.C. and 3000 B.C., new developments began to affect some Neolithic towns. Even before 4000 B.C., craftspeople discovered that by heating metal-bearing rocks they could turn the metal to liquid. The liquid metal could then be poured into molds, or casts, to make tools and weapons. The use of metals marked a new level of control over the environment.

Copper was the first metal to be used in making tools. After 4000 B.C., artisans in western Asia discovered that combining copper and tin created bronze—a metal harder and more durable than copper.

The widespread use of bronze led to the **Bronze Age** from around 3000 B.C. to 1200 B.C. After about 1000 B.C., the use of iron tools and weapons became common, an era known as the **Iron Age**.

The Neolithic Age set the stage for major changes to come. As people mastered farming, some villages developed more complex and wealthier societies. To protect their wealth they built armies and city walls. By the beginning of the Bronze Age, large numbers of people were concentrated in the river valleys of Mesopotamia, Egypt, India, and China. These farming villages led to the development of cities.

✓Reading Check **Identifying** What was the result of systematic agriculture?

# TURNING POINT

## NEOLITHIC REVOLUTION

The Neolithic Revolution was the beginning of systematic agriculture. This revolution was marked by the establishment and growth of farming villages such as Jericho. Located near a spring, which made the land especially fertile, Jericho was established by 8000 B.C. It was one of the largest Neolithic farming villages, with an estimated population over 1,000.

NATIONAL GEOGRAPHIC

### SPREAD OF FARMING

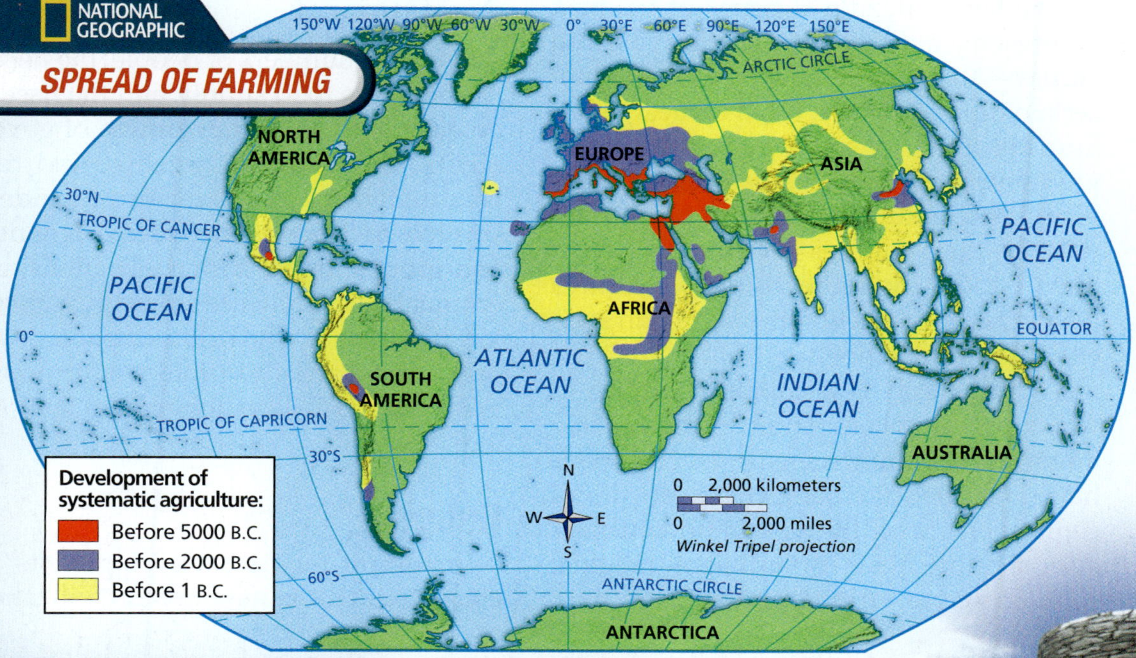

### Geography SKILLS

1. **Human-Environment Interaction** Based on the map, what patterns do you see with the spread of systematic agriculture?
2. **Location** Where were the earliest farming villages located?

**Maps In Motion** See *StudentWorks™ Plus* or glencoe.com.

# Civilization Emerges

**MAIN IDEA** Some villages grew into cities and became early civilizations.

***HISTORY & YOU*** What characteristics make our society a civilization? Learn which features defined early civilizations.

History ONLINE
**Student Web Activity—**
Visit glencoe.com and complete the activity about early peoples.

Whether analyzing societies of the past or present, anthropologists describe the **culture**—the way of life—of a people in a certain time and place. From earliest times, humans lived in small nomadic groups with simple cultures that helped them survive. When humans settled in permanent villages, their cultures became more complex. Gradually, more complex cultures developed into a new form of human society called civilization.

A **civilization** is a complex culture in which large numbers of human beings share a number of common elements. Historians have identified the basic characteristics of civilizations. Six of the most important characteristics are cities, government, religion, social structure, writing, and art.

## Cities

The first civilizations developed in river valleys where people could carry on the large-scale farming that was needed to feed a large population. As food became abundant, more people would live in the city. New patterns of living soon emerged.

## Government

Growing numbers of people, the need to maintain the food supply, and the need for defense soon led to the growth of governments. Governments organize and regulate human activity. They also provide for smooth interaction between individuals and groups. In the first civilizations, governments usually were led by **monarchs**—kings or queens who rule a kingdom—who organized armies to protect their populations and made laws to regulate their subjects' lives.

## Religion

Important religious developments also characterized the new urban civilizations.

***HISTORY & ARTS*** PRIMARY SOURCE

### *Bronze Age Artifacts*

Although these three artifacts were made during the same period, the Bronze Age, each is unique. They are different in origin, material, and subject. Each reveals valuable information about the civilization that created it.

**The Phaestos Disc, from around 1600 B.C., probably came from the Minoan civilization on Crete. The terra-cotta disc proves the existence of a written Minoan language, but no one has been able to translate the hieroglyphs.**

**This terra-cotta jug, from around 1800 B.C., was in a tomb near the settlement of Jericho. Shaped like a bird, the jug is both functional and decorative.**

**During China's Shang dynasty, rulers had a monopoly on bronze work. This gilded bronze head could be the image of a king or a god. Created about 1200 B.C., the head was found in a pit with more than 50 similar artifacts.**

**DOCUMENT-BASED QUESTIONS**

1. **Concluding** What does the presence of artwork say about a culture?
2. **Theorizing** Why might the jug and bronze head have been buried in tombs or pits?

All of them developed religions to explain the forces of nature and their roles in the world.

They believed that gods and goddesses were important to the community's success. To win their favor, **priests** supervised rituals aimed at pleasing them. This gave the priests special power and made them very important people. Rulers also claimed that their power was based on divine approval, and some rulers claimed to be divine.

## Social Structure

A new social structure based on economic power also arose. Rulers and an upper class of priests, government officials, and warriors dominated society. Below this class was a large group of free people—farmers, artisans, and craftspeople. At the bottom was a slave class.

The demand of the upper class for luxury items, such as jewelry and pottery, encouraged artisans and craftspeople to create new products. As urban populations exported finished goods to neighboring populations in exchange for raw materials, organized trade began to grow. Because trade brought new civilizations into contact with one another, it often led to the transfer of new technology, such as metals for tools and new farming techniques, from one region to another.

By and large, however, the early river valley civilizations developed independently. Each one was based on developments connected to the agricultural revolution of the Neolithic Age and the cities that this revolution helped to produce. Taken together, the civilizations of Mesopotamia, Egypt, India, and China constituted nothing less than a revolutionary stage in the growth of human society.

## Writing

Writing was an important feature in the life of these new civilizations. Above all, rulers, priests, merchants, and artisans used writing to keep accurate records. Of course, not all civilizations depended on writing to keep records. The Inca in Peru (see Chapter 11), for example, relied on well-trained memory experts to keep track of their important matters. Eventually, the earliest civilizations used writing for creative expression as well as for record keeping. This produced the world's first works of literature.

## Art

Significant artistic activity was another feature of the new civilizations. Architects built temples and pyramids as places for worship or sacrifice, or for the burial of kings and other important people. Painters and sculptors portrayed stories of nature. They also provided depictions of the rulers and gods they worshiped.

✓Reading Check **Describing** Describe the new social structure that arose in Neolithic cities.

## SECTION 2 REVIEW

### Vocabulary

1. **Explain** the significance of: Neolithic Revolution, systematic agriculture, domestication, Mesoamericans, Çatalhüyük, artisan, Bronze Age, Iron Age, culture, civilization, monarch, priest.

### Main Ideas

2. **Identify** three of the six institutions or customs that people can share in a distinct culture, or civilization.
3. **Locate** the geographic areas where the earliest civilizations developed.
4. **Create** a diagram like the one below to show how changes during the Neolithic Revolution led to the emergence of civilization.

| | | | |
|---|---|---|---|
| → | → | → | civilization |

### Critical Thinking

5. **The BIG Idea** **Explaining** Why did systematic farming make it possible for cities to develop?
6. **Describing** What was the relationship between artistic activities, religion, and government during the rise of civilization?
7. **Analyzing Visuals** Look at the Phaestos Disc on page 18. What does this piece of art reveal about the Minoan writing?

### Writing About History

8. **Expository Writing** Explain the basic features and differences between hunter-gatherer societies and those in farming villages. Use examples and information from the text.

**History ONLINE**

For help with the concepts in this section of *Glencoe World History*, go to glencoe.com and click Study Central™.

# CHAPTER 1 Visual Summary



LUNAR CALENDAR, FRANCE

About 38,000 years ago, humans carved the number of days between full moons on reindeer antlers.

## PALEOLITHIC (c. 2,500,000 B.C. to c. 10,000 B.C.) and MESOLITHIC AGES (c. 10,000 B.C. to c. 7000 B.C.)

- Early humans made stone tools and weapons.
- Paleolithic people survived by hunting and gathering.
- Small nomadic groups followed animal migrations and vegetation cycles.
- Paleolithic people found shelter in caves or covered wood poles with hides.
- Humans used fire to survive in colder climates, light caves, and cook food.
- Prehistoric artists covered caves with pictures of animals and hunting.

## NEOLITHIC AGE (c. 8000 B.C. to c. 4000 B.C.)

- The Neolithic Revolution was the shift to systematic agriculture.
- Planting crops and domesticating animals provided regular sources of food.
- Farmers settled in villages in Southeastern Europe, Asia, Africa, and Mesoamerica.
- Traditional economies based on agriculture and limited trade using the barter system developed.
- The specialization of labor began with artisans making goods for trade.

STONEHENGE, UNITED KINGDOM

Begun during the Neolithic Age, this megalith may have been used as a religious center or as an astronomical observatory.

SUMERIAN STATUE, UR

This female worshiper was carved from alabaster and decorated with shell c. 2450 B.C.

## BRONZE AGE (c. 3000 B.C. to c. 1200 B.C.)

- Artisans combined copper and tin to make bronze weapons and tools.
- Villages grew into walled cities protected by armies.
- Civilizations developed in river valleys of Mesopotamia, Egypt, India, and China.
- Monarchs created governments and laws to rule their kingdoms.
- Priests supervised rituals as religions became more structured.
- Social structure evolved with classes based on economic power and gender roles.
- The need for keeping records spurred development of writing systems.
- Art and architecture glorified kings, gods, and goddesses.

# CHAPTER 1 Assessment

## Reviewing Vocabulary

*Directions: Choose the word or words that best complete the sentence.*

**1.** Archaeologists study ________, or objects made by humans.

**A** rivers

**B** animals

**C** artifacts

**D** oceans

**2.** Donald Johanson and his team found an example of (a)n ________ in Ethiopia.

**A** *Homo habilis*

**B** *Australopithecus*

**C** *Homo erectus*

**D** Neanderthal

**3.** The keeping of animals and the growing of food on a regular basis is known as ________.

**A** systematic agriculture

**B** barter

**C** hunting and gathering

**D** Paleolithic agriculture

**4.** ________ were skilled workers who made products such as weapons and jewelry.

**A** Farmers

**B** Anthropologists

**C** Artisans

**D** Priests

**5.** A ________ has six important characteristics: cities, government, religion, social structure, writing, and art.

**A** money economy

**B** Neolithic Revolution

**C** traditional economy

**D** civilization

## Reviewing Main Ideas

*Directions: Choose the best answers to the following questions.*

### Section 1 *(pp. 4–11)*

**6.** Which type of scientist uses fossils and artifacts to study early humans?

**A** Chemist

**B** Physicist

**C** Anthropologist

**D** Geologist

**7.** Which hominids do scientists believe were probably the first to leave Africa?

**A** *Homo erectus*

**B** *Australopithecus*

**C** *Homo sapiens sapiens*

**D** Neanderthals

**8.** How did early humans adapt in order to survive?

**A** Following animal migrations

**B** Painting cave art

**C** Living in isolation

**D** Keeping records

**9.** Which invention made hunting easier for early humans?

**A** Cave art

**B** Fire

**C** The spear

**D** Farming

**TEST-TAKING TIP**

Make sure to read the entire question and each possible answer before deciding on the correct answer.

**Need Extra Help?**

| If You Missed Questions . . . | 1 | 2 | 3 | 4 | 5 | 6 | 7 | 8 | 9 |
|---|---|---|---|---|---|---|---|---|---|
| Go to Page . . . | 4 | 7 | 14 | 16 | 18 | 4 | 7 | 8 | 8 |

**GO ON**

# CHAPTER 1 Assessment

**Section 2** *(pp. 14–19)*

**10.** During which age did the agricultural revolution lead to the development of civilization?

**A** Paleolithic

**B** Ice

**C** Neolithic

**D** Bronze

**11.** What was one indicator of early farming villages?

**A** Eating cooked food

**B** Hunting

**C** Creating paintings in caves

**D** Domesticating animals

**12.** Where did many early civilizations develop?

**A** Deserts

**B** River valleys

**C** Mountain valleys

**D** Forests

**13.** Who led governments in early civilizations?

**A** Monarchs

**B** Priests

**C** Warriors

**D** Artisans

**14.** Who was farming in the Western Hemisphere by 7000 B.C.?

**A** Mesopotamians

**B** Mesoamericans

**C** Egyptians

**D** The Chinese

## Critical Thinking

*Directions: Choose the best answers to the following questions.*

**15.** Why were Paleolithic peoples nomads?

**A** Fear of enemies kept them moving.

**B** Rival groups drove each other out of settled areas.

**C** They had to follow animal migrations.

**D** They had to look for more habitable climates.

*Base your answer to questions 16 and 17 on the map below.*

**Spread of Early Humans**

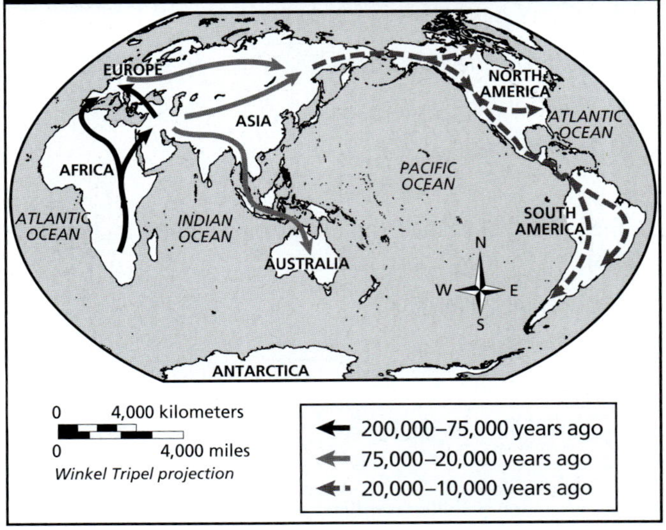


**16.** In which areas of Africa did human life begin?

**A** Eastern and southern

**B** Eastern and northern

**C** Western and southern

**D** Western and northern

**17.** Into which areas did early humans spread most recently?

**A** Asia

**B** Europe

**C** Australia

**D** North and South America

**Need Extra Help?**

| If You Missed Questions . . . | 10 | 11 | 12 | 13 | 14 | 15 | 16 | 17 |
|---|---|---|---|---|---|---|---|---|
| Go to Page . . . | 14 | 14 | 18 | 18 | 15 | 14 | 22 | 22 |

GO ON

**18.** Why was writing important to many early governments?

**A** To describe court life

**B** To express individual beliefs

**C** To keep records

**D** To write songs

*Analyze the chart and answer the question that follows. Base your answer on the chart and on your knowledge of world history.*

Before great civilizations could develop, early humans had to go through many cultural changes, movements, and technological innovations.

### Changes, Prehistory–3500 B.C.

| Event | Cultural Change | Movement | Technological Innovation |
|---|---|---|---|
| • Early humans migrate to warmer climates during the Ice Ages. | | X | |
| • Early humans learn how to control fire and make tools. | X | | X |
| • Caves are painted with religious and decorative art. | X | | |
| • Neanderthals inhabit Europe and Asia. | | X | |
| • Neolithic people domesticate animals. | X | | X |

**19.** What technological innovations were made by early humans?

**A** Neolithic peoples migrate to warmer climates and control fire.

**B** Neolithic peoples create cave paintings and domesticate animals.

**C** Neolithic peoples control fire, make tools, and domesticate animals.

**D** Neolithic peoples are first to bury their dead.

## Document-Based Questions

*Directions: Analyze the document and answer the short-answer questions that follow the document.*

The anthropologist Donald Johanson, along with his team, found a new type of hominid in Ethiopia. Johanson discusses how this *Australopithecus*, or Lucy, as she was nicknamed, presented a new view about the development of hominids:

> *"People felt that there were a number of evolutionary changes, which all went together. That our ancestors stood up to free their hands so that they could make and use stone tools. In order to make and use stone tools, they had to have large brains . . . Here comes Lucy, about 3.5 million years old . . . very small brain, . . . and we have never found any stone tool, stone artifacts, associated with her species. Yet she is walking upright. So it appears that . . . walking on two legs, precedes by perhaps as much as a million and a half years, the manufacture of stone tools and the expansion of the brain."*

**20.** According to Johanson, what did scientists believe about early hominids before the discovery of Lucy?

**21.** What does the discovery of Lucy reveal to anthropologists?

**22.** What is the time frame Johanson discusses? What does this reveal about the development of hominids?

## Extended Response

**23.** Early humans went through many stages before civilizations developed. Explain how the Neolithic revolution influenced the shift from a nomadic existence to life in a village and ultimately to a civilization. Be sure to explore the six basic characteristics of civilization.

**History ONLINE**

For additional test practice, use Self-Check Quizzes—Chapter 1 at glencoe.com.

**Need Extra Help?**

| If You Missed Questions . . . | 18 | 19 | 20 | 21 | 22 | 23 |
|---|---|---|---|---|---|---|
| Go to Page . . . | 19 | 23 | 23 | 23 | 23 | 14 |

STOP

CHAPTER 2

# Western Asia and Egypt 3500–500 B.C.



Chapter Audio

*MAKING CONNECTIONS*

## How does progress affect history?

During the 1960s, Egypt built the Aswan High Dam to control flooding of the Nile River. The lake rising behind the dam threatened to destroy ancient Egyptian monuments. An international team saved several temples including Abu Simbel—Ramses II's temple. Abu Simbel was carved into 20 ton blocks, moved 200 feet, and reassembled. In this chapter you will learn about Egyptian rulers and temples.

- Why would other countries help Egypt preserve its monuments?
- How can countries adapt to changing needs and still preserve their history?

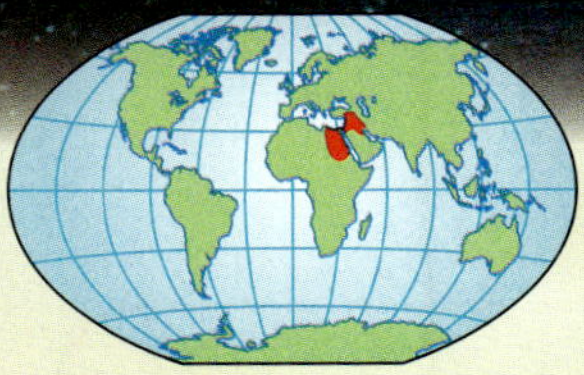

THE WORLD ▶

**c. 3000 B.C.** Sumerian cities emerge; cuneiform writing invented

**c. 2540 B.C.** Great Pyramid of King Khufu completed

3500 B.C. — 2500 B.C.

**c. 2700 B.C.** Egypt's Old Kingdom begins

**c. 1792 B.C.**
Hammurabi comes to power in Babylon

**c. 970 B.C.**
Solomon becomes King of Israel

**c. 521 B.C.**
Darius I begins expanding Persian Empire

1500 B.C. — 500 B.C.

**c. 1250 B.C.**
Queen Nefertari, wife of Ramses II, dies

**c. 539 B.C.**
Babylon falls

**FOLDABLES™**
**Study Organizer**

**Summarizing**
Create a Layered-Look Book with four layers to review the history of ancient Egypt. Summarize the important facts about each era in each layer.

**History ONLINE** Visit glencoe.com and enter *QuickPass*™ code GWHEA7447c2 for Chapter 2 resources.

SECTION 1

Section Audio    Spotlight Video

# Civilization Begins in Mesopotamia

## GUIDE TO READING

### The BIG Idea

**Physical Geography** Fertile soil between the Tigris and Euphrates Rivers allowed an early civilization to flourish in Mesopotamia.

### Content Vocabulary

- polytheistic *(p. 27)*
- city-state *(p. 28)*
- ziggurat *(p. 29)*
- theocracy *(p. 29)*
- cuneiform *(p. 30)*
- empire *(p. 32)*
- patriarchal *(p. 33)*

### Academic Vocabulary

- transport *(p. 29)*
- innovations *(p. 30)*

### People and Places

- Tigris River *(p. 26)*
- Euphrates River *(p. 26)*
- Mesopotamia *(p. 26)*
- Fertile Crescent *(p. 26)*
- Sumerians *(p. 26)*
- Uruk *(p. 28)*
- Akkadians *(p. 32)*
- Sargon *(p. 32)*
- Babylon *(p. 33)*
- Hammurabi *(p. 33)*

### Reading Strategy

**Categorizing Information** As you read, complete a chart like the one below to explain the Sumerians' contributions to civilization.

| Political Life | Cultural Life | Inventions |
|---|---|---|
| | | |
| | | |

*Mesopotamia, located in what is now southern Iraq, was one area where civilization began. The Tigris and Euphrates River valley supported agriculture and encouraged trade. Mesopotamians developed complex economic, political, and social structures. They invented written language, built the world's first empires, and codified their laws.*

## The Impact of Geography

**MAIN IDEA** The physical environment of Mesopotamia led to the development of civilization and influenced people's religious beliefs.

**HISTORY & YOU** Is your town located near a river? Read how a river valley's fertile soil supported the transition from a nomadic lifestyle to systematic agriculture and the birth of civilization.

Fertile river valleys could support a large population in permanent settlements. These farming villages grew into culture hearths, early centers of culture whose ideas and practices spread to surrounding areas. Highly organized societies then evolved in these regions.

### The Fertile Crescent

The ancient Greeks spoke of the valley between the **Tigris** and **Euphrates Rivers** as **Mesopotamia**, the land "between the rivers." Mesopotamia was at the eastern end of the **Fertile Crescent**, an arc of land from the Mediterranean Sea to the Persian Gulf. Rich soil and abundant crops allowed the land to sustain an early civilization.

Mesopotamia had little rain, but over the years its soil had been enriched by layers of silt—material deposited by the two rivers. In late spring, the Tigris and Euphrates often overflowed their banks and deposited their fertile silt. This flooding, however, was unpredictable. It depended on the melting of snows in the upland mountains where the rivers began. People in the valley could not tell exactly when the floods would come or how large they would be.

Therefore, people in ancient Mesopotamia learned to control the flow of the rivers. By using irrigation and drainage ditches, farmers were able to grow crops regularly. An abundance of food allowed many people to live together in cities, and civilization emerged.

Mesopotamian civilization refers to the achievements of people from three general areas: Assyria, Akkad, and Sumer. The **Sumerians** were the creators of the first Mesopotamian civilization.

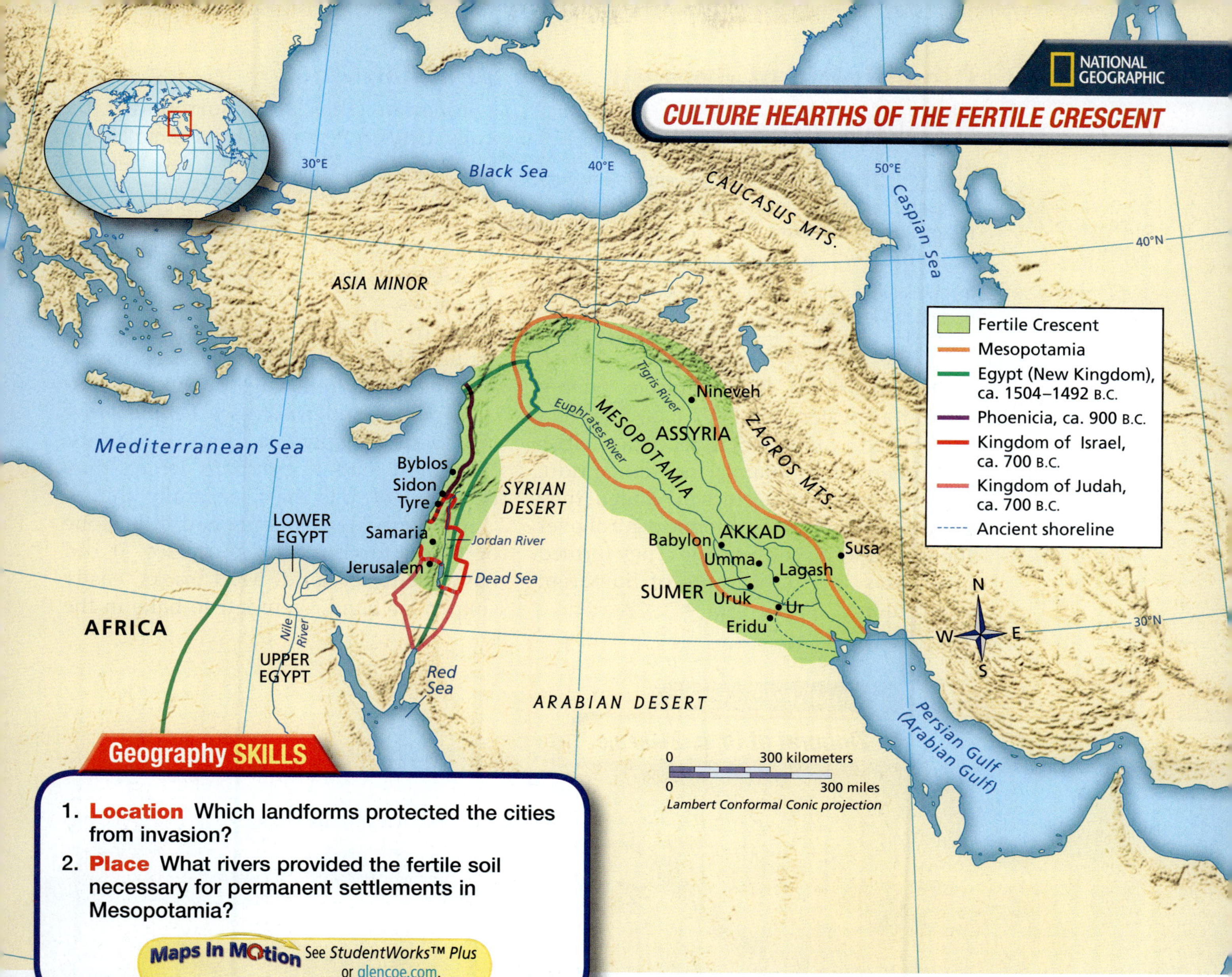


**Geography SKILLS**

1. **Location** Which landforms protected the cities from invasion?
2. **Place** What rivers provided the fertile soil necessary for permanent settlements in Mesopotamia?

Maps In Motion See *StudentWorks™ Plus* or glencoe.com.

## The Growth of Religion

The physical environment affected the way Mesopotamians viewed the world. A harsh climate and frequent famines convinced them that unreliable supernatural forces controlled this world. In the presence of nature, Mesopotamians could easily feel helpless, as this poem relates:

**PRIMARY SOURCE**

"The rampant flood which no man can oppose,
Which shakes the heavens and causes earth to tremble,
In an appalling blanket folds mother and child,
And drowns the harvest in its time of ripeness."

—in "Mesopotamia," from *Before Philosophy,* Henri Frankfort et al.

In Mesopotamia, people looked to religion to answer their questions about life. To them, powerful spiritual beings—gods and goddesses—permeated all aspects of the universe. The Mesopotamians identified nearly three thousand gods and goddesses. Their religion was **polytheistic** because of this belief in many gods. According to the beliefs of the Mesopotamians, humans were supposed to obey and serve the gods. By their nature, humans were inferior to the gods and could never be sure what the gods might do to or for them.

✓ **Reading Check** **Explaining** What role did geography play in the development of Mesopotamian civilization?

# City-States of Ancient Mesopotamia

**MAIN IDEA** Religion played a powerful role in the economic, political, and social structure of Mesopotamian city-states.

***HISTORY & YOU*** How are state and local government related in your community? Read about the connection in Mesopotamia.

The origins of the Sumerian people remain a mystery. By 3000 B.C., they had established a number of independent cities in southern Mesopotamia, including Eridu, Ur, and **Uruk.** As the cities expanded, they gained political and economic control over the surrounding countryside. They formed **city-states**, the basic units of Sumerian civilization.

## Sumerian Cities

Sumerian cities were surrounded by walls. Uruk, for example, was encircled by a wall six miles (10 km) long, with defense towers located every 30 to 35 feet (9 to 10 m) along the wall. It is estimated that Uruk had a population of around 50,000 people by 2700 B.C., making it one of the largest city-states.

City dwellings, built of sun-dried bricks, included both the small houses of peasants and the larger buildings of the city officials, priests, and priestesses. People living in city-states gained a sense of identity. They now had a group to which they belonged, beyond the basic family unit.

Although Mesopotamia had little stone or wood for building purposes, it did have plenty of mud. Mud bricks, easily shaped by hand, were left to bake in the

***HISTORY & ARTS*** PRIMARY SOURCE

***Ziggurat at Ur, c. 2100 B.C.***

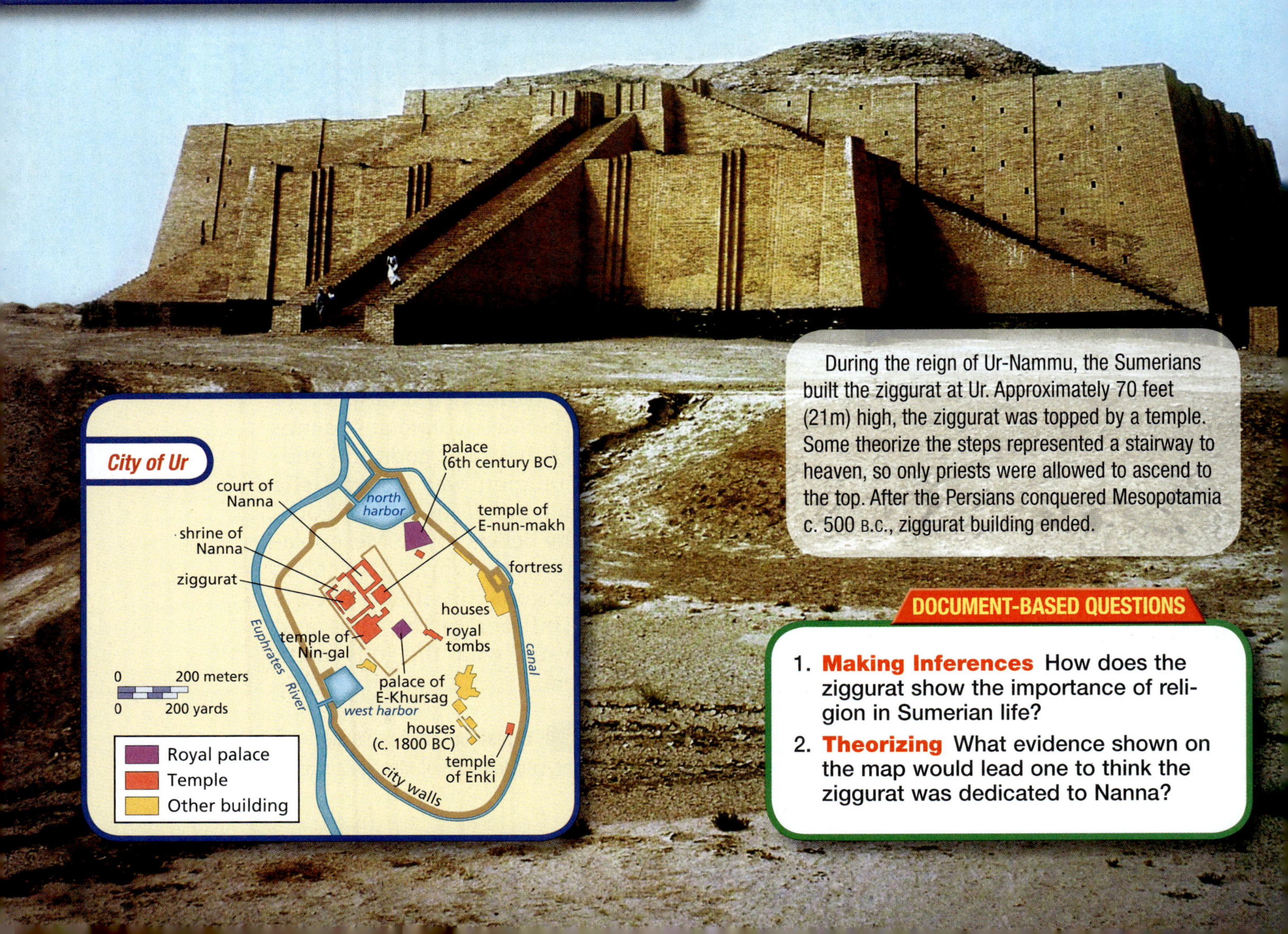


During the reign of Ur-Nammu, the Sumerians built the ziggurat at Ur. Approximately 70 feet (21m) high, the ziggurat was topped by a temple. Some theorize the steps represented a stairway to heaven, so only priests were allowed to ascend to the top. After the Persians conquered Mesopotamia c. 500 B.C., ziggurat building ended.

**DOCUMENT-BASED QUESTIONS**

1. **Making Inferences** How does the ziggurat show the importance of religion in Sumerian life?
2. **Theorizing** What evidence shown on the map would lead one to think the ziggurat was dedicated to Nanna?

hot sun until they were hard enough to use for building. People in Mesopotamia were remarkably creative with mud bricks. They invented the arch and the dome, and they built some of the largest brick buildings in the world. Mud bricks are still used in rural areas of Southwest Asia today.

## Religion and Rulers

The most prominent building in a Sumerian city was the temple dedicated to the chief god or goddess of the city. This temple was often built atop a massive stepped tower called a **ziggurat.** The Sumerians believed that gods and goddesses owned the cities. The people devoted much of their wealth to building temples and elaborate houses for the priests and priestesses who served the gods. The temples and related buildings served as the center of the city physically, economically, and even politically. Surplus food and crafts were stored in the temples, which could then be distributed or traded.

The priests and priestesses who supervised the temples held a great deal of power. In fact, historians believe that in the early stages of the city-states, priests and priestesses played an important role in ruling. The Sumerians believed that the gods ruled the cities, making the state a **theocracy**—a government by divine authority.

Even when power passed into the hands of kings, Sumerians believed that these rulers derived their power from the gods and were the agents of the gods. As one person said in a petition to his king:

**PRIMARY SOURCE**

"You in your judgement, you are the son of Anu [god of the sky]. Your commands, like the work of a god, cannot be reversed. Your words, like rain pouring down from heaven, are without number."

—anonymous Sumerian petitioner

Regardless of their origins, kings held great power. They led armies, supervised the building of public works, and organized workers for the irrigation projects on which farming depended. The army, the government, and the priests and priestesses all aided the kings in their rule. As befitted their power, Sumerian kings, their wives, and their children lived in large palaces.

## Economy and Society

Although the Sumerian city-states had a traditional economy based chiefly on farming, trade and industry became important as well. The peoples of Mesopotamia made woolen textiles and pottery, but they were particularly well known for their metalwork.

Copper, gold, and silver were already being used for jewelry and some tools. The Sumerians discovered that when tin is added to copper, it makes bronze. Bronze has a lower melting point, which makes it easier to cast than copper. Bronze is also a harder metal than copper and corrodes less. It could also be melted down and remade when it wore out.

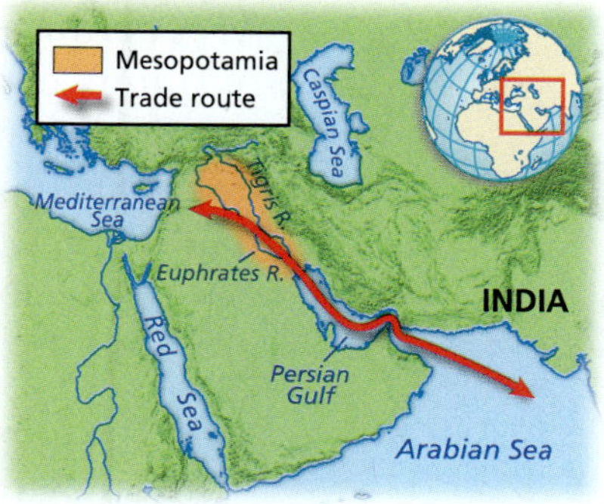


The Sumerians bartered, or exchanged, wool, barley, dried fish, wheat, and metal goods for imported copper, tin, and timber. Traders traveled by land to the eastern Mediterranean in the west and by sea to India in the east. The invention of the wheel, around 3000 B.C., led to wheeled carts, making the **transport** of goods much easier.

Sumerian city-states contained three major social groups: nobles, commoners, and slaves. Nobles included royal and priestly officials and their families. Commoners worked for palace and temple estates and as farmers, merchants, fishers, and craftspeople. Probably 90 percent or more of the people were farmers. Slaves belonged to palace officials, who used them mostly in building projects. Temple officials most often used female slaves to weave cloth and grind grain. Rich landowners also used slaves to farm their lands.

✓ Reading Check **Explaining** Why were the early Mesopotamian city-states considered to be theocracies?

## The Creativity of the Sumerians

**MAIN IDEA** The Sumerians invented writing and several new technologies that made life easier.

***HISTORY & YOU*** What are some examples of how writing makes your life better? Read about Sumerian writing innovations.

The Sumerians created many inventions that still affect our lives today. Probably their greatest invention was their writing. In addition, historians credit them with many technological **innovations.**

### Writing and Literature

Around 3000 B.C., the Sumerians created a **cuneiform** ("wedge-shaped") system of writing. Using a reed stylus (a tool for writing), they made wedge-shaped impressions on clay tablets, which were then baked or dried in the sun. Once dried, these tablets lasted a very long time. Several hundred thousand tablets have been found. They have been a valuable source of information for modern scholars.

Mesopotamian peoples used writing primarily for record keeping. Cuneiform texts, however, were also used in schools to train scribes, members of the learned class who served as copyists, teachers, and jurists.

For boys of the upper class in Mesopotamia, becoming a scribe was the key to a successful career. Men who began their careers as scribes became the leaders of their cities, temples, and armies. Scribes came to hold the most important positions in Sumerian society.

To become scribes, boys from wealthy families, many of them the sons of scribes, attended the new schools that were in operation by 2500 B.C. Young boys seeking to become scribes began school when they were small children and trained until they were young men. School days began at sunrise and ended at sunset. Discipline was harsh. The following essay, written by a teacher as a copying exercise for pupils, shows that punishments—being caned or beaten with a stick—were frequent:

**PRIMARY SOURCE**

"In the tablet-house, the monitor said to me:
'Why are you late?' I was afraid, my heart beat fast. I entered before my teacher, took my place.
My 'school-father' read my tablet to me,
said, 'The word is cut off,' caned me.
He who was in charge of drawing said 'Why when I was not here did you stand up?' caned me.
He who was in charge of the gate said 'Why when I was not here did you go out?' caned me.
My teacher said 'Your hand is not good,' caned me."

—James B. Pritchard, *Ancient Near Eastern Texts*

Scribal students spent most of their school days following the same routine. They copied and recopied standard works on clay tablets and then recited from them. Although boring, this was probably the scribe's only way of learning how to form the cuneiform writing signs neatly and correctly.

**PRIMARY SOURCE**

"'What did you do in school?'
'I read my tablet, wrote it, finished it; then my prepared lines were prepared for me and in the afternoon, my hand copies were prepared for me.'"

—James B. Pritchard, *Ancient Near Eastern Texts*

Writing was important because it allowed a society to keep records and to pass along knowledge from person to person and from generation to generation. Writing also made it possible for people to communicate ideas in new ways. This is especially evident in *The Epic of Gilgamesh.*

*Gilgamesh* is an epic poem that records the exploits of a legendary king named Gilgamesh. Gilgamesh is wise, strong, and perfect in body. He is part man and part god. Gilgamesh befriends a hairy beast named Enkidu. Together, they set off to do great deeds. When Enkidu dies, Gilgamesh feels the pain of death and begins a search for the secret of immortality. His efforts fail, and Gilgamesh remains mortal. This Mesopotamian epic makes clear that "everlasting life" is only for the gods.

HISTORY & ARTS | PRIMARY SOURCE

## The Standard of Ur

The Standard of Ur was found in a grave in the Royal Cemetery at Ur. The Standard has two main panels titled "War" and "Peace." The "War" panel, shown here, depicts a Sumerian army. It should be read from the bottom up, and left to right.

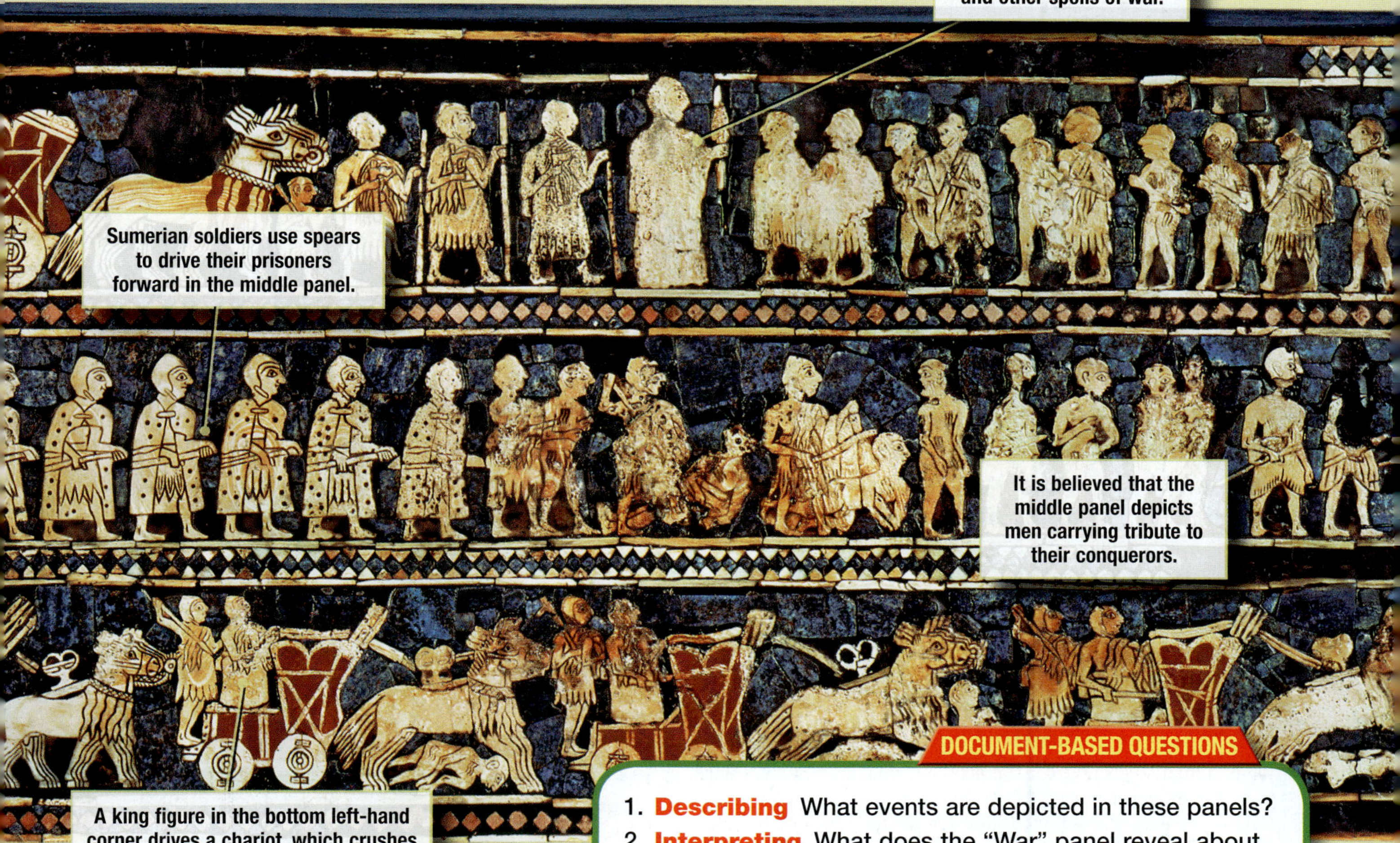


**DOCUMENT-BASED QUESTIONS**

1. **Describing** What events are depicted in these panels?
2. **Interpreting** What does the "War" panel reveal about Sumerian society?

## Technology

The Sumerians invented several tools and devices that made daily life easier and more productive. They developed the wagon wheel, for example, to help transport people and goods from place to place. The potter's wheel to shape containers, the sundial to keep time, and the arch used in construction are other examples of Sumerian technology. The Sumerians were the first to make bronze out of copper and tin, creating finely crafted metalwork. The Sumerians also made outstanding achievements in mathematics and astronomy. In math, they devised a number system based on 60. They used geometry to measure fields and to erect buildings. In astronomy, the Sumerians charted the heavenly constellations. A quick glance at your watch and its division of an hour into 60 minutes should remind you of our debt to the Sumerians.

✓**Reading Check** **Identifying** Name two major inventions of the Sumerians, and tell how those inventions affect our lives today.

## Empires in Ancient Mesopotamia

**MAIN IDEA** Strong leaders established empires and codified the laws of Mesopotamia.

***HISTORY & YOU*** How might a written code of laws change the system of justice in a country? Read about the law code Hammurabi developed.

As the number of Sumerian city-states grew and the city-states expanded, new conflicts arose. City-states fought for control of land and water. Located on flat land, the Sumerian city-states were also open to invasion by other groups.

## Akkadian and Babylonian Empires

To the north of the Sumerian city-states were the **Akkadians** (uh•KAY•dee•uhnz). They spoke a Semitic language. Around 2340 B.C., **Sargon**, leader of the Akkadians, overran the Sumerian city-states and set up the first empire in world history. An **empire** is a large political unit or state,

## TURNING POINT — HAMMURABI'S CODE

Although there were earlier Mesopotamian law codes, the Code of Hammurabi is the most complete. Written at the end of his reign, the code listed Hammurabi's accomplishments and summarized his legal rulings. The code served as a model for scribes, who copied it for more than 1,000 years.

| | COMPARING ANCIENT LAW CODES |
|---|---|
| 1 | If anyone commits a robbery and is caught, then he shall be put to death.—Hammurabi's code<br>When a man steals an ox … he shall pay double.—Hebrew Bible |
| 2 | If a man wishes to separate from a woman who has borne him children, or from his wife who has borne him children, then he shall give that wife her dowry, and a part of the usufruct [right of use] of field, garden, and property, so that she can rear her children.—Hammurabi's code<br>Those who die and leave wives, a will shall provide their wives with support for a year, provided they stay within the same household.—Quran |
| 3 | If anyone … is careless, and … water flood the field of this neighbor, then he shall pay his neighbor….—Hammurabi's code<br>When a fire is started … so that it burns stacked … grain, the one who started the fire must make restitution.— Hebrew Bible |

Hammurabi, king of Sumer and Akkad, stands in front of a seated god.

The code was carved on a basalt stela, or monument, which stood 7 feet (2 m) tall.

The text was written in cuneiform script in the Akkadian language.

*The Code of Hammurabi,* c. 1760 B.C., Louvre Museum, France

**DOCUMENT-BASED QUESTIONS**

1. **Comparing** What similarities do you see between Hammurabi's code and the Bible and the Quran?
2. **Speculating** Why do you think the images were included at the top of the stela with Hammurabi's code?

usually under a single leader, that controls many peoples or territories. Empires are often easy to create, but they can be difficult to maintain. The rise and fall of empires is an important part of history.

Attacks from neighbors caused the Akkadian Empire to fall by 2100 B.C. After that, the system of warring city-states lasted until 1792 B.C. In **Babylon**, a city-state south of Akkad, **Hammurabi** (HA•muh•RAH•bee) came to power. He gained control of Sumer and Akkad, thus creating a new Mesopotamian kingdom. After his death in 1750 B.C., however, a series of weak kings was unable to keep the empire united, and it finally fell to new invaders.

## The Code of Hammurabi

For centuries in Mesopotamia, laws had regulated people's relationships with one another. Hammurabi's collection of laws provides great insight into social conditions there. The Code of Hammurabi was based on a system of strict justice. Penalties for criminal offenses were severe, and they varied according to the social class of the victim. A crime against a noble by a commoner was punished more severely than the same offense against a member of the lower class. Moreover, the principle of retaliation ("an eye for an eye, a tooth for a tooth") was a fundamental part of this system of justice.

Hammurabi's code took seriously the duties of public officials. Officials who failed to solve crimes had to make personal restitution to the victims or their families. Judges could be penalized for ruling incorrectly on a case.

The law code also included what we would call consumer-protection laws. Builders were held responsible for the buildings they constructed. If a house collapsed and caused the owner to die, the builder was put to death.

The largest category of laws in the Code of Hammurabi focused on marriage and the family. Parents arranged marriages for their children. After marriage, the two parties signed a marriage contract, which made the marriage legal.

Mesopotamian society was **patriarchal**—that is, men dominated the society. Hammurabi's code shows that women had far fewer rights in marriage than did men.

A woman's place was definitely in the home. A husband could divorce his wife if she failed to fulfill her duties, was unable to bear children, or tried to leave home to engage in business. Even harsher, a wife who neglected her home or humiliated her husband could be drowned.

Fathers ruled their children as well. Obedience was expected: "If a son has struck his father, he shall cut off his hand." If a son committed a serious enough offense, his father could disinherit him. Hammurabi's laws clearly covered almost every aspect of people's lives.

✓Reading Check **Identifying** Identify five aspects of Mesopotamian society as revealed by the Code of Hammurabi.

## SECTION 1 REVIEW

### Vocabulary

1. **Explain** the significance of: Tigris River, Euphrates River, Mesopotamia, Fertile Crescent, Sumerians, polytheistic, Uruk, city-state, ziggurat, theocracy, transport, innovations, cuneiform, Akkadians, Sargon, empire, Babylon, Hammurabi, patriarchal.

### Main Ideas

2. **Explain** how the physical environment affected the way Mesopotamians viewed the world.
3. **Describe** how temples served as the center of Mesopotamian cities.
4. **Create** a chart like the one shown below to list Sumerian achievements and the effects of these achievements on our lives today.

| Achievements | Effects on our lives today |
|---|---|
| | |
| | |
| | |

### Critical Thinking

5. **BIG Idea** **Analyzing** How did the Tigris and Euphrates Rivers support a strong economy in Mesopotamia?
6. **Evaluating** Which type of government—separate city-states or an empire—would have been most advantageous to the people of Mesopotamia?
7. **Analyzing Visuals** Examine the image on page 31. What does it reveal about life in Sumer?

### Writing About History

8. **Descriptive Writing** Describe the lives of the people of ancient Mesopotamia. In a theocracy, what are the roles of the king, the priests, and the average citizen? How did people make a living? What were their civic responsibilities?

**History ONLINE**

For help with the concepts in this section of *Glencoe World History*, go to glencoe.com and click Study Central™.

SECTION 2

Section Audio    Spotlight Video

# Egyptian Civilization

## GUIDE TO READING

### The BIG Idea

**Order and Security** Continuity and stability were characteristics of Egyptian civilization for thousands of years.

### Content Vocabulary

- dynasty *(p. 36)*
- pharaoh *(p. 37)*
- bureaucracy *(p. 37)*
- vizier *(p. 37)*
- mummification *(p. 37)*
- hieroglyphics *(p. 42)*
- hieratic script *(p. 43)*

### Academic Vocabulary

- major *(p. 34)*
- identifying *(p. 36)*
- physical *(p. 37)*

### People and Places

- Nile River *(p. 34)*
- Lower Egypt *(p. 34)*
- Upper Egypt *(p. 34)*
- Menes *(p. 36)*
- Giza *(p. 37)*
- Hyksos *(p. 39)*
- Hatshepsut *(p. 40)*
- Akhenaten *(p. 40)*
- Tutankhamen *(p. 40)*
- Ramses II *(p. 40)*
- Cleopatra VII *(p. 40)*

### Reading Strategy

**Identifying** As you read, complete a chart like the one below listing characteristics of three major periods in Egyptian history.

| The Old Kingdom | The Middle Kingdom | The New Kingdom |
|---|---|---|
| | | |
| | | |

*Egypt, like Mesopotamia, was one of the first river-valley civilizations. Egyptian history includes three long periods of stability and achievement interspersed with shorter periods of political disorder. Egyptian society was organized in layers, but most people worked the land.*

## Geography and Religion

MAIN IDEA The Nile was fundamental to the development of Egyptian civilization.

HISTORY & YOU How does the geography of your region affect your outlook on life? Learn how the Egyptians in the Nile Valley used their geography.

The Nile River played an important role in Egyptian civilization. Egyptians wrote of their reliance on the great river in "Hymn to the Nile," praising it as the "creator of all good" in its ability to bring them food and other riches. Like their religious beliefs, the Nile provided a sense of well-being and comfort to the Egyptians.

### The Nile

The **Nile River** begins in the heart of Africa and courses northward for more than 4,000 miles (6,436 km). It is the longest river in the world. Before it empties into the Mediterranean, the Nile splits into two **major** branches. This split forms a triangular territory called a delta. The Nile Delta is called **Lower Egypt;** the land upstream, to the south, is called **Upper Egypt.** Egypt's important cities developed at the tip of the delta, the point at which the Nile divides.

The ancient Egyptians referred to the river's yearly flooding as the "miracle" of the Nile. The river rose in the summer from heavy rains in central Africa, reached its highest point in Egypt in early autumn, and left a deposit of mud that created an area of rich soil several miles wide on both sides of the river. The Egyptians called this dark-colored, fertile land the "Black Land." Beyond it lay the deserts, the "Red Land."

Farmers in the Nile Valley grew a surplus of food, which made Egypt prosperous. The river also served as a unifying factor in Egyptian history. In ancient times, the Nile was the fastest way to travel through the land, making both transportation and communication easier. North winds pushed sailboats south, and the Nile's current carried them north.

Unlike Mesopotamia, which was subject to constant invasion, Egypt was blessed by natural barriers that gave it protection from

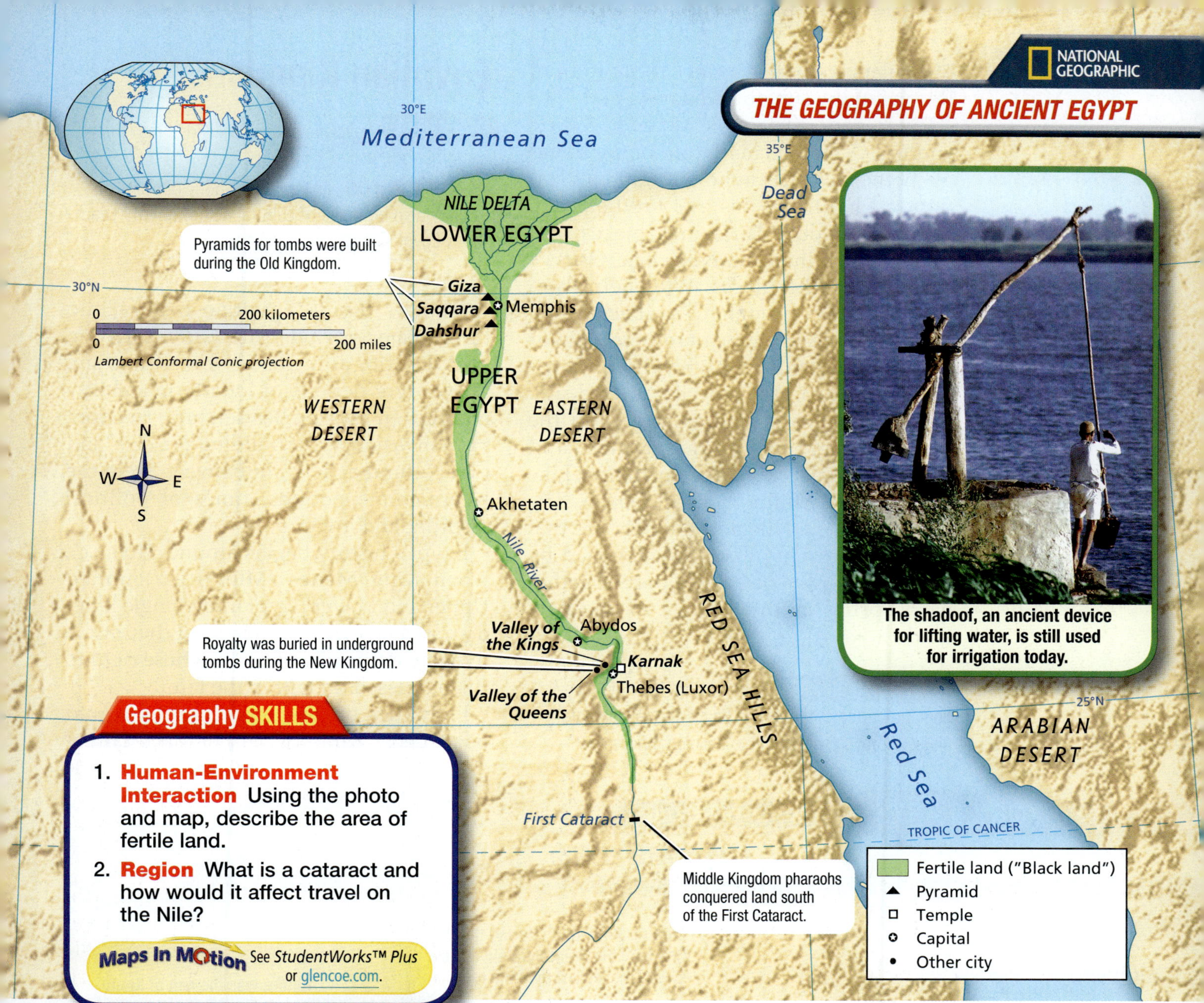


The shadoof, an ancient device for lifting water, is still used for irrigation today.

**Geography SKILLS**

1. **Human-Environment Interaction** Using the photo and map, describe the area of fertile land.
2. **Region** What is a cataract and how would it affect travel on the Nile?

**Maps In MOtion** See *StudentWorks™ Plus* or glencoe.com.

invasion and a sense of security. These barriers included the deserts to the west and east; the Red Sea to the east; the cataracts, or rapids, on the southern part of the Nile, which made defense relatively easy; and the Mediterranean Sea to the north.

The regularity of the Nile floods and the relative isolation of the Egyptians created a feeling of security and changelessness. To the ancient Egyptians, when the Nile flooded each year, "the fields laugh and people's faces light up." Unlike people in Mesopotamia, Egyptians faced life with a spirit of confidence in the stability of things. Ancient Egyptian civilization was marked by a remarkable degree of continuity over thousands of years.

## The Growth of Religion

Religion, too, provided the Egyptians with a sense of security and timelessness. They had no word for religion. For them, religious ideas represented an inseparable part of the entire world order. The Egyptians were polytheistic. They had a number of gods associated with heavenly bodies and natural forces. Two groups, sun gods and land gods (including river gods), came to have special significance in view of the importance of the sun and the fertile land along the Nile to Egypt's well-being.

The sun, the source of life, was worthy of worship. The sun god took on different forms and names based on his role. The Egyptian ruler took the title "Son of Re."

The rulers were seen as an earthly form of Re, one of the sun god's names.

River and land gods included Osiris and Isis. A famous myth told of the struggle between Osiris, who brought civilization to Egypt, and his evil brother Seth. When Seth cut Osiris into pieces and tossed them into the Nile, Isis, Osiris's wife, found the pieces. With help from other gods, she brought Osiris back to life. Osiris became a symbol of resurrection, or rebirth. By **identifying** with Osiris, Egyptians hoped to gain new life after death. The dead were placed in tombs (in the case of kings, in pyramid tombs) and through rituals would become Osiris. Like Osiris, they would then be reborn. The flooding of the Nile and the new life that it brought to Egypt were symbolized by Isis's bringing all of Osiris's parts together each spring in the festival of the new land.

✓ **Reading Check** **Contrasting** How did the flooding patterns of rivers in Egypt and Mesopotamia cause the two civilizations to develop differently?

## Egyptian Kingdoms

**MAIN IDEA** Egyptian history is divided into three major periods, called kingdoms.

***HISTORY & YOU*** Why might periods of political stability also be times of cultural achievement? Learn about Egypt's accomplishments.

Scholars divide Egyptian history into three major periods: the Old Kingdom, Middle Kingdom, and New Kingdom. These were periods of long-term stability marked by strong leadership, freedom from invasion, great building projects, and rich cultural activity. In between were the Intermediate periods, times of political disorder and invasion.

Egypt's history begins around 3100 B.C., when King **Menes** (MEE•NEEZ) united Upper and Lower Egypt into a single kingdom and created the first royal dynasty. A **dynasty** is a family of rulers whose right to rule is passed on within the family.

From then on, the Egyptian ruler would be called "King of Upper and Lower

### HISTORY & ARTS — PRIMARY SOURCE

### Pyramids at Giza

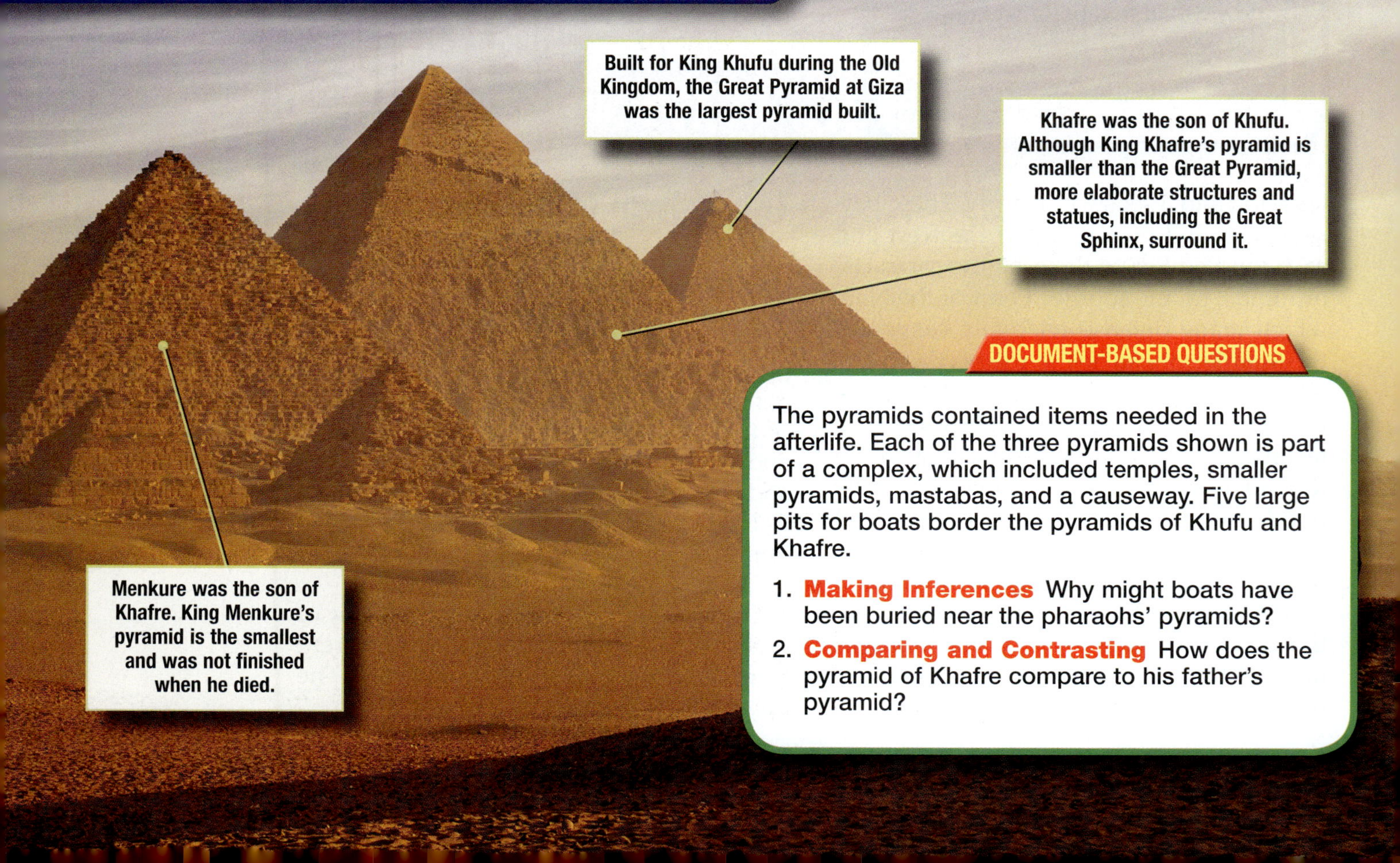

Built for King Khufu during the Old Kingdom, the Great Pyramid at Giza was the largest pyramid built.

Khafre was the son of Khufu. Although King Khafre's pyramid is smaller than the Great Pyramid, more elaborate structures and statues, including the Great Sphinx, surround it.

Menkure was the son of Khafre. King Menkure's pyramid is the smallest and was not finished when he died.

**DOCUMENT-BASED QUESTIONS**

The pyramids contained items needed in the afterlife. Each of the three pyramids shown is part of a complex, which included temples, smaller pyramids, mastabas, and a causeway. Five large pits for boats border the pyramids of Khufu and Khafre.

1. **Making Inferences** Why might boats have been buried near the pharaohs' pyramids?
2. **Comparing and Contrasting** How does the pyramid of Khafre compare to his father's pyramid?

Egypt." The crown was a double crown, indicating the unity of all Egypt. Just as the Nile served to unite Upper Egypt and Lower Egypt physically, kingship united them politically.

## The Old Kingdom

The Old Kingdom, which lasted from around 2700 B.C. to 2200 B.C., was an age of prosperity and splendor. Like the kings of the Sumerian city-states, the monarchs of the Old Kingdom were powerful rulers over a unified state. Among the various titles of Egyptian monarchs, that of **pharaoh**—originally meaning "great house" or "palace"—eventually became the most common.

Kingship was a divine institution in ancient Egypt and formed part of a universal cosmic order: "What is the king of Upper and Lower Egypt? He is a god by whose dealings one lives, the father and mother of all men, alone by himself, without an equal." In obeying their pharaoh, subjects believed that they were helping to maintain a stable world order. A breakdown in royal power could only mean that citizens were offending the gods and weakening that order.

Egyptian pharaohs possessed absolute power—that is, they had complete, unlimited power to rule their people. Nevertheless, they had help in ruling. At first, members of the pharaoh's family provided this help. During the Old Kingdom, however, a government **bureaucracy**—an administrative organization with officials and regular procedures—developed. Especially important was the office of **vizier**, the steward of the whole land. Directly responsible to the pharaoh, the vizier was in charge of the government bureaucracy. In time, Egypt was divided into 42 provinces, which were run by governors appointed by the pharaoh. Each governor was responsible to the pharaoh and vizier.

An example of the splendor of the Old Kingdom—and one of the great achievements of Egyptian civilization—is the building of pyramids. Pyramids were built as part of a larger complex of buildings dedicated to the dead—in effect, a city of the dead. The area included several structures: a large pyramid for the pharaoh's burial; smaller pyramids for his family; and several mastabas, rectangular structures with flat roofs used as tombs for the pharaoh's officials.

The tombs were well prepared for their residents. They contained rooms stocked with supplies, including chairs, boats, chests, weapons, games, dishes, and a variety of foods. The Egyptians believed that human beings had two bodies—a **physical** one and a spiritual one, which they called the *ka.* If the physical body was properly preserved and the tomb furnished with all the various objects of regular life, the *ka* could return. Surrounded by the earthly comforts, the spiritual *ka* could then continue its life despite the death of the physical body.

To preserve the physical body after death, the Egyptians practiced **mummification,** a process of slowly drying a dead body to prevent it from rotting. This process took place in workshops run by priests, primarily for the wealthy families who could afford it. Workers first removed the liver, lungs, stomach, and intestines and placed them in four special jars that were put in the tomb with the mummy. The priests also removed the brain by extracting it through the nose. They then covered the corpse with a natural salt that absorbed the body's water. Later, they filled the body with spices and wrapped it with layers of linen soaked in resin. At the end of the process, which took about 70 days, a lifelike mask was placed over the head and shoulders of the mummy. The mummy was then sealed in a case and placed in its tomb.

Pyramids were tombs for the mummified bodies of pharaohs. The largest and most magnificent of all the pyramids was built under King Khufu (KOO•FOO). Constructed at **Giza** around 2540 B.C., the famous Great Pyramid of King Khufu covers 13 acres (5.3 ha), measures 756 feet (230 m) at each side of its base, and stands 481 feet (147 m) high.

The building of the Great Pyramid was an enormous construction project. The Greek historian Herodotus reported the traditional story that it took 100,000 Egyptians 20 years to build the Great Pyramid.

# EGYPTIAN KINGDOMS

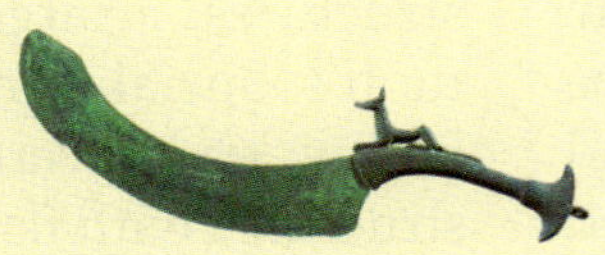

▲ Embalmer's knife

**c. 3100 B.C.**
King Menes unites the villages of Upper and Lower Egypt

**c. 2540 B.C.**
The building of the Great Pyramid of King Khufu at Giza

**c. 2055 B.C.**
Middle Kingdom begins—a golden age of stability and expansion into Africa and western Asia

3200 | 2500 | 2000

**c. 2700 B.C.**
Old Kingdom begins—a time of strong leadership and a unified Egypt

▲ Double crown of unified Egypt

**c. 2180 B.C.**
First Intermediate Period begins, consisting of nearly 150 years without centralized leadership

Herodotus wrote two thousand years after the event, however, and speculation still surrounds the building of the Great Pyramid. Especially puzzling is how the builders achieved their amazing level of precision. The stone slabs on the outside of the Great Pyramid, for example, fit so tightly side by side that even a hair cannot be pushed into the joints between them.

Guarding the Great Pyramid at Giza is a huge figure carved from rock, known as the Great Sphinx. This colossal statue is 240 feet (73 m) long and 66 feet (20 m) high. It has the body of a lion and a human head. The head is believed by many to be a likeness of Khufu's son Khafre, who ordered the statue's construction. Historians do not agree on the purpose of the Great Sphinx. Many Egyptians, however, believed that the mythical sphinx was an important guardian of sacred sites.

The Great Pyramid still stands as a visible symbol of the power of the Egyptian pharaohs of the Old Kingdom. No pyramid built later matched its size or splendor. The pyramid was not only the pharaoh's tomb but also an important symbol of royal power. It could be seen for miles and served to remind people of the glory, might, and wealth of the ruler who was a living god on Earth.

## The Middle Kingdom

The Old Kingdom eventually collapsed, followed by a period of disorder that lasted about 150 years. Finally, a new dynasty gained control of all Egypt and began the Middle Kingdom, a period of stability lasting from about 2055 B.C. to 1650 B.C. Egyptians later portrayed the Middle Kingdom as a golden age of stability.

As evidence of its newfound strength, Egypt began a period of expansion. Nubia, which was located south of Egypt, was conquered. Fortresses were built to protect the new frontier. Egypt sent armies into Canaan and Syria although they did not

◄ Akhenaten

**c. 1550 B.C.** New Kingdom begins—through military campaigns Egypt becomes the most powerful empire in Southwest Asia

**1500**

**c. 1470 B.C.** Hatshepsut dies and Thutmose III becomes pharaoh

**c. 1364 B.C.** Akhenaten (Amenhotep IV) takes the throne and establishes a monotheistic cult; religious disputes cause unrest

**c. 1347 B.C.** Tutankhamen's reign begins; he restores the old gods

**c. 1279 B.C.** The reign of Ramses II begins; he fights to regain control of lands in Africa and western Asia

**1000**

**c. 1070 B.C.** Post-empire Egypt begins

◄ Tutankhamen

**Analyzing TIME LINES**

1. **Differentiating** Which event shows how powerful the leadership was during the Old Kingdom?
2. **Making Inferences** What was the response to Akhenaten's religious reforms?

remain there. Pharaohs also sent traders to Kush, Syria, Mesopotamia, and Crete.

One feature of the Middle Kingdom was a new concern of the pharaohs for the people. In the Old Kingdom, the pharaoh had been seen as a god-king far removed from his people. Now he was portrayed as the shepherd of his people and expected to build public works and provide for the public welfare. Pharaohs of the Middle Kingdom undertook a number of helpful projects. The draining of swampland in the Nile Delta provided thousands of acres of new farmland. The digging of a canal to connect the Nile River to the Red Sea aided trade and transportation.

## The New Kingdom

The Middle Kingdom came to an end around 1650 B.C. with the invasion of Egypt by a group of people from western Asia known as the **Hyksos** (HIHK•SAHS). The Hyksos used horse-drawn war chariots to overwhelm the Egyptian soldiers, who fought from donkey carts.

For almost a hundred years, the Hyksos ruled much of Egypt. The conquered Egyptians learned a great deal from their conquerors. From the Hyksos, the Egyptians learned to use bronze in the making of their farming tools and their weapons. The Egyptians also mastered many of the military skills of the Hyksos, especially the use of horse-drawn war chariots.

Eventually, a new dynasty of pharaohs used the new weapons to drive out the Hyksos and reunite Egypt. The New Kingdom was established and lasted approximately from 1550 B.C. to 1070 B.C. This reunification launched the Egyptians along a new militaristic path. During the period of the New Kingdom, Egypt created an empire and became the most powerful state in Southwest Asia.

Massive wealth boosted the power of the New Kingdom pharaohs. They showed their wealth by building new temples.

**Hatshepsut**—one of the first women to become pharaoh—built a great temple at Deir el-Bahri, near Thebes. Hatshepsut was succeeded by her nephew Thutmose (thoot•MOH•suh) III. He led 17 military campaigns into Syria and Canaan and even reached as far east as the Euphrates River. His forces occupied Canaan and Syria and moved westward into Libya. Magnificent new buildings and temples were constructed to show the greatness of the empire.

The New Kingdom was not without troubles, however. The pharaoh Amenhotep IV introduced the worship of Aten, god of the sun disk, as the sole god. Amenhotep changed his own name to **Akhenaten**, "It is well with Aten," and closed the temples of other gods. In a society that had always been tolerant of many gods, Akhenaten's actions in destroying the old gods meant to many Egyptians the destruction of Egypt itself. Akhenaten's changes were soon undone after his death by the boy-pharaoh **Tutankhamen**, who restored the old gods.

The upheavals associated with Amenhotep's religious revolution led to a loss of Egypt's empire. Under **Ramses II**, who reigned from c. 1279 B.C. to 1213 B.C., the Egyptians went back on the offensive. They regained control of Canaan but were unable to reestablish the borders of their earlier empire. New invasions in the 1200s B.C. by the "Sea Peoples," as the Egyptians called them, drove the Egyptians back within their old frontiers and ended the Egyptian Empire. The New Kingdom itself collapsed in 1070 B.C.

For the next thousand years, Egypt was dominated periodically by Libyans, Nubians, Persians, and, finally, Macedonians after the conquest of Alexander the Great. In the first century B.C., the pharaoh **Cleopatra VII** tried to reestablish Egypt's independence. Her involvement with Rome led to her defeat and suicide, and Egypt became a province in Rome's empire.

✓Reading Check **Contrasting** What were the major differences among the Old Kingdom, the Middle Kingdom, and the New Kingdom?

## PEOPLE *in* HISTORY

### Ramses II
**Ruled c. 1279–1213 B.C. Egyptian Pharaoh**

The long reign of Ramses II brought a variety of changes to Egypt. During the early years of his reign, he fought the Hittites to regain control over land in Africa and western Asia. After a decisive battle around 1274 B.C., Ramses II claimed victory for Egypt, but signed a treaty that divided the land between the Hittites and Egyptians. He also married a Hittite princess as part of the agreement. He undertook numerous building projects during his reign, including establishing a new capital city. Ramses II also built many grand temples, such as the Ramesseum at Thebes. **Do you think Ramses II was truly victorious over the Hittites? Explain.**

### Hatshepsut
**Ruled c. 1485–1470 B.C. Egyptian Pharaoh**

Hatshepsut was the daughter of the pharaoh Thutmose I. She married the pharaoh Thutmose II. When he died, Hatshepsut assumed the full power of pharaoh. Statues show Hatshepsut clothed and bearded as a king would be. Hatshepsut's reign was a prosperous one. She exercised her power by increasing trade and completing ambitious building projects, including the temple at Deir el-Bahri on the west bank of the Nile at Thebes. She was succeeded by her stepson and nephew, Thutmose III. **Why do you think Hatshepsut had herself depicted as a man rather than a woman?**

## Life in Ancient Egypt

**MAIN IDEA** Egyptian society was organized into classes.

***HISTORY & YOU*** How does wealth or social status affect lifestyle? Learn how various classes of Egyptians lived.

Egyptian society was highly structured. The existence of a large lower class of peasants allowed a small upper class of the pharaoh and nobles to live in splendor and to build elaborate temples and pyramids. Class was important in determining individual rights.

### Egyptian Society

Over a period of thousands of years, Egyptian society maintained a simple structure. It was organized like a pyramid, with the god-king at the top. The pharaoh was surrounded by an upper class of nobles and priests, who joined in the elaborate rituals of the pharaoh's life. The members of this ruling class ran the government and managed their own landed estates, which provided much of their wealth.

Below the upper class were merchants, artisans, scribes, and tax collectors. Middle-class homes, mostly in the city, were comfortable but not elegant. Merchants carried on an active trade up and down the Nile, as well as in local markets. Some merchants also engaged in international trade. They were sent by the pharaoh to Crete and Syria to obtain wood and other products. Egyptian artisans made a huge variety of well-built, beautiful goods: stone dishes; wooden furniture; painted boxes; gold, silver, and copper tools and containers; paper and rope made of papyrus; and linen clothing.

By far, the largest number of people in Egypt simply worked the land. In theory, the pharaoh owned all the land but granted portions of it to his subjects. Large sections of land were held by nobles and by the priests who supervised the numerous temples. Most of the lower classes were peasants who farmed the land of these estates. They paid taxes in the form of crops to the pharaoh, nobles, and priests; lived in small villages; and provided military service and forced labor for building projects.

### Daily Life in Ancient Egypt

Ancient Egyptians had a positive attitude toward daily life on Earth. They married young (girls at 12 and boys at 14) and established homes and families. Monogamy (marriage to one person) was the general rule, but a husband could have additional wives if his first wife was childless.

The husband was master in the house, but wives were very well respected. Wives were in charge of the household and the education of the children. From a book of wise sayings came this advice:

See page R34 to read excerpts from Vizier Ptah-hotep's *An Egyptian Father's Advice to His Son* in the **Primary Sources and Literature Library.**

**PRIMARY SOURCE**

> "If you are a man of standing, you should love your wife at home as is fitting. Fill her belly; clothe her back. . . . Make her heart glad as long as you live."
>
> —B.G. Trigger et al., *Ancient Egypt: A Social History*

Women's property and inheritance stayed in their hands, even in marriage. Most careers and public offices were closed to women, but some women did operate businesses. Peasant women worked long hours in the fields and in the home. Upper-class women could become priestesses, and four queens became pharaohs.

Parents arranged marriages for their children. Their chief concerns were family and property. The main purpose of marriage was to produce children, especially sons. Only sons could carry on the family name. Daughters were not ignored, however, and numerous tomb paintings show the close and affectionate relationship parents had with both sons and daughters. Although marriages were arranged, the surviving love poems from ancient Egypt suggest that some marriages included an element of romance. Marriages could and did end in divorce, which included compensation for the wife.

**✓ Reading Check** **Summarizing** List the social classes of ancient Egypt and identify the contributions each class made to society.

## Egyptian Accomplishments

**MAIN IDEA** Egyptians developed complex writing and made advances in the arts and sciences.

***HISTORY & YOU*** How would society be affected if girls and boys were educated differently? Read about Egyptian education.

Although hieroglyphics is the best-known form of Egyptian writing, it was not the form people most commonly used. Writing for everyday purposes, including business, was less likely to be preserved than writing in temples and tombs. Only boys from the upper or middle classes would receive formal education in any system of writing.

### Writing and Education

One system of writing in Egypt emerged around 3000 B.C. The Greeks later called this earliest Egyptian writing **hieroglyphics**, meaning "priest-carvings" or "sacred writings."

***HISTORY & ARTS*** PRIMARY SOURCE

***Hieroglyphics***

This mural painting in Queen Nefertari's tomb contains hieroglyphs describing her life. Next to her crown is a cartouche—an oval containing a royal name.

This papyrus page from the Book of the Dead shows the ibis-headed god Thoth. Above Thoth are cursive hieroglyphs. The text on the right is hieratic script—a simplified cursive form of glyphs used by priests.

**DOCUMENT-BASED QUESTIONS**

Using hieroglyphs, ancient Egyptians recorded daily activities and the reigns of their pharaohs. Through these works we have increased our knowledge of the Egyptian way of life.

1. **Drawing Conclusions** Why might scribes have been respected in Egyptian culture?
2. **Making Inferences** How might hieratic symbols be used in trade?

The hieroglyphic system of writing, which used both pictures and more abstract forms, was complex. Learning and practicing it took much time and skill. Hieroglyphic script was used for writing on temple walls and in tombs. A highly simplified version of hieroglyphics, known as **hieratic script**, came into being. It used the same principles as hieroglyphic writing, but the drawings were simplified by using dashes, strokes, and curves to represent them. Hieratic script was used for business transactions, record keeping, and the general needs of daily life.

Egyptian hieroglyphs were at first carved in stone. Later, hieratic script was written on papyrus, a paper made from the papyrus reed that grew along the Nile. Most of the ancient Egyptian literature that has come down to us was written on rolls of papyrus.

The Egyptian scribes were masters of the art of writing and also its teachers. At the age of 10, boys of the upper classes went to schools run by scribes. Training to be a scribe took many years. Students learned to read and write by copying texts. Discipline was strict, as is evident from the following Egyptian saying: "A boy's ears are on his back. He listens only when he is beaten." Girls remained at home and learned housekeeping skills from their mothers.

## Art and Science

Pyramids, temples, and other monuments bear witness to the architectural and artistic achievements of the ancient Egyptians. Artists and sculptors were expected to follow particular formulas in style. This gave Egyptian art a distinctive look for many thousands of years. For example, the human body was often portrayed as a combination of profile, semi-profile, and frontal view to accurately represent each part.

Egyptians also made advances in mathematics. Mathematics helped them in building their massive monuments. Egyptians were able to calculate area and volume and used geometry to survey flooded land.

The Egyptians developed an accurate 365-day calendar by basing their year not only on the movements of the moon, but also the bright star Sirius. Sirius rises in the sky just before the annual flooding of the Nile River, providing a standard date from which to calculate.

The practice of embalming (preserving a dead body to protect it from decay) led to medical expertise in human anatomy. Archaeologists have recovered directions from doctors for using splints, bandages, and compresses for treating fractures, wounds, and disease. Other ancient civilizations acquired medical knowledge from the Egyptians.

**✓Reading Check** **Describing** What was distinctive about Egyptian art?

## SECTION 2 REVIEW

### Vocabulary

1. **Explain** the significance of: Nile River, major, Lower Egypt, Upper Egypt, identifying, Menes, dynasty, pharaoh, bureaucracy, vizier, physical, mummification, Giza, Hyksos, Hatshepsut, Akhenaten, Tutankhamen, Ramses II, Cleopatra VII, hieroglyphics, hieratic script.

### Main Ideas

2. **Explain** why Egyptians saw the Middle Kingdom as a golden age.
3. **Describe** some of the rights Egyptian women had.
4. **Create** a diagram like the one shown below to describe the impact the Nile had on life in ancient Egypt.

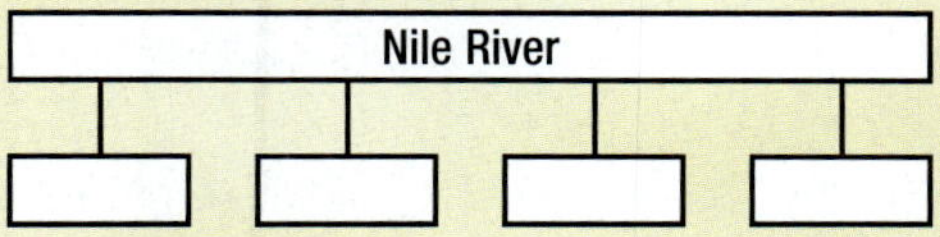


### Critical Thinking

5. **BIG Idea** **Determining Cause and Effect** How did the Hyksos both threaten and improve Egypt's security?
6. **Drawing Conclusions** What is the significance of the famous Egyptian myth of the struggle between Osiris and his evil brother Seth? Why did Osiris take on an important role for the Egyptians?
7. **Analyzing Visuals** Examine the image on page 42. How did ancient Egyptians paint the human form?

### Writing About History

8. **Descriptive Writing** Assume you are a tour guide leading a tour of the Great Pyramid. Explain to your group why the pyramids were built and what historians believe is their significance. Create an advertising brochure to promote and sell your tour.

**History ONLINE**

For help with the concepts in this section of *Glencoe World History*, go to glencoe.com and click Study Central™.

# Preparing for the Afterlife

Egyptians believed in cycles: the sun and moon, the Nile's floods, and a life cycle including death and an afterlife. They believed life in the next world would be like the life they knew, only better. Preparing for the afterlife was important to people of all social classes.

Wealthy Egyptians mummified their dead to preserve the bodies for the afterlife.

Ancient writings state that the mummification process took 70 days.

Most Egyptians were buried with personal items and food. Pharaohs were buried with extravagant items, like this chariot from the tomb of Tutankhamen.

Statues of the deceased called *ka* statues were placed in the tomb. Egyptians believed that the *ka*, or life force, of the deceased would inhabit the statue.

This *ka* statue is a depiction of Khafre, who ruled from 2558 B.C. to 2532 B.C.

Canopic jars were used to hold the organs of the deceased after they were removed during the mummification process.

## They Took It With Them

Royalty and wealthy Egyptians spent years, even decades, preparing for the afterlife. Tombs were filled with food, games, and furniture—everything needed for eternity. Artists painted scenes of daily life on the tombs. Artisans carved miniature servants, *shabtis,* to help in the underworld. Laborers and farmers could not afford these things, but their relatives brought food or buried familiar objects with them.

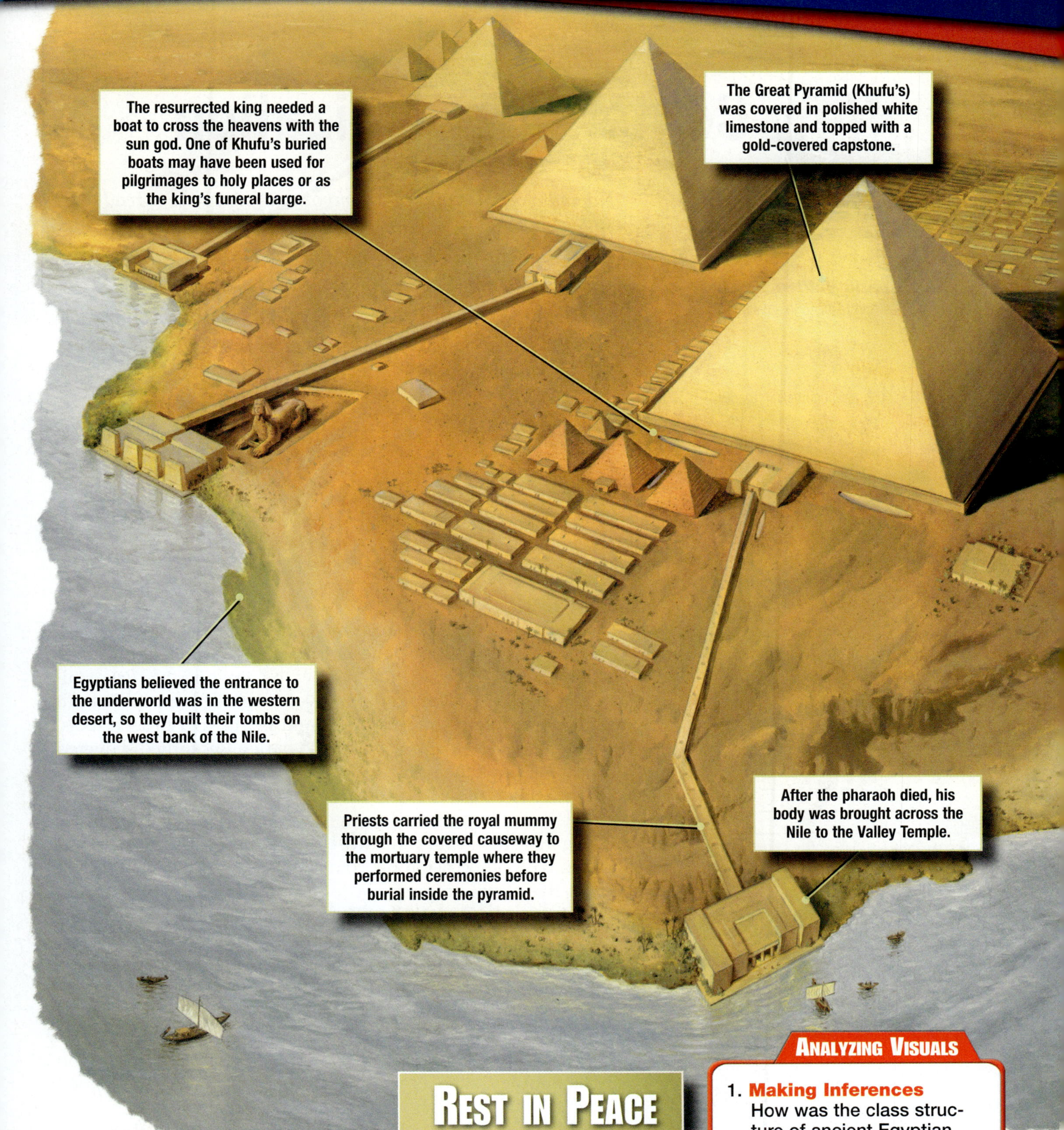


## REST IN PEACE

Mummification and tombs protected the body, which Egyptians believed the soul needed to survive. The wealthy were buried under low, rectangular structures called *mastabas.* They chose sites as close to the pharaoh's as possible. The majority of Egyptians could not afford the elaborate funerals and tombs of the upper class. Most were merely wrapped in cloth and placed in individual or communal graves.

### ANALYZING VISUALS

1. **Making Inferences** How was the class structure of ancient Egyptian society reflected in its funerary practices?
2. **Analyzing** Ancient statues often have missing heads or arms. How did the artist carve the *ka* statue to be long lasting? Why?

SECTION 3

Section Audio

Spotlight Video

# New Centers of Civilization

## GUIDE TO READING

### The BIG Idea

**Ideas, Beliefs, and Values** The Israelites' belief in one God resulted in a distinct society.

### Content Vocabulary

- pastoral nomad *(p. 46)*
- monotheistic *(p. 50)*

### Academic Vocabulary

- created *(p. 46)*
- technology *(p. 46)*
- domesticated *(p. 46)*

### People and Places

- Indo-Europeans *(p. 46)*
- Hittites *(p. 47)*
- Phoenicians *(p. 48)*
- Israelites *(p. 49)*
- King David *(p. 49)*
- King Solomon *(p. 49)*
- Jerusalem *(p. 49)*

### Reading Strategy

**Summarizing Information** As you read, complete a diagram like the one below to show how the Phoenicians affected development of civilization in Southwest Asia.

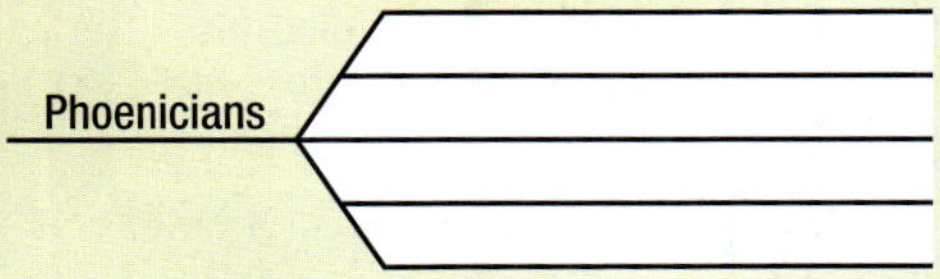


*Nomadic peoples played an important role in the spread of civilization in western and central Asia. After about 1200 B.C., there was no dominant power in the region. The Phoenicians emerged as the most important trading kingdom in the Mediterranean area. The Israelites did not create an empire, but they left a world religion, Judaism, that influenced the later religions of Christianity and Islam.*

## The Role of Nomadic Peoples

***MAIN IDEA*** Nomadic peoples, especially the Indo-Europeans, served an important function for civilized societies by spreading goods and new technology.

***HISTORY & YOU*** Why are residents of a community sometimes suspicious of or hostile to strangers? Learn how civilizations related to nomads.

Our story of civilization so far has focused on Mesopotamia and Egypt. Recent evidence suggests that another civilization flourished in central Asia (in what are now the republics of Turkmenistan and Uzbekistan) around 4,000 years ago. These people built mud-brick buildings, raised sheep and goats, had bronze tools, and used irrigation to grow wheat and barley. Recently discovered inscriptions show that these early people may have had writing.

On the fringes of these civilizations lived nomadic peoples who depended on hunting and gathering, herding, and sometimes farming for their survival. Most important were the **pastoral nomads** who on occasion overran settled communities and then **created** their own empires. Pastoral nomads **domesticated** animals for food and clothing. They followed regular migratory routes to provide food for their animals.

People who lived in settled communities often viewed nomads as hostile and barbaric. The groups did interact, however. Nomads traded animals and animal products for grains and vegetables they were unable to grow. Pastoral nomads also carried products between civilized centers. In this way nomads often passed on new **technology,** such as the use of bronze and iron, that helped strengthen civilizations. When overpopulation or drought disrupted the pastoral nomads' normal patterns, however, they often attacked the civilized communities to obtain relief.

The **Indo-Europeans** were one of the most important nomadic peoples. The term *Indo-European* refers to a particular group of people who spoke a language derived from a single parent tongue. Indo-European languages include Greek, Latin, Persian, Sanskrit, and the Germanic languages. The original Indo-Europeans were

**Some Indo-European Languages**
(Italicized languages are no longer spoken.)

| SUBFAMILY | LANGUAGES |
|---|---|
| Indo-Iranian | *Sanskrit,* Hindi, Urdu, Persian |
| Baltic | Latvian, Lithuanian |
| Slavic | Czech, Polish, Russian, Ukrainian, Serbo-Croatian, Bulgarian, Slovenian |
| Celtic | Irish, Gaelic, Welsh |
| Germanic | Dutch, English, German, Danish |
| Hellenic | Greek |
| Italic | *Latin,* Romance languages: Spanish, Italian, French, Portuguese, Romanian |

**Geography SKILLS**

1. **Movement** Which nomadic peoples moved into Anatolia?
2. **Location** How did the Hittites serve as a culture hearth?

**Maps In MOtion** See *StudentWorks™ Plus* or glencoe.com.

based somewhere in the steppe region north of the Black Sea or in Southwest Asia. Around 2000 B.C. they began to move into Europe, India, and western Asia. One group moved into Asia Minor and Anatolia around 1750 B.C. With the native peoples, they formed the Hittite kingdom with its capital at Hattushash (Bogazköy in modern Turkey).

Between 1600 B.C. and 1200 B.C., the **Hittites** created an empire in western Asia and threatened the power of the Egyptians. The Hittites were the first Indo-Europeans to use iron. Iron weapons were stronger and cheaper to make because of the widespread availability of iron ore. Around 1200 B.C. invaders, known to historians only as the "Sea Peoples," destroyed the Hittite Empire.

The end of the Hittite kingdom and the weakening of Egypt temporarily left no dominant powers in western Asia. This allowed a number of small kingdoms and city-states to emerge. The Phoenicians were one of these peoples.

**✓Reading Check** **Identifying** Who were the first Indo-Europeans to use iron?

## The Phoenicians

**MAIN IDEA** The Phoenicians created an international trade empire and invented an alphabet.

***HISTORY & YOU*** Why would using an alphabet make writing easier than using picture symbols? Learn about the Phoenician alphabet.

The **Phoenicians** lived in the area of Palestine along the Mediterranean coast on a narrow band of land 120 miles (193 km) long. After the downfall of the Hittites and the Egyptians, the newfound political independence of the Phoenicians helped them expand their trade. Trade had long been the basis of their prosperity. The chief cities of Phoenicia—Byblos, Tyre, and Sidon—were ports on the eastern Mediterranean. The Phoenicians produced a number of goods for foreign markets, including purple dye, glass, and lumber from the cedar forests of Lebanon.

The Phoenicians built ships and became great international sea traders. They eventually created a trade empire. The Phoenicians charted new routes not only in the Mediterranean but also in the Atlantic Ocean, where they reached Britain and sailed south along the west coast of Africa. They set up a number of colonies in the western Mediterranean. Carthage, on the North African coast, was their most famous colony.

Phoenician culture is best known for its alphabet. The Phoenicians, who spoke a Semitic language, simplified their writing by using 22 different signs to represent the sounds of their speech. These 22 characters, or letters, could be used to spell out all the words in the Phoenician language. Although the Phoenicians were not the only people to invent an alphabet, theirs was important because it was eventually passed on to the Greeks. From the Greek alphabet came the Roman alphabet that we still use today.

**✓ Reading Check** **Identifying** What was the most significant cultural invention of the Phoenicians?

### *HISTORY & ARTS*

### *The Phoenicians*

It is hard to separate the Phoenicians' cultural accomplishments from their economic accomplishments. Their sophisticated ships took them to far-off lands, spreading their alphabet, as well as their trade goods, throughout the Mediterranean.

**Comparing Alphabets**

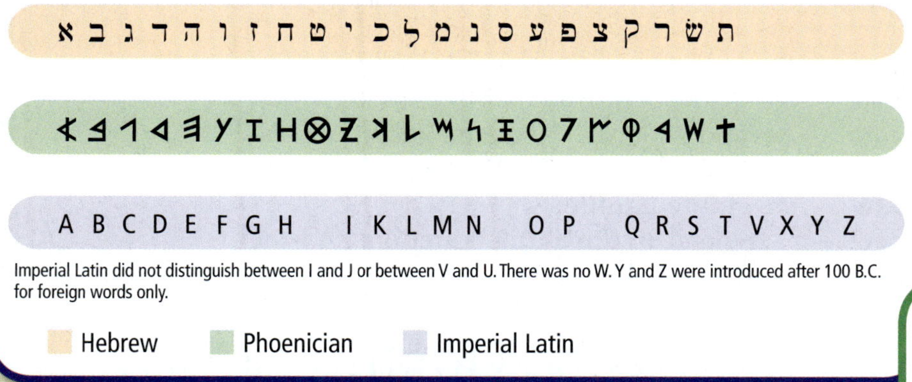


Imperial Latin did not distinguish between I and J or between V and U. There was no W. Y and Z were introduced after 100 B.C. for foreign words only.

The Phoenician alphabet influenced the Greek alphabet, which was the basis for the Latin, or Roman, alphabet.

Marker with Greek and Phoenician—bilingual—inscription on Malta

**DOCUMENT-BASED QUESTIONS**

1. **Making Inferences** Why is the Phoenician alphabet important to our society?
2. **Explaining** Why would there have been ancient bilingual documents and markers?

## The Israelites

**MAIN IDEA** The Israelites had lasting influence through their religious beliefs rather than from military power.

**HISTORY & YOU** How might religious beliefs affect the ways in which people interact? Read to learn about the interaction between religions in the eastern Mediterranean.

---

To the south of the Phoenicians lived another group of Semitic-speaking people known as the **Israelites.** They were a minor factor in the politics of the region. However, their religion—known today as Judaism—flourished and later influenced the religions of Christianity and Islam.

Much of the Israelites' history and religious beliefs was eventually written down in the Hebrew Bible, which is known to Christians as the Old Testament. According to Israelite traditions, they were descendants of the patriarch Abraham. Their ancestors migrated from Mesopotamia to Canaan. Their lifestyle was based on grazing animals rather than on farming. Then, because of drought, the Israelites moved to Egypt, where they were enslaved until Moses led them out of Egypt, probably in the first half of the thirteenth century B.C.

The Israelites wandered for many years in the desert until they returned to Canaan. It was there, between 1200 B.C. and 1000 B.C., that they organized in tribes and established a united kingdom known as Israel.

### The United Kingdom

Under **King David,** who ruled from about 1010 B.C. to 970 B.C., the Israelites had established control over all the land that came to be called Israel and made **Jerusalem** into its capital. David's son **King Solomon** expanded the government and army and encouraged trade. Solomon is best known for building a temple in the city of Jerusalem. The Israelites viewed the temple as the symbolic center of their religion and of the Israelite kingdom itself. Under King Solomon, ancient Israel reached the height of its power.

King Solomon was also known for his wisdom. Once, two women brought a child before him, each claiming that she was the child's mother. Solomon ordered his servant to cut the child in half, giving one half to each woman. The first woman objected: "Please, my lord, give her the living baby! Don't kill him!" The second woman replied, "Neither I nor you shall have him. Cut him in two!" Then Solomon said: "Give the baby to the first woman. Do not kill him; she is his mother." According to the biblical account, "When all Israel heard the verdict the king had given, they held the king in awe, because they saw that he had wisdom from God to administer justice."

### The Divided Kingdom

After Solomon's death, tension among Israel's tribes led to the creation of two separate kingdoms. The Kingdom of Israel was composed of the ten northern tribes and had its capital at Samaria. To the south, the Kingdom of Judah consisted of two tribes and had its capital at Jerusalem.

In 722 or 721 B.C., the Assyrians overran the Kingdom of Israel and sent many Israelites to other parts of the Assyrian Empire. Most of these scattered Israelites (the "ten lost tribes") merged with neighboring peoples and gradually lost their identity.

The Kingdom of Judah managed to retain its independence for a while, but a new enemy soon appeared on the horizon. The Chaldeans (kal•DEE•uhnz) defeated Assyria, conquered the Kingdom of Judah, and completely destroyed Jerusalem in 586 B.C. Many people of Judah were sent as captives to Babylonia; the exile of the people of Judah from their homeland is called the Diaspora. The words of the Psalm 137 evoke the memory of their exile:

**PRIMARY SOURCE**

"By the rivers of Babylon, we sat and wept when we remembered Zion. . . . How can we sing the songs of the Lord while in a foreign land? If I forget you, O Jerusalem, may my right hand forget its skill. May my tongue cling to the roof of my mouth if I do not remember you, if I do not consider Jerusalem my highest joy."

—Psalms 137: 1, 4–6

The Babylonian captivity did not last. New conquerors, the Persians, allowed the people of Judah to return to Jerusalem and rebuild their city and temple. The revived province of Judah was controlled by Persia until the conquests of Alexander the Great in the 300s B.C. The people of Judah survived, eventually becoming known as the Jews and giving their name to Judaism.

## Judaism

The Jews are **monotheistic**, believing in one God, who is the Creator of the world and everything in it. In the Jews' view, God rules the world; all peoples are his servants, whether they know it or not. God created nature but is not identified with it. The sun, the wind, and other natural phenomena are not gods, but God's creations to be admired but not worshiped.

This Creator is not removed from the life he created. God is just and good, and he expects goodness from his people. If they do not obey his will, they are subject to punishment. However, he is also "compassionate, slow to anger, and rich in love." Each person can have a personal relationship with him.

The covenant, law, and prophets are three aspects of Jewish religious tradition. Jews believe that during the exodus from Egypt, when Moses led his people out of bondage, God made a covenant, or contract, with them. God promised to protect them if they followed his Torah, Judaism's foundational set of precepts. The most famous laws in the Torah are the Ten Commandments that Moses is said to have received at Mount Sinai. Jews also believe that God sent additional religious teachers, or prophets, to serve as his voice to his people.

## Connecting to the United States

### The Ten Commandments

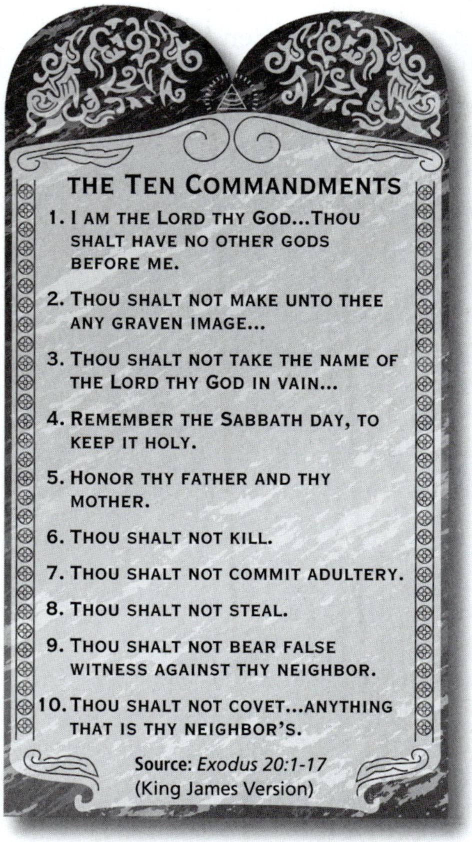


According to Jewish beliefs, God gave his laws, including the Ten Commandments, to Moses. These laws are not only fundamental to Judaism but to Christianity as well. In the United States, translations of the Ten Commandments have been posted in classrooms and carved on courthouse monuments. However, displaying the Ten Commandments in public facilities—schools, parks, and government offices—has sparked debate.

Although other countries have had a state, or official, religion, the United States does not. James Madison, drafter of the First Amendment and later president, believed the government should not tax its citizens to support religious activities or beliefs and that all religions should be treated equally and fairly. The First Amendment to the U.S. Constitution states, "Congress shall make no law respecting an establishment of religion . . ."

The debate continues. Does displaying the Ten Commandments promote law-abiding behavior or does it indicate a bias toward particular religious groups?

- **The Ten Commandments are fundamental laws of Judaism.**
- **The Commandments are part of a shared Judeo-Christian heritage.**

**Connecting to Today**

1. **Identifying Points of View** Why would some people think that posting the Ten Commandments in a courthouse shows bias?
2. **Making Connections** How do the Ten Commandments relate to the laws in the United States?

The age of prophecy lasted from the 1000s B.C. to the 400s B.C., a time when the people were threatened or conquered by powerful neighbors. The prophets declared that faithlessness to God would bring catastrophe, but that turning from evil would bring God's mercy. The prophets introduced concepts that enriched the Jewish tradition. Later prophets embraced a concern for all humanity. All nations would come to the God of Israel and find peace.

**PRIMARY SOURCE**

> "They will beat their swords into plowshares and their spears into pruning hooks. Nation will not take up sword against nation, nor will they train for war anymore."
>
> —Isaiah 2:4

The prophets also cried out against social injustice. They condemned the rich for causing the poor to suffer. They denounced excessive luxuries, and they threatened Israelites with punishments for their sins. They said that God's command was to live justly, share with others, and care for the poor and the unfortunate. These words became a source for ideals of social justice for Jews and others.

The following selection makes clear the prophets' belief that unjust actions would bring God's punishment.

**PRIMARY SOURCE**

> "The Lord enters into judgment against the elders and leaders of his people: 'It is you who have ruined my vineyard; the plunder from the poor is in your houses. What do you mean by crushing my people and grinding the faces of the poor?' . . . Your men will fall by the sword, your warriors in battle."
>
> —Isaiah 3:14–17, 25

The religion of Israel was unique among the religions of western Asia and Egypt. The biggest difference was its belief in only one God (monotheism). In other ancient religions, only priests (and some rulers) had access to the gods. In the Jewish tradition, God's wishes, though communicated to the people through prophets, had been written down. No leader of Israel could claim that he alone knew God's will. This knowledge was available to anyone who could read the Hebrew Bible.

While Judaism requires concern for all humanity, its laws also prevented complete integration into surrounding communities. Thus, unlike most other peoples of Southwest Asia, Jews would not accept the gods of their conquerors or neighbors. The social separation that this engendered may have been a factor in creating feelings of hostility toward Jews, but it also helped them maintain their identity after the loss of Jewish independence.

✓ **Reading Check** **Identifying** Which aspect of Israelite culture had the greatest impact on Western civilization?

## SECTION 3 REVIEW

### Vocabulary

1. **Explain** the significance of: pastoral nomads, created, domesticated, technology, Indo-Europeans, Hittites, Phoenicians, Israelites, King David, King Solomon, Jerusalem, monotheistic.

### Main Ideas

2. **Describe** how the Hittites used new technology to gain power.
3. **List** the areas reached by Phoenician traders. Also list the areas that were colonized by the Phoenicians.
4. **Create** a chart like the one below to show the significance of three major events in the history of the Israelites.

| Event | Significance |
|---|---|
| 1. | |
| 2. | |
| 3. | |

### Critical Thinking

5. **BIG Idea** **Contrasting** How did the Jews' religious beliefs make them different from other peoples of their time and place?
6. **Evaluating** How did nomadic peoples both contribute to and slow down the development of civilization?
7. **Analyzing Visuals** Examine the image on page 48. What similarities do you see between the three alphabets?

### Writing About History

8. **Informative Writing** Using the Internet, news magazines, and newspapers, research the current conflicts in the Middle East. Prepare a brief research report summarizing what you have learned about current events and movements toward peace in the region.

**History ONLINE**

For help with the concepts in this section of *Glencoe World History*, go to glencoe.com and click Study Central™.

NATIONAL GEOGRAPHIC

# GEOGRAPHY & HISTORY

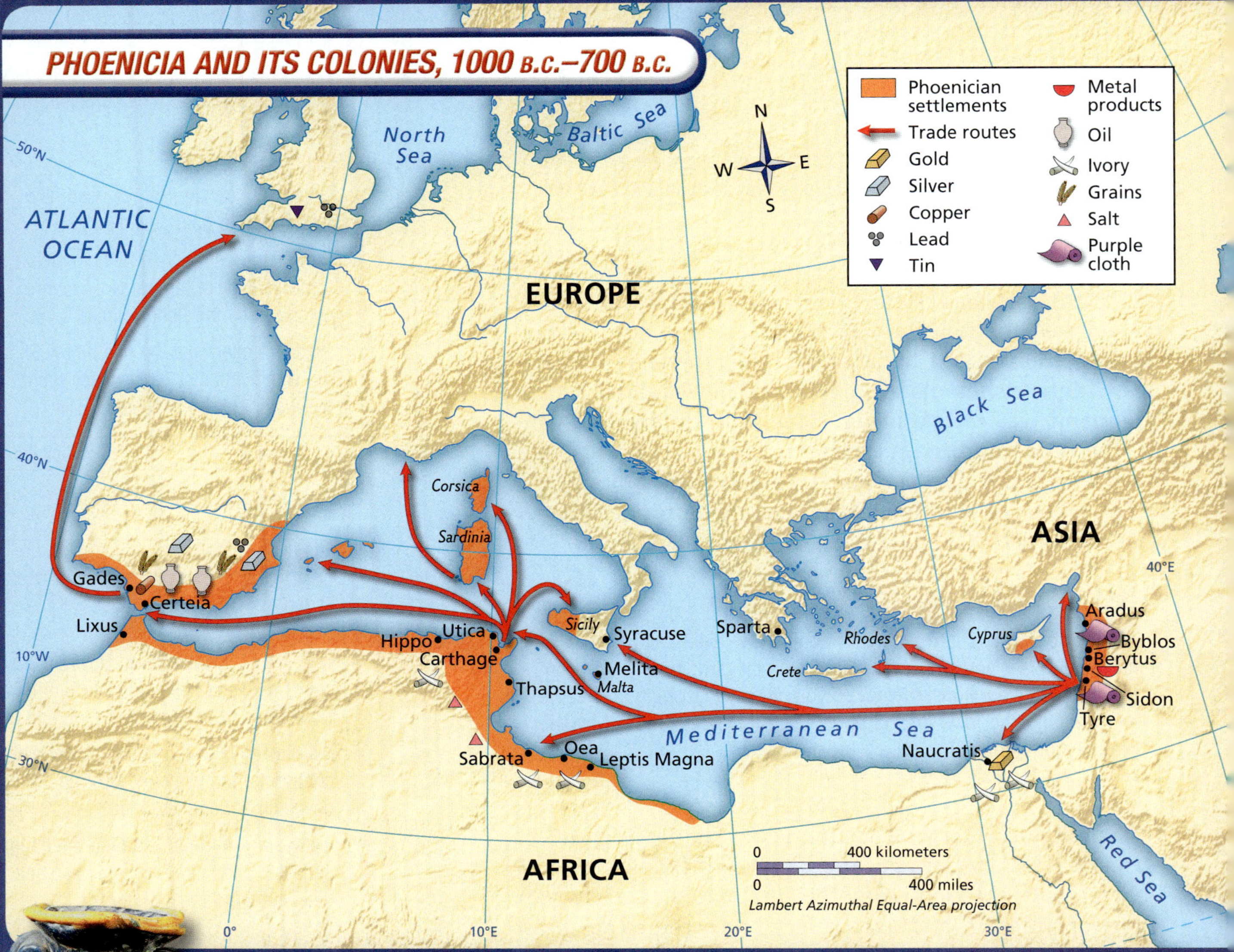

Trade goods, like this flask used for storing oils, helped Phoenicia build strong trade ties throughout the Mediterranean, 969 B.C.

Phoenician merchant ships transport cedar wood from Tyre in this Assyrian bas-relief. In the 900s B.C. and 800s B.C., Tyre became the leading Phoenician city.

PRIMARY SOURCE

▲ An Assyrian stone carving of a Phoenician warship, produced around 700 B.C.

◀ All of Phoenicia except Tyre falls to an Assyrian army led by Sennacherib, shown in this bas-relief accepting the surrender of his enemies, 701 B.C.

# THE PHOENICIANS

**A Phoenician Lake** A collection of independent city-states spread along the eastern coast of the Mediterranean Sea in an area called Canaan. Around 1200 B.C. some of the so-called "Sea Peoples" settled on the southern coast of Canaan. They may have contributed their knowledge of seafaring to the people we know as the Phoenicians. Using oars and sails for power, Phoenician ships traveled the Mediterranean. Some sailed to Britain, Spain, and West Africa. The Phoenicians became skilled at both navigation and trade.

**Colonies and Trade Goods** By around 900 B.C., Phoenician merchants had extensive trade routes and in time founded colonies on the coasts of Spain (Iberia), Sicily, and North Africa. These colonies served as trading posts and as places to resupply ships. Unlike other settlements in the ancient world, these colonies were founded for trade, not in response to overcrowding at home or desire for empire. Phoenicia's most important colony, Carthage, eventually established its own empire.

Phoenician ships carried timber, glass, tin, silver, ivory, and metalwork from its three major cities—Sidon, Tyre, and Byblos. Glassblowing is said to have originated in Sidon. Tyre's best-known luxury export was cloth colored with a purple dye made from a sea snail. Only the rich could afford Tyrian purple cloth. *Phoenicia* comes from the Greek word *phoinix,* meaning purple-red. Byblos traded Egyptian papyrus, which was used for making books. The Greek word *biblion* was applied to any book written on papyrus and was the origin of the word *Bible.*

**Spreading Culture** Phoenician religion spread along the trade routes, and the Greeks and Egyptians adopted some of their gods. The most lasting contribution of the Phoenicians was the writing system they used as they traded throughout the Mediterranean. First, the Greeks and later the Romans modified the Phoenician alphabet and spread it across their empires.

**Geography SKILLS**

1. **Location** Why did Phoenician traders create trade networks going west rather than east?
2. **Movement** Examine the map of Phoenicia and its colonies. How did trade and colonization contribute to the spread of the Phoenician alphabet?

SECTION 4

Section Audio

Spotlight Video

# The Rise of New Empires

### GUIDE TO READING

**The BIG Idea**

**Competition Among Countries** The Assyrians and the Persians established vast empires in the ancient world.

**Content Vocabulary**

- satrapy *(p. 57)*
- satrap *(p. 57)*
- monarchy *(p. 57)*

**Academic Vocabulary**

- restraint *(p. 56)*
- sought *(p. 56)*
- sustained *(p. 57)*

**People and Places**

- Assyrians *(p. 54)*
- Nebuchadnezzar *(p. 56)*
- Persians *(p. 56)*
- Cyrus *(p. 56)*
- Darius *(p. 56)*
- Royal Road *(p. 57)*
- Immortals *(p. 57)*
- Zoroaster *(p. 57)*

**Reading Strategy**

**Compare and Contrast** As you read, complete a Venn diagram like the one below identifying similarities and differences between the Assyrian Empire and Persian Empire.

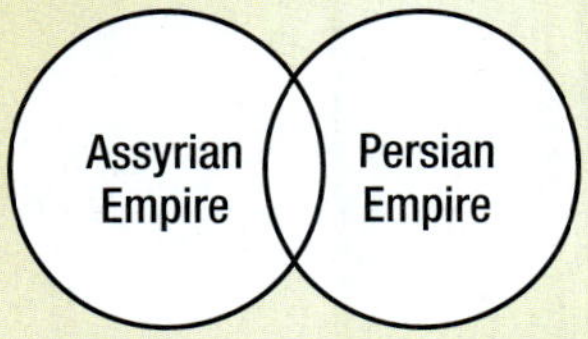


*After 700 B.C., new empires arose in western Asia that covered vast stretches of the ancient world. The Assyrians were better at conquest than at ruling, and their empire lasted less than one hundred years. The Persian Empire brought many years of peace to Southwest Asia, increasing trade and the general well-being of its people.*

## The Assyrian Empire

**MAIN IDEA** The Assyrians ruled with harsh tactics that brought about the fall of their empire.

**HISTORY & YOU** Why do you think a country that is good at fighting might not be as good at ruling? Read how the Assyrians built and lost an empire.

The first of the new empires was formed in Assyria, located on the upper Tigris River. The **Assyrians** were a Semitic-speaking people who exploited the use of iron weapons to establish an empire by 700 B.C. The Assyrian Empire included Mesopotamia, parts of the Plateau of Iran, sections of Asia Minor, Syria, Israel, and Egypt down to Thebes. In less than a hundred years, however, internal strife and resentment of Assyrian rule began to tear the Assyrian Empire apart. In 612 B.C., the empire fell to a coalition of Chaldeans and Medes (people who lived in the east), and it was divided between those powers.

At its height, the Assyrian Empire was ruled by kings whose power was seen as absolute. Under their leadership, the Assyrian Empire became well organized. Local officials were directly responsible to the king. The Assyrians also developed an efficient system of communication to administer their empire. A network of posts was established throughout the empire that used relays of horses to carry messages. The system was so effective that a governor anywhere in the empire could send a question and receive an answer from the king within a week. One of the last Assyrian kings, Ashurbanipal, established one of the world's first libraries at Nineveh. This library has provided abundant information concerning ancient Southwest Asian civilizations.

The Assyrians were good at conquering others. Through many years of practice they developed effective military leaders and fighters. The Assyrian army was large, well organized, and disciplined. A force of infantrymen was its core, joined by cavalrymen and horse-drawn war chariots that were used as platforms for shooting arrows. Moreover, the Assyrians had the first large armies equipped with iron weapons.

**PRIMARY SOURCE** **HISTORY & ARTS**

## Panel of Ashurbanipal, c. 650 B.C.

This relief of Ashurbanipal hunting lions is from his palace at Nineveh. It depicts a ceremonial hunt where King Ashurbanipal, aided by servants, hunts lions who are released from cages into a closed arena. Many reliefs depicting stories were used to decorate the king's palace.

### DOCUMENT-BASED QUESTIONS

1. **Making Inferences** Where does the hunt take place? Why might this be significant?
2. **Analyzing Visuals** Why do you think Ashurbanipal hunted lions rather than some other type of animal?

Another factor in the army's success was its ability to use different military tactics. The Assyrians could wage guerrilla warfare in the mountains, set battles on open ground, and lay siege to cities. They used battering rams and siege towers to hammer at the city's walls. Then they would tunnel under them, making them collapse.

The Assyrians used terror as an instrument of warfare. They regularly laid waste to the land in which they were fighting. They smashed dams; looted and destroyed towns; set crops on fire; and cut down trees, particularly fruit trees. The Assyrians were especially known for committing atrocities on their captives. King Ashurbanipal recorded this account of his treatment of prisoners:

**PRIMARY SOURCE**

"3,000 of their combat troops I felled with weapons. . . . Many I took alive; from some of these I cut off their hands to the wrist, from others I cut off their noses, ears, and fingers; I put out the eyes of many of the soldiers. . . . I burned their young men and women to death."

—H.W.F. Saggs, *The Might That Was Assyria*

**✓ Reading Check** **Summarizing** Why were the Assyrians so successful at conquering others?

# The Persian Empire

**MAIN IDEA** Strong Persian leaders conquered and ruled a vast empire for more than 200 years.

**HISTORY & YOU** What qualities do you think make a great leader? Read to learn why Cyrus was considered a great leader.

After the collapse of the Assyrian Empire, the Chaldean king **Nebuchadnezzar** (NEH•byuh•kuhd•NEH•zuhr) II made Babylonia the leading state in western Asia. He rebuilt Babylon as the center of his empire and gave it a reputation as one of the great cities of the ancient world, but Babylon fell to the Persians in 539 B.C.

## The Rise of the Persian Empire

The **Persians** were Indo-Europeans who lived in what is today southwestern Iran. Primarily nomadic, the Persians were eventually unified by one family. One member of this family, **Cyrus,** created a powerful Persian state that stretched from Asia Minor to India. Cyrus ruled from 559 B.C. to 530 B.C. In 539 B.C., he captured Babylon. His treatment of Babylonia showed remarkable **restraint** and wisdom. He also allowed the Jews who had been held there as captives to return to Israel.

The people of his time called Cyrus "the Great." He demonstrated wisdom and compassion in the conquest and organization of his empire. Unlike the Assyrian rulers, Cyrus had a reputation for mercy. Medes, Babylonians, and Jews all accepted him as their ruler. Cyrus had a genuine respect for other civilizations. For example, he used Assyrian, Babylonian, and Egyptian designs for building his palaces.

Cyrus's successors **sought** to extend the territory of the Persian Empire. His son Cambyses (kam•BY•SEEZ) successfully invaded Egypt.

**Darius,** who ruled from 521 B.C. to 486 B.C., added a new Persian province in

NATIONAL GEOGRAPHIC

**THE PERSIAN EMPIRE, 500 B.C.**

**Geography SKILLS**

1. **Location** Explain why the Royal Road was constructed and why it was constructed where it was.
2. **Regions** How do you think the empire was divided into satrapies? Redraw the map with boundaries for the satrapies. Explain what you have done.

western India. He then conquered Thrace in Europe, creating the world's largest empire to that time. Contact with Greece led Darius to invade the Greek mainland.

Darius strengthened the Persian government. He divided the empire into 20 provinces, called **satrapies** (SAY•truh•pees). A governor, or **satrap**, literally a "protector of the kingdom," ruled each province. Each satrap collected taxes, provided justice, and recruited soldiers.

An efficient communication system **sustained** the Persian Empire. Officials easily traveled through the empire on well-maintained roads dotted with way stations that provided food, shelter, and fresh horses. The **Royal Road** stretched from Lydia to Susa, the empire's chief capital.

In this system, the Persian king—the "Great King"—held an exalted position. He had the power of life and death. Much of the empire's power depended on the military. By the time of Darius, Persian kings had created a standing army of professional soldiers from all over the empire. At its core were a cavalry force and an elite infantry force. They were known as the **Immortals** because whenever a member was killed, he was immediately replaced.

## The Fall of the Persian Empire

After Darius, the Persian kings became isolated at their courts, surrounded by luxuries. As the kings increased taxes, loyalty to the empire declined. Struggles over the throne weakened the **monarchy** (rule by a king or queen).

Persian kings were polygamous (having many wives) and had many children. Their sons had little power, and many engaged in plots to gain the throne. Struggles for the throne weakened the empire and led to its conquest by the Greek ruler Alexander the Great during the 330s B.C.

## Persian Religion

Zoroastrianism (ZOHR•uh•WAS•tree•uh•NIH•zuhm), the Persians' religion, was their most original cultural contribution. According to tradition, **Zoroaster,** revered as a prophet of the "true religion," was born in 660 B.C. His teachings were recorded in the *Zend Avesta*, the sacred book of Zoroastrianism.

Like the Jews, Zoroastrians were monotheistic. To Zoroaster, Ahuramazda (the "Wise Lord") was a supreme god who created all things. Ahuramazda was supreme, but he was not unopposed. At the beginning of the world, the evil spirit Ahriman opposed him. Humans played a role in the struggle between good and evil. Ahuramazda gave humans the freedom to choose between right and wrong. The good person chooses the way of Ahuramazda, who would eventually triumph.

✓Reading Check **Examining** What caused the Persian Empire to decline after the death of Darius?

## SECTION 4 REVIEW

### Vocabulary

1. **Explain** the significance of: Assyrians, Nebuchadnezzar, Persians, Cyrus, restraint, sought, Darius, satrapy, satrap, sustained, Royal Road, Immortals, monarchy, Zoroaster.

### Main Ideas

2. **Describe** some of the harsh tactics used by the Assyrians.
3. **List** the duties of the satraps of the Persian government.
4. **Create** a chart like the one shown below to identify the differences between a religious system based on monotheism and one based on polytheism.

| Monotheism | Polytheism |
|---|---|
| | |
| | |
| | |

### Critical Thinking

5. **BIG Idea** **Making Inferences** Why was a strong army so important in maintaining the Persian Empire's power?
6. **Contrasting** How were the Assyrian and Persian Empires different politically and socially and in their impact on the environment?
7. **Analyzing Visuals** Examine the relief of Ashurbanipal on page 55. Describe what you see in this image. Why do you think images such as this were made of Persian rulers?

### Writing About History

8. **Persuasive Writing** Suppose that you are Cyrus ruling the Babylonians, a people you have just conquered. Explain to your government officials why you believe that mercy and tolerance are better policies than harshness.

**History ONLINE**
For help with the concepts in this section of *Glencoe World History*, go to glencoe.com and click Study Central™.

ANALYZING
PRIMARY SOURCES

# What Did Ancient Societies Believe About Creation?

**How were ancient creation accounts similar and different?** The ancient peoples of Mesopotamia, Egypt, and Israel had different accounts of the creation of the world. However, there are several similarities.

**What do creation accounts reveal about religious beliefs?** Religion played a central role in the lives of ancient peoples. Creation accounts describe the gods or God they worshiped and help explain how ancient societies interpreted the world around them.

Creation accounts provide insights into the cultures of the people who developed them. Read the excerpts and study the painting to find out what the Babylonians, Israelites, and Egyptians believed about the creation of the world.

## SOURCE 1

The Babylonian story of creation is part of an epic poem titled *Enûma elish.*

The lord **[Marduk[1]]** trod upon the hinder part
of **Tiâmat[2],**
And with his unsparing club he split her
skull. . . .
He split her open like a mussel into two parts;
Half of her he set in place and formed the sky
therewith as a roof. . . .
He fixed the crossbar and posted guards;
He commanded them not to let her waters
escape. . . .
The lord measured the dimensions of the ***Apsû[3],***
And a great structure, its counterpart, he
established, namely, **Esharra[4],**
The great structure Esharra which he made as
a canopy. . . .
As Marduk hears the words of the gods,
His heart prompts him to create ingenious
things.
He conveys his idea to **Ea[5],**
Imparting the plan which he had conceived in
his heart:
"Blood will I form and cause bone to be;
Then will I set up ***lullû[6],*** 'Man' shall be his
name!
Yes, I will create *lullû:* Man!
Upon him shall the services of the gods be
imposed that they may be at rest."

## SOURCE 2

The book of Genesis contains an Israelite account of creation.

In the beginning God created the heavens and the earth. . . .

And God said, "Let there be light," and there was light. God saw that the light was good, and he separated the light from the darkness. God called the light "day," and the darkness he called "night." And there was evening and there was morning—the first day.

And God said, "Let there be an expanse between the waters to separate water from water." So God made the expanse and separated the water under the expanse from the water above it. And it was so. God called the expanse "sky." And there was evening, and there was morning—the second day.

And God said, "Let the water under the sky be gathered to one place, and let dry ground appear." And it was so. God called the dry ground "land," and the gathered waters he called "seas." And God saw that it was good. . . .

Then God said, "Let us make man in our image, in our likeness, and let them rule over the fish of the sea and the birds of the air, over the livestock, over all the earth, and over all the creatures that move along the ground."

So God created man in his own image, in the image of God he created him; male and female he created them.

[1] **Marduk:** ruler of the gods in Babylonian mythology
[2] **Tiâmat:** monster goddess; the earliest salt water
[3] **Apsû:** husband of Tiâmat; the earliest freshwater
[4] **Esharra:** a poetic name for the Earth

▲ The sun god, Re, makes his night journey in this drawing and relief from the tomb of Horemheb in Egypt, c. 1300 B.C.

## SOURCE 3

The ancient Egyptians had several creation myths. In one account, Re, the sun god, emerged from an egg that appeared on the surface of the ocean. Re later produced gods of air, earth, and heaven. Afterward, Re made humans and all other beings and objects on Earth. In the above painting, Re, the ram-headed figure, crosses through the under-world in his boat, carrying the spirits of Egyptians who have died. When Re reappears above the horizon at the beginning of each new day, the souls of the dead are reborn into new lives with him.

Egyptians spent every day surrounded by symbols of their religion. They saw gods in the natural world, they had gods important to their hometowns, and they believed in gods of trade, justice, and prosperity. They expected the gods to care for them in the afterlife.

[5] **Ea:** god of wisdom and magic; father of Marduk

[6] **lullû:** humans

### DOCUMENT-BASED QUESTIONS

1. **Explaining** Why did the Babylonian god Marduk create humans?
2. **Clarifying** In the Israelite account, what was the expanse that separated water from water?
3. **Analyzing** How does the Egyptian god Re represent the sun?
4. **Contrasting** How is the depiction of the Israelite deity different from those in the other two creation accounts?
5. **Comparing** What similar event is found in all three creation accounts?
6. **Drawing Conclusions** What is the role of humans in each of the three creation accounts?
7. **Synthesizing** How would you describe the beliefs that ancient societies held about the creation of the world?

# CHAPTER 2 Visual Summary

You can study anywhere, anytime by downloading quizzes and flash cards to your PDA from glencoe.com.

TOMB AT SAQQARA, EGYPT

Egyptian farmers drive cattle across a river.

## ANCIENT ENVIRONMENTS

- The Egyptians received fertile soil from the floodwaters of the Nile for farming.
- The Phoenicians set up a trading empire and colonies on the Mediterranean.
- The Mesopotamians created irrigation and flood control systems.

## ANCIENT RELIGIONS

- The Mesopotamians and the Egyptians, who both were polytheistic, believed their rulers derived their power from the gods.
- The Israelites were monotheistic and believed God communicated through prophets.
- The Persians followed Zoroastrianism, a monotheistic religion.

TEMPLE AT URUK, MESOPOTAMIA

The ancient Sumerian city of Uruk was one of the first cities in the world.

ACCOUNTING TABLET, MESOPOTAMIA

Sumerians used cuneiform to keep accounts, like this tablet account of donkeys harnessed for ploughing.

## ANCIENT INNOVATIONS

- The Mesopotamians established a collection of laws, along with inventing the arch, dome, wheel, and a system of writing.
- The Phoenicians invented the alphabet.
- The Persians created the concept of a standing army.

# CHAPTER 2 Assessment

## Reviewing Vocabulary

*Directions: Choose the word or words that best complete the sentence.*

**1.** Another word for province is ________.

**A** city-state
**B** empire
**C** satrapy
**D** vizier

**2.** A ________ is a Sumerian stepped tower.

**A** ziggurat
**B** pyramid
**C** stylus
**D** papyrus

**3.** ________ is belief in one God rather than many gods.

**A** Polytheism
**B** Monotheism
**C** Theocracy
**D** Monarchy

**4.** In a ________, ruling power is passed from one generation to the next.

**A** theocracy
**B** bureaucracy
**C** dynasty
**D** patriarchy

**5.** An administrative organization with officials and regular procedures is known as a ________.

**A** dynasty
**B** bureaucracy
**C** theocracy
**D** satrapy

## Reviewing Main Ideas

*Directions: Choose the best answers to the following questions.*

### Section 1 *(pp. 26–33)*

**6.** Who created the first Mesopotamian civilization?

**A** Akkadians
**B** Assyrians
**C** Babylonians
**D** Sumerians

**7.** Which ruler set up the first empire in world history?

**A** Darius
**B** Hammurabi
**C** Sargon
**D** Solomon

**8.** What was the most important Sumerian invention?

**A** Alphabet
**B** Writing
**C** Bronze
**D** Number system

### Section 2 *(pp. 34–43)*

**9.** What god symbolized the new life brought to Egypt by the Nile?

**A** Akhenaten
**B** Osiris
**C** Re
**D** Seth

**TEST-TAKING TIP**

When a question asks for an answer related to a specific topic, such as geography, eliminate any choices that do not mention anything about that topic. Then choose the best answer from the choices that remain.

**Need Extra Help?**

| If You Missed Questions . . . | 1 | 2 | 3 | 4 | 5 | 6 | 7 | 8 | 9 |
|---|---|---|---|---|---|---|---|---|---|
| Go to Page . . . | 57 | 29 | 50 | 36 | 37 | 26 | 32 | 30 | 36 |

GO ON

# CHAPTER 2 Assessment

10. During whose reign was the Great Pyramid at Giza built?
    - **A** Khufu
    - **B** Hatshepsut
    - **C** Ramses II
    - **D** Tutankhamen

**Section 3** *(pp. 46–51)*

11. What was the common characteristic of Indo-Europeans?
    - **A** Their weapons
    - **B** Their crops
    - **C** Their language
    - **D** Their religion

12. Who invented the alphabet that influenced the Greeks and Romans?
    - **A** Chaldeans
    - **B** Hittites
    - **C** Israelites
    - **D** Phoenicians

**Section 4** *(pp. 54–57)*

13. Which statement best describes the Assyrians?
    - **A** They respected other civilizations.
    - **B** They were admired by their captives.
    - **C** They were good at conquering others.
    - **D** They had the world's largest empire.

14. Which Persian ruler was known for his wisdom and compassion?
    - **A** Ashurbanipal
    - **B** Cyrus
    - **C** Darius
    - **D** Nebuchadnezzar

## Critical Thinking

*Directions: Choose the best answers to the following questions.*

15. Which statement best reflects the principles in the Code of Hammurabi?
    - **A** Women and men are equal.
    - **B** Demand an eye for an eye.
    - **C** Let the buyer beware.
    - **D** Judges are above the law.

16. Why were the pharaohs of the Middle Kingdom different from those of earlier periods?
    - **A** They felt more responsible for taking care of their people.
    - **B** They believed in the sun god as the most important god.
    - **C** They engaged in the practice of mummification.
    - **D** They defeated the Hyksos and created an empire.

*Base your answer to question 17 on the chart below and your knowledge of world history.*

| | Mesopotamia | Egypt |
|---|---|---|
| Environment | Flat plains and river valleys allowed interaction between city-states | Deserts and Mediterranean Sea isolated Egypt |
| Economics | Traditional economy based on agriculture with some trade | Traditional economy based on agriculture with some trade |
| Government/ Politics | Theocracy—kings and priests ruled city-states | Theocracy—dynastic god-kings ruled the kingdom |
| Social Structure | Nobles, priests, merchants, scribes, farmers, slaves | Pharaohs, nobles, priests, merchants, scribes, farmers, slaves |

17. How was Mesopotamian civilization different from Egyptian?
    - **A** Unlike the Egyptians, Mesopotamian commoners had little say in the government.
    - **B** Mesopotamians trained boys to be scribes, while the Egyptians did not.
    - **C** Mesopotamia was more vulnerable to invasion than Egypt.
    - **D** Religion played an important role in Mesopotamian society, but it was unimportant in Egypt.

**Need Extra Help?**

| If You Missed Questions . . . | 10 | 11 | 12 | 13 | 14 | 15 | 16 | 17 |
|---|---|---|---|---|---|---|---|---|
| Go to Page . . . | 37 | 46 | 48 | 54 | 56 | 33 | 39 | 26 |

GO ON

**18.** Which of the following shows the correct chronological order of empires in the ancient world?

**A** Akkadian, Assyrian, Egyptian, Persian

**B** Akkadian, Egyptian, Assyrian, Persian

**C** Egyptian, Akkadian, Assyrian, Persian

**D** Assyrian, Persian, Akkadian, Egyptian

*Analyze the map and answer the question that follows. Base your answer on the map.*

**Eastern Mediterranean, 924 B.C.– 843 B.C.**

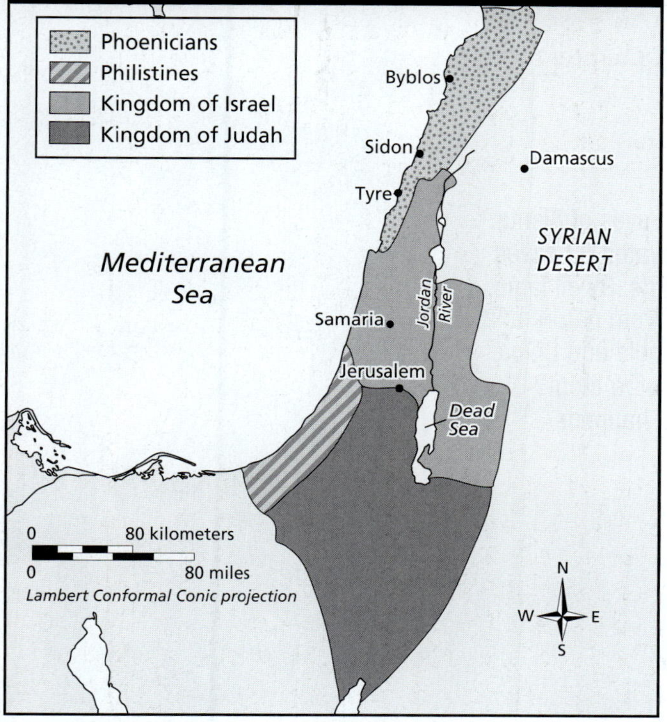


**19.** Based on the map, how did the Phoenicians probably trade with other civilizations?

**A** Along the Mediterranean Sea

**B** Across the Syrian Desert

**C** Trade was likely unimportant.

**D** Trade went through Samaria.

## Document-Based Questions

*Directions: Analyze the document and answer the short answer questions that follow the document.*

*Read the following Mesopotamian poem.*

> *"The rampant flood which no man can oppose,*
> *Which shakes the heavens and causes earth to tremble,*
> *In an appalling blanket folds mother and child,*
> *And drowns the harvest in its time of ripeness."*

**20.** How does this poem represent the Mesopotamians' attitude toward nature?

**21.** Explain the meaning of the line: "Which shakes the heavens and causes earth to tremble."

## Extended Response

**22.** Literature often reflects a people's worldview. How does this poem represent the importance of the physical environment and religion in the lives of the Mesopotamians?

**History ONLINE**

For additional test practice, use Self-Check Quizzes—Chapter 2 at glencoe.com.

**Need Extra Help?**

| If You Missed Questions . . . | 18 | 19 | 20 | 21 | 22 |
|---|---|---|---|---|---|
| Go to Page . . . | 32 | 63 | 63 | 63 | 63 |

STOP

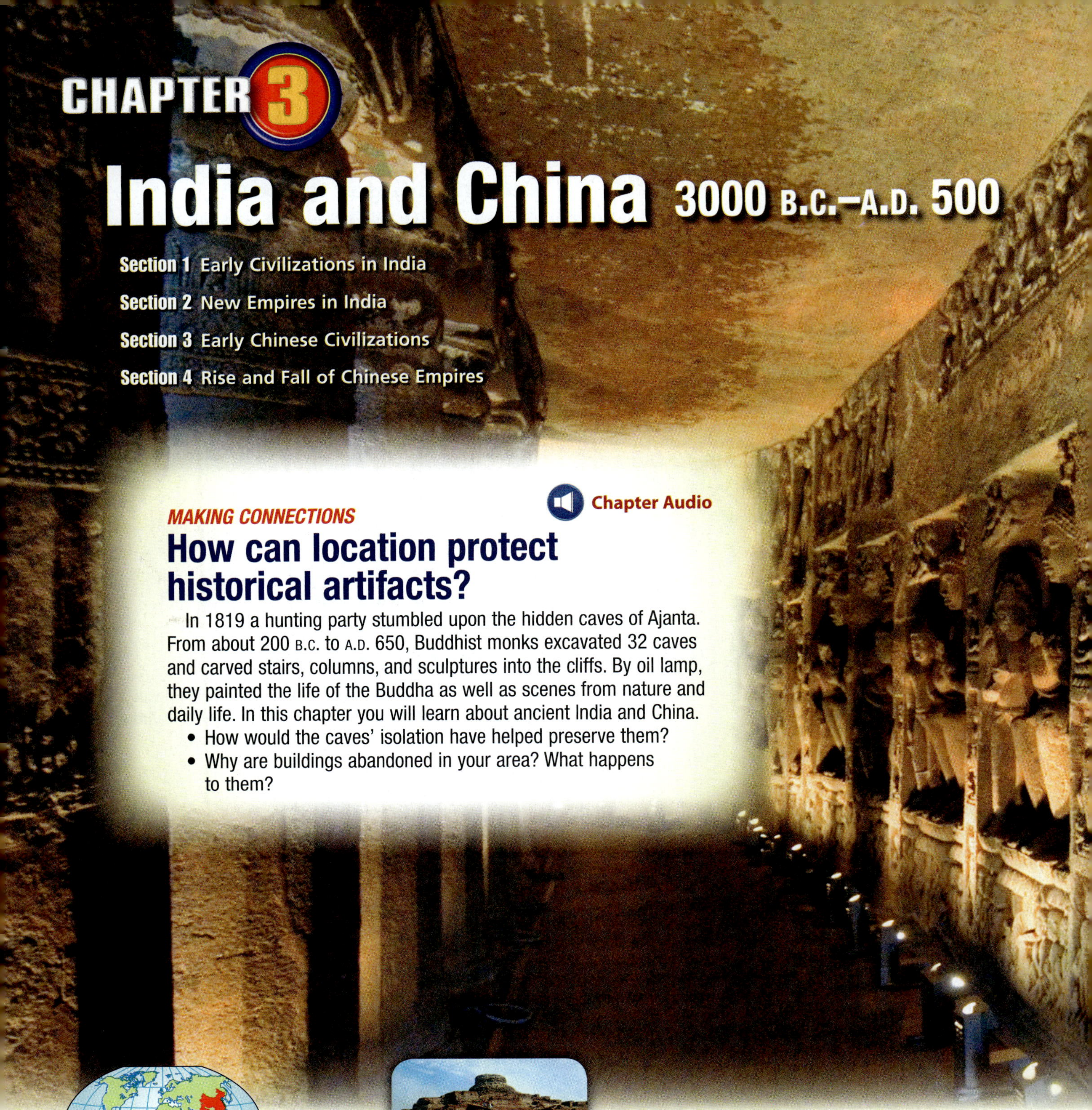

# CHAPTER 3

# India and China 3000 B.C.–A.D. 500



Chapter Audio

*MAKING CONNECTIONS*

## How can location protect historical artifacts?

In 1819 a hunting party stumbled upon the hidden caves of Ajanta. From about 200 B.C. to A.D. 650, Buddhist monks excavated 32 caves and carved stairs, columns, and sculptures into the cliffs. By oil lamp, they painted the life of the Buddha as well as scenes from nature and daily life. In this chapter you will learn about ancient India and China.

- How would the caves' isolation have helped preserve them?
- Why are buildings abandoned in your area? What happens to them?

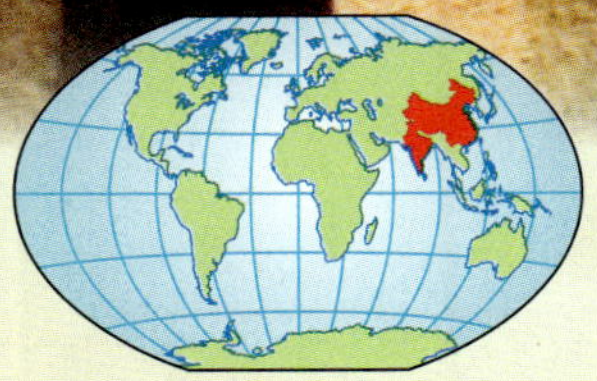

THE WORLD ▶

**c. 3000 B.C.** Cities built in Indus River valley

**c. 1500 B.C.** Aryans enter India

3500 B.C. — 2500 B.C. — 1500 B.C.

**c. 1750 B.C.** Shang dynasty begins

**c. 563 B.C.**
Birth of the Buddha, Siddhārtha Gautama

**c. 200 B.C.**
Travel on the Silk Road begins

**500 B.C.** — **A.D. 500**

**c. 551 B.C.**
Birth of Confucius

**c. A.D. 200**
Han dynasty famous for bronze sculptures

**FOLDABLES™ Study Organizer**

**Organizing** Create a Four-Tab Book to record What, Where, When, and Why/How facts while you read about the Great Wall of China or the Silk Road.

**History ONLINE** Visit glencoe.com and enter *QuickPass*™ code GWHEA7447c3 for Chapter 3 resources.

SECTION 1

Section Audio    Spotlight Video

# Early Civilizations in India

## GUIDE TO READING

### The BIG Idea

**Physical Geography** Changes to the physical environment and the migration of the Aryans led to major changes in India's culture beginning around 1800 B.C.

### Content Vocabulary

- monsoon *(p. 66)*
- Sanskrit *(p. 70)*
- *varnas* *(p. 70)*
- caste *(p. 71)*
- Hinduism *(p. 72)*
- yoga *(p. 72)*
- reincarnation *(p. 73)*
- karma *(p. 73)*
- dharma *(p. 73)*
- Buddhism *(p. 73)*
- nirvana *(p. 74)*

### Academic Vocabulary

- via *(p. 69)*
- reveal *(p. 70)*

### People and Places

- Himalaya *(p. 66)*
- Indus River *(p. 66)*
- Harappa *(p. 68)*
- Mohenjo Daro *(p. 68)*
- Aryans *(p. 69)*
- Siddhārtha Gautama *(p. 73)*

### Reading Strategy

**Sequencing Information** As you read, use a diagram like the one below to illustrate the process that led Siddhārtha Gautama to enlightenment.

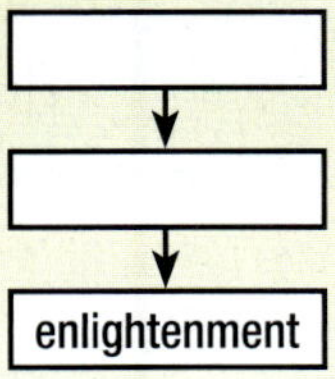


*The Indus River valley was the largest of the early river valley civilizations. An extensive river system supported agriculture, the development of cities, and widespread trade. Climate also was important to India's agriculture and development.*

## The Impact of Geography

**MAIN IDEA** India's mountains and location have played an important part in the development of the Indian subcontinent. Monsoons coming from the north and the south bring moisture to the farmers who live there.

***HISTORY & YOU*** What is the climate like in your region? How does the climate affect your clothing, activities, and architecture? Learn about the effects of monsoons on India's climate.

India is a land of diversity. Today, about 110 languages and more than 1,000 dialects—varieties of language—are spoken in India. Diversity is also apparent in India's geography. The Indian subcontinent, shaped like a triangle hanging from the southern ridge of Asia, is composed of a number of core regions, including mountain ranges, river valleys, a dry interior plateau, and fertile coastal plains.

### Mountains, Rivers, and Plains

In the far north are the **Himalaya**, the highest mountains in the world. Directly south of the Himalaya is the rich valley of the Ganges (GAN•jeez) River, one of the chief regions of Indian culture. To the west is the **Indus River** valley, a relatively dry plateau that forms the backbone of the modern state of Pakistan. In ancient times, the Indus Valley enjoyed a more moderate climate and served as the cradle of Indian civilization.

South of India's two major river valleys—the valleys of the Ganges and the Indus—lies the Deccan Plateau, which extends from the Ganges Valley to the southern tip of India. The interior of the plateau is relatively hilly and dry. India's eastern and western coasts are lush plains. These plains have historically been among the most densely populated regions of India.

### Monsoons

The primary feature of India's climate is the **monsoon**, a seasonal wind pattern in southern Asia. During the months of June through September, monsoon winds from the south and southwest blow across the Arabian Sea, part of the Indian Ocean. These summer monsoons carrying moisture-laden air cause heavy rainfall across

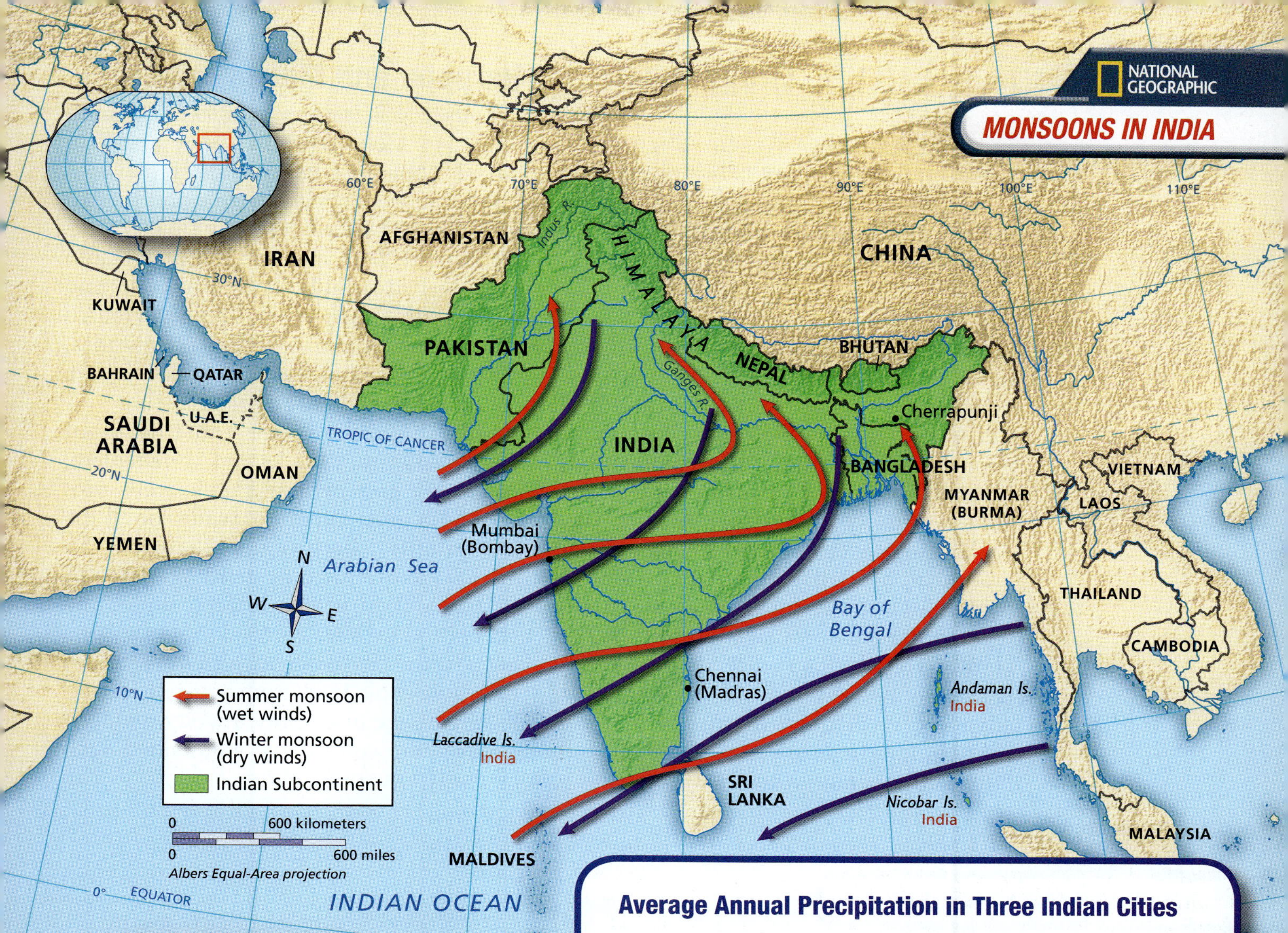


## Geography SKILLS

1. **Location** Where are Mumbai, Chennai, and Cherrapunji located?
2. **Place** How does location affect the precipitation in each city?

**Maps In MOtion** See *StudentWorks™ Plus* or glencoe.com.

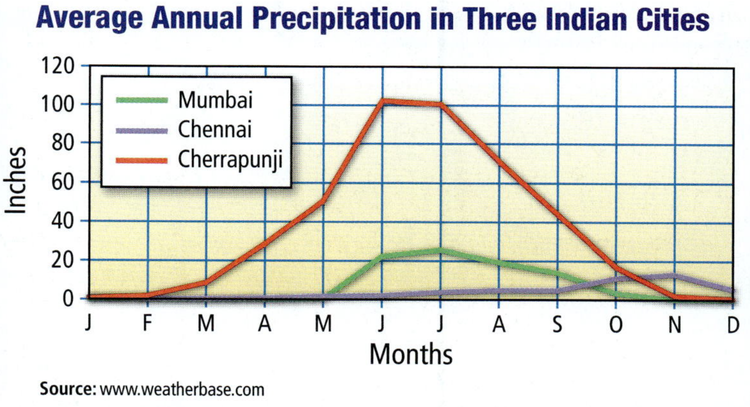


the subcontinent, especially on the west coast near Mumbai, once called Bombay.

During the cooler season, from October through February, the wind pattern reverses direction and blows from the north and northeast. Although this air is cooler and drier than the summer monsoons, the winter monsoons bring significant rainfall to the east coast of India.

The wettest place on earth is in the mountains of northeast India. Winds blow over the plains below, rise up the mountainside, cool, and release rain.

Throughout history, Indian farmers have depended on the heavy rains brought by the southwest monsoons. If the rains come early or late, or too much or too little rain falls, crops are destroyed and thousands starve.

✓ **Reading Check** **Describing** How does the monsoon affect Indian farmers?

## Indus Valley Civilization

**MAIN IDEA** The cities of the Indus Valley civilization were well planned and very advanced.

**HISTORY & YOU** What kinds of public services does your city provide? Find out about the Indus Valley cities.

As in Mesopotamia and Egypt, early civilizations in India and China emerged in river valleys. Between 3000 B.C. and 1500 B.C., the valleys of the Indus River supported a flourishing civilization that extended hundreds of miles from the Himalaya to the coast of the Arabian Sea. Archaeologists have found the remains of more than a thousand settlements in this region. Two of the ruins, about 400 miles (644 km) apart, were sites of the cities of **Harappa** (huh•RA•puh) and **Mohenjo Daro** (moh•hehn•joh DAHR•oh). An advanced civilization flourished in these cities for hundreds of years. Historians call it the Harappan or Indus civilization.

### Harappa and Mohenjo Daro

At its height, Harappa had 35,000 inhabitants, and Mohenjo Daro about 35,000 to 40,000. Both cities were carefully planned. The broad main streets ran in a north-south direction and were crossed by smaller east-west roads. Both cities were divided into large walled neighborhoods, with narrow lanes separating the rows of houses. Houses varied in size, some as high as three stories, but all followed the same plan of a square courtyard surrounded by rooms.

Most buildings were constructed of oven-baked mud bricks and were square, forming a grid pattern. Public wells provided a regular supply of water for all the inhabitants. Bathrooms featured an advanced drainage system. Wastewater flowed out to drains located under the streets and then was carried to sewage pits beyond the city walls. A system of chutes took household trash from houses to street-level garbage bins. Only a well-organized government could have maintained such carefully structured cities.

NATIONAL GEOGRAPHIC

**INDUS CIVILIZATION AND TRADE**

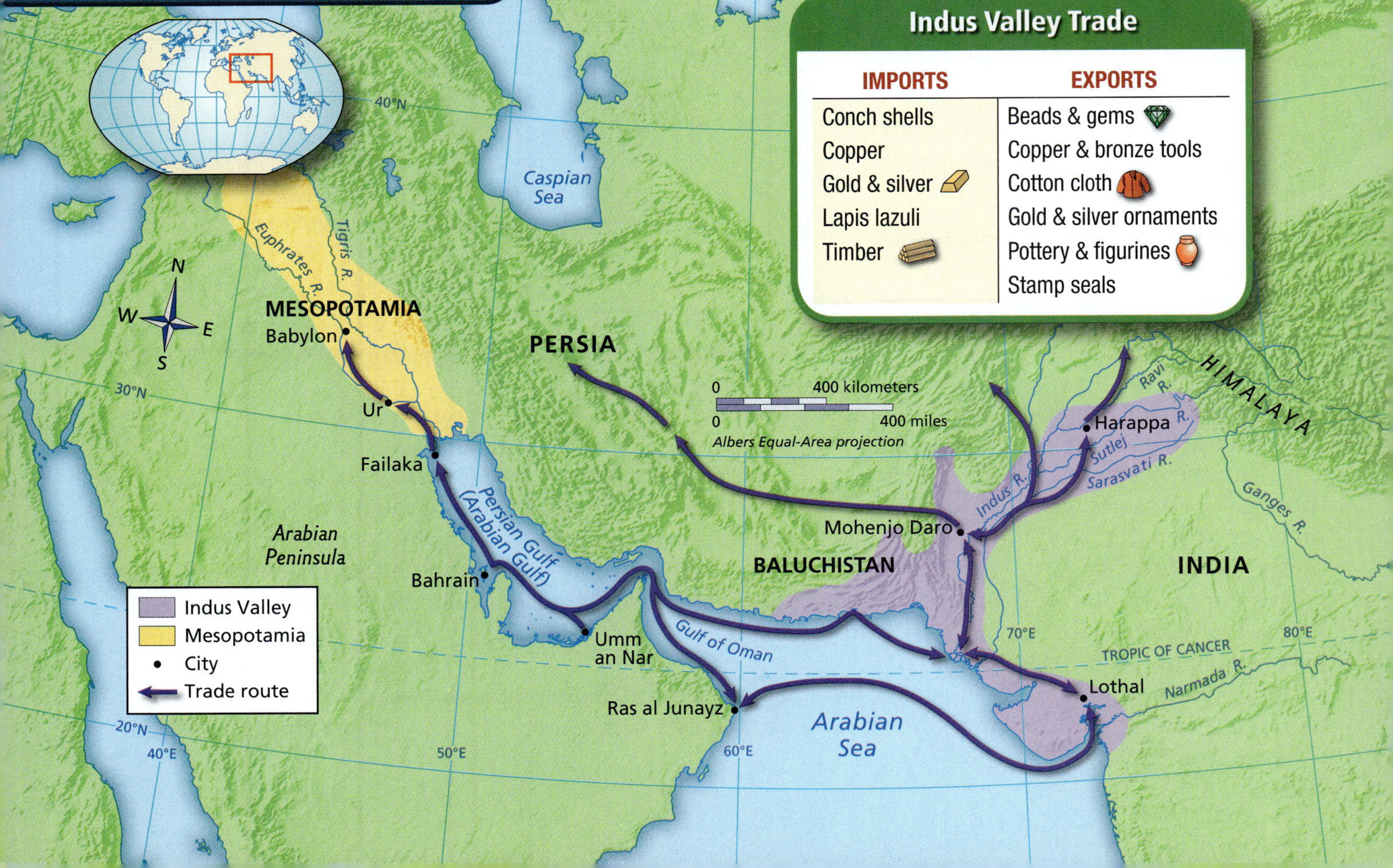

## Rulers and the Economy

As in Egypt and Mesopotamia, Harappan rulers based their power on a belief in divine assistance. Religion and political power were closely linked. That the royal palace and the holy temple were combined in the citadel, or fortress, at Harappa shows this close connection. Priests probably prayed to a fertility deity to guarantee the annual harvest.

The Harappan economy was based on farming. The Indus River flooded every year, providing rich soil to grow wheat, barley, and peas. The Indus Valley civilization also carried on trade as far away as Mesopotamia. Sumerian textiles and food were traded for Indus Valley copper, lumber, precious stones, cotton, and various luxury goods. Although some trade goods were carried overland, most goods went on ships **via** the Persian Gulf.

✓Reading Check **Explaining** What evidence indicates that there were well-organized governments in Harappa and Mohenjo Daro?

**Seals pressed into wet clay identified the owner of the goods. Unicorns were the most common animals on seals.**

**Geography SKILLS**

1. **Place** What were the dominant physical characteristics of the Indus Valley civilization?
2. **Human-Environment Interaction** How did the Indus people use their environment for trade?

# Migration and Interaction

**MAIN IDEA** Around 1500 B.C., India's culture changed, and the Indus Valley cities were abandoned.

***HISTORY & YOU*** Have you seen news stories about floods and other natural disasters? Read how climate changes may have changed India's culture.

How the Indus Valley civilization ended continues to be a mystery. Archaeologists have found signs of gradual decay in Indus Valley cities beginning around 1800 B.C. Floods, an earthquake, changes in climate, environmental changes from human settlements, and even a change in the course of the Indus River weakened the once-flourishing civilization in the Indus River valley. The final blow may have been an influx of new people. While other theories about the end of the Indus Valley civilization abound, all agree that about 1500 B.C. there was a major shift in India's culture. Many historians explain this shift as the result of a foreign migration.

## Arrival of the Aryans

Around 2000 B.C. a group of Indo-European-speaking nomadic peoples began to move out of the steppes of central Asia. Indo-Europeans all spoke similar languages. Some migrated west to Europe. Others moved south to Iran and later to the Indus Valley. One group, known as the **Aryans,** moved south across the Hindu Kush mountain range into the plains of northern India. Historians know little about the origins and early culture of the Aryans. The Aryans lived in tribal groups and had a strong warrior tradition. As they settled in northern India, the nomads came into contact with the Indus Valley civilization.

From around 1500 B.C. to 1000 B.C., the Aryan peoples gradually advanced eastward from the Indus Valley, across the fertile plain of the Ganges, and later southward into the Deccan Plateau. Eventually they extended their political control throughout all of India. The ongoing migrations and interaction between the Aryans and the Dravidians—descendants of the Indus Valley people—eventually resulted in a new and unique culture.

## A New Way of Life

In the process of settling in India, the Aryans gave up their nomadic lifestyle for farming. The introduction of iron—probably from Southwest Asia, where it had first been used by the Hittites (see Chapter 2)—played a role in this change. The creation of the iron plow, along with the use of irrigation, made it possible for farmers to clear the dense jungle growth along the Ganges River and turn it into a rich agricultural area.

The basic crops in the north were wheat, barley, and millet. Rice was most common in the fertile river valleys. In the south, grain and vegetables supplemented cotton and spices such as pepper, ginger, and cinnamon.

While there is evidence of writing in the Indus Valley, no one has yet been able to translate those symbols. Like most nomadic peoples, the early Aryans had no written language. Around 1000 B.C., they started writing in **Sanskrit,** an Indo-European language. Having a written language enabled them to record the legends and religious chants and rituals that had been passed down orally from earlier generations.

These early writings, known as the Vedas, **reveal** that between 1500 B.C. and 400 B.C., India was a world of many small kingdoms. Various leaders, known as rajas (princes), had carved out small states. These kingdoms were often at war with one another as alliances shifted between them. They attacked one another's fortresses and seized treasure. Not until the fourth century B.C. would a leader be able to establish a large Indian state.

## Daily Life in Ancient India

Life in ancient India centered on the family, the most basic unit in society. The ideal was an extended family, with three generations—grandparents, parents, and children—living under the same roof. The family was basically patriarchal, because in most of India the oldest male held legal authority over the entire family unit.

The superiority of males in ancient Indian society was evident in a number of ways. Only males could inherit property, except in a few cases where there were no sons. Women were not allowed to serve as priests, and generally, only males were educated. In high-class families, young men began their education with a guru, or teacher, and then went on to study in one of the major cities.

Upper-class young men were not supposed to marry until they completed 12 years of study. Although divorce was usually not allowed, husbands could take a second wife if the first was unable to bear children.

Children were an important product of marriage, primarily because they were expected to take care of their parents as they grew older. Marriage, arranged by the parents, was common for young girls, probably because women did not work outside the home. Parents had to support each daughter until marriage and then pay a dowry to the family of the man she married.

Perhaps the most vivid symbol of women's dominance by men was the ritual of suttee (suh•TEE). In ancient India, the dead were placed on heaps of material called pyres, which were then set on fire. Suttee required a wife to throw herself on her dead husband's flaming funeral pyre. A Greek visitor reported "that he had heard from some persons of wives burning themselves along with their deceased husbands and doing so gladly; and that those women who refused to burn themselves were held in disgrace."

## Social Class in Ancient India

The social structure of ancient India reflected Aryan ideas of the ideal society. The Aryans believed that society was divided into four ***varnas***, or social groups that ranked people from high to low.

At the top were the Brahmins, the priestly class who performed the religious ceremonies so important to Indian society. The Kshatriyas (KSHA•tree•uhz), or warriors, were considered next in importance. The Vaisyas (VYSH•yuhz) were commoners who were merchants and farmers. The lowest *varna* were the Sudras (SOO•druhz), peasants or servants who made up the great bulk of the Indian population. Sudras had only limited rights in society.

Over the centuries, a rigid social structure evolved that drew on Aryan ideas—

## INFOGRAPHICS

### Change Comes to India's Civilization

The Indus Valley civilization began a gradual decline around 2000 B.C., and its cities became deserted. By 1500 B.C., major changes had taken place in India's written language, religion, and social order. Today there is still debate among scholars surrounding the reasons for these changes.

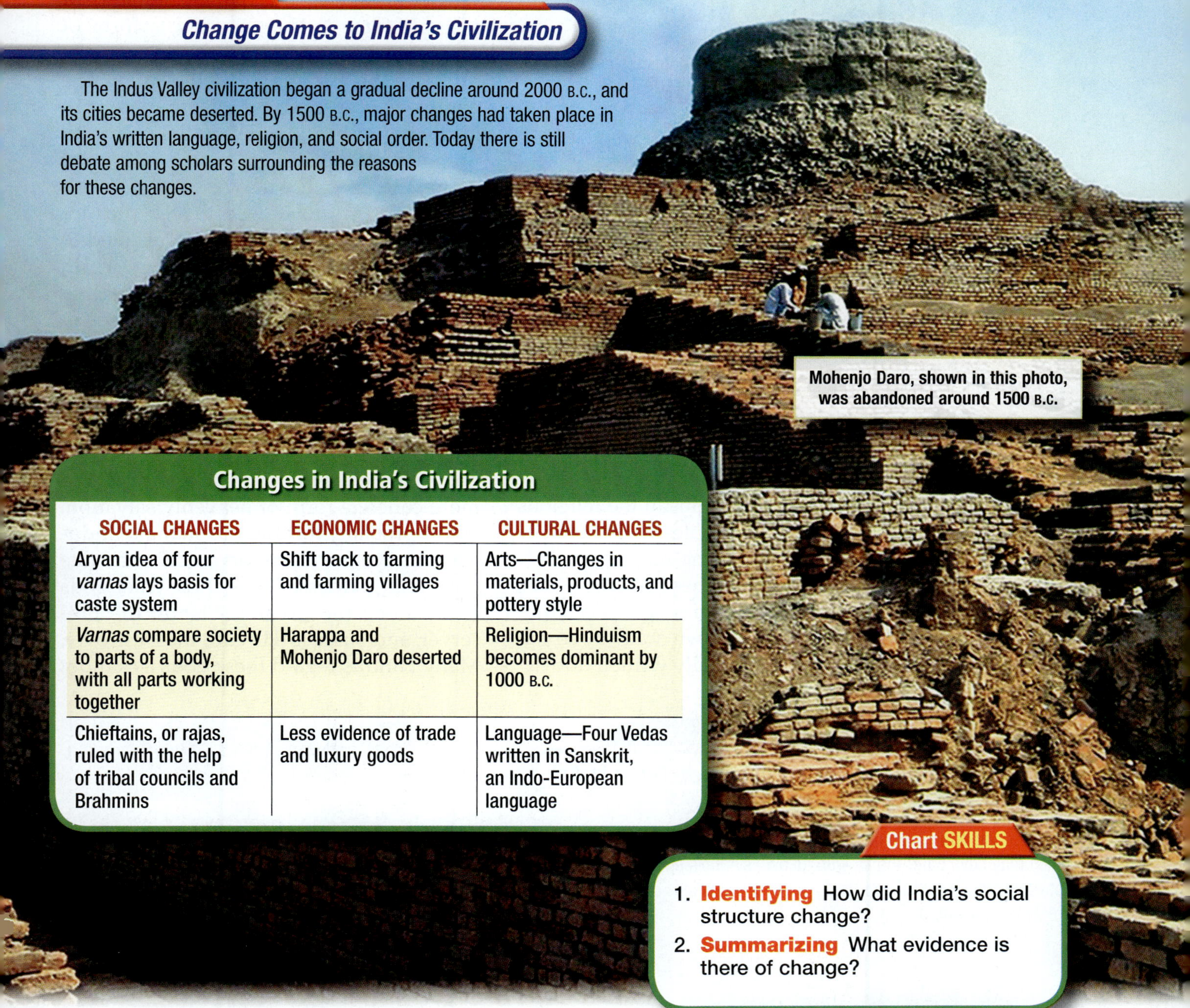

Mohenjo Daro, shown in this photo, was abandoned around 1500 B.C.

**Changes in India's Civilization**

| SOCIAL CHANGES | ECONOMIC CHANGES | CULTURAL CHANGES |
|---|---|---|
| Aryan idea of four *varnas* lays basis for caste system | Shift back to farming and farming villages | Arts—Changes in materials, products, and pottery style |
| *Varnas* compare society to parts of a body, with all parts working together | Harappa and Mohenjo Daro deserted | Religion—Hinduism becomes dominant by 1000 B.C. |
| Chieftains, or rajas, ruled with the help of tribal councils and Brahmins | Less evidence of trade and luxury goods | Language—Four Vedas written in Sanskrit, an Indo-European language |

**Chart SKILLS**

1. **Identifying** How did India's social structure change?
2. **Summarizing** What evidence is there of change?

the **caste** system. In this system, every Indian was believed to be born into a caste, a social group defined by occupation and family lineage. Caste determined what job people could have, whom they could marry, and what groups they could socialize with.

In India, no one uses the word *caste*, which is a word that Portuguese traders used to describe society. The Indian word for caste is *jati*. One reason it was difficult to escape one's *jati*, or caste, is that caste is based on beliefs about religious purity—higher castes had greater religious purity, while castes at the bottom were seen as impure.

At the lowest level of Indian society were the Untouchables, people who were viewed as so impure that they were outside the caste system completely. The Untouchables were given menial, degrading tasks, such as collecting trash and handling dead bodies. Untouchables probably made up about five percent of the population of ancient India.

✓ **Reading Check** **Summarizing** Name the *varnas* and what function they performed in Aryan society.

## Religions of India

**MAIN IDEA** Hinduism and Buddhism share some common beliefs.

**HISTORY & YOU** How has religion influenced your society? Learn how Hinduism and Buddhism were crucial in shaping the civilization of India.

Two of the world's great religions, Hinduism and Buddhism, began in India. Both were crucial in shaping civilization in India. Aryan beliefs blended with the religious practices of the Dravidians to form Hinduism. In the sixth century B.C., a new religion, known as Buddhism, emerged to rival Hinduism.

### Hinduism

**Hinduism** had its origins in the religious beliefs of the Aryan peoples who settled in India. Evidence about the religious beliefs of the Aryan peoples comes from the Vedas, collections of hymns and religious ceremonies that were passed down orally by Aryan priests and then eventually written down.

Early Hindus believed in the existence of a single force in the universe, a form of ultimate reality called *Brahman*. It was the duty of the individual self—called the *atman*—to seek to know this ultimate reality. By doing so, the self would merge with Brahman after death.

How does one achieve oneness with Brahman? Hindus developed the practice of **yoga**, a method of training designed to lead to such union. The goal of yoga, which means "union," is to leave behind earthly life and join Brahman in a kind of dreamless sleep. One Hindu text states, "When all the senses are stilled, when the mind is at rest, that, say the wise, is the highest state."

Most ordinary Indians, however, could not easily relate to this ideal and needed a more concrete form of heavenly salvation. It was probably for this reason that Hinduism came to have a number of human-like gods and goddesses. The three chief gods are Brahma the Creator, Vishnu the Preserver, and Shiva (SIH•vuh) the Destroyer. Many Hindus regard these gods as simply

**HISTORY & ARTS** PRIMARY SOURCE

**Hindu Gods in Art**

In Hindu art, the three main human forms are Brahma, Vishnu, and Shiva. Each may have other forms, with its own symbols and adherents. Artists have painted and sculpted Hindu gods for thousands of years, so the representations vary greatly.

Brahma as the creator of the universe often holds a lotus, symbol of creation. He has four heads, each reciting one of the Four Vedas. Brahma keeps track of time on a string of beads.

Shiva was first portrayed as Nataraja—the King of Dance—around A.D. 1000. The ring of flames represents the universe, and his drum symbolizes the sound of creation. Shiva's foot stamps out ignorance, portrayed as a little man.

different expressions of the one ultimate reality, Brahman. However, the various gods and goddesses give ordinary Indians a way to express their religious feelings. Through devotion at a Hindu temple, they seek not only salvation but also a means of gaining the ordinary things they need in life. Hinduism is still the religion of the majority of the Indian people.

## Principles of Hinduism

By the sixth century B.C., the idea of **reincarnation** had appeared in Hinduism. Reincarnation is the belief that the individual soul is reborn in a different form after death. As the Bhagavad Gita, India's great religious poem, says, "Worn-out garments are shed by the body / Worn-out bodies are shed by the dweller [the soul]." After a number of existences in the earthly world, the soul reaches its final goal in a union with Brahman. According to Hinduism, all living beings seek to achieve this goal.

Important to this process is the idea of **karma**, the force generated by a person's actions that determines how the person will be reborn in the next life. According to this idea, what people do in their current lives determines what they will be in their next lives. In the same way, a person's current status is not simply an accident. It is a result of the person's actions in a past existence.

The concept of karma is ruled by the **dharma**, or the divine law. The law requires all people to do their duty. People's duties vary, depending on their status in society. More is expected of those high on the social scale, such as the Brahmins, than of the lower castes. One story from the Bhagavad Gita illustrates the importance of duty. As he prepared for battle, Arjuna, a warrior, appealed to the god Krishna. Many of Arjuna's friends were in the opposing army.

**PRIMARY SOURCE**

> "O Krishna, when I see my own people . . . eager for battle, my limbs shudder, my mouth is dry, my body shivers, and my hair stands on end. I can see no good in killing my own kinsmen." Krishna replied, "Do not despair of your duty. If you do not fight this just battle, you will fail in your own law and in your honor."
>
> —Bhagavad Gita

Arjuna understood that he must do his duty regardless of the consequences.

The system of reincarnation provided a religious basis for the rigid class divisions in Indian society. It justified the privileges of those on the higher end of the scale. After all, they would not have these privileges if they did not deserve them. At the same time, the concept of reincarnation gave hope to those lower on the ladder of life. The poor, for example, could hope that if they behaved properly in this life, they would improve their condition in the next.

**Vishnu appeared in ten different avatars (forms), one the color of the clouds. The spinning disc, or *chakra*, is a weapon but also symbolizes enlightenment. Vishnu's throne is a deity in snake form, related to immortality.**

**DOCUMENT-BASED QUESTIONS**

1. **Identifying** What are the symbols for the Creation in Hindu art?
2. **Drawing Conclusions** Why is it easier to study contemporary artifacts rather than ancient ones?

## Buddhism

In the sixth century B.C., a new doctrine, called **Buddhism**, appeared in northern India and soon became a rival of Hinduism. The founder of Buddhism was **Siddhārtha Gautama** (sih•DAHR•tuh GOW•tuh•muh), known as the Buddha, or "Enlightened One."

Siddhārtha Gautama came from a small kingdom in the foothills of the Himalaya (in what is today part of southern Nepal).

**History ONLINE**
**Student Web Activity—**
Visit glencoe.com and complete the activity on Buddhism.

See page R39 to read excerpts from the Buddha's sermon in the **Primary Sources and Literature Library.**

Born around 563 B.C., he was the son of a ruling family. The young and very handsome Siddhārtha was raised in the lap of luxury and lived a sheltered life. At the age of 16, he married a neighboring princess and began to raise a family.

Siddhārtha appeared to have everything: wealth, a good appearance, a model wife, a child, and a throne that he would someday inherit. In his late twenties, however, Siddhārtha became aware of the pain of illness, the sorrow of death, and the effects of old age on ordinary people.

He exclaimed, "Would that sickness, age, and death might be forever bound!" He decided to spend his life seeking the cure for human suffering. He gave up his royal clothes, shaved his head, abandoned his family, and set off to find the true meaning of life.

At first he followed the example of the ascetics, people who practiced self-denial to achieve an understanding of ultimate reality. The abuse of his physical body, however, only led to a close brush with death from not eating. He abandoned asceticism and turned instead to an intense period of meditation. In Hinduism, this was a way to find oneness with god. One evening, while sitting in meditation under a tree, Siddhārtha reached enlightenment as to the meaning of life. He spent the rest of his life preaching what he had discovered. His teachings became the basic principles of Buddhism.

It is not certain that Siddhārtha Gautama ever intended to create a new religion or doctrine. In some ways, his ideas could be seen as an attempt to reform Hinduism. In his day, Hinduism had become complex and dependent on the Brahmins as keepers of religious secrets. Siddhārtha advised, "Do not go by what is handed down, nor by the authority of your traditional teachings. When you know of yourselves, 'These teachings are good or not good,' only then accept or reject them."

In his lifetime, the Buddha gained thousands of devoted followers. People would come to him seeking to know more about him, asking, "Are you a god?"

"No," he answered.

"Are you an angel?"

"No."

"Are you a saint?"

"No."

"Then what are you?"

The Buddha replied, "I am awake."

The religion of Buddhism began with a man who claimed that he had awakened and seen the world in a new way.

## Principles of Buddhism

Siddhārtha denied the reality of the material world. The physical surroundings of humans, he believed, were simply illusions. The pain, poverty, and sorrow that afflict human beings are caused by their attachment to things of this world. Once people let go of their worldly cares, pain and sorrow can be forgotten. Then comes *bodhi,* or wisdom. The word *bodhi* is the root of the word *Buddhism* and of Siddhārtha's usual name—Gautama Buddha. Achieving wisdom is a key step to achieving **nirvana**, or ultimate reality—the end of the self and a reunion with the Great World Soul.

## PEOPLE *in* HISTORY

**Siddhārtha Gautama**
**563–483 B.C.**

"All that we are is the result of what we have thought," said Siddhārtha Gautama. Through meditation, Gautama Buddha discovered the Middle Way—a path of moderation with worldwide appeal. Emperor Aśoka first spread the Buddha's teachings throughout India. As Buddhism spread, each region developed its own artistic vision of the Buddha. For centuries, he was represented as an icon, not as a human, so all representations of the Buddha are symbolic. Often he appears seated in meditation or reclining and is shown with signs of his enlightenment. In images of the Buddha, a bump on the top of his head symbolizes his intelligence, and long earlobes portray his perception and spirituality.
**Why does it not matter how Siddhārtha Gautama looked?**

Siddhārtha preached this message in a sermon to his followers in the Deer Park at Sarnath, outside India's holy city of Varanasi. It is a simple message based on the Four Noble Truths:

| FOUR NOBLE TRUTHS |
|---|
| 1. Ordinary life is full of suffering. |
| 2. This suffering is caused by our desire to satisfy ourselves. |
| 3. The way to end suffering is to end desire for selfish goals and to see others as extensions of ourselves. |
| 4. The way to end desire is to follow the Middle Path. |

This Middle Path is also known as the Eightfold Path, because it consists of eight steps:

| THE EIGHTFOLD PATH |
|---|
| 1. *Right view* We need to know the Four Noble Truths. |
| 2. *Right intention* We need to decide what we really want. |
| 3. *Right speech* We must seek to speak truth and to speak well of others. |
| 4. *Right action* The Buddha gave five precepts: "Do not kill. Do not steal. Do not lie. Do not be unchaste. Do not take drugs or drink alcohol." |
| 5. *Right livelihood* We must do work that uplifts our being. |
| 6. *Right effort* The Buddha said, "Those who follow the Way might well follow the example of an ox that arches through the deep mud carrying a heavy load. He is tired, but his steady, forward-looking gaze will not relax until he comes out of the mud." |
| 7. *Right mindfulness* We must keep our minds in control of our senses: "All we are is the result of what we have thought." |
| 8. *Right concentration* We must meditate to see the world in a new way. |

Siddhārtha accepted the idea of reincarnation, but he rejected the Hindu division of human beings into rigidly defined castes based on previous reincarnations. He taught instead that all human beings could reach nirvana as a result of their behavior in this life. This made Buddhism appealing to the downtrodden peoples at the lower end of the social scale.

Buddhism also differed from Hinduism in its simplicity. Siddhārtha rejected the multitude of gods that had become identified with Hinduism. He forbade his followers to worship either his person or his image after his death. For that reason, many Buddhists see Buddhism as a philosophy rather than as a religion.

Siddhārtha Gautama died in 480 B.C. at the age of 80 in what is today Nepal. After his death, his followers traveled throughout India, spreading his message. Temples sprang up throughout the countryside. Buddhist monasteries were established to promote his teaching and provide housing and training for monks dedicated to the simple life and the pursuit of wisdom.

**✓Reading Check** **Contrasting** How does Buddhism differ from Hinduism?

## SECTION 1 REVIEW

### Vocabulary

1. **Explain** the significance of: Himalaya, Indus River, monsoon, Harappa, Mohenjo Daro, via, Aryans, Sanskrit, reveal, *varnas*, caste, Hinduism, yoga, reincarnation, karma, dharma, Buddhism, Siddhārtha Gautama, nirvana.

### Main Ideas

2. **Locate** the Indian subcontinent, Himalaya, Indus River, and Deccan Plateau on a map.
3. **List** the Four Noble Truths.
4. **Describe** the relationship between karma, dharma, and reincarnation.

### Critical Thinking

5. **The BIG Idea** **Finding the Main Idea** What major changes occurred in Indian civilization around 1500 B.C.?
6. **Evaluating** How did Arjuna's decision to fight illustrate the importance of dharma in Indian life?
7. **Comparing and Contrasting** Prepare a Venn diagram like the one shown below to show the similarities and differences between Hinduism and Buddhism.

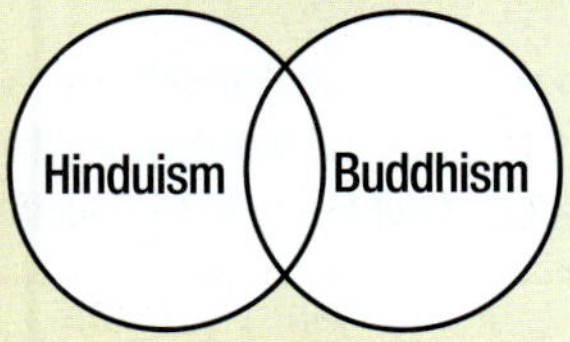


8. **Analyzing Visuals** Examine the representations of the Hindu gods and of Buddha on pages 72–73 and 74. What do they have in common?

### Writing About History

9. **Expository Writing** Most untouchables did not convert to other religions or emigrate to other countries to escape their lot in life. What social pressures might prevent a person from renouncing his or her culture?

**History ONLINE**

For help with the concepts in this section of *Glencoe World History,* go to glencoe.com and click Study Central™.

SECTION 2

Section Audio

Spotlight Video

# New Empires in India

## GUIDE TO READING

### The BIG Idea

**Ideas, Beliefs, and Values** New Indian empires grew rich through trade and left a lasting legacy of accomplishments.

### Content Vocabulary

- Silk Road *(p. 78)*
- pilgrims *(p. 79)*
- Vedas *(p. 80)*
- Bhagavad Gita *(p. 80)*

### Academic Vocabulary

- conversion *(p. 76)*
- welfare *(p. 76)*

### People

- Aśoka *(p. 76)*
- Faxian *(p. 79)*
- Kālidāsa *(p. 81)*
- Āryabhata *(p. 81)*

### Reading Strategy

**Categorizing Information** As you read this section, complete a chart identifying the indicated characteristics of the Mauryan and Gupta Empires.

| | Mauryan Empire | Gupta Empire |
|---|---|---|
| Dates | | |
| Government | | |
| Economy | | |

*While two religions—Hinduism and Buddhism—spread through India, there was little political unity. Between 1500 B.C. and 400 B.C., warring kingdoms and shifting alliances prevented a lasting peace.*

## Three New Empires

**MAIN IDEA** Warring kingdoms united to force out invaders, which led to three Indian empires.

***HISTORY & YOU*** Is it better to be loved or feared? Learn how some famous rulers held their kingdoms together.

After 400 B.C., India faced threats from invaders. First came Persia, which extended its empire into western India. Then came the Greeks and Macedonians. Alexander the Great had heard of the riches of India. After conquering Persia, he swept into India in 327 B.C., but his soldiers refused to continue fighting. His army departed almost as quickly as it came. Alexander's conquests in western India, however, gave rise to the first Indian Empire.

### The Mauryan Empire

The new Indian state was founded by Candragupta Maurya (KUHN•druh•GUP•tuh MAH•oor•yuh), who ruled from 324 B.C. to 301 B.C. He drove out the foreign forces and established the capital of his new Mauryan Empire in northern India at Pataliputra, modern Patna, in the Ganges Valley.

The first Indian Empire was highly centralized. The king divided his empire into provinces, ruled by governors he appointed. A Mauryan court official wrote, "It is power and power alone which, only when exercised by the king with impartiality, . . . maintains both this world and the next." According to Megasthenes, the Greek ambassador to the Mauryan court, Candragupta Maurya was afraid of assassination despite having a large army and a secret police. All food was tasted in his presence, and he made a practice of never sleeping two nights in a row in the same bed.

**Aśoka** (uh • SHOH • kuh), the grandson of Candragupta Maurya, is generally considered to be the greatest ruler in the history of India. After his **conversion** to Buddhism, Aśoka used Buddhist ideals to guide his rule. He set up hospitals for the **welfare** of both people and animals. He ordered trees and shelters placed along the road to provide shade and rest for weary travelers. Aśoka sponsored Buddhist missionaries, who spread Buddhism throughout India and eventually to China.

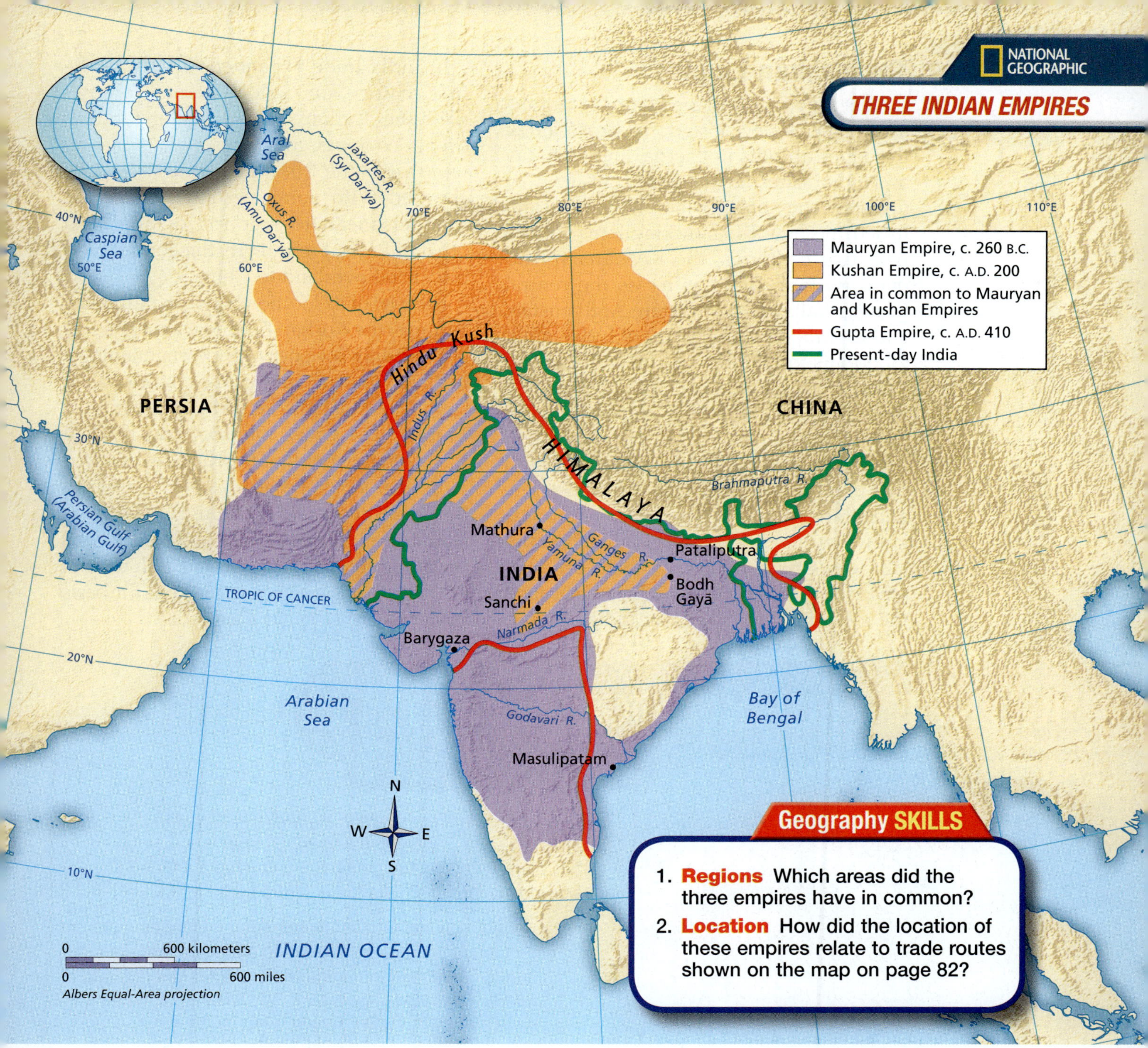


**Geography SKILLS**

1. **Regions** Which areas did the three empires have in common?
2. **Location** How did the location of these empires relate to trade routes shown on the map on page 82?

One of the decrees of Aśoka read:

**Primary Source**

"By order of the Beloved of the Gods [Aśoka] to the officers in charge: Let us win the affection of all people. All people are my children, and as I wish all welfare and happiness in this world and the rest for my own children, so do I wish it for all men. . . . For that purpose many officials are employed among the people to instruct them in righteousness and to explain it to them."

—*Aśoka Maurya,* B. G. Gokhale, 1966

Aśoka was more than a kind ruler. His kingdom prospered as India's role in regional commerce expanded. India became a major crossroads in a trade network that extended from the rim of the Pacific to Southwest Asia and the Mediterranean Sea. After Aśoka's death in 232 B.C., the Mauryan Empire began to decline. In 183 B.C., the last Mauryan ruler was killed by one of his military leaders, and India fell into disunity.

**✓Reading Check** **Evaluating** Why was Aśoka considered a great ruler?

## The Kushān Empire

After the collapse of the Mauryan Empire, a number of new kingdoms arose along the edges of India in Bactria, known today as Afghanistan. In the first century A.D., nomadic warriors seized power and established the new Kushān kingdom. For the next two centuries, the Kushāns spread over northern India as far as the central Ganges Valley into Pakistan, Afghanistan, and Central Asia. In the rest of India, other kingdoms fought for control.

The Kushāns prospered from the trade that passed through their empire between the Mediterranean countries and the countries bordering the Pacific Ocean. Most of that trade was between the Roman Empire and China. It was shipped along the route known as the **Silk Road**, so called because silk was China's most valuable product. One section of the Silk Road passed through the mountains northwest of India.

In India trade expanded rapidly in the first century A.D. Sailors learned to navigate the Indian Ocean, understanding ocean currents and seasonal monsoon winds. For the first time, goods could be shipped with some certainty from the Mediterranean to seaports on the west coast of India. From there, the goods could be carried overland to China.

Because of its location between influential cultures, the Kushān Empire was shaped by surrounding societies—while maintaining a distinctly Indian culture. The empire was in contact with China, Persia, and the Roman Empire. The Greek alphabet had reached Bactria to the west and the Kushāns adapted it for their language. The Kushāns practiced both Hinduism and Buddhism, as well as Zoroastrianism, from Persia. The Kushāns developed a calendar based on both the sun and the moon, and their calendar is the basis of the Indian calendar used today.

## SCIENCE, TECHNOLOGY, & SOCIETY

### Aryabhata: The Solar System and Pi

Statue of Aryabhata with lunar eclipse

*The Gupta Empire is often called the Golden Age of India's sciences and philosophy. A mathematician and astronomer from this period, Aryabhata (476–550), made contributions that are still in use today.*

When India launched its first satellite, it was named *Aryabhata* after India's first great astronomer. Aryabhata was one of the first to describe the rotation of Earth on its axis. He observed and identified the cause of the lunar eclipse (the sun, Earth, and moon line up with Earth's shadow falling on the moon). Today, a crater on the moon is named for Aryabhata.

Most of Aryabhata's writings were lost. Fortunately, others wrote commentaries on them, and Arab scholars translated them. His only surviving work, *Aryabhatiya*, was written in poetic verse and did not include numerals. Like other ancient Indian mathematicians, he used letters to represent numbers. Despite this, he calculated pi to five digits (3.1416), used place value, and developed algebra and trigonometry concepts.

**CRITICAL THINKING SKILLS**

1. **Clarifying** How do we know about Aryabhata's discoveries?
2. **Making Inferences** Why would a crater on the moon be named after Aryabhata?

## The Empire of the Guptas

The Kushān kingdom came to an end in the third century A.D., when invaders from Persia overran it. In 320, a new state was created in the central Ganges Valley by a local prince named Candra Gupta—no relation to the earlier Candragupta Maurya. He located his capital at Pataliputra, the site of the decaying palace of the Mauryas.

His successor, his son Samudra Gupta, expanded the empire into surrounding areas. A court official wrote of Samudra Gupta that:

**PRIMARY SOURCE**

"[He] was skillful in waging hundreds of battles with only the strength of his arms. The beauty of his charming body was enhanced by the number of wounds, caused by the blows of battle axes, arrows, spears, pikes, barbed darts, swords, lances, javelins, iron arrows, and many other weapons."

—court official

Eventually the Gupta kingdom became the dominant political force in northern India. It also established loose control over central India, thus becoming the greatest state in India since the Mauryan Empire.

Under a series of efficient monarchs—especially Candra Gupta II, who reigned from 375 to 415—the Guptas created a golden age of Indian culture shown in the flowering of Hindu and Buddhist arts. The Gupta Empire emerged as a classical civilization, a society that serves as a model of excellence and has lasting value and relevance.

The Gupta Empire actively engaged in trade with China, Southeast Asia, and the Mediterranean and also encouraged domestic trade in cloth, salt, and iron. Cities famous for their temples as well as for their prosperity rose along the main trade routes throughout India.

Much of the trade in the Gupta Empire was managed by the Gupta rulers, who owned silver and gold mines and vast lands. They earned large profits from their dealings. They lived in luxury, awakening to the sound of music and spending much time in dining with followers and guests. It was said that "the king and his companions drank wine out of ruby cups while lutes were strummed."

Much of their wealth came from religious trade as **pilgrims** (people who travel to religious places) from across India and as far away as China came to visit the major religious centers. Not surprisingly, many new Hindu and Buddhist temples and shrines were built during the Gupta era.

A Buddhist monk from China, **Faxian** (FAY•SYEN), visited India in search of documents about the teachings of the Buddha. Faxian's writings from the fifth century describe the Gupta rulers, their respect for Buddhism, and the prosperity of the empire.

**PRIMARY SOURCE**

"Beyond the deserts are the territories of western India. The kings of these territories are all firm believers in the law of [the] Buddha. They remove their caps of state when they make offerings to the priests. The members of the royal household and the chief ministers personally direct the food giving. When the distribution of food is over, they spread a carpet on the ground and sit down before it. . . .

Southward from this is the so-called middle-country. . . . The people are very well off, without poll-tax or official restrictions. Only those who farm the royal lands return a portion of profit of the land [to the king]. If they desire to go, they go; if they like to stop, they stop. The kings govern without corporal punishment; criminals are fined, according to circumstances, lightly or heavily. Even in cases of repeated rebellion they only cut off the right hand. . . . In this country they do not keep swine nor fowls, and do not deal in cattle; they have no shambles or wine-shops in their market-places."

—Faxian, *Describing Life under the Guptas*

The good fortunes of the Guptas did not last. Beginning in the late fifth century A.D., invasions by nomadic Huns from the northwest gradually reduced the power of the empire. A military commander briefly revived the empire in the middle of the seventh century, but after his death, the empire collapsed. North India would not be reunited for hundreds of years.

✓ **Reading Check** **Examining** What characteristics made the Gupta Empire great?

## Indian Accomplishments

**MAIN IDEA** India produced great works in almost all cultural fields, including literature, architecture, and science.

***HISTORY & YOU*** Have you studied algebra or geography? Learn about India's contributions to the arts and sciences.

### Literature

Few cultures are as rich and varied as India. Its literature reflects that. The earliest known Indian literature are the **Vedas**, which contain religious chants and stories. Originally passed down orally from generation to generation, the Vedas were recorded in Sanskrit after the development of writing. India's great epics, the *Mahabharata* (muh•HAH•BAH•ruh•tuh) and the *Ramayana,* were also put into written form about 100 B.C. Both of these works tell of the legendary deeds of great warriors.

The *Mahabharata,* consisting of over 90,000 stanzas, or lines of poetry, is the longest poem in any written language. Taking place around 1000 B.C., it describes a war between cousins for control of the kingdom. The most famous section of the book, called the **Bhagavad Gita** (BAH•guh•VAD•GEE•tuh), is a sermon by the god Krishna on the eve of a major battle. In this sermon, he sets forth one of the key points of Indian society: In taking action, one must not worry about success or failure. One should only be aware of the moral rightness of the act itself.

The *Ramayana,* written at about the same time, is much shorter than the *Mahabharata.* It is an account of the fictional ruler Rama. As a result of a palace plot, Rama is banished from the kingdom and forced to live in the forest. Later, he fights the demon-king of Ceylon, who had kidnapped his beloved wife Sita.

Like the *Mahabharata* and most works of the ancient world, the *Ramayana* is strongly imbued with religious and moral lessons.

**INFOGRAPHICS**

**Stupas Show Spread of Buddhism**

According to legend, the Buddha told his followers to place his relics at four sites: at his birthplace, at the bodhi tree, at the place where he preached his first sermon, and at the place where he died. Then he folded his robe into a cube and placed his begging bowl upside down on top to indicate the shape of the monuments. Over centuries in different countries, stupas changed, but five basic components remained: a square base, a dome, a spire, a crescent moon, and a circular disc; symbolizing earth, water, fire, air, and space.

a

b

c

d

*Evolution of Buddhist Architecture*
*a. third to first century B.C. Indian stupa*
*b. second century A.D. Indian stupa*
*c. fifth to seventh century A.D. Chinese pagoda*
*d. seventh century A.D. Japanese pagoda*

**CRITICAL THINKING SKILLS**

1. **Identifying** What is another name for a Buddhist stupa?
2. **Drawing Conclusions** Why did the shape and name for stupas change?

Rama is seen as the ideal hero, a perfect ruler, and ideal son. Sita projects the supreme duty of wifely loyalty to her husband. To this day, the *Mahabharata* and *Ramayana* continue to inspire the people of India.

One of ancient India's most famous authors from the Gupta era was **Kālidāsa.** His poem, *The Cloud Messenger,* remains one of the most popular Sanskrit poems. In the poem, an exiled male earth spirit shares his grief and longing for his wife.

## Architecture

Some of the earliest examples of Indian architecture stem from the time of Aśoka, when Buddhism became the state religion. The desire to spread the ideas of Gautama Buddha inspired the great architecture of the Mauryan dynasty and the period that followed.

The three main types of structures, all serving religious purposes, were the pillar, the stupa, and the rock chamber. During Aśoka's reign, many stone pillars were erected along roads to mark sites of events in the Buddha's life. The polished sandstone pillars weighed up to 50 tons (45.4 t) each and rose as high as 50 feet (15 m). Each was topped with a carved lion, uttering the Buddha's message.

A stupa was originally meant to house a relic of the Buddha, such as a lock of his hair. These structures were built in the form of burial mounds. Eventually, the stupa became a place for devotion and the most familiar form of Buddhist architecture. Each stupa rose to considerable heights and was surmounted by a spire. According to legend, Aśoka ordered the construction of 84,000 stupas throughout India.

The final development in early Indian architecture was the rock chamber, carved out of rock cliffs. This structure was developed by Aśoka to provide a series of rooms to house monks and to serve as a hall for religious ceremonies.

## Science and Mathematics

Ancient Indians possessed an impressive amount of scientific knowledge, particularly in astronomy. They charted the movements of the stars and recognized that Earth was a sphere that rotated on its axis and revolved around the sun. Their most important contribution was in the field of mathematics. **Aryabhata,** the most famous mathematician of the Gupta Empire, was one of the first scientists known to have used algebra. Indian mathematicians also introduced the concept of zero and used a symbol (0) for it.

After Arabs conquered parts of India in the eighth century A.D., Arab scholars adopted the Indian system. In turn, European traders borrowed it from the Arabs, and it spread through Europe in the 1200s. Today it is called the Indian-Arabic numerical system.

✓Reading Check **Evaluating** How have Indian advances in science and mathematics influenced our world today?

## SECTION 2 REVIEW

### Vocabulary

1. **Explain** the significance of: Aśoka, conversion, welfare, Silk Road, pilgrim, Faxian, Vedas, Bhagavad Gita, Kālidāsa, Aryabhata.

### Main Ideas

2. **Use** a table like the one below to show the parts of India the three empires controlled.

| Region/Empire | Mauryan | Kushān | Gupta |
|---|---|---|---|
| Rivers | | | |
| Plains | | | |
| Coasts | | | |

3. **Explain** what types of goods were carried on the Silk Road and why.
4. **List** three kinds of early Indian architecture and their uses.

### Critical Thinking

5. **The Big Idea** **Making Inferences** How did prosperity lead to contributions in the arts and sciences?
6. **Analyzing** How do the historic epics *Mahabharata* and *Ramayana* reflect the values of early India?
7. **Analyzing Primary Sources** What are the similarities between Aśoka's decrees and Faxian's observations of the Gupta Empire?
8. **Analyzing Visuals** Examine the diagram on page 80, and use it to explain why the shape of stupas changed.

### Writing About History

9. **Persuasive Writing** Write a short essay about whether a ruler should be loved or feared or both. Use examples from the Mauryan and Gupta Empires.

**History ONLINE**

For help with the concepts in this section of *Glencoe World History,* go to glencoe.com and click Study Central™.

# NATIONAL GEOGRAPHIC GEOGRAPHY & HISTORY

◀ This Tang dynasty statue shows a foreign trader riding a camel on the Silk Road.

Spanish map from 1375 shows the family of Marco Polo crossing Asia on the Silk Road. ▶

PRIMARY SOURCE

▲ Buddhist monks traveled the Silk Road, spreading their religion through Asia.

# THE SILK ROAD

**A Trade Route Develops** The Silk Road, which developed between 200 B.C. and A.D. 100, reached from the city of Changan in China across central Asia to Mesopotamia. The Silk Road was not a single road, but rather a network of trade routes that extended about 4,000 miles (6,436 km) and wound through mountains and deserts, ending at Antioch in Syria, a port city on the Mediterranean Sea. At Antioch, luxury goods from the West were traded for luxury goods from the East, which were then shipped across the Mediterranean to Greece and Rome. Only luxury goods were carried on the Silk Road because camel caravans were difficult, dangerous, and thus, expensive.

Chinese merchants traded silk, spices, teas, and porcelain. Indian merchants sent ivory, textiles, precious stones, and pepper. These were exchanged for woolen and linen clothes, glass, and precious stones from the Roman Empire. Silk was especially desired by the Romans, who considered it worth its weight in gold. In fact, the Romans knew China as *Serica,* which means "Land of Silk."

**Trading Ideas** The Silk Road was more than a trading route. It was also a conduit of ideas. Three great religions—Buddhism, Christianity, and Islam—spread along the Silk Road. Technical knowledge from China, including the secrets of printing, drilling wells, and making iron, gunpowder, paper, and silk reached the West along the Silk Road.

**End of an Era** Very few went the entire length of the road. Traders journeyed segments of it, made their trades, and returned home. Goods traveled farther than people. The distance, rough terrain, harsh weather, and bandits made journeys perilous. Still, traders persisted until the 1300s when more profitable sea routes developed. The era of the great Silk Road came to an end after more than a millennium. Today a highway joining Pakistan and China follows the ancient route.

▲ This porcelain bowl shows women cutting silk. Porcelain and silk were two of China's most valued exports and most carefully guarded secrets.

**Geography SKILLS**

1. **Location** How did landforms affect the route of the Silk Road?
2. **Human-Environment Interaction** How did the Silk Road change the environment?

SECTION 3

Section Audio

Spotlight Video

# Early Chinese Civilizations

## GUIDE TO READING

### The BIG Idea

**Ideas, Beliefs, and Values** China developed unique philosophies, political theories, and products.

### Content Vocabulary

- aristocracy *(p. 86)*
- Mandate of Heaven *(p. 87)*
- Dao *(p. 87)*
- filial piety *(p. 89)*
- pictographs *(p. 90)*
- ideographs *(p. 90)*
- Confucianism *(p. 90)*
- Daoism *(p. 92)*
- Legalism *(p. 93)*

### Academic Vocabulary

- cycle *(p. 88)*
- philosophy *(p. 90)*
- ethical *(p. 90)*

### People and Places

- Huang He *(p. 84)*
- Chang Jiang *(p. 84)*
- Confucius *(p. 90)*
- Laozi *(p. 92)*

### Reading Strategy

**Classifying Information** As you read this section, create a diagram like the one below that illustrates the dynastic cycle.

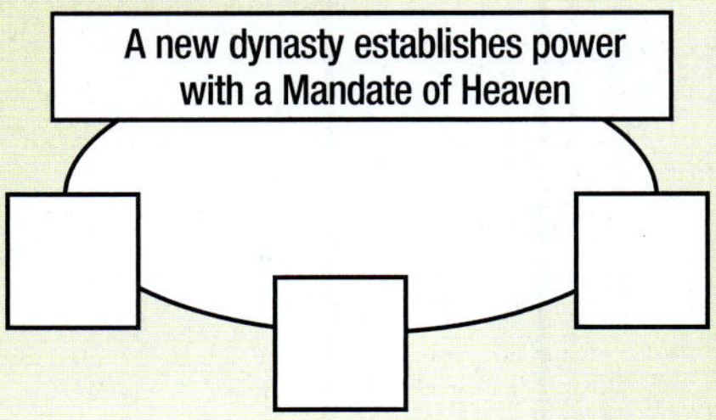


*As in Mesopotamia, Egypt, and the Indus Valley, China's early civilizations followed the spread of agriculture along the river valleys. Most of the rivers in China flow east to the Pacific Ocean, which meant China's civilizations developed near the east coast. The mountains to the west and the deserts to the north further isolated China from outside influences.*

## The Impact of Geography

**MAIN IDEA** China's physical geography influenced the location of its early civilizations.

**HISTORY & YOU** Would you rather live near the ocean or the mountains? Learn how China's geography shaped its development.

Dating back more than six thousand years, China has one of the world's oldest cultures. China also has the largest population of any nation and is made up of more than 50 ethnic groups, speaking several languages and many dialects. The diversity of its people reflects the diversity of its land and climate.

### Rivers and Mountains

The **Huang He** (HWAHNG•HUH), or Yellow River, stretches across China for more than 2,900 miles (4,666 km), carrying its rich yellow silt all the way from Mongolia to the Pacific Ocean. The **Chang Jiang** (CHAHNG•JYAHNG), or Yangtze River, is even longer, flowing for about 3,400 miles (5,470 km) across central China before emptying into the Yellow Sea. The densely cultivated valleys of these two rivers began to emerge as one of the great food-producing areas of the ancient world.

China, however, is not just a land of fertile fields. In fact, only 10 percent of the total land area is suitable for farming, compared with 19 percent of the United States. Much of the rest of the land in China consists of mountains and deserts that ring the country on its northern and western frontiers.

This forbidding landscape is a dominant feature of Chinese life and has played an important role in Chinese history. Geographical barriers—mountains and deserts—isolated the Chinese people from peoples in other parts of Asia. In the frontier regions created by these barriers lived peoples of Mongolian, Indo-European, and Turkish backgrounds. The contacts of these groups with the Chinese were often marked by conflict. The northern frontier of China became one of the areas of conflict in Asia as Chinese armies tried to protect their precious farmlands.

**Geography SKILLS**

The borders shown are modern-day China.

1. **Place** Why did China's first civilizations develop between the Huang He and the Chang Jiang?
2. **Human-Environment Interaction** Which landforms isolated the early Chinese from other cultures?

## Climate

China's climates vary from region to region based on the elevation and the monsoons. In winter, monsoons blowing from the mountainous regions are cold and dry. In summer, the monsoons blow from the south across the seas, bringing rain.

The dry season alternating with wet monsoons creates significant temperature differences in winter and summer. The Chang Jiang serves as a dividing line between the northern region and the southern region of the country.

In the north, winters are long and cold, but the short summers are sunny and hot. In the center of the country, along the Chang Jiang, there are four seasons, including hot summers and cold winters. The warmest temperatures year round are in the south, which has a subtropical climate with hot summers and mild winters.

✓ **Reading Check** **Describing** What isolated the Chinese people from peoples in other parts of Asia?

# The Shang Dynasty

**MAIN IDEA** Oracle bones, bronzes, and excavations tell about life during the Shang dynasty.

***HISTORY & YOU*** How do we show respect for our deceased family members? Learn about ancestor worship in Shang China.

Historians of China have traditionally dated the beginning of Chinese civilization to the founding of the Xia (SHYAH) dynasty over four thousand years ago. Little is known about this dynasty, which was replaced by a second dynasty, the Shang.

China under the Shang dynasty (about 1750 B.C. to 1045 B.C.) was primarily a farming society ruled by an **aristocracy** whose major concern was war. An aristocracy is an upper class whose wealth is based on land and whose power is passed from one generation to another.

Archaeologists have found evidence of impressive cities in Shang China. Shang kings may have had five different capital cities before settling Anyang (AHN•YAHNG), just north of the Huang He in north-central China. Excavations reveal huge city walls, royal palaces, and large royal tombs.

## Political and Social Structures

The Shang king ruled from the capital city Anyang. His realm was divided into territories governed by aristocratic military leaders, called warlords, but the king had the power to choose these leaders and could also remove them. The king was also responsible for defending the realm and controlled large armies, which often fought on the fringes of the kingdom. The king's importance is evident in the ritual sacrifices undertaken at his death. Like rulers in Mesopotamia and Egypt, early Chinese kings were buried in royal tombs accompanied by the corpses of their faithful servants.

NATIONAL GEOGRAPHIC

**SHANG AND ZHOU EMPIRES**

**Geography SKILLS**

1. **Regions** Which areas did these empires have in common?
2. **Location** What do you notice about the locations of the Shang and Zhou Empires in relation to physical features in China?

The royal family occupied the top of Shang society; the aristocracy came next. The aristocrats not only waged war and served as officials but also were the chief landowners. The majority of people were peasants who farmed the aristocracy's land. In addition to the aristocrats and peasants, Shang society also included a small number of merchants and artisans, as well as slaves.

### Religion and Culture

The Chinese believed in supernatural forces that could help the rulers in worldly affairs. To communicate with the gods, the priests made oracle bones. These were bones on which priests scratched questions asked by the rulers, such as: Will the king be victorious in battle? Will the king recover from his illness? Heated metal rods were stuck into the bones, causing them to crack. The priests interpreted the shapes of the cracks as answers from the gods. The priests recorded the answers on the bones. Other markings on oracle bones indicated a calendar that was based on both the sun and the moon. The inscriptions on the bones are a valuable source of information about the Shang period.

Remains of human sacrifices found in royal tombs are evidence of human efforts to win the favor of the gods. The early Chinese believed in life after death. From this belief came the veneration of ancestors commonly known in the West as "ancestor worship." The practice of burning replicas—exact copies—of physical objects to accompany the dead on their journey to the next world continues to this day in many Chinese communities. The early Chinese believed it was important to treat the spirits of their ancestors well because the spirits could bring good or bad fortune to the living family members.

The Shang are perhaps best remembered for the mastery of bronze casting. More than ten thousand bronze objects have been found in tombs from the Shang period and are among the most admired creations of Chinese art.

✓Reading Check **Identifying** How did the Shang rulers communicate with the gods?

## The Zhou Dynasty

**MAIN IDEA** The concept of the Mandate of Heaven began with the Zhou dynasty.

**HISTORY & YOU** What are your government's responsibilities? Read about the Chinese theory of effective government.

According to legend, the last of the Shang rulers was a wicked tyrant who swam in "ponds of wine" and ordered the writing of music that "ruined the morale of the nation." This led the ruler of the state of Zhou (JOH) to revolt against the Shang and establish a new dynasty. The Zhou dynasty, the longest-lasting dynasty in Chinese history, ruled for almost eight hundred years (1045 B.C. to 256 B.C.)

### Political Structure

The Zhou dynasty continued the political system of the rulers it had overthrown. At the head of the government was the Zhou king, who was served by an increasingly large and complex bureaucracy. The Zhou dynasty continued the Shang practice of dividing the kingdom into territories governed by officials. The officials of these territories were members of the aristocracy. They were appointed by the king and were subject to his authority. Like the Shang rulers, the Zhou king was in charge of defense and commanded armies throughout the country.

The Zhou dynasty claimed that it ruled China because it possessed the **Mandate of Heaven**. It was believed that Heaven—which was an impersonal law of nature—kept order in the universe through the Zhou king. The king was the link between Heaven and Earth. Thus, the king ruled by a mandate, or authority to command, from Heaven. The concept of the heavenly mandate became a basic principle of Chinese government.

The Mandate of Heaven, however, was double-edged. The king, who was chosen to rule because of his talent and virtue, was then responsible for ruling the people with goodness and efficiency. The king was expected to rule according to the proper "Way," called the **Dao** (DOW). It was the Zhou king's duty to keep the gods pleased.

This would protect the people from natural disaster or a bad harvest. If the king failed to rule effectively, he could be overthrown and replaced by a new ruler.

This theory has political side effects. It sets forth a "right of revolution" to overthrow a corrupt ruler. It also makes clear that the king, though serving as a representative of Heaven, is not a divine being himself. In practice, each founder of a new dynasty would say he had earned the Mandate of Heaven. Who could disprove it except by overthrowing the king? The saying, "He who wins is the king; he who loses is the rebel," sums up this view.

The Mandate of Heaven was closely tied to the pattern of dynastic **cycles.** From the beginning of Chinese history to A.D. 1912, China was ruled by a series of dynasties, which all went through a cycle of change. A new dynasty established its power, ruled successfully for many years, and then began to decline. The government lost power, giving rise to rebellions or invasion. When a new dynasty took over, the cycle began again.

## The Fall of the Zhou Dynasty

After almost eight hundred years, the Zhou dynasty collapsed. For centuries, the dynasty ruled wisely and efficiently, but later Zhou rule declined intellectually and morally. The Zhou kingdom had been divided into several small territories, some of which evolved into powerful states that challenged

### INFOGRAPHICS

### *Dynastic Cycles and the Mandate of Heaven*

When the Zhou overthrew the Shang dynasty, they explained their right to rule as a Mandate of Heaven. Dynasties that abused their power lost the Mandate of Heaven. The Mandate passed to another family who overthrew the old dynasty and established a new one.

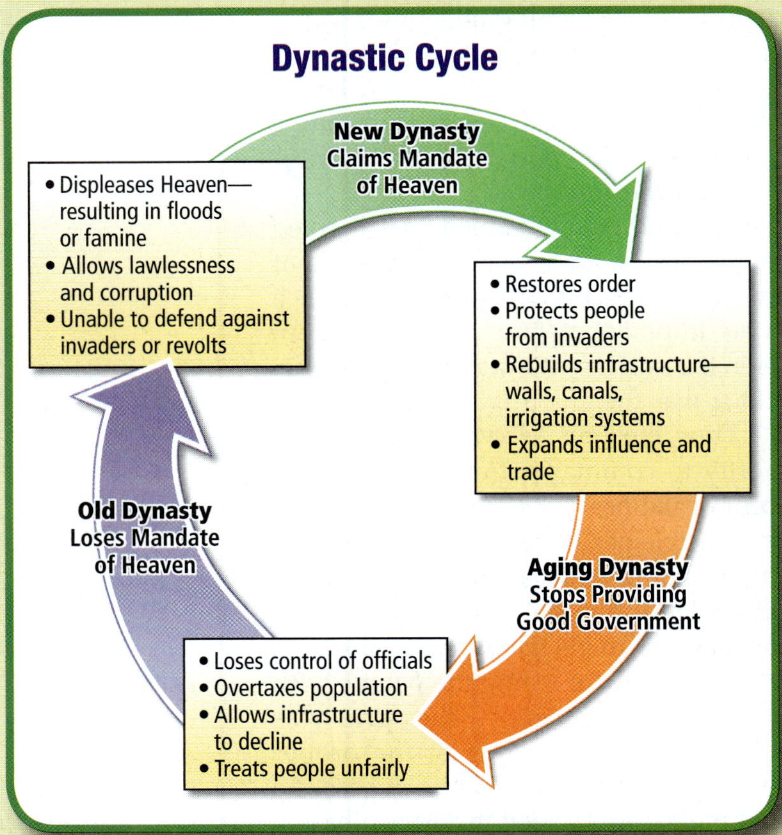


**Early Dynasties of China**

| DYNASTY | DATES | ACCOMPLISHMENTS |
|---|---|---|
| Shang | 1750–1045 B.C. | First dynasty, writing, ancestor worship, bronze |
| Zhou | 1045–256 B.C. | Classical arts, silk discovered, Daoism and Confucianism |
| Qin | 221–206 B.C. | China united, measurements and writing standardized |
| Han | 202 B.C.–A.D. 220 | Silk Road, civil service, paper invented, Buddhism |

**Analyzing VISUALS**

1. **Recognizing Bias** Why did the Zhou dynasty develop the concept of the Mandate of Heaven?
2. **Theorizing** Why do you think each of the dynasties came to an end?

the Zhou ruler. In 403 B.C., civil war broke out, beginning an age known in Chinese history as the Period of the Warring States.

Warfare had also changed in China. Iron weapons, more powerful than bronze weapons, came into use. Foot soldiers, or infantry, and soldiers on horseback, or cavalry, made their appearance. The cavalry was armed with the powerful crossbow, a Chinese invention of the seventh century B.C. Eventually, one of the warring states—the Qin (CHIHN)—took control. The Qin created a new dynasty in 221 B.C.

## Social Structure

During the Zhou dynasty, the basic features of Chinese economic and social life began to take shape. The Zhou continued the pattern of land ownership that had existed under the Shang. The peasants worked on lands owned by their lord. Each peasant family farmed an outer plot for its own use and then joined with other families to work the inner one for their lord. The system of land ownership was similar to that in the feudal order that developed later in Europe and Japan.

A class of artisans and merchants lived in walled towns under the direct control of the local lord. Merchants did not operate freely but were considered the property of the local lord. There was also a slave class.

Trade in this period involved the exchange of local products that were used on an everyday basis. Eventually, trade increased to include goods brought in from distant regions. Among these goods were salt, iron, cloth, and various luxury items.

Few social institutions have been as closely identified with China as the family. As in most agricultural societies, in ancient China the family served as the basic economic and social unit. However, the family there took on an almost sacred quality as a symbol of the entire social order.

What explains the importance of the family in ancient China? Certainly, the need to work together on the land was a significant factor. In ancient times, farming required the work of many people. This was especially true in growing rice, which had become the chief crop in the region of the Chang Jiang and the provinces to the south.

Growing rice requires hard work to plant, grow, and harvest. An irrigation network bringing water to the fields must also be kept in operation. Children were essential to the family because they worked in the fields. Later, sons were expected to take over the physical labor on the family plots and provide for their parents.

At the heart of the concept of family in China was the idea of **filial piety**. *Filial* refers to a son or daughter. *Filial piety*, then, refers to the duty of members of the family to subordinate their needs and desires to those of the male head of the family. More broadly, the term describes a system in which every family member had his or her place. This concept is important in Confucianism, covered later in this section.

Male supremacy was a key element in the social system of China, as it was in the other civilizations of the time. The male was responsible for providing food for his family. In ancient China, men worked the fields and were the warriors, scholars, and government ministers. Women raised the children and worked in the home.

Although women did not hold positions of authority, some did influence politics. This was especially true at the royal court, where female members of the royal family played a part in court affairs. These activities were clearly looked down upon by males, as this Chinese poem indicates:

**PRIMARY SOURCE**

"A clever man builds a city,
A clever woman lays one low;
With all her qualifications, that clever woman
is but an ill-omened bird."

—Herbert A. Giles, *A History of Chinese Literature*

## Zhou Accomplishments

The period from the sixth to the third centuries B.C. was an age of significant economic growth and technological change, especially in farming. For thousands of years, farmers had depended on rainfall to water crops such as rice and millet. By the sixth century B.C., irrigation was in wide use. Large-scale water projects were set in motion to control the flow of rivers and spread water evenly to the fields.

Changes in farming methods also increased food production. By the mid-sixth century B.C., the use of iron led to the development of iron plowshares to plow land that had not been farmed previously. This increased the land available for growing crops. Because of advances in farming tools and practices, China's population rose as high as fifty million people during the late Zhou period.

Improved farming methods were also a major factor in encouraging the growth of trade and manufacturing. One of the most important items of trade in ancient China was silk. Chinese silk fragments from the period have been found throughout central Asia and as far away as Athens, Greece—clear indications of a far-reaching trade network.

Perhaps the most important cultural contribution of ancient China to later Chinese society was the creation and development of the Chinese written language. By Shang times, the Chinese had developed a simple script that is the ancestor of the highly complex written language of today.

Like many other ancient languages, it was primarily pictographic and ideographic in form. **Pictographs** are picture symbols, or characters, which represent an object. For example, the Chinese characters for mountain 山, sun 日, and moon 月 were meant to represent the objects themselves. **Ideographs** are characters that combine two or more pictographs to represent an idea. For example, the word *east* 東 symbolizes the sun coming up behind the trees.

There was a sound associated with each Chinese character when a speaker read it aloud. In other cultures, people eventually stopped using pictographs and ideographs and adopted phonetic symbols representing speech sounds, such as the Roman alphabet. The Chinese, too, eventually began to attach phonetic meaning to some of their symbols. However, although the Chinese language has evolved continuously over a period of four thousand years, it has never entirely abandoned its original format.

**✓Reading Check** **Describing** What is the pattern of dynastic cycles?

## Chinese Philosophy

**MAIN IDEA** Chinese philosophers emphasized stability and order in society.

**HISTORY & YOU** What does our society value? Learn how Chinese philosophy influenced societal values.

Between 500 B.C. and 200 B.C., toward the end of the Zhou dynasty, three major schools of thought about the nature of human beings and the universe emerged in China—Confucianism, Daoism, and Legalism. While Hindus and Buddhists focused on freeing the human soul from the cycle of rebirth, Chinese philosophers were more concerned about the material world and creating a stable society.

### Confucianism

**Confucius** was known to the Chinese as the First Teacher. *Confucius* is the westernized form of Kongfuzi [KUNG•FOO•DZUH], meaning "Master Kung," as he was called by his followers. Confucius was born in 551 B.C. He hoped to get a job as a political adviser, but he had little success in finding a patron.

Upset by the violence and moral decay of his era, Confucius traveled around China in an attempt to persuade political leaders to follow his ideas. Few listened at the time, but a faithful band of followers revered him as a great teacher, recorded his sayings in the *Analects*, and spread his message. Until the twentieth century, almost every Chinese pupil studied his sayings, making **Confucianism**, or the system of Confucian ideas, an important part of Chinese culture.

Confucius lived in a chaotic time characterized by unceasing warfare and mass executions of men, women, and children by beheading. China was faced with restoring order. Confucius provided a set of ideas that eventually became widely accepted.

Confucius's interest in **philosophy** was political and **ethical,** not spiritual. He believed that it was useless to speculate on spiritual questions. It was better to assume that there was an order in the universe. If humans would act in harmony with the universe, their own affairs would prosper.

Two elements stand out in the Confucian view of the Dao (Way): duty and humanity. The concept of duty meant that people had to subordinate their own interests to the broader needs of the family and the community. Everyone should be governed by the Five Constant Relationships: parent and child, husband and wife, older sibling and younger sibling, older friend and younger friend, and ruler and subject. Each person had a duty to the other. Parents should be loving, and children should revere their parents. Husbands should fulfill their duties, and wives should be obedient. The elder sibling should be kind, and the younger sibling respectful. The older friend should be considerate, and the younger friend deferential. Rulers should be benevolent, and subjects loyal. Showing the importance of family, Confucius said: "The duty of children to their parents is the foundation from which all virtues spring." The Confucian concept of duty is often expressed in the form of a "work ethic." If each individual worked hard to fulfill his or her duties, then the affairs of society as a whole would prosper as well.

## TURNING POINT — THE RULE OF MERIT

Confucius equated education with public service and virtue. He taught that rulers should be devoted to the welfare of the people and that government officials should earn their positions through education and talent—merit. Merit-based civil service became official during the Qin dynasty and later included written examinations. Although there were periods of corruption in the 1,300-year history of the exams, testing made it possible for any male adult, regardless of social status or wealth, to become a high-ranking public official. Eventually, the Chinese civil service influenced the development of European and American systems.

Civil service exam under Emperor Jen-Tsung

A young woman applies for a civil service position.

**CRITICAL THINKING SKILLS**

1. **Making Inferences** What are some differences between ancient and modern civil service exams?
2. **Drawing Conclusions** Is the civil service still important in China today?

As Confucius stated, "If there is righteousness in the heart, there will be beauty in the character. If there is beauty in the character, there will be harmony in the home. If there be harmony in the home, there will be order in the nation. If there be order in the nation, there will be peace in the world."

Confucius taught that humans are basically good. Above all, the ruler must set a good example. If the king followed the path of goodness, then subjects would respect him, and society would prosper. Confucius said, "Let the ruler be filial and kind to all people; then they will be faithful to him. Let him advance the good and teach the incompetent; then they will eagerly seek to be virtuous."

The second key element in the Confucian view of the Dao is humanity—compassion and empathy for others. Confucius said, "Do not do unto others what you would not wish done to yourself." Confucius urged people to "measure the feelings of others by one's own," for "within the four seas all men are brothers." After his death in 479 B.C., his message spread widely throughout China.

Confucius was a harsh critic of his own times. He stressed a return to the values of the Golden Age of the early Zhou dynasty. Confucius saw it as an age of perfection. "When the Great Way was practiced, the world was shared by all alike."

Confucius, however, was not just living in the past. Many of his key ideas looked forward. Perhaps his most significant political idea was that government service should be open to all men of superior talent and not limited to those of noble birth. This concept of rule by merit was not popular with the aristocrats who held political offices based on their noble birth. Although Confucius's ideas did not have much effect in his lifetime, they opened the door to a new idea of statecraft that would later be put into widespread use.

## Daoism

**Daoism** was a system of ideas based on the teachings of **Laozi** (LOW•DZUH). According to tradition, Laozi, or the Old Master, lived around the same time period as Confucius.

## Connecting to the United States

### Civil Service Reform

By 1881, the number of people seeking presidential appointments to government jobs had gotten out of hand. That year a disappointed office seeker shot President Garfield. Public anger over Garfield's assassination led to the passage of the Civil Service Act of 1883. Civil service reform made competitive examination, not politics, the basis for filling federal jobs. In 1978, President James Carter established the U.S. Office of Personnel Management, which administers a nationwide merit system for federal employees including recruitment, examination, and training programs.

Charles J. Guiteau shoots President James Garfield

**Connecting to Today**

1. **Contrasting** What is the difference between the Chinese and the American reasons for adopting civil service examinations?
2. **Making Inferences** Why was it difficult to pass civil service reform laws?

Scholars do not know if Laozi actually existed. Nevertheless, the ideas people associate with him became popular in the fifth and fourth centuries B.C.

The chief ideas of Daoism are discussed in a short work known as *Tao Te Ching*, or *The Way of the Dao.* Scholars have argued for centuries over its meaning. Nevertheless, the basic ideas of Daoism, as interpreted by its followers, are straightforward. Daoism, like Confucianism, does not concern itself with the meaning of the universe. Rather, it sets forth proper forms of human behavior.

Daoism is also quite different from Confucianism. Followers of Confucius believe that it is the duty of human beings to work hard to improve life here on Earth. Daoists believe that the way to follow the will of Heaven is not through action but inaction:

**PRIMARY SOURCE**

"Without going outside, you may know the whole world.
Without looking through the window, you may see the ways of heaven.
The farther you go, the less you know.
Thus the sage [wise man] knows without traveling;
He sees without looking;
He works without doing."

The best way to act in harmony with the universal order is not to interfere with the natural order.

**PRIMARY SOURCE**

"The universe is sacred.
You cannot improve it.
If you try to change it, you will ruin it.
If you try to hold it, you will lose it."
—Lao Tsu, *Tao Te Ching*

## Legalism

A third philosophy that became popular was **Legalism**. Unlike Confucianism or Daoism, Legalism proposed that human beings were evil by nature. Legalists were referred to as the "School of Law" because they rejected the Confucian view that government by "superior men" could solve society's problems. Instead, they argued for a system of impersonal laws.

The Legalists believed that a strong ruler was required to create an orderly society. Confucius had said, "Lead the people by virtue and restrain them by the rules of good taste, and the people will have a sense of shame, and moreover will become good." The Legalists believed that only harsh laws and stiff punishments would cause the common people to serve the interests of the ruler. To them, people were not capable of being good. The ruler did not have to show compassion for the people.

✓Reading Check **Summarizing** What three philosophies became popular in early China?

## SECTION 3 REVIEW

### Vocabulary

1. **Explain** the significance of: Huang He, Chang Jiang, aristocracy, Mandate of Heaven, Dao, filial piety, pictographs, ideographs, Confucius, Confucianism, Daoism, Laozi, Legalism.

### Main Ideas

2. **Describe** the relationship between China's geography—including the Huang He, Chang Jiang, and the mountains—and its climate.
3. **Summarize** the relationship between the dynastic cycle and the Mandate of Heaven.
4. **Explain** the importance of filial piety to the Chinese. How does the concept of filial piety relate to the Confucian view of how society should function?
5. **List** some of the agricultural advances developed in ancient China and explain how they increased food production.

### Critical Thinking

6. **The BIG Idea** **Drawing Conclusions** How would writing with pictographs be more complex than using an alphabet?
7. **Diagramming** Create a diagram showing the Five Constant Relationships and the duty of each.

| Relationship | Duty | Duty |
|---|---|---|
| Parent and child | | |
| | | |
| | | |

8. **Contrasting** How do Chinese philosophies differ from Buddhism and Hinduism?

### Writing About History

9. **Expository Writing** Write a paper about the philosophical traditions of Confucianism, Daoism, and Legalism. Research to find examples of how these three philosophies influenced historic and contemporary world events.

**History ONLINE**

For help with the concepts in this section of *Glencoe World History*, go to glencoe.com and click Study Central™.

SECTION 4

Section Audio

Spotlight Video

# Rise and Fall of Chinese Empires

## GUIDE TO READING

### The BIG Idea

**Order and Security** The Qin and Han dynasties established strong central governments that were the basis for future dynasties.

### Content Vocabulary

- regime *(p. 96)*
- censorate *(p. 96)*

### Academic Vocabulary

- individuality *(p. 95)*
- instituted *(p. 96)*
- ideology *(p. 96)*

### People and Places

- Qin Shihuangdi *(p. 94)*
- Gobi *(p. 95)*
- Xiongnu *(p. 95)*
- Liu Pang *(p. 98)*
- Han Wudi *(p. 98)*
- South China Sea *(p. 98)*

### Reading Strategy

**Compare and Contrast** As you read this section, compare and contrast the Qin and Han dynasties using a Venn diagram.

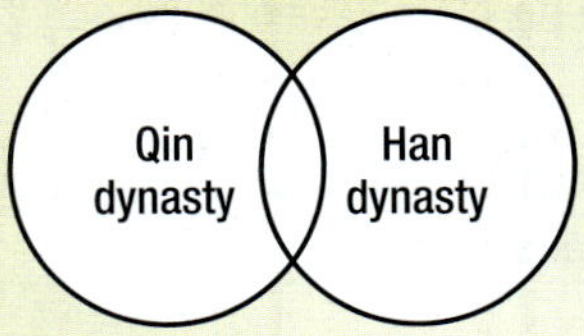


*The First Qin Emperor unified the Chinese world, though his dynasty was short-lived. The Han dynasty that followed, however, lasted more than four hundred years. These dynasties made contributions to literature, art, and technology that have endured to the present.*

## The Qin Dynasty

**MAIN IDEA** Qin Shihuangdi unified the Chinese world using force against invaders and harsh treatment of his subjects.

***HISTORY & YOU*** What makes you want to obey rules? Learn how the Chinese responded to repression.

As we have seen, from about 400 B.C. to 200 B.C., China experienced bloody civil war. Powerful states fought one another and ignored the authority of the Zhou kings. One state—that of Qin—gradually defeated its chief rivals. In 221 B.C., the Qin ruler declared the creation of a new dynasty.

### Qin Shihuangdi

The ruler of the Qin dynasty was **Qin Shihuangdi** (CHIHN SHUH•HWAHNG•DEE), meaning "the First Qin Emperor." An ambitious person, he came to the throne in 246 B.C. at the age of 13. In 221 B.C., he defeated the last of his rivals and founded a new dynasty, with himself as emperor. The famous Chinese historian Sima Qian described Qin Shihuangdi as having "the chest of a bird of prey, the voice of a jackal, and the heart of a tiger." Those were just the qualities Qin Shihuangdi used to unite China. He created a single monetary system and ordered the building of a system of roads throughout the entire empire. Many of these roads led out from his capital city of Xianyang (SHYEN•YAHNG), just north of modern-day Xi'an (SHEE•AHN).

Qin Shihuangdi was equally aggressive in foreign affairs. His armies advanced to the south, extending the border of China to the edge of the Yuan (YOO•AHN) River, or Red River, in modern-day Vietnam. To supply his armies, he had a canal dug from the Chang Jiang in central China to what is now the modern city of Guangzhou (GWAHNG•JOH).

### The Emperor's Army

Surprisingly, the emperor left behind a remarkable artistic legacy too. In 1974, farmers digging a well about 35 miles (56 km) east of Xi'an discovered an underground pit near the burial mound

PRIMARY SOURCE HISTORY & ARTS

## The Emperor's Army

Outside Xi'an is the emperor Qin Shihuangdi's tomb complex. In the emperor's tomb, archaeologists have found sculptures, buildings, and cemeteries.

East of the tomb, a museum houses the emperor's army. The infantry is lined up in one large pit. Another pit contains cavalry and chariots. A third pit holds army headquarters.

The soldiers stand between 5 feet 8 inches and 6 feet 2 inches tall; their commanders are taller. The figures are weighted—the lower half of the ceramic bodies are solid, the upper half hollow. Traces of color show the statues were once vividly painted.

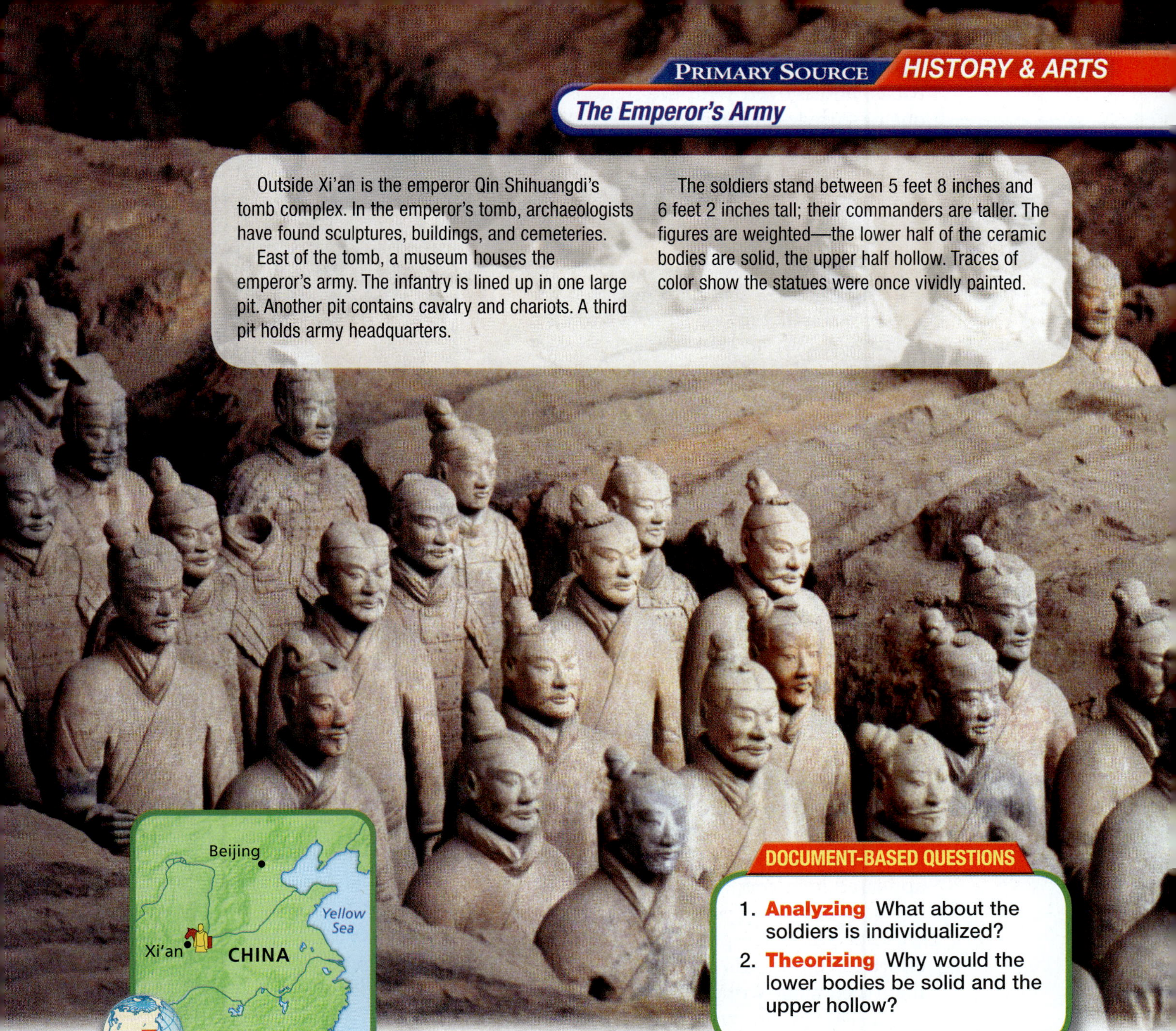


**DOCUMENT-BASED QUESTIONS**

1. **Analyzing** What about the soldiers is individualized?
2. **Theorizing** Why would the lower bodies be solid and the upper hollow?

of the First Qin Emperor. The pit contained a vast army made of terra-cotta, or hardened clay. Chinese archaeologists believe that it was a re-creation of Qin Shihuangdi's imperial guard, meant to be with the emperor on his journey to the next world.

Archaeologists estimate that there are more than six thousand figures in the first pit alone, along with horses, wooden chariots, and seven thousand bronze weapons. The figures are slightly larger than life-size. They were molded, fired, and painted in brilliant colors and then dressed in uniforms. To achieve **individuality** in the faces of the soldiers, ten different head shapes were used, which were finished by hand. Besides preparing for the next world, the Qin emperor was busy keeping out invaders.

## The Great Wall

The Qin emperor's major foreign concern was in the north. In the vicinity of the **Gobi**, there resided a nomadic people known to the Chinese as the **Xiongnu** (SHYUNG•NOO). Mounted on horses, they ranged far and wide in search of pastures.

The Xiongnu were organized loosely into tribes, and moved with the seasons from one pasture to another with their flocks of cattle, sheep, or goats. The Xiongnu had mastered the art of fighting on horseback. The historian Sima Qian remarked:

**PRIMARY SOURCE**

> "[T]he little boys start out by learning to ride sheep and shoot birds and rats with a bow and arrow, and when they get a little older they shoot foxes and rabbits, which are used for food. Thus all the young men are able to use a bow and act as armed cavalry in time of war."
>
> —Sima Qian

When the Xiongnu challenged Chinese communities near the northern frontier, a number of states constructed walls to keep the nomads out. Qin Shihuangdi's answer to the problem was to strengthen the existing system of walls and link them together to create The Wall of Ten Thousand *Li*—a *li* is about a third of a mile, or half a kilometer. Today we know Qin Shihuangdi's project as the Great Wall of China. However, the wall that we know from films and photographs was not built until 1,500 years later. Some of the walls built by Shihuangdi do remain, but most of them were built of loose stone, sand, or piled rubble and disappeared long ago.

This is not to say, of course, that the wall was not a massive project. It required the efforts of thousands of laborers. Many of them died while working there and, according to legend, are now buried within the wall. With his wall, the First Qin Emperor had some success in fighting off the nomads, but the victory was only temporary. Over the next two thousand years, China's northern frontier became one of the great areas of conflict in Asia.

## Political Changes

See page R35 to read a passage from Li Su, a chief minister of the First Qin Emperor, in the **Primary Sources and Literature Library.**

The Qin dynasty dramatically changed Chinese politics. Legalism was adopted as the **regime's**—the government in power—official **ideology**. Books presenting ideas opposed to the official views were publicly burned. Those who opposed the policies of the new regime were punished or executed.

The Qin dynasty made a number of important administrative and political changes, which served as models for future dynasties. Unlike the Zhou dynasty, the Qin dynasty ruled a highly centralized state. The central bureaucracy was divided into three parts: the civil division, the military division, and the **censorate.** The censorate had inspectors who checked on government officials to make sure they were doing their jobs. This became standard for future Chinese dynasties.

Below the central government were two levels of administration: provinces and counties. Unlike under the Zhou, these officials did not inherit their positions but were appointed and dismissed by the emperor. The censors also watched over these officials, and those found guilty of wrongdoing were executed. Qin Shihuangdi also reduced the powers of the landed aristocrats by dividing their estates among the peasants, who were now taxed directly by the state. In doing so, he eliminated possible rivals and gained tax revenues for the central government.

## Fall of the Qin Dynasty

By ruthlessly controlling the empire, Qin Shihuangdi hoped to establish a rule that "would be enjoyed by his sons for ten thousand generations." In fact, Shihuangdi was to be his dynasty's only ruler. Landed aristocrats and Confucian intellectuals, as well as the common people, groaned under the censorship of speech, harsh taxes, and forced labor projects **instituted** by the ruler. Sima Qian said of Qin Shihuangdi:

**PRIMARY SOURCE**

> "He killed men as though he thought he could never finish, he punished men as though he were afraid he would never get around to them all, and the whole world revolted against him."
>
> —Sima Qian

The emperor died in 210 B.C., and his dynasty was overthrown four years later. The fall of the Qin dynasty was followed by a period of civil war, but it did not last long. A new dynasty soon arose.

**✓Reading Check** **Identifying** What three parts of the central bureaucracy were developed by the Qin dynasty?

**INFOGRAPHICS** PRIMARY SOURCE

## The Great Wall of China: In History and Legend

The Great Wall winds across China's landscape and through its history. Over 2,000 years, piled stone gave way to elaborate watchtowers and forts. In the seventeenth century, visiting Europeans mistakenly assumed the wall was one continuous structure and called it "The Great Wall of China." Besides guarding trade routes, the wall became the source of legends.

### The Legend of Meng Jiangnu Whose Wails Split the Wall

Near Shanhaiguan Pass is a temple to Meng Jiangnu. Fan, Meng's husband, was one of thousands forced to work on the wall. With winter coming, Meng carried warm clothes to Fan. When Meng reached the place where her husband had been working, she learned that Fan had died from overwork and been buried in the wall. Hearing this awful news, Meng wept so loudly that miles of wall collapsed, exposing the bodies of laborers.

NATIONAL GEOGRAPHIC

### BUILDING THE GREAT WALL

### Geography SKILLS

1. **Location** Which border of the empires was the wall supposed to protect?
2. **Human-Environment Interaction** What physical features of the environment made it difficult to build the Great Wall?

**Maps In MOtion** See *StudentWorks™ Plus* or glencoe.com.

# The Han Dynasty

**MAIN IDEA** The Han dynasty refined the political structures of the Qin.

**HISTORY & YOU** How efficient is your government? Learn how the Chinese trained their officials.

One of the greatest dynasties in Chinese history—the Han (HAHN)—emerged in 202 B.C. The founder of the Han dynasty, **Liu Pang** (LYOO BAHNG), was of peasant origin but became known by his title of Han Gaozu—Exalted Emperor of Han. Under his strong rule, the Han quickly established control over the empire.

## Political and Social Structures

The first Han emperor discarded the Qin dynasty's harsh policies and Legalism. Confucian principles became the new state philosophy. Han Gaozu and his successors also kept some practices of the First Qin Emperor, including dividing the central government into military, civil service, and censorate. The Han rulers also kept the empire divided into provinces.

Most importantly, the Han rulers continued the Qin system of choosing government officials on the basis of merit rather than birth. As the population increased to over sixty million, the need for a large and efficient bureaucracy also increased. To create a regular system for new officials, the Han introduced the civil service examination and established a school to train these candidates. For the next two thousand years, students were expected to learn the teachings of Confucius, Chinese history, and law.

Besides providing a strong central government, the Han emperors expanded the Chinese Empire. Han rulers, especially **Han Wudi** (HAHN WOO•DEE), Martial Emperor of Han, added the regions south of the Chang Jiang. Part of what is now northern Vietnam, along the **South China Sea** coast, became part of the empire. Han armies also extended China's boundary into central Asia. Han Wudi also drove back the Xiongnu beyond the Great Wall. After his death in 87 B.C., China experienced almost another 150 years of peace.

NATIONAL GEOGRAPHIC

**QIN AND HAN EMPIRES**

**Geography SKILLS**

1. **Regions** Which areas did these empires have in common?
2. **Location** How did the location of these empires relate to trade routes shown on the map on page 82?

Although the Han period was prosperous, free peasants began to suffer. Land taxes on land-owning farmers were fairly light, but there were other demands on them, including military service and forced labor of up to one month per year. Then, too, as the population tripled, the average size of the individual farm plot was reduced to about one acre per person—barely enough for survival.

As time went on, many poor peasants were forced to sell their land and become tenant farmers, paying up to half of the annual harvest in rent. Once again aristocrats owned thousands of acres. These powerful nobles could bully free farmers into becoming tenant farmers.

## Technology and Culture

New technologies in textile manufacturing, water mills and windmills for grinding grain, and iron casting added to the economic prosperity of the Han Era. Iron casting technology led to the invention of steel. In addition, paper was developed under the Han dynasty.

With the invention of the rudder and fore-and-aft rigging, ships could sail into the wind. This made it possible for Chinese merchant ships carrying heavy cargoes to travel throughout the islands of Southeast Asia and India, leading to a major expansion of trade in the Han period.

The Han dynasty was also known for art and cultural achievements. The key works of the Confucian school were made into a set of Confucian classics, which became required reading for generations of Chinese schoolchildren. These classics introduced children to the forms of behavior that they would need as adults.

## Fall of the Han Empire

Over a period of time, the Han Empire began to fall into decay. As weak rulers amused themselves with the pleasures of court life, the power of the central government began to decline. The great noble families filled the gap, amassing huge landed estates and forcing free farmers to become their tenants. Official corruption and the concentration of land in the hands of the wealthy led to widespread peasant unrest, and nomadic raids continued in the north.

By A.D. 170, wars, intrigues at the court, and peasant uprisings brought the virtual collapse of the Han dynasty. In 190, rebel armies sacked the Han capital, Luoyang (LWAW•YAHNG). The final blow came in 220, when a general seized control but was unable to maintain his power. China again plunged into civil war, made worse by migrating nomadic people from Central Asia. The Han Empire achieved the lasting greatness of a classical civilization. The next great dynasty would not arise for 400 years.

✓Reading Check **Identifying** What new technologies developed during the Han Era?

## SECTION 4 REVIEW

### Vocabulary

1. **Explain** the significance of: Qin Shihuangdi, individuality, Gobi, Xiongnu, regime, ideology, censorate, instituted, Liu Pang, Han Wudi, South China Sea.

### Main Ideas

2. **Describe** the Great Wall, its purpose, and how it changed over the years.
3. **List** the technical and cultural achievements of the Han dynasty.
4. **Explain** how the merit system of civil service was implemented during the Han and its impact on future generations.

### Critical Thinking

5. **The BIG Idea** **Contrasting** How were the political structures and philosophies of the Qin and Han dynasties different?
6. **Organizing Information** Create a flowchart showing the government organization during the Han dynasty and the duties of each division.

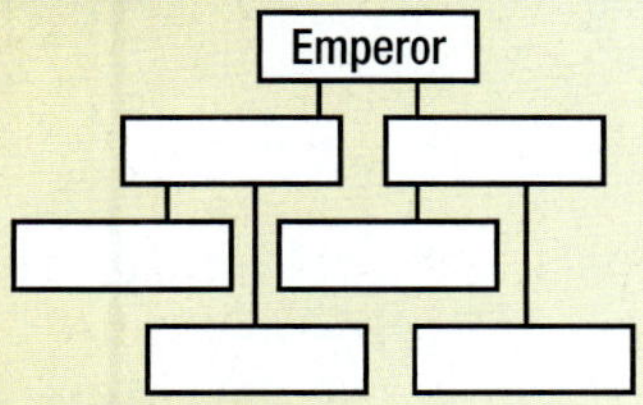


7. **Analyzing Primary Sources** Examine Sima Qian's descriptions of Qin Shihuangdi on pages 94 and 96. What is the historian's view? Why might he have that opinion?

### Writing About History

8. **Expository Writing** Write an essay that explains what the Chinese archaeological site east of Xi'an tells us about the people of the Qin dynasty. What might future historians conclude about the United States based on our monuments?

**History ONLINE**
For help with the concepts in this section of *Glencoe World History*, go to glencoe.com and click Study Central™.

STUDY TO GO You can study anywhere, anytime by downloading quizzes and flash cards to your PDA from glencoe.com.

DHAMEKH STUPA, INDIA

CONFUCIUS

## Comparing Two Ancient Cultures

3000 B.C.–A.D. 500

| INDIA | CHINA |
|---|---|
| **Geographic and Environmental Features** | |
| Himalaya<br>Indus River<br>Deccan Plateau<br>Monsoons | Himalaya<br>Gobi<br>Huang He<br>Chang Jiang |
| **Early Civilizations, Empires, Dynasties** | |
| Indus Valley Civilization<br>Mauryan Empire<br>Kushān Empire<br>Empire of Guptas | Shang Dynasty<br>Zhou Dynasty<br>Qin Dynasty<br>Han Dynasty |
| **Religions and Philosophies** | |
| Hinduism<br>Buddhism | Confucianism<br>Daoism<br>Legalism |
| **Famous People** | |
| Mauryan king Aśoka<br>Buddha | Confucius<br>Qin Shihuangdi |
| **Social and Political Structures** | |
| Caste System<br>*Varnas* | Mandate of Heaven<br>Dynastic Cycles<br>The Rule of Merit |
| **Economy and Trade** | |
| Cotton cloth<br>Ivory<br>Jewelry<br>Stamp seals<br>Pepper | Silk cloth<br>Spices<br>Teas<br>Porcelain |
| **Inventions and Accomplishments** | |
| Indus Valley script<br>The Vedas in Sanskrit<br>Algebra and zero | Silk<br>Silk Road<br>Great Wall<br>Paper |

THE RIGVEDA

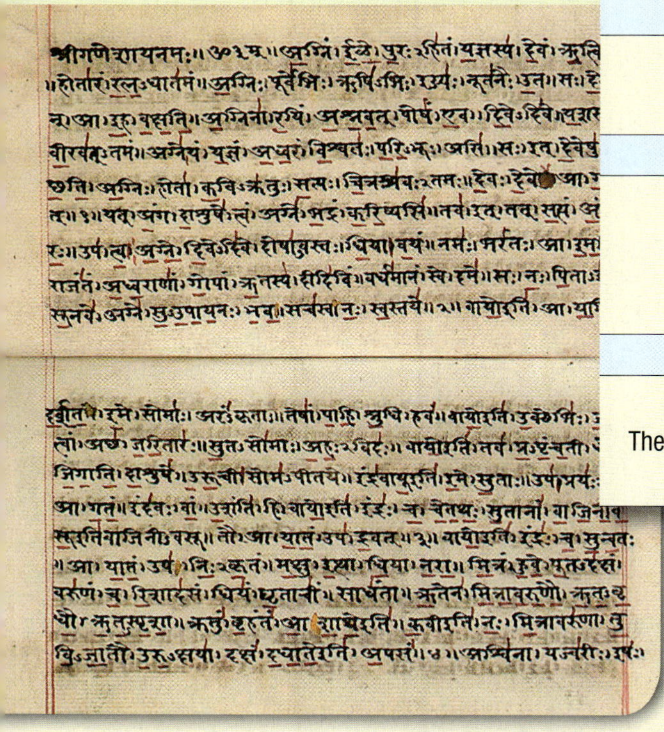

THE GREAT WALL OF CHINA

# CHAPTER 3 Assessment

## Reviewing Vocabulary

*Directions: Choose the word or words that best complete the sentence.*

**1.** Monsoons are seasonal ________ in China and the Indian subcontinent.

**A** winds

**B** thunderstorms

**C** floods

**D** cyclones

**2.** According to Confucius, the key to proper behavior was to behave in accordance with the ________ (Way).

**A** Yoga

**B** Dao

**C** Dharma

**D** Censorate

**3.** In Buddhism, reaching ________, or ultimate reality, is the end of the self and a reunion with the Great World Soul.

**A** reincarnation

**B** karma

**C** nirvana

**D** ascetic

**4.** The English word for the social divisions in India based on occupation and family is ________.

**A** caste

**B** untouchables

**C** raja

**D** reincarnation

**5.** ________ is the duty of family members to subordinate their needs to those of the male head of the family.

**A** Legalism

**B** Feudal order

**C** Individualism

**D** Filial piety

## Reviewing Main Ideas

*Directions: Choose the best answers to the following questions.*

**Section 1** *(pp. 66–75)*

**6.** Which of the following is not a characteristic of the Indus Valley civilization?

**A** Well-planned cities

**B** Large in size

**C** Easily understood writing

**D** Widespread trade

**7.** Out of what did the caste system grow?

**A** Rajas

**B** Aryans

**C** Vedas

**D** *Varnas*

**8.** What do the majority of India's people practice?

**A** Hinduism

**B** Suttee

**C** Buddhism

**D** Asceticism

**9.** Which of the following is a true statement about Buddhists?

**A** They are the majority in India.

**B** They try to follow the Middle Path.

**C** They believe in a rigid caste system.

**D** They worship the Buddha as a god.

### TEST-TAKING TIP

Even if you don't know the correct answer, you still may know which answer choices are *wrong.* Eliminate the answer choices you know are wrong. Then choose the best answer from the choices that remain.

**Need Extra Help?**

| If You Missed Questions . . . | 1 | 2 | 3 | 4 | 5 | 6 | 7 | 8 | 9 |
|---|---|---|---|---|---|---|---|---|---|
| Go to Page . . . | 66 | 90 | 74 | 70 | 89 | 68 | 70 | 72 | 73 |

GO ON

# CHAPTER 3 Assessment

## Section 2 *(pp. 76–81)*

**10.** Who is considered the greatest ruler in the history of India?

**A** Faxian

**B** Kālidāsa

**C** Aśoka

**D** Āryabhata

**11.** Which empire was known for prosperity, trade, literature, and especially for its tolerance of Buddhism?

**A** Mauryan

**B** Kushān

**C** Aryan

**D** Gupta

## Section 3 *(pp. 84–93)*

**12.** Who was known as the First Teacher or Master Kung?

**A** Confucius

**B** Han Wudi

**C** Laozi

**D** Qin Shihuangdi

**13.** The Mandate of Heaven refers to whose responsibilities?

**A** Parent to child

**B** Children to parents

**C** Husbands and wives to each other

**D** Rulers to provide good government

## Section 4 *(pp. 94–99)*

**14.** Which long-lasting dynasty was known for advances in papermaking, manufacturing textiles, water mills, and casting iron, as well as art?

**A** Shang

**B** Zhou

**C** Qin

**D** Han

## Critical Thinking

*Directions: Choose the best answers to the following questions.*

**15.** Why did the Silk Road extend from China's coast to central Asia?

**A** To move luxury goods to Western markets

**B** Because trade by ship was too dangerous

**C** To avoid trade with India

**D** To avoid bandits and deserts

*Base your answer to question 16 on the map below and on your knowledge of world history.*

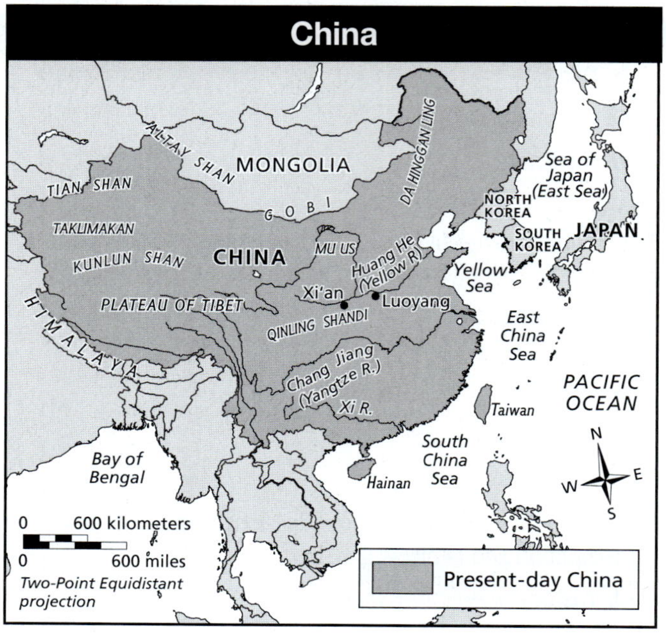


**16.** What characteristics of the Huang He and the Chang Jiang helped the development of the first Chinese civilizations?

**A** Rugged terrain protected the Chinese from invasion.

**B** Regular flooding created good conditions for farming.

**C** A cold and dry environment supported nomadic grazing.

**D** Their walls and watchtowers protected the Chinese from invasion.

**Need Extra Help?**

| If You Missed Questions . . . | 10 | 11 | 12 | 13 | 14 | 15 | 16 |
|---|---|---|---|---|---|---|---|
| Go to Page . . . | 76 | 79 | 90 | 87 | 89 | 78 | 84 |

GO ON

17. Why are Confucianism and Daoism considered philosophies, not religions?
   - **A** They do not teach proper behavior.
   - **B** They have no holy books or written code.
   - **C** They have no temples for followers.
   - **D** They do not try to explain the meaning of the universe.

18. What is distinctive about Chinese script?
   - **A** Has phonetic characters
   - **B** Was written on paper
   - **C** Used pictographs and ideographs
   - **D** Has changed over time

*Analyze the chart and answer the question that follows. Base your answer on the chart and on your knowledge of world history.*

**Average Monthly Rainfall (selected cities)**

| Months | Mumbai (inches) | Chennai (inches) |
|---|---|---|
| J | 0.0 | 1.2 |
| F | 0.0 | 0.4 |
| M | 0.0 | 0.4 |
| A | 0.0 | 0.7 |
| M | 0.5 | 1.7 |
| J | 22.3 | 2.1 |
| J | 25.6 | 3.9 |
| A | 19.2 | 4.9 |
| S | 14.0 | 4.9 |
| O | 3.5 | 11.2 |
| N | 0.2 | 13.2 |
| D | 0.0 | 5.4 |

19. What time of the year can farmers near Mumbai expect rain?
   - **A** Winter (December–February)
   - **B** Spring (March–May)
   - **C** Summer (June–August)
   - **D** Fall (September–November)

## Document-Based Questions

*Directions: Analyze the documents and answer the short-answer questions that follow the document.*

Several dynasties, especially the Han, tried to follow Confucius's teachings. The founder of the Qin dynasty followed Legalism's view.

> *Confucius taught:*
>
> *"Let the ruler be filial and kind to all people; then they will be faithful to him. Let him advance the good and teach the incompetent; then they will eagerly seek to be virtuous."*
>
> *Sima Qian said of Qin Shihuangdi:*
>
> *". . . [H]e punished men as though he were afraid he would never get around to them all, and the whole world revolted against him."*

20. Contrast the philosophies of Confucianism and Legalism and their influence on the Han and Qin dynasties.
21. What caused the downfall of the Han dynasty?

## Extended Response

22. Explain the relationship between the Mandate of Heaven, Dao, and dynastic cycles.

**History ONLINE**

For additional test practice, use Self-Check Quizzes—Chapter 3 at glencoe.com.

**Need Extra Help?**

| If You Missed Questions . . . | 17 | 18 | 19 | 20 | 21 | 22 |
|---|---|---|---|---|---|---|
| Go to Page . . . | 93 | 90 | 66 | 90 | 99 | 87 |

STOP

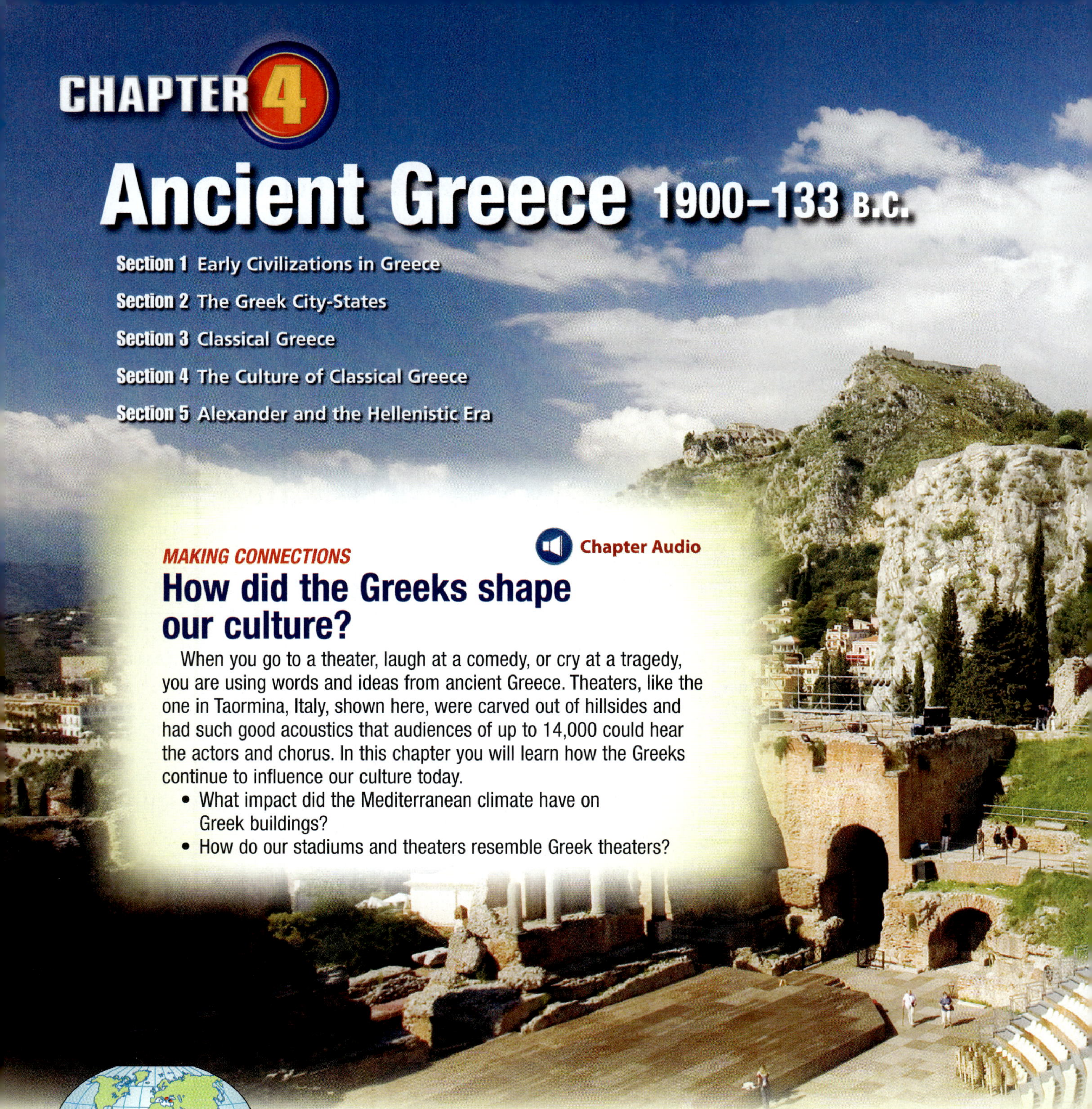

# CHAPTER 4

# Ancient Greece 1900–133 B.C.

**Section 1** Early Civilizations in Greece

**Section 2** The Greek City-States

**Section 3** Classical Greece

**Section 4** The Culture of Classical Greece

**Section 5** Alexander and the Hellenistic Era

*MAKING CONNECTIONS*

Chapter Audio

## How did the Greeks shape our culture?

When you go to a theater, laugh at a comedy, or cry at a tragedy, you are using words and ideas from ancient Greece. Theaters, like the one in Taormina, Italy, shown here, were carved out of hillsides and had such good acoustics that audiences of up to 14,000 could hear the actors and chorus. In this chapter you will learn how the Greeks continue to influence our culture today.

- What impact did the Mediterranean climate have on Greek buildings?
- How do our stadiums and theaters resemble Greek theaters?

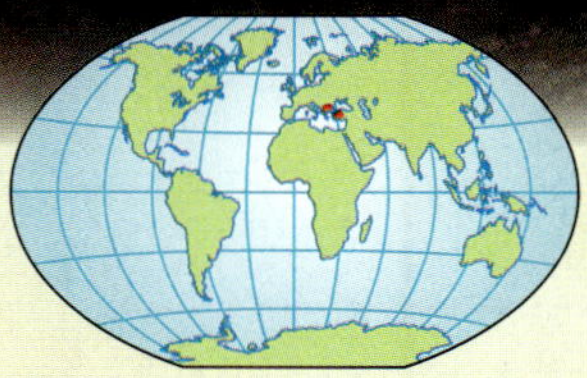

THE WORLD ▶

**c. 1900 B.C.** Peak of Minoan civilization

**776 B.C.** First Olympic Games held

1900 B.C. | 1500 B.C. | 1000 B.C.

**c. 1500 B.C.** King Agamemnon ruled Mycenae

**499–479 B.C.** Persian Wars

**323 B.C.** Death of Alexander the Great

**133 B.C.**

**500 B.C.** Height of Classical Greece

**431–404 B.C.** Spartans fought Athenians in the Peloponnesian War

**FOLDABLES™**
**Study Organizer**

**Organizing** Review the text for information about the Hellenistic Era and then create a Shutter Fold to organize facts about the era and Alexander the Great.

**History ONLINE** Visit glencoe.com and enter QuickPass™ code GWHEA7447c4 for Chapter 4 resources.

SECTION 1

Section Audio    Spotlight Video

# Early Civilizations in Greece

## GUIDE TO READING

### The BIG Idea

**Physical Geography** The earliest Greek civilizations that appeared in the second millennium B.C. were influenced by their physical environment.

### Content Vocabulary

- epic poem *(p. 111)*
- *arete (p. 111)*

### Academic Vocabulary

- participate *(p. 106)*
- debated *(p. 109)*

### People, Places, and Events

- Aegean Sea *(p. 107)*
- Black Sea *(p. 107)*
- Bronze Age *(p. 108)*
- Crete *(p. 108)*
- Minoan *(p. 108)*
- Mycenaean *(p. 109)*
- Homer *(p. 109)*
- Ionia *(p. 110)*

### Reading Strategy

**Compare and Contrast** As you read, create a diagram like the one below to help you study the Minoan and Mycenaean civilizations.

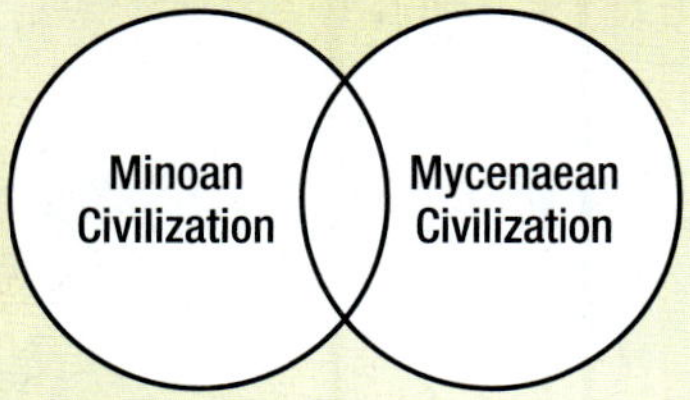


*During the third millennium B.C., the island of Crete was home to the most advanced civilization in Europe. Although Minoan Crete was not Greek, it did have some influence on the first Greek state. The story of ancient Greek civilization begins when a group of Greek-speaking Indo-European people moved into Greece around 1900 B.C. The Mycenaeans provided the inspiration for Homer's epics and paved the way for the political and cultural developments of Greece in the first millennium B.C.*

## The Impact of Geography

**MAIN IDEA** The mountains that divided Greece led to cultural and political divisions between Greeks. However, the seas linked Greece to the rest of the world.

**HISTORY & YOU** How does the physical geography of your town influence life in your community? What physical features affect your everyday life? Read about the effects of geography on development of Greek civilization.

Geography played an important role in the development of Greek civilization. Compared with the landmasses of Mesopotamia and Egypt, Greece occupies a small area. It consists of a mountainous peninsula and numerous islands that encompass about 50,000 square miles (about 129,500 square km) of territory—about the size of the state of Louisiana. The mountains and the sea played especially significant roles in the development of Greek history.

### Mountains

Two peninsulas make up much of the Greek landmass. The Isthmus of Corinth connects the Peloponnese peninsula to the mainland. About 80 percent of Greece is mountainous. Olympus is the highest peak in the Pindus Mountains, which divide the mainland. Much of Greece consists of small plains and river valleys surrounded by high mountain ranges from 8,000 to 10,000 feet (2,438 to 3,048 m) high. These mountains isolated Greeks from one another, causing different Greek communities to develop their own ways of life.

Over a period of time, these communities became fiercely independent. It is probable that the small size of these independent communities encouraged people to **participate** in political affairs. On the other hand, the rivalry between the communities led to warfare that devastated Greek society.

Corfu is one of 2,000 Greek islands.

**Geography SKILLS**

The physical geography of the Aegean basin, the area bordering the Aegean Sea, had a major impact on the development of civilizations in the area.

1. **Human-Environment Interaction** How has Greece's geography affected settlement patterns?
2. **Regions** Using the map, discuss what might account for differences in the cultures of Mycenae and Troy.

## Seas

The sea also influenced the evolution of Greek society. The **Aegean**, Mediterranean, and Ionian Seas make up the eastern, southern, and western borders of Greece. Its location on a peninsula gives Greece a long seacoast dotted by bays and inlets that provided many harbors. Although Greece is small, it has an 8,500-mile (13,700-km) coastline. In fact, no part of the Greek mainland is more than 60 miles (100 km) from a body of water. The ancient Greeks also lived on a number of islands to the west, south, and east of the Greek mainland. Surrounded by water, it was no accident that the Greeks became seafarers. They sailed out into the Aegean Sea, the Mediterranean Sea, and the **Black Sea**, making contact with the outside world. Later they established several colonies that spread Greek civilization throughout the Mediterranean world.

**✓Reading Check** **Explaining** What role did the mountains and the sea play in the development of Greek history?

## Minoans and Mycenaeans

**MAIN IDEA** The Mycenaeans created the first Greek civilization.

***HISTORY & YOU*** What do buildings say about society? Read about the Minoan and Mycenaean cultures.

By 2800 B.C., a **Bronze Age** civilization had been established on the island of **Crete.** Called the **Minoan** civilization, it flourished from 2700 B.C. to 1450 B.C. The Minoans were not Greek, but they did influence the peoples of the Greek mainland.

### Minoan Civilization

Arthur Evans, the English archaeologist who first discovered the civilization, named it after Minos, the legendary king of Crete, because some of its structures were similar to the labyrinth that King Minos was said to have built. At the beginning of the twentieth century, Evans discovered an enormous palace complex on Crete at Knossos (NAH•suhs). The remains of this complex revealed a rich culture, with Knossos as the center of a far-ranging sea empire based on trade. The ships of the Minoans took them to Egypt as well as southern Greece.

**INFOGRAPHICS** PRIMARY SOURCE

### *The Palace at Knossos*

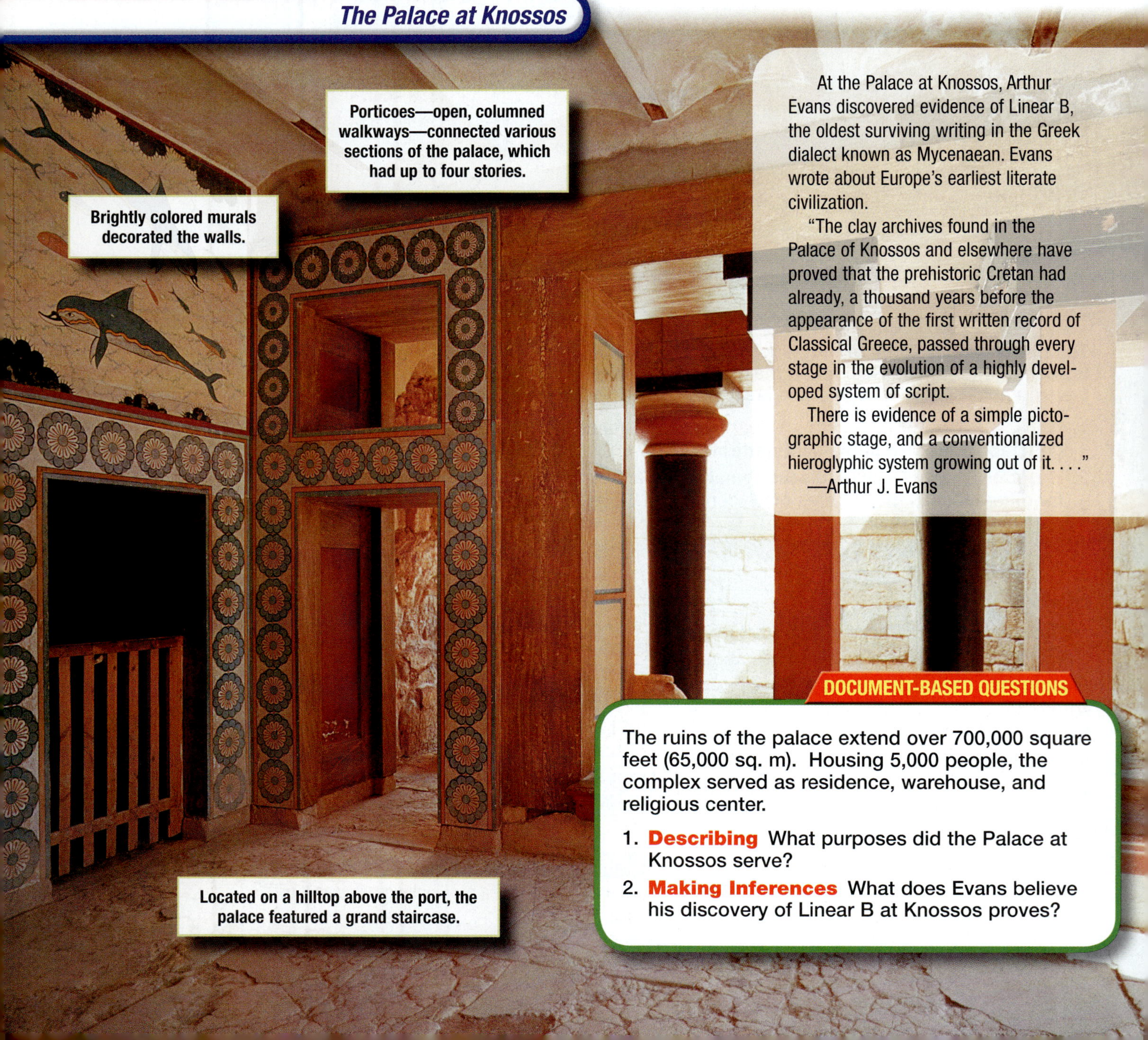


At the Palace at Knossos, Arthur Evans discovered evidence of Linear B, the oldest surviving writing in the Greek dialect known as Mycenaean. Evans wrote about Europe's earliest literate civilization.

"The clay archives found in the Palace of Knossos and elsewhere have proved that the prehistoric Cretan had already, a thousand years before the appearance of the first written record of Classical Greece, passed through every stage in the evolution of a highly developed system of script.

There is evidence of a simple pictographic stage, and a conventionalized hieroglyphic system growing out of it. . . ."

—Arthur J. Evans

**DOCUMENT-BASED QUESTIONS**

The ruins of the palace extend over 700,000 square feet (65,000 sq. m). Housing 5,000 people, the complex served as residence, warehouse, and religious center.

1. **Describing** What purposes did the Palace at Knossos serve?
2. **Making Inferences** What does Evans believe his discovery of Linear B at Knossos proves?

There, they traded finely crafted pottery and gold and silver jewelry from Crete for other goods. Trade also helped the Minoans improve the goods they produced: they drew inspiration from techniques and designs from objects from other lands. Although the Minoans built palaces on several sites in Crete, the palace at Knossos was the royal seat of the kings. This elaborate building included numerous private living rooms for the royal family and workshops for making decorated vases, ivory figurines, and jewelry. Even bathrooms, with elaborate drains, formed part of the complex. Rooms were decorated with brightly colored paintings showing sporting events and nature scenes. Storerooms held gigantic jars of oil, wine, and grain that were paid as taxes to the king.

The centers of Minoan civilization on Crete suffered a sudden and catastrophic collapse around 1450 B.C. Some historians believe that a tidal wave triggered by a powerful volcanic eruption on the island of Thera (THIHR•uh) was responsible for the devastation. Most historians, however, believe that the destruction was the result of invasion by mainland Greeks known as the Mycenaeans (my•suh•NEE•uhnz).

## Mycenae: The First Greek State

The term **Mycenaean** comes from Mycenae (my•SEE•nee), a fortified site on the Greek mainland that was first discovered by the German archaeologist Heinrich Schliemann. Mycenae was one center in a Mycenaean Greek civilization that flourished between 1600 B.C. and 1100 B.C.

The Mycenaean Greeks were part of the Indo-European family of peoples who spread into Europe and Asia. One of these groups entered Greece around 1900 B.C. and gradually gained control of the Greek mainland. Mycenaean civilization, which reached its high point between 1400 B.C. and 1200 B.C., was made up of powerful monarchies. Each resided in a fortified palace center. Like Mycenae, these centers were built on hills and surrounded by gigantic stone walls. The monarchies in these various centers of power probably formed a loose alliance of independent states. While the royal families lived within the walls of these complexes, the civilian populations lived scattered outside the walls. Among the noticeable features of these Mycenaean centers were the tombs where members of the royal families were buried. Known as *tholos* tombs, they were built into hillsides. An entryway led into a circular tomb chamber constructed of cut stone blocks in a domed shape that resembled a beehive.

The Mycenaeans were, above all, a warrior people who prided themselves on their heroic deeds in battle. Mycenaean wall murals often show war and hunting scenes, the natural occupations of a warrior aristocracy.

Archaeological evidence also indicates that the Mycenaean monarchies developed an extensive commercial network. Mycenaean pottery has been found throughout the Mediterranean area, in Syria and Egypt to the east and Sicily and southern Italy to the west. However, some historians believe that the Mycenaeans, led by Mycenae itself, also spread outward militarily, conquering Crete and making it part of the Mycenaean world. Some of the Aegean islands also fell subject to Mycenaean control.

The most famous of all their supposed military adventures is recounted in the poetry of **Homer**. According to Homer, Mycenaean Greeks, led by Agamemnon, king of Mycenae, sacked (plundered) the city of Troy on the northwestern coast of Asia Minor around 1250 B.C.

Did this event really occur? Ever since the excavations of Schliemann, begun in 1870, scholars have **debated** this question. (See discussion of archaeological methods featured in Chapter 1.) Many believe that Homer's account of the attack on Troy does have a basis in fact.

By the late thirteenth century B.C., Mycenaean Greece was showing signs of serious trouble. Mycenaean states fought one another, and major earthquakes caused widespread damage. In the twelfth century B.C., new waves of Greek-speaking invaders moved into Greece from the north. By 1100 B.C., Mycenaean civilization had collapsed.

✓Reading Check **Explaining** How was the Mycenaean government organized?

## Greeks in the Dark Age

**MAIN IDEA** Greek civilization was slow to recover from the several centuries of instability that followed the fall of the Mycenaeans.

**HISTORY & YOU** How is a society's view of its history important to its success? Read about how Homer's version of Greek history affected the Greeks.

After the collapse of Mycenaean civilization, Greece entered a difficult period in which the population declined and food production dropped. Historians call the period from approximately 1100 B.C. to 750 B.C. the Dark Age, because few records of what happened exist. Not until 850 B.C. did farming revive. At the same time, the basis for a new Greece was forming.

### Changes of the Dark Age

During the Dark Age, many Greeks left the mainland and sailed across the Aegean Sea to various islands. Many went to the western shores of Asia Minor, a strip of territory that came to be called **Ionia** (or Ionian Greece), in modern-day Turkey.

Two other major groups of Greeks settled in established parts of Greece. The Aeolian Greeks of northern and central Greece colonized the large island of Lesbos and the territory near the mainland. The Dorians established themselves in southwestern Greece, especially in the Peloponnese, as well as on some of the southern Aegean islands, including Crete.

In addition to agriculture, there was a revival of some trade and economic activity during the Dark Age. Iron replaced bronze in weaponry, making weapons affordable for more people. Iron farming tools helped reverse the decline in food production.

At some point in the eighth century B.C., the Greeks adopted the Phoenician alphabet to give themselves a new system of writing. By reducing all words to a combination of 24 letters (both consonants and vowels) the Greeks made learning to read and write simpler. The work of Homer, one of the great poets of all time, appeared near the end of the Dark Age.

**HISTORY & ARTS** PRIMARY SOURCE

***Art in the Dark Age***

**In the seventh century B.C., art began to take on a more Eastern appearance as the Greeks made contact with civilizations in Asia. The griffin's head design on pottery was found in Greece as well as throughout Southwest Asia.**

**This statue shows a traveling musician and storyteller, or bard, like Homer.**

**From 1100-700 B.C., geometric patterns were typical of Greek pottery. This amphora, or two-handled jar, decorated graves near the Dipylon gate in Athens.**

**DOCUMENT-BASED QUESTIONS**

Some art from the Dark Age has survived, giving a hint of life during that period.

1. **Making Inferences** Study these art objects. What conclusion might you draw about life during the Dark Age?
2. **Drawing Conclusions** What practical purpose do you think the object with the griffin's head served?

## Homer: Poet of the Dark Age

The *Iliad* and the *Odyssey* were the first great epic poems of early Greece. An **epic poem** is a long poem that tells the deeds of a great hero. The *Iliad* and the *Odyssey* were based on stories that had been passed from generation to generation. Both poems are hundreds of pages long, but not because they tried to preserve an entire account of history as earlier oral poets did. Instead, Homer focuses his imagination on the dramatic events of a few days of the Trojan War.

Homer used stories of the Trojan War to compose the *Iliad* and the *Odyssey*. The war is caused by Paris, a prince of Troy. By kidnapping Helen, the wife of the king of the Greek state of Sparta, Paris outrages all the Greeks. Under the leadership of the Spartan king's brother, King Agamemnon, the Greeks attack Troy.

Ten years later, the Greeks devise a plan to take the city. They trick the Trojans by building a huge hollow wooden horse. The best Mycenaean soldiers hide inside the horse, while the rest board their ships and pretend to sail away. The joyful Trojans, thinking themselves victorious, bring the gift horse into the city. That night, the Greeks creep out of the horse, slaughter the Trojan men, enslave the women and children, and burn the city to the ground. The *Iliad* is not so much the story of the war itself, however, as it is the tale of the Greek hero Achilles (uh•KIH•leez) and how the anger of Achilles led to disaster.

The *Odyssey* recounts the journeys of one of the Greek heroes, Odysseus, after the fall of Troy, and his ultimate return to his wife. It has long been considered Homer's other masterpiece. Some scholars believe that it was composed later than the *Iliad*.

Homer proved to be of great value to later Greeks. He did not so much record history; he created it. The Greeks looked on the *Iliad* and the *Odyssey* as true history and as the works of one poet, Homer. These masterpieces gave the Greeks an ideal past with a cast of heroes. The epics came to be used as basic texts for the education of generations of Greek males. As one ancient Athenian stated, "My father was anxious to see me develop into a good man . . . and as a means to this end he compelled me to memorize all of Homer."

The values Homer taught were courage and honor. A hero strives for excellence, which the Greeks called ***arete*** (ahr•ah•TEE). *Arete* is won in a struggle or contest. Through his willingness to fight, the hero protects his family and friends, preserves his own honor and that of his family, and earns his reputation. Homer gave to later generations of Greek males a model of heroism and honor. For example, in an exciting description of men marching to war, the *Iliad* taught students to be proud of their Greek heritage and the actions of their heroic ancestors.

✓ Reading Check **Summarizing** Why is Homer thought to have created Greek history?

## SECTION 1 REVIEW

### Vocabulary

1. **Explain** the significance of: participate, Aegean Sea, Black Sea, Bronze Age, Crete, Minoan, Mycenaean, Homer, debated, Ionia, epic poem, *arete*.

### Main Ideas

2. **Explain** how the geography of Greece affected Greek development.
3. **List** the troubles affecting Mycenaean Greece before its collapse.
4. **Summarize** the changes that occurred in Greece during the Dark Ages. Record your answer in a chart like the one below.

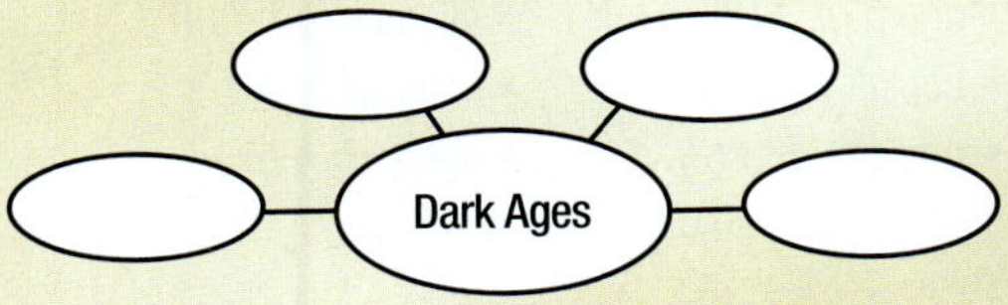


### Critical Thinking

5. **BIG Idea** **Analyzing** How did the Minoan and Mycenaean civilizations provide order and security?
6. **Evaluating** Why was the Dark Age of Greece considered "dark"?
7. **Analyzing Visuals** Examine the mural on page 108. What conclusions can you draw about the Minoans' environment from the colors and the content of the mural? Explain your reasoning.

### Writing About History

8. **Expository Writing** What archaeological evidence might support scholars' differing views of the collapse of the Minoan and Mycenaean cultures? Explain your opinions in a well-reasoned essay.

**History ONLINE**

For help with the concepts in this section of *Glencoe World History*, go to glencoe.com and click Study Central™.

# The Greek City-States

## GUIDE TO READING

### The BIG Idea

**Ideas, Beliefs, and Values** Differences between Athenian and Spartan values led to different forms of government.

### Content Vocabulary

- polis *(p. 112)*
- acropolis *(p. 112)*
- agora *(p. 112)*
- hoplite *(p. 113)*
- phalanx *(p. 113)*
- tyrant *(p. 114)*
- democracy *(p. 114)*
- oligarchy *(p. 114)*
- helot *(p. 115)*
- ephor *(p. 116)*

### Academic Vocabulary

- assemble *(p. 112)*
- implies *(p. 114)*

### People and Places

- Hellespont *(p. 114)*
- Bosporus *(p. 114)*
- Byzantium *(p. 114)*
- Sparta *(p. 115)*
- Athens *(p. 117)*
- Solon *(p. 117)*
- Cleisthenes *(p. 117)*

### Reading Strategy

**Categorizing Information** As you read, create a chart like the one below to help you study. Identify the advantages and disadvantages of each of the three types of government used in Greek city-states.

| | Advantage | Disadvantage |
|---|---|---|
| Tyranny | | |
| Democracy | | |
| Oligarchy | | |

*Greece slowly recovered during the late part of the Dark Age. Several Greek centers of trade established themselves during the ninth century* B.C., *and population growth in the following century fueled a growth in agriculture. Increased trade stimulated craftwork and shipbuilding. Greek communities were growing and gaining wealth.*

## Polis: The Center of Greek Life

*MAIN IDEA* The polis or city-state was the central focus of Greek life. The citizens of a polis had defined rights and responsibilities, as well as a strong identity and loyalty that kept the city-states divided.

*HISTORY & YOU* How is your community organized? Read about the organization of the Greek polis.

By 750 B.C., the city-state—or what the Greeks called a **polis**—became the central focus of Greek life. Our word *politics* is derived from the Greek word *polis*. In a physical sense, the polis was a town, a city, or even a village, along with its surrounding countryside. The town, city, or village served as the center of the polis where people could meet for political, social, and religious activities.

### Organization of the City-State

The main gathering place in the polis was usually a hill. At the top of the hill was a fortified area called an **acropolis.** The acropolis served as a place of refuge during an attack and sometimes came to be a religious center on which temples and public buildings were built. Below the acropolis was an **agora,** an open area that served as a place where people could **assemble** and as a market.

City-states varied greatly in size, from a few square miles to a few hundred square miles. They also varied in population. Athens had a population of more than 300,000 by the fifth century B.C., but most city-states were much smaller, consisting of only a few hundred to several thousand people.

### Community of the City-State

The polis was, above all, a community of people who shared a common identity and common goals. As a community, the polis consisted of citizens with political rights (adult males), citizens with no political rights (women and children), and noncitizens

PRIMARY SOURCE HISTORY & ARTS

## Ancient Athens

**CRITICAL THINKING SKILLS**

Ancient Athens was a powerful Greek city-state and is considered to be the birthplace of Western civilization.

1. **Describing** Describe the location of the Agora in relation to the Acropolis.
2. **Drawing Conclusions** Why were temples and public buildings located within the Acropolis?

(including agricultural laborers, slaves, and resident aliens).

Citizens had rights, but these rights were coupled with responsibilities. The Greek philosopher Aristotle argued that a citizen did not belong just to himself or herself: "We must rather regard every citizen as belonging to the state." However, the loyalty that citizens had to their city-states had a negative side. City-states distrusted one another, and the division of Greece into fiercely patriotic, independent units helped to bring about its ruin.

As the polis developed, so too did a new military system. In earlier times, nobles on horseback fought wars in Greece. These aristocrats, who were large landowners, also dominated the political life of their city-states.

By 700 B.C., however, the military system was based on **hoplites,** who were heavily armed infantry soldiers, or foot soldiers. Each carried a round shield, a short sword, and a thrusting spear about 9 feet (2.7 m) long. Hoplites went into battle as a unit, marching shoulder to shoulder in a rectangular formation known as a **phalanx.** This close formation created a wall of shields to protect the hoplites. As long as they kept their order, it was difficult for enemies to harm them.

✓ **Reading Check** **Defining** Describe the characteristics of a Greek city-state.

## Greek Expansion

**MAIN IDEA** The search for farmland and the growth of trade resulted in colonization and the spread of Greek culture and political ideas.

**HISTORY & YOU** How does your community choose its leaders? Read about how new leaders came to power in Greek city-states.

Between 750 B.C. and 550 B.C., large numbers of Greeks left their homeland to settle in distant lands. A desire for good farmland, overpopulation at home, and the growth of trade were important factors in deciding to settle new places. Each Greek colony became a new polis, independent of the polis that had founded it.

### Greek Colonies

Across the Mediterranean, new Greek colonies were established along the coastlines of southern Italy, southern France, eastern Spain, and northern Africa west of Egypt. At the same time, to the north the Greeks set up colonies in Thrace, where they sought good farmland to grow grains. The Greeks also settled along the shores of the Black Sea, setting up cities on the **Hellespont** and the **Bosporus** straits. The most notable of these cities was **Byzantium** (buh•ZAN•shuhm), the site of what later became Constantinople and is now İstanbul. In establishing these colonies, the Greeks spread their culture and political ideas throughout the Mediterranean.

Securing control of the straits and waterways between the Mediterranean and Black Seas also gave the Greeks great economic advantages. Colonization in these prime port locations led to increased trade and industry. The Greeks on the mainland exported pottery, wine, and olive oil. In return, they received grains and metals from the west and fish, timber, wheat, metals, and slaves from the Black Sea region.

The expansion of trade and industry created a new group of wealthy individuals in many of the Greek city-states. These men wanted political power, but found it difficult to gain because of the power of the ruling aristocrats. The landowners would not willingly give up their political power to the newly rich merchants.

### Tyranny in the City-States

The creation of this new group of rich men fostered the rise of tyrants in the seventh and sixth centuries B.C. Tyrants were not necessarily oppressive or wicked, as our word *tyrant* **implies.** Greek **tyrants** were rulers who seized power by force from the aristocrats. They were unique in Greek history, and in fact, the Greeks did not have a word for them: the Greek term *tyrannos* was developed from another language, probably one from Asia Minor.

Support for the tyrants came from the newly rich who had made their money in trade and industry. These people were hungry for the social prestige and political influence that aristocrats had denied them. Poor peasants who were in debt to landholding aristocrats also supported the tyrants. Both the newly rich and the peasants were tired of aristocratic domination of their city-states.

The tyrants gained power and kept it by using hired soldiers. Once in power, the tyrants tried to help the poor and launched public works projects. They built new marketplaces, temples, and walls. These efforts glorified the city but, more importantly, increased the tyrants' popularity. Despite their achievements, however, the tyrants eventually came to be seen as oppressive. The tyrants had fallen out of favor by the end of the sixth century B.C. Greeks believed in the rule of law, and tyranny was an insult to that ideal.

Although tyranny did not last, it played an important role in Greek history. The rule of the tyrants ended the rule of the aristocrats in many city-states. The end of tyranny then allowed many new people to participate in government. In some Greek city-states, this led to the development of **democracy**, which is government by the people or rule of the many. Other city-states remained committed to government by an **oligarchy**, rule by the few.

✓ Reading Check **Evaluating** What role did tyrants play in the development of Greek forms of government?

## Two Rival City-States

**MAIN IDEA** Sparta and Athens developed different systems of government.

**HISTORY & YOU** How can strict rules affect people? Read about the Spartans' strict rules.

The differences in the Greek city-states can be understood by examining the two most famous and powerful city-states, Sparta and Athens.

### Sparta

Like other Greek city-states, **Sparta** needed more land. Instead of starting new colonies, as some states did, the Spartans conquered the neighboring Laconians. Later, beginning around 730 B.C., the Spartans undertook the conquest of neighboring Messenia despite its larger size and population.

After their conquest, the Messenians and Laconians became serfs and were made to work for the Spartans. These captured people were known as **helots,** a name derived from a Greek word for "capture." To ensure control over the conquered helots, the Spartans made a conscious decision to create a military state.

Between 800 B.C. and 600 B.C., the lives of Spartans were rigidly organized and tightly controlled —thus, our word *spartan,* meaning "highly self-disciplined." Males spent their childhood learning military discipline. Then they enrolled in the army for regular military service at age 20. Although allowed to marry, they continued to live in the military barracks until age 30. All meals were eaten in public dining halls with fellow soldiers. Meals were simple: the famous Spartan black broth consisted of a piece of pork boiled in animal blood, salt, and vinegar. A visitor who ate some of the black broth once remarked that he now understood why Spartans were not afraid to die. At 30, Spartan males were allowed to vote in the assembly (discussed later).

NATIONAL GEOGRAPHIC

**GREEK COLONIES AND TRADE, 750–550 B.C.**

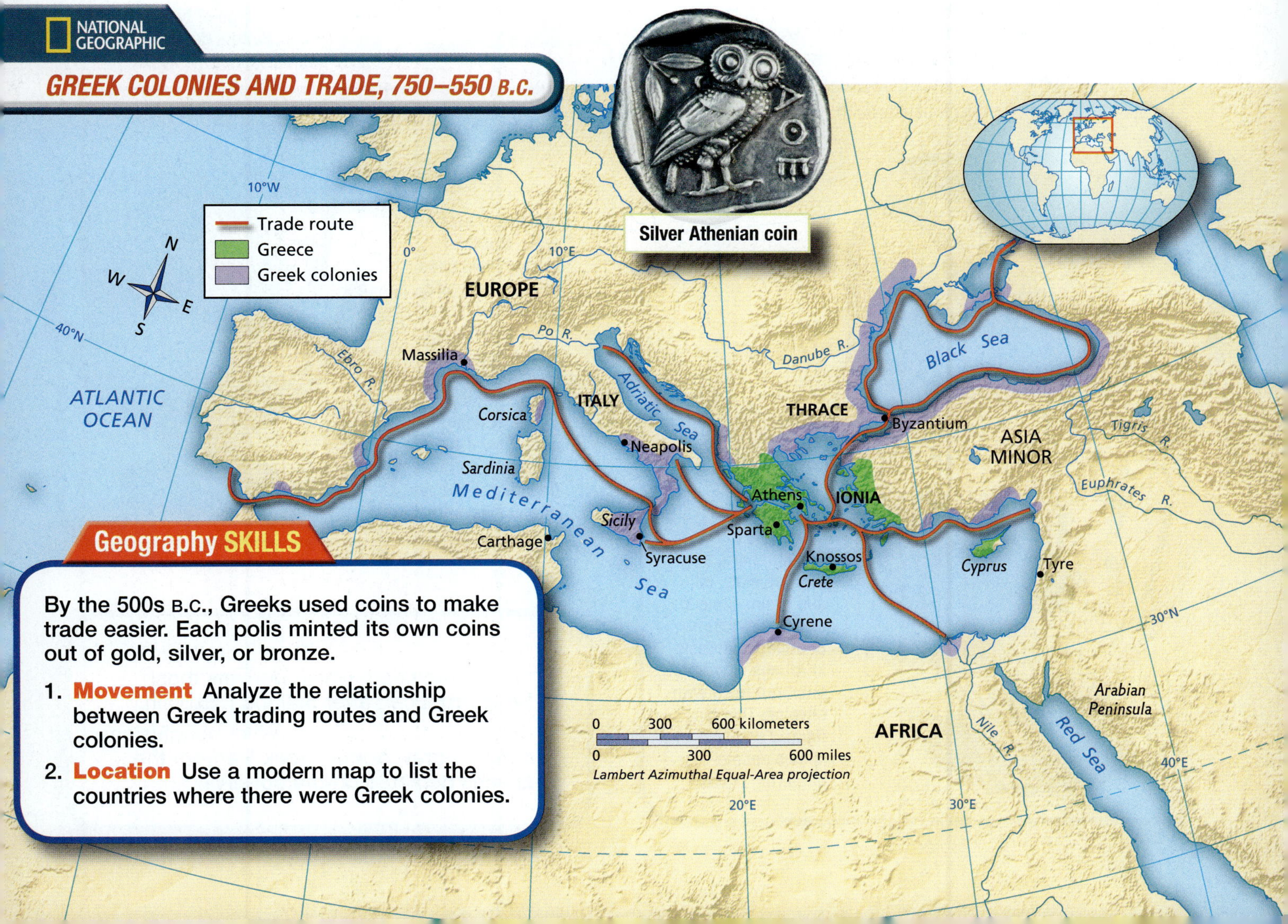


**Geography SKILLS**

By the 500s B.C., Greeks used coins to make trade easier. Each polis minted its own coins out of gold, silver, or bronze.

1. **Movement** Analyze the relationship between Greek trading routes and Greek colonies.
2. **Location** Use a modern map to list the countries where there were Greek colonies.

They could live at home, but they stayed in the army until the age of 60.

While their husbands lived in the barracks, Spartan women lived at home. Because of this separation, Spartan women had greater freedom of movement and greater power in the household than was common elsewhere in Greece. Spartan women were expected to remain fit to bear and raise healthy children.

Many Spartan women upheld the strict Spartan values, expecting their husbands and sons to be brave in war. The story is told of a Spartan mother who, as she handed her son his shield, told him to come back carrying his shield or being carried on it. In other words, he was not to drop his shield in retreat, but to be victorious or to die bravely.

The Spartan government was an oligarchy headed by two kings, who led the Spartan army on its campaigns. A group of five men, known as the **ephors** (EH•fuhrs), were elected each year and were responsible for the education of youth and the conduct of all citizens. A council of elders, composed of the two kings and 28 citizens over the age of 60, decided on the issues that would be

## HISTORY & ARTS — PRIMARY SOURCE

### Everyday Art in Athens

The Greeks made pottery for every possible use. The best Greek pottery came from Athens because the clay found there was easy to bake in a kiln. At first, the pottery was decorated with geometric shapes. Later scenes from everyday life, stories of the gods, wars, and Olympic events decorated the pottery. Before 500 B.C., the pottery was red with figures that appeared black after they were baked. After 500 B.C., craftsmen discovered how to create red figures on a black background.

**The *kylix* was a type of two-handled drinking cup. Potters decorated the inside and outside of the *kylix*.**

**The krater was a wide-mouthed mixing bowl used to mix water with wine—the most popular beverage with meals. A special krater on a stand was part of the wedding ceremony. This red-figured krater depicts the winner of a music contest.**

**The amphora, a jar to store wine, oil, and grain, came in all sizes. Winners of athletic contests in Athens won an amphora filled with olive oil. This black-figured amphora shows people gathering olives.**

**DOCUMENT-BASED QUESTIONS**

1. **Making Inferences** Based on the information provided, which pot was most likely produced after 500 B.C.? Explain.
2. **Drawing Conclusions** What conclusions can you draw about Greek life from the scenes depicted on the pottery?

presented to an assembly made up of male citizens. This assembly did not debate; it only voted on the issues.

To make their new military state secure, the Spartans turned their backs on the outside world. Foreigners, who might have brought in new ideas, were discouraged from visiting. Except for military reasons, Spartans were not allowed to travel abroad, where they might encounter ideas dangerous to the stability of the state. Likewise, Spartan citizens were discouraged from studying philosophy, literature, or the arts. The art of war was the Spartan ideal. All other arts were frowned upon.

## Athens

By 700 B.C., **Athens** had become a unified polis on the peninsula of Attica. Early Athens was ruled by a king. By the seventh century B.C., however, Athens had become an oligarchy under the control of its aristocrats. These aristocrats owned the best land and controlled political life. The assembly of all the citizens had few powers.

By the end of the 600s B.C., economic problems caused political turmoil in Athens. Draco, a politician, codified the laws, adding harsh penalties, including slavery for debtors. Many Athenian farmers were sold into slavery when they were unable to pay their debts. There was an outcry to cancel the debts and give land to the poor. Civil war seemed likely.

The ruling Athenian aristocrats reacted to this crisis in 594 B.C. by giving full power to **Solon**, a reform-minded aristocrat. Solon canceled all land debts and freed people who had fallen into slavery for debts. He refused, however, to take land from the rich and give it to the poor. Despite Solon's reforms aristocrats were still powerful and poor peasants could not obtain land. Internal strife finally led to the very thing Solon had hoped to avoid—tyranny.

Peisistratus (pih•SIHS•truh•tuhs), an aristocrat, seized power in 560 B.C. He then aided Athenian trade as a way of pleasing the merchants. He also gave aristocrats' land to the peasants in order to gain the favor of the poor.

The Athenians rebelled against Peisistratus's son, who had succeeded him, and ended the tyranny in 510 B.C. Two years later, with the backing of the Athenian people, **Cleisthenes** (KLYS•thuh•NEEZ), another reformer, gained the upper hand.

Cleisthenes created a council of 500 that supervised foreign affairs, oversaw the treasury, and proposed laws. The Athenian assembly, composed of male citizens, was given authority to pass laws after free and open debate. Because the assembly now had the central political role, the reforms of Cleisthenes created the basis for Athenian democracy.

**✓Reading Check** **Contrasting** How was a Spartan man's life different from an Athenian man's?

## SECTION 2 REVIEW

### Vocabulary

1. **Explain** the significance of: polis, acropolis, agora, assemble, hoplite, phalanx, Hellespont, Bosporus, Byzantium, implies, tyrant, democracy, oligarchy, Sparta, helot, ephor, Athens, Solon, Cleisthenes.

### Main Ideas

2. **Summarize** how the city-states' military system had changed by 700 B.C.
3. **Sequence** the causes and effects of Greek colonization, trade, and industry. Create a cause-and-effect sequence chart like the one below to record your answer.

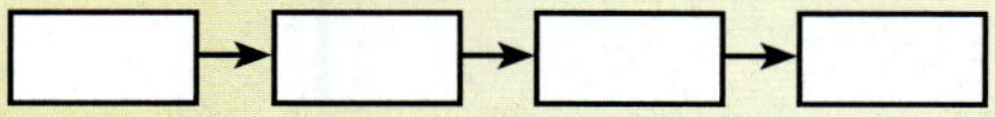

4. **Compare** Athens and Sparta by identifying the social structure and role of slavery and by explaining the differences between the political systems and role of citizens.

### Critical Thinking

5. **Big Idea** **Making Generalizations** Discuss the ideas, beliefs, and values that are implied in forms of government that the Spartans and Athenians adopted.
6. **Comparing and Contrasting** In what way(s) is Athenian democracy similar to American democracy? In what way(s) is it different?
7. **Analyzing Visuals** Examine the photograph of the Acropolis on page 113 of your text. Why do you think the Athenians decided to place their important buildings on top of a hill?

### Writing About History

8. **Descriptive Writing** Imagine that you are a 25-year-old male living in Sparta in 700 B.C. Create a diary in which you record your activities for one week. Write one diary page for each day.

**History ONLINE**

For help with the concepts in this section of *Glencoe World History*, go to glencoe.com and click Study Central™.

SECTION 3

Section Audio    Spotlight Video

# Classical Greece

## GUIDE TO READING

### The BIG Idea

**Competition Between Countries**

Athens's growing power led to conflict with Sparta.

### Content Vocabulary

- Age of Pericles *(p. 121)*
- direct democracy *(p. 121)*
- ostracism *(p. 121)*

### Academic Vocabulary

- classical *(p. 121)*
- strategy *(p. 123)*

### People and Places

- Asia Minor *(p. 118)*
- Darius *(p. 118)*
- Xerxes *(p. 118)*
- Delian League *(p. 121)*
- Delos *(p. 121)*
- Pericles *(p.121)*
- Thebes *(p. 123)*
- Macedonia *(p. 123)*

### Reading Strategy

**Organizing Information** As you read, create a concept map like the one below to help you study. Identify the elements that contributed to the classical age of Greece.

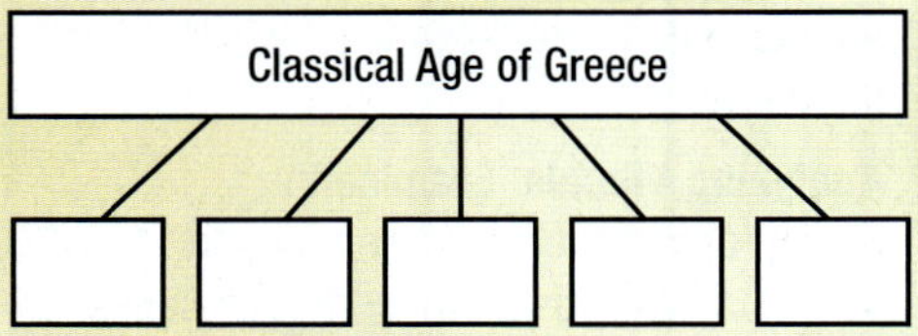


*Classical Greece is the name given to the period of Greek history from around 500 B.C. to the conquest of Greece by the Macedonian king Philip II in 338 B.C. This period was marked not only by a brilliant culture but also by a disastrous war among the Greeks, the Peloponnesian War.*

## The Challenge of Persia

***MAIN IDEA*** The Greek states of Athens and Sparta formed alliances to defeat the Persian invaders.

***HISTORY & YOU*** What are some stories of American soldiers' bravery and struggle in combat? Read about the Greek forces in battle.

As the Greeks spread throughout the Mediterranean, they came in contact with the Persian Empire to the east. The Ionian Greek cities in western **Asia Minor** had fallen to the Persian Empire by the mid-sixth century B.C. In 499 B.C., an unsuccessful revolt by the Ionian cities—assisted by the Athenian navy—led the Persian ruler **Darius** to seek revenge. It is said that Darius ordered one of his slaves to say to him at every meal, "Sire, remember the Athenians."

In 490 B.C., the Persians landed on the plain of Marathon, only 26 miles (42 km) from Athens. There, an outnumbered Athenian army attacked and defeated the Persians decisively. The Persians returned to Asia. According to legend, news of Persia's defeat was brought by an Athenian runner named Pheidippides, who raced from Marathon to Athens. With his last breath, he announced, "Victory, we win," before dropping dead. Today's marathon race is based on this heroic story. Although the Battle of Marathon was a minor defeat to the Persians, to the Athenians it proved that the Persians could be beaten and gave them new confidence in their city-state.

After Darius died in 486 B.C., **Xerxes** (ZUHRK•SEEZ) became the new Persian monarch. Xerxes vowed revenge and planned to invade Greece. In preparation for the attack, some of the Greek states formed a defensive league under the Spartans. The Athenians, however, followed a new military policy insisted on by Themistocles, one of the Athenian leaders, and built a navy. By the time the Persians invaded in 480 B.C., the Athenians had a fleet of about 200 vessels.

Xerxes led a massive invasion force into Greece. His forces included about 180,000 troops and thousands of warships and supply vessels. In spite of their differences, Athenians, Spartans, and other Greeks were united by a common goal of defeating the

**Geography SKILLS**

1. **Movement** How did the strategy of the first Persian campaign differ from the second Persian campaign?
2. **Location** What do the locations of the major battles have in common? Why do you think this is?

Persian invaders. The Greeks tried to delay the Persians at the pass of Thermopylae, along the main road into central Greece. A Greek force of about 7,000 held off the Persian army for two days. The 300 Spartans in the Greek army were especially brave.

When told that Persian arrows would darken the sky in battle, one Spartan responded, "That is good news. We will fight in the shade!" Unfortunately, a traitor told the Persians how to use a mountain path to outflank the Greek force.

The Athenians, threatened by Persian forces, abandoned their city. Near the island of Salamis, the outnumbered Greek fleet defeated the Persians. A few months later, early in 479 B.C., the Greeks formed the largest Greek army up to that time. With their defeat of the Persian army at Plataea (pluh•TEE•uh), northwest of Athens, the Greeks took control of the Aegean Sea.

**✓Reading Check** **Identifying** What did victory over the Persians cost the Greeks?

TURNING POINT

# PERICLES EXPANDS ATHENIAN DEMOCRACY

Pericles was a prominent political leader in Athens from 461 B.C. to 429 B.C. During this time, he expanded Athenian democracy to enable all citizens to play a role in government. In his famous speech, the Funeral Oration, given to honor those who perished in Athens's war with Sparta, Pericles describes the Greek ideal of democracy:

> "Our constitution does not copy the laws of neighboring states; we are rather a pattern to others than imitators ourselves. Its administration favors the many instead of the few; this is why it is called a democracy. If we look to the laws, they afford equal justice to all in their private differences; if no social standing, advancement in public life falls to reputation for capacity, class considerations not being allowed to interfere with merit; nor again does poverty bar the way. . . . The freedom which we enjoy in our government extends also to our ordinary life. . . . [W]e do not feel called upon to be angry with our neighbor for doing what he likes. . . . But all this ease in our private relations does not make us lawless as citizens. Against this fear is our chief safeguard, teaching us to obey the magistrates and the laws. . . ."
>
> —Pericles, as quoted in *History of the Peloponnesian War,* Book 2, Thucydides

**Pericles, here giving his famous Funeral Oration, encouraged all citizens to participate in the government of Athens.**

## Comparing Democratic Systems

| | ATHENIAN DEMOCRACY | MODERN U.S. DEMOCRACY |
|---|---|---|
| Citizenship | Only adult male citizens of Athens were eligible to participate. | All adult male and female citizens of the United States are eligible to vote. |
| Participation | Athenian population = 300,000<br>Eligible male voters = 43,000<br>Direct—Male citizens voted on all issues of government. | U.S. population = 300,000,000<br>Eligible voters = 203,000,000<br>Representative—Citizens elect officials to vote on issues. |
| Freedom and Justice | "Justice . . . in democracy is equality" and "for democracy is . . . defined by two things: by the majority having authority and by freedom." from *Politics,* Aristotle | "With liberty and justice for all" from *The Pledge of Allegiance* |

### DOCUMENT-BASED QUESTIONS

Classical Greece laid the foundation for Western democracy and political ideals.

1. **Analyzing** What does Pericles say about freedom and lawlessness?
2. **Comparing** How do participation and eligibility in Athenian democracy differ from participation and eligibility in modern U.S. democracy?

## The Athenian Empire

**MAIN IDEA** During the Age of Pericles, Athens became the center of Greek culture.

**HISTORY & YOU** What are your rights in society? Read about life in Greece during the Age of Pericles.

After the defeat of the Persians, Athens took over the leadership of the entire Greek world. In 478 B.C., the Athenians formed a defensive alliance against the Persians known as the **Delian League.** Its main headquarters was on the island of **Delos.** However, its chief officials, including the treasurers and commanders of the fleet, were Athenian. Under Athenian leadership, the Delian League pursued the attack against the Persian Empire, eventually liberating virtually all of the Greek states in the Aegean from Persian control. In 454 B.C., the Athenians moved the treasury of the league from the island of Delos to Athens on the mainland. By controlling the Delian League, Athens had created an empire.

Under **Pericles,** a dominant figure in Athenian politics between 461 B.C. and 429 B.C., Athens expanded its empire abroad while democracy flourished at home. This period of **classical** Athenian and Greek history, which historians have called the **Age of Pericles,** saw the height of Athenian power and brilliance.

### The Age of Pericles

By creating a **direct democracy,** Pericles expanded the involvement of Athenians in their democracy. In this system, every male citizen participated directly in government decision making through mass meetings. In Athens, every male citizen participated in the governing assembly and voted on all major issues.

Every ten days the assembly met on a hillside east of the Acropolis. The assembly passed all laws, elected public officials, and made decisions concerning war and foreign policy. Anyone attending the assembly could speak, but usually only respected leaders did so. Pericles made it possible for poor citizens to take part in public affairs by paying officeholders.

A large body of city officials ran the government on a daily basis. Ten officials, or generals, directed policy. The generals could be reelected, so individual leaders could play an important political role.

Athenians devised the practice of **ostracism** to protect against ambitious politicians. On a pottery fragment *(ostrakon)*, members of the assembly could write the name of a person they considered harmful. A person named by at least 6,000 members was banned from the city for 10 years.

Under Pericles, Athens became the center of Greek culture. Since the Persian Wars had destroyed much of the city, Pericles began a massive rebuilding program with new temples (including the Parthenon) and statues that signified the greatness of Athens. Art, architecture, and philosophy flourished. Pericles proudly called Athens the "school of Greece."

### Daily Life in Classical Athens

By the fifth century B.C., Athens had the largest population of the Greek city-states. Before the plague in 430 B.C., there were about 300,000 people living in Athens and the surrounding area. About 60,000 of them were adult males with political power. Most residents of Athens were not citizens. Adult male foreigners living in Athens, numbering about 10,000, received the protection of the laws. They were also subject to some of the responsibilities of citizens—military service and the funding of festivals. Slaves numbered around 100,000.

Slavery was common in the ancient world. Most people in Athens—except the very poor—owned at least one slave. The very wealthy might own large numbers. Those who did usually employed them in industry. Most often, slaves worked in the fields or in the home as cooks and maids. Some slaves were owned by the state and worked on public construction projects.

### Economy and Society

The Athenian economy was largely based on farming and trade. Athenians grew grains, vegetables, and fruit for local use. Grapes and olive trees were cultivated for wine and olive oil, for local use and for export.

Bronze helmet and breastplate from the time of the Peloponnesian War

**Geography SKILLS**

1. **Place** Analyze the pattern of alliances. What geographical factors affected the ways in which the states were allied?
2. **Regions** From a geographic standpoint, which side, Sparta or Athens, had an advantage in the war? Explain your answer.

Athenians raised sheep and goats for wool, milk, and dairy products.

Because of the number of people and the lack of fertile land, Athens had to import from 50 to 80 percent of its grain, a basic item in the Athenian diet. This meant that trade was highly important to the Athenian economy. The building of a port at nearby Piraeus (py•REE•uhs) helped Athens become the leading trade center in the fifth-century B.C. Greek world.

The family was an important institution in ancient Athens. It was composed of a husband, wife, and children, although Athenians also regarded other dependent relatives and even slaves as parts of their families. The family's primary function was to produce new citizens by having children.

Women who were citizens could take part in most religious festivals but otherwise were excluded from public life. They were expected to remain at home, out of sight in special quarters, unless attending funerals or festivals. If they left the house, women had to have a companion.

An Athenian woman was expected to be a good wife. Her chief obligation was to bear children, especially male children who would preserve the family line. She was also expected to take care of her family and her house. She either did the housework herself or supervised the slaves who did the work.

Women were strictly controlled. Women could not own property other than personal items. They always had a male guardian: if unmarried, a father; if married, a husband; if widowed, a son or male relative. Because they married at 14 or 15, girls learned their responsibilities early. Their mothers taught them how to run a home, including how to spin and weave cloth. Although many learned to read and to play musical instruments, girls were not provided with any formal education. Women did not work outside the home unless they were poor. Then they could only work at unskilled jobs, not skilled trades.

✓ **Reading Check** **Examining** What was the family's most important role?

## The Great Peloponnesian War

**MAIN IDEA** The creation of an Athenian empire led to tensions with Sparta and, eventually, war.

**HISTORY & YOU** How can differences between societies lead to conflict? Read to learn about the war between Sparta and Athens.

After the defeat of the Persians, the Greek world divided into two main camps: the Athenian Empire (Athens and the Delian League, which it controlled) and Sparta and its supporters (Peloponnesian League). Athens and Sparta had very different societies, and neither was able to tolerate the other's system. Sparta and its allies feared the growing Athenian Empire, and a series of disputes finally led to the outbreak of the Great Peloponnesian War in 431 B.C.

At the beginning of the war, both sides believed they had winning **strategies.** The Athenians planned to remain behind the city's protective walls and receive supplies from their colonies and navy. The Spartans and their allies surrounded Athens, hoping that the Athenians would send out their army to fight beyond the walls. Pericles knew, however, that the Spartan forces could beat the Athenians in open battles. The Athenians had a better navy, but the Spartans had a stronger army. Pericles also believed that Athens was secure behind its walls, so the Athenians stayed put.

In the first winter of the war, the Athenians held a public funeral to honor those who had died in combat. Pericles spoke about the greatness of Athens and the strength of its political system. (Read more on page 120.)

In the second year of the war, a plague broke out in the overly crowded city of Athens. The plague killed more than a third of the people. Pericles himself died the following year (429 B.C.). Despite these severe losses, the Athenians fought on for about another 25 years.

A crushing blow to the Athenians came in 405 B.C., when their fleet was destroyed at Aegospotami (ee•guh•SPAH•tuh•mee) on the Hellespont. Within the next year, Athens surrendered. Its walls were torn down, the navy disbanded, and the Athenian Empire destroyed. The great war was finally over, but so was the age of classical Greek culture and government.

The Great Peloponnesian War weakened the major Greek states and ruined any possibility of cooperation among them. During the next 67 years, Sparta, Athens, and **Thebes** (a new Greek power) struggled to dominate Greek affairs. In continuing their petty wars, the Greeks ignored the growing power of **Macedonia** to their north. This oversight would cost them their freedom.

**✓ Reading Check** **Explaining** How did the Great Peloponnesian War weaken the Greek states?

## SECTION 3 REVIEW

### Vocabulary

1. **Explain** the significance of: Asia Minor, Darius, Xerxes, Delian League, Delos, Pericles, classical, Age of Pericles, direct democracy, ostracism, strategy, Thebes, Macedonia.

### Main Ideas

2. **Specify** the cause of the Persian attacks on Athens.
3. **List** the accomplishments of the Athenians during the Age of Pericles.

| Accomplishments During the Age of Pericles |
|---|
| |
| |
| |
| |

4. **Identify** the results of the Persian and the Peloponnesian Wars.

### Critical Thinking

5. **BIG Idea** **Analyzing** How might the Athenians' leadership of the Delian League have contributed to the Great Peloponnesian War?
6. **Analyzing Visuals** Examine the image of Pericles giving the Funeral Oration during the Peloponnesian War on page 120. Describe the crowd's reaction to their leader's speech.
7. **Defining** A "classical civilization" serves as a model of excellence and has enduring relevance. How does fifth century B.C. Athens fit that definition?

### Writing About History

8. **Descriptive Writing** Write three short journal entries about a particular day or event. Write one entry from the perspective of an Athenian male citizen, one as a female citizen, and one as a slave, contrasting their daily lives.

**History ONLINE**

For help with the concepts in this section of *Glencoe World History,* go to glencoe.com and click Study Central™.

SECTION 4

Section Audio

Spotlight Video

# The Culture of Classical Greece

## GUIDE TO READING

### The BIG Idea

**Ideas, Beliefs, and Values** Ideas from the classical age of Greece helped to shape Western civilization.

### Content Vocabulary

- ritual *(p. 124)*
- oracle *(p. 124)*
- tragedy *(p. 126)*
- philosophy *(p. 128)*
- Socratic method *(p. 129)*

### Academic Vocabulary

- ethics *(p. 129)*
- method *(p. 129)*

### People and Places

- Olympus *(p. 124)*
- Delphi *(p. 124)*
- Aeschylus *(p. 126)*
- Sophocles *(p. 126)*
- Euripides *(p. 126)*
- Herodotus *(p. 127)*
- Thucydides *(p. 127)*
- Pythagoras *(p. 128)*
- Sophists *(p. 129)*
- Socrates *(p. 129)*
- Plato *(p. 129)*
- Aristotle *(p. 130)*

### Reading Strategy

**Summarizing Information** As you read, create a chart like the one below to help you study. Identify the major Greek contributions to Western civilization.

| | |
|---|---|
| Major Greek Contributions | |
| | |
| | |
| | |
| | |

*Classical Greece, especially Athens under Pericles' rule, witnessed a period of remarkable intellectual and cultural growth that became the main source of Western culture. Aristotle, Socrates, and Plato established the foundations of Western philosophy.*

## Greek Religion

**MAIN IDEA** Greek religion was fundamental to Greek society and is remembered today for the Olympic Games and Greek drama, which were part of religious festivals.

**HISTORY & YOU** What is the role of religion in your society's government? Read about religious practices in Greece.

Religion affected every aspect of Greek life. Greeks considered religion necessary to the well-being of the state. Temples dedicated to gods and goddesses were the major buildings in Greek cities.

Homer described the gods worshiped in the Greek religion. Twelve chief gods and goddesses were thought to live on **Olympus**, the highest mountain in Greece. Among the twelve were Zeus, the chief god and father of the gods; Athena, goddess of wisdom and crafts; Apollo, god of the sun and poetry; Artemis, the sister of Apollo, who was goddess of the moon and of the hunt; Ares, god of war; Aphrodite, goddess of love; and Poseidon, brother of Zeus and god of the seas and earthquakes.

Greek religion did not have a body of doctrine, nor did it focus on morality. The spirits of most people, regardless of what they had done in life, went to a gloomy underworld ruled by the god Hades. Because the Greeks wanted the gods to look favorably upon their activities, rituals became important. **Rituals** are ceremonies or rites. Greek religious rituals involved prayers often combined with gifts to the gods based on the principle "I give so that you [the gods] will give [in return]."

Festivals also developed as a way to honor the gods and goddesses. Certain festivals were held at special locations, such as those dedicated to the worship of Zeus at Olympia or to Apollo at Delphi. Numerous events, including athletic games, took place in honor of the gods at the Greek festivals. The first such games were held at the Olympic festival in 776 B.C.

The Greeks also had a great desire to learn the will of the gods. To do so, they made use of the **oracle**, a sacred shrine where a god or goddess revealed the future through a priest or priestess. The most famous was the oracle of Apollo at **Delphi**, located on the side of Mount Parnassus overlooking the Gulf of Corinth. At Delphi, a

**PRIMARY SOURCE** **INFOGRAPHICS**

## Greek Religion and Mythology

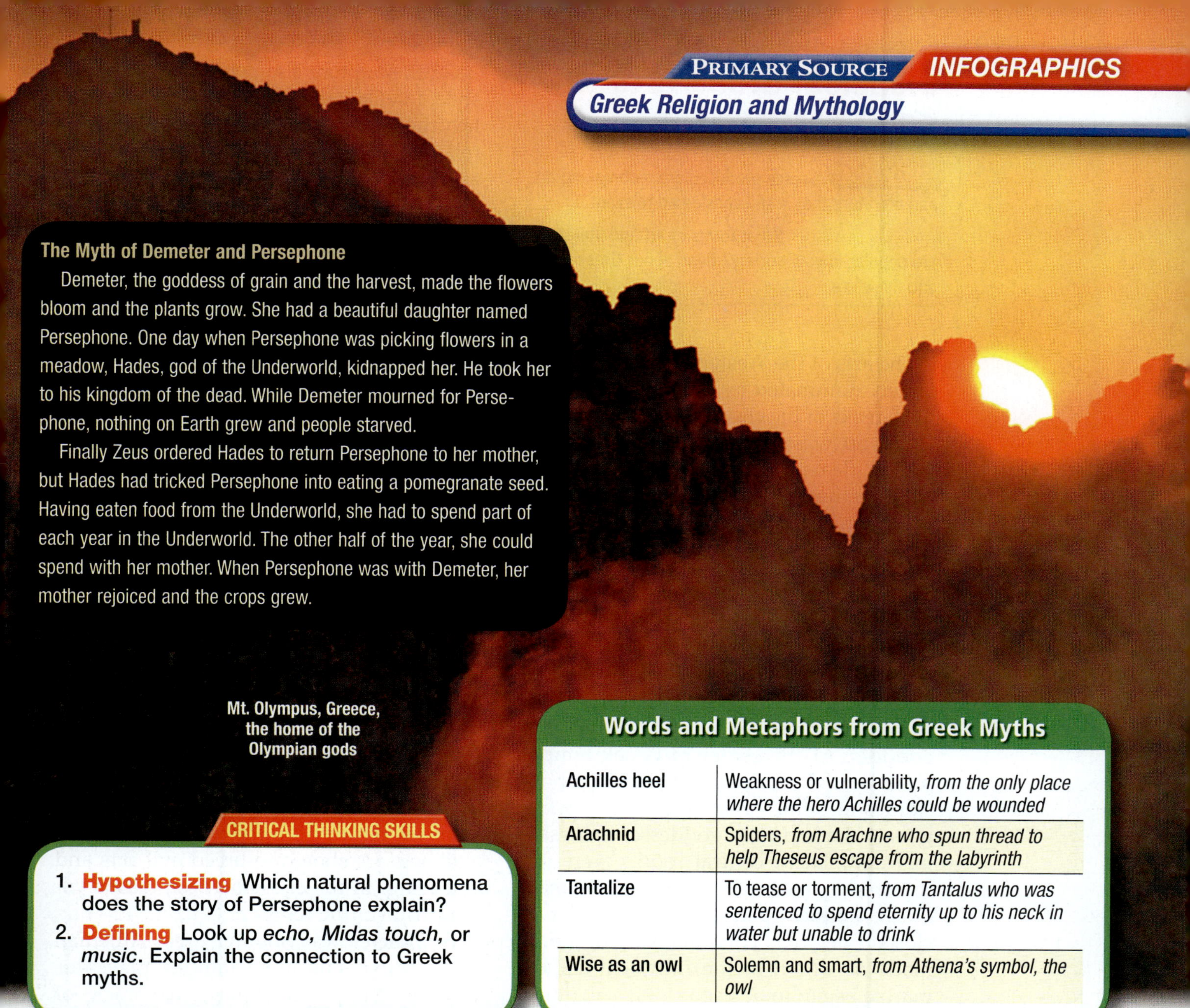

Mt. Olympus, Greece, the home of the Olympian gods

### The Myth of Demeter and Persephone

Demeter, the goddess of grain and the harvest, made the flowers bloom and the plants grow. She had a beautiful daughter named Persephone. One day when Persephone was picking flowers in a meadow, Hades, god of the Underworld, kidnapped her. He took her to his kingdom of the dead. While Demeter mourned for Persephone, nothing on Earth grew and people starved.

Finally Zeus ordered Hades to return Persephone to her mother, but Hades had tricked Persephone into eating a pomegranate seed. Having eaten food from the Underworld, she had to spend part of each year in the Underworld. The other half of the year, she could spend with her mother. When Persephone was with Demeter, her mother rejoiced and the crops grew.

### Words and Metaphors from Greek Myths

| | |
|---|---|
| Achilles heel | Weakness or vulnerability, *from the only place where the hero Achilles could be wounded* |
| Arachnid | Spiders, *from Arachne who spun thread to help Theseus escape from the labyrinth* |
| Tantalize | To tease or torment, *from Tantalus who was sentenced to spend eternity up to his neck in water but unable to drink* |
| Wise as an owl | Solemn and smart, *from Athena's symbol, the owl* |

### CRITICAL THINKING SKILLS

1. **Hypothesizing** Which natural phenomena does the story of Persephone explain?
2. **Defining** Look up *echo, Midas touch,* or *music*. Explain the connection to Greek myths.

priestess, thought to be inspired by Apollo, listened to questions. Her responses were then interpreted by priests and given in verse form to the persons asking the questions. Representatives of states and individuals traveled to Delphi to consult the oracle of Apollo.

The responses provided by the priests and priestesses were often puzzling and could be interpreted in more than one way. For example, Croesus (KREE•suhs), king of Lydia and known for his incredible wealth, sent messengers to the oracle at Delphi asking "whether he shall go to war with the Persians." The oracle replied that if Croesus attacked the Persians, he would destroy a mighty empire. Overjoyed to hear these words, Croesus made war on the Persians but was crushed by his enemy. A mighty empire—that of Croesus—was destroyed!

Although Greek religion is no longer practiced, it was the source of most Greek drama and art. Not only did the Romans adopt the Greek gods, but many stories and references about Greek gods appear in European and American literature.

✓ **Reading Check** **Describing** In what ways did the Greeks honor their gods and goddesses?

# Classical Greek Arts and Literature

**MAIN IDEA** Greece produced groundbreaking art and literature that is still considered relevant.

**HISTORY & YOU** What forms of art and literature are popular in your society? Read about Greek art and literature.

The arts of the Western world have been largely dominated by the standards set by the Greeks of the classical period. Classical Greek art was concerned with expressing eternal ideals. The subject matter of this art was the human being, presented as an object of great beauty. The classic style, with its ideals of reason, moderation, balance, and harmony in all things, was meant to civilize the emotions.

## Architecture and Sculpture

In architecture, the most important form was the temple, dedicated to a god or goddess. At the center of Greek temples were walled rooms that housed both the statues of deities and treasuries in which gifts to the gods and goddesses were safeguarded. These central rooms were surrounded by a screen of columns that made Greek temples open structures rather than closed ones. The columns were originally made of wood. In the fifth century B.C., marble began to be used.

Some of the finest examples of Greek classical architecture were built in Athens in the fifth century B.C. The most famous building on the Acropolis, the Parthenon is regarded as the greatest example of the classical Greek temple. It was built between 447 B.C. and 432 B.C. Dedicated to Athena, the patron goddess of Athens, the Parthenon was an expression of Athenians' pride in their city-state. Indeed, it was dedicated not only to Athena but also to the glory of Athens and the Athenians. The Parthenon shows the principles of classical architecture: the search for calmness, clarity, and freedom from unnecessary detail. The Parthenon today is a revered ruin. It was damaged by an explosion in 1687 and has been partially restored.

Greek sculpture also developed a classical style. Lifelike statues of the male nude, the favorite subject of Greek sculptors, showed relaxed attitudes. Their faces were self-assured, their bodies smooth and muscled.

Classical Greek sculptors did not seek to achieve realism, however, but rather a standard of ideal beauty. Polyclitus (PAH•lih•KLY•tuhs), a fifth-century sculptor, wrote down systematic rules for proportions that he illustrated in a work known as the *Doryphoros*. His theory maintained that the use of ideal proportions, based on mathematical ratios found in nature, could produce an ideal human form.

## Drama

Drama as we know it in Western culture was created by the Greeks. Plays were presented in outdoor theaters as part of religious festivals. The first Greek dramas were **tragedies**, which were presented in a trilogy—a set of three plays—built around a common theme. The only complete trilogy we possess today, called the *Oresteia*, was composed by **Aeschylus.** This set of three plays relates the fate of Agamemnon, a hero in the Trojan War, and his family after his return from the war. In the plays, evil acts are shown to breed evil acts and suffering. In the end, however, reason triumphs over the forces of evil.

**Sophocles** was another great Athenian playwright. His most famous play was *Oedipus Rex*. In this play, the oracle of Apollo accurately foretells that Oedipus will kill his own father and marry his mother. Despite all attempts to prevent this, Oedipus does commit these tragic acts.

A third outstanding Athenian dramatist, **Euripides**, tried to create more realistic characters. His plots became more complex and showed a greater interest in real-life situations. Euripides was controversial. He questioned traditional values. He portrayed war as brutal and barbaric and expressed deep compassion for the women and children who suffered as a result of it.

Greek tragedies dealt with universal themes still relevant today. They examined such problems as the nature of good and evil, the rights of the individual, the nature of divine forces, and the nature of human beings. In the world of the Greek tragedies, striving to do the best thing may not always lead to success, but the attempt is a worthy endeavor. Greek pride in accomplishment and independence was real.

As the chorus chanted in Sophocles' *Antigone,* "Is there anything more wonderful on earth, our marvelous planet, than the miracle of man?"

Greek comedy developed later than tragedy. Comedies were used to criticize politicians and intellectuals and were meant to both entertain and provoke a reaction. The plays of Aristophanes are good examples, using puns and satire.

## The Writing of History

In the Western world, the Greeks were the first people to present history as a systematic analysis of past events. **Herodotus** (hih•RAH•duh•tuhs) wrote *History of the Persian Wars,* often seen as the first real history in Western civilization. Its central theme is the conflict between the Greeks and the Persians, which Herodotus viewed as a struggle between Greek freedom and Persian despotism. Herodotus traveled widely and questioned many people as a means of obtaining his information. He was a master storyteller.

Many historians today consider **Thucydides** (thoo•SIH•duh•DEEZ) the greatest historian of the ancient world. Thucydides was an Athenian general who fought in the Great Peloponnesian War and later wrote its history. Unlike Herodotus, Thucydides saw war and politics as the activities of human beings, not gods. He examined the Peloponnesian War clearly and fairly, placing much emphasis on accuracy.

PRIMARY SOURCE **HISTORY & ARTS**

### Greek Architecture and Sculpture

In the center of the Parthenon was a statue of Athena and the treasury of the Delian League. The sculptor Phidias created the Athena from ivory and gold leaf on a wooden frame. Larger than life-sized sculptures on the pediments narrated the birth of Athena and the contest between Athena and Poseidon.

***Discobolus*** **by Myron, 450 B.C.**

Most of the bronze statues by Myron and other classical sculptors have been lost. All that remains are marble copies, and most of those were damaged. When this Roman copy of the discus thrower was restored, its head was placed facing the wrong direction—front instead of toward the discus.

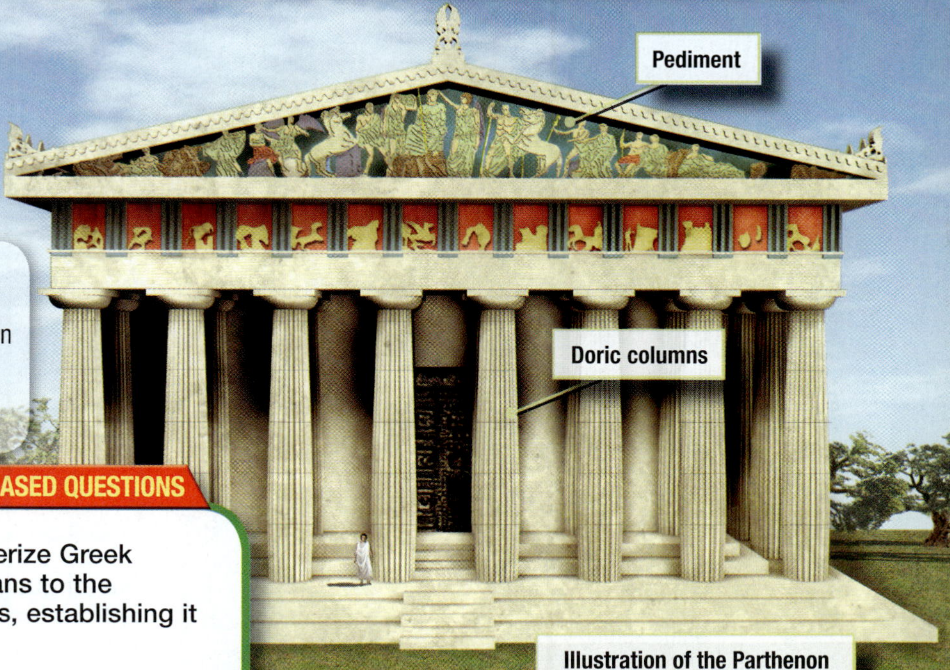

**Illustration of the Parthenon as it appeared around 432 B.C.**

**DOCUMENT-BASED QUESTIONS**

Balance, harmony, and proportion characterize Greek sculpture and architecture. From the Romans to the Americans, civilizations imitated the Greeks, establishing it as the "classic," or standard, of style.

1. **Analyzing Visuals** Compare the Parthenon on the cover of your book with this illustration. Which features have been lost over time?
2. **Summarizing** How is the *Discobolus* different from the *ka* statue on page 44?

As Thucydides stated in his history:

**PRIMARY SOURCE**

"And with regard to my factual reporting of the events of the war I have made it a principle not to write down the first story that came my way, and not even to be guided by my own general impressions; either I was present myself at the events which I have described or else I heard of them from eye-witnesses whose reports I have checked with as much thoroughness as possible."

—Thucydides, *History of the Peloponnesian War*

Thucydides was not a modern historian, of course. For example, he wrote set speeches for the leading actors in the war, but these words were based on a careful judgment of facts he tried to verify. Like many later historians, Thucydides believed that the study of history was of great value in understanding the present.

**✓Reading Check** **Summarizing** What forms of literature were developed in ancient Greece?

## Greek Philosophy

**MAIN IDEA** Three great Greek philosophers—Socrates, Plato, and Aristotle—established the foundations of Western philosophy.

**HISTORY & YOU** How do people in your society try to answer questions about the nature of the universe? Read about philosophy in Greece.

**Philosophy** refers to an organized system of thought. The term comes from a Greek word that means "love of wisdom." Early Greek philosophers focused on the development of critical or rational thought about the nature of the universe.

Many early Greek philosophers tried to explain the universe on the basis of unifying principles. In the sixth century B.C., for example, **Pythagoras**, familiar to geometry students for his Pythagorean theorem, taught that the essence of the universe could be found in music and numbers. In the fifth and fourth centuries B.C., Socrates,

### INFOGRAPHICS

### Greek Myths and Theater

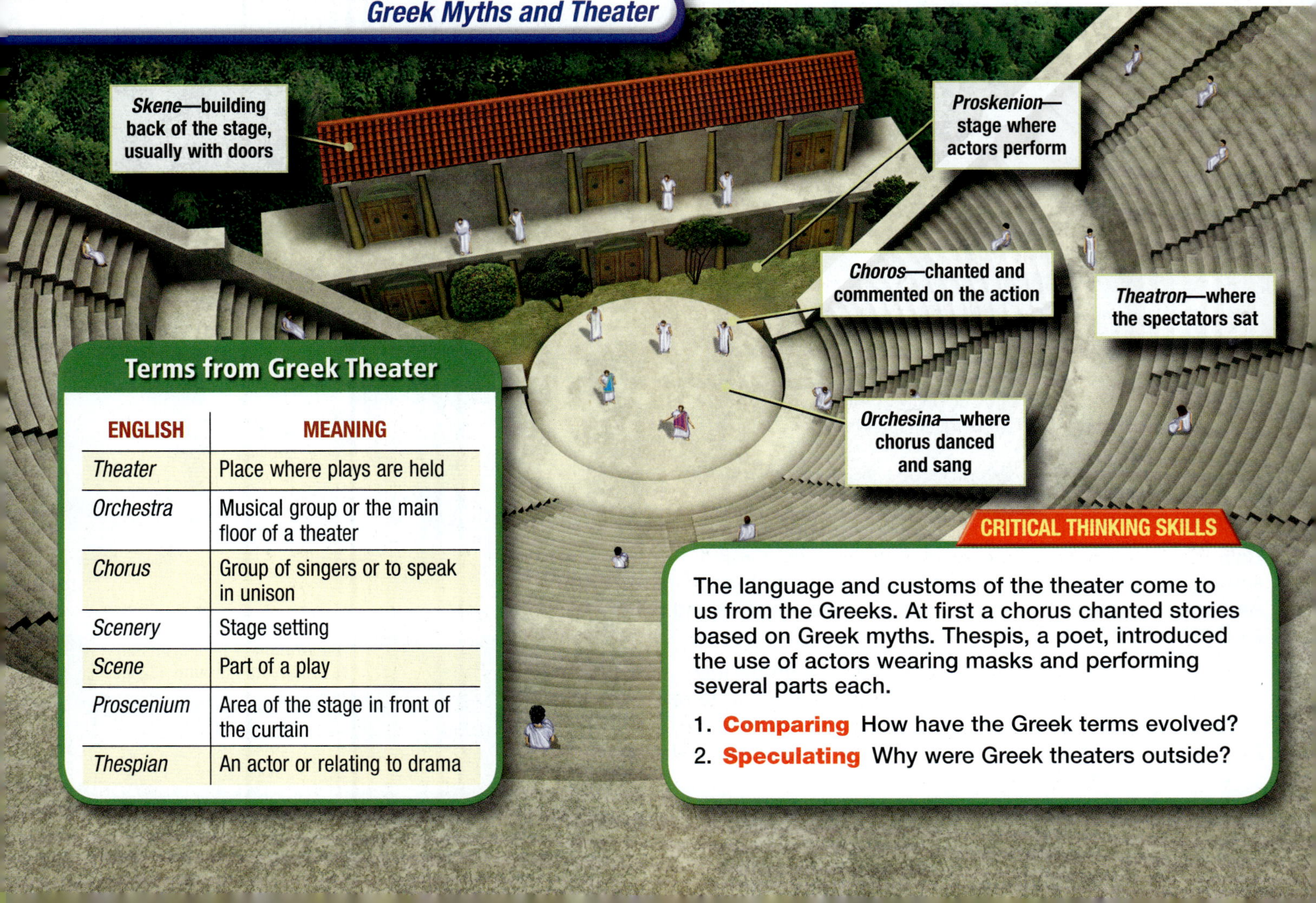


**Terms from Greek Theater**

| ENGLISH | MEANING |
|---|---|
| *Theater* | Place where plays are held |
| *Orchestra* | Musical group or the main floor of a theater |
| *Chorus* | Group of singers or to speak in unison |
| *Scenery* | Stage setting |
| *Scene* | Part of a play |
| *Proscenium* | Area of the stage in front of the curtain |
| *Thespian* | An actor or relating to drama |

**CRITICAL THINKING SKILLS**

The language and customs of the theater come to us from the Greeks. At first a chorus chanted stories based on Greek myths. Thespis, a poet, introduced the use of actors wearing masks and performing several parts each.

1. **Comparing** How have the Greek terms evolved?
2. **Speculating** Why were Greek theaters outside?

Plato, and Aristotle raised basic questions that have been debated for two thousand years.

## Sophists

The **Sophists** were a group of traveling teachers in ancient Greece who rejected speculation such as that of Pythagoras as foolish. They argued that it was simply beyond the reach of the human mind to understand the universe. It was more important for individuals to improve themselves.

The Sophists sold their services as professional teachers to the young men of Greece, especially those of Athens. The Sophists stressed the importance of rhetoric (the art of persuasive speaking in winning debates and swaying an audience). This skill was especially valuable in democratic Athens.

The Sophists' goal was to argue effectively, not to promote particular beliefs or ideas. They were known for their ability to argue for both sides of an issue. To the Sophists, there was no absolute right or wrong. What was right for one individual might be wrong for another. True wisdom consisted of being able to perceive and pursue one's own good. Because of these ideas, many people viewed the Sophists as harmful to society and especially dangerous to the values of young people.

## Socrates

One of the critics of the Sophists was **Socrates**, a sculptor whose true love was philosophy. Because Socrates left no writings, we know about him only what we have learned from the writings of his pupils, such as Plato. Socrates taught many pupils, but he accepted no pay. He believed that the goal of education was only to improve the individual.

Greek philosophers before Socrates were most concerned with issues of natural science. However, Socrates taught his students how to live their lives by a code of **ethics.** He believed that people could be happy by living moral lives, and that they could also be taught how to behave morally.

Socrates used a teaching **method** that is still known by his name. The **Socratic method** of teaching uses a question-and-answer format to lead pupils to see things for themselves by using their own reason. Socrates believed that all real knowledge is already present within each person. Only critical examination is needed to call it forth. This is the real task of philosophy, because, as Socrates said, "The unexamined life is not worth living." This belief in the individual's ability to reason was an important contribution of the Greeks.

Socrates questioned authority, and this soon led him into trouble. Athens had had a tradition of free thought and inquiry, but defeat in the Peloponnesian War changed the Athenians. They no longer trusted open debate. Socrates was accused and convicted of corrupting the youth of Athens by teaching them to question and think for themselves. An Athenian jury sentenced him to die by drinking hemlock, a poison.

## Plato

One of Socrates' students was **Plato**, considered by many the greatest philosopher of Western civilization. Unlike his teacher Socrates, who did not write down his thoughts, Plato wrote a great deal. He was fascinated with the question of reality. How do we know what is real?

According to Plato, a higher world of eternal, unchanging Forms has always existed. These ideal Forms make up reality and only a trained mind— the goal of philosophy—can become aware of or understand these Forms. To Plato, the objects that we perceive with our senses (trees, for example) are simply reflections of the ideal Forms (treeness). They (the trees) are but shadows. Reality is found in the Form (treeness) itself.

Plato explained his ideas about government in a work entitled *The Republic.* Based on his experience in Athens, Plato had come to distrust the workings of democracy. To him, individuals could not achieve a good life unless they lived in a just and rational state. Plato described how he would explore the nature and value of justice, as follows:

**PRIMARY SOURCE**

"[Justice is]... sometimes spoken of as the virtue of an individual, and sometimes as the virtue of a State... And is not a State larger than an individual?... I propose therefore that we enquire into the nature of justice and injustice, first as they appear in the State, and secondly in the individual, proceeding from the greater to the lesser and comparing them."

—Plato, *The Republic, Book II*

Plato's search for the just state led him to construct an ideal state in which people were divided into three basic groups. At the top was an upper class of philosopher-kings.

**PRIMARY SOURCE**

"Unless either philosophers become kings in their countries or those who are now called kings and rulers come to be sufficiently inspired with a genuine desire for wisdom; unless, that is to say, political power and philosophy meet together . . . there can be no rest from troubles . . . for states, nor for all mankind."

—Plato, *The Republic, Book II*

The second group in Plato's ideal state were warriors. The third group contained all the rest, people driven not by wisdom or courage but by desire. They were society's producers—artisans, tradespeople, and farmers. When each of these groups performed its appropriate role in society—and did not try to take on the roles of others—the society would function smoothly and be just. Contrary to Greek custom, Plato also believed that men and women should have the same education and equal access to all positions.

In *The Republic,* he concluded that justice could be achieved in the same manner by both a state and an individual. He argued that just as the different groups in a society need to work together, the different parts of a person's soul—reason, courage (or will), and desire—need to come together to create a just and ethical individual.

## Aristotle

Plato established a school at Athens that was known as the Academy. His most famous pupil was **Aristotle**, who studied

# PEOPLE *in* HISTORY

### Socrates

c. 470 B.C.–c. 399 B.C. Greek philosopher

Born in Athens to a sculptor and a midwife, Socrates received the standard elementary education of literature, music, and gymnastics. He later served as a soldier with the Athenian army in the Peloponnesian War. Socrates believed in the power of argument over writing. Unlike many of his contemporaries, he did not travel to other cities to pursue his intellectual interests. He spent much of his adult life in public places around Athens engaging in debate with anyone who would participate. **How was Socrates different from other philosophers of his time?**

### Plato

c. 428 B.C.–c. 347 B.C. Greek philosopher

Plato was from a noble Greek family and had planned a career in politics. However, he was so horrified by the death of his teacher Socrates that he left politics and spent many years traveling and writing. When Plato returned to Athens in 387 B.C., he founded an academy where he taught using the Socratic method. His academy drew bright young students from Athens and other Greek city-states. Plato looked for truth beyond the appearance of everyday objects, a philosophy reflected in his teachings. **How did Socrates' death impact Plato?**

there for 20 years. Aristotle did not accept Plato's theory of ideal forms. He thought that by examining individual objects (trees), we could perceive their form (treeness). However, he did not believe that these forms existed in a separate, higher world of reality beyond material things. Rather, he thought of forms as a part of things themselves. (In other words, we know what treeness is by examining trees.)

Like Plato, Aristotle believed that people's happiness was tied to their behavior. He taught that happiness resulted from living a life filled with virtue, and that virtue was a midpoint between extreme behaviors. For example, courage would be a midpoint between reckless behavior and cowardice.

Aristotle's many interests lay in analyzing and classifying things based on observation and investigation. He defined entire categories of study, such as logic, biology, and physics, and wrote about a range of subjects, including ethics, politics, poetry, and the sciences.

Aristotle studied natural science by making and recording observations. Although these methods are now part of the scientific method, they were groundbreaking in Aristotle's day. Until the seventeenth century, science in the Western world remained largely based on Aristotle's ideas.

Aristotle often wrote about the importance of intellectual life:

**PRIMARY SOURCE**

> "The activity of the mind is not only the highest . . . but also the most continuous: we are able to study continuously more easily than to perform any kind of action. . . . It follows that the activity of our intelligence constitutes the complete happiness of man. In other words, a life guided by intelligence is the best and most pleasant for man, inasmuch as intelligence, above all else, is man. Consequently, this kind of life is the happiest."
>
> —Aristotle, from *Western Civilization*, Margaret King

Like Plato, Aristotle wanted an effective form of government that would rationally direct human affairs. Unlike Plato, he did not seek an ideal state but tried to find the best form of government by analyzing existing governments. For his *Politics,* Aristotle looked at the constitutions of 158 states and found three good forms of government: monarchy, aristocracy, and constitutional government. He slightly favored constitutional government, which can be democratic, as the best form for most people.

Aristotle is often viewed as the most influential thinker in the Western world. He wrote a vast number of works on a wide range of subjects. His most famous pupil, Alexander the Great, spread his ideas across a vast empire. Students and scholars study Aristotle's works to this day.

**✓Reading Check** **Contrasting** How did Aristotle's idea of government differ from Plato's?

## SECTION 4 REVIEW

### Vocabulary

1. **Explain** the significance of: Olympus, ritual, oracle, Delphi, tragedy, Aeschylus, Sophocles, Euripides, Herodotus, Thucydides, philosophy, Pythagoras, Sophists, Socrates, ethics, method, Socratic method, Plato, Aristotle.

### Main Ideas

2. **Explain** why Olympus was important to the Greeks.
3. **Organize** the bodies of knowledge that the Greeks explored in a web diagram.

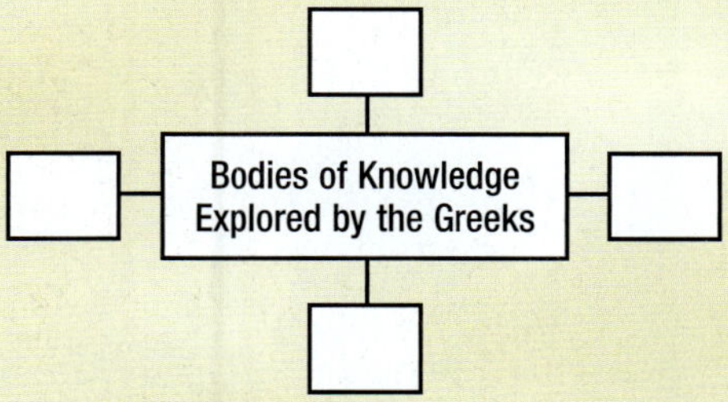


4. **List** the three basic groups of people in Plato's ideal state.

### Critical Thinking

5. **Big Idea** **Making Generalizations** How have ideas from Greece helped shape Western civilization?
6. **Summarizing** How does Plato's theory of ideal forms differ from Aristotle's? Which view makes more sense to you? Why?
7. **Analyzing Visuals** Examine the illustration of the Parthenon shown on page 127. In what modern buildings would you find examples of classical architecture?

### Writing About History

8. **Summarizing** How does Plato's view of government differ from Aristotle's? What was Aristotle's view?

**History ONLINE**
For help with the concepts in this section of *Glencoe World History,* go to glencoe.com and click Study Central™.

# The Olympics: Festival and Games in Ancient Greece

The Olympic Games of ancient Greece began in 776 B.C. and were held between the city-states every four years until they were banned in A.D. 393 by the Roman emperor Theodosius. The Greeks honored both their athletes and Greek gods at the games. A special truce was declared throughout the land as a matter of religious respect and as a practical step to allow people to travel to the games safely. In their heyday, the games lasted for five days and included standard events.

**Day 1** The athletes and spectators gather to prepare for the games. They have come from city-states all over Greece. Officials make sacrifices and offer prayers to the gods in opening ceremonies.

**Day 2** The games begin. First are the equestrian events: horse and chariot racing. Later the pentathlon is held. It is a competition of five events: discus throw, javelin throw, jumping, running, and wrestling.

## Olympia

The games were held at Olympia, one of the oldest and most venerated religious centers in the Greek world. By classical times, the Greeks had constructed temples and altars there in an area called the *altis*, or "sacred grove." Outside the *altis* stood buildings for the games themselves, including a stadium, a gymnasium, and a hippodrome. The Olympic Games honored Zeus, but games were also held in other cities for other gods. These were held in cycles, so individuals could participate in a festival every year.

**Day 3** There are prayers, a feast, and a procession to the altar of Zeus, whom the games honor. The 40-foot statue of the ruler of the gods was one of the wonders of the ancient world.

**Day 4** A day of intense competition. There are a variety of foot races, wrestling and boxing matches, and the brutal *pankration,* a sort of combination of wrestling and boxing in which almost anything is allowed.

**Day 5** The closing day is another one of celebration and ceremony. After a great feast, the spectators and athletes begin the journey home. Spectators have tales to tell, losers perhaps a resolve to return, and winners the anticipation of a hero's welcome back home.

## Superstars of the Ancient World

A victor in the games was awarded a crown of olive leaves pulled from a sacred tree and permission to have a statue of himself placed at Olympia. But winning athletes often received much more from their home city-states, grateful for the glory, fame, and heightened reputation the community gained by producing an Olympic winner. Like modern sports stars, these athletes were rewarded with celebrity and a wide variety of gifts.

### Analyzing Visuals

1. **Making Inferences** Why do you think religious practices were such a large part of the ancient Greek Olympics?
2. **Comparing** How were the ancient Greek Olympic Games similar to the modern Olympics?

SECTION 5

Section Audio    Spotlight Video

# Alexander and the Hellenistic Era

## GUIDE TO READING

### The BIG Idea

**Ideas, Beliefs and Values** Greek culture spread to new lands.

### Content Vocabulary

- Hellenistic Era *(p. 137)*
- Stoicism *(p. 139)*
- Epicureanism *(p. 139)*

### Academic Vocabulary

- subsidizing *(p. 138)*
- founder *(p. 139)*

### People and Places

- Macedonia *(p. 134)*
- Philip II *(p. 134)*
- Alexander the Great *(p. 134)*
- Alexandria *(p. 135)*
- Pergamum *(p. 137)*
- Eratosthenes *(p. 138)*
- Euclid *(p. 138)*
- Archimedes *(p. 139)*

### Reading Strategy

**Compare and Contrast** As you read, create a diagram like the one below to help you study. Compare and contrast the characteristics of the classical and Hellenistic periods.

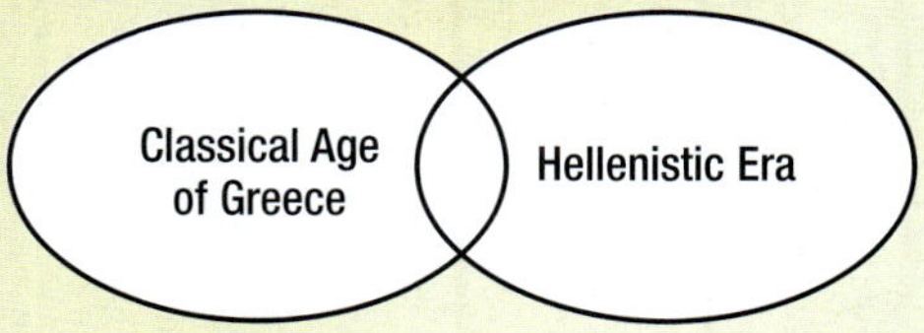


*Under the leadership of Alexander the Great, Macedonians and Greeks united to invade and conquer the Persian Empire. In the conquered lands, Greeks and non-Greeks formed a new society in what is known as the Hellenistic Era.*

## Macedonians Invade Greece

MAIN IDEA Under Alexander the Great, Macedonians and Greeks conquered the Persian Empire.

***HISTORY & YOU*** Who are some of the military leaders you know about in American history? Read about how Alexander the Great led his army to create an empire.

The Greeks viewed their northern neighbors, the Macedonians, as barbarians. They were a rural people of farmers and agricultural laborers, organized into groups, not in city-states like the Greeks. They were probably not Greek, and they had not been involved in the rivalries of Greek city-states—their leaders focused mostly on defending their northern borders. By the end of the fifth century B.C., however, **Macedonia** emerged as a powerful kingdom.

### Philip and Alexander

In 359 B.C., **Philip II** came to the throne. He built a powerful army and turned Macedonia into the chief power of the Greek world. Philip was soon drawn into Greek affairs. A great admirer of Greek culture, he longed to unite all of Greece under Macedonia.

Fearing Philip, the Athenians allied with a number of other Greek states and fought the Macedonians at the Battle of Chaeronea (KEHR•uh•NEE•uh), near Thebes, in 338 B.C. The Macedonian army crushed the Greeks.

Philip quickly gained control of all Greece, bringing an end to the freedom of the Greek city-states. He insisted that the Greek states form a league and then cooperate with him in a war against Persia. Before Philip could undertake his invasion of Asia, however, he was assassinated, leaving the task to his son Alexander.

**Alexander the Great** was only 20 years old when he became king of Macedonia. Philip had carefully prepared his son for kingship. By taking Alexander along with him on military campaigns, Philip taught Alexander the basics of military leadership. After his father's death, Alexander moved quickly to fulfill his father's dream—the invasion of the Persian Empire. He was motivated by the desire for glory and empire but also by the desire to avenge the Persian burning of Athens in 480 B.C.

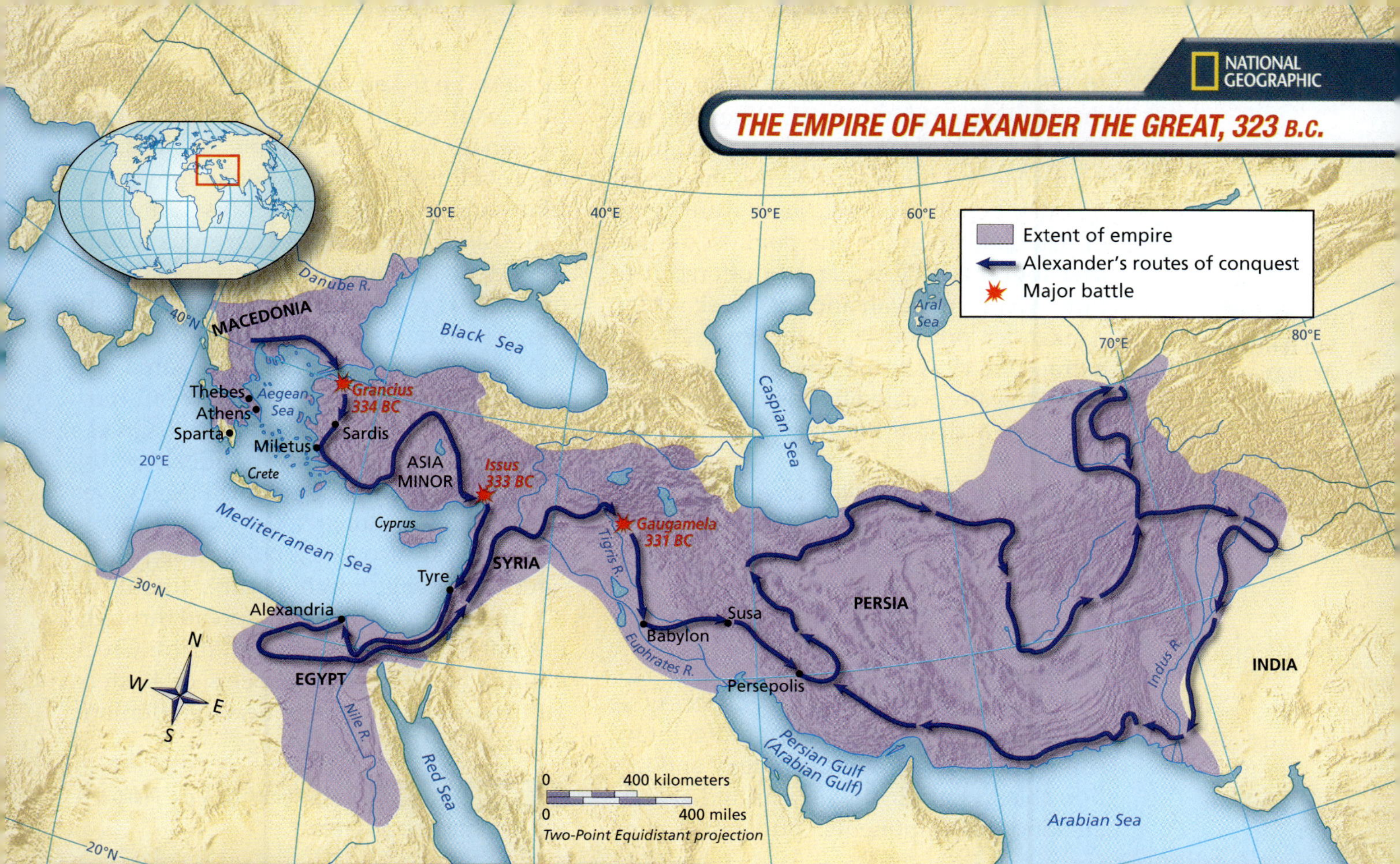

**Geography SKILLS**

**The empire of Alexander the Great stretched across three continents and over 200,000 miles. The inset map shows the present-day equivalent of Alexander's empire.**

1. **Human-Environment Interaction** **Does it appear that physical boundaries limited the extent of Alexander's empire? Explain.**
2. **Place** **Compare the inset map to the large map. What modern states correspond to Alexander's empire?**

## Alexander's Conquests

Alexander was taking a chance in attacking the Persian Empire. Although weakened, it was still a strong state in the spring of 334 B.C. when Alexander entered Asia Minor with an army of some 37,000 men, both Macedonians and Greeks. The cavalry, which would play an important role as a striking force, numbered about 5,000.

By the next year, Alexander had freed the Ionian Greek cities of western Asia Minor from the Persians and defeated a large Persian army at Issus. He then turned south. By the winter of 332 B.C., Alexander had Syria, Palestine, and Egypt under his control. He built **Alexandria** as the Greek capital of Egypt. It became and remains today one of the most important cities in both Egypt and the Mediterranean world. It was also the first of a series of cities named after him.

In 331 B.C., Alexander turned east and fought the decisive battle with the Persians at Gaugamela, not far from Babylon. Soon after, Alexander controlled the rest of the Persian Empire. Over the next three years, Alexander moved as far as modern Pakistan.

History ONLINE
**Student Web Activity—**
Visit glencoe.com and complete the activity about Alexander the Great and his conquests.

In 326 B.C., Alexander reached India, where the campaigning was hard. When his soldiers refused to go farther, he agreed to go home. He led his troops across the desert of today's southern Iran. Many were dying of heat and thirst. At one point, some soldier found a little water and offered it to him. According to an ancient Greek writer, Alexander poured it on the ground: "So extraordinary was the effect of this action that the water wasted by Alexander was as good as a drink for every man in the army."

Alexander returned to Babylon, planning more conquests. But in 323 B.C., exhausted from wounds, fever, and too much alcohol, he died. He was 32 years old.

## Alexander's Legacy

Alexander's extraordinary success is explained by his leadership and military skills. He was a master of strategy and tactics, able to fight in all terrains and against all kinds of opponents. Brave and even reckless, he risked his own life, an example that inspired his soldiers to follow him. Alexander sought to imitate Achilles, the hero of Homer's *Iliad.* He kept a copy of the *Iliad*—and a dagger—under his pillow.

Alexander created an enormous legacy. He extended Greek and Macedonian rule over a vast area, which brought large quantities of gold and silver into their economies.

Alexander's successors used force and claims of divine rule to create military monarchies. Although mainland Greeks remained committed to the ideals of the city-state, Alexander's political legacy was the creation of monarchies.

Alexander also left a cultural legacy as Greek language, architecture, literature, art, and religious diversity spread throughout parts of Asia and North Africa. Greek culture blended with aspects of Eastern culture to become a new Hellenistic culture.

✓Reading Check **Identifying** How did Philip II and Alexander change Greece?

### HISTORY & ARTS — PRIMARY SOURCE
### Alexander's Army

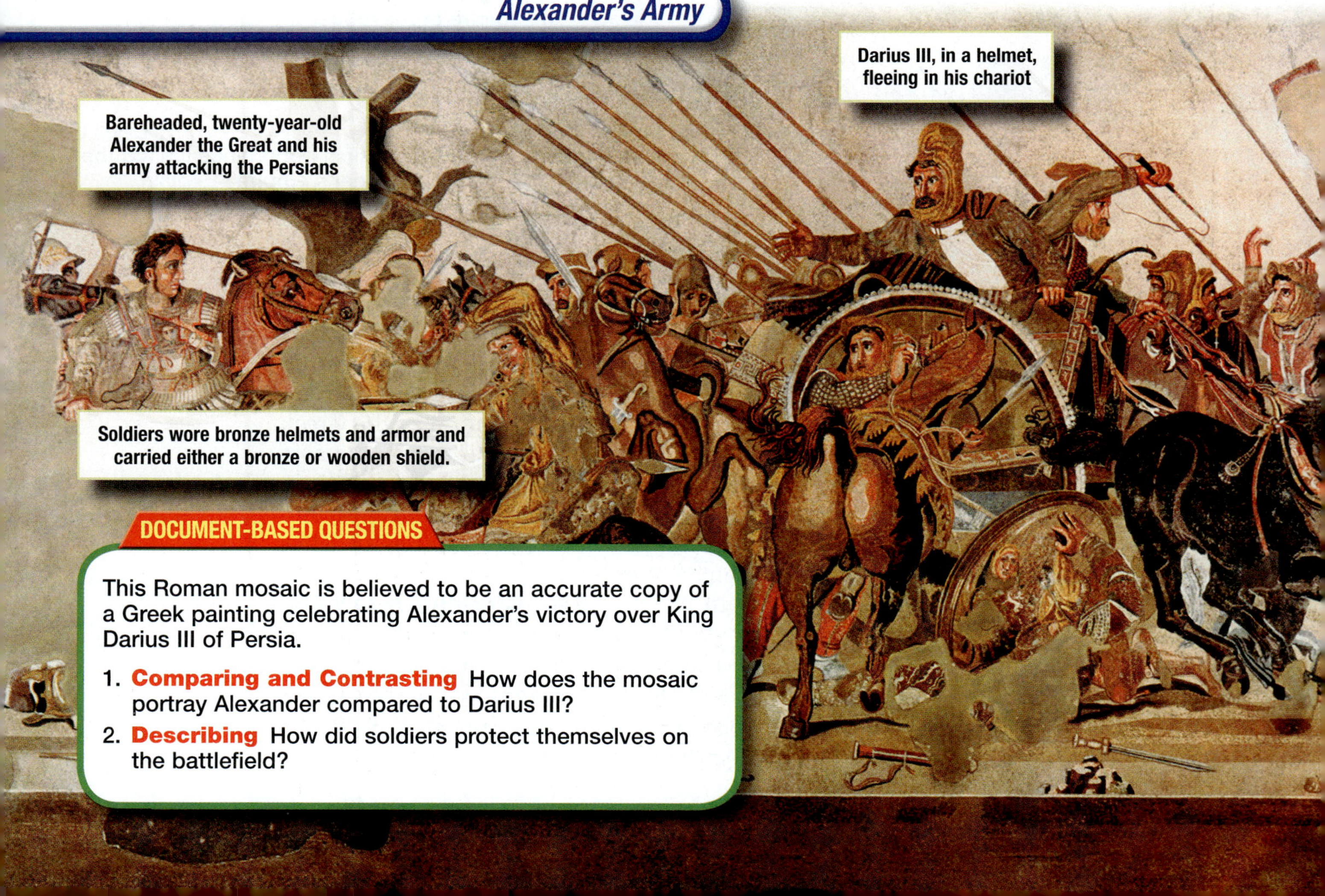

Darius III, in a helmet, fleeing in his chariot

Bareheaded, twenty-year-old Alexander the Great and his army attacking the Persians

Soldiers wore bronze helmets and armor and carried either a bronze or wooden shield.

**DOCUMENT-BASED QUESTIONS**

This Roman mosaic is believed to be an accurate copy of a Greek painting celebrating Alexander's victory over King Darius III of Persia.

1. **Comparing and Contrasting** How does the mosaic portray Alexander compared to Darius III?
2. **Describing** How did soldiers protect themselves on the battlefield?

## The Hellenistic Era

**MAIN IDEA** As a result of Alexander's conquests, Hellenistic cities became centers for the spread of Greek language, art, architecture, and literature.

***HISTORY & YOU*** How many different cultures do you encounter in your daily life? Read about the Hellenistic world.

---

Alexander created a new age, the **Hellenistic Era.** The word *Hellenistic* comes from a Greek word meaning "to imitate Greeks." It is an appropriate way to describe an age that saw the expansion of the Greek language and ideas to the non-Greek world of Southwest Asia and beyond.

### Hellenistic Kingdoms

The united empire that Alexander created by his conquests fell apart soon after his death as the most important Macedonian generals engaged in a struggle for power. By 300 B.C., any hope of unity was dead. Eventually, four Hellenistic kingdoms emerged as the successors to Alexander: Macedonia, Syria in the east, the kingdom of **Pergamum** in western Asia Minor, and Egypt. All were eventually conquered by the Romans.

Alexander the Great had planned to fuse Macedonians, Greeks, and Persians in his new empire by using Persians as officials and encouraging his soldiers to marry native women. The Hellenistic monarchs who succeeded him, however, relied only on Greeks and Macedonians to form the new ruling class. Even those from eastern regions who did advance to important government posts had learned Greek, for all government business was transacted in Greek. The Greek ruling class was determined to maintain its position.

In his conquests, Alexander had created a series of new cities and military settlements. Hellenistic kings did likewise. These new population centers varied in size from military settlements of only a few hundred men to cities with thousands of people. Alexandria, which Alexander had founded in Egypt, was the largest city in the Mediterranean region by the first century B.C.

Hellenistic rulers encouraged a spread of Greek colonists to Southwest Asia. Greeks (and Macedonians) provided not only new recruits for the army but also a pool of civilian administrators and workers. Architects, engineers, dramatists, and actors were all in demand in the new Greek cities. Through trade, the new Greek cities spread Hellenistic culture to Southwest and Central Asia—as far as modern Afghanistan and India.

### Hellenistic Arts and Literature

The Hellenistic Era was a period of considerable cultural accomplishment in many areas, especially science and philosophy. These achievements occurred throughout the Hellenistic world. Certain centers, however—especially the great Hellenistic city of Alexandria—stood out. Alexandria became home to poets, writers, philosophers, and scientists—scholars of all kinds.

The library in Alexandria became the largest in ancient times, with more than 500,000 scrolls. The library encouraged the careful study of literature and language. There was also a museum that welcomed scholarly research.

Pergamum, the most important city in Asia Minor, also became a leading cultural center. As a result, Pergamum also attracted both scholars and artists. The library at Pergamum was second only to Alexandria's library.

The founding of new cities and the rebuilding of old ones presented many opportunities for Greek architects and sculptors. Hellenistic kings were very willing to spend their money to beautify the cities within their states. The buildings characteristic of the Greek homeland—baths, theaters, and temples—lined the streets of these cities.

Both Hellenistic kings and rich citizens patronized sculptors. Thousands of statues were erected in towns and cities all over the Hellenistic world. Hellenistic sculptors maintained the technical skill of the classical period, but they moved away from the idealism of earlier classicism to a more emotional and realistic art. This is especially evident in the numerous statues of old women and little children.

## HISTORY & ARTS — PRIMARY SOURCE

### Jason and the Golden Fleece

Apollonius of Rhodes told the story of Jason and the Golden Fleece, around the third century B.C., in the epic poem *Argonautica.* Jason is a hero who must complete impossible tasks to take his place in society. In this particular task, Jason must capture the Golden Fleece, which is guarded by a serpent in a garden, so that he can become king. He accomplishes this with the help of Medea, as Apollonius describes:

> "And they two by the pathway came to the sacred grove, seeking the huge oak tree on which was hung the fleece, like to a cloud that blushes red with the fiery beams of the rising sun. But right in front the serpent with his keen sleepless eyes saw them coming, and stretched out his long neck and hissed in awful wise. . . . And as he writhed, the maiden came before his eyes, with sweet voice calling to her aid sleep, highest of gods, to charm the monster . . . so at that time did Jason uplift the mighty fleece in his hands. . . . And he strode on now with the fleece covering his left shoulder from the height of his neck to his feet, and now again he gathered it up in his hands; for he feared exceedingly, lest some god or man should meet him and deprive him thereof."

**DOCUMENT-BASED QUESTIONS**

**This marble piece from the Hellenistic period shows Medea charming the serpent while Jason captures the Golden Fleece.**

1. **Restating** What is happening in Apollonius's description?
2. **Drawing Conclusions** Why was a heroic tale appealing in the Hellenistic Era?

The Hellenistic Age also produced a great quantity of literature. Writing talent was held in high esteem, especially by Hellenistic leaders, who spent large amounts of money **subsidizing** writers. Unfortunately, very little of this literature has survived.

Apollonius of Rhodes wrote the epic poem *Argonautica,* which tells the story of Jason's search for the Golden Fleece. Theocritus wrote short poems that expressed a love of nature and an appreciation of its beauty. Unlike Apollonius, Theocritus believed that it was best not to attempt epic poems, for which Homer had established a standard that many scholars felt could not be matched.

Athens remained the center of Greek theatre. A new type of comedy developed that sought only to entertain and amuse and avoided political commentary. Menander was perhaps the most successful of these new playwrights.

## Science and Philosophy

The Hellenistic Age witnessed considerable advances in the sciences. Astronomy and mathematics were two areas of progress. One astronomer, Aristarchus (AR•uh•STAHR•kuhs) of Samos, developed the theory that the sun is at the center of the universe while the Earth rotates around the sun in a circular orbit. The prevailing view, in contrast, held that Earth was at the center of the universe. The new theory was not widely accepted at the time.

**Eratosthenes** (EHR•uh•TAHS•thuh•NEEZ) was another important astronomer. He determined that Earth was round and calculated Earth's circumference at 24,675 miles (39,702 km), an estimate that was within 185 miles (298 km) of the actual figure. The mathematician **Euclid** wrote the *Elements,* a textbook on plane geometry. This work has been used up to modern times.

The most famous scientist of the Hellenistic Era was **Archimedes** (AHR•kuh•MEE•deez) of Syracuse. He worked on the geometry of spheres and cylinders and also established the value of the mathematical constant pi. A practical inventor, too, he may have devised the "Archimedes' screw," a machine used to pump water out of mines and to lift irrigation water.

Archimedes' achievements inspired a number of stories. Supposedly, he discovered specific gravity by observing the water he displaced in his bath. He then became so excited by his realization that he jumped out of the water and ran home naked, shouting, "Eureka!" ("I have found it!"). He is said to have emphasized the importance of levers by proclaiming to the king of Syracuse, "Give me a lever and a place to stand on and I will move the earth." The king encouraged Archimedes to lower his sights and build defensive weapons instead.

Athens remained the chief center for philosophy in the Hellenistic Era, attracting famous thinkers from all over who established schools there. The development of two new systems of thought, Epicureanism and Stoicism, strengthened Athens's reputation as a philosophical center.

Epicurus, the **founder** of **Epicureanism**, began a school in Athens at the end of the fourth century B.C. He believed that human beings were free to follow their own self-interest and make happiness their goal. The means to happiness was the pursuit of pleasure, the only true good.

Epicurus did not speak of the pursuit of pleasure in a physical sense (which is what our word *epicurean* has come to mean). Instead, pleasure was freedom from emotional turmoil and worry. To achieve this, people had to free themselves from public activity. However, they were not to give up all social life. To Epicurus, a life could only be complete when it was centered on the ideal of friendship.

Another school of thought was **Stoicism.** It became the most popular philosophy of the Hellenistic world and later flourished in the Roman Empire as well. Stoicism was the product of a teacher named Zeno. A Syrian who came to Athens as a merchant, Zeno lost his possessions on the sea voyage. A philosopher in Athens consoled Zeno by teaching him that material possessions were not necessary to be happy. After learning from other philosophers, Zeno began to teach in a building known as the Painted Portico (the *Stoa Poikile*—hence, the word *Stoicism*).

Like Epicureans, Stoics wanted to find happiness, but they thought it could be found only by living in harmony with the will of God. Then they could bear whatever life offered (hence, our word *stoic*). Unlike Epicureans, Stoics did not want to separate themselves from the world. Public service was regarded as noble. The real Stoic was a good citizen.

**✓Reading Check** **Summarizing** In which fields did Hellenistic scholars make advancements?

## SECTION 5 REVIEW

### Vocabulary

1. **Explain** the significance of: Macedonia, Philip II, Alexander the Great, Alexandria, Hellenistic Era, Pergamum, subsidizing, Eratosthenes, Euclid, Archimedes, founder, Epicureanism, Stoicism.

### Main Ideas

2. **Describe** the role of Alexander the Great's empire in creating the Hellenistic world and in spreading Hellenistic culture.
3. **List** the three most famous scientists of the Hellenistic Age and describe their contributions.
4. **Organize** information using a cluster diagram to show Alexander's goals for his empire.

### Critical Thinking

5. **BIG Idea** **Defending** What was the most important effect of Macedonia's conquest of Greece? Explain your answer.
6. **Evaluating** Why is Alexander called "the Great"? Do you think the title is justified? Why or why not?
7. **Analyzing Visuals** View the image on page 136 of Alexander the Great. What does this tell you about the style of warfare during his conquests?

### Writing About History

8. **Persuasive Writing** Choose an Epicurean or Stoic perspective and argue whether an individual should participate in government and civic affairs.

**History ONLINE**

For help with the concepts in this section of *Glencoe World History*, go to glencoe.com and click Study Central™.

# CHAPTER 4 Visual Summary

STUDY TO GO You can study anywhere, anytime by downloading quizzes and flash cards to your PDA from glencoe.com.

## EARLY GREECE AND THE POLIS

- Greek civilization emerged with the Mycenaeans, who reflected aristocratic and warrior values; later these were celebrated in Homer's epics.
- A difficult Dark Age dispersed Greeks in colonies around the Mediterranean.
- The polis, or city-state, became the central unit of Greek political and social life.
- Sparta and Athens, the leading city-states, followed very different ideals; in Athens democracy emerged.

MYCENAEAN KING AGAMEMNON

**Agamemnon led the attack on Troy in Homer's *Iliad*.**

DETAIL FROM THE NORTH FRIEZE OF THE PARTHENON

**These water carriers are a clear example of Greek classical principles in the arts.**

## CLASSICAL GREECE

- To defend their lands, the Greeks fought and defeated the Persians.
- Under Pericles, Athens embraced democracy at home, but not in the empire.
- Sparta destroyed Athenian domination, ending the classical age.
- Greek drama probed eternal questions while Greek philosophy pioneered rational thought.
- Greeks wrote the first analytical history, while balance and harmony guided their art and architecture.

## THE HELLENISTIC AGE

- Alexander the Great unified Greece, then spread its culture as he conquered other lands.
- Four Hellenistic kingdoms developed after Alexander's death.
- Hellenistic kingdoms in Egypt, Persia, and elsewhere absorbed Greek language and culture.
- Alexandria and Pergamum became important Hellenistic cities.
- Hellenistic mathematicians, scientists, writers, and philosophers developed new ideas and inventions.

HELLENISTIC MASTERPIECE

***Nike of Samothrace* embodies the artistic movement of Hellenistic Greece.**

# CHAPTER 4 Assessment

## Reviewing Vocabulary

*Directions: Choose the word or words that best complete the sentence.*

**1.** Heavily armed infantrymen or foot soldiers are known as ________.

**A** phalanx
**B** Spartans
**C** cavalry
**D** hoplites

**2.** Athenians devised the practice of ________ to protect themselves against overly ambitious politicians.

**A** tyranny
**B** ostracism
**C** democracy
**D** warfare

**3.** In order to know the will of the gods, the Greeks consulted a(n) ________.

**A** oracle
**B** Delphi
**C** festival
**D** temple

**4.** ________ comes from the Greek word that means "love of wisdom."

**A** Literature
**B** Theatre
**C** Philosophy
**D** Mathematics

**5.** A Greek city-state, including the town, city, or village and the surrounding countryside, is called a(n)________.

**A** polis
**B** ephor
**C** agora
**D** *arete*

## Reviewing Main Ideas

*Directions: Choose the best answers to the following questions.*

### Section 1 *(pp. 106–111)*

**6.** How did the physical geography of Greece affect the Greeks?

**A** It helped to make their city-states fiercely independent.
**B** It encouraged them to focus on truth and beauty.
**C** It was one of the factors that made them fierce, skilled warriors.
**D** It prevented contact with other civilizations.

### Section 2 *(pp. 112–117)*

**7.** Which of the following best describes Sparta?

**A** A city-state that valued alliances with other cultures
**B** A Macedonian democracy
**C** A strict society run by helots
**D** A military state focused on the art of war

**8.** How did Cleisthenes create the foundation for democracy in Athens?

**A** By declaring war on Sparta
**B** By giving the Athenian assembly a central political role
**C** By giving aristocrats' land to the poor
**D** By discouraging the study of the arts

### Section 3 *(pp. 118–123)*

**9.** What brought Sparta and Athens together as allies?

**A** Their common values, beliefs, and culture
**B** The movement of the Delian League to Athens
**C** The threat of the Persian Empire
**D** The Great Peloponnesian War

### TEST-TAKING TIP

Look for key words such as *best, always,* and *never* in questions and answer choices.

**Need Extra Help?**

| If You Missed Questions . . . | 1 | 2 | 3 | 4 | 5 | 6 | 7 | 8 | 9 |
|---|---|---|---|---|---|---|---|---|---|
| Go to Page . . . | 113 | 121 | 124 | 128 | 112 | 106 | 115 | 117 | 118 |

GO ON

**10.** Who benefited from the power struggles of Athens, Sparta, and Thebes?

**A** Philip II of Macedonia

**B** The Delian League

**C** Women in all three societies

**D** Pericles of Athens

## Section 4 *(pp. 124–131)*

**11.** Which of the following is true of Aristotle?

**A** He developed the Pythagorean theorem.

**B** He designed the Parthenon, the greatest example of the classical Greek temple.

**C** He defined the subject of logic.

**D** He is considered the greatest historian of the ancient world.

**12.** What do Aeschylus and Sophocles have in common?

**A** They developed mathematical proofs.

**B** They studied under Plato.

**C** They wrote tragedies.

**D** They were gifted historians.

## Section 5 *(pp. 134–139)*

**13.** How did Alexander's father prepare him for kingship?

**A** By having him brought up in Athens

**B** By bringing him on military campaigns

**C** By enlisting him in the Spartan army

**D** By sending for Socrates to tutor him

**14.** What was Alexander's cultural legacy?

**A** The gold and silver that his conquests brought to Greece and Macedonia

**B** The spread of Greek language, architecture, literature, and art

**C** The possession of the entire Persian Empire

**D** His strong skills as a military leader

## Critical Thinking

*Directions: Choose the best answers to the following questions.*

*Use the following information to answer question 15.*

**Ancient Civilizations of Greece**

| | Minoans | Mycenaeans | Spartans | Athenians |
|---|---|---|---|---|
| **Location** | Crete | Peloponnese | Peloponnese | Attica |
| **Values** | sports, nature | heroic deeds | discipline, military arts | philosophy, art |
| **Trade** | sea trading empire | pottery | trade discouraged | pottery |

**15.** Which of the following statements is supported by the information in the table?

**A** The Spartans and the Athenians had many common interests.

**B** The Minoans and the Mycenaeans were allies.

**C** All four civilizations existed at the same time.

**D** The Spartans had more in common with the Mycenaeans than with the other civilizations.

**16.** A Greek dramatist would most likely be a citizen of which of the following?

**A** The Minoan civilization

**B** The Mycenaean civilization

**C** Sparta

**D** Athens

**17.** How did the formation of the Delian League give proof to the saying that strength lies in unity?

**A** After the collapse of the Delian League, the Greeks were conquered.

**B** When the Macedonians and Greeks worked together, they ended the Persian Empire.

**C** The Delian League led to the spread of Greek language in modern-day Pakistan.

**D** The Delian League provided a democratic forum for all Greek city-states.

**Need Extra Help?**

| If You Missed Questions . . . | 10 | 11 | 12 | 13 | 14 | 15 | 16 | 17 |
|---|---|---|---|---|---|---|---|---|
| Go to Page . . . | 123 | 131 | 126 | 134 | 136 | 142 | 126 | 121 |

GO ON

18. What event blinded the major Greek states to the threat from Macedonia?

**A** The Age of Pericles

**B** The establishment of Sparta

**C** The Great Peloponnesian War

**D** The end of the Persian Empire

*Analyze the map and answer the question that follows. Base your answer on the map.*

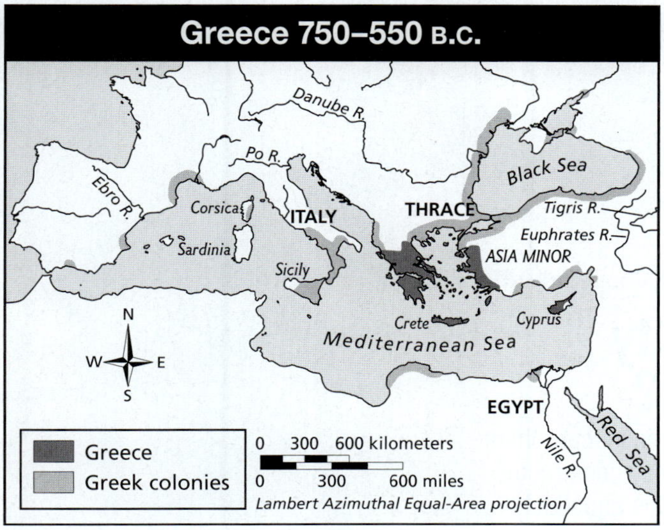


19. Based on the map, which of the following is most likely true?

**A** The Greeks relied heavily on their navy.

**B** The Greeks planned to conquer all of Western Europe.

**C** The Greeks had little interest in colonization.

**D** Greece was the largest colony in the empire.

20. Excepting the Mediterranean Sea, around which body of water was there a major presence of Greek colonies?

**A** Red Sea

**B** Ebro River

**C** Black Sea

**D** Danube River

## Document-Based Questions

*Directions: Analyze the document and answer the short-answer questions that follow the document. Base your answers on the document and on your knowledge of world history.*

While Athens was at war with Sparta, Pericles spoke at a public funeral to honor those who had died in combat. He spoke of the greatness of Athens and the strength of its political system. Read the following excerpt.

> *"Our Constitution is called a democracy because the power is in the hands not of a minority but of the whole people. When it is a question of settling private disputes, everyone is equal before the law. Just as our political life is free and open, so is our day-to-day life in our relations with each other. . . . Here each individual is interested not only in his own affairs but in the affairs of the state as well."*
>
> —Pericles

21. According to Pericles, what is the relationship between the individual and the state in a democracy?

22. What is the historical significance of this speech in Pericles' own day and now?

## Extended Response

23. What role did tyrants play in the development of Greek democracy? What does the word *tyrant* mean today? How did its meaning evolve?

24. Analyze how the Greek world divided into Spartan and Athenian camps after defeating the Persians. To what did this split eventually lead?

**History ONLINE**
For additional test practice, use Self-Check Quizzes—Chapter 4 at glencoe.com.

**Need Extra Help?**

| If You Missed Questions . . . | 18 | 19 | 20 | 21 | 22 | 23 | 24 |
|---|---|---|---|---|---|---|---|
| Go to Page . . . | 123 | 143 | 143 | 143 | 121 | 114 | 123 |

STOP

# CHAPTER 5

# Rome and the Rise of Christianity 600 B.C.–A.D. 500



*MAKING CONNECTIONS*

Chapter Audio

## What did we learn about city planning from the Romans?

The Romans built cities from England to Africa and connected them with roads. Using concrete, the dome, and the arch, they constructed amphitheaters, temples, law courts, and aqueducts. This aqueduct brought water 31 miles (50 km) to the city of Nîmes. The upper level was the waterway, the lower a road. In this chapter you will learn how the Romans influenced the development of cities.

- Why was it important to build aqueducts?
- How does your city supply water to its residents?

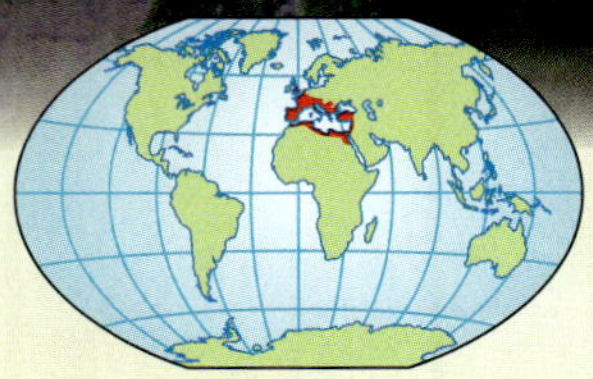

THE WORLD ▶

**650 B.C.** Etruscans rule Rome

**509 B.C.** Start of Roman Republic

**264–146 B.C.** The Punic Wars

**27 B.C.** Augustus becomes Roman emperor

600 B.C. — 300 B.C. — A.D. 1

**A.D. 33**
Death of Jesus in Jerusalem

**A.D. 79**
Volcano destroys Pompeii

A.D. 300

**A.D. 313**
Constantine legalizes Christianity

**A.D. 476**
Fall of the Western Roman Empire

A.D. 500

**FOLDABLES™**
**Study Organizer**

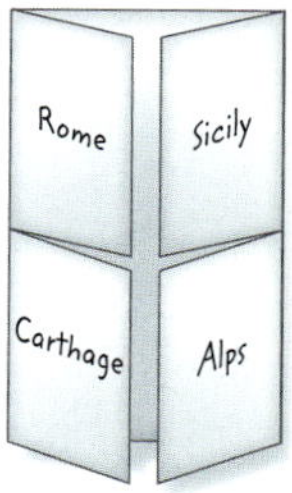


**Analyzing** Create a Four-Door Book to analyze the impact of geography on the rise of Rome. On the inside of the book, write descriptive phrases explaining the geographic importance of Rome, Sicily, Carthage and the Alps to Rome's rise.

**History ONLINE** Visit glencoe.com and enter *QuickPass*™ code GWHEA7447c5 for Chapter 5 resources.

SECTION 1

Section Audio

Spotlight Video

# The Rise of Rome

## GUIDE TO READING

### The BIG Idea

**Order and Security** The Romans conquered and controlled the Italian peninsula and then the entire Mediterranean world.

### Content Vocabulary

- republic *(p. 148)*
- patrician *(p. 148)*
- plebeian *(p. 148)*
- consul *(p. 148)*
- praetor *(p. 148)*

### Academic Vocabulary

- virtually *(p. 148)*
- institutions *(p. 148)*
- inadequate *(p. 149)*

### People and Places

- Rome *(p. 146)*
- Latins *(p. 146)*
- Sicily *(p. 147)*
- Etruscans *(p. 147)*
- Livy *(p. 148)*
- Roman Senate *(p. 148)*
- Carthage *(p. 150)*
- Hannibal *(p. 151)*
- Alps *(p. 151)*

### Reading Strategy

**Categorizing Information** As you read this section, complete a chart like the one shown below listing the government officials and the legislative bodies of the Roman Republic.

| Officials | Legislative Bodies |
|---|---|
| | |
| | |

*Roman history is the story of the Romans' conquest of Italy and the entire Mediterranean world. The Romans were conquerors, but they also governed, using republican forms that have been passed down to us.*

## The Land and Peoples of Italy

**MAIN IDEA** Rome's central location and geographic features made it a desirable location from which to expand.

**HISTORY & YOU** What geographic features led people to settle in your area? Read about the conquest of the Italian peninsula.

Italy is a peninsula extending about 750 miles (1,207 km) from north to south. It is not very wide, averaging about 120 miles (193 km) across. The Apennine (A•puh•NYN) mountain range forms a ridge from north to south, dividing west from east. Italy has some fairly large fertile plains ideal for farming. Most important are the Po River valley in the north; the plain of Latium, where **Rome** is located; and the region of Campania, south of Latium.

As in other civilizations, geography had an impact on Rome's development. The Apennines, less rugged than the mountain ranges of Greece, did not divide the Italian peninsula into many small, isolated communities. Italy also had more land for farming than did Greece, enabling it to support a large population.

Rome's location about 18 miles (29 km) inland on the Tiber River was especially favorable. The river gave Rome a route to the sea, but Rome was far enough inland to be safe from pirates. Because it was built on seven hills, it was easily defended. In addition, it was situated where the Tiber could be forded, making it a natural crossroads. All in all, Rome had a good central location in Italy from which to expand.

The Italian peninsula juts into the Mediterranean Sea, making it an important crossroads between the western and eastern Mediterranean. After the Romans had established their empire around the Mediterranean, governing it was easier because of Italy's location.

Indo-European peoples moved into Italy from about 1500 B.C. to 1000 B.C. We know little about them, but we do know that one group called the **Latins** lived in the region of Latium. These people spoke Latin, which, like Greek, is an Indo-European language.

The Latins were herders and farmers who lived in settlements on the tops of Rome's hills. After about 800 B.C., other people also began settling in Italy—the two most notable being the Greeks and the Etruscans.

**Geography SKILLS**

In 500 B.C., the Etruscans and Greeks occupied much of Italy.

1. **Location** How did Rome's location help the Latins conquer Italy?
2. **Movement** Which geographic features protected the Italian Peninsula from invasion?

The Greeks came to Italy in large numbers during the age of Greek colonization (750 B.C. to 550 B.C.). Starting in southern Italy, they slowly migrated up the peninsula. They also occupied eastern **Sicily**, an island south of the Italian peninsula. The Greeks had much influence on the people of Rome. They cultivated olives and grapes, passed on their alphabet, and gave the Romans artistic and cultural models through their sculpture, architecture, and literature.

It was the **Etruscans,** however, who most influenced the early development of Rome. Located north of Rome in Etruria, they came to control Rome and most of Latium after 650 B.C. The Etruscans found Rome a village and turned it into a city. The Romans adopted Etruscan dress—the toga and short cloak. The Roman army also borrowed its organization from the Etruscans.

**✓Reading Check** **Evaluating** What role did geography play in Rome's prosperity and defensibility?

## The Roman Republic

**MAIN IDEA** The Romans were practical and skillful in politics and military matters.

**HISTORY & YOU** Is the United States a republic? Learn how the Romans governed.

In 509 B.C., the Romans overthrew the last Etruscan king and established a **republic**. In a republic, the leader is not a monarch and some citizens have the right to vote. This was the beginning of a new era in Rome's history.

### War and Conquest

At the beginning of the republic, Rome was surrounded by enemies. For the next two hundred years, the city was engaged in almost continuous warfare. In 338 B.C., Rome crushed the Latin states. During the next 50 years, the Romans waged a fierce struggle against people from the central Apennines. Rome was again victorious, giving the Romans control over a large part of Italy.

History ONLINE
**Student Web Activity—** Visit glencoe.com and complete the activity about the Roman Republic.

It also brought them into direct contact with the Greek communities of southern Italy. By 264 B.C., the Romans had overcome the Greeks and completed their conquest of southern Italy. After defeating the remaining Etruscan states to the north, Rome had conquered **virtually** all of Italy.

To rule Italy, the Romans devised the Roman Confederation. Under this system, Rome allowed some peoples—especially Latins—to have full Roman citizenship. Most of the remaining communities were made allies. They remained free to run their own local affairs but were required to provide soldiers for Rome. The Romans made it clear that loyal allies could improve their status and become Roman citizens. The Romans made the conquered peoples feel they had a stake in Rome's success.

### Successful Strategies

Romans believed that their early ancestors were successful because of their sense of duty, courage, and discipline. The Roman historian **Livy**, writing in the first century B.C., provided a number of stories to teach Romans the virtues that had made Rome great. His account of Cincinnatus (SIHN•suh•NA•tuhs), a simple farmer who was chosen as a temporary ruler to save Rome from attack, is one such example.

What other characteristics made Rome successful? First, the Romans were good diplomats. They were shrewd in extending Roman citizenship and allowing states to run their own internal affairs. Second, the Romans excelled in military matters. They were not only accomplished soldiers but also persistent ones. The loss of an army or a fleet did not cause them to quit but instead spurred them on to build new armies and new fleets. In addition, they were brilliant strategists. As they conquered, the Romans built colonies—fortified towns—throughout Italy. By building roads to connect these towns, the Romans could move troops quickly throughout their conquered territory.

Finally, in law and politics, as in conquest, the Romans were practical. They did not try to build an ideal government but instead created political **institutions** in response to problems, as the problems arose.

### Roman Political Structure

Early Rome was divided into two groups or orders—the patricians and the plebeians (plih•BEE•uhns). The **patricians** were wealthy landowners who became Rome's ruling class. Less wealthy landowners farmers, artisans, and merchants made up the larger group, **plebeians**. Men in both orders were citizens who paid taxes, owed military service, and could vote. Only patricians, however, could be elected to office.

The chief executive officers of the Roman Republic were the **consuls** and **praetors** (PREE•tuhrz). Two consuls, chosen every year, ran the government and led the Roman army into battle. The praetor was in charge of civil law—laws that applied to Roman citizens. As Roman territory expanded, another praetor was added to judge cases involving noncitizens. The Romans also had officials who had special duties, such as supervising the treasury.

The **Roman Senate** came to hold an especially important position in the Roman Republic. It was a select group of about three hundred patricians who served for life. At first, the Senate's only role was to advise government officials. By the third century B.C., however, it had the force of law.

The Roman Republic had several assemblies in addition to the Senate. By far the most important of these was the centuriate assembly, which elected the chief officials, such as consuls and praetors, and passed laws. Because it was organized by classes based on wealth, the wealthiest citizens always had a majority. Another assembly, the council of the plebs, came into being as a result of the struggle between the two Roman social orders.

## The Struggle of the Orders

There was often conflict between the two orders in the early Roman Republic. Children of patricians and plebeians were forbidden to marry each other. Plebeians resented this situation, especially since they served in the Roman army that protected the Republic. They thought that they deserved both political and social equality with the patricians.

The struggle between the patricians and plebeians dragged on for hundreds of years. Ultimately, it led to success for the plebeians. A popular assembly for plebeians only, the council of the plebs, was created in 471 B.C. New officials, known as tribunes of the plebs, had the power to protect the plebeians. In the fourth century B.C., plebeians were permitted to marry patricians and to become consuls.

Finally, in 287 B.C., the council of the plebs received the right to pass laws for all Romans. All male Roman citizens were now supposedly equal under the law. In reality, a few wealthy patrician and plebeian families formed a new senatorial ruling class. The Roman Republic had not become a democracy.

## Roman Law

One of Rome's chief gifts to the Mediterranean world of its day and to later generations was its system of law. Rome's first code of laws was the Twelve Tables, adopted in 450 B.C. This code was a product of a simple farming society and proved **inadequate** for later Roman needs.

### INFOGRAPHICS

### Roman Law

The Twelve Tables were the first written set of laws that were publicly displayed in Rome. Prior to the Twelve Tables the patricians, who both made the laws and served as judges, had clear advantages over plebeians in Roman society. Having the Twelve Tables established and protected certain rights for both patricians and plebeians in the Roman Republic. The original tablets that contained the laws were destroyed when Rome fell, but the idea of establishing rights and procedures in legal systems was adopted by later cultures. The influence of the Twelve Tables can still be seen in legal systems today.

**CRITICAL THINKING SKILLS**

1. **Evaluating** Why would it be important to record and display the laws for citizens to see?
2. **Comparing** Explain how the laws in the table are similar to laws in the United States.

**Twelve Tables of Rome 449 B.C.**

**Table I: Proceedings Preliminary to Trial**
9. If both parties are present, sunset shall be the time limit of the proceedings.

**Table II: Trial**

**Table III: Execution of Judgment**
1. Thirty days shall be allowed by law for payment of confessed debt and for settlement of matters adjudged in court.

**Table IV: Paternal Power**

**Table V: Inheritance and Guardianship**

**Table VI: Ownership and Possession**

**Table VII: Real Property**

**Table VIII: Torts or Delicts**

**Table IX: Public Law**
6. For anyone whomsoever to be put to death without a trial and unconvicted . . . is forbidden.

**Table X: Sacred Law**

**Table XI: Supplementary Laws**

**Table XII: Supplementary Laws**
5. Whatever the people ordain last shall be legally valid.

From the Twelve Tables, the Romans developed a more sophisticated system of civil law. This system applied only to Roman citizens, however, and, as Rome expanded, legal questions arose that involved both Romans and non-Romans. In these cases, special rules were needed. These rules gave rise to a body of law known as the Law of Nations, which the Romans identified with natural law, or universal law based on reason. This enabled them to establish standards of justice that applied to all people.

These standards of justice included principles still recognized today. A person was innocent until proved otherwise. People accused of wrongdoing were allowed to defend themselves before a judge. A judge, in turn, was expected to weigh evidence carefully before arriving at a decision. These principles lived on long after the fall of the Roman Empire.

**✓Reading Check** **Explaining** How were plebeians and patricians different in early Rome?

## Roman Expansion

***MAIN IDEA*** After their conquest of Italy, the Romans faced the state of Carthage.

***HISTORY & YOU*** What causes conflict? Learn why the Romans and Carthaginians fought three wars.

The Phoenicians founded **Carthage** around 800 B.C. on the coast of North Africa. By the third century B.C., Carthage had an enormous trading empire in the western Mediterranean. With colonies from Spain to Sicily, Carthage was the largest and richest state in the area.

### The First Punic War

Rome's first war with Carthage began in 264 B.C. It is called the First Punic War, after the Latin word for Phoenician, *punicus.* The presence of Carthaginians in Sicily, an island close to the Italian coast, made the Romans fearful. The Romans sent an army to Sicily, and the Carthaginians responded. Both sides were determined to control Sicily.

NATIONAL GEOGRAPHIC

**PUNIC WARS, 264–146 B.C.**

**Carthaginian Empire, 264 B.C.**

**Geography SKILLS**

From 264 B.C. to 146 B.C. the Romans fought the Carthaginians in the Punic Wars.

1. **Location** Compare the maps. Which territory did Carthage lose to Rome in the First Punic War?
2. **Movement** Why might Hannibal choose to cross the Alps to get to Rome?

The Romans—a land power—realized that they could not win the war without a navy and built a large fleet. After a long struggle, a Roman fleet defeated the Carthaginian navy, and the war came to an end. Rome gained control over many sea trade routes. In 241 B.C., Carthage gave up all rights to Sicily and paid a fine to the Romans. Sicily became the first Roman province.

Carthage vowed revenge, however, and added new lands in Spain to make up for the loss of Sicily. The Romans encouraged one of Carthage's Spanish allies to revolt against Carthage. **Hannibal**, the greatest Carthaginian general, struck back, beginning the Second Punic War.

## The Second Punic War

Hannibal decided to bring the war to Rome. Hannibal entered Spain, moved east, and crossed the **Alps** with an army of about 46,000 men, a large number of horses, and 37 battle elephants. The Alps took a toll on the Carthaginian army; most of the elephants did not survive, but the remaining army posed a real threat. In 216 B.C., the Romans made a serious mistake; they met Hannibal head-on. At Cannae (KA•nee), the Romans lost an army of almost 40,000 men. On the brink of disaster, the Romans refused to surrender and raised yet another army.

Rome gradually recovered. Although Hannibal remained free to roam Italy, he had neither the men nor the equipment to attack the major cities. The Romans began to reconquer some of the Italian cities that had been taken by Hannibal. They also sent troops to Spain and, by 206 B.C., they had pushed the Carthaginians out of Spain.

Rome invaded Carthage rather than fight Hannibal in Italy, forcing the Carthaginians to recall Hannibal from Italy. At the Battle of Zama in 202 B.C., the Romans, led by Scipio Africanus, crushed Hannibal's forces, and the war was over. Spain became a Roman province. Rome had become the dominant power in the western Mediterranean.

## More Conquests

Fifty years later, the Romans fought their third and final battle with Carthage, the Third Punic War. For years, a number of prominent Romans had called for the complete destruction of Carthage. In 146 B.C., it was destroyed. For ten days, Roman soldiers burned and demolished the city. The inhabitants were sold into slavery. The territory of Carthage became a Roman province called Africa.

During its struggle with Carthage, Rome also battled the Hellenistic states in the eastern Mediterranean. By 129 B.C., Macedonia, Greece, and Pergamum were under Roman control. Rome was now master of the Mediterranean.

✓**Reading Check** **Evaluating** What is the historical and cultural significance of the Roman destruction of Carthage?

## SECTION 1 REVIEW

### Vocabulary

1. **Explain** the significance of: Rome, Latins, Sicily, Etruscans, republic, virtually, Livy, institutions, patrician, plebeian, consul, praetor, Roman Senate, inadequate, Carthage, Hannibal, Alps.

### Main Ideas

2. **List** in order the major events of the Punic Wars.
3. **Describe** the significance of the Twelve Tables and the Law of Nations.
4. **List** ways in which the Greeks influenced the Romans.

### Critical Thinking

5. **The BIG Idea** **Analyzing** What was the importance of the Senate, the centuriate assembly, and council of the plebs to the Roman Republic?
6. **Contrasting** Create a chart that shows the major differences between the patricians and the plebeians.

| Patricians | Plebeians |
|---|---|
| | |
| | |

7. **Assessing** What were the reasons for the conflicts between the patricians and the plebeians, and what were the outcomes?
8. **Analyzing Visuals** Use the maps on pages 147 and 150 and the text to describe the growth of Rome through the era of the Roman Republic.

### Writing About History

9. **Informative Writing** Imagine that you are a journalist covering the Second Punic War. Using the text or outside authoritative sources, write an account of one of the major battles of the war. Be sure to pose and answer questions for both Hannibal and the Roman generals in your account.

**History ONLINE**

For help with the concepts in this section of *Glencoe World History,* go to glencoe.com and click Study Central™.

SECTION 2

Section Audio Spotlight Video

# From Republic to Empire

## GUIDE TO READING

### The BIG Idea

**Struggle for Rights** The internal instability of the Roman Empire eventually led to civil wars and increased power for the military.

### Content Vocabulary

- triumvirate *(p. 154)*
- dictator *(p. 154)*
- imperator *(p. 156)*

### Academic Vocabulary

- financial *(p. 152)*
- instability *(p. 152)*
- whereas *(p. 159)*

### People and Places

- Crassus *(p. 154)*
- Pompey *(p. 154)*
- Julius Caesar *(p. 154)*
- Rubicon River *(p. 154)*
- Octavian *(p. 155)*
- Antony *(p. 155)*
- Augustus *(p. 156)*
- Nero *(p. 157)*
- Pax Romana *(p. 157)*
- Dacia *(p. 158)*
- Sinai Peninsula *(p. 158)*
- Rhine River *(p 158)*
- Danube River *(p. 158)*

### Reading Strategy

**Determining Cause and Effect** As you read, create a diagram like the one below to identify the factors that led to the end of the Roman Republic.

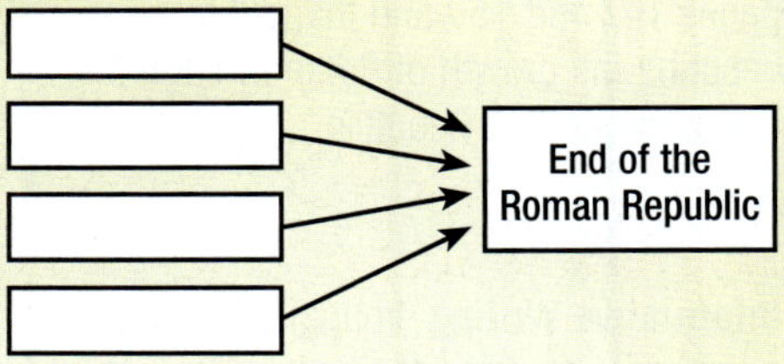


*Early in the days of the Roman Republic, farmers fulfilled their duty to Rome by serving in the army. As Rome grew, the landed aristocracy became more powerful, and the ideals of the Republic changed. By 129 B.C., Rome stood supreme over the Mediterranean Sea, but problems arose in Rome itself.*

## The End of the Roman Republic

**MAIN IDEA** Political and social unrest led to civil wars, ending the Republic.

**HISTORY & YOU** What values do you expect from your leaders? Read how greed helped bring an end to the Republic.

By the second century B.C., the Senate had become the real governing body of the Roman state. Members of the Senate were drawn mostly from the landed aristocracy. They remained senators for life and held the chief offices of the republic. The Senate directed the wars and took control of both foreign and domestic policy, including **financial** affairs.

### Growing Unrest

The Senate and political offices were increasingly controlled by a small circle of wealthy and powerful families. Of course, these aristocrats formed only a tiny minority of the Roman people. The backbone of the Roman state and army had always been the small farmers. Over a period of time, however, many small farmers were unable to compete with large, wealthy landowners and lost their lands. By taking over state-owned land and by buying out small peasant owners, these landed aristocrats had developed large estates that used slave labor. As a result, many of these small farmers drifted to the cities, especially Rome, forming a large class of landless poor.

Some aristocrats tried to remedy the growing economic and social crisis caused by the decline of the small farmer. Two brothers, Tiberius and Gaius Gracchus (GRA•kuhs), urged the council of the plebs to pass land-reform bills that called for the government to take back public land held by large landowners and give it to landless Romans.

Many senators, themselves large landowners whose estates included large areas of public land, were furious. A group of senators took the law into their own hands and killed Tiberius in 133 B.C. His brother Gaius later suffered the same fate. The attempts of the Gracchus brothers to bring reforms had opened the door to more **instability** and more violence. Changes in the Roman army soon brought even worse problems.

PRIMARY SOURCE INFOGRAPHICS

## Martyrs of the Roman Republic

The Gracchus brothers, or the Gracchi, were at the center of the social conflict that eventually destroyed the Roman Republic. After Tiberius Gracchus returned from the Third Punic War, he was elected tribune in 133 B.C. His land reforms aimed to reduce unemployment and save the Roman Republic. When Tiberius bypassed the Senate and took his legislation to the Assembly, he made enemies. In 133 B.C., Tiberius was clubbed to death by a mob, some of whom were members of the Senate.

Elected to the tribunate in 123 B.C., Gaius Gracchus's political and social agenda was more radical. He proposed extending citizenship to non-Romans, lowering food prices, and giving farmers more legal rights. Gaius died at the hands of political opponents in 121 B.C. A new era of political and social conflict followed with some politicians advocating for the urban poor and the landless farmers. The ongoing social struggle resulted in the fall of the Republic.

### The Roman Republic

- **509 B.C.** Foreign ruler overthrown (according to tradition)
- **471 B.C.** Council of the plebs created
- **450 B.C.** Senate publishes Roman law codes: Twelve Tables
- **376 B.C.** Praetors preside over civil trials
- **287 B.C.** Decrees of plebeian assembly have force of law
- **264–133 B.C.** Conquest of Mediterranean: Carthage, Spain, North Africa, Greece, Pergamum
- **60 B.C.** Crassus, Pompey, and Julius Caesar form the First Triumvirate
- **44 B.C.** Assassination of Julius Caesar
- **27 B.C.** Octavian Caesar named Augustus, first emperor of Roman Empire

**CRITICAL THINKING SKILLS**

Bronze double portrait of the Gracchi sculpted by Jean-Baptiste Guillaume in 1800s.

1. **Summarizing** At what time in the history of the Roman Republic did the Gracchi live?
2. **Hypothesizing** Why might a French sculptor create a work honoring Romans who died about 2,000 years before he lived?

## A New Role for the Army

In 107 B.C., a Roman general named Marius became consul and began to recruit his armies in a new way. For a long time, the Roman army had been made up of small farmers who were landholders. Now Marius recruited volunteers from the urban and rural poor who owned no property. To recruit them, he promised them land. These volunteers swore an oath of loyalty to the general, not to the Roman state. As a result, Marius created a new type of army that was not under government control. In addition, generals were forced to become involved in politics to get laws passed that would provide the land they needed for their veterans.

Marius left a powerful legacy. He created a new system of military recruitment that placed great power in the hands of the individual generals.

Lucius Cornelius Sulla was the next general to take advantage of the new military system. The Senate had given him command of a war in Asia Minor. The council of the plebs tried to transfer command to Marius, and a civil war broke out.

Sulla won and seized Rome itself in 82 B.C., conducting a reign of terror to wipe out all opposition. Then Sulla restored power to the hands of the Senate and eliminated most of the powers of the popular assemblies.

Sulla hoped that he had created a firm foundation to restore a traditional Roman republic governed by a powerful Senate. His real legacy was quite different from what he had intended, however. His example of using an army to seize power would prove most attractive to ambitious men.

## The First Triumvirate

For the next 50 years (82–31 B.C.), Roman history was characterized by civil wars as many individuals competed for power. As the Roman historian Sallust observed:

**PRIMARY SOURCE**

"But when our country had grown great through toil, when great kings had been vanquished in war, when Carthage, the rival of Rome's sway, had perished root and branch, then Fortune began to grow cruel. . . . Hence the lust for power first, then for money, grew upon them; these were, I may say, the root of all evils. For greed destroyed honor, integrity, and all other noble qualities. Ambition drove many men to become false; to have one thought locked in the breast, another ready on the tongue; to value friendships and enmities not on their merits but by the standard of self-interest."

—*Sallust*, J. C. Rolfe, trans., 1921

Three men—Crassus, Pompey, and Julius Caesar—emerged as victors of the civil wars. **Crassus** was known as the richest man in Rome. **Pompey** had returned from a successful command in Spain as a military hero. **Julius Caesar** also had a military command in Spain. The combined wealth and power of these three men was enormous and enabled them to dominate the political scene and achieve their basic aims.

In 60 B.C., Caesar joined with Crassus and Pompey to form the First Triumvirate. A **triumvirate** is a government by three people with equal power.

Pompey received a command in Spain, Crassus was given a command in Syria, and Caesar was granted a special military command in Gaul—modern France—where he achieved success and distinction as a military leader. When Crassus was killed in battle in 53 B.C., only two powerful men were left. Fearing Caesar's popularity, leading senators decided that rule by Pompey alone would be to their benefit. They voted for Caesar to lay down his command.

Caesar refused to obey the Senate. While serving in Gaul, he had gained military experience, as well as an army of loyal veterans. He chose to keep his army and to enter Italy by illegally crossing the **Rubicon**, the river that formed the southern boundary of his province. The phrase "crossing the Rubicon" means to take a decisive action that cannot be taken back. Disobeying the Senate was serious. As Judas Maccabees, a Jewish military leader, said of Romans a century earlier:

**PRIMARY SOURCE**

"They had defeated Antiochus the Great, king of Asia. . . . Yet for all this not one of the Romans has put on a crown, but they have built for themselves a senate chamber, and every day three hundred senators constantly deliberate concerning the people, to govern them well."

—Margaret L. King, *Western Civilization*, 2000

Caesar's march on Rome started a civil war between his forces and those of Pompey. Pompey's defeat left Caesar in complete control of the Roman government.

Caesar was officially made **dictator**, or absolute ruler, in 45 B.C. This position was usually temporary, only used in emergencies. Realizing the need for reforms, Caesar gave land to the poor and vastly enlarged the Senate. By filling the Senate with his supporters and increasing the number of Senators, he weakened the Senate's power. He granted citizenship to his supporters in the provinces and introduced the solar calendar. (The Julian calendar is the basis for the one we use today.) Caesar had plans for building projects and military campaigns to the east. Many Senators thought he had plans to continue as dictator. That is why, in 44 B.C., a group of leading senators assassinated him.

## The Second Triumvirate

A new power struggle followed the death of Caesar. Three men—**Octavian**, Caesar's heir and grandnephew; **Antony**, Caesar's ally and assistant; and Lepidus, who had been commander of Caesar's cavalry—joined forces to form the Second Triumvirate. Within a few years after Caesar's death, however, only two men divided the Roman world between them. Octavian took the west; Antony, the east.

The empire of the Romans, large as it was, was still too small for two masters. Octavian and Antony soon came into conflict. Antony allied himself with the Egyptian queen Cleopatra VII. At the Battle of Actium in Greece in 31 B.C., Octavian's forces smashed the army and the navy of Antony and Cleopatra. Both fled to Egypt, where they committed suicide a year later. The Roman historian Florus, writing 40 years later, described the scene.

**PRIMARY SOURCE**

"Antony was the first to commit suicide, by the sword. Cleopatra threw herself at Octavian's feet . . . It was not her life she was after . . . but a portion of her kingdom. When she realized this was hopeless . . . she took advantage of her guard's carelessness to get herself into the royal tomb. Once there, she put on the royal robes . . . lay down in a richly perfumed coffin beside her Antony. Then she applied poisonous snakes to her veins and passed into death as though into a sleep."

—Florus, *Epitome of Roman History*

Octavian, at the age of 32, stood supreme over the Roman world. The civil wars had ended. So had the republic. The period beginning in 31 B.C. and lasting until A.D. 14 came to be known as the Age of Augustus.

✓Reading Check **Summarizing** Why did the Roman Republic fail to survive challenges by Julius Caesar?

# PEOPLE in HISTORY

### Julius Caesar
c. 100 B.C.–44 B.C.

Although he was born into an undistinguished family, Julius Caesar made a name for himself in Roman society. His ambition helped him in his pursuit. He became a great military man and politician. His brilliant military and political careers were aided by his skills as an expert orator and author. He used these skills as political tools to communicate his ideas and shape his political identity. He was an energetic and tireless ruler who helped reform Rome. **How were Caesar's personal qualities important to his success?**

### Augustus
63 B.C.–A.D. 14

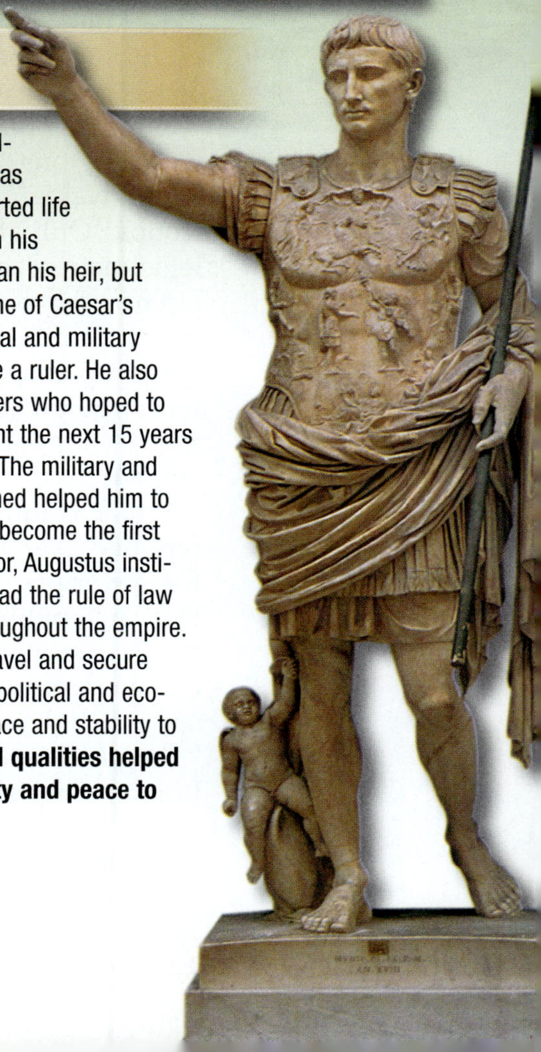

As Julius Caesar's grandnephew, Octavian—who was later called Augustus—started life with more advantages than his uncle. Caesar made Octavian his heir, but only 18 years old at the time of Caesar's death, he lacked the political and military experience necessary to be a ruler. He also had to be content with others who hoped to control the empire. He spent the next 15 years eliminating his opponents. The military and political experience he gained helped him to consolidate his power and become the first Roman emperor. As emperor, Augustus instituted civil service and spread the rule of law and common currency throughout the empire. His armies assured safe travel and secure trade. During his reign his political and economic reforms brought peace and stability to the empire. **What personal qualities helped Augustus to bring stability and peace to the empire?**

## The Beginning of the Roman Empire

**MAIN IDEA** Octavian, titled Caesar Augustus, created a new order that began the Roman Empire.

**HISTORY & YOU** What makes a good government? Learn how the Roman Empire expanded and grew prosperous.

In 27 B.C., Octavian proclaimed the "restoration of the Republic." He knew that only traditional republican forms would satisfy the Senate. At the same time, he was aware that the republic could not be fully restored. Although he gave some power to the Senate, Octavian in fact became the first Roman emperor.

### The Age of Augustus

In 27 B.C., the Senate awarded Octavian the title of **Augustus**—the revered one, a fitting title in view of his power. Augustus proved to be highly popular. No doubt people were glad the civil wars had ended, but his continuing control of the army was the chief source of his power. The Senate gave Augustus the title **imperator**, or commander in chief. The English word *emperor* comes from *imperator*.

Augustus maintained a standing army of 28 legions, or about 151,000 men. A legion was a military unit of about 5,000 troops. Only Roman citizens could be legionnaires—members of a legion. Subject peoples could serve as auxiliary forces, which numbered around 130,000 under Augustus. Augustus also instituted a praetorian guard of roughly 9,000 men who had the important task of guarding the emperor.

While claiming to have restored the republic, Augustus began a new system for governing the provinces. Under the Roman Republic, the Senate had appointed the governors of the provinces. Now, the emperor controlled certain provinces and appointed deputies to govern them.

Augustus stabilized the frontiers of the Roman Empire, conquering many new areas. His attempt to conquer Germany failed, however, when three Roman legions led by the Roman general Varus were massacred by German warriors. These defeats in Germany taught Augustus that Rome's power was not unlimited. This knowledge devastated him. For months, he would beat his head on a door, shouting, "Varus, give me back my legions!"

After the death of Augustus in A.D. 14, a series of new emperors ruled Rome. This period, ending in A.D. 180, is called the Early Empire.

### Emperors and the Early Empire

Augustus's new political system allowed the emperor to select his successor from his natural or adopted family. The first four emperors after Augustus came from his family. They were Tiberius, Caligula, Claudius, and Nero. During their reigns, these emperors took over more and more of the responsibilities that Augustus had given to the Senate. As the emperors grew more powerful, many became more corrupt.

Wherever the Romans went, they built baths. This one in Bath, England, has the original Roman lead pipes.

**Nero**, for example, had people killed if he wanted them out of the way, including his own mother. Without troops, the senators were unable to oppose his excesses, but the Roman legions finally revolted. Nero, abandoned by his guards, committed suicide after allegedly uttering these final words: "What an artist the world is losing in me."

After Nero's death, a civil war broke out in A.D. 69. It soon became obvious that the Roman Empire had a major flaw. Without a system for selecting a new emperor, emperors could be made and deposed by the Roman legions.

At the beginning of the second century, a series of five so-called good emperors came to power. They were Nerva, Trajan, Hadrian, Antoninus Pius, and Marcus Aurelius. These emperors concluded a period of peace and prosperity known as the **Pax Romana**—the Roman Peace. The Pax Romana lasted for almost 200 years (27 B.C.–A.D. 180). These rulers treated the ruling classes with respect, ended arbitrary executions, maintained peace in the empire, and supported domestic policies generally helpful to the empire. Although they were absolute rulers, they were known for their tolerance. By adopting capable men as their sons and successors, the first four good emperors reduced the chances of succession problems.

Under the five good emperors, the powers of the emperor continued to expand at the expense of the Senate's powers. Officials appointed and directed by the emperor took over the running of the government. The good emperors also created new social programs. Trajan, for example, provided state funds to assist poor parents in the raising and educating of their children. The good emperors were widely praised for their building programs. Trajan and Hadrian were especially active in building public works—aqueducts, bridges, roads, and harbor facilities—throughout the provinces and in Rome.

INFOGRAPHICS

## The Five Good Emperors

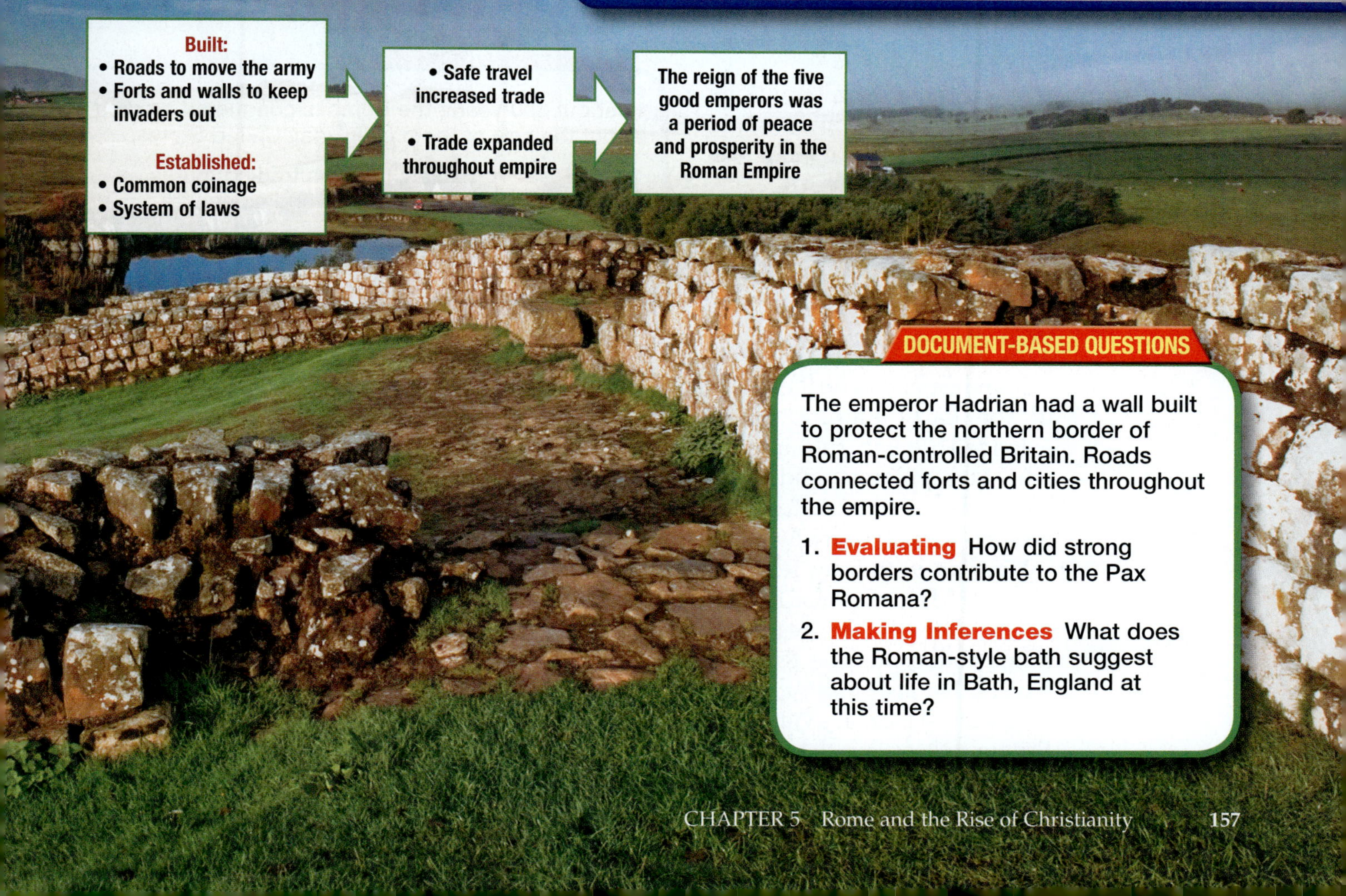


**DOCUMENT-BASED QUESTIONS**

The emperor Hadrian had a wall built to protect the northern border of Roman-controlled Britain. Roads connected forts and cities throughout the empire.

1. **Evaluating** How did strong borders contribute to the Pax Romana?
2. **Making Inferences** What does the Roman-style bath suggest about life in Bath, England at this time?

**Geography SKILLS**

In about 350 years, the Romans conquered an area about the size of the present-day United States.

1. **Movement** Explain how the trading routes helped to strengthen Rome and its empire.
2. **Regions** Why did control of the Mediterranean region benefit Rome's economy?

## The Empire Expands

Rome expanded further during the period of the Early Empire. Although Trajan extended Roman rule into **Dacia** (Romania), Mesopotamia, and the **Sinai Peninsula,** his successors realized that the empire was too large to be easily governed.

Hadrian withdrew Roman forces from much of Mesopotamia. To protect the frontier, he strengthened the fortifications along a line connecting the **Rhine** and **Danube Rivers**. He also built a 74-mile-(118-km-) long wall—Hadrian's Wall—across northern Britain to keep out the Picts and the Scots.

By the end of the second century, it became apparent that it would be more and more difficult to defend the empire. Roman forces were located in permanent bases behind the frontiers. When one frontier was attacked, however, troops were drawn from another, leaving those frontiers open to attack.

At its height in the second century, the Roman Empire was one of the greatest states the world had ever seen. It covered about three and a half million square miles (9.1 million square km) and had a population that has been estimated at more than 50 million.

The emperors and the imperial government provided a degree of unity throughout the empire. At the same time, the Romans gave much leeway to local customs. The privileges of Roman citizenship were granted to many people in the provinces. In A.D. 212, the emperor Caracalla gave Roman citizenship to every free person in the empire.

The administration of the Roman Empire depended greatly on cities and towns. A provincial governor's staff was not large, so local officials acted as Roman agents, performing many government duties, especially taxation.

Most cities were not large by modern standards. Provincial cities resembled each other because they followed a Roman plan. Each Roman-built city contained temples, markets, and public buildings, such as law courts and baths. These cities were important in the spread of Roman culture, Roman law, and the Latin language. (Romance languages, Italian, French, Spanish, Portuguese, and Romanian, are based on Latin and spoken throughout the former Roman Empire.) Latin was the language of the western part of the empire, **whereas** Greek was used in the east as a result of Alexander the Great's earlier conquests. Roman culture spread and freely mixed with Greek culture. The result has been called Greco-Roman civilization.

## Economy and Society

The Early Empire was a period of much prosperity, with internal peace leading to high levels of trade. Merchants from all over the empire came to the chief Italian ports of Puteoli (pyu•TEE•uh•LY) on the Bay of Naples and Ostia at the mouth of the Tiber.

Trade went beyond the Roman frontiers as well and included even silk goods from China. Large quantities of grain were imported, especially from Egypt, to feed the people of Rome. Luxury items poured in to satisfy the desires of the wealthy. It could be said the Roman Empire was the first consumption-oriented society in the West.

Despite the active trade and commerce, however, farming remained the chief occupation of most people and the underlying basis of Roman prosperity. Large landed estates, called latifundia (LA•tuh•FUHN•dee•uh), dominated farming in southern and central Italy. These estates mostly used slaves to raise sheep and cattle on a large scale. Small peasant farms continued to exist in northern Italy.

An enormous gulf separated rich and poor in Roman society. The upper classes lived lives of leisure and luxury in their villas and on their vast estates. Small farmers became dependent on the huge estates of their wealthy neighbors. In the cities, many poor citizens worked in shops and markets. Thousands of unemployed depended on the emperor's handouts of grain to survive.

✓Reading Check **Summarizing** What were the economic conditions and chief occupations in Rome during the Early Empire?

## SECTION 2 REVIEW

### Vocabulary

1. **Explain** the significance of: financial, instability, Crassus, Pompey, Julius Caesar, triumvirate, Rubicon River, dictator, Octavian, Antony, Augustus, imperator, Nero, Pax Romana, Dacia, Sinai Peninsula, Rhine River, Danube River, whereas.

### Main Ideas

2. **Describe** the problems that led to the end of the Roman Republic.
3. **Explain** how Augustus's political system provided for succession of rulers in the empire.
4. **List** the differences between the Roman Republic and the Roman Empire.

### Critical Thinking

5. **The BIG Idea** **Analyzing** What qualities made the "good emperors" good in comparison to Augustus's successors?
6. **Comparing and Contrasting** Create a Venn diagram like the one shown below to compare and contrast the accomplishments of the three men.

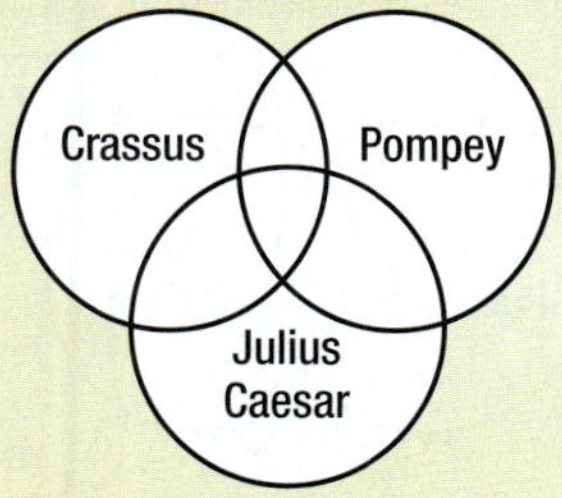


7. **Analyzing Visuals** Examine the statues on page 155. How are they similar? Why might this be true?

### Writing About History

8. **Persuasive Writing** Pretend you are part of the council of the plebs. Argue for or against the land reforms instituted by Tiberius and Gaius Gracchus.

History ONLINE
For help with the concepts in this section of *Glencoe World History,* go to glencoe.com and click Study Central™.

SECTION 3

Section Audio    Spotlight Video

# Roman Culture and Society

## GUIDE TO READING

**The BIG Idea**

**Ideas, Beliefs, and Values** The Romans spread both Greek and Roman contributions to art, architecture, and literature throughout the empire.

**Content Vocabulary**

- paterfamilias *(p. 162)*
- *insulae (p. 165)*

**Academic Vocabulary**

- primary *(p. 162)*
- contractor *(p. 164)*

**People and Places**

- Virgil *(p. 161)*
- Livy *(p. 162)*
- Horace *(p. 161)*
- Spartacus *(p. 164)*

**Reading Strategy**

**Compare and Contrast** As you read this section, create a Venn diagram like the one shown below comparing and contrasting the lifestyle of a wealthy Roman with that of a poor citizen.

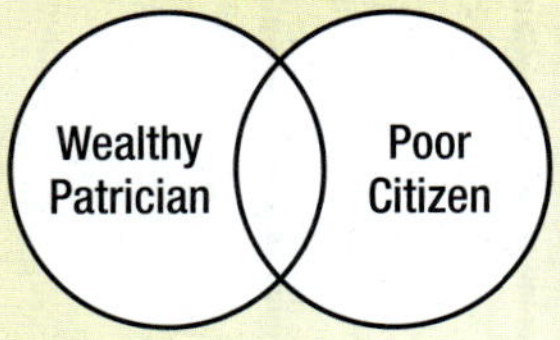


*After they conquered Greece, the Romans adopted many aspects of Greek culture and society. As the Roman poet Horace said, "Captive Greece took captive her rude conqueror."*

## Roman Arts and Literature

**MAIN IDEA** The Romans spread Greco-Roman arts and culture throughout the empire.

**HISTORY & YOU** Have you ever borrowed a style from someone you admire? Learn how Rome borrowed from Greece.

As part of their plunder, Roman military commanders shipped Greek manuscripts and artworks back to Rome. By adapting Greek styles, the Romans spread Greco-Roman civilization throughout their empire.

### Art and Architecture

During the third and second centuries B.C., the Romans adopted many features of the Greek style of art. They developed a taste for Greek statues, which they placed in public buildings and in their houses. Reproductions of Greek statues became popular once the supply of original works ran low. While Greek sculptors aimed for an ideal appearance in their figures, Roman sculptors produced more realistic works that included even unattractive physical details. They painted portraits and landscapes on the walls of villas.

The Romans excelled in architecture, a highly practical art. Although they continued to use Greek styles such as colonnades and rectangular buildings, the Romans also used curved forms: the arch, the vault, and the dome. The Romans were the first people in antiquity to use concrete on a massive scale. Using concrete along with the new architectural forms made it possible for the Romans to construct huge buildings undreamed of by the Greeks.

The Romans were superb builders. Their remarkable engineering skills were put to use constructing roads, bridges, and aqueducts. The Romans built a network of some 50,000 miles (80,450 km) of roads throughout the empire. In Rome, almost a dozen aqueducts kept a population of one million supplied with water.

### Literature

Although there were many talented writers, the high point of Latin literature was reached in the Age of Augustus. Indeed, the

# Connecting to the United States

## Washington, D.C.

When Pierre Charles L'Enfant developed the plan for Washington, D.C., he based it on Roman city planning. Streets were laid out in a grid, and government buildings arranged around an open area—The Mall.

Many of the capital's buildings are also based on Roman models. The United States Capitol dome and the Jefferson Memorial borrow from the Pantheon in Rome. Roman temples had a raised base, or podium, with steps leading to a columned porch. The best preserved Roman temple is the Maison Carrée in Nîmes, France, the model for the United States Supreme Court Building.

- **The layout of the city reflects the influence of Roman city planning.**
- **Roman building styles influenced much of the architecture in Washington, D.C.**

Supreme Court Building, Washington, D.C.

Maison Carrée in Nîmes, France

**Connecting to Today**

1. **Identifying** Name three other buildings in Washington, D.C., that may have been based on Roman architecture.
2. **Hypothesizing** Based on what you know about the Roman Republic, why do you think the architects of Washington, D.C., based the city plan and buildings on Roman models?

Augustan Age has been called the golden age of Latin literature.

The most distinguished poet of the Augustan Age was **Virgil**. The son of a small landholder in northern Italy near Mantua, he welcomed the rule of Augustus and wrote his masterpiece, the *Aeneid* (ih•NEE•uhd), in honor of Rome. Virgil's epic poem was meant to rival the work of Homer. The character Aeneas is the ideal Roman whose virtues are duty, piety, and faithfulness. Aeneas fulfilled his purpose by establishing the Romans in Italy and starting Rome on its mission to rule the world. The poem was also meant to express that Rome's gift was the art of ruling.

### Primary Source

"Let others fashion from bronze more lifelike, breathing images—For so they shall—and evoke living faces from marble; Others excel as orators, others track with their instruments the planets circling in heaven and predict when stars will appear. But, Romans, never forget that government is your medium! Be this your art: to practise men in the habit of peace, generosity to the conquered, and firmness against aggressors."

—*Aeneid*, C. Day Lewis, trans., 1952

Another prominent Augustan poet was **Horace**, a friend of Virgil's. He was a sophisticated writer who enjoyed pointing out some of the "follies and vices of his age."

In his works, Horace mostly laughs at the weaknesses of humans. In the *Satires*, Horace directs attacks against job dissatisfaction and greed: "How does it happen, Maecenas, that no man alone is content with his lot?"

The most famous Latin prose work of the golden age was written by the historian **Livy**, whose masterpiece was *The Early History of Rome*. In 142 books, of which only 35 survive, Livy traced Roman history to 9 B.C. Livy saw history in terms of moral lessons.

**PRIMARY SOURCE**

> "The study of history is the best medicine for a sick mind; for in history you have a record of the infinite variety of human experience plainly set out for all to see; and in that record you can find for yourself and your country both examples and warnings: fine things to take as models, base things, rotten through and through, to avoid."
>
> —Livy, *The Early History of Rome*

His stories revealed the character of the chief figures and demonstrated the virtues that had made Rome great. Livy had a serious weakness as a historian: he was not always concerned about the factual accuracy of his stories. He did tell a good tale, and his work became the standard history of Rome for a long time. One such tale is about a simple farmer, Cincinnatus, whom the Senate names dictator to save Rome.

**PRIMARY SOURCE**

> "A delegation from the city found him at work on his land—digging a ditch, maybe, or ploughing. Greetings were exchanged, and he was asked . . . to put on his toga and hear the Senate's instructions. . . he told his wife to run to their cottage and fetch his toga . . . and wiping the grimy sweat from his hands and face he put it on; at once the envoys from the city saluted him, with congratulations, as Dictator. . ."
>
> —Livy, *The Early History of Rome*

After Cincinnatus led the army to victory, he resigned as dictator and returned to his farm.

✓ Reading Check **Evaluating** Why are Livy's histories considered important to historians?

## Life in Ancient Rome

MAIN IDEA City life in ancient Rome had problems similar to life today.

HISTORY & YOU Have you visited a city that was beautiful, noisy, and crowded? Read about life in ancient Rome.

At the heart of the Roman social structure stood the family, headed by the **paterfamilias**—the dominant male. The household also included the wife, sons with their wives and children, unmarried daughters, and slaves.

### Family Life and Women's Roles

Unlike the Greeks, the Romans raised their children at home. All Roman upper-class children—boys and girls—were expected to learn to read. The father was the chief figure in providing for the education of his children. He decided whether to teach his children himself, acquire a teacher for them, or send them to school. Teachers were often Greek slaves because upper-class Romans had to learn Greek to prosper in the empire.

Roman boys learned reading and writing, moral principles and family values, law, and physical training to prepare them to be soldiers. At age 16, childhood ended for Roman males. At a special ceremony, a young Roman exchanged his purple-edged toga for a plain white toga—the toga of manhood.

Some parents in upper-class families provided education for their daughters by hiring private tutors or sending the girls to **primary** schools. However, at the age when boys were entering secondary schools, girls were entering into marriage.

Like the Greeks, Roman males believed that the weakness of females made it necessary for women to have male guardians. The paterfamilias had that responsibility. When he died, his sons or nearest male relatives assumed the role of guardian. Fathers also arranged the marriages of their daughters.

For females, the legal minimum age for marriage was 12, although 14 was a more common age. For males, the legal minimum age was 14, although most men married later. Traditionally, Roman marriages were meant to be for life, but divorce was introduced in the third century B.C. and became fairly easy to obtain. Either husband or wife could ask for a divorce.

By the A.D. 100s, changes were occurring in the Roman family. The paterfamilias no longer had absolute authority over his children. He could not sell his children into slavery or have them put to death. The husband's absolute authority over his wife also disappeared. Women were no longer required to have guardians.

Upper-class Roman women in the Early Empire had considerable freedom and independence. They had the right to own, inherit, and sell property. Unlike Greek wives, Roman wives were not segregated from males in the home. Outside their homes, upper-class women could attend races, the theater, and the amphitheater; however, they had to sit in separate female sections. When they went out, women of rank were still accompanied by maids and companions. Women could not participate in politics but influenced politics through their husbands.

**HISTORY & ARTS** **PRIMARY SOURCE**

## Roman Life

Most Roman meals were meatless, but bread was served with every meal. Seafood, cheese, fruits, olives, and vegetables made up the bulk of the Roman diet. Archaeologists have found few ovens inside homes, concluding that many families bought their bread from community bakeries that supplied many types of bread. Ancient Roman writers recorded some recipes in their works.

**Recipe: pear dessert**
**Grind boiled and cored pears with pepper, cumin, honey, passum [wine], garum [fish sauce], and a bit of oil. When the eggs have been added, make a patina [pudding], sprinkle pepper over, and serve.**
**—reprinted from "A Taste of Ancient Rome," by Ilaria Gozzini Giacosa**

Mosaic showing bread going into an oven

**DOCUMENT-BASED QUESTIONS**

Mosaics are made of small pieces of colored tiles. This mosaic of a servant in a kitchen was discovered in Pompeii.

1. **Identifying** What foods are pictured in the mosaics?
2. **Drawing Conclusions** What do the mosaics tell us about food in Rome and the provinces?

HISTORY & ARTS PRIMARY SOURCE

## Circus Maximus

Chariot races, horse races, and athletic contests were held at the Circus Maximus, Latin for *great circle.* Enlarged over a period of 600 years, at its largest the Circus Maximus was more than 2,000 feet long, could hold 300,000 people, and had three tiers.

Chariot racing was dangerous, with serious crashes sometimes resulting in death. Four teams, or factions, participated in the races. Winnings from the races went to the owner of the faction, but the winning charioteer often received a portion. Many charioteers were slaves who used the money to purchase their freedom.

**DOCUMENT-BASED QUESTIONS**

1. **Describing** How did the Circus Maximus resemble stadiums today?
2. **Evaluating** What about the chariot races appealed to the audience?

## Slavery and Slave Revolts

Slavery was common throughout the ancient world, but no people had more slaves or relied so much on slave labor as the Romans did. Before the third century B.C., a small Roman farmer might possess one or two slaves, who would help farm his few acres and work in the house. These slaves would most likely be from Italy and be regarded as a part of the family household. The very rich would have many slaves.

The Roman conquest of the Mediterranean brought a change in the use of slaves. Large numbers of foreign peoples who had been captured in wars were brought back to Italy as slaves.

Greek slaves were in much demand as tutors, musicians, doctors, and artists. Roman businessmen would employ them as shop assistants or craftspeople. Slaves of all nationalities were used as household workers, such as cooks, valets, waiters, cleaners, and gardeners. Slaves were used as farm laborers on the large estates of the wealthy. Roads, aqueducts, and other public structures were built by **contractors** using slave labor.

The conditions under which these slaves lived were often pitiful. One Roman writer argued that it was cheaper to work slaves to death and then replace them than it was to treat them well.

Some slaves revolted against their owners and even murdered them, causing some Romans to live in great fear of their slaves. The murder of a master by a slave might mean the execution of all the other household slaves.

The most famous slave revolt in Italy occurred in 73 B.C. Led by the gladiator **Spartacus**, the revolt broke out in southern Italy and involved 70,000 slaves. Spartacus managed to defeat several Roman armies before being trapped and killed in 71 B.C. The Romans crucified—put to death by nailing to a cross—6,000 of Spartacus's followers.

## Living Conditions in Rome

At the center of the colossal Roman Empire was Rome. Truly a capital city, Rome had the largest population of any city in the empire—close to one million by the time of Augustus. People from all over the empire resided there. Rome was the place to be.

Rome boasted public buildings unequaled anywhere in the empire. Its temples, markets, baths, theaters, governmental buildings, and amphitheaters gave parts of the city an appearance of grandeur and magnificence. On the other hand, Rome was an overcrowded and noisy city. Because of the congestion, cart and wagon traffic was banned from the streets during the day. However, the noise from the traffic at night often made sleep difficult. Walking in Rome at night was also dangerous. Although Augustus had organized a police force, people were assaulted or robbed. They could also be soaked by filth thrown out of the upper-story windows of Rome's massive apartment buildings.

A large gulf existed between rich and poor. The rich had comfortable villas, while the poor lived in apartment blocks called ***insulae***, which might be six stories high. Constructed of concrete walls with wooden beam floors, these buildings were usually poorly built and often collapsed.

Fire was a constant threat in the insulae where stoves, torches, candles, and lamps were used for heat and light. Once started, fires were extremely difficult to put out. The famous fire of A.D. 64, which Nero was falsely accused of starting, destroyed a large part of the city.

High rents forced entire families to live in one room. There was no plumbing or central heating. These conditions made homes uncomfortable, so many poor Romans spent most of their time outdoors in the streets.

Although it was the center of a great empire, Rome had serious problems. Beginning with Augustus, the emperors provided food for the city poor. About two hundred thousand people received free grain. Even so, conditions remained grim for the poor.

Large-scale entertainment was provided for the inhabitants of Rome. The poet Juvenal said of the Roman masses, "But nowadays, with no vote . . . , their motto is 'Couldn't care less.' Time was when their vote elected generals, heads of state, commanders of legions: but now . . . there's only two things that concern them: Bread and Circuses."

Public spectacles were provided by the emperor as part of the great religious festivals celebrated by the state. The festivals included three major types of entertainment. At the Circus Maximus, horse and chariot races attracted hundreds of thousands. Dramatic performances were held in theaters. The most famous of all the public spectacles, however, were the gladiatorial shows.

✓ **Reading Check** **Evaluating** Why did the Roman emperors provide free grain to the poor?

## SECTION 3 REVIEW

### Vocabulary

1. **Explain** the significance of: Virgil, Horace, Livy, paterfamilias, primary, contractor, Spartacus, *insulae*.

### Main Ideas

2. **Discuss** the role of slaves in Roman society. Why did some Romans live in great fear of their slaves?
3. **Explain** Why do historians not find Livy a reliable source of information?
4. **Describe** the lives of males and females in Roman society.

### Critical Thinking

5. **The BIG Idea** **Comparing** How is life in a modern city similar to life in ancient Rome?
6. **Summarizing Information** Create a table like the one below describing the contributions of the Greeks and the Romans to Western civilization.

| Greek Contributions | Roman Contributions |
|---|---|
| | |
| | |

7. **Analyzing Visuals** Examine the mosaic on page 163. How is the servant portrayed? Can you identify the servant's age or gender?

### Writing About History

8. **Expository Writing** In this section there are several excerpts from Roman writers. What does each passage reveal about Roman life and society?

**History ONLINE**

For help with the concepts in this section of *Glencoe World History*, go to glencoe.com and click Study Central™.

# Games of Death in Ancient Rome

Public spectacles have always been a part of civilization. The earliest city-states held ceremonies where the punishment of criminals, the awarding of honors, and parades of soldiers were conducted for all to see. Such events reinforced cultural values and the existing social order. In ancient Rome, the most mesmerizing public spectacles were of gladiators fighting to the death. They embodied the Roman virtues of bravery, honor, and glory in a world that was cruel and unpredictable.

## The Arena

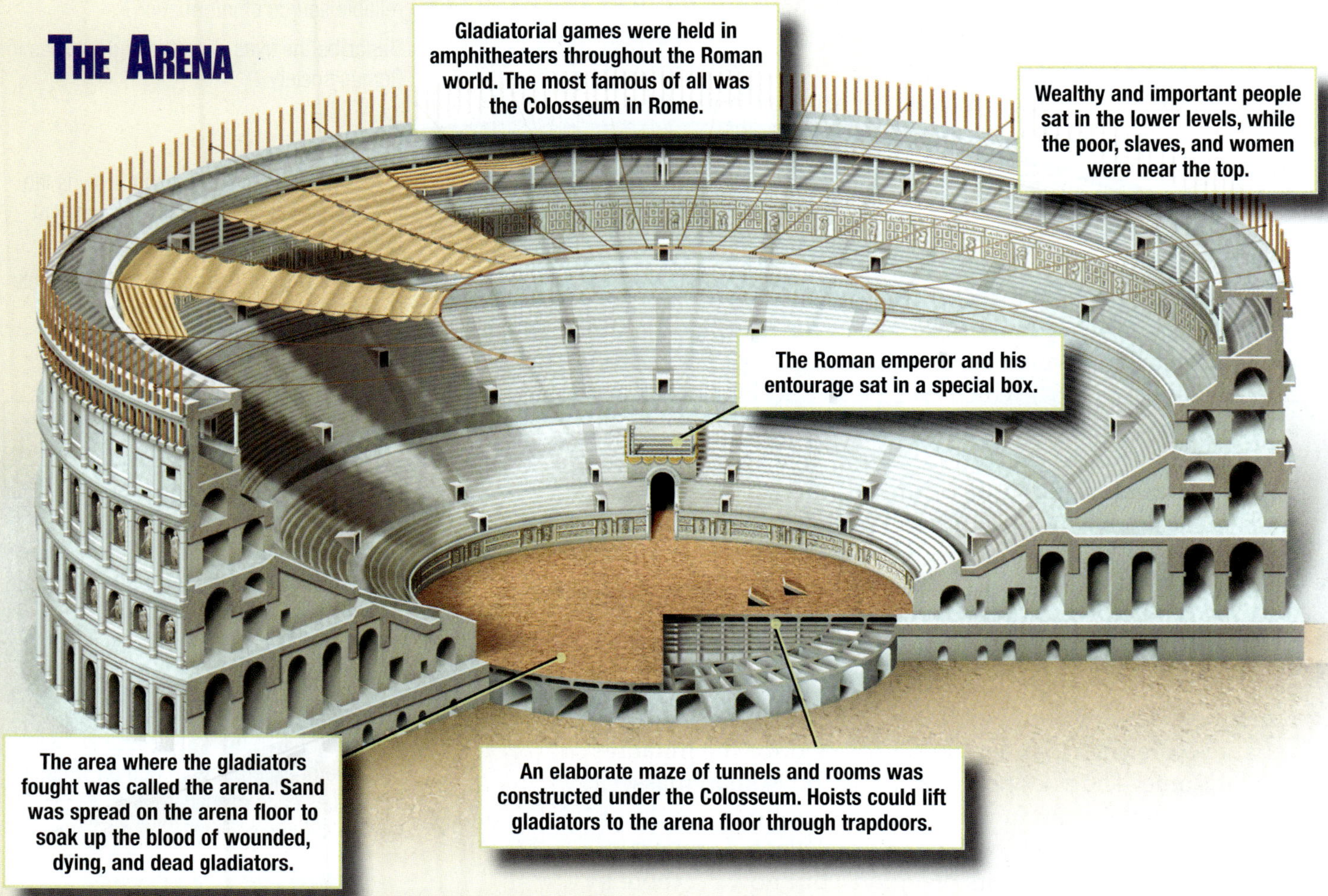


## Gladiators in Roman Society

Gladiatorial combat began as funerary rites and evolved into spectacles sponsored by the wealthy to gain prestige. The fights were wildly popular, and so were taken over by the government and later by the emperor himself. The Roman view of gladiatorial combat was complex. Men who ran training schools for gladiators were wealthy, but were looked down upon socially. The gladiators were admired as kinds of heroes, but most of them were slaves, prisoners of war, or criminals.

## The Combatants

## A Retiarius ("Net-man")

His strategy is to keep his distance, strike with the trident when he can, capture his opponent with the net, and then finish him off with the dagger. His lack of armor is both an advantage—he is mobile—and a disadvantage—he is vulnerable.

## A Secutor ("Pursuer")

He plans to pursue his opponent and strike him down with the sword. His equipment provides protection, but he must come in close to attack, making him vulnerable to the reach of his opponent's trident and net.

## Gladiatorial Styles

**The *secutor* and the *retiarius* were but two of many types of gladiators. Each type was equipped with unique equipment for different fighting styles. Many of the gladiatorial types were supposed to emulate Rome's enemies. The *Thraex* type, for example, represented the fighting man of Thrace. Arguments about the advantages and disadvantages of each gladiator type added to the sheer spectacle of the bloody duels.**

### Analyzing Visuals

1. **Comparing and Contrasting** What modern events are comparable to gladiatorial combat? How are they similar to or different from the Roman events?
2. **Making Judgments** How might you explain the existence of gladiatorial combat in the highly developed Roman civilization?

SECTION 4

Section Audio    Spotlight Video

# The Development of Christianity

## GUIDE TO READING

### The BIG Idea

**Ideas, Beliefs, and Values**

Christianity spread throughout the Roman Empire and eventually became the state religion of Rome.

### Content Vocabulary

- procurator *(p.169)*
- New Testament *(p. 170)*
- clergy *(p. 173)*
- laity *(p. 173)*

### Academic Vocabulary

- guarantee *(p. 168)*
- transformation *(p. 170)*
- structure *(p. 173)*

### People and Places

- Judaea *(p. 169)*
- Jerusalem *(p. 169)*
- Jesus *(p. 170)*
- Simon Peter *(p. 170)*
- Paul *(p. 170)*
- Aegean Sea *(p. 170)*
- Constantine *(p. 173)*
- Theodosius the Great *(p. 173)*

### Reading Strategy

**Summarizing Information** In the diagram below, identify the political views held by the three groups.

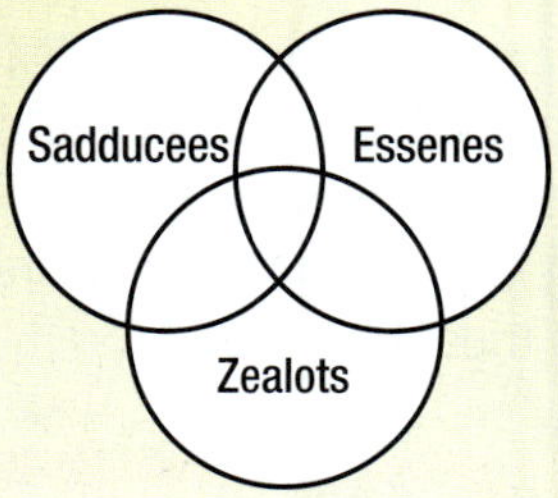


*Christian views on God, human beings, and the world were quite different from those of the Greeks and Romans. For example, Christian beliefs held that one would be taken care of and his or her needs met by seeking righteousness from one God. In contrast, Romans believed in many gods, even accepting foreign gods and philosophical practices into their culture. The rise of Christianity marked an important break with the dominant values of the Greek and Roman worlds.*

## Religion in the Roman Empire

**MAIN IDEA** Prior to Christianity, Roman religion involved the worship of a number of gods and goddesses and the belief that Rome had earned the favor of the gods.

***HISTORY & YOU*** How has the immigration of people from other parts of the world influenced religion in the United States? Read to learn how various religions and beliefs from the Hellenistic east affected religion in the Roman Empire.

Augustus brought back traditional festivals and ceremonies to revive the Roman state religion, which had declined during the turmoil of the late Roman Republic. The official state religion focused on the worship of a number of gods and goddesses, including Jupiter, Juno, Minerva, and Mars. In addition, beginning with Augustus, emperors were often officially made gods by the Roman Senate, thus bolstering support for the emperors.

### Roman Religion

The Romans believed that the observance of proper ritual by state priests brought them into a right relationship with the gods. This **guaranteed** peace and prosperity. Indeed, the Romans believed that their success in creating an empire meant that they had earned the favor of the gods. As the politician Cicero claimed in the first century B.C., "We have overcome all the nations of the world, because we have realized that the world is directed and governed by the gods."

At the same time, the Romans were tolerant of other religions. They allowed the worship of native gods and goddesses throughout their provinces. They even adopted some of the local gods.

After the Romans conquered the states of the Hellenistic east, religions from those regions flooded the western Roman world. The desire for a more emotional spiritual experience drew many people to these religions. They promised their followers an entry

INFOGRAPHICS

## Roman Religion and Mythology

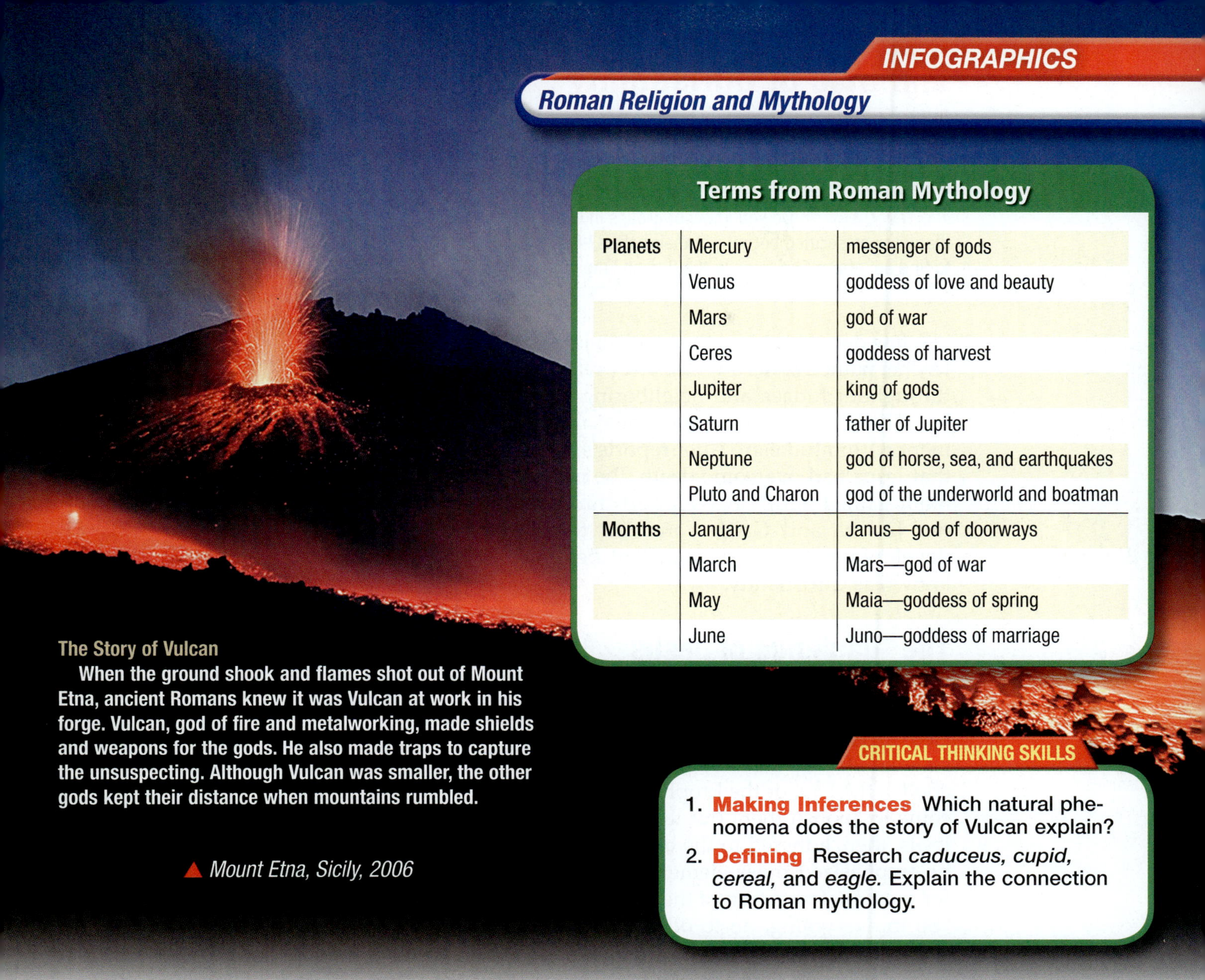

**Terms from Roman Mythology**

| | | |
|---|---|---|
| **Planets** | Mercury | messenger of gods |
| | Venus | goddess of love and beauty |
| | Mars | god of war |
| | Ceres | goddess of harvest |
| | Jupiter | king of gods |
| | Saturn | father of Jupiter |
| | Neptune | god of horse, sea, and earthquakes |
| | Pluto and Charon | god of the underworld and boatman |
| **Months** | January | Janus—god of doorways |
| | March | Mars—god of war |
| | May | Maia—goddess of spring |
| | June | Juno—goddess of marriage |

**The Story of Vulcan**

**When the ground shook and flames shot out of Mount Etna, ancient Romans knew it was Vulcan at work in his forge. Vulcan, god of fire and metalworking, made shields and weapons for the gods. He also made traps to capture the unsuspecting. Although Vulcan was smaller, the other gods kept their distance when mountains rumbled.**

▲ *Mount Etna, Sicily, 2006*

**CRITICAL THINKING SKILLS**

1. **Making Inferences** Which natural phenomena does the story of Vulcan explain?
2. **Defining** Research *caduceus, cupid, cereal,* and *eagle.* Explain the connection to Roman mythology.

into a higher world of reality and the promise of a future life superior to the present one. It was believed that, by participating in these ceremonies, a person could communicate with spiritual beings and open the door to life after death.

## Judaism in the Empire

In Hellenistic times, the Jewish people had been given considerable independence. By A.D. 6, however, **Judaea**, which embraced the lands of the old Jewish kingdom of Judah, had been made a Roman province placed under the direction of an official called a **procurator**.

Unrest was widespread in Judaea, but the Jews differed among themselves about Roman rule. The priestly Sadducees (SA•juh•SEEZ) favored cooperation with Rome. The scholarly Pharisees (FAR•uh•SEEZ) held that close observance of religious law would protect them from Roman influences. The Essenes lived apart from society, sharing goods in common. Like many other Jews, they waited for God to save Israel from oppression. The Zealots, however, called for the violent overthrow of Roman rule. In fact, a Jewish revolt began in A.D. 66, only to be crushed by the Romans four years later. The Jewish temple in **Jerusalem** was destroyed.

✓ Reading Check **Explaining** How were religion and government connected in the Roman Empire?

## The Rise of Christianity

**MAIN IDEA** Although Christians were initially persecuted, Christianity grew in importance and spread throughout the Roman Empire.

**HISTORY & YOU** Do you know of groups in history that were persecuted because of their beliefs? Read to find out about Christians in the Roman Empire.

A few decades before the revolt, a Jewish teacher named **Jesus** traveled and preached throughout Judaea and neighboring Galilee. These teachings began a new movement within Judaism. After reports spread that Jesus had overcome death, the movement gained additional support throughout Judaea and Galilee and led to the development of a new faith that became known as Christianity.

### The Teachings of Jesus

Jesus believed that his mission was to complete the salvation that God had promised to Israel throughout its history. He stated: "Do not think that I have come to abolish the Law or the Prophets; I have not come to abolish them but to fulfill them." Jesus, then, adhered to the entire Law, but he emphasized those elements that called for the **transformation** of the inner person: "So in everything, do to others what you would have them do to you, for this sums up the Law and the Prophets."

Citing verses from the Hebrew Bible, Jesus said, "Love the Lord your God with all your heart and with all your soul and with all your mind and with all your strength. This is the first commandment. The second is this: Love your neighbor as yourself." Jesus shared these and related ethical concepts with other prominent Jewish teachers, but he gave them particularly eloquent and influential expression. The concepts—humility, charity, and love toward others—later shaped the value system of Western civilization.

Jesus' preaching stirred controversy. Some people saw him as a potential revolutionary who might lead a revolt against Rome. His opponents finally turned him over to Roman authorities. The procurator Pontius Pilate ordered Jesus' crucifixion.

After the death of Jesus, his followers proclaimed that he had risen from death and had appeared to them. They believed Jesus to be the Messiah (anointed one), the long-expected deliverer who would save Israel from its foes and inaugurate an age of peace, prosperity, and monotheism.

### Christianity Spreads Through the Empire

Prominent apostles, or leaders, arose in early Christianity. One was **Simon Peter,** a Jewish fisherman who had become a follower of Jesus during Jesus' lifetime. Peter was recognized as the leader of the apostles. Another major apostle was **Paul,** a highly educated Jewish Roman citizen who joined the movement later. Paul took the message of Jesus to Gentiles—non-Jews—as well as to Jews. He founded Christian communities in Asia Minor and along the shores of the **Aegean Sea.**

At the center of Paul's message was the belief that Jesus was the Savior, the Son of God who had come to Earth to save humanity. Paul taught that Jesus' death made up for the sins of all humans. By accepting Jesus as Christ (from Christos, the Greek term for Messiah) and Savior, people could be saved from sin and reconciled to God.

The teachings of early Christianity were passed on orally. Written materials also appeared, however. Paul and other followers of Jesus had written letters, or epistles, outlining Christian beliefs for communities they had helped found around the eastern Mediterranean. Also, some of Jesus' disciples, or followers, may have preserved some of the sayings of Jesus in writing. Later, between A.D. 40 and A.D. 100, these accounts became the basis of the written Gospels—the "good news" concerning Jesus. These writings give a record of Jesus' life and teachings, and they form the core of the **New Testament,** the second part of the Christian Bible.

By A.D. 100, Christian churches had been established in most of the major cities of the eastern empire and in some places in the western part of the empire. Most early Christians came from the Jews and the Greek-speaking populations of the east. In the second and third centuries, however, an increasing number of followers were Latin-speaking people.

## Roman Persecution

The basic values of Christianity differed markedly from those of the Greco-Roman world. In spite of that, the Romans at first paid little attention to the Christians, whom they regarded as simply another sect of Judaism. As time passed, however, the Roman attitude toward Christianity began to change.

The Romans tolerated the religions of other peoples unless these religions threatened public order or public morals. Many Romans came to view Christians as harmful to the Roman state because Christians refused to worship the state gods and emperors. The Romans saw the Christians' refusal to do so as an act of treason, punishable by death. The Christians, however, believed there was only one God. To them, the worship of state gods and the emperors meant worshiping false gods and endangering their own salvation.

**Geography SKILLS**

When Constantine converted to Christianity, it had already begun spreading through the Roman Empire.

1. **Regions** Which city clusters had the most growth in Christianity up to A.D. 325?
2. **Movement** How did Roman roads help the spread of Christianity?

The Roman government began persecuting (harassing to cause suffering) Christians during the reign of Nero (A.D. 54–68). The emperor blamed the Christians for the fire that destroyed much of Rome and subjected them to cruel deaths. In contrast, in the second century, persecution of Christians diminished.

By the end of the reigns of the five good emperors (A.D. 180), Christians still represented a small minority, but one of considerable strength.

## Roman Empire Adopts Christianity

Although Christians were persecuted in the first and second centuries, this did not stop the growth of Christianity. In fact, it strengthened Christianity by forcing it to become more organized. Missionaries used the Roman language and organizational structures to spread their message. Fear of persecution meant that only the most committed would follow the faith.

## TURNING POINT: THE SPREAD OF CHRISTIANITY IN THE ROMAN EMPIRE

The conversion of Emperor Constantine aided in the spread of Christianity. Although he did not make Christianity the official religion of the empire, he took an active role in protecting Christians and in shaping the religion. With the Edict of Milan and later edicts, Constantine made Christianity a "permitted" religion and gave Christians back confiscated property. He also convened the Council at Nicaea to organize and unify Christianity. Constantine also ordered the construction of churches. In A.D. 380 Emperor Theodosius I made Christianity the official religion of the empire.

When the empire began to decline in the 400s, Christianity replaced the Roman Empire as the main unifying force in Western Europe. Citizens looked to the church for moral authority when Rome's authority seemed to be decaying. When people lost faith in the emperor to protect them, they turned their loyalty to the church.

### DOCUMENT-BASED QUESTIONS

This fresco, completed in 1520, shows Constantine being baptized, an event which may not have occurred. The painting illustrates the significance of Constantine's role in the spread and legitimization of Christianity.

1. **Summarizing** How did Constantine support the Christian movement?
2. **Speculating** What do you think might have happened to Christianity if it had not been officially recognized before the Roman Empire fell?

### CONSTANTINE'S CONTRIBUTIONS TO THE SPREAD OF CHRISTIANITY

| | |
|---|---|
| 312 | Constantine's conversion |
| 313 | Constantine issues the Edict of Milan proclaiming the official tolerance of Christianity in the empire |
| 325 | Constantine convenes the Council of Nicaea to organize and unify Christianity |
| 333 | Constantine orders the construction of churches. The Church of the Holy Sepulchre is completed. |

Crucial to this change was the emerging role of the bishops, who began to assume more control over church communities. The Christian church was creating a new **structure** in which the **clergy**, or church leaders, had distinct functions separate from the **laity**, or the regular church members.

Christianity grew quickly in the first century. It took root in the second century, and by the third century, it had spread widely. Why was Christianity able to attract and maintain so many followers?

First, the Christian message had much to offer the Roman world. The Roman state-based religion was impersonal and existed for the good of Rome. Christianity is personal and offers salvation and eternal life to individuals. Christianity gave Romans meaning and purpose to life.

Second, Christianity seemed familiar. It was viewed by some as similar to other religions, offering immortality as the result of the sacrificial death of a savior-god. However, Christianity does not require painful or expensive initiation rites like some other religions at that time. Also, Jesus had been a human figure, making him easy to relate to.

Finally, Christianity fulfills the human need to belong. Christians formed communities bound to one another. In these communities, people could express their love by helping one another and offering assistance to the poor and the sick. Christianity satisfied the need to belong in a way that the huge Roman Empire could never provide.

Christianity proved attractive to all classes, but especially to the poor and powerless. Eternal life is promised to all—rich, poor, aristocrats, slaves, men, and women. As Paul stated in his letters to the Colossians and the Galatians, "And [you] have put on the new self . . . . Here there is no Greek nor Jew . . . barbarian, Scythian, slave or free, but Christ is all, and is in all." Although Christianity did not call for revolution, it stresses a sense of spiritual equality for all people—a revolutionary idea at the time.

Some emperors began new persecutions of the Christians in the third century, but their schemes failed. The last great persecution was by Diocletian (DY•uh•KLEE•shuhn) at the beginning of the fourth century. Even he had to admit, however, what had become obvious in the course of the third century: Christianity and its followers were too strong to be blotted out by force.

In the fourth century, Christianity prospered as never before when **Constantine** became the first Christian emperor. Although he was not baptized until the end of his life, in 313 Constantine issued the Edict of Milan, which proclaimed official tolerance of Christianity. Then, under **Theodosius the Great** (A.D. 378–395), the Romans adopted Christianity as the official religion of the Roman Empire.

**✓Reading Check** **Explaining** Why and how did the Christian church become more organized in the second and third centuries?

## SECTION 4 REVIEW

### Vocabulary

1. **Explain** the significance of: guarantee, Judaea, procurator, Jerusalem, Jesus, transformation, Simon Peter, Paul, Aegean Sea, New Testament, structure, clergy, laity, Constantine, Theodosius the Great.

### Main Ideas

2. **Describe** the beliefs and practices of Roman religion prior to the spread of Christianity.
3. **List** the ethical concepts voiced by Jesus.
4. **Contrast** the beliefs of the Roman state religion with the beliefs of Christianity in a chart like the one below.

| Roman State Religion | Christianity |
|---|---|
| | |
| | |

### Critical Thinking

5. **The BIG Idea** **Explaining** Explain why Romans began to accept Christianity and why it took so long for it to be accepted by the state.
6. **Drawing Conclusions** Explain why the Romans persecuted Christians despite their general religious tolerance.
7. **Analyzing Visuals** Examine the fresco on page 172. Compare the figures standing at the top of the steps on the left and right side of the fresco. Which one represents the Roman era? What era might the other represent?

### Writing About History

8. **Expository Writing** Research why Romans thought Christianity was dangerous to their empire. Compare these arguments to actual Christian doctrine and practices. Present your findings in an essay. Show that your sources corroborate your position.

**History ONLINE**

For help with the concepts in this section of *Glencoe World History*, go to glencoe.com and click Study Central™.

SECTION 5 Section Audio Spotlight Video

# Decline and Fall

## GUIDE TO READING

### The BIG Idea

**Order and Security** Although two strong emperors temporarily revived the Roman Empire, Germanic tribes from central Europe helped bring it to an end.

### Content Vocabulary

- plague *(p. 174)*
- inflation *(p. 176)*

### Academic Vocabulary

- military *(p. 174)*
- collapse *(p. 174)*
- economic *(p. 174)*

### People and Places

- Diocletian *(p. 174)*
- Constantine *(p. 174)*
- Byzantium *(p. 175)*
- Bosporus *(p. 175)*
- Huns *(p. 176)*
- Visigoths *(p. 176)*
- Danube River *(p. 177)*
- Vandals *(p. 177)*
- Romulus Augustulus *(p. 177)*

### Reading Strategy

**Cause and Effect** Complete a chart describing the events that led to the decline and fall of the Roman Empire.

| Decline | Fall |
|---|---|
| | |
| | |

*In A.D. 410, the Visigoths sacked Rome. The scholar Jerome wrote, "A terrible rumor had arrived from the West. Rome is besieged. . . . The City is taken which took the whole world."*

## The Decline

**MAIN IDEA** Political upheavals, the plague, and the division of the empire led to its decline.

**HISTORY & YOU** Can cities or countries become too large to run effectively? Learn about the decline of the Roman Empire.

Marcus Aurelius, the last of the five good emperors, died in A.D. 180. A period of conflict, confusion, and civil wars followed.

### Problems and Upheavals

Following a series of civil wars, a **military** government under the Severan rulers restored order. Septimius Severus told his sons "to pay the soldiers, and ignore everyone else," setting the tone for the new dynasty. After the Severan rulers there was more disorder. For almost 50 years, from 235 to 284, the Roman throne was occupied by whoever had military strength to seize it. During this period there were 22 emperors, most of whom died violently.

At the same time, the empire was troubled by a series of invasions. In the east, the Sassanid (suh•SAH•nuhd) Persians made inroads into Roman territory. Germanic tribes poured into the Balkans, Gaul, and Spain.

Invasions, civil wars, and plague almost caused an **economic collapse** in the third century. A labor shortage created by **plague**—an epidemic disease—affected both military recruiting and the economy. There was a decline in trade and small industry. Farm production declined as crops were ravaged by invaders or the defending Roman army. Armies were needed more than ever, but financial strains made it difficult to enlist and pay more soldiers. By the mid-third century, the state had to hire Germans to fight. These soldiers did not understand Roman traditions and had little loyalty to either the empire or the emperors.

### Reforms by Diocletian and Constantine

At the end of the third and the beginning of the fourth centuries, the Roman Empire gained a new lease on life through the efforts of two emperors, **Diocletian** and **Constantine**. The empire changed into a new state: the Late Roman Empire, which included

A carving of the tetrarchs at St. Mark's in Venice, Italy

## Geography SKILLS

The emperor Diocletian divided the Roman Empire into western and eastern halves. In 293 he created a *tetrarchy*—a government made up of four rulers.

1. **Explaining** How would establishing four different capitals help to protect Rome?
2. **Comparing and Contrasting** How does the establishment of the tetrarchy compare and contrast to the United States's division of power between state and local governments?

Maps In MOtion See *StudentWorks™ Plus* or glencoe.com.

a new governmental structure, a rigid economic and social system, and a new state religion—Christianity. Believing that the empire had grown too large for a single ruler, Diocletian, who ruled from 284 to 305, divided it into four units, each with its own ruler. Diocletian's military power enabled him to hold ultimate authority.

Constantine, who ruled from 306 to 337, continued and even expanded the policies of Diocletian. Constantine's biggest project was the construction of a new capital city in the east, on the site of the Greek city of **Byzantium** on the shores of the **Bosporus**. The city, eventually renamed Constantinople (now İstanbul, Turkey) was developed for defensive reasons. Its strategic location provided protection of the eastern frontier. Constantinople, the "New Rome," became the center of the Eastern Roman Empire and one of the great cities of the world.

Diocletian's and Constantine's political and military reforms enlarged two institutions—the army and civil service—which drained public funds. The population was not growing so the tax base could not pay for the bureaucracy and the army. Roman money, or currency, began to lose value.

Both rulers devised new economic and social policies to deal with these financial burdens. To fight **inflation**—a rapid increase in prices—Diocletian issued a price edict in 301 that set wage and price controls for the empire. Despite severe penalties, it failed.

To ensure the tax base and keep the empire going despite the labor shortage, the emperors issued edicts forcing workers to remain in their vocations. Hence, jobs, such as bakers and shippers, became hereditary. Large landowners took advantage of depressed agricultural conditions to enlarge their estates.

In general, the economic and social policies of Diocletian and Constantine were based on control and coercion. Although temporarily successful, such policies in the long run stifled the very vitality the Late Empire needed to revive its sagging fortunes.

✓Reading Check **Describing** Describe the conditions in the Roman Empire prior to Diocletian and Constantine.

# The Fall

**MAIN IDEA** The migration of Germanic tribes helped bring an end to the Roman Empire.

***HISTORY & YOU*** Have you heard about migrations that bring down governments? Learn about the end of the Roman Empire.

The restored empire of Diocletian and Constantine limped along for more than a century. The empire continued to be divided into western and eastern parts. The capital of the Western Roman Empire remained in Rome. Constantinople remained the capital of the Eastern Roman Empire. The Western Roman Empire came under increasing pressure from migrating Germanic tribes.

## Germanic Tribes

The major breakthrough of Germanic tribes into the west came in the second half of the fourth century. The **Huns**, who came from Asia, moved into eastern Europe and put pressure on the Germanic **Visigoths**.

NATIONAL GEOGRAPHIC

**MIGRATIONS INTO THE ROMAN EMPIRE, A.D. 200–500**

**Geography SKILLS**

1. **Movement** Which groups of Germanic tribes made the most limited incursions?
2. **Place** Which parts of the Roman Empire seem to have been more secure from the migrations? Why do you think this was?

The Visigoths, in turn, moved south and west, crossed the **Danube River** into Roman territory, and settled down as Roman allies, until they revolted. The Romans attempted to stop the revolt at Adrianople in 378, but the Visigoths defeated them.

Increasing numbers of Germans now crossed the frontiers. In 410, the Visigoths sacked Rome. Another group, the **Vandals**, poured into southern Spain and Africa. They crossed into Italy from northern Africa and, in 455, they too sacked Rome. The words *vandal* and *vandalize* come from this ruthless tribe.

In 476, the western emperor, **Romulus Augustulus**, was deposed by the Germanic head of the army. This is usually taken as the date of the fall of the Western Roman Empire. As we shall see in Chapter 9, a series of German kingdoms replaced the Western Roman Empire. The Eastern Roman Empire, or the Byzantine Empire, however, continued to thrive with its center at Constantinople.

## Theories

Many theories have been proposed to explain the decline and fall of the Roman Empire. They include:

- Christianity's emphasis on a spiritual kingdom weakened Roman military virtues.
- Traditional Roman values declined as non-Italians gained prominence in the empire.
- Lead poisoning through leaden water pipes and cups caused a mental decline in the population.
- Plague wiped out one-tenth of the population.
- Rome failed to advance technologically due to slavery.
- Rome could not create a workable political system.

There may be an element of truth in each of these theories, but history is an intricate web of relationships, causes, and effects. No single explanation can sufficiently explain the fall of a great empire.

For example, both the Han dynasty in China and the Roman Empire lasted for centuries. Both of these empires were able to govern large areas of land effectively. They instituted and maintained laws and a language. In spite of their attempts at unifying conquered territories, both empires experienced problems that came from acquiring so much land. Both tried to protect their borders with walls, forts, and troops. Both, however, eventually fell to new peoples. The Han dynasty fell to the Xiongnu. The Roman army in the west was not able to fend off the hordes of people moving into Italy and Gaul, and the Western Roman Empire collapsed. In contrast, the Eastern Roman Empire, which would survive for another thousand years, was able to withstand invaders.

**✓Reading Check** **Identifying** Which groups moved into the Western Roman Empire?

## SECTION 5 REVIEW

### Vocabulary

1. **Explain** the significance of: military, economic, collapse, plague, Diocletian, Constantine, Byzantium, Bosporus, inflation, Huns, Visigoths, Danube River, Vandals, Romulus Augustulus.

### Main Ideas

2. **Describe** the Roman rulers from 235 to 284.
3. **Explain** why the decline in population was so harmful to the Roman Empire.
4. **List** the economic and military problems that contributed to the decline of the Roman Empire.

### Critical Thinking

5. **The BIG Idea** **Evaluating** Summarize the theories why the Roman Empire fell and then tell which theories seem more reasonable than others.
6. **Summarizing Information** Create a chart like the one below to list ways that Diocletian and Constantine strengthened the Roman Empire.

| Diocletian | Constantine |
|---|---|
| | |
| | |

7. **Analyzing Visuals** Examine the statue on page 175. Why are the tetrarchs shown with their hands on their swords? What is the symbolism of placing their hands on each other's shoulders?

### Writing About History

8. **Persuasive Writing** Imagine you are the adviser to a benevolent Roman emperor. Write a letter to the emperor describing the steps he should take to preserve the Roman Empire.

**History ONLINE**

For help with the concepts in this section of *Glencoe World History*, go to glencoe.com and click Study Central™.

# CHAPTER 5 Visual Summary

STUDY TO GO You can study anywhere, anytime by downloading quizzes and flash cards to your PDA from glencoe.com.

THE ETRUSCANS

Etruscan art demonstrates their influence on the Romans.

## ROMAN REPUBLIC

- The Romans learned from, then overthrew, Etruscan rule and established a republic.
- The Romans controlled the Italian peninsula but allowed some non-Romans to be citizens of Rome.
- After defeating Carthage, Rome became master of the Mediterranean.

FORUM OF AUGUSTUS IN ROME

Many Roman cities had forums.

## ROMAN EMPIRE

- The Republic died as generals competed to rule Rome.
- The "Good Emperors" brought prosperity through trade and expansion.
- Public works, a shared culture, and architecture unified Rome's far-flung cities.
- A new religion—Christianity—spread through the empire, becoming the official religion.

CONSTANTINE'S ARCH IN ROME

Monuments told stories to the public about rulers.

## DECLINE AND FALL of the Western Empire

- Outside threats, civil strife, and economic woes weakened Rome's ability to hold the empire together.
- Diocletian and Constantine could not revive the divided empire's economy.
- The migration of Germanic tribes helped bring about an end to the Roman Empire.
- The Eastern Empire survived as the Byzantine Empire.

# CHAPTER 5 Assessment

## Reviewing Vocabulary

*Directions: Choose the word or words that best complete the sentence.*

**1.** The term ________ refers to the idea in Roman society that males should be dominant because females were too weak.

**A** patriarch
**B** patrilineal
**C** paterfamilias
**D** matriarch

**2.** Judaea became a Roman province under the direction of an official called a(n) ________.

**A** dictator
**B** praetor
**C** procurator
**D** imperator

**3.** Caesar, Crassus, and Pompey formed a powerful governmental coalition called a(n) ________.

**A** triumvirate
**B** consul
**C** republic
**D** *insulae*

**4.** A form of government in which the leader is not a monarch and certain citizens have the right to vote is called a(n) ________.

**A** dictatorship
**B** monarchy
**C** empire
**D** republic

**5.** ________ is a rapid increase in prices, which causes currency to lose its value.

**A** Depression
**B** Inflation
**C** Money economy
**D** Barter

## Reviewing Main Ideas

*Directions: Choose the best answers to the following questions.*

### Section 1 *(pp. 146–151)*

**6.** What is the Law of Nations primarily based on?

**A** Sacrifice
**B** Civil law
**C** Reason
**D** Democracy

**7.** Who influenced the way Rome organized its army?

**A** Sicilians
**B** Greeks
**C** Latins
**D** Etruscans

### Section 2 *(pp. 152–159)*

**8.** Who became the first Roman emperor known as Augustus?

**A** Crassus
**B** Julius Caesar
**C** Antony
**D** Octavian

**9.** What was the Pax Romana a time of?

**A** Peace
**B** War
**C** Creativity
**D** Oppression

### TEST-TAKING TIP

Do not pick an answer just because it sounds good. Sometimes a choice is deliberately meant to sound correct but is not. Read all of the answer choices very carefully before you select the best one and avoid making any hasty decisions.

**Need Extra Help?**

| If You Missed Questions . . . | 1 | 2 | 3 | 4 | 5 | 6 | 7 | 8 | 9 |
|---|---|---|---|---|---|---|---|---|---|
| Go to Page . . . | 162 | 169 | 154 | 148 | 176 | 150 | 147 | 155 | 157 |

GO ON

### Section 3 *(pp. 160–165)*

**10.** What culture influenced Roman art and architecture?

**A** American

**B** Persian

**C** Egyptian

**D** Greek

**11.** Who wrote *The Early History of Rome*?

**A** Virgil

**B** Horace

**C** Livy

**D** Plato

### Section 4 *(pp. 168–173)*

**12.** What was one lasting contribution of the Roman Empire?

**A** The idea of the triumvirate

**B** The Christian church

**C** The gladiatorial shows

**D** Pax Romana

### Section 5 *(pp. 174–177)*

**13.** What did the reforms of Diocletian and Constantine do for the Roman Empire?

**A** Revived the Roman Empire

**B** Caused a decline in trade

**C** Brought on additional civil wars and invasions

**D** Placed the empire in a state of political unrest

**14.** What finally caused the fall of the Roman Empire?

**A** Migration of Germanic tribes

**B** An increase in taxes

**C** The rise of the Christian religion

**D** Death of Constantine

## Critical Thinking

*Directions: Choose the best answers to the following questions.*

*Use the following map to answer questions 15 and 16.*

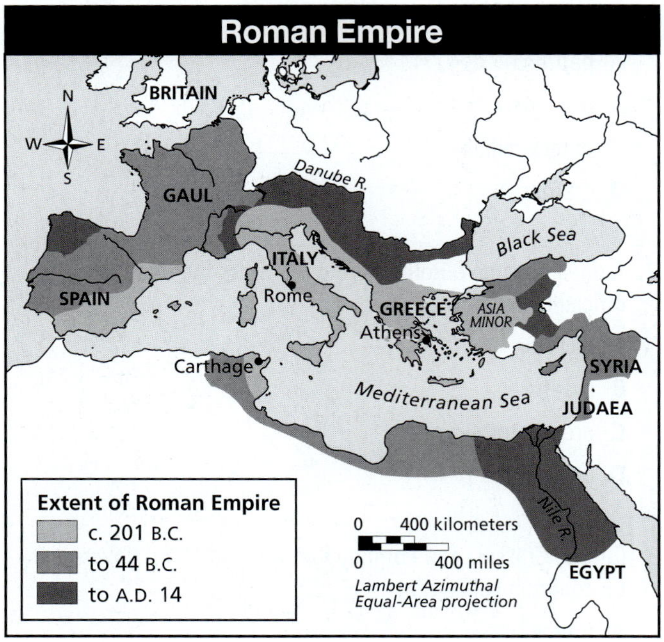


**15.** Around what body of water did the Roman Empire expand?

**A** Danube River

**B** Mediterranean Sea

**C** Black Sea

**D** Nile River

**16.** What region was added to the Roman Empire from 44 B.C. to A.D. 14?

**A** Egypt

**B** Italy

**C** Britain

**D** Gaul

**Need Extra Help?**

| If You Missed Questions . . . | 10 | 11 | 12 | 13 | 14 | 15 | 16 |
|---|---|---|---|---|---|---|---|
| Go to Page . . . | 160 | 162 | 173 | 174 | 176 | 180 | 180 |

GO ON

# CHAPTER 5 Assessment

*Use the following time line to answer question 17.*

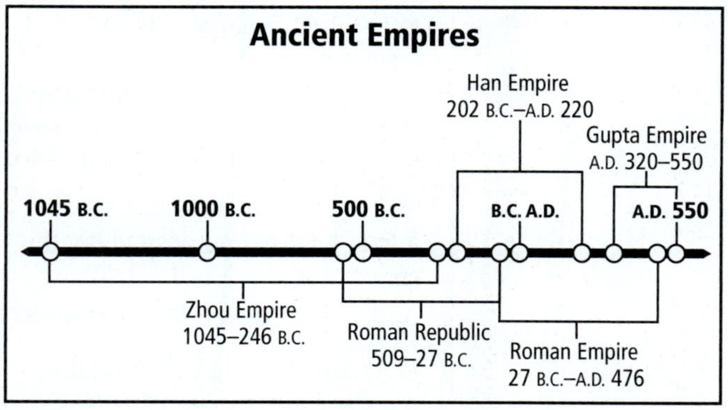


**17.** How long did the Roman civilization last?

**A** Almost 1,000 years

**B** 2,000 years

**C** 50 years

**D** About 500 years

**18.** On which group of people were Romans dependent for manual labor on farms and to help build roads and buildings?

**A** Women

**B** Greeks

**C** Slaves

**D** Children

**19.** Which Roman emperor helped spread Christianity?

**A** Crassus

**B** Constantine

**C** Antony

**D** Octavian

## Document-Based Questions

*Directions: Analyze the document and answer the questions that follow the document. Base your answers on the document and on your knowledge of world history.*

*Read the following poem by Virgil, and answer the questions.*

> *Let others fashion from bronze more lifelike, breathing images—*
> *For so they shall—and evoke living faces from marble;*
> *Others excel as orators, others track with their instruments*
> *The planet circling in heaven and predict when stars will appear.*
> *But, Romans, never forget that government is your medium!*
> *Be this your art: to practise men in the habit of peace,*
> *Generosity to the conquered, and firmness against aggressors."*

**20.** What did the poet feel was Rome's gift? Who are the "others" mentioned in the poem?

**21.** How does this poem summarize the fundamental ideas of Western civilization that originated in Rome?

## Extended Response

**22.** Compare and contrast the causes and effects of the rise and decline of Rome with other ancient civilizations, such as Greece, Egypt, Persia, Han China, or Gupta India.

**History ONLINE**

For additional test practice, use Self-Check Quizzes—Chapter 5 at glencoe.com.

**Need Extra Help?**

| If You Missed Questions . . . | 17 | 18 | 19 | 20 | 21 | 22 |
|---|---|---|---|---|---|---|
| Go to Page . . . | 181 | 164 | 172 | 181 | 181 | 161 |

**STOP**

MARY EVANS PICTURE LIBRARY/ALAMY

## What a Blast!

*In A.D. 79* **PLINY THE YOUNGER,** *an 18-year-old Roman, was vacationing in southern Italy when a nearby volcano, Vesuvius, erupted. It eventually buried the cities of Herculaneum and Pompeii. Pliny described the event in letters to the historian Tacitus. Here is a terrifying excerpt.*

"Being at a convenient distance from the houses, we stood still, in the midst of a most dangerous and dreadful scene. . . . The sea seemed to roll back upon itself, and to be driven from its banks by the convulsive motion of the earth. . . . On the other side, a black and dreadful cloud . . . revealed behind it various shaped masses of flame. . . .

"The ashes now began to fall upon us. . . . I looked back: a dense dark mist seemed to be following us, spreading itself over the country like a cloud. . . . The night came upon us, [like] that of a room when it is shut up, and all the lights put out. You might hear the shrieks of women, the screams of children, and the shouts of men. . . . [A] heavy shower of ashes rained upon us, which we were obliged to stand up to shake off, otherwise we should have been crushed and buried in the heap."

## VERBATIM

"The truth is always the strongest argument."

**SOPHOCLES,** *Greek playwright, in his tragedy Phaedra*

"To everything there is a season, a time for every purpose under the sun."

**BOOK OF ECCLESIASTES**

"A man should practice what he preaches but should also preach what he practices."

**CONFUCIUS,** *Chinese philosopher and founder of Confucianism*

"Where there's life, there's hope."

**CICERO,** *Roman senator and famed orator*

"You are young again. You live again. . . . Forever."

**BOOK OF THE DEAD,** *a series of prayers written on the walls of Egyptian tombs*

## ATHENS VS. SPARTA

ROLF RICHARDSON/ALAMY

Spartan warrior Leonidas

*Everyone knows that the Greek city-states of Athens and Sparta are as alike as, well, oil and water. Athens is known as a city of culture, Sparta as a burg that likes to battle. This chart describes some differences between the two places. Which town would you prefer to call home?*

| Sparta | Athens |
|---|---|
| Trains boys to become soldiers from age 7 | Trains boys in the arts and sciences from age 7 |
| Allows women to move about the city | Expects women to stay at home |
| Values physical superiority | Values intellectual superiority |
| Builds mostly military barracks | Builds beautiful buildings |
| Produces good warriors | Produces good citizens |

SCALA/ART RESOURCE

Athenian thinkers Plato and Aristotle

## All Wrapped Up

*To Egyptians, death is the final frontier. They believe that a dead person can live on in the afterworld—but only if that person's body is well preserved, through embalming. Special priests are in charge of the process of mummification, which takes 70 days. Below we've scrambled the steps it takes to make a mummy. Can you put them in the right order?*

1. Innards are dried out, wrapped in linen, and placed in containers called canopic jars to be preserved forever.
2. The body is wrapped in linen bandages and placed in a coffin called a sarcophagus.
3. All the inner organs, except the heart, are removed through a slit in the abdomen.
4. The body is covered inside and out with a kind of salt called natron. It dries out the body.
5. A small hook draws out the brain through the nose.
6. The body is covered with myrrh and other fragrant spices.

Answers: 5, 3, 1, 4, 6, 2

## Milestones

**HELD. FIRST OLYMPIC GAMES,** in 776 B.C., in the city of Olympia. Male athletes competed in events that included boxing, wrestling, and chariot racing. Winners received a crown of olive leaves. Koroibos of Elis won the first prize at these games, which are scheduled to take place every four years.

**CONQUERED.** By **ALEXANDER THE GREAT,** most of the known world. A legend in his own time, Alexander had defeated Persia, Egypt, India, and other empires before his untimely death in 323 B.C. at age 32.

**ASSASSINATED. CALIGULA,** unpopular Roman emperor, in A.D. 41 by members of his security force. Caligula's strange behavior and cruelty were factors in his murder. The final straw came when he declared himself a god. In a move that surprised political observers, Claudius was named the new emperor.

**DIED. ZHANG HENG,** an engineer, mathematician, inventor, artist, and scholar in the Eastern Han Dynasty, in A.D. 139. Among his innovations were a more accurate calendar and the world's first seismograph, to measure the force of earthquakes.

**INVENTED. THE WHEEL,** by potters in the Mesopotamian city of Ur, around 3500 B.C. This flat, circular piece of wood sits atop a wooden stick called an axle. As the axle spins, so does the wheel, allowing very uniform pots to be made more quickly. Experts speculate that the wheel may have many potential uses.

## BY THE NUMBERS

**50,000** Number of people who can fit into the Roman Colosseum

**37,000** Approximate number of men in Alexander the Great's army when he attacked the Persian Empire

**450** Height in feet of the lighthouse built in the harbor of Alexandria, Egypt

**12** Number of years it takes for a Sumerian student of cuneiform to become a scribe

**7** Number of "Wonders of the Ancient World," which include the Great Pyramid of Giza, the Hanging Gardens of Babylon, the Statue of Zeus at Olympia, the Temple of Artemis at Ephesus, the Mausoleum at Halicarnassus, the Colossus at Rhodes, and the Lighthouse of Alexandria

## CRITICAL THINKING

1. **Comparing and Contrasting** What are the differences between living in Athens and living in Sparta?
2. **Drawing Conclusions** What is causing the darkness that Pliny the Younger describes?

# UNIT 2

# New Patterns of Civilization

## A.D. 400–1500

### ▶ Why It Matters

As civilizations and empires emerged in different parts of the world, new political systems, religions, arts, and sciences developed. These new systems and these new ways of life continue to influence societies in the modern world.

*The city of Machu Picchu, nestled high in the Andes of Peru, provides archaeological clues to the Inca civilization.*

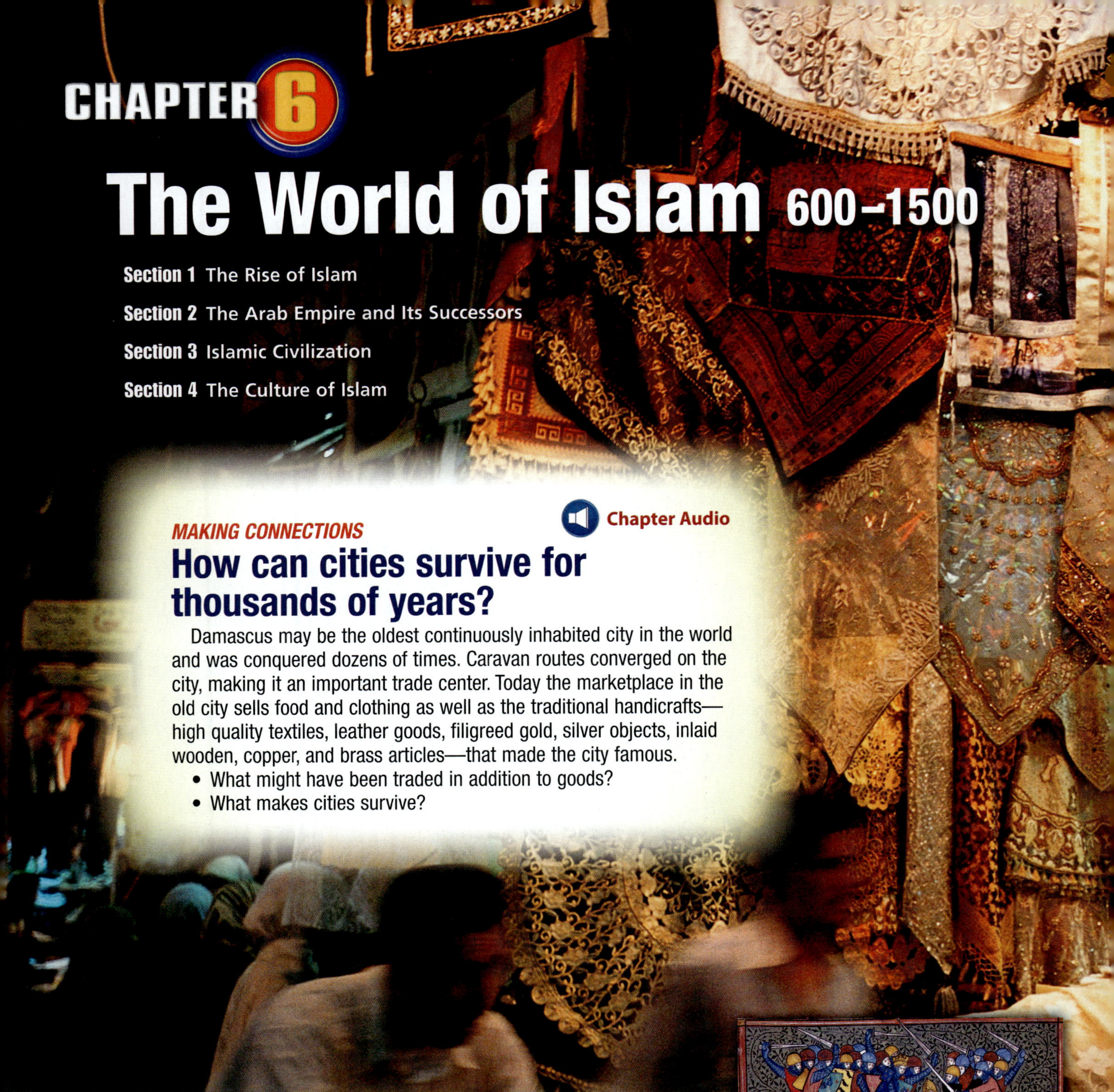

CHAPTER 6

# The World of Islam 600–1500



Chapter Audio

*MAKING CONNECTIONS*

## How can cities survive for thousands of years?

Damascus may be the oldest continuously inhabited city in the world and was conquered dozens of times. Caravan routes converged on the city, making it an important trade center. Today the marketplace in the old city sells food and clothing as well as the traditional handicrafts—high quality textiles, leather goods, filigreed gold, silver objects, inlaid wooden, copper, and brass articles—that made the city famous.

- What might have been traded in addition to goods?
- What makes cities survive?

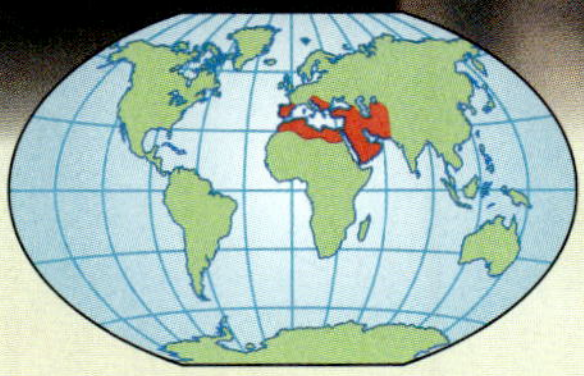

ISLAMIC WORLD ▶

**630** Muhammad returns to Makkah

**732** Charles Martel defeats Arab forces at Battle of Tours

**852** Great Mosque of Sāmarrā' finished

600 — 700 — 800 — 900

THE WORLD ▶

**618** Tang dynasty begins in China

**c. 800** Civilization at Teotihuacán collapses

**1187**
Saladin's army invades Jerusalem

**1382**
Ibn-Khaldūn teaches at university in Cairo

1000 — 1200 — 1500

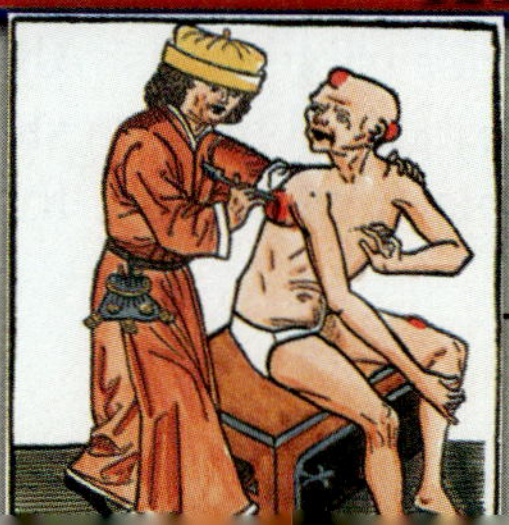

**1347**
Plague spreads to Italy and France

**FOLDABLES™**
**Study Organizer**

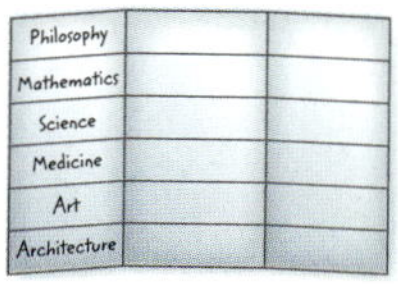


**Analyzing** Create a Folded Chart to record the advancements made by Muslims in philosophy, mathematics, science, medicine, art, and architecture. Names, places, and dates should be included on the chart.

**History ONLINE** Visit glencoe.com and enter *QuickPass*™ code GWHEA7447c6 for Chapter 6 resources.

SECTION 1

Section Audio    Spotlight Video

# The Rise of Islam

## GUIDE TO READING

### The BIG Idea

**Ideas, Beliefs, and Values** In the 600s, an Arab merchant named Muhammad created the religion of Islam, which led to great changes in the social and political systems of Southwest Asia.

### Content Vocabulary

- sheikh *(p. 188)*
- Allah *(p. 188)*
- Quran *(p. 190)*
- Islam *(p. 190)*
- *Hijrah (p. 190)*
- hajj *(p. 190)*
- Five Pillars of Islam *(p. 191)*
- *shari'ah (p. 191)*

### Academic Vocabulary

- revelations *(p. 189)*
- submission *(p. 190)*

### People and Places

- Arabian Peninsula *(p. 188)*
- Makkah *(p. 189)*
- Muhammad *(p. 189)*
- Khadija *(p. 189)*
- Muslims *(p. 190)*
- Madinah *(p. 190)*
- bedouin *(p. 190)*

### Reading Strategy

**Summarizing Information** As you read, create a diagram like the one below to help you study. List the main characteristics of the Islamic religion. Your diagram can list more characteristics than this example.

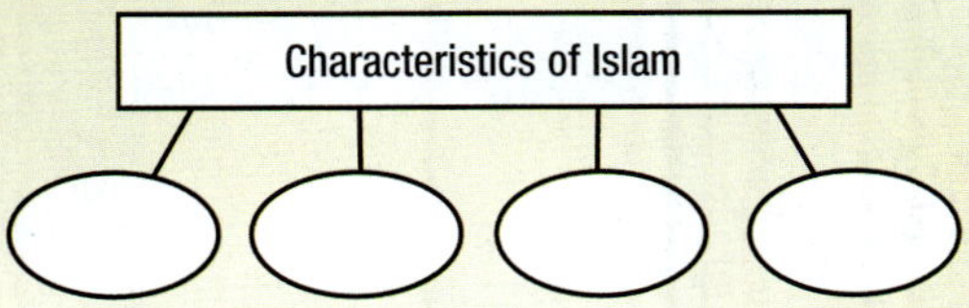


*Early Arabs were nomads who believed in many gods. In the seventh century, an Arab merchant named Muhammad founded the Islamic religion. Today, more than one billion people around the world are Muslims, and Islam is one of the world's leading faiths. Over a thousand years after Islam began, the cultural, artistic, and scientific contributions of Muslims continue to enrich our daily lives.*

## The Arabs

**MAIN IDEA** After the domestication of the camel, the trade routes of the Arabs expanded. Communities prospered, but tension among the rich and poor increased.

**HISTORY & YOU** How does political disorder affect where you travel? Learn how political disorder affected trade routes in early Southwest Asia.

Beginning with the Sumerians and continuing with the Assyrians, the Babylonians, the Persians, and the brief conquests of Alexander the Great, Western Asia has given birth to some of the most powerful civilizations in history. In the seventh century, another force—the Arabs—arose in the Arabian Peninsula and spread their influence throughout Western Asia and beyond.

Like the Israelites and the Assyrians, the Arabs were a Semitic-speaking people who lived in the **Arabian Peninsula**, a desert land sorely lacking in rivers and lakes. The Arabs were nomads who, because of their hostile surroundings, moved constantly to find water and food for their animals.

Survival in such a harsh environment was not easy, and the Arabs organized into tribes to help one another. Each tribe was ruled by a **sheikh** (SHAYK) who was chosen from one of the leading families by a council of elders. Although each tribe was independent, all the tribes were loosely connected to one another.

The Arabs lived as farmers and sheepherders on the oases and rain-fed areas of the Arabian Peninsula. After the camel was domesticated in the first millennium B.C., the Arabs populated more of the desert. They also expanded the caravan trade into these regions. Towns developed along the routes as the Arabs became major carriers of goods between the Indian Ocean and the Mediterranean, where the Silk Road ended.

Most early Arabs were polytheistic—they believed in many gods. The Arabs recognized a supreme god named **Allah** (*Allah* is Arabic for "God"), but they also believed in other tribal gods. Allah was symbolized by a sacred stone, and each tribe had its own stone. All tribes, however, worshiped a massive black meteorite, the Black

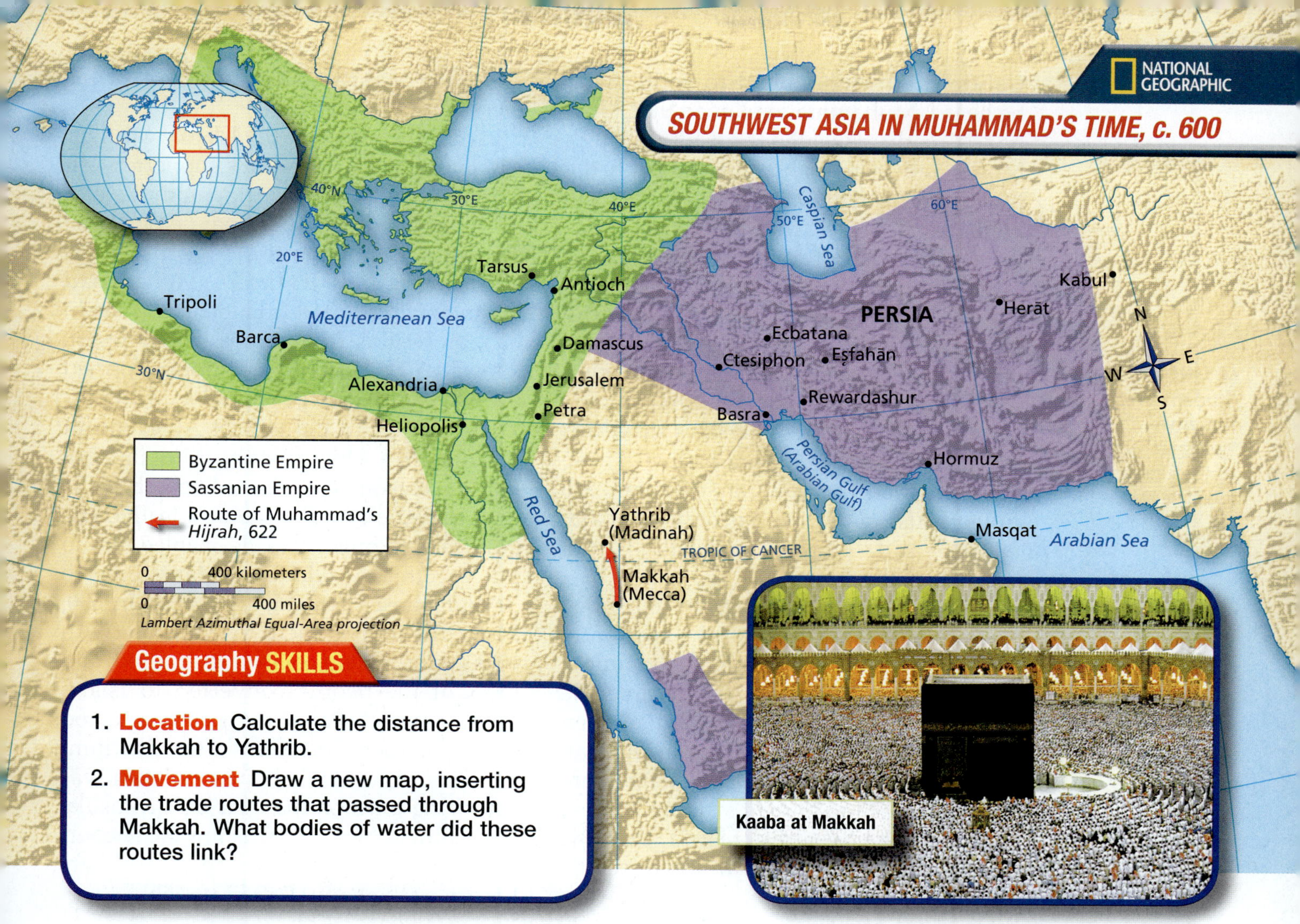


**Geography SKILLS**

1. **Location** Calculate the distance from Makkah to Yathrib.
2. **Movement** Draw a new map, inserting the trade routes that passed through Makkah. What bodies of water did these routes link?

Kaaba at Makkah

Stone, which had been placed in a central shrine called the Kaaba (KAW•buh). This shrine is in the city of **Makkah** (Mecca), which is located in the Arabian Peninsula.

The Arabian Peninsula took on a new importance when political disorder in Mesopotamia and Egypt made the usual trade routes in Southwest Asia too dangerous to travel. A safer route through Makkah to present-day Yemen and then by ship across the Indian Ocean became popular.

Camel caravans transported highly prized frankincense and myrrh along this route. The journey was long and camels had to stop over 60 times.

Communities along this route prospered from the increased trade. Tensions arose, however, as increasingly wealthy merchants showed little concern for the welfare of poorer clans people and slaves.

✓Reading Check **Explaining** Why did the communities on the Arabian Peninsula prosper?

## The Life of Muhammad

*MAIN IDEA* The revelations of Muhammad led to the creation of the Islamic religion.

***HISTORY & YOU*** What do you do when people behave unfairly? Learn how Muhammad dealt with tension in his community.

Into this world of tension stepped a man named **Muhammad**. Born in Makkah to a merchant family, he was orphaned at five. He grew up to become a caravan manager and married a rich widow named **Khadija**. Over time, Muhammad became troubled by the growing gap between the generosity of most Makkans and the greediness of the wealthy elite. Deeply worried, he began to visit the hills to meditate. During one of these visits, Muslims believe, Muhammad received **revelations** from God. According to Islamic teachings, the messages were given by the angel Gabriel.

**History ONLINE**
**Student Web Activity—**
Visit glencoe.com and complete the activity about the practice of hajj.

Gabriel told Muhammad to recite what he heard. Muhammad believed that Allah had already revealed himself through Moses and Jesus—and thus through the Jewish and Christian traditions. He believed, however, that the final revelations of Allah were now being given to him. Out of these revelations, which were eventually written down, came the **Quran,** the holy book of **Islam.** The word *Islam* means "peace through **submission** to the will of Allah." The Quran contains the ethical guidelines and laws by which the followers of Allah are to live. Those who practice the religion of Islam are called **Muslims.** Islam has only one God, Allah, and Muhammad is God's prophet.

After returning home from the hills, Muhammad reflected on his experience. His wife, Khadija, urged him to follow Gabriel's message, and she became the first convert to Islam. Muhammad then set out to convince the people of Makkah of the truth of the revelations. Many were surprised at Muhammad's claims to be a prophet. The wealthy feared that his attacks on corrupt society would upset the established social and political order. After three years of preaching, he had only 30 followers. Muhammad was discouraged by the persecution of his followers, as well as by the Makkans' failure to accept his message.

In 622, the year 1 of the Islamic calendar still in use today, he and his supporters left Makkah and moved north to Yathrib, later renamed **Madinah** (Medina; "city of the prophet"). The journey to Madinah is known as the ***Hijrah*** (HIH•jruh). Muhammad began to win support from people in Madinah, as well as from Arabs in the desert, known as **bedouin**. These groups formed the first community of practicing Muslims.

Submission to the will of Allah meant submission to his prophet, Muhammad. For this reason, Muhammad soon became both a religious and a political leader. His political and military skills enabled him to put together a reliable military force to defend himself and his followers. In 630, Muhammad returned to Makkah with 10,000 men. After the city surrendered, and most of the people converted to Islam, Muhammad declared the Kaaba a sacred shrine of Islam. Two years after his triumphal return to Makkah, just as Islam was spreading through the Arabian Peninsula, Muhammad died. All Muslims are encouraged to make a pilgrimage to Makkah, known as the **hajj** (HAJ), if possible.

**✓Reading Check** **Identifying** What do Muslims conclude from Muhammad's experience?

## The Five Pillars of Islam

**Chart SKILLS**

Muslims practice acts of worship called the Five Pillars of Islam.

1. **Describing** What behaviors are encouraged by the Five Pillars of Islam?

## The Teachings of Muhammad

**MAIN IDEA** Islam, like Christianity and Judaism, is a monotheistic religion comprising both a set of religious beliefs and a whole way of life.

***HISTORY & YOU*** What principles of behavior do you follow? Who or what influences your behavior? Learn how Muslims practice their principles of behavior.

Like Christianity and Judaism, Islam is a monotheistic religion. In Islam, Allah is the all-powerful being who created the universe and everything in it. Islam emphasizes salvation and offers the hope of an afterlife. Those who desire to achieve life after death must subject themselves to the will of Allah.

Unlike Christianity, Islam does not believe that its first preacher was divine. Muhammad is considered a prophet, similar to Moses, but he was also a man like other men. Muslims believe that because humans rejected Allah's earlier messengers, Allah sent his final revelation through Muhammad.

Islam is a direct and simple faith, stressing the need to obey the will of Allah. This means practicing acts of worship known as the **Five Pillars of Islam:** belief, prayer, charity, fasting, and pilgrimage. Muslims believe there is no deity but the One God, and Muhammad is his messenger (belief). They perform prescribed prayers five times a day (prayer) and give part of their wealth to the poor (charity). During Ramadan, Muslims refrain from food and drink from dawn to sunset (fasting). Finally, believers are expected to make a pilgrimage to Makkah at least once in their lifetime (pilgrimage).The faithful who follow the law go to an eternal paradise.

Islam is not just a set of religious beliefs but a way of life as well. After Muhammad's death, Muslim scholars developed a law code known as the ***shari'ah*** (shuh•REE•uh). It provides believers with a set of practical laws to regulate their daily lives. It is based on scholars' interpretations of the Quran and the example set by Muhammad in his life. The *shari'ah* applies the teachings of the Quran to daily life. It regulates all aspects of Muslim life including family life, business practice, government, and moral conduct. The *shari'ah* does not separate religious matters from civil or political law.

Believers are expected to follow sound principles for behavior. In addition to acts of worship called the Five Pillars, Muslims must practice honesty and justice in dealing with others. Muslims are forbidden to gamble, eat pork, drink alcoholic beverages, or engage in dishonest behavior. Family life is based on marriage.

✓ **Reading Check** **Comparing** How is Islam similar to Christianity and Judaism?

## SECTION 1 REVIEW

### Vocabulary

1. **Explain** the significance of: Arabian Peninsula, sheikh, Allah, Makkah, Muhammad, Khadija, revelations, Quran, Islam, submission, Muslims, Madinah, *Hijrah*, bedouin, hajj, Five Pillars of Islam, *shari'ah.*

### Main Ideas

2. **Locate** the expanded trade routes of the early Arab Empire.
3. **List** the Five Pillars of Islam.
4. **Create** a chart like the one below showing the changes that Islam brought to the peoples of the Arabian Peninsula.

| Early Arabs | Islam |
|---|---|
| | |
| | |
| | |
| | |

### Critical Thinking

5. **Discussing** What problems did Muhammad encounter while trying to spread the message of Islam?
6. **The BIG Idea** **Contrasting** How is the *shari'ah* different from the Five Pillars of Islam?
7. **Analyzing Visuals** Examine the photograph of the Kaaba on page 189. How are the people arranged as they pray? Why?

### Writing About History

8. **Descriptive Writing** Imagine that you are a former bedouin who now lives in Makkah. Write a letter to your bedouin cousin describing how your life has changed since the move to the city.

**History ONLINE**

For help with the concepts in this section of *Glencoe World History,* go to glencoe.com and click Study Central™.

SECTION 2

Section Audio    Spotlight Video

# The Arab Empire and Its Successors

## GUIDE TO READING

### The BIG Idea

**Order and Security** After the death of Muhammad, his successors organized the Arabs and set in motion a great expansion.

### Content Vocabulary

- caliph *(p. 192)*
- jihad *(p. 192)*
- Shia *(p. 194)*
- Sunni *(p. 194)*
- vizier *(p. 196)*
- sultan *(p. 197)*
- mosque *(p. 199)*

### Academic Vocabulary

- oriented *(p. 192)*
- complex *(p. 196)*

### People, Places, and Events

- Abū Bakr *(p. 192)*
- Mu'āwiyah *(p. 194)*
- Umayyad dynasty *(p. 194)*
- Battle of Tours *(p. 194)*
- Abbasid dynasty *(p. 196)*
- Baghdad *(p. 196)*
- Hārūn al-Rashīd *(p. 196)*
- Seljuk Turks *(p. 197)*
- Saladin *(p. 198)*
- Mongols *(p. 199)*

### Reading Strategy

**Comparing** As you read, create a chart like the one below to help you study. Compare and contrast the characteristics of the early caliphs with the caliphs of the Umayyad and Abbasid dynasties.

| Early Caliphs | Caliphs of the Umayyad and Abbasid Dynasties |
|---|---|
| | |
| | |

*The successors to Muhammad were known as caliphs, rulers who became the secular and spiritual leaders of the Islamic community. As the empire grew, caliphs became more like kings or emperors who wore expensive and elaborate clothes and jewels. This finery was an indication of the strength and power of the growing Arab Empire.*

## Creation of an Arab Empire

**MAIN IDEA** Islam grew under the rule of Muhammad's successors, but there was constant tension over choosing who should rule the empire.

**HISTORY & YOU** What happens when people are dissatisfied with the leaders in your community? Learn how dissatisfaction with leadership caused problems in the Islamic Empire.

Muhammad had been accepted as both the political and religious leader of the Islamic community. The death of Muhammad left his followers with a problem: Muhammad had never named a successor. Although he had several daughters, he had left no son. In a male-**oriented** society, who would lead the community of the faithful?

Shortly after Muhammad's death, some of his closest followers chose **Abū Bakr** (uh•BOO BA•kuhr), a wealthy merchant and Muhammad's father-in-law, to be their leader. Abū Bakr had been Muhammad's companion on the journey to Madinah in 622. There Abū Bakr had functioned as Muhammad's chief adviser and also led the public prayers during Muhammad's final illness. In 632 Abū Bakr was named **caliph** (KAY•luhf), the religious and political successor to Muhammad.

### Arab Conquest

Under Abū Bakr's leadership, the Islamic movement grew. He suppressed tribal political and religious uprisings, thereby uniting the Muslim world. As the Romans had slowly conquered Italy, so also the Muslims expanded over Arabia and beyond.

Muhammad had overcome military efforts by the early Makkans to defeat his movement. The Quran permitted fair, defensive warfare as **jihad** (jih•HAHD), or "struggle in the way of God." Muhammad's successors expanded their territory.

Unified under Abū Bakr, the Arabs began to turn the energy they had once directed toward each other against neighboring peoples. At Yarmūk in 636, the Arab army defeated the Byzantine army in a dust storm that let the Arabs take their enemy by surprise. Four

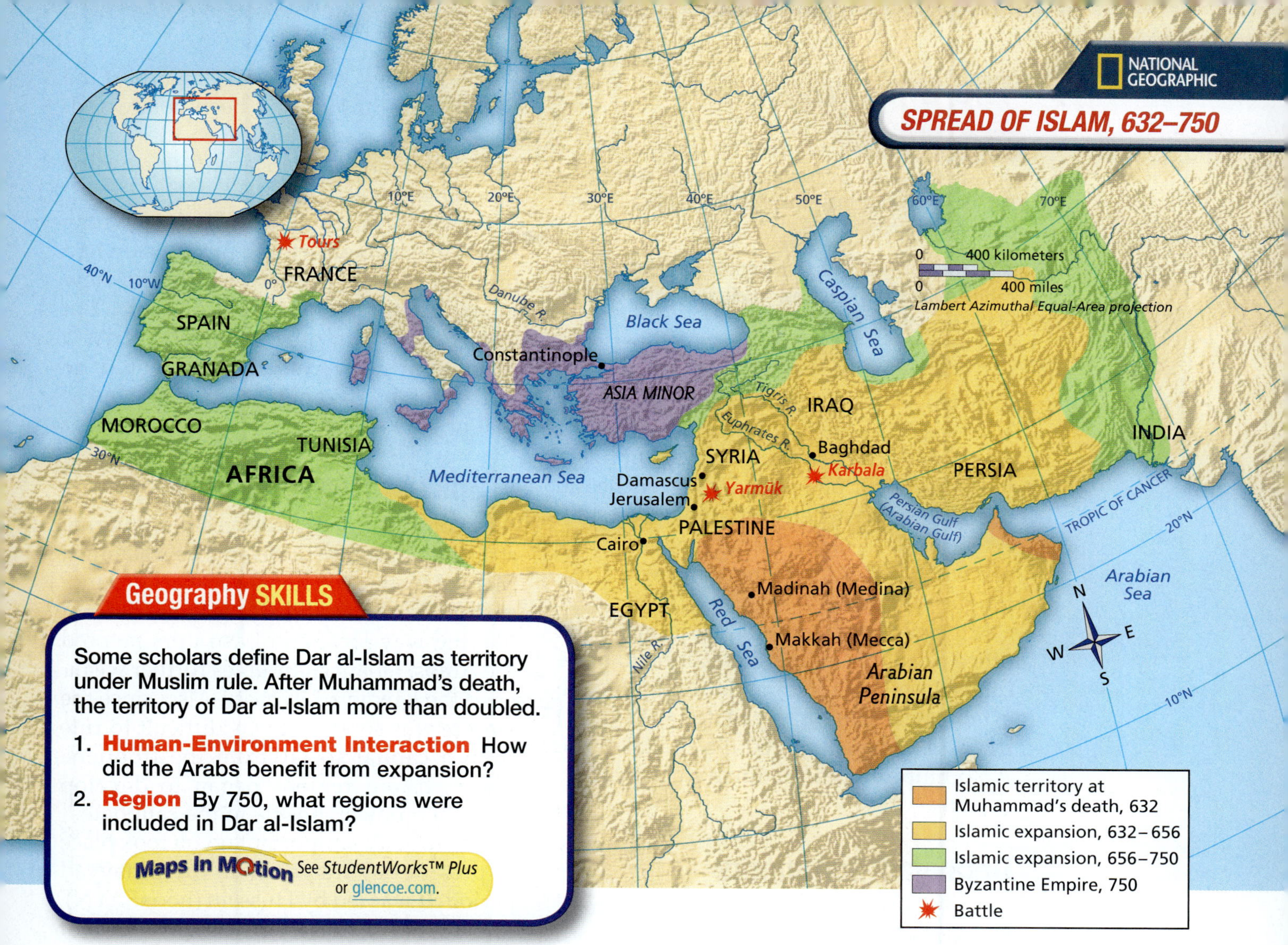


**Geography SKILLS**

Some scholars define Dar al-Islam as territory under Muslim rule. After Muhammad's death, the territory of Dar al-Islam more than doubled.

1. **Human-Environment Interaction** How did the Arabs benefit from expansion?
2. **Region** By 750, what regions were included in Dar al-Islam?

**Maps In Motion** See *StudentWorks™ Plus* or glencoe.com.

years later, they took control of the Byzantine province of Syria. By 642, Egypt and other areas of northern Africa had been added to the new Arab Empire. To the east, the Arabs had conquered the entire Persian Empire by 650.

The Arabs, led by a series of brilliant generals, had put together a large, dedicated army that traveled long distances and crossed mountains and harsh terrain. The courage of the Arab soldiers was enhanced by the belief that Muslim warriors were assured a place in paradise if they died in battle.

## Arab Rule

Early caliphs ruled their far-flung empire from Madinah. After Abū Bakr died, problems arose over who should become the next caliph. There were no clear successors to Abū Bakr, and the first two caliphs to rule after his death were assassinated. In 656, Ali, Muhammad's son-in-law and one of the first converts to Islam, was chosen to be caliph, but he too was assassinated after ruling for five years.

In the conquered territories, Muslim administrators were relatively tolerant, sometimes allowing local officials to continue to govern. Both Christians and Jews were allowed to practice their religions, with some restrictions, because they were "People of the Book." Islam recognizes the "People of the Book" as those who had written scriptures revealed to them by God before the time of Muhammad. Those who chose not to convert were required to be loyal to Muslim rule and to pay special taxes.

**✓Reading Check** **Explaining** How did the various achievements and policies of Muhammad's successors help the Arab world to grow?

## The Umayyads

**MAIN IDEA** Under the rule of the Umayyad dynasty, the Islamic Empire made many conquests, but there were internal struggles that led to a division of the community.

**HISTORY & YOU** How have governments divided earlier civilizations you have studied? Learn the cause of the split of Islam.

In 661, the general **Mu'āwiyah** (moo•UH•wee•uh), the governor of Syria and one of Ali's chief rivals, became caliph. He was known for one outstanding virtue: he used force only when absolutely necessary. As he said, "I never use my sword when my whip will do, nor my whip when my tongue will do."

Mu'āwiyah moved quickly to make the office of caliph, called the caliphate, hereditary in his own family. In doing this, he established the **Umayyad** (oo•MY•uhd) **dynasty**. He then moved the capital of the Arab Empire from Madinah to Damascus, in Syria.

### Umayyad Conquests

At the beginning of the eighth century, the Arabs carried out new attacks at both the eastern and western ends of the Mediterranean world. Arab armies moved across North Africa and conquered and converted the Berbers, a pastoral people living along the Mediterranean coast.

Around 710, combined Berber and Arab forces crossed the Strait of Gibraltar and occupied southern Spain. By 725, most of Spain had become a Muslim state with its center at Córdoba. In 732, however, Arab forces were defeated at the **Battle of Tours** in Gaul (now France). Arab expansion in Europe came to a halt.

In 717, another Muslim force had launched an attack on Constantinople with the hope of defeating the Byzantine Empire. The Byzantines survived, however, by destroying the Muslim fleet. This created an uneasy frontier in southern Asia Minor between the Byzantine Empire and the Islamic world.

By 750, the Arab advance had finally come to an end, but not before the southern and eastern Mediterranean parts of the old Roman Empire had been conquered. Arab power also extended to the east in Mesopotamia and Persia and northward into central Asia.

The Umayyad dynasty at Damascus now ruled an enormous empire. Expansion had brought not only great wealth and new ethnic groups into the fold of Islam, but also contact with other civilizations. As a result, the new Arab Empire would be influenced by Byzantine culture, as well as that of the Persians.

### A Split in Islam

In spite of Umayyad successes, internal struggles threatened the empire's stability. Many Muslims of non-Arab background, such as Persians and Byzantines, did not like the way local administrators favored the Arabs. Financial troubles further weakened the Umayyad dynasty. Also, since the empire was so vast, it was difficult to rule from a capital so far from the frontiers. These distant regions began to develop their own power, hostile to the caliphate.

An especially important revolt took place in present-day Iraq early in the Umayyad period. It was led by Hussein (hoo•SAYN), second son of Ali—the son-in-law of Muhammad.

Hussein encouraged his followers to rise up against Umayyad rule in 680. He set off to do battle, but his soldiers defected, leaving him with an army of 72 warriors against 10,000 Umayyad soldiers. Hussein's tiny force fought courageously, but all died.

This struggle led to a split of Islam into two groups. The **Shia** (SHEE•AH) Muslims accept only the descendants of Ali as the true rulers of Islam. The **Sunni** (SU•NEE) Muslims did not all agree with Umayyad rule but accepted the Umayyads as rulers, or caliphs. This political split led to the development of two branches of Muslims that persist to the present. The Sunnis are a majority in the Muslim world, but most of the people in Iraq and neighboring Iran consider themselves to be Shia.

✓Reading Check **Evaluating** What weakness in Arab rule led to revolts against the Umayyads?

TURNING POINT

# THE BATTLE OF TOURS

Encouraged by their success in Spain, Arab armies crossed the Pyrenees and marched northward into southern France. The forces led by ʻAbd ar-Raḥmān easily captured Bordeaux in Aquitaine, and then continued north toward Poitiers and Tours.

The defeated Duke of Aquitaine called on Charles Martel, the Frankish mayor of Austrasia, to help stop the Arab advance. In October 732, Charles's army met ʻAbd ar-Raḥmān's forces on the road between Poitiers and Tours. The Franks killed ʻAbd ar-Raḥmān and routed the Arabs, who fled south. The Franks' defeat of Arab forces at the Battle of Tours ended Arab expansion in Europe.

**ʻAbd ar-Raḥmān is shown using an Arab scimitar, or long sword with a curved blade.**

**Charles Martel (mounted), also called "Charles the Hammer" for the hammer-like shape of his weapon and his victory at Tours.**

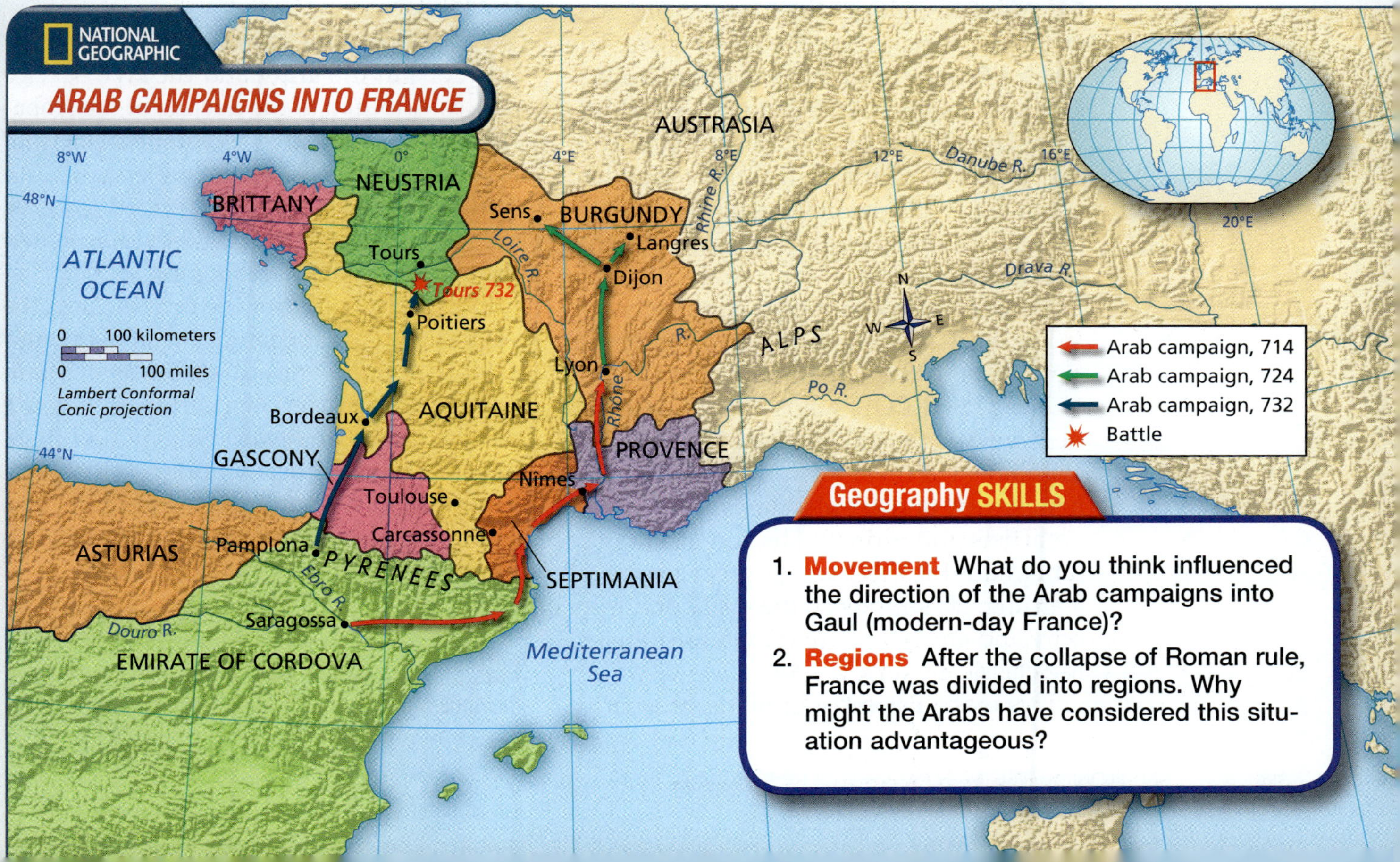


**Geography SKILLS**

1. **Movement** What do you think influenced the direction of the Arab campaigns into Gaul (modern-day France)?
2. **Regions** After the collapse of Roman rule, France was divided into regions. Why might the Arabs have considered this situation advantageous?

# The Abbasid Dynasty

**MAIN IDEA** Under the Abbasid dynasty, Islam experienced prosperity and a new cultural outlook.

**HISTORY & YOU** How do leaders in your community or state support the arts? Learn how the caliph Hārūn al-Rashīd helped further the arts in early Islam.

Resentment against Umayyad rule grew among non-Arab Muslims who resented the favoritism shown to Arabs. The Umayyads also helped to bring about their end by corrupt behavior. Abū al-'Abbās, a descendant of Muhammad's uncle, overthrew the Umayyad dynasty in 750 and set up the **Abbasid** (uh•BA•suhd) **dynasty,** which lasted until 1258.

## Abbasid Rule

In 762, the Abbasids built a new capital city at **Baghdad,** on the Tigris River, far to the east of the Umayyad capital at Damascus. Baghdad's location took advantage of river traffic in the Persian Gulf and the caravan route from the Mediterranean to central Asia.

The move eastward increased Persian influence and encouraged a new cultural outlook. Under the Umayyads, warriors had been seen as the ideal citizens. Under the Abbasids, judges, merchants, and government officials were the new heroes. The Abbasid rulers tried to break down the distinctions between Arab and non-Arab Muslims. This change opened Islamic culture to the influence of the civilizations they had conquered. All Muslims, regardless of ethnic background, could now hold both civil and military offices. Many Arabs began to intermarry with conquered peoples.

The best known of the caliphs of the time was **Hārūn al-Rashīd** (ha•ROON ahl•rah•SHEED), whose reign is often described as the golden age of the Abbasid caliphate. Hārūn al-Rashīd was known for his charity, and he also lavished support on artists and writers. His son al-Ma'mūn (ahl•mah•MOON) was a great patron of learning. He supported the study of astronomy and created a foundation for translating classical Greek works.

This was a period of growing prosperity. The Arabs had conquered many of the richest provinces of the Roman Empire, and they now controlled the trade routes to the East. Baghdad became the center of an enormous trade empire that helped spread products and knowledge from the Islamic world to Asia, Africa, and Europe. For example, from Persia the knowledge of planting sugarcane and building windmills spread west along the trade routes.

Under the Abbasids, the caliph began to act more regally. The bureaucracy assisting the caliph grew more **complex.** A council headed by a prime minister, known as a **vizier,** advised the caliph. During council meetings, the caliph sat behind a screen listening to the council's discussions and then whispered his orders to the vizier.

## Decline and Division

Despite its prosperity, all was not well in the empire of the Abbasids. There was much fighting over the succession to the caliphate. When Hārūn al-Rashīd died, his two sons fought to succeed him, almost destroying the city of Baghdad.

Vast wealth gave rise to financial corruption. Members of Hārūn al-Rashīd's clan were given large sums of money from the state treasury. His wife was reported to have spent vast amounts on a pilgrimage to Makkah.

The shortage of qualified Arabs for key positions in the army and the civil service also contributed to the decline of the Abbasids. Caliphs began to recruit officials from among non-Arabs, such as Persians and Turks. These people were trained to serve the caliphs, but gradually they dominated the army and the bureaucracy.

Eventually, rulers of the provinces of the Abbasid Empire began to break away and establish independent dynasties. Spain had established its own caliphate when a prince of the Umayyad dynasty fled there in 750. Morocco became independent, and a new dynasty under the Fatimids was established in Egypt, with its capital at Cairo, in 973. The Muslim Empire was now politically divided.

✓ **Reading Check** **Describing** What changes did the Abbasid rulers bring to the world of Islam?

# Seljuk Turks and the Crusades

**MAIN IDEA** Political turmoil disrupted Southwest Asia after the Seljuk Turks became a powerful military force.

**HISTORY & YOU** Have you ever had to challenge a leader? Learn how the Byzantines and the Christian states of Europe challenged the Seljuk Turks.

The Fatimid dynasty in Egypt soon became the dynamic center of Islamic civilization. From their position in the heart of the Nile delta, the Fatimids played a major role in trade from the Mediterranean to the Red Sea. They created a strong army by hiring nonnative soldiers. One such group was the **Seljuk** (SEHL•JOOK) **Turks**.

## The Seljuk Turks

The Seljuk Turks were a nomadic people from central Asia. They had converted to Islam and prospered as soldiers for the Abbasid caliphate. As the Abbasids grew weaker, the Seljuk Turks grew stronger, moving gradually into Iran and Armenia. By the eleventh century, they had taken over the eastern provinces of the Abbasid Empire.

In 1055, a Turkish leader captured Baghdad and took command of the empire. His title was **sultan**—or "holder of power." The Abbasid caliph was still the chief religious authority, but, after they captured Baghdad, the Seljuk Turks held the real military and political power of the state.

By the second half of the eleventh century, the Seljuks were putting military pressure on the Byzantine Empire. In 1071, the Byzantines foolishly challenged the Turks, and the Byzantine army was routed at Manzikert in modern-day eastern Turkey. The Turks now took over most of the Anatolian Peninsula. In desperation, the Byzantine Empire turned to the West for help.

NATIONAL GEOGRAPHIC

**ABBASID EMPIRE, 800**

**Geography SKILLS**

1. **Place** What factors influenced the placement of the Abbasid capital, Baghdad?
2. **Movement** How did trade spread Islamic culture, religion, and language?

**Maps In MOtion** See *StudentWorks™ Plus* or glencoe.com.

## The Crusades

The Byzantine emperor Alexius I asked the Christian states of Europe for help against the Turks. Because the Christian states and the Islamic world feared and disliked each other, many Europeans agreed, beginning a series of crusades in 1096.

At first, Muslim rulers lost to the invading crusaders, who conquered areas and established crusader states. In 1169, however, **Saladin**, a new Muslim ruler, took control of Egypt and made himself sultan, thus ending the Fatimid dynasty. He also established control over Syria and took the offensive against the Christian states in the area. In 1187, Saladin's army invaded the kingdom of Jerusalem and destroyed the Christian forces there. The Christians were left with only a handful of fortresses along the coast of Palestine. Saladin did not allow a massacre of the population. He even allowed Christian religious services to continue.

The Crusades had little lasting impact on Southwest Asia, except to breed centuries of mistrust between Muslims and Christians. Far more important was the threat posed by new invaders—the Mongols.

✓Reading Check **Explaining** How did the Seljuk Turks affect Southwest Asia?

## OPPOSING VIEWPOINTS

# How Did the Arab Empire Succeed?

### PRIMARY SOURCE 1

"They were aided by the weakness of the two contemporary empires, the Sassanian (Persian) and the Byzantine, which had largely exhausted themselves by their wars on one another. . . . Nor were these Arabs simply zealots fired by the ideal of a Holy War. They were by long tradition tough fighters, accustomed to raiding out of hunger and want; many or perhaps even most of them were not ardent followers of Mohammed. Yet there can be little question that what got the Arabs started, and kept them going, was mainly the personality and the teaching of the Prophet."

**—*The Loom of History,***
**Herbert J. Muller, 1958**

### PRIMARY SOURCE 2

"Perhaps . . . another kind of explanation can be given for the acceptance of Arab rule by the population of the conquered countries. To most of them it did not matter whether they were ruled by Iranians, Greeks or Arabs. Government impinged for the most part on the life of cities and . . . city-dwellers might not care much who ruled them, provided they were secure, at peace and reasonably taxed. The people of the countryside . . . lived under their own chiefs and . . . with their own customs, and it made little difference to them who ruled the cities. For some, the replacement of Greeks and Iranians by Arabs even offered advantages."

**—*A History of the Arab Peoples,***
**Albert Hourani, 1991**

### DOCUMENT-BASED QUESTIONS

During the early eighth century, the Muslims swiftly extended their empire, conquering Southwest Asia.

1. **Drawing Conclusions** Do you believe that most people easily accepted outside rule as Hourani suggests?
2. **Making Inferences** Was the success of the Arabs due to religious fervor, military strength, or other reasons?

## The Mongols

**MAIN IDEA** The violent invasion of the Mongols destroyed the old Islamic Empire established by the Arabs and created a new center of Islamic civilization in Cairo, Egypt.

***HISTORY & YOU*** How can one aggressive group terrify a community? Where has this happened in your state or country? Learn how the Mongols' aggression created terror.

The **Mongols** were a pastoral, horse-riding people who swept out of the Gobi in the early thirteenth century to seize control over much of the known world (see Chapter 8). Unlike the Seljuk Turks, the Mongols were not Muslims. As nomadic peoples, they often found it difficult to adapt to the settled conditions they found in major cities in the region. These invaders were destructive in their conquests. They burned cities to the ground, destroyed dams, and reduced farming villages to the point of mass starvation. Their goal was to create such terror that people would not fight back.

Beginning with the advances led by Genghis Khan in North China, Mongol armies spread across central Asia. By the time of Genghis Khan's death in 1227, the Mongol Empire covered land from the Caspian Sea to the Sea of Japan. In 1258, under the leadership of Hülegü (hoo•LAY•GOO), brother of the more famous Kublai Khan (KOO•BLUH•KAHN), the Mongols seized Persia and Mesopotamia. The Abbasid caliphate at Baghdad was brought to an end. Hülegü had a strong hatred of Islam. After his forces captured Baghdad in 1258, he decided to destroy the city. Schools, libraries, **mosques** (Muslim houses of worship), and palaces were burned to the ground. Possibly a million Muslims were killed, along with members of the Abbasid dynasty.

The Mongols advanced as far as the Red Sea. Their attempt to seize Egypt failed, however, in part because of resistance from the Mamluks. The Mamluks were enslaved Turkish soldiers who had overthrown the administration set up by Saladin and seized power for themselves.

Like the Arabs, Berbers, and Turks, the Mongols became involved in city life through the caravan trade. Over time, the Mongol rulers converted to Islam and began to intermarry with local peoples. Where once they had aggressively destroyed the cities, they now began to rebuild them. By the fourteenth century, the Mongol Empire had begun to split into separate kingdoms. The old Islamic Empire established by the Arabs in the seventh and eighth centuries had come to an end. As a result of the Mongol destruction of Baghdad, the new center of Islamic civilization became Cairo, in Egypt.

✓**Reading Check** **Summarizing** How did the Mongols seize control of the Arab Empire in the early thirteenth century?

## SECTION 2 REVIEW

### Vocabulary

1. **Explain** the significance of: oriented, Abū Bakr, caliph, jihad, Muʻāwiyah, Umayyad dynasty, Battle of Tours, Shia, Sunni, Abbasid dynasty, Baghdad, Hārūn al-Rashīd, complex, vizier, Seljuk Turks, sultan, Saladin, Mongols, mosque.

### Main Ideas

2. **List** the successors to Muhammad through the year 656.
3. **Explain** the positive and negative results of the Umayyad dynasty.
4. **Create** a chart comparing causes for the decline of the the Abbasid dynasty and the end of the Western Roman Empire.

| Abbasid Dynasty | Roman Empire |
|---|---|
| | |
| | |
| | |

5. **Identify** the event that prompted the Byzantine emperor to ask for help against the Seljuk Turks.

### Critical Thinking

6. **The BIG Idea** **Comparing and Contrasting** How did the different rulers of the Arab Empire create order and security?
7. **Making Inferences** The initial Mongol reaction to Islam changed over time. Why do you think the Mongols gradually accepted Islam?
8. **Analyzing Visuals** Examine the painting on page 195. Does this work represent the European or the Arab point of view? Why?

### Writing About History

9. **Persuasive Writing** Imagine you are General Muʻāwiyah and have just become caliph. Write a speech that outlines how you will rule and why you believe the caliphate should be hereditary.

**History ONLINE**

For help with the concepts in this section of *Glencoe World History,* go to glencoe.com and click Study Central™.

SECTION 3 Section Audio Spotlight Video

# Islamic Civilization

## GUIDE TO READING

### The BIG Idea

**Struggle for Rights** Though Islamic teaching says that all people are equal under Allah, this was not strictly the case in the Arab Empire.

### Content Vocabulary

- bazaar *(p. 201)*
- dowry *(p. 203)*

### Academic Vocabulary

- compiled *(p. 202)*
- eroded *(p. 203)*

### People and Places

- Morocco *(p. 200)*
- Caspian Sea *(p. 200)*
- Fatimids *(p. 200)*
- Córdoba *(p. 200)*

### Reading Strategy

**Comparing** As you read, create a chart like the one below to help you study. Compare the urban areas of the Arab Empire to the more rural areas of the empire.

| Urban areas | Rural areas |
|---|---|
| | |
| | |

*An extensive trade network brought prosperity to the Islamic world, which necessitated the creation of new rules. The Quran provided fundamental guidelines for all Muslims, not only in spiritual affairs, but also in politics, economics, and social life.*

## Prosperity in the Islamic World

**MAIN IDEA** Growing trade and favorable geography allowed both urban and rural areas to flourish during the period of the Arab Empire.

**HISTORY & YOU** What do you like best about where you live? Learn about the different lifestyles of people in the Arab Empire.

Overall, the period of the Arab Empire was prosperous. The Arabs carried on extensive trade, not only within the Islamic world but also with China, the Byzantine Empire, India, and Southeast Asia. Trade was carried both by ship and by camel caravans, which traveled from **Morocco** in the far west to the countries beyond the **Caspian Sea.**

Starting around 750, trade flourished under the Abbasid dynasty. From south of the Sahara came gold and slaves; from China, silk and porcelain; from eastern Africa, gold and ivory; and from Southeast Asia and India, sandalwood and spices. Within the empire, Egypt contributed grain; Iraq provided linens, dates, and precious stones; and western India supplied textiles. The development of banking and the use of coins made it easier to exchange goods.

### The Role of Cities

With flourishing trade came prosperous cities. While the Abbasids were in power, Baghdad, the Abbasid capital known as the City of Peace, was probably the greatest city in the empire and one of the greatest cities in the world. After the rise of the **Fatimids** in Egypt, however, the focus of trade shifted to Cairo. A traveler described Cairo as "one of the greatest and most famous cities in all the whole world, filled with stately and admirable palaces . . . and most sumptuous temples." Another great trading city was Damascus in modern-day Syria. Baghdad, Cairo, and Damascus were the centers of administrative, cultural, and economic activity for their regions. Aside from these capital cities, travelers did not find Islamic cities to be especially grand, though the cities did outshine those of mostly rural Europe.

This is exemplified by **Córdoba,** the capital of Umayyad Spain. With a population of two hundred thousand, Córdoba was Europe's largest city after Constantinople.

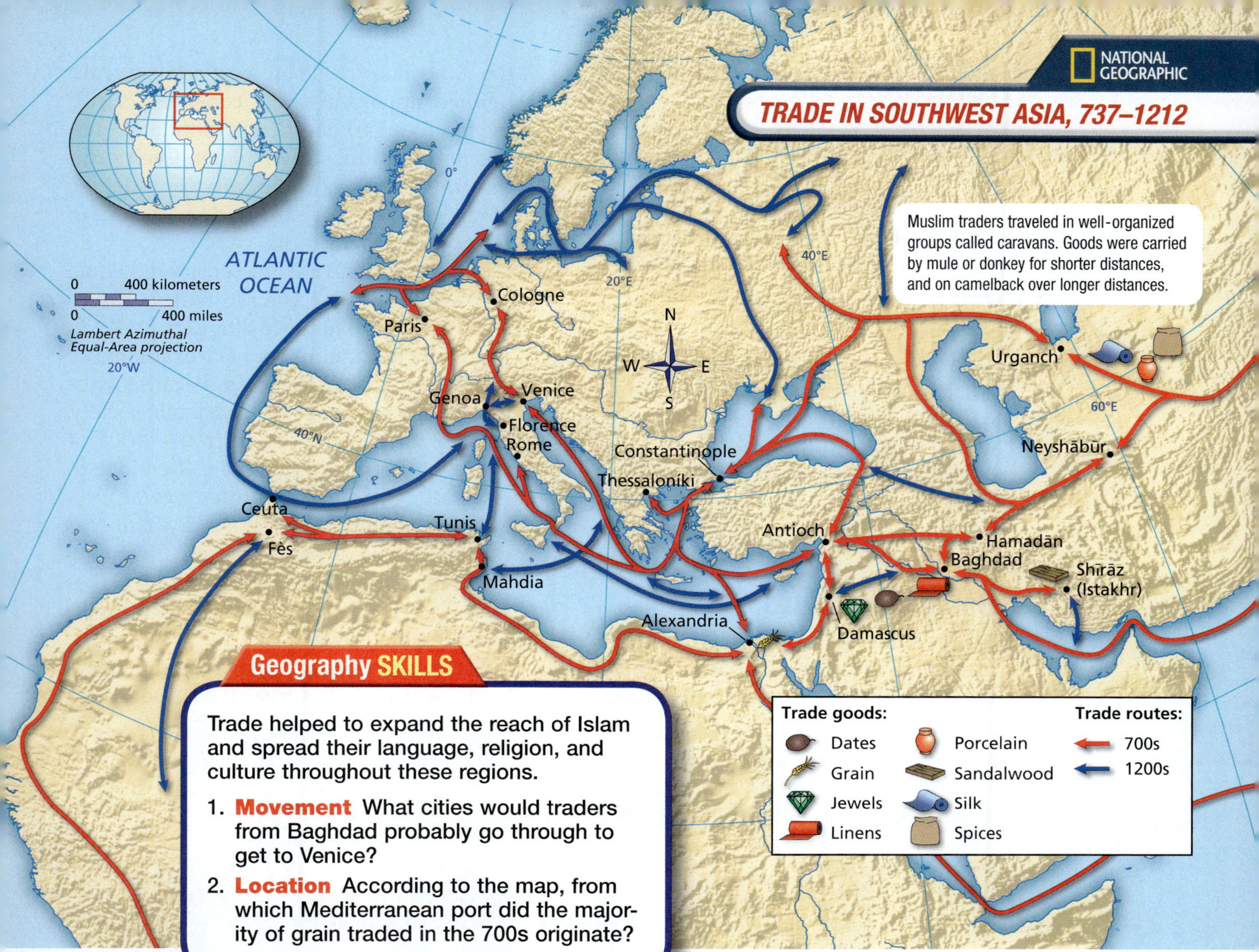


**Geography SKILLS**

Trade helped to expand the reach of Islam and spread their language, religion, and culture throughout these regions.

1. **Movement** What cities would traders from Baghdad probably go through to get to Venice?
2. **Location** According to the map, from which Mediterranean port did the majority of grain traded in the 700s originate?

Islamic cities had a distinctive physical appearance. Usually, the most impressive urban buildings were palaces for caliphs or local governors and mosques for worship. There were also public buildings with fountains and secluded courtyards, public baths, and bazaars or marketplaces.

The **bazaar**, or covered market, was an important part of every Muslim city or town. Customers could compare prices and seek the best bargains. To guarantee high standards, inspectors enforced rules, such as the daily washing of counters and containers. One rule stated, "Grilled meats should only be made with fresh meat and not with meat coming from a sick animal and bought for its cheapness." The bazaar housed many craftspeople's shops, as well as services like laundries and bathhouses.

## The Importance of Farming

The Arab Empire was more urbanized than most other areas of the known world at the time. Nevertheless, a majority of people still lived in the country, making their living by farming or herding animals.

During the early stages of the empire, most of the farmland was owned by independent peasants. Later, wealthy landowners began to amass large estates. Some lands were owned by the state or the court and were farmed by slave labor. In river valleys like those of the Tigris, Euphrates, and Nile, however, most farmers remained independent peasants and continued to farm the way their ancestors had.

✓ **Reading Check** **Identifying** List major Islamic cities and the activities centered there.

## Islamic Society

**MAIN IDEA** According to Islamic teaching, all groups are equal under the eyes of Allah. However, this was not strictly the case in the Arab Empire.

***HISTORY & YOU*** What are some rights you enjoy? Learn about the lack of rights for early Islamic women.

To be a Muslim is not simply to worship Allah but also to live one's life according to Allah's teachings as revealed in the Quran, which was **compiled** in 635. As Allah has decreed, so must humans live. Politics, economics, and social life are covered in Islamic teachings.

### Social Structure

According to Islam, all Muslim people are equal in the eyes of Allah. In reality, however, this was not strictly the case in the Arab Empire. There was a fairly well-defined upper class that consisted of ruling families, senior officials, nomadic elites, and the wealthiest merchants. Even ordinary merchants, however, enjoyed a degree of respect that merchants did not receive in Europe, China, or India.

Non-Muslims were not considered equal to Muslims in the Islamic world. Slaves were one of the non-Muslim groups. As in the other civilizations we have examined so far, slavery was widespread. Because Muslims could not be slaves in Islamic society, most of their slaves came from Africa or from non-Islamic populations elsewhere in Asia. Many had been captured in war.

Slaves often served in the army. This was especially true of slaves recruited from the Turks of central Asia. Many military slaves were freed. Some even came to exercise considerable power.

Many slaves, especially women, were used as domestic servants. These slaves

**INFOGRAPHICS**

### *Understanding the Hijab*

Women in Arab societies wore veils to cover themselves before the time of Islam. In ancient west Asia, some wealthy women wore veils and lived secluded lives in urban areas. Women of ancient Mesopotamia viewed wearing a veil as a sign of status and of a woman deserving respect. Under Assyrian law, slaves were not permitted to wear veils. A veil was a symbol of status, purity, and moral character.

*Hijab* is often used as a general term for the veil of Muslim women. In the Quran, however, *hijab* has different meanings. In some verses, it is a curtain or partition dividing rooms. In other verses, it is a sacred divide between two things, such as earthly and holy, god and humans, light and dark, and men and women.

***Hijab***
*A headscarf covering the head and neck.*

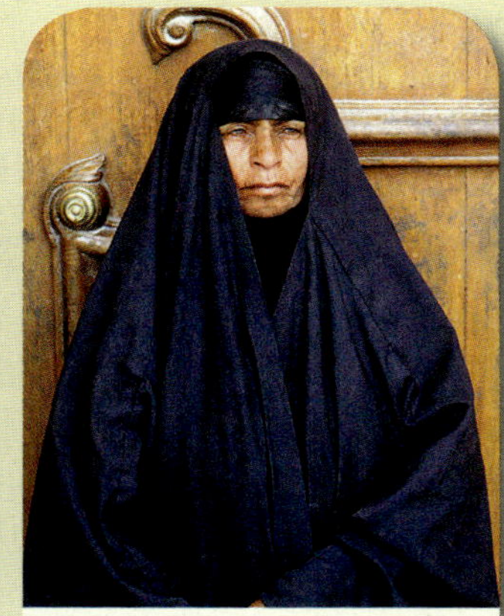

***Chador***
*A cloak that covers the full body, with a head-scarf worn underneath.*

***Burka***
*A veil that completely covers the face and body.*

**CRITICAL THINKING SKILLS**

1. **Recognizing Bias** How can the tradition of wearing a veil be interpreted to promote either women's equality or inequality?
2. **Making Connections** In what other religions or cultures do women cover their heads?

were sometimes permitted to purchase their freedom. Islamic law made it clear that slaves should be treated fairly, and it was considered a good act to free them.

## The Role of Women

The Quran granted women spiritual and social equality with men. Believers, men and women, were to be friends and protectors of one another. Women had the right to the fruits of their work and to own and inherit property. Women had played prominent roles in the rise of Islam during the time of Muhammad.

Islamic teachings did account for differences between men and women in the family and social order. Both had duties and responsibilities. As in most societies of the time, however, men were dominant in Muslim society.

Every woman had a male guardian, be it father, brother, or other male relative. Parents or guardians arranged marriages for their children. The Quran allowed Muslim men to have more than one wife, but no more than four. Most men, however, were unable to afford more than one, because they were required to pay a **dowry** (a gift of money or property) to their brides. Women had the right to freely enter into marriage, but they also had the right of divorce under some circumstances. Adultery was forbidden to both men and women.

After the spread of Islam, older customs **eroded** the rights enjoyed by early Muslim women. For example, some women were secluded and kept from social contacts with males outside their own families. One jurist wrote that

**PRIMARY SOURCE**

> "some . . . have said that a woman should leave her house on three occasions only: when she is conducted to the house of her bridegroom, on the deaths of her parents, and when she goes to her own grave."
>
> —Albert Hourani, *A History of the Arab Peoples*

The custom of requiring women to cover virtually all parts of their bodies when appearing in public was common in the cities and is still practiced today in many Islamic societies. It should be noted, however, that these customs owed more to traditional Arab practice than to the Quran. Despite the restrictions, the position of women in Islamic society was better than it had been in former times, when women had often been treated like slaves.

Even today the rights and customs related to Islamic women are still under debate. Traditional Muslims argue that the meaning of the sacred texts is being manipulated by those who advocate reform, and that the will of Allah, and not social needs, should be the ultimate law.

✓Reading Check **Describing** Describe how life in the Arab Empire did and did not reflect the principle of equality.

## SECTION 3 REVIEW

### Vocabulary

1. **Explain** the significance of: Morocco, Caspian Sea, Fatimids, Córdoba, bazaar, compiled, dowry, eroded.

### Main Ideas

2. **Create** a chart like the one below to list the characteristics of farming during the Arab Empire.

| | |
|---|---|
| Characteristics of Farming | |
| | |
| | |
| | |

3. **Describe** the basic differences in the roles of Muslim men and women.

### Critical Thinking

4. **The BIG Idea** **Analyzing** Explain how Islamic beliefs influenced the treatment of slaves.
5. **Making Inferences** How might flourishing trade routes and the spread of Islam have influenced the beliefs of early Muslims?
6. **Analyzing Visuals** Examine the photographs on page 202. Which covering allows the most freedom of movement? What advantages would cloaks have?

### Writing About History

7. **Descriptive Writing** Imagine that you are an inspector at a bazaar. Describe what is sold at the bazaar. Then describe the types of violations that you are searching for and ways you use to spot violations.

**History ONLINE**

For help with the concepts in this section of *Glencoe World History,* go to glencoe.com and click Study Central™.

SECTION 4

Section Audio

Spotlight Video

# The Culture of Islam

## GUIDE TO READING

### The BIG Idea

**Ideas, Beliefs, and Values** Islamic achievements in philosophy, science, history, and the arts had an important influence on European civilization.

### Content Vocabulary

- astrolabe *(p. 205)*
- muezzin *(p. 207)*
- minaret *(p. 207)*
- arabesques *(p. 207)*

### Academic Vocabulary

- commentary *(p. 204)*
- transform *(p. 207)*

### People and Places

- Ibn-Rushd *(p. 204)*
- Ibn Sīnā (Avicenna) *(p. 205)*
- Ibn-Khaldūn *(p. 205)*
- Omar Khayyám *(p. 206)*
- Sāmarrā' *(p. 207)*
- Granada *(p. 207)*

### Reading Strategy

**Summarizing Information** As you read, create a chart like the one below to help you study. Identify the achievements of Islamic civilization.

| Achievements of Islam |
|---|
| |
| |
| |
| |

*Muslim scholars made great advances in the areas of mathematics and the natural sciences. Islamic art and architecture incorporated innovative, geometric decoration, and early Muslim literature continues to be enjoyed today.*

## Philosophy, Science, and History

**MAIN IDEA** Islamic advancements in philosophy, science, and history contributed to the world's knowledge.

**HISTORY & YOU** How has the knowledge or achievements of others helped you learn new things? Learn how Islamic achievements contributed to civilization.

During the first few centuries of the Arab Empire, the ancient Greek philosophers were largely unknown in Europe. The Arabs, however, were not only aware of Greek philosophy, they were translating works by Plato and Aristotle into Arabic. The translations were put in a library called the House of Wisdom in Baghdad, where they were read and studied by Muslim scholars. Similarly, texts on mathematics were brought to Baghdad from India.

### Preservation of Knowledge

Muslim scholars helped preserve Greek and Roman culture by translating works and making them available to other scholars. It was through the Muslim world that Europeans recovered the works of Aristotle and other Greek philosophers. In the twelfth century, the Arabic translations were translated into Latin, making them available to the West. This process was aided by papermaking, which was introduced from China in the 700s. By the end of the century, paper factories had been established in Baghdad. Booksellers and libraries soon followed.

### Islamic Advancements

Islamic civilization contributed more intellectually to the West than translations. When Aristotle's works arrived in Europe in the second half of the twelfth century, they were accompanied by commentaries written by outstanding Arabic philosophers. One such philosopher was **Ibn-Rushd** (IH•buhn•RUSHT). He lived in Córdoba and wrote a **commentary** on virtually all of Aristotle's surviving works.

Islamic scholars also made contributions to mathematics and the natural sciences that were passed on to the West. The Muslims adopted and passed on the numerical system of India, including the use of the zero. In Europe, it became known as the "Arabic" system.

# SCIENCE, TECHNOLOGY, & SOCIETY

## Ibn Sīnā's Medical Encyclopedia

Twentieth-century painting of Ibn Sīnā

*Ibn Sīnā (980–1037), also known as Avicenna, was an accomplished Arabic physician, philosopher, and scientist.*

His masterwork, *The Canon of Medicine,* is recognized as the single most famous work in the history of medicine. Translations of the *Canon* were used as medical textbooks into the seventeenth century. To write *The Canon of Medicine,* Ibn Sīnā drew on the work of Greek physicians, Arabic treatises, and his own experience as a physician. The book consists of:

1. a discussion of general medical principles,
2. a description of simple drugs and materials,
3. information about specific ailments, organized by the affected sites in the body,
4. information about diseases that affect the body as a whole, and
5. recipes for remedies.

**CRITICAL THINKING SKILLS**

1. **Evaluating** Why is it significant that the *Canon* was used as a textbook for so long?
2. **Theorizing** Why do you think the *Canon*'s information about ailments was organized according to the affected body part?

A ninth-century Arab mathematician developed the mathematical discipline of algebra, still taught in schools today.

In astronomy, Muslims set up an observatory at Baghdad to study the position of the stars. They knew that Earth was round, and they named many stars. They also perfected an instrument called the **astrolabe**, an instrument used by sailors to determine their location by observing the positions of stars and heavenly bodies. The astrolabe made it possible for Europeans to sail to the Americas.

Muslim scholars developed medicine as a field of scientific study. Especially well known was the philosopher and scientist, **Ibn Sīnā** (IH•buhn SEE•nuh). He wrote a medical encyclopedia that, among other things, stressed the contagious nature of certain diseases. Ibn Sīnā showed how diseases could be spread by contaminated water supplies. After it was translated into Latin, Ibn Sīnā's work became a basic medical textbook for university students in medieval Europe. Ibn Sīnā was only one of many Arabic scholars whose work was translated into Latin and thus helped the development of intellectual life in Europe in the twelfth and thirteenth centuries.

Islamic scholars also took an interest in writing history. **Ibn-Khaldūn** (IH•buhn KAL•DOON), who lived in the fourteenth century, was the most prominent Muslim historian of the age. Disappointed in his career in politics, he began to devote his time to the study and writing of history.

In his most famous work, *Muqaddimah (Introduction to History),* he argued for a cyclical view of history. Civilizations, he believed, go through regular cycles of birth, growth, and decay. He tried to find a scientific basis for the political and social factors that determine the course of history.

✓**Reading Check** **Identifying** What were the major contributions of Islamic scholars?

## Literature

**MAIN IDEA** The *Rubaiyat* and *The 1001 Nights* are two major early Islamic works of literature that are still enjoyed today.

***HISTORY & YOU*** What are some of your favorite poems about? Learn about the poetry of Omar Khayyám.

Islam brought major changes to the culture of Southwest Asia, including its literature. Though Muslims regarded the Quran as their greatest literary work, pre-Islamic traditions continued to influence writers. One of the most familiar works of Middle Eastern literature is the *Rubaiyat* (ROO•bee•AHT) of **Omar Khayyám** (KY•YAHM). Another is *The 1001 Nights* (also called *The Arabian Nights*).

We know little of the life and poetry of twelfth-century Persian poet, mathematician, and astronomer, Omar Khayyám. We do know that he composed his poetry orally. His simple, direct poetry was recorded later by friends or scribes. In the following lines, Khayyám wondered about life's meaning:

**PRIMARY SOURCE**

"Yesterday and today go on without us;
Tomorrow what's the charge against me, pray?
In youth I studied for a little while;
Later I boasted of my mastery.
Yet this was all the lesson that I learned:
We come from dust, and with the wind are gone.
Of all the travelers on this endless road
No one returns to tell us where it leads,
There's little in this world but greed and need;
Leave nothing here, for you will not return."

—Ehsan Yarshatar, *Persian Literature*

The anonymous stories of *The Arabian Nights* are a collection of folktales, fables, and romances that blend the natural with the supernatural. The earliest stories were told orally and recorded later, with many additions, in Arabic and Persian. The famous story of Aladdin and the magic lamp was added in the eighteenth century. *The Arabian Nights* is full of unusual plots, comic and tragic situations, and unforgettable characters.

**✓Reading Check** **Comparing** What are the similarities between the *Rubaiyat* and *The Arabian Nights*?

### HISTORY & ARTS — PRIMARY SOURCE

### *Islamic Art and Architecture*

Islamic art and architecture is guided by the Quran, which forbids the representation of living beings. Islamic mosques and palaces are decorated with floral motifs, geometric patterns, and Arabic script. Intricate mosaics cover domes and arches. These repetitive patterns are said to represent the infinite nature of God.

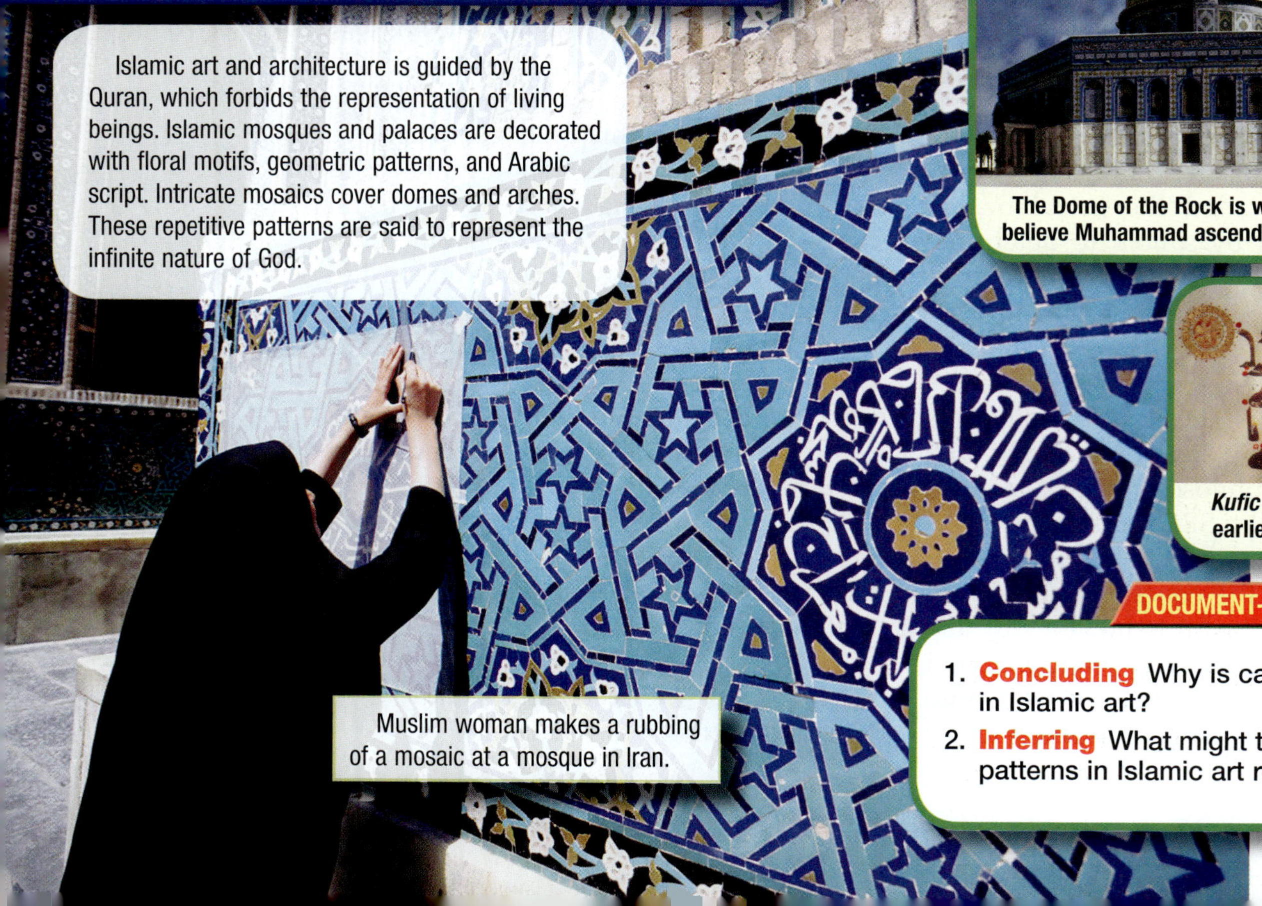

Muslim woman makes a rubbing of a mosaic at a mosque in Iran.

The Dome of the Rock is where Muslims believe Muhammad ascended into heaven.

*Kufic* script was used on the earliest copies of the Quran.

**DOCUMENT-BASED QUESTIONS**

1. **Concluding** Why is calligraphy prevalent in Islamic art?
2. **Inferring** What might the use of repetitive patterns in Islamic art represent?

## Art and Architecture

**MAIN IDEA** Muslim art and architecture reflect the spiritual glory of Islam.

***HISTORY & YOU*** How would you describe the architecture in your community? Learn about the unique features of Islamic architecture.

Islamic art is a blend of Arab, Turkish, and Persian traditions. The best expression of Islamic art is found in the way Muslim mosques represent the spirit of Islam.

The Great Mosque of **Sāmarrā'** in present-day Iraq was the world's largest mosque at the time it was built (848 to 852), covering 10 acres (more than 40,000 square m). The most famous section of the Sāmarrā' mosque, its **minaret**, is nearly 90 feet (27 m) tall and has an unusual outside spiral staircase. The **muezzin** (moo•EH•zuhn), or crier, calls the faithful to prayer five times a day from the minaret.

The famous ninth-century mosque at Córdoba in southern Spain is still in remarkable condition today. Its hundreds of columns, which support double-horseshoe arches, **transform** this building into a unique "forest of trees."

Because the Muslim religion unites spiritual and political power, palaces also reflected the glory of Islam. Beginning in the eighth century with the castles of Syria, Islamic rulers built large brick palaces with protective walls, gates, and baths.

Designed around a central courtyard surrounded by two-story arcades and massive gate-towers, Islamic castles resembled fortresses. The castles even had a gallery over the entrance gate with holes through which boiling oil could be poured down on the heads of attacking forces. This feature was later adopted by the crusaders for the castles of Europe.

The finest example of the Islamic palace is the Alhambra in **Granada**, Spain. Built in the fourteenth century, every inch of the castle's surface is decorated in floral and abstract patterns. Much of the decoration is finely carved plasterwork that looks like lace. The Alhambra is an excellent expression of Islamic art.

Most decorations on Islamic art consisted of Arabic letters, natural plants, and abstract figures. These decorations were repeated over and over in geometric patterns called **arabesques** that completely covered the surfaces of objects. The Hadith, an early collection of Muhammad's sayings, warns against any attempt to imitate God by creating pictures of living beings. As a result, no representations of figures, including Muhammad, appear in Islamic religious art.

**✓Reading Check** **Summarizing** What distinguishes the Great Mosque of Sāmarrā' from other mosques of its time?

## SECTION 4 REVIEW

### Vocabulary

1. **Explain** the significance of: Ibn-Rushd, commentary, astrolabe, Ibn Sīnā, Ibn-Khaldūn, Omar Khayyám, Sāmarrā', minaret, muezzin, transform, Granada, arabesque.

### Main Ideas

2. **Explain** how Muslim contributions to mathematics were spread throughout the world.
3. **Create** a table like the one below to identify and describe two important Islamic works of literature.

| Literary Work | Description |
|---|---|
| | |
| | |

4. **List** the other cultures that influenced Islamic art and architecture.

### Critical Thinking

5. **The BIG Idea** **Defending** Argue against the viewpoint that Islamic civilization was mainly a preserver and transmitter of culture, rather than a creator of culture.
6. **Making Inferences** What does the poetry of Omar Khayyám tell you about his character?
7. **Analyzing Visuals** Examine the photographs on page 206. What designs do you see in the mosaics? Which colors are dominant?

### Writing About History

8. **Expository Writing** Using your knowledge of Rome from Chapter 5, compare and contrast Islamic and Roman cultures. How were the art and architecture, the role of women, and the spread of religion of these cultures similar? How were they different?

**History ONLINE**

For help with the concepts in this section of *Glencoe World History,* go to glencoe.com and click Study Central™.

# The House of Wisdom

Science, mathematics, and intellectual pursuits flourished in the Arab Empire, and Islamic scholarship blossomed. Caliph al-Ma'mūn founded the "House of Wisdom," a library and learning academy, in Baghdad in 830. There, translators preserved many of the greatest writings from classical Greece—including works on mathematics and the works of Plato and Aristotle. These works, and many original treatises by Muslim scholars, form much of the foundation of Western civilization.

## Holy Months and Days

**A decree in the Quran was interpreted to mean that the calendar should be lunar, or based on the phases of the moon. Muslim astronomers created a calendar that has 12 months, each beginning when a crescent moon, or new moon, first appears in the west.**

**Muslim astronomers used astronomy to identify holy days and the beginning and end of holy months.**

**According to the Islamic calendar, each month has 29 or 30 days. A year has 354 or 355 days, so the months do not correspond to the seasons.**

## Advances in Mathematics

**Solving the complex astronomical problems required making sophisticated geometrical and other mathematical calculations. Muslim mathematicians became experts at trigonometry, developing it far beyond what the Greeks and Indians had achieved. They also made great strides in algebra. Our use of "Arabic" numerals (actually Indian) is a testament to Muslim mathematicians, as are the words *algebra, algorithm, azimuth,* and *zenith.***

## An Islamic Astrolabe

The astrolabe—essentially a model of the sky—was invented by the Greeks but perfected by Muslim astronomers. Because it can be used to make predictions and solve problems, the astrolabe is a type of computer. Islamic scholars found hundreds of uses for the astrolabe, including:

- calculating the length of the day
- telling time and predicting the time of sunrise and sunset
- determining the beginning and ending of months and years
- locating objects in the sky
- locating the direction of Makkah for prayer

These nested plates are called the *umm,* or womb.

The upper plate has marks that indicate the position of stars. It's called the *'ankabut,* or spider.

By turning the spider around the central point, the location of heavenly bodies can be simulated or represented—and predicted.

The other plates contain a kind of coordinate system for locating heavenly bodies. Inscribed on them are the names of the stars and the planets.

## Advances in Astronomy

People have always been fascinated by the sky. The path of the sun, the cycle of the moon, and the slow procession of the stars are awe-inspiring. These movements also denote time. Measuring the passage of time, whether for planting or for sacred ceremonies, has been crucial to all civilizations. Muslims are required to pray at specific times each day, so time had to be calculated accurately. For astronomers of the Arab Empire, understanding the movement of the heavens was a religious imperative that made them the masters of the sky.

### Analyzing Visuals

1. **Comparing** What modern devices serve the purposes that astrolabes once did?
2. **Making Predictions** How might European history have differed if Islamic scholars had not preserved ancient works?

# CHAPTER 6 Visual Summary

You can study anywhere, anytime by downloading quizzes and flash cards to your PDA from glencoe.com.

## MUHAMMAD'S VISION and a Powerful New Faith

- In A.D. 622, Muhammad began preaching a new religion—Islam.
- Arab leaders persecuted Muslims, but Muhammad led an army against them; for Muslims, he was a political, along with a religious, leader.
- Muslims believe the revelations of Allah (God) to Muhammad are written down in the Quran, or holy book of Islam.

A NEW FAITH

The Quran is the sacred text of Islam.

BUILDING AN EMPIRE

The Seljuk Turks defeated the Byzantine army.

## ARAB MUSLIMS Build an Empire

- In time, issues about who should be the caliph, or successor to Muhammad, resulted in a split between Sunni and Shia Muslims.
- Islamic zeal and territorial ambition led to vast conquests and an empire ruled first from Makkah, then Baghdad.
- The Seljuk Turks established a new Islamic dynasty in 1055, and in 1071 they defeated the Byzantine rulers, who asked the European states for help.

ISLAMIC ARCHITECTURE

The Mosque of Córdoba is famous for the symmetry of its arches.

## ISLAM Focuses On All Aspects of Muslim Life

- Commerce and scholarship throve in the Islamic cities of Baghdad, Cairo, and Damascus.
- Social classes existed, but Islam granted merchants and women more status than most other cultures of the era.
- Muslim scholars preserved Greek and Roman learning while making significant advances in mathematics and medicine.
- Mosques and palaces testified to Islamic architectural innovation.

# CHAPTER 6 Assessment

## Reviewing Vocabulary

*Directions: Choose the word or words that best complete the sentence.*

**1.** _______ is a Muslim house of worship.

**A** Hajj
**B** Mosque
**C** Madinah
**D** Allah

**2.** _______ is the journey of Muhammad from Makkah to Madinah.

**A** *Shari'ah*
**B** Quran
**C** *Hijrah*
**D** Hajj

**3.** _______ is a covered market that is a crucial part of every Muslim city or town.

**A** Five Pillars
**B** Bazaar
**C** Mosque
**D** Minaret

**4.** _______ was the Islamic philosopher credited with writing commentary on Aristotle's surviving works.

**A** Omar Khayyám
**B** Ibn-Khaldūn
**C** Ibn-Rushd
**D** Ibn Sīnā

**5.** _______ is the crier that calls the Muslim faithful to prayer five times a day from a mosque's minaret.

**A** Astrolabe
**B** Muezzin
**C** Sultan
**D** Caliph

## Reviewing Main Ideas

*Directions: Choose the best answers to the following questions.*

### Section 1 *(pp. 188–191)*

**6.** How did trade route expansion negatively affect the early Arab Empire?

**A** Tensions increased between rich and poor.
**B** All bazaars were shut down.
**C** Many camels died during long journeys.
**D** Many traders were killed by the Mongols.

**7.** Why did Muhammad have few followers in the beginning?

**A** Most people were Christians.
**B** He only wanted to help wealthy people.
**C** He did not believe in politics.
**D** The wealthy feared he would upset the established social and political order.

**8.** What is common between Judaism, Christianity, and Islam?

**A** They were founded at the same time.
**B** They are all monotheistic.
**C** They were all founded by Muhammad.
**D** Members of each religion were persecuted by the Romans.

### Section 2 *(pp. 192–199)*

**9.** How was Abū Bakr able to unite the Muslim world?

**A** By forcing everyone to follow the Quran
**B** By leading prayers when Muhammad was sick
**C** By suppressing tribal political and religious uprisings
**D** By conquering new land

**TEST-TAKING TIP**

When a question asks for an answer that is supported by information presented in a table, find the answer choice that is *proven true* by the information in the table.

**Need Extra Help?**

| If You Missed Questions . . . | 1 | 2 | 3 | 4 | 5 | 6 | 7 | 8 | 9 |
|---|---|---|---|---|---|---|---|---|---|
| Go to Page . . . | 199 | 190 | 201 | 204 | 207 | 189 | 190 | 190 | 192 |

GO ON

10. Which of the following factors weakened the Umayyad dynasty?

**A** Financial troubles and a capital far from the frontiers

**B** Christianity

**C** The Berbers

**D** Too many taxes

**Section 3** *(pp. 200–203)*

11. What happened to farming in the Nile, Tigris, and Euphrates river valleys as urban centers prospered?

**A** There were fewer farmers.

**B** The government controlled all the farms.

**C** Most farmers remained independent.

**D** There were serious food shortages.

12. What does Islamic law say about slaves?

**A** They could never buy their freedom.

**B** They were required to serve in the military.

**C** They could never exercise any power.

**D** They should be treated fairly.

**Section 4** *(pp. 204–207)*

13. What are some examples of Islamic advancements?

**A** Translations of Aristotle's works, paper, and the use of zero

**B** Commentaries on Aristotle's works, the astrolabe, and algebra

**C** Paper, silk, and algebra

**D** Medicine, the astrolabe, and the telescope

14. Which piece of literature is enjoyed today for its unusual plots and unforgettable characters?

**A** The Quran

**B** *The Rubaiyat*

**C** *The 1001 Nights*

**D** Omar Khayyám

## Critical Thinking

*Directions: Choose the best answers to the following questions.*

*Use the following table to answer question 15.*

### Muslim Conquests and Defeats

| YEAR | PLACE | VICTOR |
|---|---|---|
| 636 | Yarmūk | Muslim |
| 640 | Syria | Muslim |
| 650 | Persian Empire | Muslim |
| 710 | southern Spain | Muslim |
| 717 | Constantinople | Byzantine |

15. Which of the following statements is supported by the information in the table?

**A** In 717, the Byzantines forced the Muslims to give up all their territories.

**B** By 710, the Arab Empire had conquered all of Spain.

**C** By 640, the Arab Empire had conquered Syria.

**D** In less than 100 years, the Muslim Empire had conquered all the territories it had invaded.

16. In what way could slaves in the Muslim world find a way out?

**A** Under Islamic law, it was considered a good act to free them.

**B** Muslims had to pay their slaves.

**C** Under Islamic law, no women could be slaves.

**D** The Quran states that no one can be a slave for more than a year.

17. Ibn Sīnā is best known for his contributions in which area?

**A** Astronomy

**B** Algebra

**C** Cartography

**D** Medicine

**Need Extra Help?**

| If You Missed Questions . . . | 10 | 11 | 12 | 13 | 14 | 15 | 16 | 17 |
|---|---|---|---|---|---|---|---|---|
| Go to Page . . . | 194 | 201 | 203 | 204 | 206 | 212 | 203 | 201 |

GO ON

18. How did tension between rich and poor people lead to the start of Islam?

   **A** Poor people demanded a new religion that was not based on material possessions.

   **B** Wealthy people wanted a religion through which they could control the poor.

   **C** Muhammad was disturbed by this problem and sought a way to resolve it.

   **D** Muhammad wanted to help his wealthy wife, Khadija.

*Analyze the map and answer the question that follows. Base your answer on the map.*

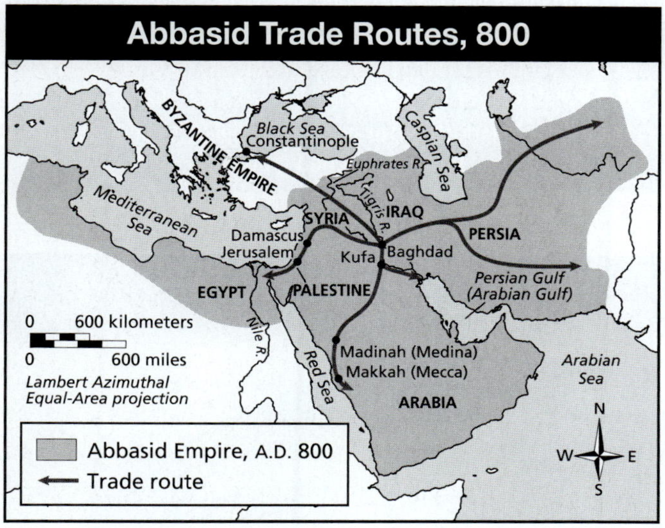


19. Why might the Abbasid Empire have established their capital in Baghdad?

   **A** Baghdad was isolated from any trade routes.

   **B** Baghdad was located on the Mediterranean Sea.

   **C** Baghdad was close to the center of the empire and was an important location for trade.

   **D** Baghdad was located on the Red Sea.

## Document-Based Questions

*Directions: Analyze the document and answer the short-answer questions that follow the document. Base your answers on the document and on your knowledge of Chapter 6.*

Known in the West as Avicenna, Ibn Sīnā was an eleventh-century Islamic scholar. In his *Autobiography,* he described his early training. Read the following excerpt.

> *"By the time I was [10] I had mastered the Quran and a great deal of literature. There followed training in philosophy . . . then I took to reading texts by myself . . . mastering logic, geometry and astronomy. I now occupied myself with mastering the various texts and commentaries on natural science and metaphysics, until all the gates of knowledge were open to me. Next I desired to study medicine, and proceeded to read all the books that have been written on this subject. At the same time I continued to study and dispute on law, being now sixteen years of age."*

20. What can you infer about Ibn Sīnā from this passage?

21. How might Ibn Sīnā's *Autobiography* have helped people to understand and value his other writings?

## Extended Response

22. *The 1001 Nights* incorporates tales from many cultures. What does this tell us about the nature of Islamic society?

**History ONLINE**

For additional test practice, use Self-Check Quizzes—Chapter 6 at glencoe.com.

**Need Extra Help?**

| If You Missed Questions . . . | 18 | 19 | 20 | 21 | 22 |
|---|---|---|---|---|---|
| Go to Page . . . | 189 | 213 | 213 | 213 | 206 |

STOP

# World Religions

A *religion* is a set of beliefs in an ultimate reality and a set of practices used to express those beliefs. Religion is a key component of culture.

Each religion has its own special celebrations and worship styles. Most religions also have their own sacred texts, symbols, and sites. All of these aspects of religion help to unite followers regardless of where in the world they live.

**TERMS**

**animism**–belief that spirits inhabit natural objects and forces of nature

**atheism**–disbelief in the existence of any god

**monotheism**–belief in one God

**polytheism**–belief in more than one god

**secularism**–belief that life's questions can be answered apart from religious belief

**sect**–a subdivision within a religion that has its own distinctive beliefs and/or practices

**tenet**–a belief, doctrine, or principle believed to be true and held in common by members of a group

NATIONAL GEOGRAPHIC **World Religions Today**

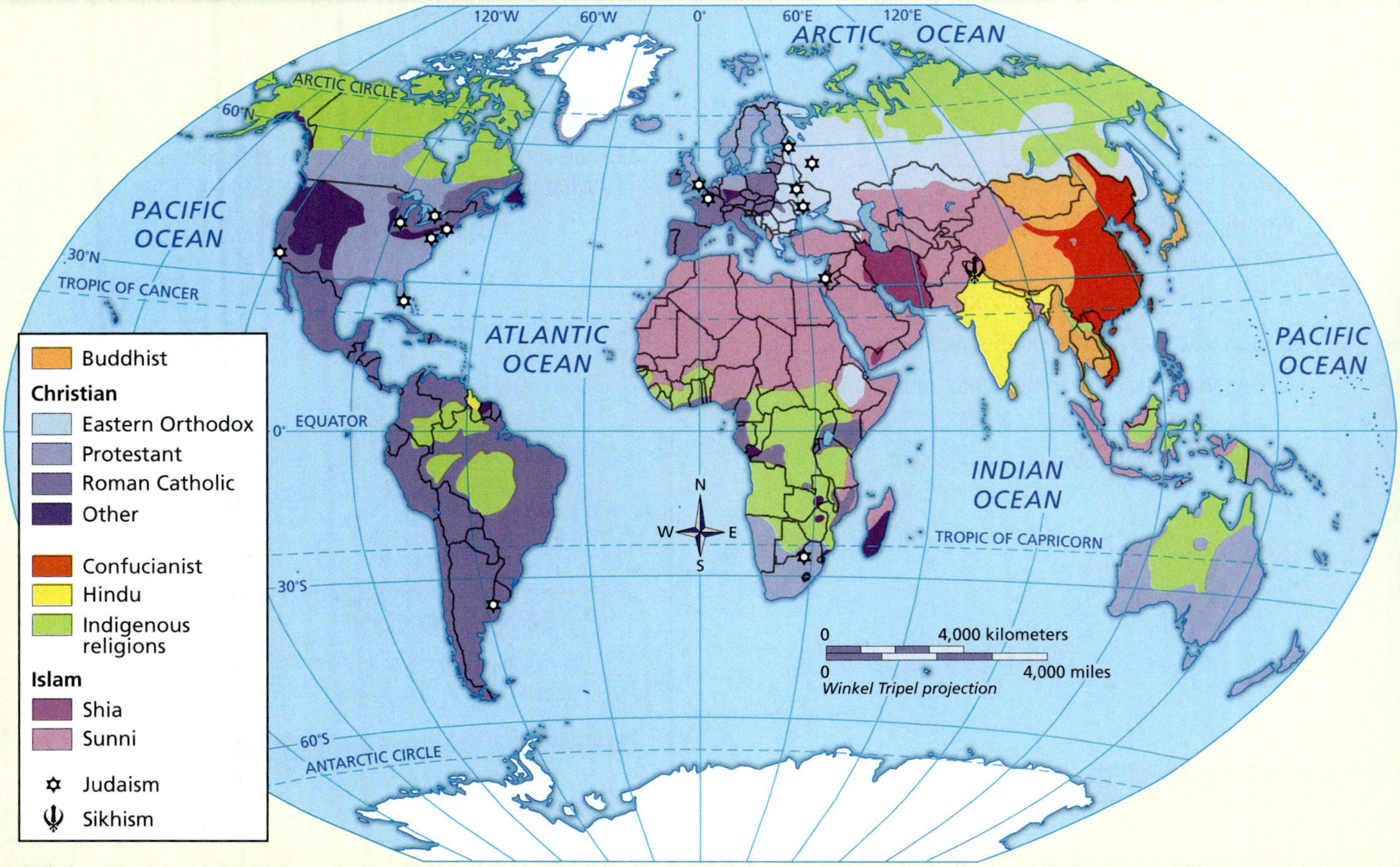

We study religion because it is an important component of civilization, shaping how people interact with one another, dress, and eat. Religion is at the core of the belief system of a civilization.

The diffusion of religion throughout the world has been caused by a variety of factors including migration, missionary work, trade, and war. Buddhism, Christianity, and Islam are the three major religions that spread their religion through missionary activities. Religions such as Hinduism, Sikhism, and Judaism are associated with a particular culture group. Followers are usually born into these religions. Sometimes close contact and differences in beliefs have resulted in conflict between religious groups.

**Percentage of World Population**

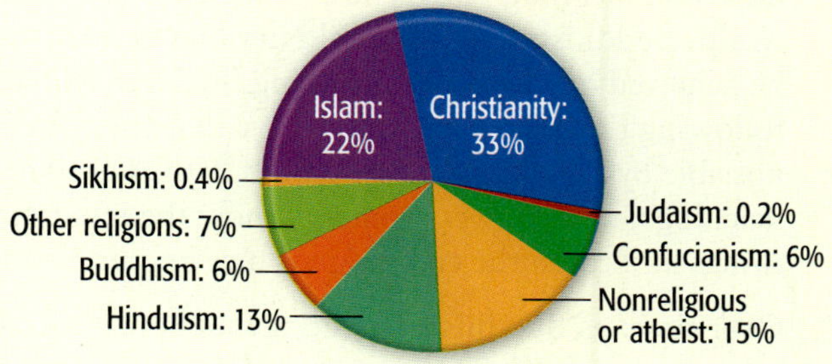


Note: Total exceeds 100% because numbers were rounded.
**Sources:** www.cia.gov, The World Factbook 2006; www.adherents.com.

NATIONAL GEOGRAPHIC **Early Diffusion of Major World Religions**

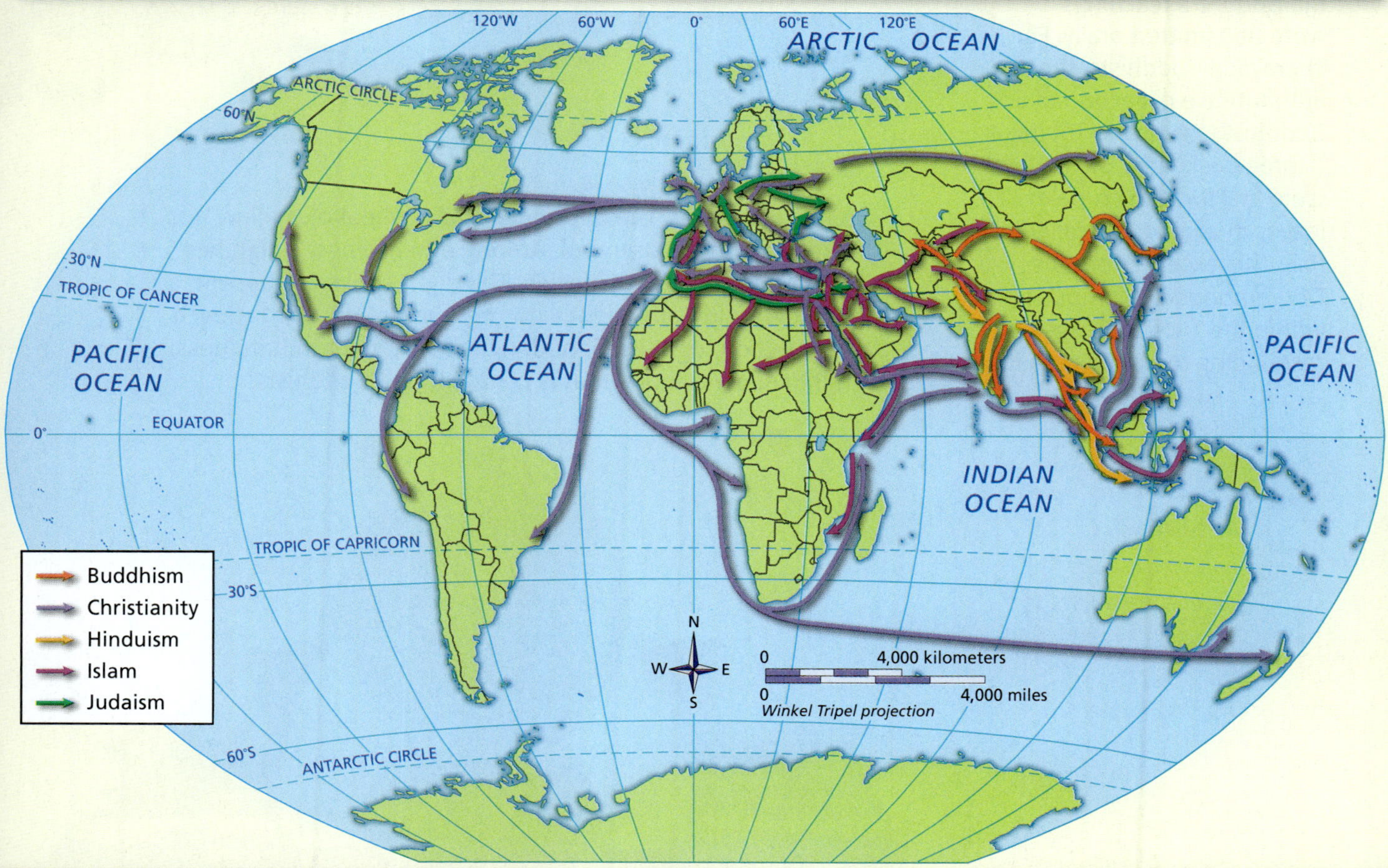

# BUDDHISM

Siddhārtha Gautama, known as the Buddha ("the Awakened") after his enlightenment at the age of 35, was born some 2,500 years ago in what is now Nepal. The Buddha's followers adhere to his teachings (dharma, meaning "divine law"), which aim to end suffering in the world. Buddhists call this goal Nirvana; and they believe that it can be achieved only by understanding the Four Noble Truths and by following the 4th Truth, which says that freedom from suffering is possible by practicing the Eightfold Path. Through the Buddha's teachings, his followers come to know the impermanence of all things and reach the end of ignorance and unhappiness.

Over time, as Buddhism spread throughout Asia, several branches emerged. The largest of these are Theravada Buddhism, the monk-centered Buddhism that is dominant in Sri Lanka, Burma, Thailand, Laos, and Cambodia; and Mahayana, a complex, more liberal variety of Buddhism that has traditionally been dominant in Tibet, Central Asia, Korea, China, and Japan.

*Statue of the Buddha, Kamakura, Japan*

**Sacred Text** For centuries the Buddha's teachings were transmitted orally. For Theravada Buddhists, the authoritative collection of Buddhist texts is the Tripitaka ("three baskets"). These texts were first written on palm leaves in a language called Pali. This excerpt from the *Dhammapada,* a famous text within the Tripitaka, urges responding to hatred with love:

> *"Never in this world is hate*
> *Appeased by hatred.*
> *It is only appeased by love—*
> *This is an eternal law."*
>
> —*Dhammapada I.5*

**Sacred Symbol** The *dharmachakra* ("wheel of the law") is a major Buddhist symbol. Among other things, it signifies the overcoming of obstacles. The eight spokes represent the Eightfold Path—right view, right intention, right speech, right action, right livelihood, right effort, right mindfulness, right concentration—that is central for all Buddhists.

**Sacred Site** Buddhists believe that Siddhārtha Gautama achieved enlightenment beneath the Bodhi Tree in Bodh Gayā, India. Today, Buddhists from around the world flock to Bodh Gayā in search of their own spiritual awakening.

**Worship and Celebration** The ultimate goal of Buddhists is to achieve Nirvana, the enlightened state in which individuals are free from ignorance, greed, and suffering. Theravada Buddhists believe that monks are most likely to reach Nirvana because of their lifestyle of renunciation, moral virtue, study, and meditation.

# Christianity

Christianity claims more members than any of the other world religions. It dates its beginning to the death of Jesus in A.D. 33 in what is now Israel. It is based on the belief in one God and on the life and teachings of Jesus. Christians believe that Jesus, who was born a Jew, is the son of God and is fully divine and human. Christians regard Jesus as the Messiah (Christ), or savior, who died for humanity's sins. Christians feel that people are saved and achieve eternal life by faith in Jesus.

The major forms of Christianity are Roman Catholicism, Eastern Orthodoxy, and Protestantism. All three are united in their belief in Jesus as savior, but have developed their own individual theologies.

Stained glass window depicting Jesus

**Sacred Text** The Christian Bible is the spiritual text for all Christians and is considered to be inspired by God. This excerpt, from Matthew 5:3-12, is from Jesus' Sermon on the Mount.

*"Blessed are the poor in spirit, for theirs is the kingdom of heaven.*
*Blessed are those who mourn, for they shall be comforted.*
*Blessed are the meek, for they shall inherit the earth.*
*Blessed are those who hunger and thirst for righteousness, for they shall be satisfied.*
*Blessed are the merciful, for they shall obtain mercy.*
*Blessed are the pure in heart, for they shall see God.*
*Blessed are the peacemakers, for they shall be called sons of God.*
*Blessed are those who are persecuted for righteousness' sake, for theirs is the kingdom of heaven.*
*Blessed are you when men revile you and persecute you and utter all kinds of evil against you falsely on my account.*
*Rejoice and be glad, for your reward is great in heaven, for so men persecuted the prophets who were before you."*

**Sacred Symbol** Christians believe that Jesus died for their sins. His death redeemed those who follow his teachings. The statue *Christ the Redeemer,* located in Rio de Janeiro, Brazil, symbolizes this fundamental belief.

**Sacred Site** The Gospels affirm that Bethlehem was the birthplace of Jesus. It consequently holds great importance to Christians. The Church of the Nativity is located in the heart of Bethlehem. It houses the spot where Christians believe Jesus was born.

**Worship and Celebration** Christians celebrate many events commemorating the life and death of Jesus. Among the most widely known and observed are Christmas, Good Friday, and Easter. Christmas is often commemorated by attending church services to celebrate the birth of Jesus. As part of the celebration, followers often light candles.

# Confucianism

Confucianism began more than 2,500 years ago in China. Although considered a religion, it is actually a philosophy. It is based upon the teachings of Confucius, which are grounded in ethical behavior and good government.

The teachings of Confucius focused on three areas: social philosophy, political philosophy, and education. Confucius taught that relationships are based on rank. Persons of higher rank are responsible for caring for those of lower rank. Those of lower rank should respect and obey those of higher rank. Eventually his teachings spread from China to other East Asian societies.

*Students studying Confucianism, Chunghak-dong, South Korea*

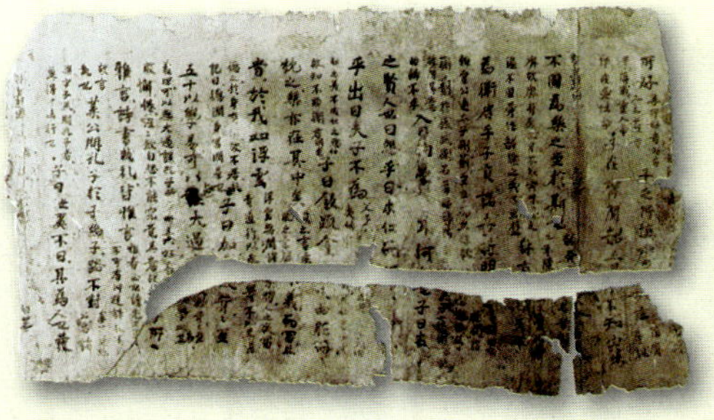

*The* Analects

**Sacred Text** Confucius was famous for his sayings and proverbs. These teachings were gathered into a book called the *Analects* after Confucius's death. Below is an example of Confucius's teachings.

*Confucius said:*

> *"To learn and to practice what is learned time and again is pleasure, is it not? To have friends come from afar is happiness, is it not? To be unperturbed when not appreciated by others is gentlemanly, is it not?"*
>
> —*The* Analects

**Sacred Symbol** Yin-yang, associated with both Confucianism and Daoism, symbolizes the harmony offered by the philosophies. The light half represents *yang*, the creative, firm, strong elements in all things. The dark half represents *yin*, the receptive, yielding, weak elements. The two act together to balance one another.

**Sacred Site** The temple at Qufu is a group of buildings dedicated to Confucius. It is located on Confucius's ancestral land. It is one of the largest ancient architectural complexes in China. Every year followers gather at Qufu to celebrate the birthday of Confucius.

**Worship and Celebration** Confucianism does not have a god or clergy, but there are temples dedicated to Confucius, the spiritual leader. Those who follow his teachings see Confucianism as a way of life and a guide to ethical behavior and good government.

# HINDUISM

Hinduism is the oldest of the world's major living religions. It developed among the cultures in India as they spread out over the plains and forests of the subcontinent. It has no single founder or founding date. Hinduism is complex: it has numerous sects and many different divinities are honored. Among the more famous Hindu gods are Brahma, Vishnu, and Shiva, who represent respectively the creative, sustaining, and destructive forces in the universe. Major Hindu beliefs are reincarnation, karma, and dharma.

Hindus believe the universe contains several heavens and hells. According to the concept of rebirth or reincarnation, which is central to their beliefs, souls are continually reborn. In what form one is reborn is determined by the good and evil actions performed in his or her past lives. Those acts are karma. A soul continues in the cycle of rebirth until release is achieved.

Statue of Vishnu

**Sacred Text** The Vedas consist of hymns, prayers, and speculations composed in ancient Sanskrit. They are the oldest religious texts in an Indo-European language. The Upanishads are part of the Vedas and describe the nature of ultimate reality. The Rig Veda, Sama Veda, Yajur Veda, and Atharva Veda are the four great Vedic collections. Together, they make up one of the most significant and authoritative Hindu religious texts.

*"Now, whether they perform a cremation for*
*such a person or not,*
*people like him pass into the flame,*
*from the flame into the day,*
*from the day into the fortnight of the waxing moon*
*from the fortnight of the waxing moon into the six*
*months when the sun moves north,*
*from these months into the year,*
*from the year into the sun,*
*from the sun into the moon, and from*
*the moon into the lightning.*
*Then a person who is not human—*
*he leads them to Brahman.*
*This is the path to the gods, the path to Brahman.*
*Those who proceed along this path do not*
*return to this human condition."*

*—The Chandogya Upanishad 4:15.5*

**Sacred Symbol** One important symbol of Hinduism is actually a symbol for a sound. "Om" is a sound that Hindus often chant during prayer, mantras, and rituals.

**Sacred Site** Hindus believe that when a person dies his or her soul is reborn. This is known as reincarnation. Many Hindus bathe in the Ganges and other sacred rivers to purify their soul and to be released from rebirth.

**Worship and Celebration** Holi is a significant North Indian Hindu festival celebrating the triumph of good over evil. As part of the celebration, men, women, and children splash colored powders and water on each other. In addition to its religious significance, Holi also celebrates the beginning of spring.

# Islam

Followers of Islam, known as Muslims, believe in one God, whom they call Allah. The word *Allah* is Arabic for "the god." The spiritual founder of Islam, Muhammad, began his teachings in Makkah (Mecca) in A.D. 610. Eventually the religion spread throughout much of Asia, including parts of India to the borders of China, and a substantial portion of Africa. According to Muslims, the Quran, their holy book, contains the direct word of God, revealed to their prophet Muhammad sometime between A.D. 610 and A.D. 632. Muslims believe that God created nature and without his intervention, there would be nothingness. God serves four functions: creation, sustenance, guidance, and judgment.

Central to Islamic beliefs are the Five Pillars. These are affirmation of the belief in Allah and Muhammad as his prophet; group prayer; tithing, or the giving of money to charity; fasting during Ramadan; and a pilgrimage to Makkah once in a lifetime if physically and financially able. Within Islam, there are two main branches, the Sunni and the Shia. The differences between the two are based on the history of the Muslim state. The Shia believed that the rulers should descend from Muhammad. The Sunni believed that the rulers need only be followers of Muhammad. Most Muslims are Sunni. Some Muslims are Sufis, members of a mystical movement that developed in the 600s.

**Sacred Text** The sacred text of Islam is the Quran. Preferably, it is written and read only in Arabic, but translations have been made into many languages. The excerpt below is a verse repeated by all Muslims during their five daily prayers.

> "*In the Name of Allah, the Compassionate,*
> *the Merciful,*
> *Praise be to Allah, the Lord of the World,*
> *The Compassionate, the Merciful,*
> *Master of the Day of Judgment,*
> *Only You do we worship, and only You*
> *Do we implore for help.*
> *Lead us to the right path,*
> *The path of those you have favored*
> *Not those who have incurred*
> *Your wrath or*
> *Have gone astray.*"
>
> —*The Quran*

*The Dome of the Rock, Jerusalem*

*The Quran*

**Sacred Symbol** Islam is often symbolized by the crescent moon. It is an important part of Muslim rituals, which are based on the lunar calendar.

**Sacred Site** Makkah is a sacred site for all Muslims. One of the Five Pillars of Islam states that all those who are physically and financially able must make a hajj, or pilgrimage, to the holy city once in their life. Practicing Muslims are also required to pray facing Makkah five times a day.

**Worship and Celebration** Ramadan is a month-long celebration commemorating the time during which Muhammad received the Quran from Allah. It is customary for Muslims to fast from dawn until sunset all month long. Muslims believe that fasting helps followers focus on spiritual rather than bodily matters and creates empathy for one's fellow men and women. Ramadan ends with a feast known as Eid-al-Fitr, or Feast of the Fast.

# Judaism

Judaism is a monotheistic religion. In fact, Judaism was the first major religion to believe in one God. Jews trace their national and religious origins back to God's call to Abraham. Jews have a covenant with God. They believe that God, who expects them to pursue justice and live ethical lives, will one day usher in an era of world peace.

Over time Judaism has separated into branches, including Orthodox, Reform, Conservative, and Reconstructionist. Orthodox Jews are the most traditional of all the branches.

El Ghriba Synagogue, Jerba, Tunisia

**Sacred Text** The Torah is the five books of Moses, which tell the story of the origins of the Jews and explain Jewish laws. The remainder of the Hebrew Bible contains the writings of the prophets, Psalms, and ethical and historical works.

> *"I am the Lord your God, who brought you out of the land of Egypt, out of the house of slavery; you shall have no other gods before me."*
>
> —Exodus 20:2–3

**Sacred Symbol** The menorah is used in the celebration of Hanukkah, commemorating the rededication of the Temple of Jerusalem following the Maccabees' victory over the Syrian Greeks.

The Torah scroll

**Sacred Site** The Western Wall is what remains of the structure surrounding the Second Jerusalem Temple, built after the Jews' return from the Babylonian captivity. It is considered the most sacred spot in Jewish religious tradition. Prayers are offered at the wall morning, afternoon, and evening.

**Worship and Celebration** The day-long Yom Kippur service ends with the blowing of the ram's horn (shofar). Yom Kippur is the holiest day in the Jewish calendar. During Yom Kippur, Jews do not eat or drink for 25 hours. The purpose is to reflect on the past year and gain forgiveness from God for one's sins. It falls in September or October, ten days after Rosh Hashanah, the Jewish New Year.

# Sikhism

Sikhism emerged in the mid-1500s in the Punjab, in northwest India, rising from the religious experience and teachings of Gurū Nānak. The religion exhibits influences from Islam and Hinduism, but it is distinct from both. Sikh traditions teach that Nānak encountered God directly and was commissioned by Him to be His servant.

Sikhs ("students, disciples") believe in one almighty god who is formless and without qualities (*nirguna*) but can be known through meditation and heard directly. Sikhism forbids discrimination on the basis of class, color, religion, caste, or gender. While 80 percent of the world's 20 million Sikhs live in the Punjab, Sikhism has spread widely as many Sikhs have migrated to new homes around the world.

*Sikh man, Chapeltown, England*

*The Adi Granth*

**Sacred Text** The great authoritative sacred text for Sikhs is the Adi Granth ("Principal Book," also known as the Guru Granth Sahib). Compiled from the mid-1500s through the 1600s, it includes contributions from Sikh gurus and from some persons also claimed as saints by Hindus and Muslims, such as Namdev, Ravidas, and Kabir.

> *"Enshrine the Lord's Name within your heart. The Word of the Guru's Bani prevails throughout the world, through this Bani, the Lord's Name is obtained."*
>
> —*Gurū Amar Dās, page 1066*

**Sacred Symbol** The sacred symbol of the Sikhs is the *khanda.* It is composed of four traditional Sikh weapons: the *khanda* or double-edged sword (in the center), from which the symbol takes its name; the *cakkar* (disk), and two curved daggers (*kirpan*) representing temporal and spiritual power, respectively Piri and Miri.

**Sacred Sites** Amritsar is the spiritual capital of Sikhism. The Golden Temple (*Harimandir Sahib*) in Amritsar is the most sacred of Sikh shrines.

**Worship and Celebration** Vaisakhi is a significant Punjabi and Sikh festival in April celebrating the new year and the beginning of the harvest season. Celebrations often take place along riverbanks with participants dancing and wearing brightly colored clothes.

# Indigenous Religions

There are many varieties of religious belief that are limited to particular ethnic groups. These local religions are found in Africa as well as isolated parts of Japan, Australia, and the Americas.

Most local religions reflect a close relationship with the environment. Some groups teach that people are a part of nature, not separate from it. Animism is characteristic of many indigenous religions. Natural features are sacred, and stories about how nature came to be are an important part of religious heritage. Although many of these stories have been written down in modern times, they were originally transmitted orally.

**Africa** The continent of Africa is home to a variety of local religions. Despite their differences, most African religions recognize the existence of one creator in addition to spirits that inhabit all aspects of life. Religious ceremonies are often celebrated with music and dance.

1 These Turkana women from Kenya are performing a traditional jumping dance.

2 Rituals are an important part of African religions. These Masai boys are wearing ceremonial dress as part of a ritual.

3 Masks are a component of ritual and ceremony. This mask from Cameroon is used to celebrate harvest.

**Japan** Shinto, founded in Japan, is the largest indigenous religion. It dates back to prehistoric times and has no formal doctrine. The gods are known as kami. Ancestors are also revered and worshiped. Its four million followers often practice Buddhism in addition to practicing Shinto.

**4** This Shinto priest is presiding over a ritual at a Japanese temple. These priests often live on shrine grounds.

**5** Shinto shrines, like this one, are usually built in places of great natural beauty to emphasize the relationship between people and nature.

**Australia** The Australian Aboriginal religion has no deities. It is based upon a belief known as the Dreaming, or Dreamtime. Followers believe that ancestors sprang from the Earth and created all people, plant, and animal life. They also believe that these ancestors continue to control the natural world.

**6** These Aborigine women are blessing a newborn with smoke during a traditional ritual intended to ensure the child's health and good fortune.

**7** Aborigines, like these young girls, often paint their faces with the symbols of their clan or family group.

# Indigenous Religions

**Native Americans** The beliefs of most Native Americans center on the spirit world; however, the rituals and practices of individual groups vary. Most Native Americans believe in a Great Spirit who, along with other spirits, influences all aspects of life. These spirits make their presence known primarily through acts of nature.

The rituals, prayers, and ceremonies of Native Americans are often centered on health and good harvest and hunting. Rituals used to mark the passage through stages of life, including birth, adulthood, and death, are passed down as tribal traditions. Religious ceremonies often focus on important points in the agricultural and hunting seasons. Prayers, which are offered in song and dance, also concentrate on agriculture and hunting themes as well as health and well-being.

**1** Rituals are passed down from generation to generation. These Native Americans are performing a ritual dance in Utah.

**2** There are many different Native American groups throughout the United States and Canada. This Pawnee is wearing traditional dress during a celebration in Oklahoma.

**3** Totem poles, like this one in Alaska, were popular among the Native American peoples of the Northwest Coast. They were often decorated with mythical beings, family crests, or other figures. They were placed outside homes.

# Assessment

## Reviewing Vocabulary

Match the following terms with their definition.

| | |
|---|---|
| **1.** sect | **a.** belief that spirits inhabit natural objects and forces of nature |
| **2.** monotheism | **b.** belief in one God |
| **3.** polytheism | **c.** a subdivision within a religion that has its own distinctive belief and/or practices |
| **4.** animism | **d.** belief in more than one god |
| **5.** atheism | **e.** disbelief in the existence of any god |

## Reviewing the Main Ideas

### World Religions (pp. 214–215)

**6.** Which religion has the most followers worldwide? Which has the second-largest group of followers?

**7.** **Analyzing Visuals** Compare the maps at the bottom of pages 214 and 215. Which religions have spread throughout the world? What factors may have contributed to this spread?

**8.** On a separate sheet of paper, make a table of the major world religions. Use the chart below to get you started.

| Name | Founder | Geographic distribution | Sacred sites |
|---|---|---|---|
| Buddhism | | | |
| Christianity | | | |
| Confucianism | | | |
| Hinduism | | | |
| Islam | | | |
| Judaism | | | |
| Sikhism | | | |
| Indigenous | | | |

### Buddhism (pp. 216–217)

**9.** According to Buddhism, how can the end of suffering in the world be achieved?

**10.** What is Nirvana? According to Buddhists, who is most likely to achieve Nirvana and why?

### Christianity (pp. 218–219)

**11.** In what religion was Jesus raised?

**12.** Why do Christians regard Jesus as their savior?

### Confucianism (pp. 220–221)

**13.** What is Confucianism based on? Why might some not consider it a religion?

**14.** What does yin-yang symbolize?

### Hinduism (pp. 222–223)

**15.** What type of religion is Hinduism? Where did it develop?

**16.** Describe reincarnation. What role do Hindus believe karma plays in this process?

### Islam (pp. 224–225)

**17.** What are the two branches of Islam? What is the main difference between the two groups?

**18.** What role does Makkah play in the Islamic faith?

### Judaism (pp. 226–227)

**19.** What is the Torah?

**20.** What is the purpose of Yom Kippur?

### Sikhism (pp. 228–229)

**21.** Where do most Sikhs live? Why?

**22.** What other religions have contributed to the Adi Granth?

### Indigenous Religions (pp. 230–232)

**23.** Many of the sacred stories in local religions explain the creation of people, animals, and plant life. Why would religions feature such stories?

**24.** Which of the indigenous religions has the largest membership?

## Critical Thinking

**25.** **Drawing Conclusions** How are major religions similar? How are they different?

**26.** **Analyzing Information** How do people's religious beliefs affect what people eat and how they dress?

**27.** **Making Inferences** How do religious beliefs influence a society's laws?

## Writing About History

**28.** **Expository Writing** Select one of the religions profiled and write an essay on how that religion has affected the history of a particular country.

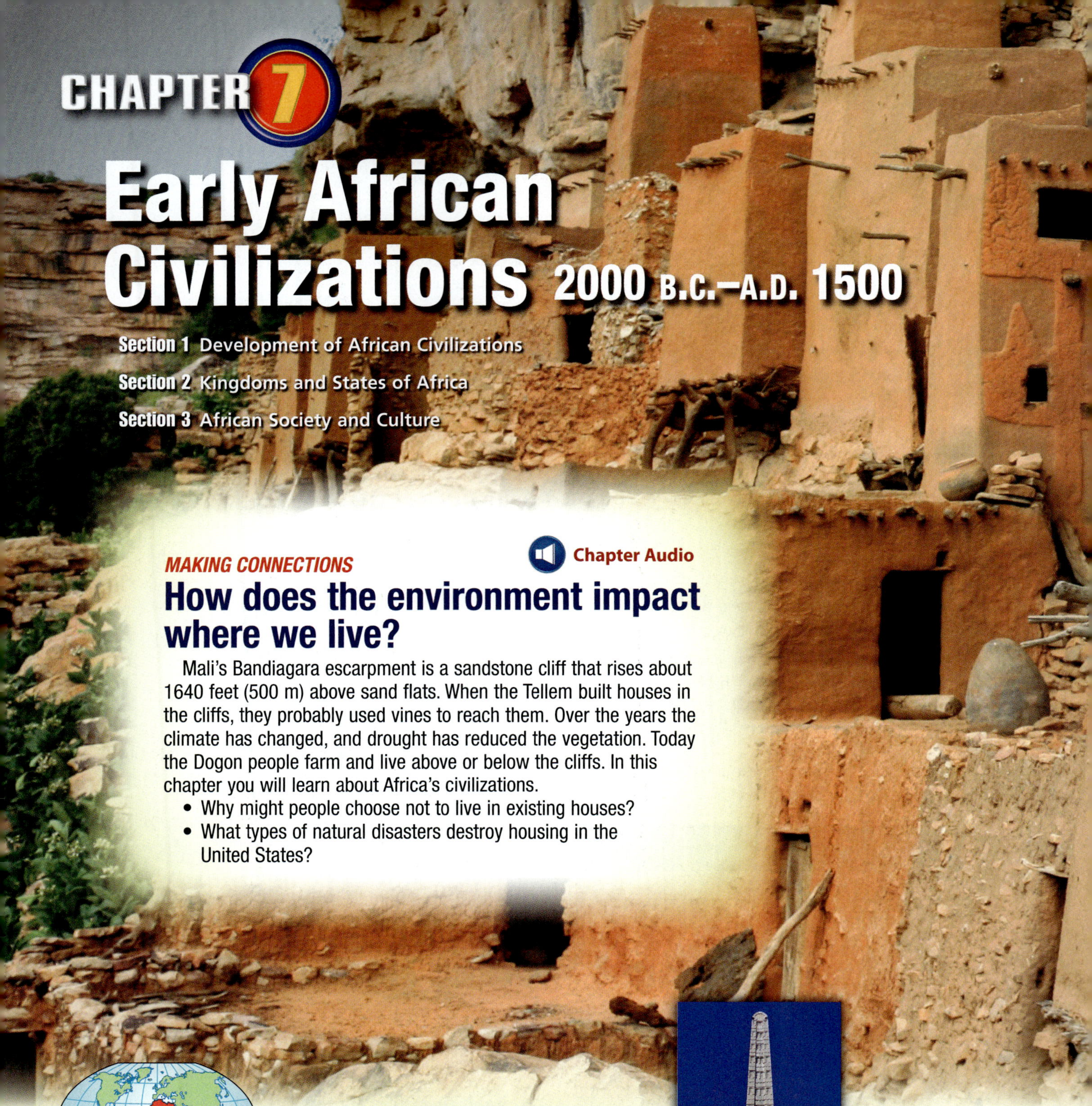

# CHAPTER 7

# Early African Civilizations 2000 B.C.–A.D. 1500

**Section 1** Development of African Civilizations

**Section 2** Kingdoms and States of Africa

**Section 3** African Society and Culture

*MAKING CONNECTIONS*

Chapter Audio

## How does the environment impact where we live?

Mali's Bandiagara escarpment is a sandstone cliff that rises about 1640 feet (500 m) above sand flats. When the Tellem built houses in the cliffs, they probably used vines to reach them. Over the years the climate has changed, and drought has reduced the vegetation. Today the Dogon people farm and live above or below the cliffs. In this chapter you will learn about Africa's civilizations.

- Why might people choose not to live in existing houses?
- What types of natural disasters destroy housing in the United States?

AFRICA ▶

**2000 B.C.** Trade thrives between Egypt and Nubia

**A.D. 330** Stele of King 'Ezānā, who converts to Christianity

**C. A.D. 1000** Bantu spread ironworking across Africa

2000 B.C. | A.D. 100 | A.D. 1000

THE WORLD ▶

**A.D. 630** Muhammad returns to Makkah

**A.D. 800** Charlemagne crowned Roman Emperor

**A.D. 1312**
Mansa Mūsā becomes King of Mali

**C. A.D. 1490**
Area south of Sahara accepts Islam

**A.D. 1500**

**A.D. 1279**
Kublai Khan establishes the Yuan dynasty in China

## FOLDABLES™ Study Organizer

**Comparing and Contrasting**
Create a Three-Pocket Book and use it to store notes about the people, places, and events of the kingdoms of Ghana, Mali, and Songhai. Organize the notes in the appropriate pocket.

**History ONLINE** Visit glencoe.com and enter *QuickPass*™ code GWHEA7447c7 for Chapter 7 resources.

SECTION 1

Section Audio    Spotlight Video

# Development of African Civilizations

### GUIDE TO READING

**The BIG Idea**

**Physical Geography** The widely varied geography of Africa influenced its culture and trade.

**Content Vocabulary**

- plateau *(p. 236)*
- savanna *(p. 237)*

**Academic Vocabulary**

- so-called *(p. 236)*
- resources *(p. 239)*

**People and Places**

- Sahara *(p. 236)*
- Great Rift Valley *(p. 236)*
- Congo River *(p. 236)*
- Kalahari Desert *(p. 237)*
- Nubia *(p. 238)*
- Kushites *(p. 238)*
- Ethiopia *(p. 239)*
- King 'Ezānā *(p. 239)*

**Reading Strategy**

**Cause and Effect** As you read, create a chart like the one below showing how trade affected Kush and Axum.

| | Effects of Trade |
|---|---|
| Kush | |
| Axum | |

*The second-largest continent on Earth, Africa includes a dazzling array of landforms, from rugged mountains to vast river basins and deep canyons. Its climate varies from region to region, from mild climates suitable for farming to rain forests and arid deserts. Both Africa's landforms and climate zones influence the ways in which its people live.*

## The Impact of Geography

**MAIN IDEA** Africa includes a wide variety of landforms and a number of different climate zones that have influenced its history and culture.

**HISTORY & YOU** What examples can you give of how landforms and climate zones vary across North America? Learn why various regions of Africa developed differently.

The landforms and climates of Africa presented both challenges and opportunities to its early civilizations.

### Landforms

After Asia, Africa is the largest of the continents. It stretches nearly 5,000 miles (around 8,000 km) from the Mediterranean Sea in the north to the Cape of Good Hope in the south. The continent is almost completely surrounded by two oceans and two seas.

As diverse as it is vast, Africa includes several distinct geographical zones. The northern fringe, on the coast washed by the Mediterranean Sea, is mountainous along much of its length. South of the mountains lies the largest desert on Earth, the **Sahara**, which stretches from the Atlantic Ocean to the Indian Ocean. To the east is the Nile River, heart of the ancient Egyptian civilization. Beyond that lies the Red Sea, separating Africa from Asia.

Africa south of the Sahara is divided into a number of major regions. In the west is the **so-called** hump of Africa, which juts like a massive shoulder into the Atlantic Ocean. Here the Sahara gradually gives way to grasslands in the interior and then to tropical jungles along the coast.

Far to the east is a very different terrain of snow-capped mountains, upland plateaus, and lakes. A distinctive feature is the **Great Rift Valley**, where mountains loom over deep canyons. Much of this region is grassland populated by wild animals. Farther to the south lies the Congo basin, with its dense vegetation watered by the mighty **Congo River**. The tropical rain forests of this area then fade gradually into the hills, **plateaus** (relatively high, flat land areas), and deserts of the south.

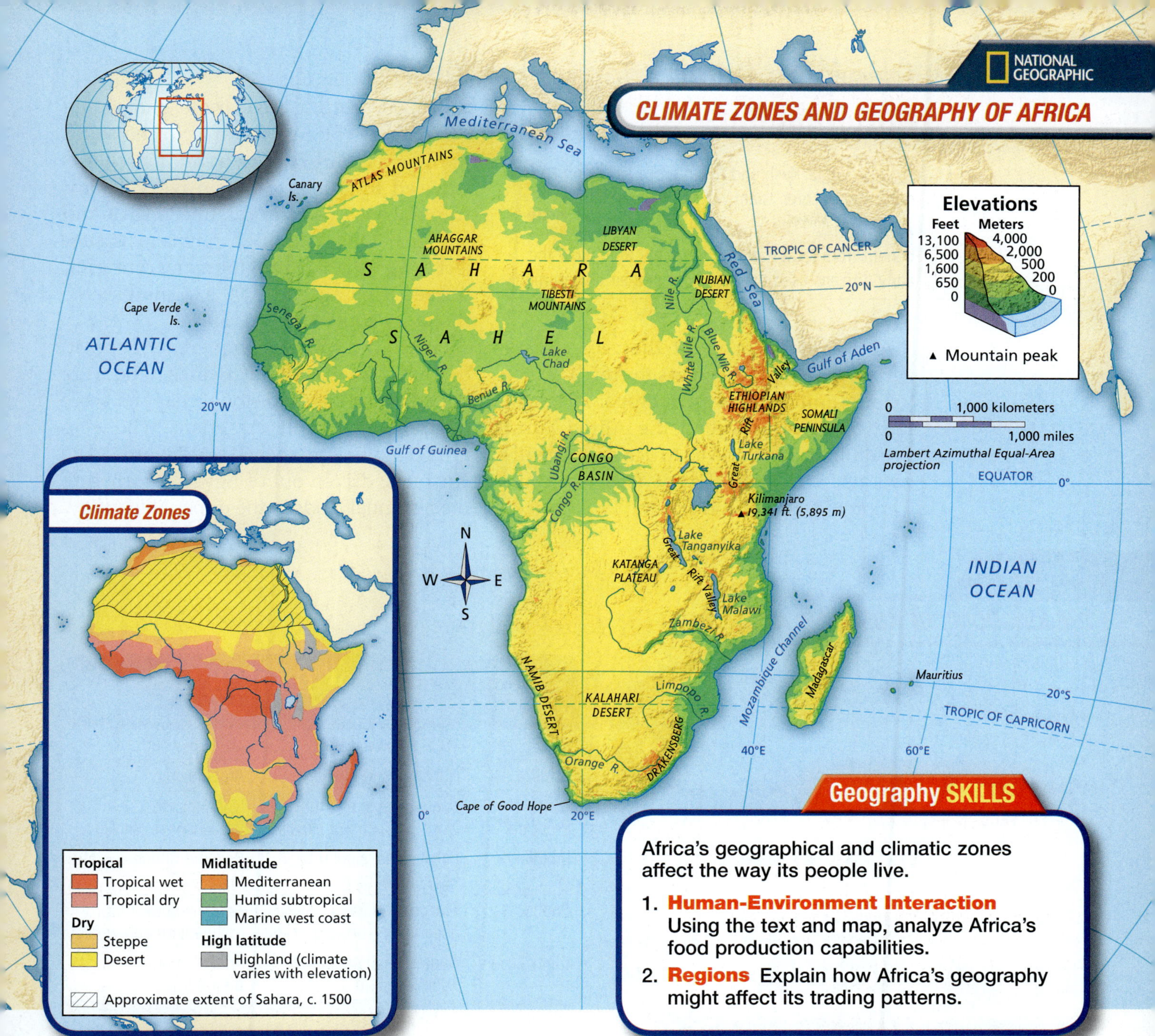


**Geography SKILLS**

Africa's geographical and climatic zones affect the way its people live.

1. **Human-Environment Interaction** Using the text and map, analyze Africa's food production capabilities.
2. **Regions** Explain how Africa's geography might affect its trading patterns.

## Climate

Africa includes four distinct climate zones. A mild climate zone stretches across the northern coast and southern tip of Africa. Moderate rainfall, warm temperatures, and fertile land produce abundant crops that can support large populations.

Deserts form another climate zone, covering about 40 percent of Africa. The Sahara in the north and the **Kalahari** in the south are the two largest deserts.

A third climate zone is the rain forest that stretches along the equator and makes up about 10 percent of the continent. Heavy rains and warm temperatures produce dense forests where little farming and little travel are possible. The rain forest is home to the tsetse (SET•see) fly, which infects both animals and humans with sleeping sickness.

**Savannas**, broad grasslands dotted with small trees and shrubs, exist both north and south of the rain forest. They cover perhaps 40 percent of Africa's land area. The savannas get enough rainfall for farming and herding, but the rain is unreliable.

✓**Reading Check** **Identifying** What are Africa's four climate zones?

# Emerging Civilizations and Religions

**MAIN IDEA** Kush and Axum arose as strong early civilizations. Later, Islam would influence Africa.

**HISTORY & YOU** How do people in your region benefit from local natural resources? Read how the early Africans used the resources in their environment.

About seven or eight thousand years ago, hunters and gatherers in Africa began to tame animals and grow crops. The mastery of farming, called the Agricultural Revolution, gave rise to Africa's first civilizations, including Egypt (discussed in Chapter 2), Kush, and Axum.

## Kush

By 2000 B.C., a busy trade had arisen between Egypt and the area to the south known as **Nubia**. Egyptian merchants traveled to Nubia to obtain ivory, ebony, frankincense (a fragrant tree resin), and leopard skins. Although Nubia was subject to Egyptian control for many centuries, it freed itself around 1000 B.C. and became the independent state of Kush.

In 750 B.C., Kush conquered Egypt. In 663 B.C., however, the **Kushites,** who were still using bronze and stone weapons, were overwhelmed by the Assyrians, who were armed with iron spears and swords. The Kushites, driven out of Egypt, returned to their original lands in the upper Nile valley.

NATIONAL GEOGRAPHIC

### THE KINGDOMS OF KUSH AND AXUM

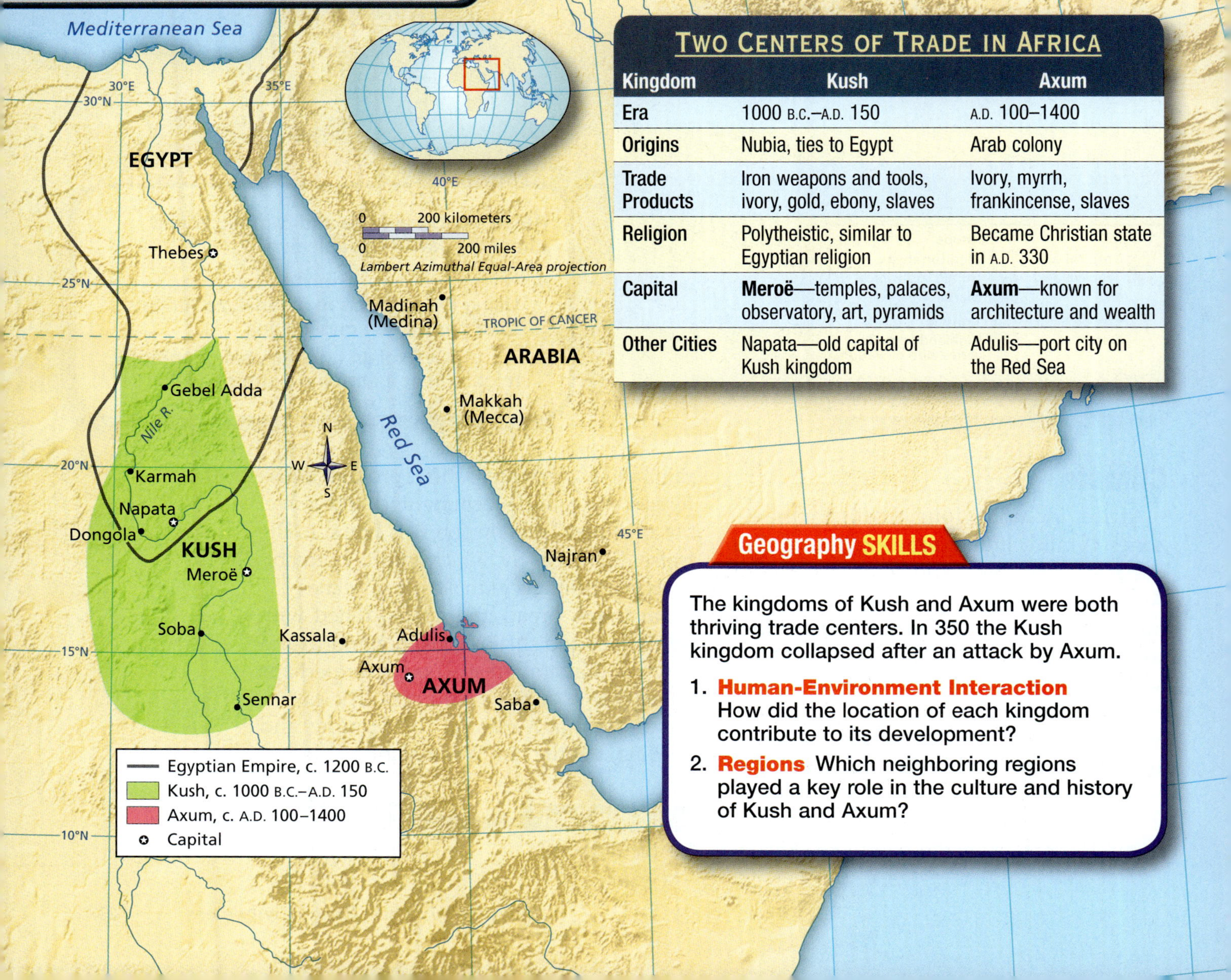


**TWO CENTERS OF TRADE IN AFRICA**

| Kingdom | Kush | Axum |
|---|---|---|
| Era | 1000 B.C.–A.D. 150 | A.D. 100–1400 |
| Origins | Nubia, ties to Egypt | Arab colony |
| Trade Products | Iron weapons and tools, ivory, gold, ebony, slaves | Ivory, myrrh, frankincense, slaves |
| Religion | Polytheistic, similar to Egyptian religion | Became Christian state in A.D. 330 |
| Capital | **Meroë**—temples, palaces, observatory, art, pyramids | **Axum**—known for architecture and wealth |
| Other Cities | Napata—old capital of Kush kingdom | Adulis—port city on the Red Sea |

**Geography SKILLS**

The kingdoms of Kush and Axum were both thriving trade centers. In 350 the Kush kingdom collapsed after an attack by Axum.

1. **Human-Environment Interaction** How did the location of each kingdom contribute to its development?
2. **Regions** Which neighboring regions played a key role in the culture and history of Kush and Axum?

The economy of Kush was based on farming at first. Kush soon emerged, however, as one of the major trading states in the region, with its center at the city of Meroë (MEHR•oh•WEE). Meroë was located where a newly opened land route across the desert to the north crossed the Nile. Meroë had abundant iron ore **resources.** Having learned iron ore smelting from the Assyrians, the Kushites made iron weapons and tools.

For the next several hundred years, Kush was a major trading empire. Kush provided iron products, ivory, gold, ebony, and slaves from central and eastern Africa to the Roman Empire, Arabia, and India. In return, the Kushites received luxury goods from India and Arabia.

It seems likely that Kushite society was mostly urban. At first, state authorities probably controlled foreign trade. Extensive luxury goods found in private tombs indicate that material prosperity was relatively widespread.

## Axum

Kush flourished from about 250 B.C. to about A.D. 150 but declined because of the rise of Axum. Located in what is now **Ethiopia,** Axum was founded by Arabs and combined Arab and African cultures.

Axum owed its prosperity to its location along the Red Sea, on the trade route between India and the Mediterranean. Axum exported ivory, frankincense, myrrh, and slaves. It imported textiles, metal goods, wine, and olive oil.

For a time, Axum competed with the neighboring state of Kush for control of the ivory trade. Probably as a result of this competition for ivory, in the fourth century A.D., **King 'Ezānā,** the Axumite ruler, invaded and conquered Kush.

Perhaps the most distinctive feature of Axumite civilization was its religion. About A.D. 330, King 'Ezānā converted to Christianity, which was first brought to Axum by shipwrecked Syrians. The king made Christianity Axum's official religion. Within a few centuries, a new religion—Islam—brought profound challenges to the kingdom.

## Rise of Islam

Islam rose from the Arabian Peninsula and then spread across the region. In 641, Arab forces captured Egypt. By the early 700s, Arabs ruled North Africa's coast west to the Strait of Gibraltar. Muslim states also occupied lands along the Red Sea. Their relationship with Christian Axum was relatively peaceful. Beginning in the twelfth century, Muslim states moved inland to gain control over the trade in slaves and ivory. Axum fought back. By the early fifteenth century, Axum had become involved in a growing conflict with the Muslim state of Adal, located at the point where the Indian Ocean meets the Red Sea.

✓Reading Check **Summarizing** How did conquest and trade affect the people of Kush and Axum?

## SECTION 1 REVIEW

### Vocabulary

1. **Explain** the significance of: Sahara, so-called, Great Rift Valley, Congo River, plateau, Kalahari, savanna, Nubia, Kushites, resources, Ethiopia, King 'Ezānā

### Main Ideas

2. **List** the major landforms found in Africa.
3. **Identify** the trade product that affected relations between Kush and Axum.
4. **Create** a chart like the one below to compare the occupations, natural resources, imports, and exports of Kush and Axum.

| Kush | Axum |
|---|---|
| | |
| | |

### Critical Thinking

5. **The BIG Idea** **Making Connections** How did trade help facilitate the spread of Islam across Africa?
6. **Analyzing** How did the technology of iron ore smelting help Kush to become a powerful trading state?
7. **Analyzing Visuals** Examine the map on page 238. How did the size (land area) of Axum compare to that of Kush?

### Writing About History

8. **Narrative Writing** Describe how Meroë's location and its natural resources contributed to the rise of Kush as a major trading empire.

**History ONLINE**

For help with the concepts in this section of *Glencoe World History,* go to glencoe.com and click Study Central™.

NATIONAL GEOGRAPHIC

# GEOGRAPHY & HISTORY

The Great Mosque of Kilwa, built of coral limestone from the Indian Ocean, dates from the 11th–13th centuries.

Trading made Great Zimbabwe the wealthy capital of an inland African society around 1290.

PRIMARY SOURCE

▲ Manuscript showing 13th-century sailing ship, called a dhow, used by Arab traders to travel the Indian Ocean trade routes.

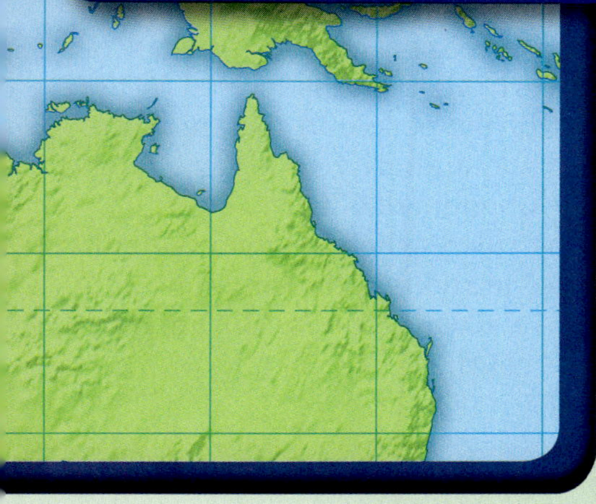

◀ Arab merchants brought Chinese porcelains to East Africa in the early 1400s.

# TRADE NETWORKS FROM EAST AFRICA TO ASIA

**Crossing the Indian Ocean** For over one thousand years Arab traders controlled the sea routes from East Africa to Asia. They began to sail these routes as early as A.D. 500 and kept their hold on the valuable Indian Ocean trade until 1500.

As they sailed the Indian Ocean, Arab traders and sailors took advantage of the seasonal wind patterns known as monsoons. Air warming or cooling over the Asian continent formed the monsoons, which blow in a northeasterly direction in the spring and summer and in a southwesterly direction in the fall and winter. Traders relied on the monsoon winds to cross the Indian Ocean to Asia in the late spring and to return speedily to East Africa in the late fall. The traders also used the lateen, or triangular sail, which allowed them to sail into the wind. From China, they learned to use a magnetic compass to guide them.

**Inland Networks** Swahili traders built regional trade links between inland African kingdoms and states and coastal cities to obtain local goods for trade with Asia. These goods included natural resources such as ivory, copper, and iron, as well as rhinoceros horns. Gold came from an area near Great Zimbabwe.

**Portuguese Take Control** In the early 1500s, Arab traders lost control of trade with Asia. In 1498 Portuguese explorer Vasco da Gama established a sea route to Asia across the Indian Ocean. The Portuguese moved quickly to take control of trading at the East African ports. Lacking large armies, weapons, or forts for protection, the traders were no match for their Portuguese attackers. The disruption of the long-established networks ended East African trading.

**Geography SKILLS**

1. **Place** How did the location of the East African cities contribute to their success as trading ports?
2. **Movement** How did the movement of goods along the Indian Ocean trade networks contribute to the spread of ideas?

SECTION 2 Section Audio Spotlight Video

# Kingdoms and States of Africa

## GUIDE TO READING

### The BIG Idea

**Order and Security** The expansion of trade enabled the kingdoms and states of Africa to protect their people and to prosper.

### Content Vocabulary

- subsistence farming *(p. 247)*
- Swahili *(p. 248)*
- stateless society *(p. 249)*

### Academic Vocabulary

- factor *(p. 243)*
- administrative *(p. 244)*
- security *(p. 245)*

### People and Places

- Ghana *(p. 242)*
- Berbers *(p. 243)*
- Sundiata Keita *(p. 244)*
- Mali *(p. 244)*
- Timbuktu *(p. 244)*
- Mansa Mūsā *(p. 244)*
- Sunni Ali *(p. 245)*
- Muhammad Ture *(p. 245)*
- Bantu *(p. 247)*
- Mogadishu *(p. 247)*
- Mombasa *(p. 247)*
- Kilwa *(p. 247)*
- Ibn Battuta *(p. 247)*
- Zimbabwe *(p. 249)*

### Reading Strategy

**Categorizing Information** As you read, create a chart like the one below describing the rulers, government, and economy of each kingdom.

| Ghana | Mali | Songhai |
|---|---|---|
| | | |
| | | |

*As African civilizations developed, great trading states arose. Traveling across the desert and over the wide Indian Ocean, traders from these states helped make their people rich and powerful. Trade not only resulted in a transfer of ivory, gold, and other valuable merchandise, but also in a transfer of cultures, spreading religion, languages, and new ideas.*

## The Kingdom of Ghana

***MAIN IDEA*** Trade in gold helped create a strong economy in Ghana, bringing wealth to its merchants and its kings.

***HISTORY & YOU*** Would you be willing to trade a lump of gold for a pile of salt? Read why salt was so valuable to the Africans.

**Ghana**, the first great trading state in West Africa, emerged as early as A.D. 500. The kingdom of Ghana was located in the upper Niger River valley, a grassland region between the Sahara and the tropical forests along the West African coast. (The modern state of Ghana takes its name from this early state, but is located in the forest region to the south.) Most of the people in the area were farmers living in villages under the authority of a local ruler. Together, the villages formed the kingdom of Ghana.

The kings of Ghana were strong rulers who governed without any laws. They played active roles in running the kingdom, and their wealth was vast. Al-Bakri, an eleventh-century Muslim traveler, wrote of the Ghanaian king's court:

**PRIMARY SOURCE**

"The king sits in audience or to hear grievances against officials in a domed pavilion around which stand ten horses covered with gold-embroidered materials. Behind the king stand ten pages holding shields and swords decorated with gold, and on his right are the sons of subordinate kings of his country wearing splendid garments and their hair mixed with gold."

—Al-Bakri

To protect their kingdom and enforce their wishes, Ghanaian kings relied on a well-trained regular army of thousands of men.

The people of Ghana had lived off the land for centuries. In addition they prospered from their possession of both iron and gold. The region had an abundant supply of iron ore. The skilled blacksmiths of Ghana were highly valued because of their ability to turn this ore into tools and weapons.

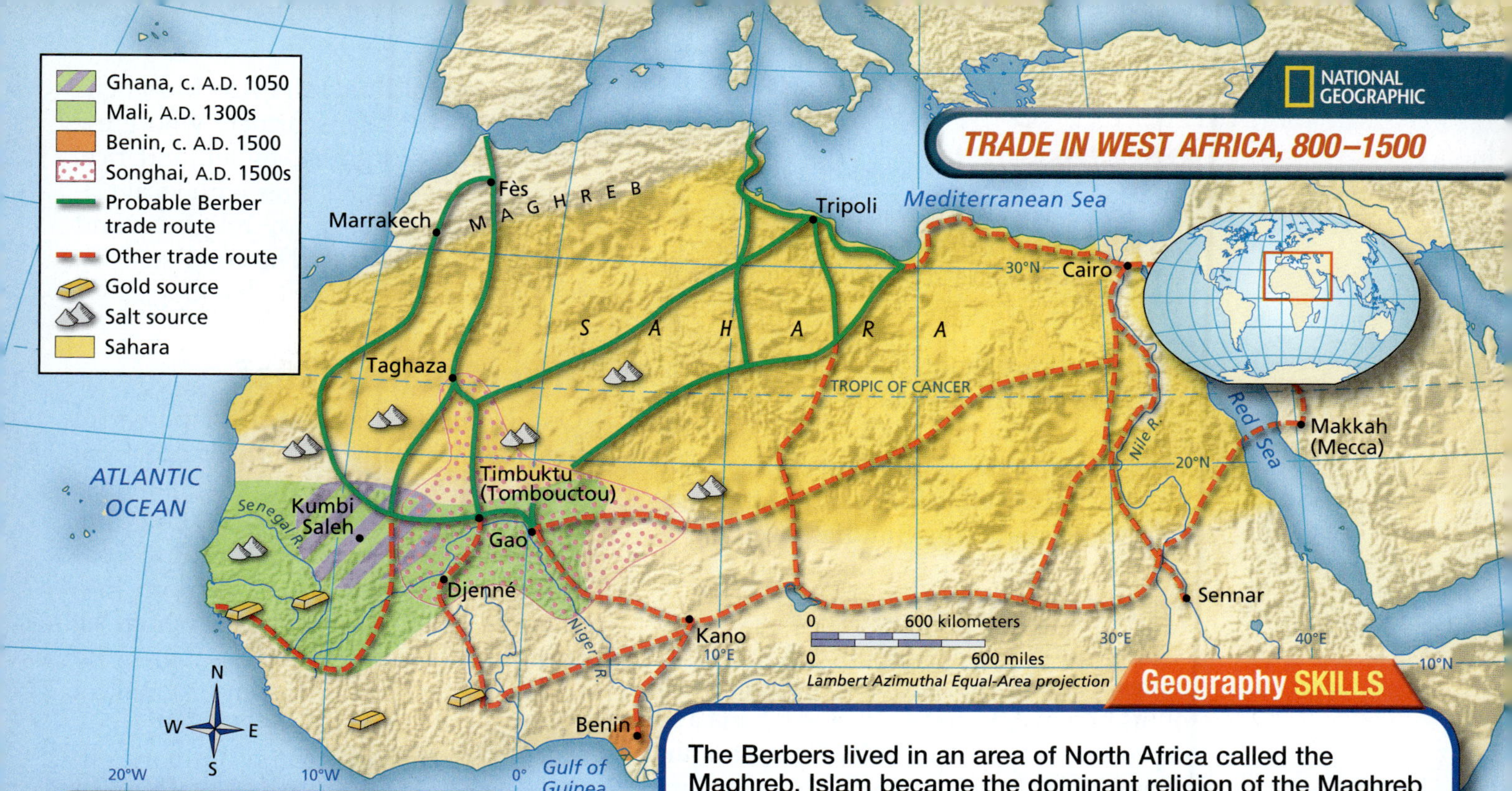


## Geography SKILLS

The Berbers lived in an area of North Africa called the Maghreb. Islam became the dominant religion of the Maghreb in the 600s. The Berbers, who had become Muslim, traded with the sub-Saharan kingdoms.

1. **Location** Why were the locations of Gao, Timbuktu, and Kumbi Saleh important?
2. **Human-Environment Interaction** How did the resources in West Africa lead to its importance at this time?

Maps In MOtion See *StudentWorks™ Plus* or glencoe.com.

Descendents of Berbers in modern-day Morocco

Ghana also had an abundance of gold. The heartland of the state was located near one of the richest gold-producing areas in all of Africa. Ghana's gold made it the center of an enormous trade empire.

Ghanaians traded their abundant gold for products brought from North Africa. Muslim merchants from North Africa exchanged metal goods, textiles, horses, and salt with the Ghanaians. Salt, a highly desired item, was used to preserve food and to improve food's taste. It was also important because people needed extra salt to replace what their bodies lost in the hot climate. Other Ghanaian exports, including ivory, hides, and slaves, were carried to the markets of the Mediterranean and beyond.

Trade across the desert was carried by the **Berbers,** nomadic peoples whose camel caravans became known as the "fleets of the desert." Camels became a crucial **factor** in trade across the Sahara, since they were well-adapted to desert conditions.

As many as a hundred camels would be loaded with goods and supplies for the journey across the desert. The caravan moved at a rate of about three miles (4.8 km) per hour. A caravan might take 40 to 60 days to reach its destination.

The trading merchants of Ghana often became wealthy. Kings also prospered because they imposed taxes on goods that entered or left the kingdom. By the eighth and ninth centuries, however, much of this trade was carried by Muslim merchants. They bought the goods from local traders, using iron or copper or items from as far away as Southwest Asia. They then sold them to Berbers, who carried them across the desert.

✓Reading Check **Examining** What role did the Berbers play in African trade?

## The Kingdom of Mali

**MAIN IDEA** Powerful leadership helped Mali thrive.

***HISTORY & YOU*** Why do some empires and countries expand more easily than others? Read how West African rulers were able to expand their empires.

Ghana flourished for several hundred years. Eventually weakened by wars, it collapsed during the 1100s. In its place rose new trading states in West Africa. The greatest was **Mali,** established in the mid-thirteenth century by **Sundiata Keita.**

### Founding and Economy

Like George Washington in the United States, Sundiata is considered the founder of his nation. Sundiata defeated Ghana and captured its capital in 1240. He united the people of Mali and created a strong government. Extending from the Atlantic coast inland as far as the famous trading city of **Timbuktu** (TIHM•BUHK•TOO), present-day Tombouctou, Mali built its wealth and power on the gold and salt trade. Most of its people, however, were farmers who grew grains such as sorghum, millet, and rice. The farmers lived in villages with local rulers, who served as both religious and **administrative** leaders. The ruler sent tax revenues from the village to the king.

### PEOPLE *in* HISTORY

**Sundiata Keita**
c. 1210–1255 Malian ruler

Sundiata belonged to a family that had ruled in Mali for about two centuries. Born with a disability, he was still unable to walk at seven years old. Eventually, a blacksmith made braces for Sundiata's legs and he gradually and painfully learned to walk. When his half-brother became ruler, Sundiata and his mother fled. While in exile, he became headman of a village and raised a personal army. After the kingdom of Susu conquered Mali and killed Sundiata's brothers, Sundiata marched on Susu and killed their king. Because of bravery and courage, he became ruler, or mansa, of Mali. Sundiata ruled Mali from 1230 to 1255. As a powerful warrior-king and the founder of the kingdom of Mali, Sundiata Keita became revered as the father of his country.

**How did Sundiata become ruler of Mali?**

### Reign of Mansa Mūsā

One of the richest and most powerful kings was **Mansa Mūsā,** who ruled from 1312 to 1337 (*mansa* means "king"). Mansa Mūsā doubled the size of the kingdom of Mali. He created a strong central government and divided the kingdom into provinces ruled by governors whom he appointed. Once he felt secure, he decided—as a devout Muslim—to make a pilgrimage to Makkah.

A king, of course, was no ordinary pilgrim. Mansa Mūsā was joined by thousands of servants and soldiers on this journey. Accompanying the people were hundreds of camels carrying gold, as well as food, clothing, and other supplies. Everywhere he went, Mansa Mūsā lavished gold gifts on his hosts and bought hundreds of items with gold. In fact, by putting so much gold into circulation in such a short time, he caused its value to fall.

Mansa Mūsā's pilgrimage demonstrated his wealth and power. His journey also had another legacy. Mansa Mūsā was inspired to make Timbuktu a center of Islamic learning and culture. In Timbuktu, he built mosques and libraries. He brought scholars to the city to study the Quran.

Timbuktu became recognized as one of the intellectual capitals of the Muslim world. The city attracted religious leaders, scholars, and artists from all over the Middle East and Africa. As many as 20,000 students may have attended the famous Sankore mosque.

Mansa Mūsā proved to be the last powerful ruler of Mali. By 1359, civil war divided Mali. Within another hundred years a new kingdom—that of Songhai—was beginning to surpass Mali.

✓**Reading Check** **Summarizing** What were Mansa Mūsā's accomplishments?

## The Kingdom of Songhai

**MAIN IDEA** Situated along the Niger River, the Songhai became powerful traders.

**HISTORY & YOU** How do rivers promote trade? Read how the Niger River helped the development of Songhai.

Like the Nile, the Niger River floods, providing a rich soil for raising crops and taking care of cattle. East of Timbuktu, the Niger makes a wide bend. Along the river, south of that bend, a people known as the Songhai established themselves there.

In 1009, a ruler named Kossi converted to Islam and established the Dia dynasty. This first Songhai state benefited from the Muslim trade routes linking Arabia, North Africa, and West Africa. An era of prosperity ensued with Gao as the chief trade center.

Under **Sunni Ali**, who created a new dynasty—the Sunni—in 1464, Songhai began to expand. Sunni Ali spent much of his reign on horseback and on the march as he led his army in one military campaign after another. His armies both defended Songhai territory from attacks by outsiders and conquered new territories.

Two of Sunni Ali's conquests, Timbuktu and Djenné, were especially important. They gave Songhai control of the trading empire—especially trade in salt and gold—that had made Ghana and Mali so prosperous. Sunni Ali not only controlled the military, but the government of Songhai.

Among his most important administrative accomplishments was uniting rural and city dwellers, who often had differing interests, under a single government.

The Songhai Empire reached the height of its power during the reign of **Muhammad Ture.** A military commander and devout Muslim, Muhammad Ture overthrew the son of Sunni Ali and seized power in 1493, thus creating a new dynasty, the Askia. *Askia* means "usurper."

Muhammad Ture continued Sunni Ali's policy of expansion, creating an empire that stretched a thousand miles along the Niger River. He was an able administrator who divided Songhai into provinces. Muhammad Ture maintained the peace and **security** of his kingdom with a navy and soldiers on horseback. The chief cities of the empire prospered as never before from the expanding salt and gold trade.

Under Askia Dawud, or Daud, (1549–1582), Songhai became the largest empire in African history. After his reign, Songhai entered a period of slow decline. Near the end of the 1500s, that decline quickened when the forces of the sultan of Morocco occupied much of Songhai. One observer wrote, "From that moment on, everything changed. Danger took the place of security, poverty [took the place] of wealth. Peace gave way to distress, disaster, and violence." By 1600, the Songhai Empire was a remnant of its former glorious self.

✓Reading Check **Summarizing** What were the key factors in Songhai's rise to power?

### West African Kingdoms

| | GHANA | MALI | SONGHAI |
|---|---|---|---|
| **Exports** | Iron tools and weapons, gold, copper, slaves | Gold, salt, slaves | Gold, salt, kola nuts, slaves |
| **Economy** | Farming and trade | Trade and farming: millet, sorghum, rice | Farming, fishing, trade |
| **Religion** | Traditional religion | Islam | Islam |
| **Cities** | Kumbi Saleh: center of trade, taxation, Muslim schools | Timbuktu: center of Islamic learning | Gao: tomb of Mohammad Ture, who converted Gao to Islam |
| **Social Structure** | King, Muslim scholars as administrators, craftsmen | King, courtiers, scholars, artisans | King, scholars, judges, doctors, craftsmen |
| **End of Kingdom** | Drought, lost trade monopoly, wars with Berbers | Civil wars | North Africans took control of gold trade |

# TURNING POINT

# THE BANTUS SPREAD IRONWORKING

The Bantu migrated out of West Africa across the sub-Saharan grasslands and through rainforests. Some theorize that the Bantu migrated because of pressure from North African groups. Over a period of more than 2,000 years small groups of Bantu spread their language, agricultural skills, and ironworking south and east across the continent.

Iron smelting gave the Bantu many advantages. Their iron weapons allowed them to conquer other peoples. Their iron farm implements were superior to wooden or stone tools. With these tools, the Bantu settled in farming villages. When the Bantu came across existing groups, they may have conquered, intermarried, and traded with them. In their wake, the Bantu left a trail of ironworking technology, language, and systematic agriculture.

Iron smelting using a traditional furnace, 1897 drawing

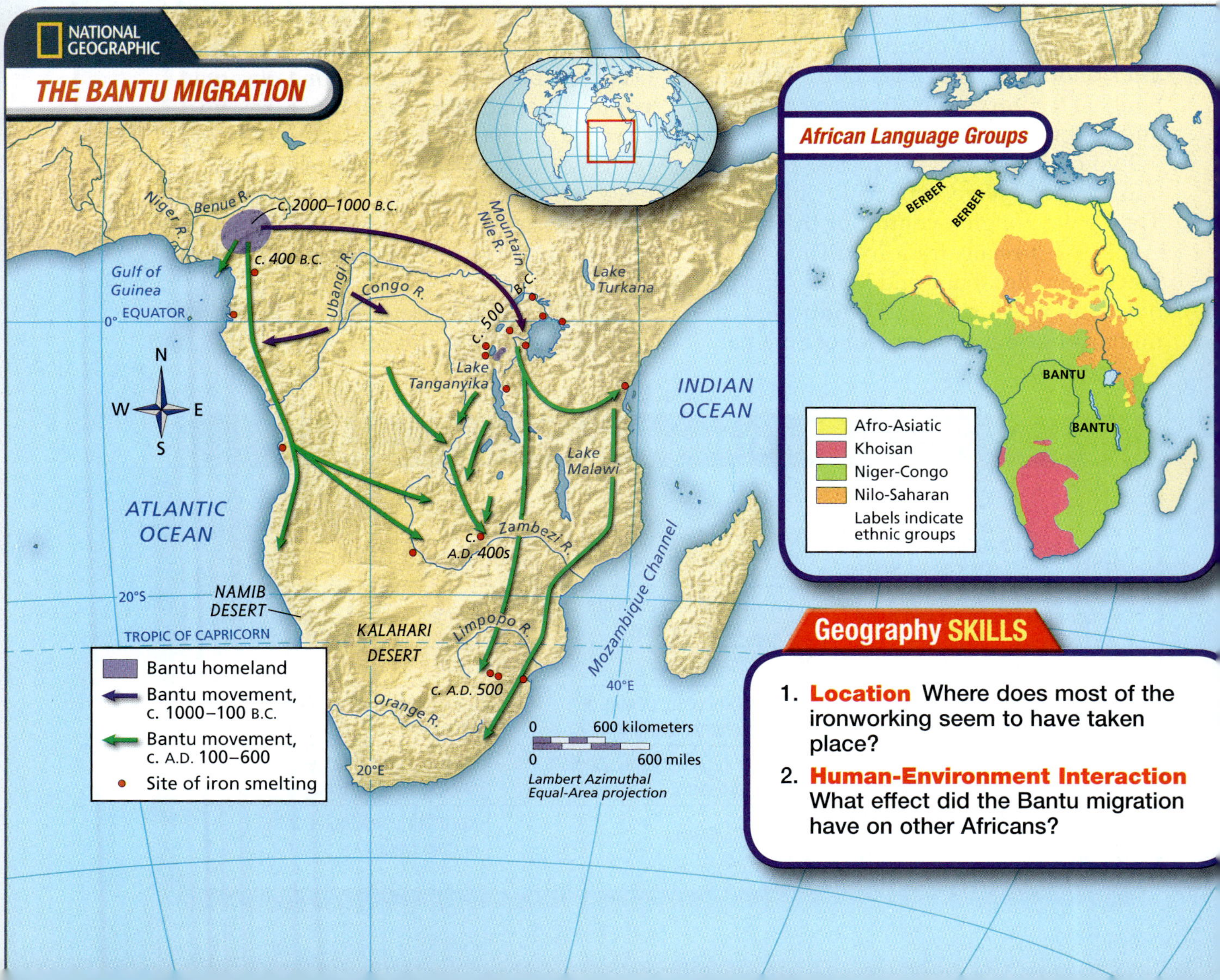


## Geography SKILLS

1. **Location** Where does most of the ironworking seem to have taken place?
2. **Human-Environment Interaction** What effect did the Bantu migration have on other Africans?

## Societies in East Africa

**MAIN IDEA** The migration of the Bantu and Indian Ocean trade changed East Africa.

**HISTORY & YOU** Why do people migrate to new regions? Read how the Bantus spread their culture.

In eastern Africa, a variety of states and societies took root. Islam strongly influenced many of them. Some became extremely wealthy through trade.

### Migration of the Bantus

South of Axum, along the shores of the Indian Ocean and inland from the mountains of Ethiopia, lived a mixture of peoples. Some lived by hunting and food gathering, while others raised livestock.

In the first millennium B.C., farming peoples who spoke dialects of the **Bantu** (BAN•TOO) family of languages began to move from the Niger River region into East Africa. They moved slowly, not as invading hordes, but as small communities.

Recent archaeological work has provided many insights into Bantu society. Their communities were based on **subsistence farming**—growing crops for personal use, not for sale. Grains like millet and sorghum were the primary crops, along with yams, melons, and beans. Iron and stone tools were used to farm the land. Men hunted or conducted local trade in salt, copper, and iron ore, while women tilled the fields and cared for the children.

The Bantus spread iron-smelting techniques across Africa and the knowledge of high-yield crops like yams and bananas. Sometime after A.D. 1000, descendants of a Bantu group established the prosperous city of Great Zimbabwe. The center of a thriving state, Great Zimbabwe dominated the trade route to the coast.

### Indian Ocean Trade and Ports

On the eastern fringe of the continent, the Bantu-speaking peoples began to take part in the regional sea trade up and down the East African coast.

With the growth in regional trade following the rise of Islam during the seventh and eighth centuries A.D., the eastern coast of Africa became a part of the trading network along the Indian Ocean. Beginning in the eighth century, Muslims from the Arabian Peninsula and the Persian Gulf began to settle at ports along the coast.

The result was the formation of a string of trading ports that included **Mogadishu** (MOH•guh•DEE•shoo), **Mombasa**, and **Kilwa** in the south. Merchants in these cities grew very wealthy. One of the most magnificent cities was Kilwa, which was located in what is now Tanzania.

In the fourteenth century, two monumental buildings were constructed in Kilwa of coral cut from the cliffs along the shore. One was the Great Mosque of Kilwa. Even grander was the Husuni Kubwa palace, an enormous clifftop building that contained more than a hundred rooms.

Members of Kilwa's wealthy elite built their houses near the palace and the Great Mosque. With imported Chinese porcelain and indoor plumbing, these homes provided a luxurious lifestyle.

Arab traveler **Ibn Battuta**, who lived in the fourteenth century, was among those who visited the cities of Kilwa, Mogadishu, and Mombasa. One of the most widely traveled people of his time period, Battuta traveled as many as 75,000 miles, visiting almost all Muslim countries and even reaching China. As Battuta traveled, he recorded his impressions about the places he visited.

No stranger to the architectural wonders of his time, Battuta called Kilwa, which he visited in 1331, "one of the most beautiful towns in the world." Kilwa's splendor did not last long, however. Kilwa began to decline, and the Portuguese finished the job in 1505 by sacking the city and destroying its major buildings.

Located just north of the Equator, Mogadishu was also founded by Arab traders. Arising in the tenth century, this trading port enjoyed hundreds of years of prosperity, but declined in the sixteenth century.

Arab traders settled Mombasa, which is located on the coast of present-day Kenya, in the eleventh century. Like Mogadishu and Kilwa, Mombasa played a key role in trade across the Indian Ocean.

**INFOGRAPHICS** **PRIMARY SOURCE**

## Swahili Trading Cities

▲ Portuguese map of Kilwa from 1500s

### Common Features of Kilwa, Mombasa, Mogadishu

| | |
|---|---|
| **Founded by** | Arab traders |
| **Ruled by** | Sultans |
| **Religion** | Islam |
| **Language** | Swahili: combination of Arabic and Bantu |
| **Economy** | Trade between Africa, Asia, Europe |
| **Exports to Asia** | Gold, ivory, iron, tortoise shell, slaves, precious stones |
| **Imports from Asia** | Porcelain, spices, cloth |

▼ Fort Kilwa Kisiwani in present-day Tanzania

**CRITICAL THINKING SKILLS**

1. **Summarizing** Why was the location of the trading cities advantageous?
2. **Making Inferences** The illustrated map is Portuguese. What was the Portuguese impression of Kilwa?

As time passed, a mixed African-Arabian culture, eventually known as **Swahili** (swah•HEE•lee), began to emerge throughout the coastal area. Intermarriage was common among the ruling groups. Gradually, the Muslim religion and Arabic architectural styles became part of a society that was still largely African.

The term *Swahili* (from *sahel,* meaning "coast" in Arabic, and thus "peoples of the coast") was also applied to the major language used in the area. The Swahili language arose as a result of trade between people from Arab lands and the Bantu people who lived along Africa's eastern coast. The language incorporated words from both Bantu and Arabic. It enabled these two groups of people without a common language to communicate and trade. As Arab trade in ivory and slaves spread north and west, the Swahili language spread there, too.

✓**Reading Check** **Describing** How did the arrival of Arab traders influence life in eastern Africa?

## Societies in South Africa

**MAIN IDEA** In southern Africa, independent villages organized into states, the most powerful of which was Zimbabwe.

***HISTORY & YOU*** Why might groups of villages organize into a unified state? Read how the organization of villages in southern Africa was different from the rest of the continent.

In the southern half of the African continent, states formed more slowly than in the north. Until the eleventh century A.D., most of the peoples in this region lived in what are sometimes called **stateless societies**—groups of independent villages organized by clans and led by a local ruler or clan head.

In the grassland regions south of the Zambezi River, a mixed economy of farming, cattle herding, and trade had developed over a period of many centuries. Villages were usually built inside walls to protect the domestic animals from wild animals at night. Beginning in the eleventh century, some of these villages in southern Africa gradually united.

From about 1300 to about 1450, **Zimbabwe** (zihm•BAH•bwee) was the wealthiest and most powerful state in the region. It prospered from the gold trade with the Swahili trading communities on the eastern coast of Africa. Indeed, Zimbabwe's gold ended up in the court of Kublai Khan, emperor of China.

The ruins of Zimbabwe's capital, known as Great Zimbabwe, illustrate the kingdom's power and influence. The town sits on a hill overlooking the Zambezi River and is surrounded by stone walls. Ten thousand residents would have been able to live in the area enclosed by the walls. Artifacts found at the site include household implements, ornaments made of gold and copper, and porcelain imported from China.

The Great Enclosure, whose exact purpose is not known, dominated the site. It was an oval space surrounded by a wall 800 feet long, 17 feet thick, and 32 feet high (about 244 m long, 5 m thick, and 10 m high). Near the Great Enclosure were smaller walled enclosures that contained round houses built of a mudlike cement on stone foundations. In the valley below was the royal palace, surrounded by a high stone wall.

The massive walls of Great Zimbabwe are unusual. The local people stacked granite blocks together without mortar to build the walls. By the middle of the fifteenth century, however, the city was abandoned, possibly because of damage to the land through over-grazing or natural disasters such as droughts and crop failures.

**✓Reading Check** **Evaluating** What do the walled enclosures tell us about Great Zimbabwe?

## SECTION 2 REVIEW

### Vocabulary

1. **Explain** the significance of: Ghana, Berbers, factor, Mali, Sundiata Keita, Timbuktu, administrative, Mansa Mūsā, Sunni Ali, Muhammad Ture, security, Bantu, subsistence farming, Mogadishu, Mombasa, Kilwa, Ibn Battuta, Swahili, stateless societies, Zimbabwe.

### Main Ideas

2. **Identify** the mineral that gave Ghana its trading power.
3. **Name** the river on which the Songhai Empire was located.
4. **Create** a chart like the one below describing the economic, religious, political, and social structures of Ghana, Mali, Swahili Coast, and Zimbabwe.

| Kingdoms | Structures |
|---|---|
| Ghana | |
| Mali | |
| Swahili Coast | |
| Zimbabwe | |

### Critical Thinking

5. **The BIG Idea** **Determining Cause and Effect** What motivated the people of Africa to trade?
6. **Making Inferences** Why might an anthropologist be interested in Ibn Battuta's writings?
7. **Analyzing Visuals** Examine the photo on page 248. What does this tell us about Kilwa?

### Writing About History

8. **Narrative Writing** Imagine you are a trader in a Berber caravan. Describe the preparations you must make and thoughts about your journey.

**History ONLINE**

For help with the concepts in this section of *Glencoe World History,* go to glencoe.com and click Study Central™.

SECTION 3

Section Audio

Spotlight Video

# African Society and Culture

## GUIDE TO READING

### The BIG Idea

**Ideas, Beliefs, and Values** African society was centered on village and family life, with distinct religious beliefs and a rich culture.

### Content Vocabulary

- lineage group *(p. 251)*
- matrilineal *(p. 252)*
- patrilineal *(p. 252)*
- diviner *(p. 253)*
- griot *(p. 255)*

### Academic Vocabulary

- founding *(p. 253)*
- culture *(p. 254)*

### People and Places

- Yoruba *(p. 253)*
- Nigeria *(p. 253)*
- Ashanti *(p. 253)*
- Ife *(p. 255)*
- Benin *(p. 255)*

### Reading Strategy

**Compare and Contrast** As you read this section, use the chart below to compare and contrast the duties and rights of women and men in African society.

| | Duties | Rights |
|---|---|---|
| Women | | |
| Men | | |

*African societies were based on extended family units, with most people living in rural villages. Most Africans shared common traditional religious beliefs and customs, especially the honoring of their ancestors. Through unique musical forms and storytelling, Africa's rich cultural heritage was passed from one generation to the next—influencing world culture today.*

## Aspects of African Society

**MAIN IDEA** African society was strongly influenced by values and customs, such as the importance of the family, common ancestors, and community education.

**HISTORY & YOU** There is a traditional African saying that it takes a village to educate a child. Read how African society was set up to achieve this goal.

African towns often began as fortified walled villages and gradually grew into larger communities serving several purposes. These towns were the centers of government and trade, with markets filled with goods from faraway regions. African towns were also home to artisans skilled in metalworking, woodworking, pottery making, and other crafts, as well as farmers who tilled the soil in the neighboring fields.

Because most African societies did not have written languages, much of what we know about these societies comes from descriptions recorded by foreign visitors, such as the Arab traveler Ibn Battuta. These reports provide much information, but the visitors usually saw things from their own perspectives and only came into contact with the wealthy and the powerful. The visitors' accounts do not tell us much about the lives of ordinary people.

### King and Subject

In most Asian societies, the royal family and the aristocracy were largely isolated from the rest of the people. In Africa, the gulf between king and common people was not as great. Frequently, the ruler would hold an audience (meeting) to let people voice their complaints. Nevertheless, the king was still held in a position high above all others.

The relationship between king and subject in many African states helped both sides. Merchants received favors from the king, and the king's treasury was filled with taxes paid by merchants. It was certainly to the benefit of the king to maintain law and order in the kingdom so that the merchants could practice their trade.

PRIMARY SOURCE HISTORY & ARTS

## Kinship with Ancestors in African Societies

Many peoples placed mother-and-child figures in shrines near graves.

Spirits of ancestors were believed to participate in family life and were honored at festivals.

Masks were worn during initiation and funerary rites and linked the living to their ancestors.

**DOCUMENT-BASED QUESTIONS**

Art was a fundamental part of African life. Headdresses and masks were worn by dancers as part of ceremonies. Paintings decorated homes and sculptures marked graves. Much of the wood and leather artwork did not survive in the sub-Saharan climate.

1. **Drawing Conclusions** Why would it be difficult to find many examples of ancient African art?
2. **Making Inferences** Why is African art stylized and abstract, not realistic?

## Family and Lineage

Few Africans, of course, ever had an audience with their kings. Most people lived in small villages in the countryside. Their sense of identity was determined by their membership in an extended family and a lineage group.

At the basic level was the extended family, made up of parents, children, grandparents, and other family dependents. They lived in small, round dwellings made of packed mud, with a thatch roof of plant material such as straw. These extended family units were in turn combined into larger communities known as **lineage groups**.

Lineage groups served as the basic building blocks of African society. All members of a lineage group could claim to be descended from a real or legendary common ancestor. As in China, the elders—the leading members of the lineage group—had much power over the others in the group. A lineage group provided mutual support for all its members. Members of extended families and lineage groups were expected to take care of one another.

## The Role of Women

Women were usually subordinate to men in Africa, as they were in most early societies around the world. In some cases, they were valued for the work they could do or for their role in having children and thus increasing the size of the lineage group. Women often worked in the fields while the men of the village tended the cattle or hunted. In some communities, women were merchants.

There were some key differences between the role of women in Africa and elsewhere.

History ONLINE
**Student Web Activity—** Visit the Glencoe World History Web site at glencoe.com to learn more about African culture.

In many African societies, lineage was based on the mother rather than the father. In other words, these were **matrilineal** societies (societies in which descent is traced through the mother), rather than **patrilineal** societies (societies in which descent is traced through the father).

One Arab traveler noted, "A man does not pass on inheritance except to the sons of his sister to the exclusion of his own sons." Women were often permitted to inherit property, and the husband was often expected to move into his wife's house.

## Community Education and Initiation

In a typical African village, a process existed for educating young people and preparing them to become part of the community. For example, in the Congo, by the 1400s, both boys and girls were raised by their mothers until the age of six. From their mothers, they learned language, their family history, and the songs that gave meaning to their lives. At six, boys and girls went their separate ways: girls to the "house of the women," boys to the "house of the men."

Fathers then took control of their sons' education. Boys learned how to hunt and fish, how to grow plants, and how to clear the fields for planting. By experience, young males learned how to live and survive in the natural world.

Girls continued to learn what they needed from their mothers. This included how to take care of the home and work in the fields. Girls also learned what they would need to be good wives and mothers. Marriage and motherhood would be their entry into the world of the community for females.

As the children matured, they played a larger role in the community. Boys cleared the fields, built houses, and took part in village discussions and ceremonies. Girls took over more responsibility for household tasks, took care of younger brothers and sisters, and attended village ceremonies, especially those connected to marriages and funerals.

Finally, young people reached a point in their upbringing where they were expected to enter the community fully. This transition—which occurred at the time of puberty—was marked by an initiation ceremony in which young people were kept isolated from the community. They then underwent a ritual ceremony in which they symbolically died and were reborn. Young females were then considered fully women; young males fully men. Both entered completely into the life of the community.

## Slavery

When we use the term African slavery, we usually think of the period after 1500, when European slave ships carried millions of Africans in bondage to Europe or the Americas (see Chapter 13). Slavery, however, did not begin with the coming of the Europeans. It had been practiced in Africa since ancient times. Furthermore, as we have seen, slavery was not unique to Africa, but was common throughout the world.

Berber groups in North Africa regularly raided farming villages south of the Sahara for captives. The captives were then taken northward and sold throughout the Mediterranean. The use of captives for forced labor or for sale was also common in African societies further south and along the coast of East Africa.

Slaves included people captured in war, debtors, and some criminals. They were not necessarily seen as inferior but as trusted servants. Some were even respected for their special knowledge or talents.

Life was difficult for most slaves. Those who worked on farmlands owned by the royal family or other wealthy landowners toiled hard, long hours. Others were enrolled as soldiers and were sometimes better off.

Many slaves were used in the royal household or as domestic servants in private homes. These slaves usually had the best existence, with decent living conditions. In Muslim societies in Southwest Asia, slaves might at some point even win their freedom.

✓Reading Check **Summarizing** Describe the role of lineage groups in African society.

## Religious Beliefs

**MAIN IDEA** Most African societies held similar, traditional beliefs; the spread of Islam challenged these African beliefs.

**HISTORY & YOU** Do you know about religious practices in Africa? Read about the development of religions in Africa.

Early African religious beliefs varied from place to place. Most African societies shared some common religious ideas. One of these was a belief in a single creator god. The **Yoruba** peoples in **Nigeria**, for example, believed that their chief god sent his son Oduduwa down from Heaven in a canoe to create the first humans. The Yoruba religion was practiced by many of the slaves transported to the Americas.

Sometimes, the creator god was joined by a whole group of lesser gods. The **Ashanti** people of Ghana, for example, believed in a supreme being called Nyame, whose sons were lesser gods. Because the Ashanti gods could not always be trusted, humans needed to appease them to avoid their anger. Some peoples believed that the creator god had lived on Earth but left in disgust at human behavior. However, the god was also merciful and could be pacified by proper behavior.

One way to communicate with the gods was through ritual. This process was usually carried out by a special class of **diviners**, people who believe they have the power to foretell events, usually by working with supernatural forces. Many diviners were employed by the king. This was done to guarantee a bountiful harvest or to protect the interests of the ruler and his subjects.

Another key element in African religion was the importance of ancestors. Each lineage group could trace itself back to a **founding** ancestor or group of ancestors. Ritual ceremonies were dedicated to ancestors because the ancestors were believed to be closer to the gods. They had the power to influence, for good or evil, the lives of their descendants.

NATIONAL GEOGRAPHIC

### RELIGIOUS SYNCRETISM

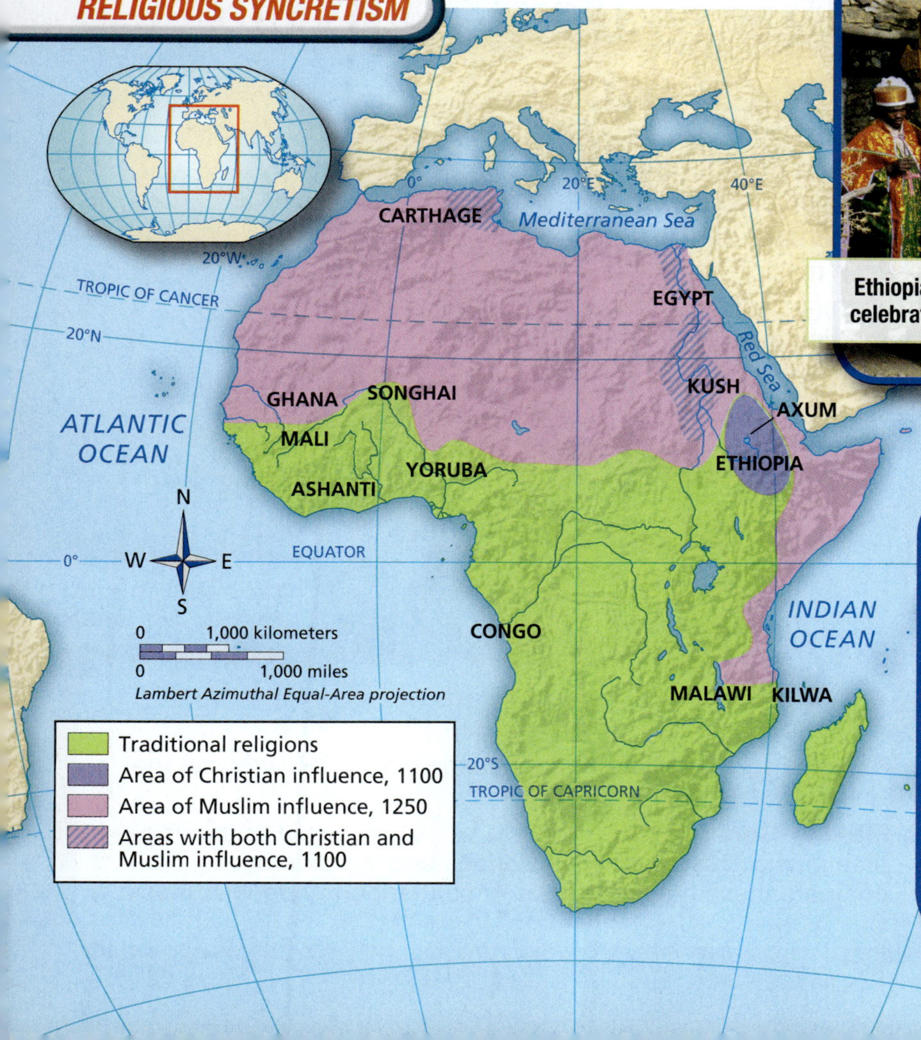

Ethiopian Christians celebrate Holy Week.

**Geography SKILLS**

Syncretism is the blending of two or more beliefs systems. In some areas, African traditional religion fused with Islam or Christianity. Today in the Congo, half the people are Roman Catholic, and the rest belong to syncretic sects.

1. **Movement** Islam spread to which early African kingdoms by 1250?
2. **Location** Which kingdoms had not been introduced to Islam or Christianity by 1250?

Many African religions shared a belief in an afterlife. Human life, it was thought, consisted of two stages. The first stage was life on Earth. The second stage was an afterlife. Ancestral souls would live on in the afterlife as long as the lineage group continued to perform rituals in their names.

African religious beliefs were challenged, but not always replaced, by the arrival of Islam. Islam swept across northern Africa in the wake of the Arab conquest. It was slower to penetrate the lands south of the Sahara. The process likely began as a result of trade, as merchants introduced Muslim beliefs to the trading states south of the desert.

At first, conversion took place on an individual basis. Initially, African rulers did not convert to Islam themselves, although they welcomed Muslim traders and did not try to keep their subjects from adopting the new faith. The first rulers to convert were the royal family of Gao at the end of the tenth century. By the end of the fifteenth century, much of the population south of the Sahara had accepted Islam.

The process was even more gradual in East Africa. It had less success in areas of Ethiopia, where, as we have seen, Christianity continued to gain followers. Islam was first brought to East Africa by Muslim traders from Arabia, but it did not gain many converts there until the twelfth and thirteenth centuries. At that time, Swahili **culture** emerged, and many upper-class people converted to Islam.

In some ways, the beliefs of Islam were in conflict with traditional African beliefs and customs. Islam's rejection of spirit worship ran counter to the beliefs of many Africans and was often ignored in practice. Likewise, Islam's insistence on distinct roles for men and women was contrary to the relatively informal relationships in many African societies. As elsewhere, in Africa, imported ideas were combined with native beliefs to create a unique brand of Africanized Islam.

✓Reading Check **Describing** What role do ancestors play in African religion?

## CONNECTING TO THE UNITED STATES

### AFRICAN RHYTHMS TO ROCK AND ROLL

Music and dance were fundamental to African festivals and religious observances. African musical traditions included call-and-response (lead singer with chorus), improvisation, and polyrhythmic (multiple beats at once) percussion. African Americans incorporated these traditions with European music, creating new vocal and instrumental forms. Blues (solo and guitar) and ragtime (piano) became popular in the 1890s. Blues, ragtime, brass band, and syncopated dance music fused into jazz. Beginning in the 1940s and 1950s, American popular music was dominated by African American forms: rhythm and blues, rock and roll, soul, funk, disco, hip-hop, and rap.

- **The complex rhythms and improvisation of Africans' musical heritage enriched American music.**
- **African music has been an important ingredient in the development of American musical styles.**

Charles Lloyd performs at Monterey Jazz Festival

**CONNECTING TO TODAY**

1. **Explaining** How did African rhythms make their way into the United States?
2. **Making Connections** Listen to blues, gospel, jazz, and ragtime music. Describe the similarities and the differences, then compare these types of music to contemporary popular music.

## African Culture

**MAIN IDEA** Africa's rich culture of paintings, carvings, sculpture, music, and dance often served a religious purpose.

***HISTORY & YOU*** How has African culture influenced world culture? Read about early African cultural practices.

In early Africa, as in much of the rest of the world at the time, the arts—whether painting, literature, or music—were a means of serving religion. A work of art was meant to express religious conviction.

The earliest art forms in Africa were rock paintings. The most famous examples are in the Tassili Mountains in the central Sahara. These paintings show the life of the peoples of the area as they shifted from hunting to herding and eventually to trade.

Wood-carvers throughout Africa made remarkable masks and statues. The carvings often represented gods, spirits, or ancestral figures and were believed to embody the spiritual powers of the subjects. Terra-cotta (clay) and metal figurines served a similar purpose. For example, terra-cotta human figures and human heads found near the Nigerian city of Nok are thought to have had religious significance. The Nok culture is the oldest known West African culture to have created sculpture.

In the thirteenth and fourteenth centuries, metalworkers at **Ife** (EE•feh), the capital of the Yoruba people, in what is now Nigeria, produced handsome bronze and iron statues. The Ife sculptures may have influenced artists in **Benin** in West Africa, who produced equally impressive works in bronze during the same period. The Benin sculptures include bronze heads, many of kings, and figures of various types of animals.

Like wood carving and sculpture, African music and dance often served a religious purpose. African dancing served as a way to communicate with the spirits. It was also "the great popular art of the African people." With its strong rhythmic beat, African music would influence modern Western music.

African music also had a social purpose. It was used to pass on to young people information about the history of the community. In the absence of written language, the words to songs served to transmit folk legends and religious traditions from generation to generation.

Storytelling, usually by priests or a special class of storytellers known as **griots** (GREE•OHZ), served the same purpose. Storytellers were historians who kept alive a people's history. For example, much of what we know about Sundiata Keita—the founder of the kingdom of Mali—has come down to us from the oral traditions of the griot.

**✓Reading Check** **Explaining** Why were storytellers important in African society?

## SECTION 3 REVIEW

### Vocabulary

1. **Explain** the significance of: lineage groups, matrilineal, patrilineal, Yoruba, Nigeria, Ashanti, diviner, founding, culture, Ife, Benin, griot.

### Main Ideas

2. **Describe** how children were educated in early African societies.
3. **Explain** the importance of honoring ancestors in traditional African religious practices.
4. **Identify** the ways that religion was expressed in African culture, using a web diagram like the one below.

### Critical Thinking

5. **The BIG Idea** **Comparing and Contrasting** Choose one early society you previously studied. Compare and contrast it to early African society. How were they similar? Different?
6. **Defending** Explain the role of art, music, and dance in African society. Explain why you think these subjects should or should not be part of every school's curriculum.
7. **Analyzing Visuals** Examine the images on page 251. What can you deduce from them about the role of the family in African society?

### Writing About History

8. **Expository Writing** Music, dance, and storytelling do not leave archaeological evidence in the same way as buildings or roads. Describe how historians have been able to determine the significance of the performing arts in African society.

**History ONLINE**

For help with the concepts in this section of *Glencoe World History,* go to glencoe.com and click Study Central™.

# Preserving the Past

Some of what we know about the distant past, in almost all parts of the world, comes from stories passed down orally over countless generations. In some cases, the stories are preserved with such rigor that they rival written accounts in veracity. Such is the case of the stories of the history of West Africa, preserved over the years by a remarkable group of people who devote their lives to remembering and reciting their cultures' histories: the griots (GREE•ohs).

## Becoming a Griot

**A Lifetime of Training**—Griots spent years and decades memorizing the long and complex histories they spent their lifetimes telling. Most began as children.

**A Family Affair**—Most griots learned the craft, at least initially, from their griot parents. In various times and places, griot schools trained apprentices.

**Griots and *Griottes***—Traditionally, most griots were male. However, female griots, sometimes called *griottes*, played an important role in West African society as well.

## The Oral Tradition

The word *literature* often refers to written works such as books, plays, and poetry. In West Africa there is a long tradition of oral literature. These hero stories, fables, poems, and other "literary" works have been passed on for centuries. In the 1900s, scholars began publishing written translations of these works. By doing so, the universal nature of the messages in these tales has been appreciated well beyond West Africa.

# MANY ROLES

## GRIOTS TODAY

The tradition of the griot is alive and well in West Africa today. Many modern griots perform all of the traditional roles. But today's griots are more often popular entertainers who put on shows, appear on television, record CDs, and sing people's praises in exchange for payment or gifts. Their work often mixes traditional stories and modern commentary.

### ANALYZING VISUALS

1. **Making Inferences** What qualities do you think an outstanding griot would need to possess?
2. **Explaining** Why do people find it important to preserve stories of the past?

# CHAPTER 7 Visual Summary

You can study anywhere, anytime by downloading quizzes and flash cards to your PDA from glencoe.com.

THE LION TEMPLE, KUSH

Societies that traded also exchanged cultural ideas, as seen in this Kush temple built in an Egyptian style.

## EARLY AFRICAN SOCIETIES

- For centuries until A.D. 150, Kush's advanced civilization in the upper Nile thrived on trading ivory and ebony with Egypt, India, and Arabia.
- Evolving from an Arab colony, Axum succeeded Kush as a major trading power in East Africa.
- Once the Muslims conquered Egypt, they began to set up Islamic states in Northern Africa, transforming the culture.

TERRACOTTA HORSE AND RIDER, MALI

Art flourished in the kingdom of Mali. This figure may represent an official or visitor to the court.

## AFRICAN KINGDOMS

- In the upper Niger River valley, the kings of Ghana ruled a trading empire based on gold.
- With legendary rulers Sundiata Keita and Mansa Mūsā, the kingdom of Mali replaced Ghana's dominance in the 1200s.
- Bantu-speaking peoples slowly migrated east and south, spreading the use of iron tools in farming.
- In the 1300s and 1400s, cities on the eastern coast traded with India and Arabia while the wealthy state of Zimbabwe prospered in the south.

NOK HEAD, THE NIGER RIVER

It is not clear what the Nok heads were used for, but they were most likely ritualistic.

## AFRICAN SOCIETY AND CULTURE

- In Africa extended families and lineage groups were the basic units for village societies.
- Communication with a creator god through rituals and ancestors typified many African religions.
- Arab merchants brought Islam to East and Southern Africa, and it began to gain converts in the 1300s.
- Religion drove artistic expression, exemplified in West African sculptures, while griots or storytellers preserved literature and history.

# CHAPTER 7 Assessment

## Reviewing Vocabulary

*Directions: Choose the word or words that best complete the sentence.*

**1.** ______ are broad grasslands that cover about 40 percent of Africa's land area.

**A** Savannas

**B** Plateaus

**C** Lowlands

**D** Highlands

**2.** ______ farming means growing crops for personal use, not for sale.

**A** Organic

**B** Home

**C** Domesticated

**D** Subsistence

**3.** ______ are societies in which descent is traced through the mother, not the father.

**A** Patrilineal societies

**B** Matrilineal societies

**C** Lineage groups

**D** Ashanti groups

**4.** Another word for *griot* is ______.

**A** merchant

**B** ruler

**C** storyteller

**D** ancestor

**5.** Extended family units are called ______.

**A** lineage groups

**B** syncretic

**C** askias

**D** diviners

## Reviewing Main Ideas

*Directions: Choose the best answers to the following questions.*

### Section 1 *(pp. 236–239)*

**6.** What is the name of a major desert in Africa other than the Sahara?

**A** Great Rift

**B** Mombasa

**C** Kalahari

**D** Ashanti

**7.** What was the name of the major trading center in Kush?

**A** Mogadishu

**B** Cairo

**C** Timbuktu

**D** Meroë

**8.** To which body of water did Axum owe much of its prosperity?

**A** Indian Ocean

**B** Mediterranean Sea

**C** Red Sea

**D** Niger River

### Section 2 *(pp. 242–249)*

**9.** Which was the first great trading state to emerge in West Africa?

**A** Kush

**B** Ghana

**C** Mali

**D** Ethiopia

### TEST-TAKING TIP

Look for clues in a question before you make an answer choice. You can use these hints to help you eliminate incorrect answer choices.

**Need Extra Help?**

| If You Missed Questions . . . | 1 | 2 | 3 | 4 | 5 | 6 | 7 | 8 | 9 |
|---|---|---|---|---|---|---|---|---|---|
| Go to Page . . . | 237 | 247 | 252 | 255 | 251 | 237 | 238 | 239 | 242 |

GO ON

10. Under whose reign did the Songhai Empire reach the height of its power?
   **A** Muhammad Ture
   **B** Sunni Ali
   **C** Mansa Mūsā
   **D** Sundiata Keita

11. What was the name of the mixed African-Arabian culture that emerged along East Africa's coast?
   **A** Bantu
   **B** Swahili
   **C** Kilwa
   **D** Gao

## Section 3 *(pp. 250–255)*

12. What served as the most basic building blocks for African society?
   **A** Matrilineal societies
   **B** Farming villages
   **C** Trade centers
   **D** Lineage groups

13. Which class of people, who believed they could foretell events, were employed by many African rulers?
   **A** Ancestors
   **B** Diviners
   **C** Drummers
   **D** Oracles

14. What was "the great popular art of the African people"?
   **A** Bronze sculpture
   **B** Wood carving
   **C** Dance
   **D** Call and response

## Critical Thinking

*Directions: Choose the best answers to the following questions.*

15. Which of the following statements is the best reason why Africans who live in the rain forest do not keep cattle or other farm animals?
   **A** The rain forest is home to the tsetse fly.
   **B** There is not enough dependable rainfall.
   **C** The land is better suited to growing crops.
   **D** The rain forest is home to predators, which prey on cattle and other farm animals.

*Base your answer to question 16 on the time line below and your knowledge of world history.*

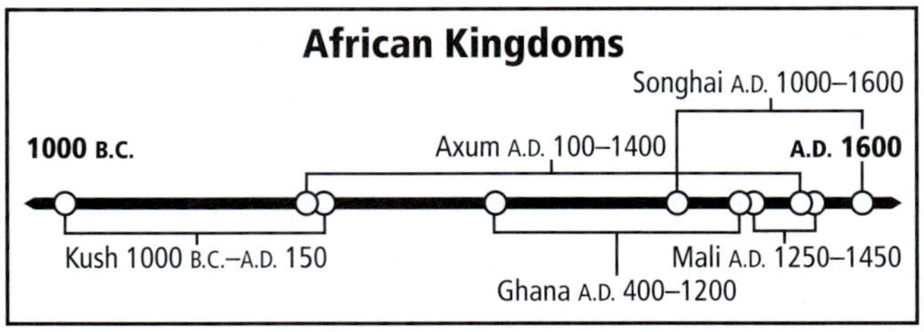


16. Which African kingdom would most likely have come into contact with Kush?
   **A** Songhai
   **B** Mali
   **C** Axum
   **D** Ghana

17. Why did the value of gold fall under Mansa Mūsā?
   **A** He kept gold in short supply.
   **B** He put too much gold into circulation.
   **C** He increased the value of salt.
   **D** He built too many palaces and libraries.

**Need Extra Help?**

| If You Missed Questions . . . | 10 | 11 | 12 | 13 | 14 | 15 | 16 | 17 |
|---|---|---|---|---|---|---|---|---|
| Go to Page . . . | 245 | 248 | 251 | 253 | 255 | 237 | 260 | 244 |

GO ON

*Use the following map and your knowledge of world history to answer questions 18 and 19.*

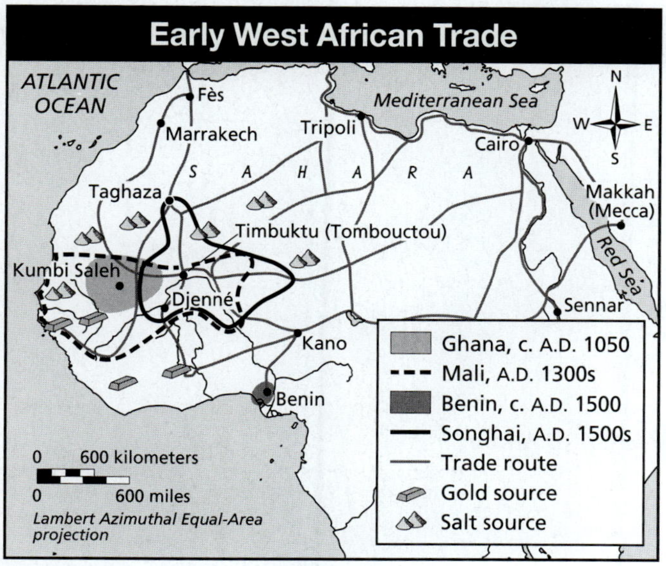


**18.** Which kingdom might have competed with Benin for trade?

**A** Ghana

**B** Songhai

**C** Mali

**D** None of the kingdoms competed for trade.

**19.** Why were Sunni Ali's conquests of Timbuktu and Djenné especially important?

**A** They were vital port cities.

**B** They ensured that his son would rule after him.

**C** They gave his empire control of the trade in salt and gold.

**D** They gave his empire control of the trade in ivory and iron ore.

## Document-Based Questions

*Directions: Analyze the document and answer the short-answer questions that follow the document. Base your answers on the document and on your knowledge of Chapter 7.*

The exchange of goods in Ghana was done by a method of silent trade. Read the following account of this trade by a tenth-century Arabian traveler.

> *"Great people of the Sudan [the Arab name for West Africa] lived [in Ghana]. They had traced a boundary which no one who sets out to them ever crosses. When the merchants reach this boundary, they place their wares and cloth on the ground and then depart, and so the people of the Sudan come bearing gold which they leave beside the merchandise and then depart. The owners of the merchandise then return, and if they were satisfied with what they had found, they take it. If not, they go away again, and the people of the Sudan return and add to the price until the bargain is concluded."*

**20.** Why would a silent trade be an effective way to exchange goods?

**21.** Do you think a silent trade method would be useful today? Defend your opinion.

## Extended Response

**22.** Through trade, many civilizations came into contact with each other. What civilizations outside of Africa did African kingdoms and states contact? How did these civilizations influence each other?

**History ONLINE**

For additional test practice, use Self-Check Quizzes—Chapter 7 at glencoe.com.

**Need Extra Help?**

| If You Missed Questions . . . | 18 | 19 | 20 | 21 | 22 |
|---|---|---|---|---|---|
| Go to Page . . . | 261 | 261 | 242 | 242 | 248 |

STOP

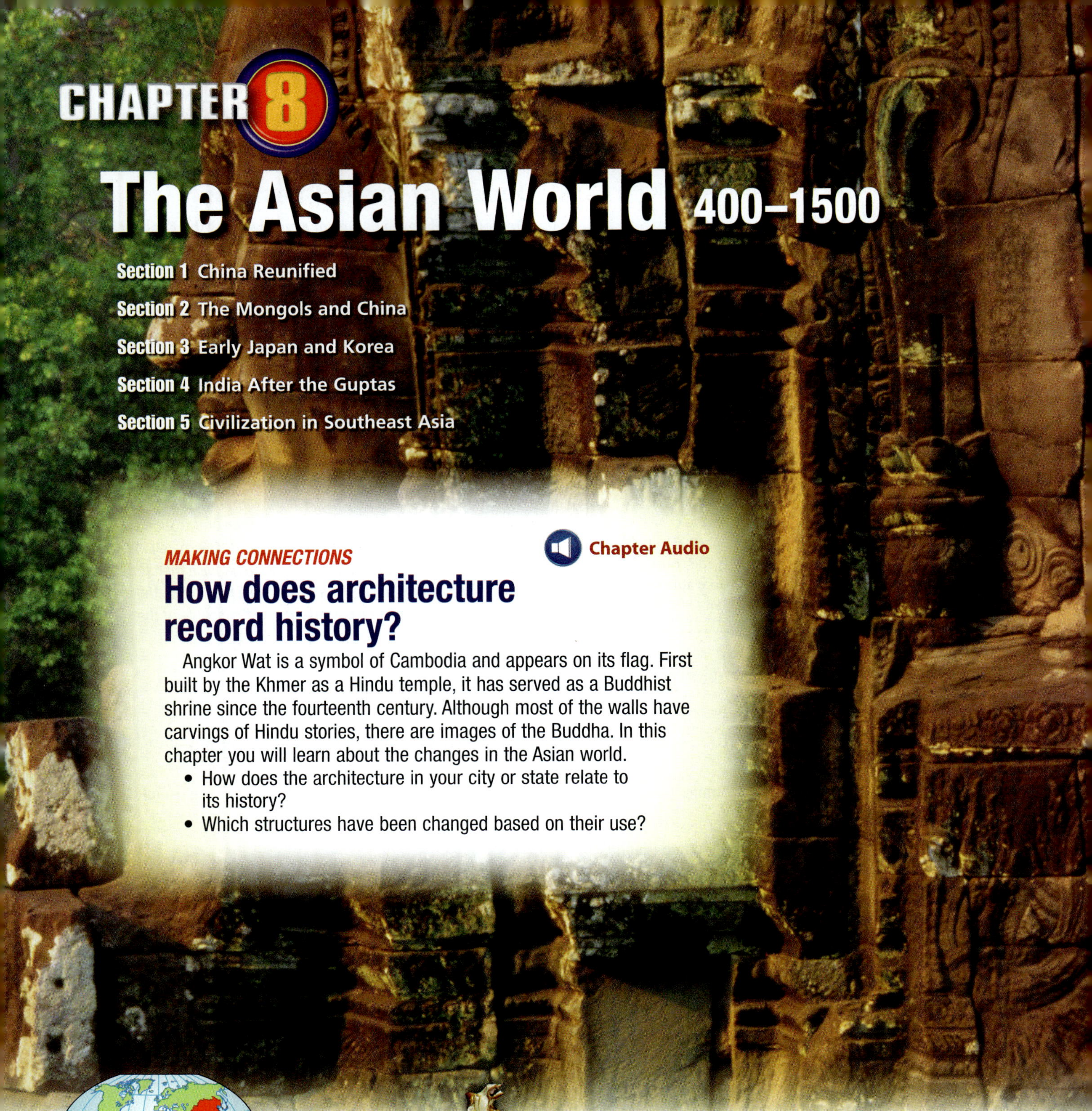

# CHAPTER 8

# The Asian World 400–1500



*MAKING CONNECTIONS*

Chapter Audio

## How does architecture record history?

Angkor Wat is a symbol of Cambodia and appears on its flag. First built by the Khmer as a Hindu temple, it has served as a Buddhist shrine since the fourteenth century. Although most of the walls have carvings of Hindu stories, there are images of the Buddha. In this chapter you will learn about the changes in the Asian world.

- How does the architecture in your city or state relate to its history?
- Which structures have been changed based on their use?

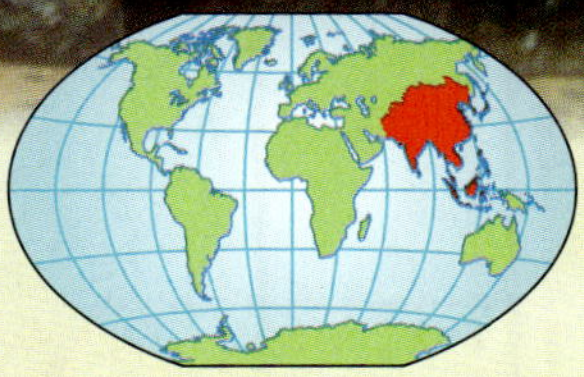

**ASIA ▶**

**c. 600** Silk Road trade flourishes during Tang dynasty

**802** Jayavarman II unites Khmer of Angkor

**c. 1000** Chinese invent movable type

500 — 700 — 900

**THE WORLD ▶**

**565** Roman Emperor Justinian dies

**c. 800** Maya civilization declines

**1192**
Minamoto Yoritomo establishes Kamakura shogunate

**1369**
Timur Lenk begins conquest of northern India

1100 — 1300 — 1500

**1325**
Mansa Mūsā begins Timbuktu mosque

**FOLDABLES™**
**Study Organizer**

**Identifying** Create a Four-Tab Book to record Who, What, When, and Where facts while you read about Kublai Khan or Genghis Khan.

**History ONLINE** Visit glencoe.com and enter QuickPass™ code GWHEA7447c8 for Chapter 8 resources.

SECTION 1

Section Audio

Spotlight Video

# China Reunified

## GUIDE TO READING

### The BIG Idea

**Order and Security** After centuries of chaos and civil war, three dynasties unified China, bringing peace, stability, and technological progress.

### Content Vocabulary

- scholar-gentry *(p. 269)*
- dowry *(p. 269)*

### Academic Vocabulary

- period *(p. 266)*
- complexity *(p. 267)*

### People and Places

- Sui Yangdi *(p. 264)*
- Tibet *(p. 265)*
- Tang Xuanzang *(p. 265)*
- Uighurs *(p. 265)*
- Hangzhou *(p. 266)*
- Changan *(p. 268)*
- Marco Polo *(p. 269)*
- Wu Zhao *(p. 269)*

### Reading Strategy

**Summarizing Information** As you read, create three charts like the one shown below to help you study. Summarize the time periods, the most important rulers, and the reasons for decline of the Sui, Tang, and Song dynasties.

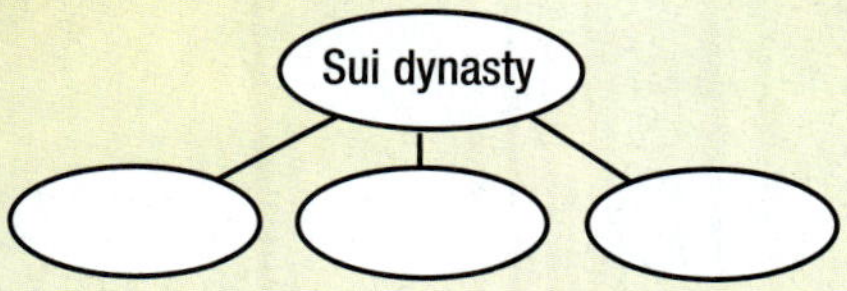


*In 581 the Sui dynasty unified China for the first time in hundreds of years. Over the next several centuries, with only a brief period of disorder in the 900s, three dynasties would bring progress and stability to China. During this period, China would invent block printing and gunpowder, participate in increased foreign trade, and restore a merit-based civil service system.*

## Three Dynasties

**MAIN IDEA** The Sui, Tang, and Song dynasties restored peace to China in between periods of chaos and disorder.

***HISTORY & YOU*** Do you know what tests are required to qualify for government jobs in the United States? Learn about merit-based civil service in early China.

The Han dynasty is considered to have set the standard for the Chinese dynasties that followed. In fact, the Chinese word for someone who is Chinese means "a man of Han."

### The Sui Dynasty

The Han dynasty ended in 220, and China fell into chaos. For the next three hundred years, the Chinese suffered through disorder and civil war. Then, in 581, a new empire was set up under a dynasty known as the Sui (SWAY). The Sui dynasty (581–618) did not last long, but it unified China once again under the emperor's authority.

**Sui Yangdi**, the second emperor of the dynasty, completed the Grand Canal, built to link the two great rivers of China, the Huang He (Yellow River) and the Chang Jiang (Yangtze River). Both rivers flowed from west to east. The new canal linked north and south, making it easier to ship rice from the south to the north.

Sui Yangdi was a cruel ruler. He used forced labor to build the Grand Canal, which he used to keep an eye on his empire. This practice, together with high taxes, his extravagant and luxurious lifestyle, and military failures, caused a rebellion. The emperor was murdered, and his dynasty came to an end.

### The Tang Dynasty

A new dynasty, the Tang (TAHNG), soon emerged. It would last for nearly three hundred years, from 618 until 907. The early Tang rulers began their reigns by instituting reforms, as rulers often did in the early days of new dynasties. They created a more stable economy by giving land to the peasants and breaking up the power

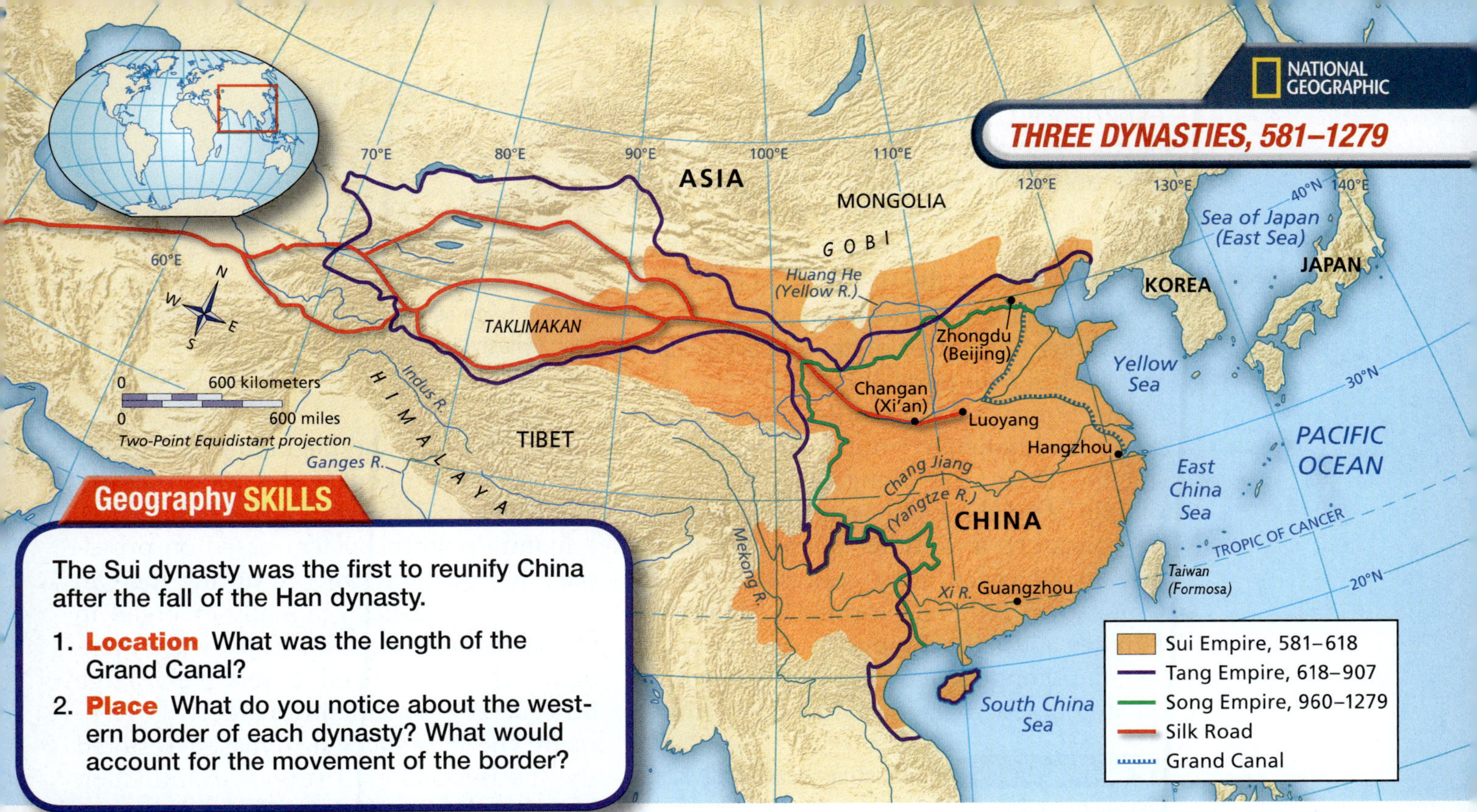


**Geography SKILLS**

The Sui dynasty was the first to reunify China after the fall of the Han dynasty.

1. **Location** What was the length of the Grand Canal?
2. **Place** What do you notice about the western border of each dynasty? What would account for the movement of the border?

of the owners of the large estates. They also restored the civil service examination to serve as the chief method of recruiting officials for the civilian bureaucracy.

The civil service examination tested a student's grasp of Confucian principles. Young men prepared to take the examination by memorizing all the Confucian classics. They had little free time and were forbidden to take part in any strenuous physical activities. They were taught never to use their hands except for painting or writing. Even after many years of education, only about one in five students managed to pass the examination and receive a position in the civil service.

Tang rulers worked hard to restore the power of China in East Asia. They brought peace to northwestern China and gained control of parts of Central Asia north of the Himalaya from **Tibet.** Neighboring states, including Korea, offered tribute to China. The Chinese imperial court also set up trade and diplomatic relations with the states of Southeast Asia.

Like the Han, however, the Tang sowed the seeds of their own destruction. Tang rulers were unable to prevent plotting and government corruption. One emperor was especially unfortunate.

Emperor **Tang Xuanzang** (SHWAHN•DZAHNG) is remembered for his devotion to a commoner's daughter, Yang Guifei. To entertain her, he kept hundreds of dancers and musicians at court. He also ordered riders to travel thousands of miles to bring her fresh fruit.

Finally, the emperor's favorite general led a bloody revolt. The army demanded that someone be held accountable for the war and strife in the country. For this reason the emperor invited his true love to hang herself from a nearby tree, although it is said that for the rest of his life, the emperor "washed his face everyday with a fountain of tears."

During the eighth century, the Tang dynasty weakened and became prey to rebellions. Tang rulers hired **Uighurs** (WEE•gurz), a northern tribal group of Turkic-speaking people, to fight for the dynasty. Continued unrest, however, led to the collapse of Tang rule in 907.

## The Song Dynasty

In 960 a new dynasty known as the Song (SUNG) rose to power. The Song ruled during a **period** of economic prosperity and cultural achievement, from 960 to 1279.

From the start, however, the Song also experienced problems, especially from northern neighbors. These groups crossed into northern China and occupied large parts of Chinese territory. Because of this threat, Song rulers were forced to move the imperial court farther south to **Hangzhou** (HAHNG•JOH), on the coast just south of the Chang Jiang river delta. The Song also lost control over parts of Central Asia.

The Song dynasty could never overcome the challenge from the north. During the 1200s, the Mongols—a nomadic people from the Gobi—carried out wars of conquest and built a vast empire. Within 70 years, they controlled all of China. The Song had formed a defensive alliance with the Mongols. As we shall see, the Mongols overthrew the Song and created a new Mongol dynasty in China.

✓Reading Check **Contrasting** How did the Tang and Sui rulers differ?

## Government and Economy

*MAIN IDEA* For 700 years, the Chinese economy grew in size and sophistication.

*HISTORY & YOU* Would you be able to survive as a farmer? Learn about the lives of peasants during the Tang dynasty and the Song dynasty.

The era from the beginning of the Sui dynasty to the end of the Song dynasty lasted nearly 700 years. During that **period,** a mature political system based on principles first put into practice during the Qin and Han dynasties gradually emerged in China. As in the Han Era, China was a monarchy that employed a relatively large bureaucracy to maintain an orderly government. The Tang and Song dynasties restored the merit-based civil service examination begun in the Qin dynasty. The examination

### SUI TO MONGOL DYNASTIES

◄ Figures of female musicians from Sui dynasty tomb

**581** Sui dynasty begins

**618** Tang dynasty begins

500 | 600 | 700 | 800

▲ Emperor with attendants

**589** Emperor and former general Sui Wendi reunites China; ends centuries of chaos

**610** Emperor Sui Yangdi completes construction of the Grand Canal

**618** Sui Yangdi assassinated in military coup

**690** Wu Zhao becomes first female emperor of China

**755** General An Lushan starts rebellion; millions die in resulting civil war gave China a more efficient government staffed by a literate bureaucracy.

Beyond the capital, government was based on provinces, districts, and villages. Confucian ideals were still the cement that held the system together.

During the long period between the Sui and Song dynasties, the Chinese economy grew in size and **complexity.** Agriculture flourished, and manufacturing and trade grew dramatically.

China was still primarily a farming society. In the long period of civil war, aristocratic families had taken control of most of the land, and the majority of peasants had become serfs or slaves. The Song government, however, worked to weaken the power of the large landholders and help poor peasants obtain their own land. These reform efforts and improved farming techniques led to an abundance of food.

In Chinese cities, technological developments added new products and stimulated trade. During the Tang dynasty, for example, the Chinese began to make steel by mixing cast iron and wrought iron in a blast furnace, which was heated by burning coal. The steel was then used to make swords and sickles. The introduction of cotton made it possible to make new kinds of clothes.

Another important Chinese invention, gunpowder, was created during the Tang dynasty. It was used to make explosives and a primitive flamethrower called a fire-lance. The fire-lance could spit out a mixture of flame and projectiles that could travel 40 yards (36.6 m).

The nature of trade also changed. State officials had controlled most long-distance trade. By the time of the Song, private merchants were active in commerce and trade. Guilds (merchant associations) began to appear, along with a new money economy (an economic system based on money rather than barter). The use of paper money began in the 700s and 800s.

▲ Buddhist sculpture from the Song dynasty

▲ Kublai Khan founds Yuan dynasty

900 1000 1100 1200 1300

**907** Tang dynasty collapses

**960** Song dynasty begins

**960** General Chao K'uang-yin reunifies China under his rule

**1127** Beginning of Southern Song period

**1211** China invaded by Genghis Khan

**1279** Mongols led by Kublai Khan defeat Song dynasty and absorb China into Mongol Empire

▲ General becomes Emperor T'ai Tsu

**Analyzing TIME LINES**

1. **Summarizing** What pattern is shown by the rise and fall of the dynasties between 581 and 1279?
2. **Making Inferences** Why did generals play such a large role in the formation of these dynasties?

## INFOGRAPHICS

### The Role of Women in the Tang and Song Dynasties

During the Tang dynasty, Wu Zhao began as the emperor's concubine and became Empress Wu, ruling in her own right after 690.

One of the most famous women of the Tang dynasty is Empress Wu. Born Wu Zhao, she became mistress to the emperor in 649. She so longed for power that she accused the empress of a crime. The emperor deposed his wife and chose Wu Zhao as his new empress. After his death she gained supreme power.

Known for her ruthlessness, she was also a strong leader. She was the first ruler to give graduates of the civil service examinations the highest government positions. She also formed an alliance with Korea and lowered taxes.

In accordance with Confucianism, most women, however, had few rights and privileges during the Tang dynasty. Women were allowed to join in sports such as horseback riding and polo, and activities such as dancing and playing music. Most marriages were arranged, and a woman was permitted to marry only once in her lifetime.

During the Song dynasty, the practice of foot binding became popular among upper-class women. Foot binding, which made feet unnaturally small, permanently deformed women's feet, caused great pain, and often made women unable to stand or walk without assistance. A woman's willingness to bind her feet was considered a sign of her virtue. On the other hand, two-thirds of aristocratic women in the Song dynasty were literate and well-educated. Some women benefited from new inheritance rights. If there was no male heir, the estate could pass to a woman in the family.

#### DOCUMENT-BASED QUESTIONS

1. **Making Generalizations** How did the roles of women compare to the roles of men during the Tang and Song dynasties in China?
2. **Drawing Conclusions** How did foot binding affect women's roles in society?

Merchants found that strings of copper coins were too heavy to carry for their business deals, so they used paper money. With the increased flow of paper money, banking began to develop.

Long-distance trade, both by land and by sea, expanded. Trade had declined between the 300s and 500s as a result of the collapse of both the Han dynasty and the Roman Empire. Trade began to revive under the Tang dynasty and the unification of much of Southwest Asia under the Arabs. The Silk Road was renewed and thrived as caravans carried goods between China and the regions of Southwest Asia and South Asia. Improvements in ships helped increase sea trade.

Trade with regions near China, such as Japan and Korea, also increased during the Tang and Song dynasties. The Chinese exported tea, silk, and porcelain to the countries beyond the South China Sea. In return, they received exotic woods, precious stones, and various tropical goods.

As a result of trade, **Changan**, with a population of about two million, became the wealthiest city in the world. Changan was filled with temples and palaces, and its markets were filled with goods from all over Europe, Africa, and Asia.

✓Reading Check **Comparing** In what ways did trade improve during the time between the Sui and Song dynasties?

## Chinese Society

**MAIN IDEA** The political stability established by the three dynasties allowed Chinese society to grow in complexity.

***HISTORY & YOU*** How does the status of women today compare with the status of women in early China? Read about Chinese society and the status of women.

Economic changes had an impact on Chinese society. For wealthier city dwellers, the Tang and Song eras were an age of prosperity. There was probably no better example than the Song capital of Hangzhou. In the late 1200s, the Italian merchant **Marco Polo** described the city to European readers as one of the largest and wealthiest cities on Earth. "So many pleasures may be found," he said, "that one fancies himself to be in Paradise."

For rich Chinese during this period, life offered many pleasures. There were new forms of entertainment, such as playing cards and chess (brought from India). The paddlewheel boat and horseback riding (made possible by the introduction of the stirrup) made travel easier. The invention of block printing in the eighth century provided new ways to communicate.

The vast majority of the Chinese people still lived off the land in villages. Most peasants never left their villages except for an occasional visit to a nearby market town. Changes were taking place in the countryside, however. Before, there had been a great gulf between wealthy landowners and poor peasants. A more complex mixture of landowners, free peasants, sharecroppers, and landless laborers now emerged.

Most significant was the rise of the landed gentry. This group controlled much of the land and at the same time produced most of the candidates for the civil service. The **scholar-gentry**, as this class was known, replaced the old landed aristocracy as the political and economic elite of Chinese society.

Few Chinese women had any power. An exception was **Wu Zhao** (WOO JOW), known as Empress Wu. The concubine of the second Tang emperor, she then became empress of China and ruled for half a century.

As in other parts of the world, female children were considered less desirable than male children. In times of famine, female infants might be killed if there was not enough food to feed the whole family. When a girl married, she became part of her husband's family. In addition, a girl's parents were expected to provide a **dowry**—money, goods, or property—to her husband when she married. Poor families often sold their daughters to wealthy villagers.

**✓Reading Check** **Identifying** Which group in Chinese society replaced the landed aristocracy?

## SECTION 1 REVIEW

### Vocabulary

1. **Explain** the significance of: Sui Yangdi, Tibet, Tang Xuanzang, Uighurs, period, Hangzhou, complexity, Changan, Marco Polo, scholar-gentry, Wu Zhao, dowry

### Main Ideas

2. **Describe** the process of studying for the civil service examination during the Tang and Song dynasties.
3. **List** China's main exports and imports during the Tang and Song dynasties.
4. **Create** a diagram like the one shown below to compare and contrast the status of women in early China with the status of women in the United States today.

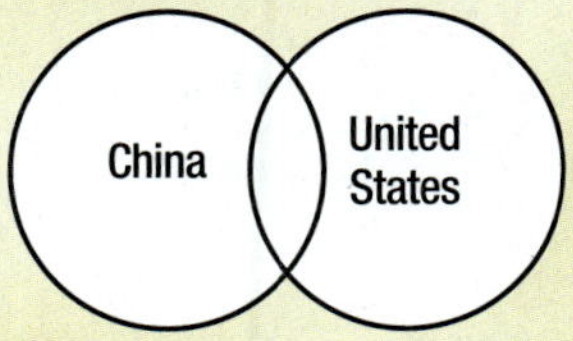


### Critical Thinking

5. **The BIG Idea** **Hypothesizing** If China had never been unified by the dynasties, how might society in China have been different during this period?
6. **Assessing** The Chinese form of government was adopted by many other countries. Describe the basis for the Chinese form of government and evaluate its effectiveness.
7. **Analyzing Visuals** Examine the painting of Wu Zhao on page 268. What indicates her status in Chinese society?

### Writing About History

8. **Expository Writing** Suppose that you have just heard about one of the Tang dynasty innovations, perhaps the process of making steel, but you do not understand it. Write a letter of inquiry to the Tang emperor asking for more information.

**History ONLINE**

For help with the concepts in this section of *Glencoe World History*, go to glencoe.com and click Study Central™.

SECTION 2

Section Audio | Spotlight Video

# The Mongols and China

### GUIDE TO READING

**The BIG Idea**

**Order and Security** The Mongol conquest of China brought political stability to much of Asia and central Europe, which allowed trade to flourish.

**Content Vocabulary**

- khanate *(p. 271)*
- porcelain *(p. 275)*
- neo-Confucianism *(p. 273)*

**Academic Vocabulary**

- acquired *(p. 273)*
- vision *(p. 275)*
- available *(p. 274)*

**People and Places**

- Mongolia *(p. 270)*
- Beijing *(p. 271)*
- Genghis Khan *(p. 270)*
- Li Bo *(p. 274)*
- Gobi *(p. 270)*
- Du Fu *(p. 274)*
- Kublai Khan *(p. 271)*

**Reading Strategy**

**Cause and Effect** As you read, use a chart like the one below to help you study how the Mongols acquired the world's largest land empire.

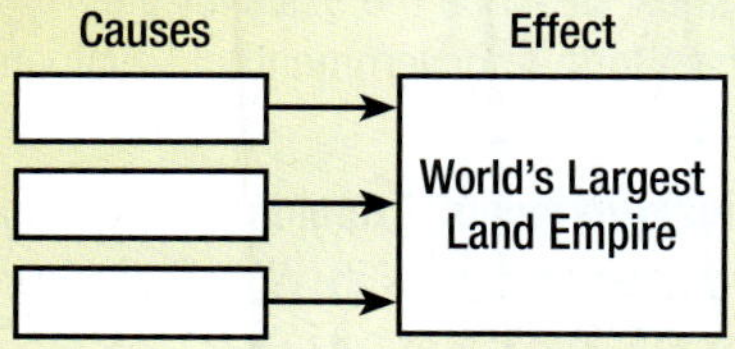


*At the time of the Mongol invasion, art and literature in China were in the middle of a golden age, spurred, in part, by the invention of porcelain and the printing press. Also, religious attitudes were changing in favor of a revived Confucianism, which would remain the basis of Chinese government for centuries.*

## The Mongols

**MAIN IDEA** The Mongols created the world's largest land empire by conquering all of China.

***HISTORY & YOU*** What do you think drove rulers to expand their empires? How would the lives of the citizens of these conquered lands have to change?

Due in large part to their military prowess, the Mongols rose to power in Asia with stunning speed. The Mongols were a pastoral people from the region of modern-day **Mongolia** who were organized loosely into clans. Temüjin (TEHM•yuh•juhn), born during the 1160s, gradually unified the Mongols. In 1206 he was elected **Genghis Khan**—strong ruler—at a massive meeting somewhere in the **Gobi.** From that time on, he devoted himself to conquest.

The army that Genghis Khan unleashed on the world was not unusually large; it totaled less than 130,000 in 1227. It was the Mongols' military tactics, which were devastatingly effective, that set them apart from their enemies. John of Plano Carpini, a Franciscan friar, wrote:

**PRIMARY SOURCE**

> "As soon as they discover the enemy they charge and each unleashes three or four arrows. If they see they cannot break him, they retreat in order to entice the enemy to pursue, thus luring him into an ambush prepared in advance. If they conclude that the enemy army is stronger, they retire for a day or two and ravage neighboring areas. Or they [set up] camp in a well chosen position, and when the enemy army begins to pass by, they appear unexpectedly."
>
> —John of Plano Carpini, in *L'Empire des Steppes,* Rene Grousset, 1939

The Mongols brought much of the Eurasian landmass under a single rule, creating the largest land empire in history. To rule the new Mongol Empire, Genghis Khan set up a capital city at Karakorum. Mongol armies traveled both to the west and to the east. Some went as far as central Europe.

After the death of Genghis Khan in 1227, the empire began to change. Following Mongol custom, upon the death of the ruling

# PEOPLE *in* HISTORY

### Kublai Khan
**1215–1294 Mongol Leader**

As leader of the Yuan dynasty, Kublai Khan ruled—rather than conquered—China. To improve communication with other parts of the empire, Kublai Khan asked a Buddhist monk to create a new written language that could transcribe all of the languages used throughout the Mongol Empire. He passed laws, trying to force people to use the language, but it never gained popularity outside some official uses, like stamps, passports, and paper money. Kublai Khan was also a patron of the arts, and theater and painting flourished in China under his rule. **Why would it be difficult to force people to use a new written language?**

### Genghis Khan
**c. 1162–1227 Mongol Leader**

Genghis Khan's early life is described mostly in myth. According to one myth, he came from divine origin, descending from a gray wolf. From an early age, Temüjin, who later took the title of Genghis Khan, learned to survive in the harsh climate of the Gobi. His family was part of the royal Mongol clan. When he was nine, his father was poisoned. The clan abandoned Temüjin's family. Temüjin's mother raised her family alone, living in extreme poverty and teaching her children how to survive in the Mongolian desert. **Why do you think myths would give Genghis Khan a divine origin?**

khan, his heirs divided the territory. The once-united empire of Genghis Khan was split into several separate territories called **khanates**, each under the rule of one of his sons. It may be that only the death of Genghis Khan kept the Mongols from attacking western Europe. In 1231 the Mongols attacked Persia and then defeated the Abbasids at Baghdad in 1258. Mongol forces attacked the Song dynasty in China in the 1260s.

In their attack on the Chinese, the Mongols encountered the use of gunpowder and the fire-lance. By the end of the thirteenth century, the fire-lance had evolved into the much more effective handgun and cannon. These inventions came too late to save China from the Mongols, however. By the early fourteenth century, foreigners employed by the Mongol rulers of China had introduced the use of gunpowder and firearms into Europe.

In 1279 one of Genghis Khan's grandsons, named **Kublai Khan** (KOO•bluh KAHN), completed the conquest of the Song and established a new Chinese dynasty, the Yuan (YWAHN). Kublai Khan, who ruled China until his death in 1294, established his capital at Khanbalik—the city of the Khan—later known by the Chinese name **Beijing**.

The new Chinese dynasty was at first a dynamic one. Under the leadership of the talented Kublai Khan, the Yuan, or Mongol, dynasty continued to expand the empire. Mongol armies advanced into Vietnam, and Mongol fleets were launched against Java and Sumatra and twice against the islands of Japan. Only parts of northern Vietnam were conquered, however, and then only for a while. The capital at Hanoi was destroyed. The other campaigns failed. On one occasion, a massive storm destroyed the Mongol fleet that attacked Japan, killing thousands. The Mongols used tactics such as cavalry charges and siege warfare. These were not very effective in tropical and hilly regions.

**History ONLINE**
**Student Web Activity—**
Visit glencoe.com and complete the activity about the Mongol dynasty.

The Mongols had more success in ruling China. Mongol rulers adapted to the Chinese political system and made use of Chinese bureaucrats. Culturally the Mongols were quite different from the Chinese and became a separate class with their own laws. The highest positions in the bureaucracy were usually staffed by Mongols.

The Mongol dynasty won the support of many Chinese people, who respected the stability and prosperity that the Mongols had brought. By bringing the entire Eurasian landmass under a single rule, the Mongols increased trade, especially along the Silk Road. The capital at Khanbalik reflected this prosperity. It was a magnificent city, and foreign visitors were impressed by its splendor. One visitor was Marco Polo, who lived in Khanbalik during the reign of Kublai Khan. Polo's stories of the glories of China seemed unbelievable to the Europeans.

## Primary Source

"The streets are so straight and wide that you can see right along them from end to end and from one gate to the other. And up and down the city there are beautiful palaces, and many great and fine hostelries, and fine houses in great numbers."

—Marco Polo, Italian traveler

The Mongol dynasty eventually fell victim to the same problems that had plagued other dynasties: too much spending on foreign conquests, corruption at court, and growing internal instability. In 1368 Zhu Yuanzhang (JOO YWAHN•JAHNG), the son of a peasant, put together an army, ended the Mongol dynasty, and set up a new dynasty, the Ming.

**✓Reading Check** **Summarizing** Why were the Mongols so successful in ruling China?

NATIONAL GEOGRAPHIC

### MONGOL EMPIRE, 1294

## Religion and Government

**MAIN IDEA** Between the Han and Yuan dynasties, religion's role in Chinese government changed.

**HISTORY & YOU** Throughout history, all religions have tried to answer some basic questions. What do you think some of these questions are?

Confucian principles became the basis for Chinese government during the Han dynasty. By the time of the Sui and Tang dynasties, Buddhism and Daoism rivaled the influence of Confucianism.

### Buddhism and Daoism

Buddhism was brought to China in the first century A.D. by merchants and missionaries from India. At first, only merchants and intellectuals were intrigued by the new ideas. However, as a result of the insecurity that prevailed after the collapse of the Han dynasty, both Buddhism and Daoism became more attractive to many people. Both philosophies gained support among the ruling classes.

The growing popularity of Buddhism continued into the early years of the Tang dynasty. Early Tang rulers lent their support to Buddhist monasteries that were set up throughout the country. Buddhists even became advisers at the imperial court but ultimately lost favor.

Buddhism was criticized for being a foreign religion. Like Christian monasteries in Europe during the Middle Ages, Buddhist monasteries had **acquired** thousands of acres of land and serfs. With land came corruption. The government reacted strongly. During the later Tang period, it destroyed countless Buddhist temples and monasteries and forced more than 260,000 monks and nuns to leave the monasteries and return to secular life.

Buddhists taught that the material world was not real, but an illusion. By teaching this, Buddhism was denying the very essence of Confucian teachings—the need for devotion to family and hard work. These were virtues that the Chinese state had reason to support.

### Neo-Confucianism

From the Song dynasty to the end of the dynastic system in the twentieth century, official support went to a revived Confucianism, which became the heart of the state government. This new doctrine, called **neo-Confucianism**, served as a Confucian response to Buddhism and Daoism. It teaches that the world is real, not an illusion, and that fulfillment comes from participation in the world.

Neo-Confucianists divide the world into a material world and a spiritual world. Humans live in the material world but are also linked with the Supreme Ultimate. The goal is to move beyond the material world to reach union with the Supreme Ultimate. Humans do this through a careful examination of the moral principles that rule the universe.

**✓Reading Check** **Explaining** What caused Buddhism to lose favor with the Chinese government?

See page R39 to read excerpts from The Buddha's Sermon in the **Primary Sources and Literature Library.**

### *Pax Mongolia*

*Stability, Trade, and Economic Growth*

The Mongol Empire brought political stability to much of Asia and central Europe from the mid-1200s to the mid-1300s. This stability allowed trade to flourish along the Silk Road and across the empire, and increased cultural contacts between Europe and Asia.

Because the Mongols were a nomadic people, they relied on trade with other cultures and recognized the importance of commerce. Merchants were respected members of society, and Mongol rulers encouraged trade. To achieve this, they increased the use of paper money in China and guaranteed its value with precious metals. They also lowered taxes for merchants and developed merchant associations, which pooled the resources of individual members to finance caravans along the Silk Road.

**Geography SKILLS**

1. **Place** Which geographic factors might have determined the boundaries of the khanates?
2. **Location** How many miles did Marco Polo travel on his journeys?

See page R40 to read five poems by Li Bo in the **Primary Sources and Literature Library.**

## A Golden Age in Literature and Art

**MAIN IDEA** With the invention of printing, a golden age of literature and art emerged in China.

**HISTORY & YOU** In what way does the creation of the Internet compare to the invention of printing? Read about the impact of printing on Chinese art and literature.

The period between the Tang and Ming dynasties was in many ways the great age of Chinese literature. The invention of printing during the Tang dynasty helped to make literature more readily **available** and more popular among the educated elite. Most Chinese, however, were illiterate until modern times. Art, especially landscape painting and ceramics, flourished during this period.

### Poetry

It was in poetry, above all, that the Chinese of this time best expressed their literary talents. The Tang dynasty is viewed as the great age of poetry in China. At least 48,000 poems were written by some 2,200 authors. Poetry was expected to encourage high moral ideals and served as a means of self-expression. Chinese poems celebrated the beauty of nature, the changes of the seasons, and the joys of friendship. They expressed sadness at the shortness of life and the necessity of parting.

**Li Bo** (LEE BWAW) and **Du Fu** (DOO FOO) were two of the most popular poets during the Tang era. Li Bo was a free spirit whose writing often centered on nature. Probably the best-known poem in China, "Quiet Night Thoughts" has been memorized by schoolchildren for centuries.

## SCIENCE, TECHNOLOGY, & SOCIETY

### The Development of Printing in China

Pi Sheng invented movable type in the eleventh century.

Woodblock printing began in the seventh century A.D., during the Tang dynasty. Each page of a text required its own wooden block, with each character, carved in reverse into it. The block was then inked and a piece of paper applied. The printer rubbed the sheet of paper with a brush to transfer inked text. Each block could be reused to make thousands of copies.

Woodblock printing's drawback was that no changes could be made to a page once it was carved. In the eleventh century, Pi Sheng solved this problem by inventing movable type. This allowed individual characters to be moved, making changes easier. Printing had an economic impact during the Song dynasty (960–1279), when the government printed the world's first paper money.

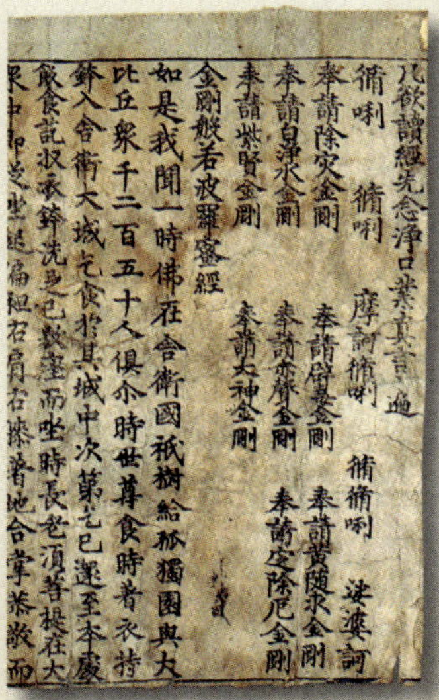

▲ The earliest known printed book is a Chinese translation of the Diamond Sutra, a Buddhist text from A.D. 868.

**CRITICAL THINKING SKILLS**

1. **Drawing Inferences** What effect would the invention of movable type have upon the availability of books? How would societies be affected?
2. **Explaining** Explain why movable type was an improvement over woodblocks.

**PRIMARY SOURCE**

"Beside my bed the bright moonbeams bound
Almost as if there were frost on the ground.
Raising up, I gaze at the Mountain moon;
Lying back, I think of my old home town."
—Li Bo

Where Li Bo was carefree, Du Fu was a serious Confucian. In "Spring Prospect," the poet has returned to his home in the capital after a rebellion has left the city in ruins.

**PRIMARY SOURCE**

"The capital is taken. The hills and streams are left,
And with spring in the city the grass and trees grown dense.
Mourning the times, the flowers trickle their tears;
Saddened with parting, the birds make my heart flutter.
The army beacons have flamed for three months;
A letter from home would be worth ten thousand in gold.
My white hairs have I anxiously scratched ever shorter;
But such disarray! Even hairpins will do no good."
—Du Fu

## Painting and Ceramics

During the Song and Mongol dynasties, landscape painting reached its high point. Influenced by Daoism, artists went into the mountains to find the Dao, or Way, in nature. The word *landscape* in Chinese means "mountain-water" and reflects the Daoist search for balance between the earth and water. Chinese artists tried to reveal the hidden forms of the landscape. Rather than depicting the realistic shape of a specific mountain, for example, they tried to portray the idea of "mountain." Empty spaces were left in the paintings because in the Daoist **vision,** one cannot know the whole truth. Daoism also influenced the portrayal of humans as insignificant in the midst of nature. Chinese artists painted people as tiny figures fishing in small boats or wandering up a hillside trail, living in but not dominating nature.

Tang artisans perfected the making of **porcelain**—a ceramic made of fine clay baked at very high temperatures. Porcelain-making techniques did not reach Europe until the eighteenth century. An Arab traveler in 851 described Chinese porcelain:

**PRIMARY SOURCE**

"There is in China a very fine clay from which are made vases having the transparency of glass bottles; water in these vases is visible through them, and yet they are made of clay."

**✓Reading Check** **Summarizing** What invention helped make literature both more available and more popular?

## SECTION 2 REVIEW

### Vocabulary

1. **Explain** the significance of: Mongolia, Genghis Khan, Gobi, khanate, Kublai Khan, Beijing, acquired, neo-Confucianism, available, Li Bo, Du Fu, vision, porcelain.

### Main Ideas

2. **Explain** how neo-Confucianism differs from Confucianism.
3. **List** the ways in which Daoism is represented in Chinese art of the Song and Yuan dynasties.
4. **Create** a time line like the one shown below that illustrates the Mongols' rise to power.

Mongols' Rise to Power

### Critical Thinking

5. **The BIG Idea** **Making Connections** How did the Mongol dynasty continue and expand the economic and political changes begun under the Tang and Song dynasties?
6. **Evaluating** During the Yuan dynasty, how did the Mongols and Chinese affect each other's cultures?
7. **Analyzing Visuals** Examine the illustration of Genghis Khan on page 271. Compare and contrast it with the illustration of the Empress Wu on page 268. How do their expressions differ? What is similar about the portraits?

### Writing About History

8. **Persuasive Writing** Write a letter to Marco Polo. Tell him why he should hire you for his next expedition to China. Include the reasons you want to go as well as how you would be a helpful member of his crew.

**History ONLINE**

For help with the concepts in this section of *Glencoe World History,* go to glencoe.com and click Study Central™.

# Life in Genghis Khan's Army

Most states that have disappeared into history met their demise in the same way: they were conquered by a foreign army. There have always been outsiders who threaten force to take territories and goods away from other groups. One of the most feared of these outside forces was the army of the Mongol ruler Genghis Khan. It was an army and state in one—and it could move. What was it like to march with him on his conquests that built the largest empire in history?

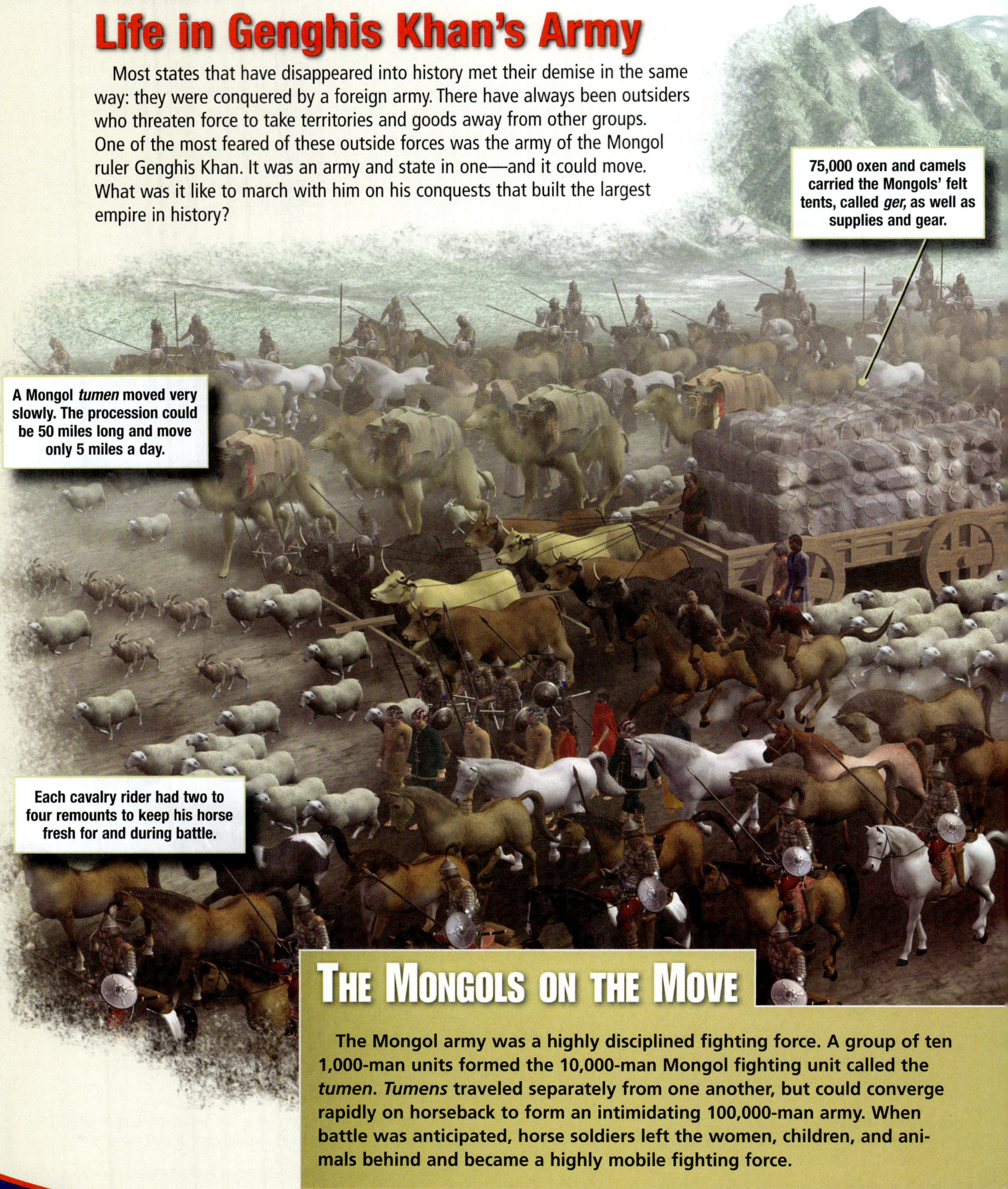


## The Mongols on the Move

The Mongol army was a highly disciplined fighting force. A group of ten 1,000-man units formed the 10,000-man Mongol fighting unit called the *tumen. Tumens* traveled separately from one another, but could converge rapidly on horseback to form an intimidating 100,000-man army. When battle was anticipated, horse soldiers left the women, children, and animals behind and became a highly mobile fighting force.

## Mongol Meals

"An army," Napoleon Bonaparte was believed to have said, "marches on its stomach." Genghis Khan knew as much 500 years earlier. Not surprisingly, meat and dairy products formed the basis of the marching Mongols' diet. They cooked mutton and lamb over rocks heated by dung fires. Milk tea and fermented mare's milk were common drinks.

### Analyzing Visuals

1. **Evaluating** What do you think the *tumen's* main strengths were? Its greatest weaknesses?
2. **Comparing and Contrasting** How was life for Mongol children similar to and different from the life of children in other cultures you have read about?

SECTION 3

Section Audio

Spotlight Video

# Early Japan and Korea

## GUIDE TO READING

### The BIG Idea

**Physical Geography** The geography of Japan, a string of islands, and of Korea, a peninsula bordering China, have had a huge impact on their respective histories.

### Content Vocabulary

- samurai *(p. 280)*
- Bushido *(p. 280)*
- shogun *(p. 281)*
- daimyo *(p. 281)*
- Shinto *(p. 282)*
- Zen *(p. 282)*

### Academic Vocabulary

- revenue *(p. 279)*
- code *(p. 280)*

### People and Places

- Ōsaka *(p. 278)*
- Kyōto *(p. 278)*
- Shōtoku Taishi *(p. 279)*
- Minamoto Yoritomo *(p. 281)*
- Murasaki Shikibu *(p. 282)*
- Yi Sŏng-gye *(p. 283)*

### Reading Strategy

**Categorizing Information** As you read, create a chart like the one below to help you study which elements of Chinese culture were adopted by Korea and Japan.

**Chinese Culture in . . .**

| Japan | Korea |
|---|---|
| | |
| | |
| | |

*Early Japan was unified by a noble family that gave rise to a line of emperors. Over time, power passed from the hands of the emperor to powerful aristocratic families, then to military leaders called shoguns. Finally, centralized power disappeared altogether. Korea's history during this period is one of a struggle for independence against the neighboring Chinese.*

## Early Japan

**MAIN IDEA** Japan's history has been marked by power struggles between rulers and independent families.

**HISTORY & YOU** How has geography played an important role in the growth of your area? Read about geography's role in the development of Japan.

The ancestors of present-day Japanese settled in the Yamato Plain near the location of the modern cities of **Ōsaka** and **Kyōto** in the first centuries A.D. Their society was made up of clans. The people were divided between a small aristocratic class (the rulers) and a large population of rice farmers, artisans, and household servants. The local ruler protected his clan in return for a share of the annual harvest. Eventually, one ruler of the Yamato clan (named for the Yamato Plain where they lived) achieved supremacy over the others and became, in effect, ruler of Japan.

### The Impact of Geography

Chinese and Japanese societies have historically been very different. One of the reasons for these differences is geography. Whereas China is located on a vast continent, Japan is a mountainous archipelago, or chain of many islands. The population is concentrated on four main islands: Hokkaidō, the main island of Honshū, and the two smaller islands of Kyūshū and Shikoku. Japan's total land area is approximately 146,000 square miles (378,000 square km)—about the size of Montana.

Like China, much of Japan is mountainous. Only about 11 percent of the total land area can be farmed. The mountains are volcanic in origin. Volcanic soils are very fertile, which has helped Japanese farming. The area, however, is prone to earthquakes. In 1923 an earthquake nearly destroyed the entire city of Tokyo.

The fact that Japan is an island nation has also affected its history. Because of their geographical isolation, the Japanese developed a number of unique qualities. These qualities contributed to the Japanese belief that they had a destiny separate from that of the peoples on the continent.

**Early Japanese Rule**

- **c. 600–622** Shōtoku Taishi begins to centralize Japan
- **710** Shōtoku reforms continue, Nara period begins
- **794** Capital moves to Heian-kyo, central power begins to decline
- **1192** Minamoto Yoritomo founds Kamakura shogunate
- **1333** Ashikaga family overthrows Kamakura shogunate
- **1467–1477** Onin War leads to the destruction of Kyōto

**Geography SKILLS**

1. **Location** What three major islands made up early Japan?
2. **Regions** What geographic features contributed to the importance of Heian-kyo (Kyōto), Ōsaka, and Edo (Tokyo)?

## Chinese Influences

In the early seventh century, **Shōtoku Taishi**, a Yamato prince, tried to unify the various clans so that the Japanese could more effectively resist an invasion by the Chinese. To do this, Prince Shōtoku sent representatives to the Tang capital of China to learn how the Chinese organized their government. He then began to create a new centralized system of government in Japan, based roughly on the Chinese model.

Prince Shōtoku wanted a centralized government under a supreme ruler. His objective was to limit the powers of the aristocrats and enhance the Yamato ruler's (his own) authority. As a result, the ruler was portrayed as a divine figure and the symbol of the Japanese nation.

Shōtoku Taishi's successors continued to make reforms based on the Chinese model. The territory of Japan was divided into administrative districts, and the senior official of each district was selected from among the local nobles. As in China, the rural village was the basic unit of government. A new tax system was set up. Now all farmland technically belonged to the state. All taxes were to be paid directly to the central government rather than to local aristocrats.

## The Nara Period

After Shōtoku Taishi's death in 622, political power fell into the hands of the Fujiwara clan. A Yamato ruler was still emperor. He was, however, strongly influenced by the Fujiwara family. In 710 a new capital was established at Nara. The emperor began to use the official title "Son of Heaven."

Though the reforms begun by Prince Shōtoku continued during this period, Japan's central government could not overcome the power of the aristocrats. These powerful families were able to keep the taxes from the lands for themselves. Unable to gain tax **revenues,** the central government steadily lost power and influence.

## The Heian Period

In 794 the emperor moved the capital from Nara to nearby Heian-kyo, on the site of present-day Kyōto. At Heian-kyo, the emperor continued to rule in name, but actual power remained in the hands of the Fujiwara clan. In fact, the government was returning to the decentralized system that had existed before the time of Shōtoku Taishi. Powerful families whose wealth was based on the ownership of tax-exempt farmland dominated the rural areas.

With the decline of central power, local aristocrats took justice into their own hands. They turned to military force, and a new class of military servants emerged whose purpose was to protect the security and property of their employers. Called the **samurai** ("those who serve"), these warriors fought on horseback, clad in helmet and armor, and carried a sword and a bow. Like knights, the samurai were supposed to live by a strict warrior **code,** known in Japan as **Bushido** ("the way of the warrior").

# TURNING POINT — JAPANESE ISOLATION

Mongol emperor Kublai Khan first attempted to conquer Japan in 1274. Strengthened with Korean and Chinese troops, the Mongols seized the beach at Hakata. Heavy storms decimated the Mongol fleet and its manpower.

In 1281 Kublai Khan attacked with a larger fleet, but most of the ships were destroyed by a typhoon. The Japanese called the storms *kamikaze,* or "divine wind." They took this as a sign that they were invincible because they were protected by divine powers. After defeating the Mongol invaders, Japan isolated itself from major foreign influence until the Meiji Restoration, beginning in 1867.

Japanese samurai attacking a Mongol ship

**DOCUMENT-BASED QUESTIONS**

1. **Determining Cause and Effect** How did the Mongol attacks change Japan?
2. **Evaluating** How did Japan's policy of isolation help the country? How was it detrimental to the country?

## The Kamakura Shogunate

By the end of the twelfth century, rivalries among Japanese aristocratic families had led to almost constant civil war. Finally, a powerful noble named **Minamoto Yoritomo** defeated several rivals and set up his power near the modern city of Tokyo.

To strengthen the state, he created a more centralized government under a military leader known as the **shogun** (general). In this new system—called the shogunate—the emperor remained ruler in name only, and the shogun exercised the actual power. The Kamakura shogunate, founded by Yoritomo, lasted from 1192 to 1333.

Although the shogunate was a military government, it was unprepared when Mongol ruler Kublai Khan sent 23,000 troops to invade Japan in 1274. The Mongols were winning until a storm sank their fleet. In 1281, Kublai Khan sent nearly 150,000 troops. Fighting from behind stone walls they had built, the Japanese forced the Mongols to retreat. A typhoon (violent storm) then devastated the Mongol fleet. The wars strained the political system. In 1333, several powerful families led by the Ashikagas overthrew the Kamakura shogunate.

## Collapse of Central Rule

The power of the local aristocrats grew during the fourteenth and fifteenth centuries. Heads of noble families, now called **daimyo** (DY•mee•OH), "great names," controlled vast landed estates that owed no taxes to the government. As family rivalries continued, the daimyo relied on the samurai for protection, and political power came into the hands of a loose coalition of noble families.

By 1500, Japan was close to chaos. A disastrous civil war known as the Onin War, which lasted from 1467 to 1477, led to the virtual destruction of the capital city of Kyōto. Central authority disappeared. Powerful aristocrats in rural areas seized control over large territories, which they ruled as independent lords. Their rivalries caused almost constant warfare.

✓Reading Check **Summarizing** What were the effects of the Onin War?

# Life in Early Japan

MAIN IDEA Japan's small size and relative isolation have had a major effect on the development of its economy, religion, and culture.

**HISTORY & YOU** Have you read any books categorized as "women's literature"? Read about female authors in early Japan.

Early Japan was mostly a farming society. Its people took advantage of the limited amount of farmland and abundant rainfall to grow wet rice (rice grown in flooded fields). Trade in Japan was slow to develop. Barter, rather than money, was used until the twelfth century.

Manufacturing began to develop during the Kamakura period. Markets appeared in the larger towns, and industries such as the making of paper and porcelain and iron casting emerged. Trade between regions also grew. Goods were carried in carts, on boats, or on human backs. Foreign trade, mainly with Korea and China, began during the eleventh century. Japan shipped raw materials, paintings, swords, and other manufactured items in return for silk, porcelain, books, and copper coins.

## The Role of Women

In early Japan, women may have had a certain level of equality with men. An eighth-century law code, for example, guaranteed the inheritance rights of women. Wives who were abandoned could divorce and remarry. Later practices, however, show women were considered subordinate to men. A husband could divorce his wife if she did not produce a son or if she committed adultery, talked too much, was jealous, or had a serious illness.

Although women did not possess the full legal and social rights of men, they played an active role at various levels of society. Aristocratic women were prominent at court. Some became known for their artistic or literary talents.

Women often appear in the paintings of the period along with men. The women are doing the spring planting, threshing and hulling rice, and acting as salespersons and entertainers.

**HISTORY & ARTS** PRIMARY SOURCE

## *Murasaki Shikibu and* The Tale of Genji

*The Tale of Genji* covers four generations of a fictitious imperial family and reveals much about the culture of the aristocracy in Heian-era Japan. Most of the book focuses on the nobleman Genji's life, his many love affairs, and the consequences of these relationships upon his career as a government official. An excerpt from *The Tale of Genji,* translated by Suyematz Kenchio, describes the young Genji:

> "The young Prince, whom we now style Genji (the Gen), was still with the Emperor. . . . When he attained the age of twelve the ceremony of Gembuk (or crowning) took place. . . .
>
> About ten o'clock in the forenoon Genji appeared on the scene. The boyish style of his hair and dress excellently became his features; and it almost seemed matter for regret that it should be altered. The Okura-Kiô-Kurahito, whose office it was to rearrange the hair of Genji, faltered as he did so. . . . After he had been crowned the Prince withdrew to a dressing-room, where he attired himself in the full robes of manhood. Then descending to the Court-yard he performed a measured dance in grateful acknowledgment. This he did with so much grace and skill that all present were filled with admiration; and his beauty, which some feared might be lessened, seemed only more remarkable from the change."

Three-part woodblock illustration from *The Tale of Genji*

**DOCUMENT-BASED QUESTIONS**

Little is known about the life of Lady Murasaki Shikibu, the author of *The Tale of Genji*—even her real name is unknown. She began writing *Genji* around 1001. In 1006 she was called to serve in the court of the empress and probably completed writing *The Tale of Genji* a few years later.

1. **Analyzing** How did the circumstances of Shikibu's life help her write *Genji*?
2. **Making Inferences** What does the excerpt tell us about the aristocracy of Heian-era Japan?

## Religion in Early Japan

Early Japanese people worshiped spirits, called *kami,* whom they believed resided in trees, rivers, streams, and mountains. The Japanese also believed that the spirits of their ancestors were present in the air around them. In Japan, these beliefs evolved into a religion called **Shinto** ("the Sacred Way" or "the Way of the Gods"), which is still practiced today. Over time, Shinto became a state doctrine linked to a belief in the divinity of the emperor and the sacredness of the Japanese nation.

Shinto, however, did not satisfy the spiritual needs of all the Japanese people. Some turned to Buddhism, which Buddhist monks from China brought to Japan during the A.D. 500s. Among the aristocrats in Japan, one sect, known as **Zen**, became the most popular. Zen beliefs about self-discipline became part of the samurai warrior's code. The two main schools of Zen teach that nirvana either comes by instantaneous enlightenment or through a long process of meditation.

## Culture in Early Japan

During much of the history of early Japan, aristocratic men believed that prose fiction was merely "vulgar gossip" and was thus beneath them. Consequently, from the ninth to the twelfth centuries, women were the most productive writers of prose fiction in Japanese. From this tradition appeared one of the world's great novels, *The Tale of Genji,* written by court author **Murasaki Shikibu**. Her novel traces the life of nobleman Genji as he moves from youthful adventures to a life of compassion in his later years.

In Japanese art and architecture, landscape serves as an important means of expression. The landscape surrounding the Golden Pavilion in Kyōto displays a harmony of garden, water, and architecture that makes it one of the treasures of the world.

✓**Reading Check** **Summarizing** Why were the Shinto and Buddhist religions important to the development of Japanese culture?

## The Emergence of Korea

**MAIN IDEA** The early history of Korea was marked by the presence of dominating neighbors.

**HISTORY & YOU** Recall the Chinese response to the Mongol invasion. As you read, compare it with the Korean response.

The Korea Peninsula, only slightly larger than the state of Minnesota, is relatively mountainous. Its closeness to both China and Japan has greatly affected its history. Indeed, no society in East Asia was more strongly influenced by the Chinese model than Korea.

In 109 B.C., the northern part of the Korea Peninsula came under the control of the Chinese. The Koreans, however, drove them out in the A.D. 200s. Eventually, three separate kingdoms emerged: Koguryo in the north, Paekche (PAK•chuh) in the southwest, and Silla in the southeast. Each of the kingdoms was governed by the combination of a hereditary monarch and powerful aristocratic families. From the fourth to the seventh centuries, the three kingdoms were bitter rivals. This period also saw the introduction of Buddhism to Korea, which quickly became the state religion of each of the kingdoms. After 527 Silla kings adopted Buddhist names and sponsored the building of many Buddhist temples. One was a nine-story wooden pagoda, which was perhaps the tallest in East Asia. As the Silla kingdom became more allied with the Chinese, the monarchy turned to Confucian ideals to run the country.

Gradually, with the support of the Tang dynasty of China, the kingdom of Silla gained control of the peninsula. After the king of Silla was assassinated, however, Korea sank into civil war. Finally, in the early tenth century, a new dynasty called Koryo (the root of the modern word *Korea*) arose in the north. This kingdom adopted Chinese political institutions in order to unify its territory and remained in power for four hundred years.

In the thirteenth century, the Mongols seized the northern part of Korea. By accepting Mongol authority, the Koryo dynasty managed to remain in power. Mongol rule led to much suffering for the Korean people, especially the thousands of peasants and artisans who were forced to build ships for Kublai Khan's invasion of Japan.

After the collapse of the Mongol dynasty in China, the Koryo dynasty broke down. In 1392 **Yi Sŏng-gye**, a military commander, seized power and founded the Yi dynasty, which would rule Korea for over five hundred years. The Korean people were once again in charge of their own destiny.

**✓Reading Check** **Identifying** Which Asian country had the greatest influence on Korean political institutions?

## SECTION 3 REVIEW

### Vocabulary

1. **Explain** the significance of: Ōsaka, Kyōto, Shōtoku Taishi, revenue, samurai, code, Bushido, Minamoto Yoritomo, shogun, daimyo, Shinto, Zen, Murasaki Shikibu, Yi Sŏng-gye.

### Main Ideas

2. **List** the reforms in government made by Shōtoku Taishi and his successors.
3. **Create** a cluster diagram like the one below that clarifies the role of women in early Japan.

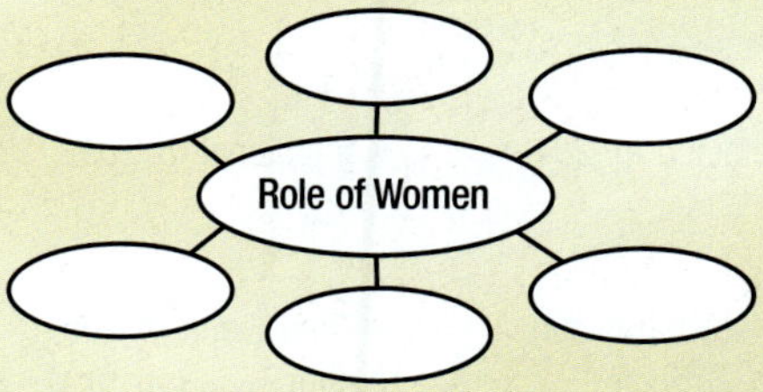


4. **Explain** why China had such a large role in Korea's history.

### Critical Thinking

5. **The BIG Idea** **Hypothesizing** If Korea had been an island instead of a peninsula, how might its history have been different?
6. **Assessing** How did the samurai and shogun affect the government of early Japan?
7. **Analyzing Visuals** Examine the color woodblock on page 282. What does the illustration tell us about the clothing, customs, and living conditions among the nobility in Heian-era Japan?

### Writing About History

8. **Descriptive Writing** Imagine you are a samurai living in Japan during the fourteenth century. Explain why you became a samurai and describe your duties.

**History ONLINE**

For help with the concepts in this section of *Glencoe World History*, go to glencoe.com and click Study Central™.

SECTION 4

Section Audio

Spotlight Video

# India After the Guptas

## GUIDE TO READING

### The BIG Idea

**Ideas, Beliefs, and Values** When Islamic peoples conquered much of India, tension arose between the Muslim rulers and the majority Hindu population.

### Content Vocabulary

- Theravada *(p. 284)*
- Mahayana *(p. 284)*

### Academic Vocabulary

- retained *(p. 284)*
- traditional *(p. 289)*

### People and Places

- Ghazna (Ghaznī) *(p. 286)*
- Maḥmūd of Ghazna *(p. 286)*
- Rajputs *(p. 286)*
- sultanate of Delhi *(p. 286)*
- Timur Lenk *(p. 286)*
- Samarqand *(p. 286)*
- Moguls *(p. 286)*
- Daṇḍin *(p. 289)*

### Reading Strategy

**Contrasting** As you read, use a chart like the one below to help you study the main differences between Theravada and Mahayana Buddhism.

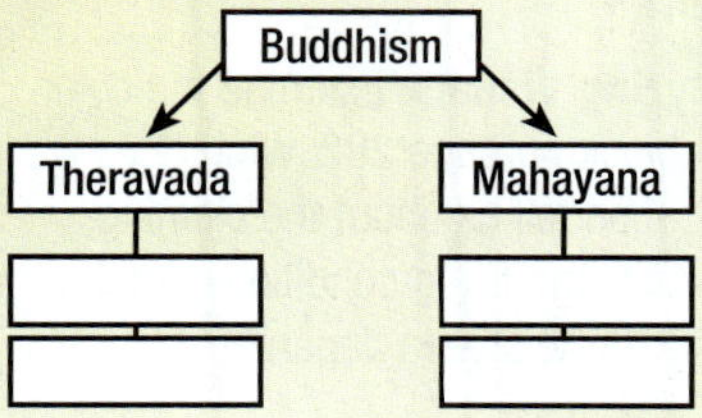


*After the Gupta Empire collapsed, Muslim conquerors moved into India, eventually taking control of nearly all of the subcontinent. The majority of the population in India remained Hindu, which often led to tension and open conflict.*

## The Impact of Religion

**MAIN IDEA** Buddhism, Hinduism, and Islam all influenced the development of India.

***HISTORY & YOU*** How have patterns of religious belief changed in your own state or region? Read about the patterns of religion in India.

For hundreds of years, Buddhism had **retained** widespread acceptance among the Indian people. The teachings of the Buddha came to be interpreted in different ways, however. People did not always agree on the meaning of the Buddha's teachings. As a result, a split developed among Buddhists in India.

One group believed that they were following the original teachings of the Buddha. They called themselves the school of **Theravada**, "the teachings of the elders." Followers of Theravada see Buddhism as a way of life, not a religion that is centered on individual salvation. They insist that an understanding of oneself is the chief way to gain nirvana, or release from the "wheel of life." Theravada is best suited to a monastic life so that followers can spend most of their time in meditation.

Another view of Buddhist doctrine was emerging in northwest India. This school, known as **Mahayana** Buddhism, said that Theravada teachings were too strict for ordinary people. To Mahayana Buddhists, Buddhism is a religion, not a philosophy. The Buddha is not just a wise man, but also a divine figure. Nirvana is not just a release from the wheel of life, but a true heaven. Through devotion to the Buddha, people can achieve salvation in this heaven after death.

### The Decline of Buddhism

In the end, neither the Mahayana nor the Theravada sect of Buddhism remained popular in Indian society. By the 600s, Theravada had declined rapidly. Mahayana was absorbed by a revived Hinduism and later by a new arrival, Islam. Despite their decline in India, though, both schools of Buddhism found success abroad. Carried by monks to China, Korea, Southeast Asia, and Japan, the practice of Buddhism has remained active in all four areas to the present.

### The Impact of Religions on India

*Om symbol*

*Dharma wheel*

*Star and crescent*

| | HINDUISM | BUDDHISM | ISLAM |
|---|---|---|---|
| Origin | India | India | Arabian Peninsula |
| Introduced | c. 1500 B.C. | c. 600–400 B.C. | A.D. 700 |
| Cultural Contributions | • Temples with towers<br>• Astronomy<br>• Epic poems and prose<br>• Mathematics | • Stupas and pillars<br>• Ajanta Caves | • Architecture<br>• Mathematics<br>• Medicine |
| Important Historical Figures | • Religious toleration by Kushān and Gupta rulers<br>• Rajputs resisted the rule of Maḥmūd of Ghazna | • Siddhārtha Gautama established Buddhism<br>• Mauryan king Aśoka established Buddhism | • Abbasid dynasty, spread Islam into India<br>• Maḥmūd of Ghazna, expanded the rule of Islam into southeast<br>• Timur Lenk |
| Population in Modern India | More than 80% | Less than 1% | More than 12% |

**Chart SKILLS**

1. **Analyzing** Why would Buddhism and Hinduism share many similarities?
2. **Making Inferences** Why might it be difficult to trace the religious history of India?

## The Eastward Expansion of Islam

In the early eighth century, Islam became popular in the northwestern part of the Indian subcontinent and had a major impact on Indian civilization. This impact is still evident today in the division of the subcontinent into mostly Hindu India and two Islamic states, Bangladesh and Pakistan. One reason for Islam's success was the state of political disunity in India when it arrived. The Gupta Empire had collapsed, and no central authority had replaced it. India was divided into about 70 states, which fought constantly. During this time, warriors were held in very high esteem. One Indian poet wrote:

**PRIMARY SOURCE**

"When you see a fight, rush to the front, divide your enemy's forces, stand before them, and get your body scarred by the deep cuts of their swords; thus your fame is pleasant to the ear, not your body to the eye. As for your enemies, when they see you, they turn their backs, and with bodies whole and unscarred, they are pleasant to the eye, not so their shame to the ear."

When the Arab armies reached India in the early eighth century, they did little more than move into the frontier regions. At the end of the tenth century, however, a new phase of Islamic expansion took place when a group of rebellious Turkish slaves founded a new Islamic state known as **Ghazna (Ghaznī)**, located in what is now Afghanistan.

When the founder of the new state died in 997, his son, **Maḥmūd of Ghazna**, succeeded him. Maḥmūd, an ambitious man, began to attack neighboring Hindu kingdoms to the southeast. Before his death in 1030, he was able to extend his rule throughout the upper Indus Valley and as far south as the Indian Ocean.

Resistance against the advances of Maḥmūd and his successors into northern India was led by the **Rajputs**, who were Hindu warriors. They fought bravely, but their military tactics, based on infantry supported by elephants, were no match for the cavalry of the invaders. Maḥmūd's cavalry was able to strike with great speed. Maḥmūd's successors continued their advances. By 1200, Muslim power had reached over the entire plain of northern India, creating a new Muslim state known as the **sultanate of Delhi**. In the fourteenth century, this state extended its power into the Deccan Plateau.

## PEOPLE *in* HISTORY

**Timur Lenk**
Turkic Conqueror 1330s–1405

Timur Lenk was a shrewd warrior who built an empire that stretched from modern-day Iraq to India, and from the Arabian Sea to modern-day Kazakhstan. His initial rise to power involved first rebelling against the khan to whom he had vowed allegiance, then turning on the brother-in-law who had helped him overthrow the khan. His cruelty toward his enemies and the people he conquered was legendary. For example, when conquered Persians tried to rebel against Timur's forces in 1395, the residents of entire cities were killed and towers built of the victims' skulls. **Why might Timur's life have been the subject of legends?**

## The Impact of Timur Lenk

During the latter half of the fourteenth century, the sultanate of Delhi began to decline. Near the end of the century, a new military force crossed the Indus River from the northwest. The invaders raided the capital of Delhi, and then withdrew. As many as 100,000 Hindu prisoners were massacred before the gates of the city. It was India's first meeting with **Timur Lenk** (Tamerlane).

Timur Lenk was the ruler of a Mongol state based in **Samarqand**, to the north of the Pamirs. Born sometime during the 1330s in Samarqand, Timur Lenk seized power in 1369 and immediately launched a program of conquest. It took more than a century for the city of Delhi to recover from the destruction caused by the invasion.

During the 1380s, Timur Lenk placed the entire region east of the Caspian Sea under his authority and then occupied Mesopotamia. After his brief foray into northern India, he turned to the west. He died in 1405 in the midst of a military campaign.

The death of Timur Lenk removed a major menace from the various states of the Indian subcontinent, but the calm did not last long. By the early sixteenth century, two new challenges had appeared from beyond the horizon. One came from the north in the form of the **Moguls**, a newly emerging nomadic power. The other came from Europe, from Portuguese traders arriving by sea in search of gold and spices. Both the Moguls and the Portuguese would exert a major impact on the later course of Indian civilization.

✓Reading Check **Evaluating** What was the impact of the introduction of Islam in India?

## Indian Society and Culture

**MAIN IDEA** The ruling class of India was made up of Muslims, but some members of the Hindu population also prospered. The rich culture of India was reflected in its art, literature, architecture, and technological advances.

***HISTORY & YOU*** Recall the interaction between Aryans and Dravidians. Read to compare with the interaction between Hindus and Muslims.

The imposition of Islamic rule by Maḥmūd of Ghazna and his successors created a level of general tension in Indian society. The life of the typical Indian, however, remained about the same as it had been for the past several hundred years.

### Islam and Indian Society

The Muslim rulers in India viewed themselves as foreign conquerors. They tried to maintain a strict separation between the Muslim ruling class and the Hindu population.

Like rulers elsewhere at this time, many Muslim rulers in India were intolerant of other faiths. They generally used peaceful means, however, to encourage people to convert to Islam. Still, some could be fierce when their religious zeal was aroused. Said one,

**PRIMARY SOURCE**

"I forbade the infliction of any severe punishment on the Hindus in general, but I destroyed their idol temples and raised mosques in their place."

—a Muslim ruler

Most Muslim rulers realized that there were simply too many Hindus to convert them all. They reluctantly accepted the need to tolerate religious differences. Nevertheless, Muslim rulers did impose many Islamic customs on Hindu society. Overall, the relationship between Muslims and Hindus was that of conqueror and conquered, a relationship marked by suspicion and dislike rather than friendship and understanding.

**PRIMARY SOURCE** ***HISTORY & ARTS***

***Islamic Architecture***

Adhai-Din-Ka Jhonpra was built by the Jains, a minority religious group in India with similarities to both Hinduism and Buddhism. The building may have been a temple and college for teaching Sanskrit. In 1198, the sultan of Delhi turned it into a mosque and built a seven-arched wall inscribed with verses in Arabic. The wall and minarets may have been built with mortar from Hindu and Jain temples that the Sultan destroyed. The interior of the Jhonpra resembles a Hindu temple more than a mosque. The pointed arches and minarets are characteristic of Islamic architecture.

**DOCUMENT-BASED QUESTIONS**

1. **Drawing Conclusions** Why did the sultan of Delhi destroy Hindu and Jain temples?
2. **Describing** How does this mosque represent Indo-Islamic architecture?

## Economy and Daily Life

Between 500 and 1500, most Indians lived on the land and farmed their own tiny plots. These peasants paid a share of their harvest each year to a landlord, who in turn sent part of the payment to the local ruler. In effect, the landlord worked as a tax collector for the king, who in theory owned all the land in his state.

The rents paid by the farmers funded the sumptuous lifestyle, the wars, and the grand temples of the rich and high born. At best the peasants scraped by. At worst, they fell into debt and were victims of moneylenders who charged high rates of interest.

Although the vast majority of Indians were peasants, reports by foreign visitors between 500 and 1500 indicate that many people lived in the cities. It was here that the landed elites and rich merchants lived, often in conditions of considerable wealth.

Rulers naturally had the most wealth. One maharaja (great king) of a small state in southern India, for example, had more than 100,000 soldiers in his pay, along with 900 elephants and 20,000 horses. Another ruler kept a thousand high-caste women to sweep his palace. Each carried a broom and a brass basin holding a mixture of cow dung and water.

**PRIMARY SOURCE**

"When the King goes from one house to another, or to a house of prayer, he goes on foot, and these women go before him with their brooms and basins in their hands, plastering the path where he is to tread."

Agriculture was not the only source of wealth in India. Since ancient times, India's location had made it a center for trade between Southwest Asia and East Asia. It had also been a source for other goods shipped throughout the world.

Internal trade within India probably declined during this period, primarily

### HISTORY & ARTS

### *Hindu Temple at Khajuraho*

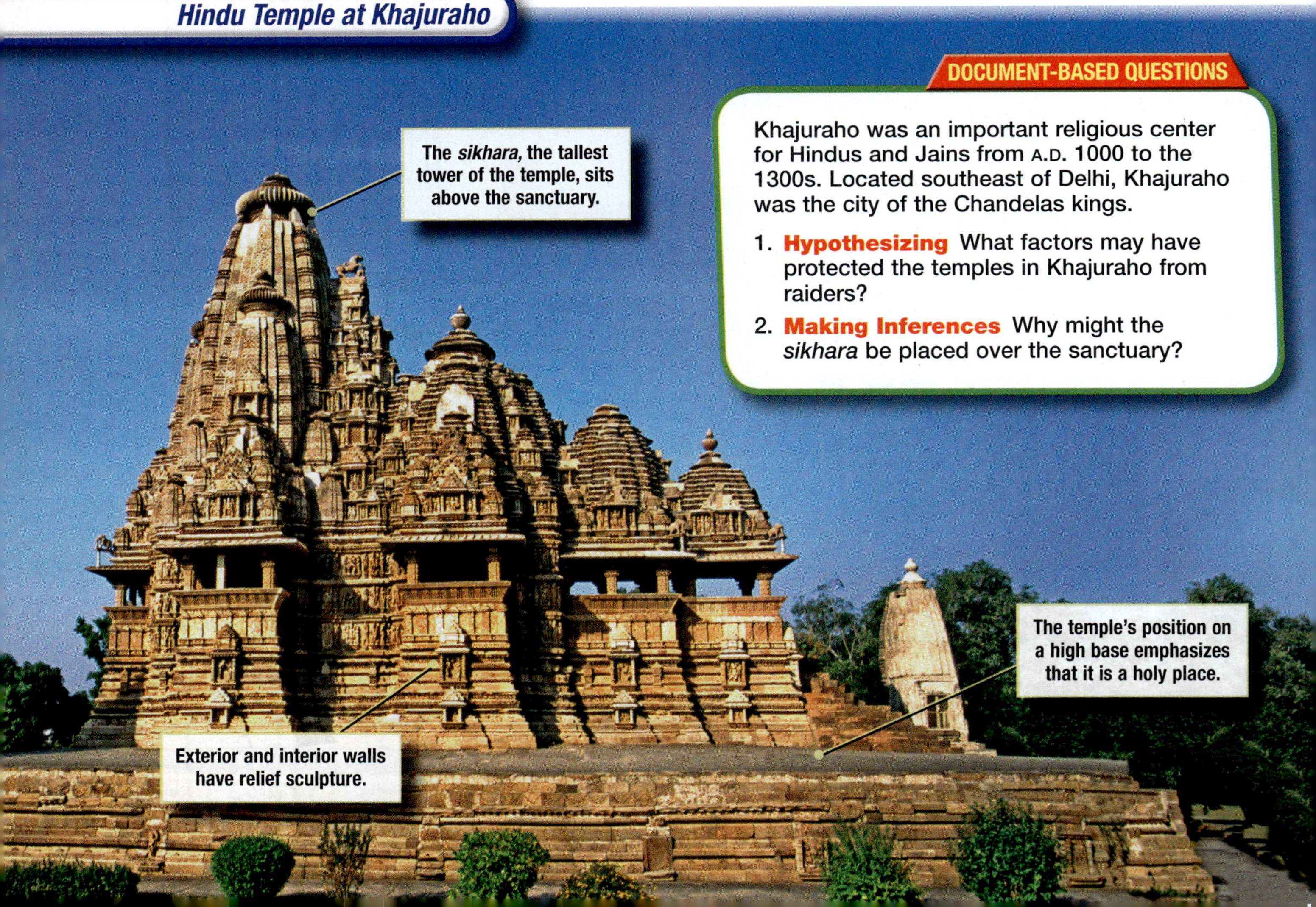


**DOCUMENT-BASED QUESTIONS**

Khajuraho was an important religious center for Hindus and Jains from A.D. 1000 to the 1300s. Located southeast of Delhi, Khajuraho was the city of the Chandelas kings.

1. **Hypothesizing** What factors may have protected the temples in Khajuraho from raiders?
2. **Making Inferences** Why might the *sikhara* be placed over the sanctuary?

because of the fighting among the many states of India. The level of foreign trade, however, remained high, especially in the south and along the northwestern coast. Both areas were located along the **traditional** trade routes to Southwest Asia and the Mediterranean Sea region.

Wealthy Hindu merchants with close ties to the royal courts carried on much of the foreign trade. Others, including Muslims, also participated in this trade. Sometimes, traders from other lands settled in India; in other cases Indian traders traveled elsewhere.

## Culture in India

Between 500 and 1500, Indian artists and writers built on the achievements of their predecessors while making innovations in all fields of creative endeavor, both secular and religious. Here, we examine two such fields: architecture and prose literature.

During this period, religious architecture in India developed from caves to new, magnificent structures. From the eighth century on, Indian architects built monumental Hindu temples. Each temple consisted of a central shrine surrounded by a tower, a hall for worshipers, an entryway, and a porch, all set in a rectangular courtyard. Temples became ever more ornate. The towers became higher and the temple complexes more intricate. Some became walled compounds set one within the other, resembling a town.

Probably the greatest examples of Hindu temple art of this period are found at Khajuraho. Of the 80 temples originally built there in the tenth century, 20 remain standing today. All of the towers on these temples are buttressed (supported by stone walls) at various levels on the sides. This gives the whole temple a sense of unity and creates an upward movement similar to that of Gandisê (Kailas) in the Himalaya, a sacred place to Hindus.

The use of prose in fiction was well established in India by the sixth and seventh centuries. This is truly astonishing in light of the fact that the novel did not appear in Japan until the tenth or eleventh century and in Europe until the seventeenth century.

One of the greatest masters of Sanskrit prose was **Daṇḍin**, a seventh-century author. In *The Adventures of the Ten Princes,* he relates the exploits of 10 princes as they search for love and power. He created a fantastic world, fusing realistic portrayal of human behavior with supernatural occurrences, including the direct intervention of gods in worldly affairs. His powers of observation, details of everyday life, and humor give his writing much vitality.

✓Reading Check **Describing** How does Indian architecture reflect Hindu ideals?

## SECTION 4 REVIEW

### Vocabulary

1. **Explain** the significance of: retained, Theravada, Mahayana, Ghazna (Ghaznī), Maḥmūd of Ghazna, Rajputs, sultanate of Delhi, Timur Lenk, Samarqand, Moguls, traditional, Daṇḍin.

### Main Ideas

2. **Create** an outline like the one shown below to describe the impact of Timur Lenk.

I. Timur Lenk
   A. born during 1330s in Samarqand
   B. ______________________
   C. ______________________

3. **Summarize** the principal sources of wealth in India.

### Critical Thinking

4. **The BIG Idea** **Evaluating** What was the impact of the introduction of Islam into the Indian culture? Give reasons to support whether the impact was a positive or negative one.
5. **Making Connections** How do you think India's expansive foreign trade affected its development?
6. **Analyzing Visuals** Contrast the temple on page 288 with the mosque on page 287. How do they differ in decoration and layout from each other?

### Writing About History

7. **Expository Writing** Using the information contained in Chapters 3, 6, and 8 describe the differences and similarities in Hindu, Buddhist, and Muslim arts.

**History ONLINE**
For help with the concepts in this section of *Glencoe World History,* go to glencoe.com and click Study Central™.

SECTION 5

Section Audio    Spotlight Video

# Civilization in Southeast Asia

## GUIDE TO READING

### The BIG Idea

**Physical Geography** The mountains, river valleys, and islands of Southeast Asia had a major effect on its political, cultural, and economic development.

### Content Vocabulary

- archipelago *(p. 290)*
- agricultural society *(p. 294)*
- trading society *(p. 294)*

### Academic Vocabulary

- region *(p. 290)*
- area *(p. 290)*

### People and Places

- Malay Peninsula *(p. 290)*
- Vietnam *(p. 291)*
- Angkor *(p. 292)*
- Jayavarman *(p. 292)*
- Pagan *(p. 292)*
- Thai *(p. 292)*
- Thailand *(p. 292)*
- Strait of Malacca *(p. 293)*
- Melaka *(p. 294)*

### Reading Strategy

**Categorizing Information** As you read, create a chart like the one below to help you study characteristics of the states in Southeast Asia.

| | Government | Economy | Culture |
|---|---|---|---|
| Vietnam | | | |
| Angkor | | | |
| Thailand | | | |
| Burma | | | |
| Malay | | | |

*Unlike most of the other regions of Asia, Southeast Asia was never unified under a single government, largely due to its formidable geographic barriers. Therefore, the history of the area tells of the competition and interaction between several small states.*

## The Formation of States

**MAIN IDEA** The geography of Southeast Asia led to the development of distinct cultures throughout the region.

***HISTORY & YOU*** Millions of people have visited the monuments in Southeast Asia. Which structures would you be most interested in seeing?

Between 500 and 1500, a number of organized states developed throughout Southeast Asia. When the peoples of the region began to form states, they used models from China and India. At the same time, they adapted these models to their own needs and created their own unique states.

### The Impact of Geography

Between China and India lies the **region** that today is called Southeast Asia. It has two major parts. One is the mainland region, extending southward from the Chinese border down to the tip of the **Malay Peninsula**. The other is an extensive **archipelago**, or chain of islands, most of which is part of present-day Indonesia and the Philippines.

Ancient mariners called the **area** the "golden region" or "golden islands." Located between India and China—two highly advanced and densely populated regions—Southeast Asia contains a vast mixture of races, cultures, and religions.

Mainland Southeast Asia consists of several north-south mountain ranges. Between these ranges are fertile river valleys that run in a southerly or southeasterly direction. The mountains are densely forested and often infested with malaria-bearing mosquitoes. Thus, the people living in the river valleys were often cut off from one another and had only limited contact with the people living in the mountains.

These geographical barriers may help explain why Southeast Asia is one of the few regions in Asia that was never unified under a single government. The geographical barriers encouraged the development of separate, distinctive cultures within Southeast Asia, with diverse cultural practices, such as different religions and languages.

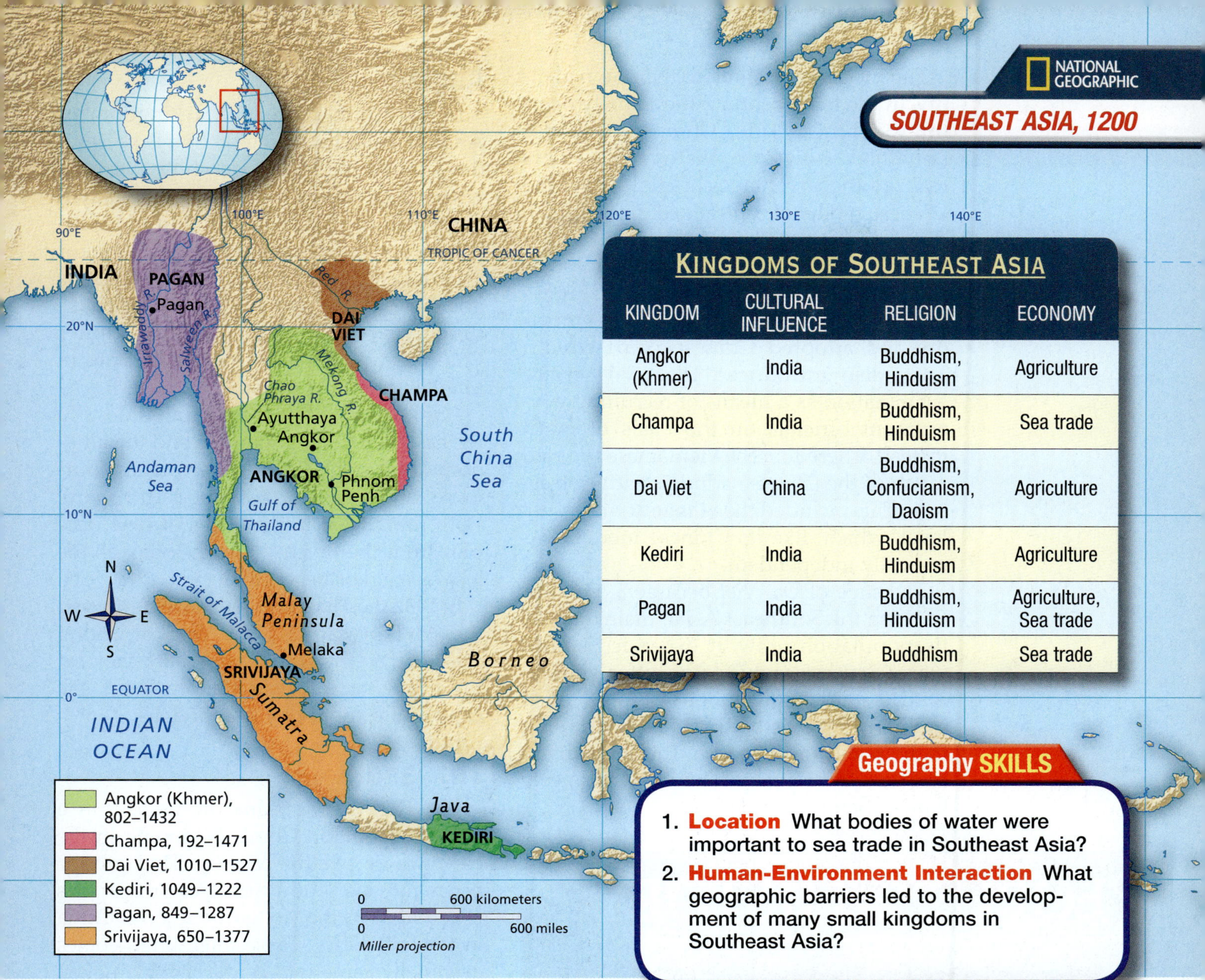


### Kingdoms of Southeast Asia

| Kingdom | Cultural Influence | Religion | Economy |
|---|---|---|---|
| Angkor (Khmer) | India | Buddhism, Hinduism | Agriculture |
| Champa | India | Buddhism, Hinduism | Sea trade |
| Dai Viet | China | Buddhism, Confucianism, Daoism | Agriculture |
| Kediri | India | Buddhism, Hinduism | Agriculture |
| Pagan | India | Buddhism, Hinduism | Agriculture, Sea trade |
| Srivijaya | India | Buddhism | Sea trade |

**Geography SKILLS**

1. **Location** What bodies of water were important to sea trade in Southeast Asia?
2. **Human-Environment Interaction** What geographic barriers led to the development of many small kingdoms in Southeast Asia?

## Vietnam

The Vietnamese were one of the first peoples in Southeast Asia to develop their own state and their own culture. This strong sense of cultural identity caused difficulties for would-be conquerors. China, larger and more powerful than Vietnam, first attempted an invasion in the 200s B.C., but quickly ran into problems:

**PRIMARY SOURCE**

"The Viet people fled into the depths of the mountains and forests, and it was not possible to fight them. The soldiers were kept in garrisons to watch over abandoned territories. This went on for a long time, and the soldiers grew weary. Then the Viet came out and attacked; the Chinese soldiers suffered a great defeat; the dead and wounded were many. After this, the emperor deported convicts to hold the garrisons against the Viet people."

— Keith W. Taylor, *The Birth of Vietnam*

After over a hundred years of warfare, the Chinese finally conquered **Vietnam** in 111 B.C. They tried for centuries to make Vietnam part of China; however, Chinese officials were often frustrated by the Vietnamese. As one official said,

**PRIMARY SOURCE**

"The people are like birds and beasts; they wear their hair tied up and go barefoot, while for clothing they simply cut a hole in a piece of cloth for their head or they fasten their garments on the left side. It is useless to try to change them."

— Chinese official, *The Birth of Vietnam*

The Vietnamese clung to their own identity. In the tenth century, they finally overthrew Chinese rule. Chinese influence remained, however. Vietnamese rulers realized the advantages of taking over the Chinese model of centralized government. The new Vietnamese state, which called itself Dai Viet—Great Viet—adopted state Confucianism. Following the Chinese model, the rulers called themselves emperors and adopted Chinese court rituals. They also introduced the civil service examination as a means of recruiting government officials on the basis of merit instead of heredity. The Vietnamese adopted much of the Chinese administrative structure. This included the village at the lowest level, which, like its Chinese model, was basically independent.

The state of Dai Viet became a dynamic force on the Southeast Asian mainland. As its population grew, it expanded southward. Several centuries of bitter warfare with its southern neighbor, Champa, ended in Vietnamese victory by 1500. Continuing their march to the south, the Vietnamese reached the Gulf of Thailand (formerly Gulf of Siam) by 1600.

## PEOPLE *in* HISTORY

**Jayavarman II**
c. 770–850 Founder of Khmer Empire

Although he is believed to have been a Khmer descendent, Jayavarman spent much of his early life in Java. Around 800, he was sent to rule the Khmer people as a puppet of the Javanese. In 802 he declared independence from Java and had himself crowned *devaraja,* or god-king, of the Khmer and made the *devaraja* cult the official state religion. The *devaraja* cult combined Hindu and local religious traditions and revered the king as divine. The cult produced a line of *devarajas* who ruled the Khmer for hundreds of years. **Why might Jayavarman have been accepted by the Khmer people as their god-king?**

## Angkor

In the ninth century, the kingdom of **Angkor** arose in the region that is present-day Cambodia. The kingdom was formed when a powerful figure named **Jayavarman** united the Khmer (kuh•MEHR) people and established a capital at Angkor Thom. In 802 Jayavarman was crowned as god-king of his people. For several hundred years, Angkor—or the Khmer Empire—was the most powerful state in mainland Southeast Asia.

Angkor faced enemies on all sides. To the east were the Vietnamese and the kingdom of Champa. To the west was the Burmese kingdom of **Pagan** (modern Bagan). With the arrival in the 1300s of new peoples from the north—known today as the **Thai**—Angkor began to decline.

In 1432 the Thai from the north destroyed the Angkor capital. The Angkor ruling class fled to the southeast, where they set up a new capital near Phnom Penh, the capital of present-day Cambodia.

## Thailand

The Thai first appeared in the 500s as a frontier people in China. Beginning in the eleventh or twelfth century, Thai groups began moving southward. This process was encouraged by the Mongol invasion of China in the mid-1200s. These migrating peoples eventually came into conflict with Angkor, destroying the Angkor capital in 1432.

The Thai set up their own capital at Ayutthaya (AH•yoo•TY•uh) on the Chao Phraya River, where they remained as a major force in the region for the next 400 years. Although many converted to Buddhism, the Thai were also influenced by Hindu religion and Indian culture in their political practices, dance, and literature. This unique blend eventually became the modern-day culture of **Thailand.**

## Burma

The Thai were also threatened from the west by the Burmese peoples, who had formed their society along the Salween and Irrawaddy Rivers. The Burmese had migrated from Tibet beginning in the 600s, probably to escape Chinese armies.

**INFOGRAPHICS**

## Southeastern Asian Civilizations, 800–1500

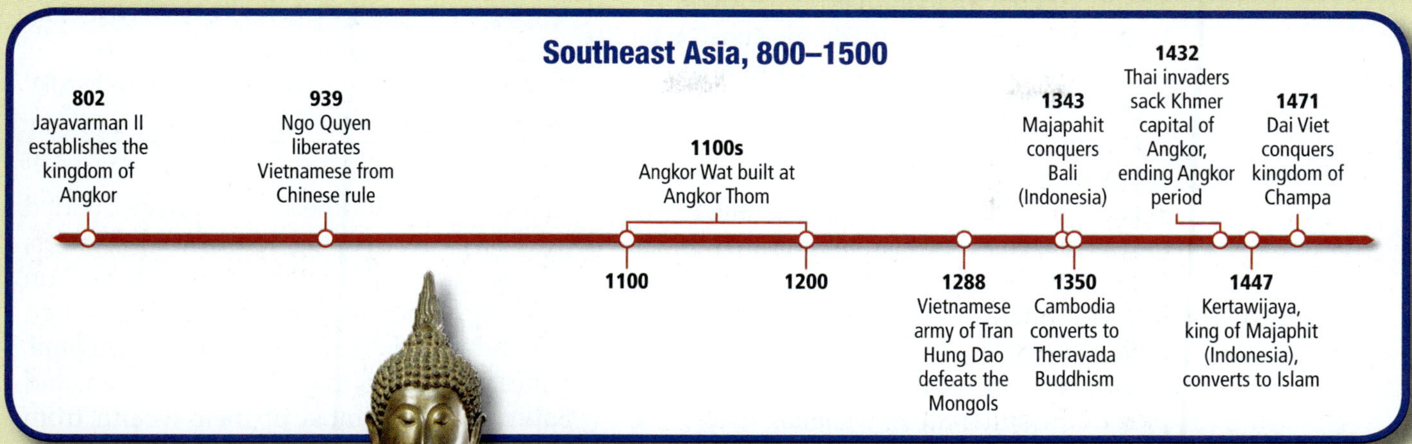

**Bronze Buddha from fifteenth-century Thailand**

**Analyzing TIME LINES**

1. **Analyzing** Based on the dates on the time-line, how long did the kingdom of Angkor last?
2. **Locating** On which two dates did the Vietnamese defeat foreign invaders?

The Burmese were pastoral peoples, but they adopted farming soon after their arrival in Southeast Asia. In the eleventh century, they founded the first great Burmese state, the kingdom of Pagan. Like the Thai, they converted to Buddhism and adopted Indian political institutions and culture.

During the next two hundred years, Pagan became a major force in the western part of Southeast Asia. The capital city was at the center of a network of highways, which allowed it to exert power over large distances. It also played an active role in sea trade throughout the region. Attacks by the Mongols in the late 1200s, however, weakened Pagan, causing it to decline.

## The Malay World

In the Malay Peninsula and the Indonesian archipelago, a different pattern emerged. For centuries, this area had been tied to the trade that passed from East Asia into the Indian Ocean. The area had never been united under a single state, however. The vast majority of the people of the region were of Malay background, but the peoples were divided into numerous separate communities.

Two organized states eventually emerged in the region. In the eighth century, the state of Srivijaya (SREE•wih•JAW•yuh) came to dominate the trade route passing through the **Strait of Malacca**.

At the same time, the kingdom of Sailendra emerged in eastern Java. Both states were influenced by Indian culture. Whereas Srivijaya depended on trade, the wealth of Sailendra was based primarily on farming.

In the late 1200s, the new kingdom of Majapahit (MAH•jah•PAH•hiht) was founded. It became the greatest empire the region had yet seen. In the mid-fourteenth century, Majapahit incorporated most of the archipelago and perhaps even parts of the mainland under a single rule. Majapahit did not have long to enjoy its status, however. By the 1400s, a new state was beginning to emerge in the region.

After the Muslim conquest of northern India, Muslim merchants—either Arabs or Indian converts—settled in port cities in the region and began to convert the local population. Around 1400, an Islamic state began to form in **Melaka**, a small town on the western coast of the Malay Peninsula. Traders found it a natural place to replenish their supplies of food and water. Melaka soon became the major trading port in the region and a chief rival to Majapahit. From Melaka, Muslim traders and the Muslim faith moved into the interior of the peninsula. Eventually, almost the entire population of the region was converted to Islam and became part of the sultanate of Melaka.

✓Reading Check **Examining** Why was Southeast Asia never unified under a single government?

## Life in Southeast Asia

**MAIN IDEA** The growth of the states of Southeast Asia depended largely on trade and agriculture.

***HISTORY & YOU*** What is the most impressive building in the United States? Read about the temple of Angkor Wat in Southeast Asia.

The states of Southeast Asia can be divided into two groups: **agricultural societies**, whose economies were largely based on farming, and **trading societies**, which depended primarily on trade for income. States such as Vietnam, Angkor, Pagan, and Sailendra drew most of their wealth from the land. Others, such as Srivijaya and the sultanate of Melaka, supported themselves chiefly through trade.

### HISTORY & ARTS — PRIMARY SOURCE

### Angkor Wat

Angkor Wat was originally a Hindu temple but was taken over by Buddhists during the sixteenth century.

Angkor Wat is a model of the Hindu universe, with a shrine at its hub, enclosed by three courtyards, and topped by five towers.

The walls are decorated with hundreds of statues and bas-reliefs showing scenes from ancient Indian stories.

A 3-mile (5-km) moat surrounds Angkor Wat.

**DOCUMENT-BASED QUESTIONS**

Angkor was the capital of the Khmer Empire. The most famous of the temples in the area, Angkor Wat, was built in the 1100s.

1. **Making Connections** How does Angkor Wat show the influence of Indian culture?
2. **Making Inferences** What protection might the moat have provided Angkor Wat?

Trade through Southeast Asia expanded after the emergence of states in the area and reached even greater heights after the Muslim conquest of northern India. The rise in demand for spices also added to the growing volume of trade. As the wealth of Europe and Southeast Asia increased, demand grew for the products of East Asia.

At the top of the social ladder in most Southeast Asian societies were the hereditary aristocrats. They held both political power and economic wealth. Most aristocrats lived in the major cities. Angkor Thom, for example, was a city with royal palaces and parks, a massive parade ground, reservoirs, and numerous temples.

Beyond the major cities lived the rest of the population, which consisted of farmers, fishers, artisans, and merchants. In most Southeast Asian societies, the majority of people were probably rice farmers who lived at a bare level of subsistence and paid heavy rents or taxes to a landlord or local ruler.

Most of the societies in Southeast Asia gave greater rights to women than did their counterparts in China and India. Women worked side by side with men in the fields and often played an active role in trading activities.

Chinese culture made an impact on Vietnam. In many other areas of Southeast Asia, Indian cultural influence prevailed. The most visible example of this influence was in architecture. Of all the existing structures at Angkor Thom, the temple of Angkor Wat is the most famous and most beautiful. It combines Indian architectural techniques with native inspiration in a structure of impressive grace. Surrounded by walls measuring 1,700 by 1,500 feet (518 by 457 m), Angkor Wat rises like a 200-foot-high (61-m-high) mountain in a series of three great terraces. The construction of Angkor Wat, which took 40 years to complete, required an enormous quantity of stone—as much as it took to build Egypt's Great Pyramid.

Hindu and Buddhist ideas began to move into Southeast Asia in the first millennium A.D. However, the new religions did not entirely replace existing beliefs. In all Southeast Asian societies, as in China and Japan, old beliefs were blended with those of the new faiths. In this process, the king played a central role. The ruler of Angkor, for example, was seen as a living link between the people and the gods.

Buddhism also spread to Southeast Asia. Monks returning from Sri Lanka introduced Theravada Buddhism to Burma in the eleventh century. From Burma, Theravada spread rapidly to other areas of Southeast Asia.

Eventually, Theravada Buddhism became the religion of the masses in much of Southeast Asia. Why did it have such appeal? For one thing, it teaches that people can seek nirvana through their own efforts; they do not need priests or rulers. Moreover, it tolerated local gods and posed no threat to established faith.

✓ **Reading Check** **Identifying** Which countries most influenced the cultural development of Southeast Asia?

## SECTION 5 REVIEW

### Vocabulary

1. **Explain** the significance of: region, Malay Peninsula, archipelago, area, Vietnam, Angkor, Jayavarman, Pagan, Thai, Thailand, Strait of Malacca, Melaka, agricultural society, trading society.

### Main Ideas

2. **Explain** the importance of Islam in the development of Melaka.
3. **Create** a diagram like the one shown below to represent the social hierarchy in most Southeast Asian societies discussed in this section.

**Social Hierarchy**

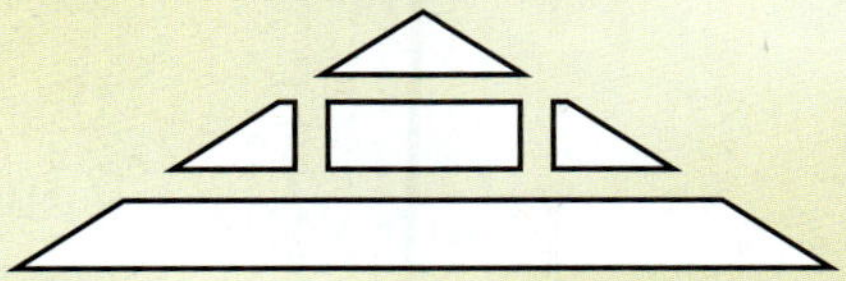

### Critical Thinking

4. **The Big Idea** **Contrasting** How did the development of the Malay Peninsula and the Indonesian archipelago differ from the development of Southeast Asia?
5. **Considering** How would an increase in trade and exporting cause a region to develop more complex forms of political and social organization? Use examples from the text to support your answer.
6. **Analyzing Visuals** Compare the temple on page 288 with Angkor Wat on page 294. What features do they have in common?

### Writing About History

7. **Descriptive Writing** When Vietnam was conquered by China, the people clung to their own identity. Write a paragraph describing the aspects of conquered peoples that conquerors would want to change and why.

**History ONLINE**

For help with the concepts in this section of *Glencoe World History*, go to glencoe.com and click Study Central™.

# CHAPTER 8 Visual Summary

You can study anywhere, anytime by downloading quizzes and flash cards to your PDA from glencoe.com.

## CHINA'S DYNASTIES

- The Tang dynasty, stable for 300 years, renewed trade in silk and porcelain over the Silk Road.
- The Song dynasty took over in the 900s and vastly increased crop yields and trade.
- In the 800s, the scholar-gentry class emerged, an influential group down to 1911, while a revived, practical Confucianism was dominant in religion.
- Northern invaders, always a threat, finally triumphed with the Mongol Invasion in 1270.
- Chinese poetry and ceramics were inspired by nature and Confucian philosophy.

THE SONG DYNASTY

**Silk played an important role in China's economy and society.**

THE KAMAKURA PERIOD

**This Japanese battle scene reflects the frequent civil chaos of the 1200s.**

## JAPAN AND KOREA

- The islands of Japan are isolated and mountainous.
- The heads of Japanese noble families, daimyos, competed for power with fighting samurai, which led to frequent civil wars.
- The religion of Shinto contributed to emperor worship, while Buddhism's spirituality appealed to other Japanese.
- Korea, dominated by nearby China, and borrowing many cultural elements, finally gained its independence in the 900s.

BUDDHISM IN SOUTHEAST ASIA

**Wat Arun, in Bangkok, is one of the thousands of Buddhist temples in Thailand.**

## SOUTH AND SOUTHEAST ASIA

- India fragmented into many states in the medieval period; later rulers from the north introduced Islam, but Hinduism remained the religion of most Indians.
- In Southeast Asia, new states were influenced by the Chinese and Indian examples in both government and religion.
- The trade in spices was profitable for several southeastern Asian states.

# CHAPTER 8 Assessment

## Reviewing Vocabulary

*Directions: Choose the word or words that best complete the sentence.*

**1.** ________ is a type of translucent ceramic made from very fine clay.

**A** Dowry
**B** Archipelago
**C** Porcelain
**D** Daimyo

**2.** The heirs of Genghis Khan divided up his empire into ________.

**A** khanates
**B** samurais
**C** dowries
**D** trading societies

**3.** ________ was the name for the strict code of behavior followed by the warrior class of early Japan.

**A** Bushido
**B** Shogunate
**C** Daimyo
**D** Mahayana

**4.** In early Chinese society, ________ produced most of the candidates for civil service.

**A** artisans
**B** farmers
**C** scholar-gentry
**D** traders

**5.** From 1192 to 1333, the Japanese military leader with greater power than the emperor was called the ________.

**A** daimyo
**B** shogun
**C** rajput
**D** samurai

## Reviewing Main Ideas

*Directions: Choose the best answers to the following questions.*

### Section 1 *(pp. 264–269)*

**6.** What emperor used forced labor to build the Grand Canal?

**A** Wu Zhao
**B** Sui Yangdi
**C** Tang Xuanzang
**D** Kublai Khan

**7.** When a girl in early China married, how would her life change?

**A** She became part of her husband's family.
**B** She remained with her parents.
**C** She was able to participate in business and trade.
**D** She was able to take the civil service examination.

### Section 2 *(pp. 270–275)*

**8.** Which of the following best describes the Mongol Empire?

**A** Militarily powerful, but poor
**B** The largest land empire in history
**C** The last government to control China
**D** An Islamic state

**9.** Which of these was most often the philosophical basis of Chinese government?

**A** Buddhism
**B** Daoism
**C** Islam
**D** Confucianism

**TEST-TAKING TIP**

If you do not immediately know the right answer to a question, look at each answer choice carefully. Try to recall the context in which these events were discussed in class. Remembering this context may help you eliminate incorrect answer choices.

**Need Extra Help?**

| If You Missed Questions . . . | 1 | 2 | 3 | 4 | 5 | 6 | 7 | 8 | 9 |
|---|---|---|---|---|---|---|---|---|---|
| Go to Page . . . | 275 | 270 | 280 | 269 | 281 | 264 | 269 | 270 | 273 |

GO ON

# CHAPTER 8 Assessment

**Section 3** *(pp. 278–283)*

**10.** Who was the author of *The Tale of Genji,* one of the finest achievements of world literature?

**A** Yi Sŏng-gye
**B** Minamoto Yoritomo
**C** Shōtoku Taishi
**D** Murasaki Shikibu

**11.** After a long struggle, which kingdom gained control over the Korea Peninsula?

**A** Silla
**B** Paekche
**C** Koguryo
**D** Kamakura

**Section 4** *(pp. 284–289)*

**12.** Which of these introduced the idea that the Buddha was not just a wise man, but a divine figure?

**A** Theravada Buddhism
**B** Mahayana Buddhism
**C** Zen Buddhism
**D** Daoism

**13.** Who were the Hindu warriors who led the resistance against the advances of Maḥmūd and his successors into northern India?

**A** Moguls
**B** Samurai
**C** Uighurs
**D** Rajputs

**Section 5** *(pp. 290–295)*

**14.** Who founded the kingdom of Angkor?

**A** Jayavarman
**B** Dai Viet
**C** Timur Lenk
**D** Daṇḍin

## Critical Thinking

*Directions: Choose the best answers to the following questions.*

*Use the following quote about the Japanese Samurai to answer question 15.*

> *"I spurred my horse on, careless of death in the face of the foe.*
> *I braved the dangers of wind and wave, not reckoning that my body*
> *might sink to the bottom of the sea, and be devoured by monsters of the deep."*

**15.** How does this quote reflect the code of the samurai?

**A** It describes the riding ability of the samurai.
**B** It shows the importance placed on honor and loyalty, above all other concerns.
**C** It portrays the most common initiation ritual of the samurai.
**D** It displays the samurai's hatred of the sea.

**16.** Which of the following religions did not play a major role in the history of Southeast Asia?

**A** Islam
**B** Theravada Buddhism
**C** Mahayana Buddhism
**D** Hinduism

**17.** In early Japan, why was prose fiction written primarily by women?

**A** All men were samurai and therefore had little time for artistic pursuits.
**B** Women were better educated than men.
**C** Men believed prose fiction was beneath them.
**D** The Shinto religion forbade the writing of fiction by men.

**18.** What was a major cause of the expansion of trade throughout Southeast Asia?

**A** The construction of stronger vessels
**B** The blessings of important religious figures
**C** The growing demand for spices
**D** The construction of beautiful temples

**Need Extra Help?**

| If You Missed Questions . . . | 10 | 11 | 12 | 13 | 14 | 15 | 16 | 17 | 18 |
|---|---|---|---|---|---|---|---|---|---|
| Go to Page . . . | 282 | 283 | 284 | 286 | 292 | 298 | 295 | 282 | 294 |

GO ON

**19.** Which of the following images would you most likely see in an early Chinese painting?

**A** A small figure in the midst of a nature scene

**B** An aristocrat at home with his family

**C** Warriors in battle

**D** People worshiping at a temple

*Analyze the map and answer the question that follows. Base your answer on the map.*

**Population Growth in China, 750–1250**

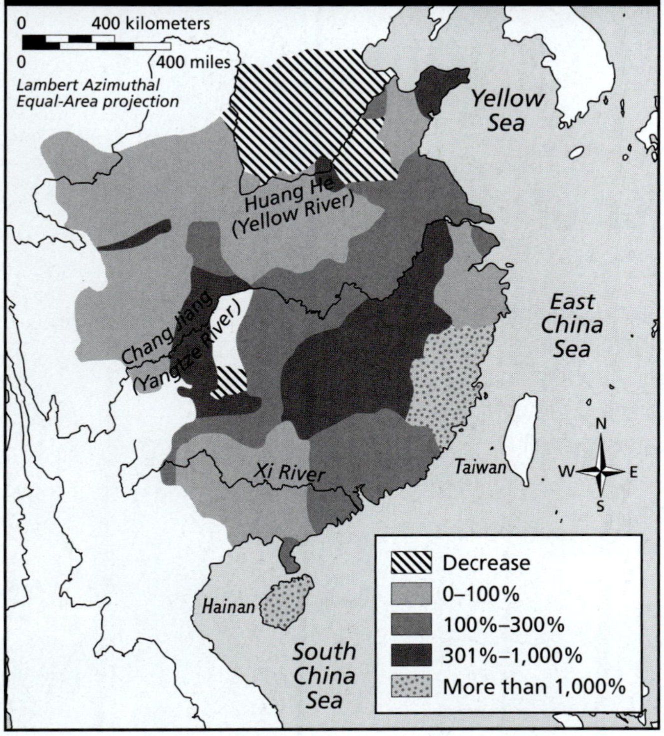


**20.** Which statement best describes changes in population growth in China from A.D. 750 to A.D. 1250?

**A** A large increase in the far west and decrease in Hainan

**B** An increase everywhere except the south

**C** A decline north of the Huang He and increase in the southeast

**D** A decline on the east coast and increase north of the Chang Jiang

## Document-Based Questions

*Directions: Analyze the document and answer the short-answer questions that follow the document. Base your answers on the document and on your knowledge of world history.*

Chang Tsai, a neo-Confucian philosopher, wrote the following in the eleventh century:

> *"Heaven is my father and Earth is my mother, and even such a small being as I finds a central abode in their midst. Therefore that which fills the universe I regard as my body and that which directs the universe I consider as my nature. All people are my brothers and sisters, and all things are my companions."*
>
> —Chang Tsai

**21.** Can you detect any echoes of Daoism in this excerpt? What are they?

**22.** How do the ideas in this quotation conflict with the basic ideas of Buddhism?

## Extended Response

**23.** Imagine that you are a Korean person who is traveling through the states of Southeast Asia during the fifteenth century. Which states will seem most familiar to you? Which will seem most foreign? Why?

**24.** How did the civil service examinations aid in the development of a strong central government in China?

**25.** Describe the development of trade from the Tang through the Yuan dynasties.

**History ONLINE**

For additional test practice, use Self-Check Quizzes—Chapter 8 at glencoe.com.

**Need Extra Help?**

| If You Missed Questions . . . | 19 | 20 | 21 | 22 | 23 | 24 | 25 |
|---|---|---|---|---|---|---|---|
| Go to Page . . . | 275 | 299 | 299 | 299 | 290 | 267 | 265–272 |

STOP

CHAPTER 9

# Emerging Europe and the Byzantine Empire 400–1300

**Section 1** Transforming the Roman World

**Section 2** Feudalism

**Section 3** The Growth of European Kingdoms

**Section 4** Byzantine Empire and Crusades

Chapter Audio

*MAKING CONNECTIONS*

## How important is the location of a city?

From ancient times, Carcassonne was important because of its location near the Pyrenees Mountains. The Romans built fortifications on the hilltop, and each ruler added to them until the 1600s. A fortified city like Carcassonne, with a double ring of defensive walls and 53 towers, could hold out for months against an army. In this chapter you will learn about the beginning of the Middle Ages.

- What was the advantage of locating a city on a hilltop?
- Why might castles and fortified towns become impractical?

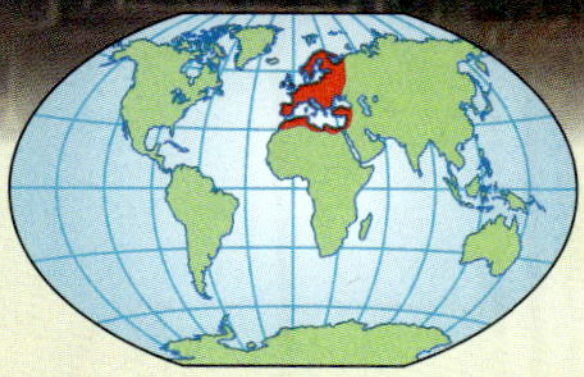

EUROPE ▶

**800** Charlemagne crowned Roman emperor

**1066** William of Normandy invades England

400 | 700 | 1000

THE WORLD ▶

**762** Abbasids build capital at Baghdad

**960** Song dynasty comes to power in China

**1096**
Crusades begin

**1215**
King John signs Magna Carta

1100 — 1300

**1187**
Saladin's army invades Jerusalem

**c. 1300**
Yorubas produce metal and terra-cotta sculptures

**FOLDABLES™ Study Organizer**

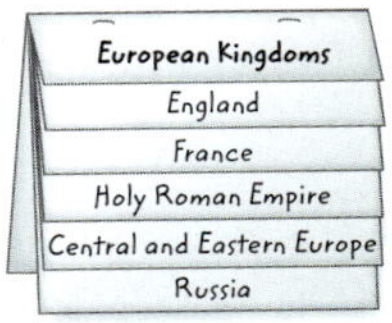


**Identifying** Create a Layered-Look Book to identify important people, events, and government institutions of England, France, the Holy Roman Empire, Central and Eastern Europe, and Russia.

History ONLINE Visit glencoe.com and enter QuickPass™ code GWHEA7447c9 for Chapter 9 resources.

SECTION 1

Section Audio

Spotlight Video

# Transforming the Roman World

## GUIDE TO READING

### The BIG Idea

**Ideas, Beliefs, and Values** The new European civilization combined Germanic, Roman, and Christian elements.

### Content Vocabulary

- wergild *(p. 304)*
- ordeal *(p. 304)*
- bishopric *(p. 304)*
- pope *(p. 304)*
- monk *(p. 305)*
- monasticism *(p. 305)*
- missionary *(p. 306)*
- nun *(p. 306)*
- abbess *(p. 306)*

### Academic Vocabulary

- excluded *(p. 302)*
- ensure *(p. 307)*

### People and Places

- Clovis *(p. 302)*
- Gregory I *(p. 304)*
- Benedict of Nursia *(p. 305)*
- Pépin *(p. 306)*
- Charlemagne *(p. 306)*
- Carolingian Empire *(p. 307)*

### Reading Strategy

**Summarizing Information** Create a diagram like the one below to list the reasons why monasticism was an important factor in the development of European civilization.

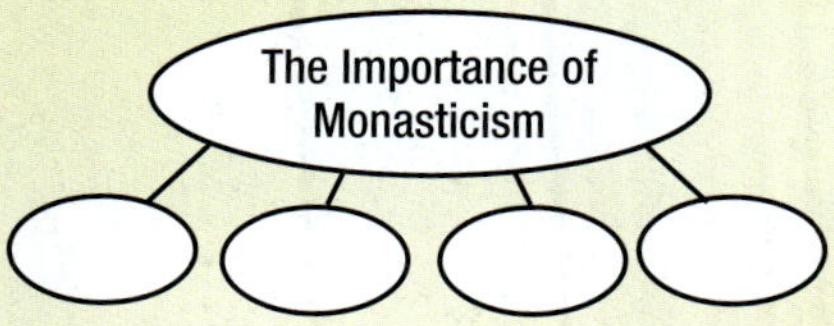


*Germanic tribes became the dominant political force in Europe during the Early Middle Ages, while Christianity became the dominant religion. Rome became the center of the Catholic Church's power. Ultimately a new empire emerged that was linked to the idea of a lasting Roman Empire.*

## The New Germanic Kingdoms

***MAIN IDEA*** The Frankish kingdom was the strongest of the early German states and developed new laws based on the importance of family in Germanic society.

***HISTORY & YOU*** How might laws be different if they were based on settling personal feuds rather than on protecting society as a whole? Read about Germanic laws and wergild.

The Germanic peoples had begun to move into the lands of the Roman Empire by the third century. The Visigoths occupied Spain and Italy until the Ostrogoths, another Germanic tribe, took control of Italy in the fifth century. By 500, the Western Roman Empire had been replaced by a number of states ruled by German kings. The merging of Romans and Germans took different forms in the various Germanic kingdoms.

Both the kingdom of the Ostrogoths in Italy and the kingdom of the Visigoths in Spain retained the Roman structure of government. However, a group of Germanic warriors came to dominate the considerably larger native populations and eventually **excluded** Romans from holding power.

Roman influence was even weaker in Britain. When the Roman armies abandoned Britain at the beginning of the fifth century, the Angles and Saxons, Germanic tribes from Denmark and northern Germany, moved in and settled there. Eventually, these peoples became the Anglo-Saxons.

### The Kingdom of the Franks

Only one of the German states on the European continent proved long lasting—the kingdom of the Franks. The Frankish kingdom was established by **Clovis**, a strong military leader who around 500 became the first Germanic ruler to convert to Christianity. At first, Clovis had refused the pleas of his Christian wife to adopt Christianity as his religion. According to Gregory of Tours, a sixth-century historian, Clovis had remarked to his wife, "Your God can do nothing."

During a battle with another Germanic tribe, however, Clovis's army faced certain destruction. Clovis was reported to have cried

**Geography SKILLS**

New Germanic kingdoms developed in areas that had once belonged to the Western Roman Empire.

1. **Regions** Which Germanic kingdoms were the largest in 500? Which Germanic group west of the Pyrenees survives today?
2. **Movement** What geographic factors kept Constantinople from being conquered?

out, "Jesus Christ, if you shall grant me victory over these enemies, I will believe in you and be baptized." After he uttered these words, the enemy began to flee, and Clovis soon became a Christian.

Clovis found that his conversion to Christianity won him the support of the Roman Catholic Church, as the Christian church in Rome was now known. Not surprisingly, the Catholic Church was eager to gain the friendship of a major ruler in the Germanic states.

By 510, Clovis had established a powerful new Frankish kingdom that stretched from the Pyrenees in the southwest to German lands in the east—modern-day France and western Germany. He defeated the many Germanic tribes surrounding him and unified the Franks as a people. After Clovis's death his sons followed Frankish custom and divided his newly created kingdom among themselves. The once-united Frankish kingdom came to be divided into three major areas.

## Germanic Society

Over time, Germans and Romans intermarried and began to create a new society. As they did, some of the social customs of the Germanic people came to play an important role.

The crucial social bond among the Germanic peoples was the family, especially the extended family of husbands, wives, children, brothers, sisters, cousins, and grandparents. This extended family worked the land together and passed it down to future generations. The family also provided protection, which was much needed in the violent atmosphere of the time.

The German concept of family affected the way Germanic law treated the problem of crime and punishment. In the Roman system, as in our own, a crime such as murder was considered an offense against society or the state. Thus, a court would hear evidence and arrive at a decision. Germanic law, on the other hand, was personal. An injury by one person against another could mean a blood feud, and the feud could lead to savage acts of revenge.

To avoid bloodshed, a new system developed, based on a fine called **wergild** (WUHR•gihld). Wergild was the amount paid by a wrongdoer to the family of the person he or she had injured or killed. Wergild, which means "money for a man," was the value of a person in money. The value varied according to social status. An offense against a member of the nobility, for example, cost considerably more than an offense against an ordinary person or a slave. Germanic laws were now established by custom, not at the whim of a king or codified like Roman law.

One means of determining guilt in Germanic law was the ordeal. The **ordeal** was based on the idea of divine intervention. All ordeals involved a physical trial of some sort, such as holding a red-hot iron. It was believed that divine forces would not allow an innocent person to be harmed. If the accused person was unharmed after a physical trial, or ordeal, he or she was presumed innocent.

✓Reading Check **Analyzing** What was the significance of Clovis's conversion to Christianity?

# The Role of the Church

MAIN IDEA The Bishop of Rome became the leader of the Christian Church.

HISTORY & YOU How does someone take over the leadership of an organization? Read how the Bishop of Rome claimed to be the leader of the Christian Church.

By the end of the fourth century, Christianity had become the supreme religion of the Roman Empire. As the official Roman state fell apart, the Church played an increasingly important role in the growth of the new European civilization.

## Organization of the Church

By the fourth century, the Christian Church had developed a system of organization. Priests led local Christian communities called parishes. These priests also met the social needs of their parishes, as the church often was the center of village social life. A group of parishes was headed by a bishop, whose area of authority was called a **bishopric**, or diocese. An archbishop joined together the bishoprics.

Over time the Bishop of Rome began to claim that he was the leader of what had become the Roman Catholic Church. Catholics believed that Jesus gave the keys to the kingdom of Heaven to Peter, who was considered the chief apostle and the first bishop of Rome. Later bishops of Rome were viewed as Peter's successors. They came to be known as **popes** (from the Latin word *papa,* "father") of the Catholic Church.

Western Christians came to accept the bishop of Rome—the pope—as head of the Church, but they did not agree on how much power he should have. In the sixth century, a strong pope, **Gregory I**, known as Gregory the Great, strengthened the power of the papacy (office of the pope) and the Church.

Gregory I, pope from 590 to 604, was also leader of the city of Rome and its surrounding territories (later called the Papal States), thus giving the papacy a source of political power. Gregory I increased his spiritual authority over the Church in the West. He was especially active in converting non-Christian peoples of Germanic

Europe to Christianity. He did this through the monastic movement.

## Monks and Monasteries

A **monk** is a man who separates himself from ordinary society to dedicate himself to God. The practice of living the life of a monk is known as **monasticism**. At first, Christian monasticism was based on the hermit who led an isolated spiritual life. In the sixth century, **Benedict of Nursia** wrote a set of rules to guide a community of monks he founded. This community became the model for monasticism in the Catholic Church, and the Benedictine rule came to be used by other monastic groups.

Benedict's rule divided each day into a series of activities, with primary emphasis on prayer and manual labor. Physical work was required of all monks for several hours a day, because idleness was "the enemy of the soul." At the very heart of community practice was prayer, the proper "Work of God." Although prayer included private meditation and reading, all monks gathered together seven times during the day for common prayer and the chanting of Psalms—sacred songs. A Benedictine life was a communal one. Monks ate, worked, slept, and worshiped together.

Each Benedictine monastery was led by an abbot or "father," whom the monks were expected to obey. The abbot had complete authority over the monks. Each monastery owned lands that enabled it to be self-sustaining and isolated from the world. In the monastery, monks were to fulfill their vow of poverty.

Monks became the new Christian heroes, an important force in the new European civilization. The monastic community set the highest ideal of Christian life and provided a moral example to all. Monks were the social workers of their communities, providing schools for the young, hospitality for travelers, and hospitals for the sick. They also taught peasants carpentry and weaving and made agricultural improvements that they passed on to others.

### INFOGRAPHICS

### Monastic Centers of Learning

Monks were men who devoted their lives to the Church and took vows of poverty, chastity, and obedience. Although Benedict of Nursia envisioned monasteries as a place to withdraw from the world, many monasteries became central to medieval society. Monasteries became centers of learning and produced most medieval scholars prior to the founding of European universities. Monasteries educated scribes, political advisors, and church officials.

Many monasteries also contained a scriptorium, where monks studied ancient Greek and Arabic texts on philosophy, medicine, and science. Monks preserved these texts, along with biblical works, by copying them by hand into Latin. Many of the works contained not only copied text, but also beautiful illustrations either on their own pages or alongside the text. Perhaps the most famous works to come out of scriptoriums were illuminated manuscripts, books of the Bible with illustrations or decorated letters.

**Monk illustrating a manuscript, *Eadwine Psalter*, c. 1150, which contained psalms in Latin, Old English, and Anglo-Norman**

**CRITICAL THINKING SKILLS**

1. **Making Inferences** How might the work done in a scriptorium preserve ancient texts?
2. **Drawing Conclusions** Why would it be difficult for the people in a monastery to remain closed off from the rest of the medieval world?

Monasteries became centers of learning. Monks also spread Christianity and the Latin alphabet to all of Europe. English and Irish monks were **missionaries**—people sent out to carry a religious message—who undertook the conversion of non-Christian peoples, especially in German lands. By 1050 most western Europeans had become Catholics.

Although the first monks were men, women, called **nuns**, also began to withdraw from the world to dedicate themselves to God. These women played an important role in the monastic movement. Nuns lived in convents headed by **abbesses**. Many of the abbesses belonged to royal houses, especially in Anglo-Saxon England. In the kingdom of Northumbria, for example, Hilda founded the monastery of Whitby in 657. As abbess, she was responsible for giving learning an important role in the life of the monastery and helped educate five future bishops.

✓Reading Check **Describing** How did the Catholic Church affect the new European civilization?

## The Carolingian Empire

**MAIN IDEA** Charlemagne expanded the Frankish kingdom and created the Carolingian Empire.

**HISTORY & YOU** Who provides your education? Read how Charlemagne promoted learning.

During the 600s and 700s, the Frankish kings gradually lost their power to the mayors of the palace, chief officers of the king's household. One of them, **Pépin**, finally took the logical step of assuming the kingship for himself and his family. Pépin was the son of Charles Martel, the leader who defeated the Muslims at the Battle of Tours in 732. Upon Pépin's death in 768, his son became the new Frankish king. This powerful ruler is known to history as Charles the Great, or **Charlemagne**. He was a determined and decisive man who was highly intelligent and curious. Charlemagne was a fierce warrior, a strong statesman, and a pious Christian. Although possibly unable to write, he was a wise patron—supporter—of learning.

**INFOGRAPHICS**

### The Carolingian Empire

**Charlemagne, King of the Franks**

| CHARLES THE MAN | CHARLES THE ADMINISTRATOR | CHARLES THE CONQUEROR | CHARLES THE PATRON OF LEARNING |
|---|---|---|---|
| Was athletic, well-spoken, and charismatic | Delegated authority to the nobles | Was an aggressive warrior | Revived classical studies |
| Married four times | Retained local laws of conquered areas | Strengthened the Frankish military | Preserved Latin culture |
| Understood Greek, spoke Latin, but possibly could not write | Divided kingdom into districts | Expanded and consolidated the Frankish kingdom | Established monastic and palace schools |
| Left an empire to his sole surviving son | Used *missi dominici* ("messengers of the lord king") to inspect and report on provinces | | |

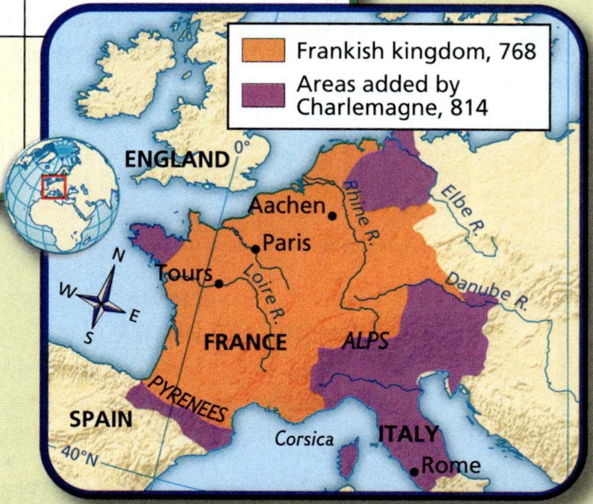


**CRITICAL THINKING SKILLS**

1. **Evaluating** Which of Charlemagne's actions helped strengthen his empire?
2. **Drawing Conclusions** Which of Charlemagne's actions continue to affect civilization today?

During his long rule from 768 to 814, Charlemagne greatly expanded the Frankish kingdom and created what came to be known as the **Carolingian** (KAR•uh•LIN•jee•uhn) **Empire**. At its height, this empire covered much of western and central Europe. Not until Napoleon Bonaparte's time in the nineteenth century would an empire its size be seen again in Europe.

The administration of the empire depended both on Charlemagne's household staff and on counts (German nobles) who acted as the king's chief local representatives. In order to limit the counts' powers, Charlemagne set up the *missi dominici* (messengers of the lord king)—two men sent out to local districts to **ensure** that the counts carried out the king's wishes.

## Charlemagne as Roman Emperor

As Charlemagne's power grew, so too did his prestige as the most powerful Christian ruler. One monk even described Charlemagne's empire as the "kingdom of Europe." In 800, Charlemagne acquired a new title—emperor of the Romans.

Charlemagne's coronation as Roman emperor showed the strength of the idea of an enduring Roman Empire. After all, his coronation took place 300 years after the collapse of the Western Roman Empire.

The coronation also symbolized the joining of Roman, Christian, and Germanic elements. A Germanic king had been crowned emperor of the Romans by the pope, the spiritual leader of Western Christendom. A new civilization had emerged.

## Carolingian Renaissance

Charlemagne had a strong desire to promote learning in his kingdom. This desire stemmed from his own intellectual curiosity and from the need to educate Catholic clergy and government officials. His efforts led to an intellectual revival sometimes called the Carolingian Renaissance, or rebirth. This revival involved renewed interest in Latin culture and classical works—the works of the Greeks and Romans.

The monasteries, many of which had been founded by Irish and English missionaries, played a central role in this cultural renewal. By the 800s, the work asked of Benedictine monks included copying manuscripts. Monasteries established scriptoria, or writing rooms, where monks copied not only the works of early Christianity, such as the Bible, but also the works of classical Latin authors. Their work was a crucial factor in the preservation of the ancient legacy. Most of the ancient Roman works we have today exist because they were copied by Carolingian monks.

✓Reading Check **Explaining** What was the importance of the *missi dominici?*

## SECTION 1 REVIEW

### Vocabulary

1. **Explain** the significance of: excluded, Clovis, wergild, ordeal, bishopric, pope, Gregory I, monk, monasticism, Benedict of Nursia, missionary, nun, abbess, Pépin, Charlemagne, Carolingian Empire, ensure.

### Main Ideas

2. **Explain** how the *missi dominici* helped Charlemagne establish a strong empire.
3. **Summarize** the crucial social bond among the Germanic peoples, along with one area of its application.
4. **List** contributions monasteries made to medieval society.

### Critical Thinking

5. **The BIG Idea** **Describing** How did the Roman Empire, Germanic tribes, and the Church impact the foundation of early medieval society?

| | Roman Empire | Germanic Tribes | Catholic Church |
|---|---|---|---|
| Ideas | | | |
| Beliefs | | | |
| Values | | | |

6. **Summarizing Information** Identify the rulers discussed in the chapter and explain how they were significant in both religious and political realms.
7. **Analyzing Visuals** Analyze the chart on page 306. Which of Charlemagne's accomplishments is the most significant? Why?

### Writing About History

8. **Expository Writing** Write an essay describing how Christianity supported stability and political structure in medieval Europe. Compare your conclusions with the political role of religion in another area of the world.

**History ONLINE**

For help with the concepts in this section of *Glencoe World History,* go to glencoe.com and click Study Central™.

SECTION 2

Section Audio | Spotlight Video

# Feudalism

## GUIDE TO READING

### The BIG Idea

**Order and Security** The collapse of central authority in Europe led to a new political order known as feudalism.

### Content Vocabulary

- feudalism *(p. 310)*
- vassal *(p. 310)*
- knight *(p. 310)*
- fief *(p. 310)*
- feudal contract *(p. 311)*
- tournament *(p. 312)*
- chivalry *(p. 313)*

### Academic Vocabulary

- enabled *(p. 309)*
- contract *(p. 311)*

### People and Places

- Magyars *(p. 308)*
- Hungary *(p. 308)*
- Vikings *(p. 308)*
- Normandy *(p. 309)*
- Eleanor of Aquitaine *(p. 313)*

### Reading Strategy

**Identifying Information** Use a diagram like the one below to show the system of loyalties created under feudalism.

| Rulers | Religious Realm | Political Realm |
|---|---|---|
| | | |
| | | |

*The Carolingian Empire was weakened from within by division after Charlemagne's death and from outside by enemy attacks. Local nobles became more important as people turned to them for the protection that the empire could no longer provide. The result was feudalism, a new political and social order in Europe.*

## The End of the Carolingian Empire

**MAIN IDEA** Vikings, Magyars, and Muslims invaded Europe during the ninth and tenth centuries.

**HISTORY & YOU** Why might the death of a strong leader make a country vulnerable to attack? Read how the death of Charlemagne left his kingdom vulnerable.

Charlemagne held his empire together with his personal power and prestige as a leader and the strong administrative system he established. His death created a vacuum of leadership that left the empire vulnerable. The Frankish tradition of dividing an estate among the surviving heirs also weakened the empire. As the Germanic tribes had moved into the Roman Empire and helped create a new European civilization, new invaders entered Europe and influenced its culture.

### Invaders

The Carolingian Empire began to fall apart soon after Charlemagne's death in 814. Less than 30 years later, it was divided among his grandsons into three major sections: the west Frankish lands, the eastern Frankish lands, and the Middle Kingdom. Local nobles gained power while the Carolingian rulers fought each other. Invasions in different parts of the old Carolingian world added to the process of disintegration.

In the ninth and tenth centuries, western Europe was beset by a wave of invasions. The Muslims attacked the southern coasts of Europe and sent raiding parties into southern France. The **Magyars**, a people from western Asia, moved into central Europe at the end of the ninth century, settled on the plains of **Hungary**, and invaded western Europe.

The most far-reaching attacks of the time, however, came from the Norsemen or Northmen of Scandinavia, also called the **Vikings**. The Vikings were a Germanic people. Their great love of adventure and their search for spoils of war and new avenues of trade may have been what led them to invade other areas of Europe.

**Geography SKILLS**

1. **Location** How did invasions by the Angles, Saxons, Magyars, and Vikings influence the development of Europe?
2. **Regions** Describe how the presence of invaders would have disrupted everyday life in Europe.

**Maps In Motion** See StudentWorks™ Plus or glencoe.com.

In the ninth century, Vikings sacked villages and towns, destroyed churches, and easily defeated small local armies. The Vikings were warriors, and they were superb shipbuilders and sailors. Their ships were the best of the period. Long and narrow with beautifully carved, arched prows, the Viking dragon ships carried about 50 men. The construction of the ships **enabled** them to sail up European rivers and attack places far inland. By the mid-ninth century, the Vikings had begun to build various European settlements.

Beginning in 911, the ruler of the west Frankish lands gave one band of Vikings land at the mouth of the Seine River, forming a section of France that came to be known as **Normandy**. The Frankish policy of settling the Vikings and converting them to Christianity was a deliberate one. As a result of their conversion to Christianity, the Vikings were soon made a part of European civilization.

**✓Reading Check** **Evaluating** What factors helped the Vikings invade Europe successfully?

## The Development of Feudalism

**History ONLINE**
**Student Web Activity—**
Visit glencoe.com and complete the activity about medieval Europe.

**MAIN IDEA** A system of lords and vassals spread throughout Europe after the collapse of the Carolingian Empire.

**HISTORY & YOU** What do you think of when you hear the term *knight*? Learn about the social order of feudalism.

Invaders posed a large threat to the safety of people and a disruption in trade throughout Europe. Rulers found it increasingly difficult to defend their subjects and economies as centralized governments such as the Carolingian Empire were torn apart.

Thus, people began to turn to local landed aristocrats, or nobles, to protect them. To survive, it became important to find a powerful lord who could offer protection in return for service. This led to a new political and social order known as **feudalism**.

### Knights and Vassals

At the heart of feudalism was the idea of vassalage. In Germanic society, warriors swore an oath of loyalty to their leaders and fought in battles for them. The leaders, in turn, took care of the warriors' needs. By the eighth century, a man who served a lord in a military capacity was known as a **vassal**.

The Frankish army had originally consisted of foot soldiers dressed in coats of mail (armor made of metal links or plates) and armed with swords. Horsemen had been throwers of spears. In the eighth century, however, larger horses and the stirrup were introduced. Now, horsemen were armored in coats of mail (the larger horses could carry the weight). They wielded long lances that enabled them to act as battering rams (the stirrups kept them on their horses). For almost five hundred years, warfare in Europe was dominated by heavily armored cavalry, or **knights**, as they came to be called. The knights had great social prestige and formed the backbone of the European aristocracy.

It was expensive to have a horse, armor, and weapons. It also took more time and practice to learn to use these instruments skillfully. With the breakdown of royal governments, the more powerful nobles took control of large areas of land. When these lords wanted men to fight for them, they granted each vassal a piece of land that supported the vassal and his family. In the society of the Early Middle Ages, where there was little trade and wealth was based primarily on land, land was the most important gift a lord could give to a vassal.

### The Feudal Contract

In feudal society, having loyalty to one's lord was the chief virtue. The relationship between lord and vassal was made official by a public ceremony. To become a vassal, a man performed an act of homage to his lord:

**PRIMARY SOURCE**

"The man should put his hands together as a sign of humility, and place them between the two hands of his lord as a token that he vows everything to him and promises faith to him; and the lord should receive him and promise to keep faith with him. Then the man should say: 'Sir, I enter your homage and faith and become your man by mouth and hands [that is, by taking the oath and placing his hands between those of the lord], and I swear and promise to keep faith and loyalty to you against all others.'"

—*A Source Book for Medieval History*

By the ninth century, the grant of land made to a vassal had become known as a **fief** (FEEF). Vassals who held fiefs came to hold political authority within them. As the Carolingian world fell apart, the number of separate, powerful lords and vassals increased. Instead of a single government, many different people were responsible for keeping order.

Feudalism became increasingly complicated. The vassals of a king, who were great lords, might also have vassals who would owe them military service in return for a grant of land taken from their estates. Those vassals, in turn, might likewise have vassals. At that level, the vassals would be simple knights with barely enough land to provide income for their equipment.

The lord-vassal relationship bound together greater and lesser landowners. It was an honorable relationship between free men and implied no sense of servitude. Feudalism came to be characterized by a set of unwritten rules—known as the **feudal contract**—that determined the relationship between a lord and his vassal. The major obligation of a vassal to his lord was to perform military service, usually about 40 days a year.

When summoned, a vassal had to appear at his lord's court to give advice. Vassals were responsible for making payments to the lord on certain occasions, for example, the knighting of the lord's eldest son or marriage of his eldest daughter.

Under the feudal **contract**, the lord also had responsibilities to his vassals. Of course, he supported a vassal by granting him land but he also had to protect his vassal by defending him militarily or by taking his side in a dispute.

✓Reading Check **Explaining** Why was land the most important gift a lord could give a vassal?

## Feudal Society

**MAIN IDEA** Men and women of the nobility were guided by a code of ethical behavior and society's expectations of their roles.

**HISTORY & YOU** How do sports provide people with an outlet? Read how tournaments provided an outlet for knights.

Feudal society was built around a culture of warfare as vassals prepared to fight for their lords when called upon. However, such a society also needed to find ways to prevent conflicts and violence from tearing the society apart.

### Nobility and Chivalry

In the Middle Ages, European society, like Japanese society during the same period, was dominated by men whose chief concern was warfare. Like the Japanese samurai, many European nobles loved war. As one nobleman wrote in a poem on the subject:

**INFOGRAPHICS**

**Feudal and Manorial Relationships**

From roughly 800 to 1500, the social system of feudalism provided security for most of Europe. Manorialism, often tied together with feudalism, was an economic system in which a lord held rights over land and tenants. Both feudalism and manorialism involved a complex web of obligations for people at all levels of society.

Kings awarded tracts of land, called fiefs, to nobles. As vassals to the king, nobles pledged their loyalty and promised military services as a knight. Wealthier nobles subdivided their land into fiefs for lesser nobles and thus had vassals of their own. Peasants and serfs were not a formal part of feudalism. They were tied to the land. For them, the feudal order meant security.

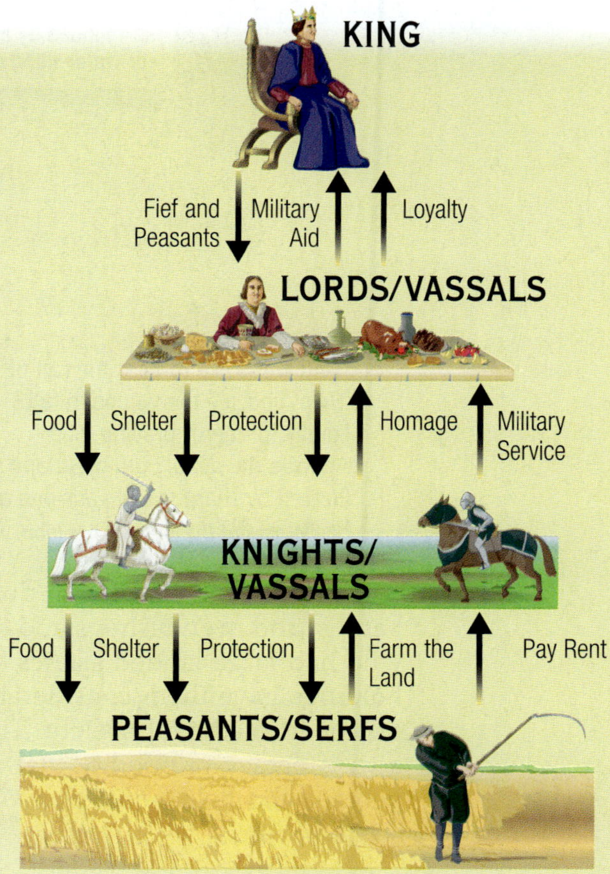


**CRITICAL THINKING SKILLS**

1. **Comparing and Contrasting** How did the obligations of the serfs differ from those of lords and knights?
2. **Evaluating** What does the chart reveal about feudal values?

## INFOGRAPHICS

### Medieval Castle

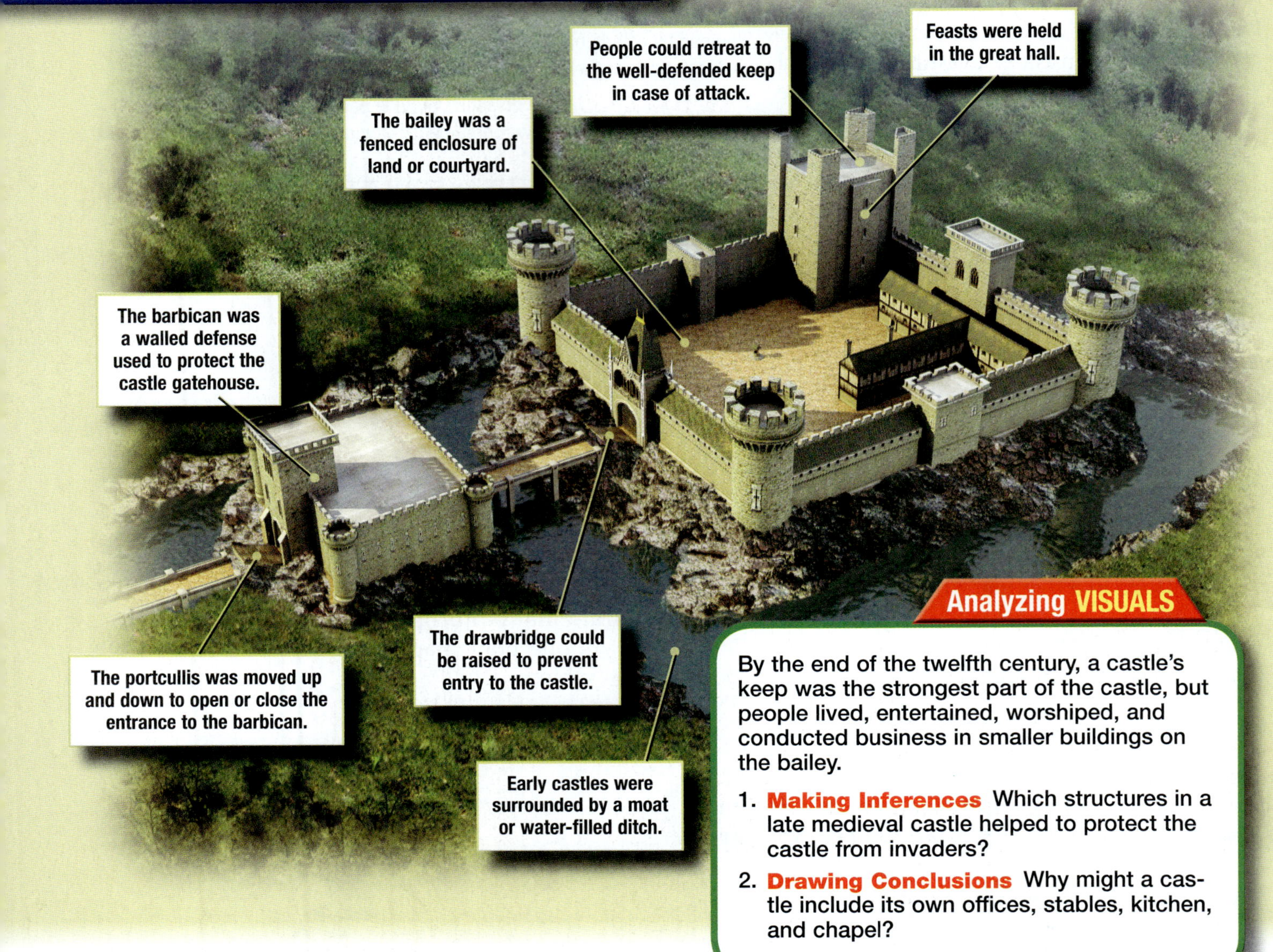


**Analyzing VISUALS**

By the end of the twelfth century, a castle's keep was the strongest part of the castle, but people lived, entertained, worshiped, and conducted business in smaller buildings on the bailey.

1. **Making Inferences** Which structures in a late medieval castle helped to protect the castle from invaders?
2. **Drawing Conclusions** Why might a castle include its own offices, stables, kitchen, and chapel?

**PRIMARY SOURCE**

> "And well I like to hear the call of
> 'Help' and see the wounded fall,
> Loudly for mercy praying,
> And see the dead, both great and small,
> Pierced by sharp spearheads one and all."
>
> —*Sources of the Western Tradition, vol. 1*

The nobles were the kings, dukes, counts, barons, and even bishops and archbishops who had large landed estates. Their landholdings gave them considerable political power in medieval society. They formed an aristocracy, or nobility, that consisted of people who held political, economic, and social power.

Great lords and ordinary knights came to form a common group within the aristocracy. They were all warriors, and the institution of knighthood united them all. However, there were also social divisions among them based on extremes of wealth and landholdings.

Trained to be warriors but with no adult responsibilities, young knights had little to do but fight. In the twelfth century, **tournaments**—contests where knights could demonstrate their fighting skills—began to appear. By the late twelfth century, the joust—individual combat between two knights—had become the main part of the tournament.

Knights saw tournaments as an excellent way to train for war. One knight expressed it in these words: "A knight cannot distinguish himself in war if he has not trained for it in tourneys."

In the eleventh and twelfth centuries, under the influence of the Catholic Church, there gradually evolved among the nobility an ideal of civilized behavior, called **chivalry**. Chivalry was a code of ethics that knights were supposed to uphold. In addition to their oath to defend the Church and defenseless people, knights were expected to treat captives as honored guests instead of putting them in dungeons. In terms of the treatment of women, chivalry put the aristocratic woman on a pedestal. A knight was to treat her with tenderness and respect.

Chivalry also implied that knights should fight only for glory and not for material rewards. Of course, this ideal was not always followed.

## Aristocratic Women's Roles

Although women could legally hold property, most remained under the control of men—of their fathers until they married and of their husbands after they married. Still, aristocratic women had many opportunities to play important roles.

Because the lord was often away at war or court, the lady of the castle had to manage the estate. Households could include large numbers of officials and servants, so this was no small responsibility. Care of the financial accounts alone took considerable knowledge. The lady of the castle was also responsible for overseeing the food supply and maintaining all the other supplies needed for the smooth operation of the household.

Women were expected to be subservient to their husbands, but there were many strong women who advised, and even dominated, their husbands. Perhaps the most famous of these was **Eleanor of Aquitaine**. Eleanor was one of the most remarkable personalities of twelfth-century Europe. Heiress to the duchy of Aquitaine in southwestern France, she was married at the age of 15 to King Louis VII of France. The marriage was not a happy one, and Louis had their marriage annulled. Eleanor married again, only eight weeks later, to Duke Henry of Normandy, who soon became King Henry II of England.

Henry II and Eleanor had a stormy relationship. She spent much time abroad in her native Aquitaine, where she created a brilliant court dedicated to cultural activities. She and Henry had eight children (five were sons). Two of her sons—Richard and John—became kings of England.

As Eleanor aged, she continued to travel to arrange royal and noble weddings and to manage her estates. She lived until her eighties, dying in 1204 in an abbey.

✓Reading Check **Summarizing** List three features of chivalry.

## SECTION 2 REVIEW

### Vocabulary

1. **Explain** the significance of: Magyars, Hungary, Vikings, enabled, Normandy, feudalism, vassal, knight, fief, feudal contract, contract, tournament, chivalry, Eleanor of Aquitaine.

### Main Ideas

2. **Explain** how Frankish traditions weakened the Carolingian Empire following Charlemagne's death.
3. **Describe** the benefits granted a vassal under feudalism. What was a vassal's primary obligation to his lord?
4. **List** the invasions that besieged the Carolingian Empire throughout the ninth and tenth centuries.

### Critical Thinking

5. **The BIG Idea** **Summarize** What factors helped feudalism develop in western Europe throughout the ninth and tenth centuries?
6. **Contrasting Information** Use a table like the one below to list the differences between the social order of feudalism and empires.

| Feudalism | Empires |
|---|---|
| | |
| | |

7. **Analyzing Visuals** Analyze the castle on page 312. What does its structure reveal about medieval life?

### Writing About History

8. **Descriptive Writing** Describe a twelfth-century tournament, using details to create vivid images. Use your local library or the Internet to supplement the text information. What questions would you ask about tournaments, knights, and jousting?

**History ONLINE**
For help with the concepts in this section of *Glencoe World History,* go to glencoe.com and click Study Central™.

# Social History

## The Code of Chivalry

Beginning in the eleventh and twelfth centuries, the idea of chivalry developed. This was an idealized set of rules and behaviors that knights were called on to follow. These rules varied according to time and place, but generally the ideal heroic knight was influenced by courtesy, fairness, piety, and devotion to an honorable idea.

The word "chivalry" comes from *cheval,* the French word for horse.

In the feudal system, a knight swore his oath of loyalty to his liege (feudal) lord. This oath helped form a basis for the ideals of chivalry.

The code of chivalry was reserved for wealthy and noble horse soldiers, called knights.

### More Romance than Reality

Chivalry existed to a certain degree, but it hardly controlled the way knights behaved or courts were run. It was first a literary movement—troubadours and bards (musicians and poets) spread romantic tales of noble, usually fictitious knights. The stories were also based on the ideas of "courtly love," in which courtesy toward women was considered the most important quality. It began in the "courts of love" in southern France and then spread, but was never adopted by any large numbers of the nobility. It was a romanticized idea, but, as one historian states, chivalry was "more playacting than real."

# A Chivalrous Knight Pledged Loyalty and Service...

**To the Church**
The Roman Catholic Church was a major influence on life in the Middle Ages. Rigorous observance of Church doctrine was expected, although Church practices varied across the continent.

**To His Lord**
The knight was a soldier. Loyalty to his lord was essential in a feudal society, and a central element of chivalry.

**To Women**
Knights were expected to be honorable in their dealing with noblewomen. In time, a romantic idea developed: a knight was supposed to pledge his devotion and service to a noble lady, who might be married to someone else.

**To the Weak**
Ideally, a knight would be expected to use his military skill and social standing to protect the most vulnerable people in society.

## Periods of Chivalry

The history of chivalry is sometimes viewed in four periods. The first was during the Crusades, when knights pledged themselves to their holy task. The second was in the Crusades' aftermath, when military orders, like the Knights Templar, were formed, and member knights took chivalric oaths. The third was during the Hundred Years' War, when the concepts of honor in battle and with women dominated chivalric ideals. The fourth period was during the 1400s, when chivalry was carried out in ceremonies in royal courts.

### Analyzing Visuals

1. **Evaluate** How important do you think chivalry was in the history of Europe? Explain your answer.
2. **Comparing** Are there any modern equivalents of chivalry? Give some examples.

SECTION 3

Section Audio    Spotlight Video

# The Growth of European Kingdoms

## GUIDE TO READING

### The BIG Idea

**Order and Security** During the High Middle Ages, monarchs began to extend their power and build strong states.

### Content Vocabulary

- common law *(p. 317)*
- Magna Carta *(p. 318)*
- Parliament *(p. 318)*
- estate *(p. 319)*

### Academic Vocabulary

- challenge *(p. 317)*
- document *(p. 317)*

### People and Places

- William of Normandy *(p. 316)*
- Henry II *(p. 316)*
- Thomas à Becket *(p. 317)*
- Paris *(p. 319)*
- Philip II Augustus *(p. 319)*
- Otto I *(p. 319)*
- Slavs *(p. 320)*
- Kiev *(p. 321)*
- Alexander Nevsky *(p. 321)*

### Reading Strategy

**Cause and Effect** Use a chart like the one below to show the main reasons why eastern Slavs developed separately from western Europe.

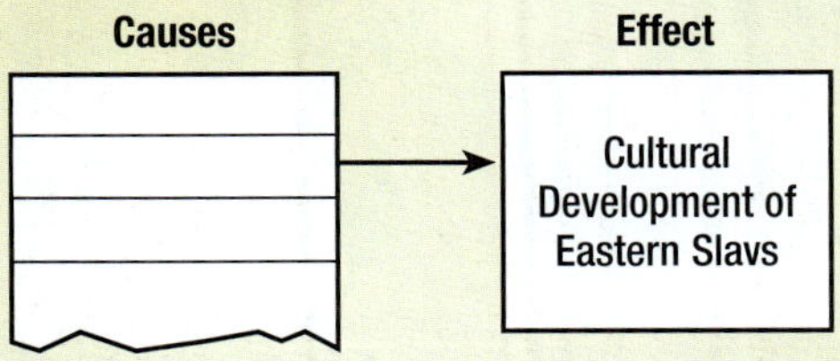


*The domination of society by the nobility reached its high point between 1000 and 1300—the High Middle Ages. At the same time, monarchs began extending their power. This frequently led to conflict between the two.*

## England in the High Middle Ages

**MAIN IDEA** King John of England put his seal on the Magna Carta in 1215, recognizing the rights of his nobles, and keeping the English monarch from ever becoming an absolute ruler.

**HISTORY & YOU** What other famous documents granting rights can you name? Read how the nobles and the kings clashed.

Angles and Saxons, Germanic peoples from northern Europe, had invaded England early in the fifth century. King Alfred the Great had united various kingdoms in the late ninth century, and since then England had been ruled by Anglo-Saxon kings.

### The Norman Conquest

On October 14, 1066, an army of heavily armed knights under **William of Normandy** landed on the coast of England and soundly defeated King Harold and his foot soldiers at the Battle of Hastings. William was crowned king of England. Norman knights received parcels of land, which they held as fiefs, from the king. William made all nobles swear an oath of loyalty to him as sole ruler of England.

The Norman ruling class spoke French, but the marriage of the Normans with the Anglo-Saxon nobility gradually merged Anglo-Saxon and French into a new English language. The Normans also took over existing Anglo-Saxon institutions, such as the office of sheriff. William took a census, known as the Domesday Book. It was the first census taken in Europe since Roman times and included people, manors, and farm animals. William also developed more fully the system of taxation and royal courts begun by earlier Anglo-Saxon kings.

### Henry II and the Church

The power of the English monarchy was enlarged during the reign of **Henry II**, from 1154 to 1189. Henry increased the number of criminal cases tried in the king's court and also devised means for taking property cases from local courts to the royal courts. By expanding the power of the royal courts, Henry expanded the king's power. In addition, because the royal courts were now

**Geography SKILLS**

Strong monarchies developed in France and England, while Germany and Italy consisted of independent states.

1. **Location** Locate Runnymede. In which kingdom is it located?
2. **Place** Create a bar graph comparing the sizes of the kingdoms on this map.

found throughout England, a body of **common law**—law that was common to the whole kingdom—began to replace law codes that varied from place to place.

Henry was less successful at imposing royal control over the Church. He claimed the right to punish clergymen in royal courts. **Thomas à Becket**, archbishop of Canterbury and the highest-ranking English cleric, claimed that only Roman Catholic Church courts could try clerics. An angry king publicly expressed the desire to be rid of Becket: "Who will free me of this priest?" Four knights took the **challenge,** went to Canterbury, and murdered the archbishop in the cathedral. Faced with public outrage, Henry backed down in his struggle with the Church.

## The Magna Carta

Many English nobles resented the ongoing growth of the king's power and rebelled during the reign of King John. At Runnymede in 1215, John was forced by the nobles to put his seal on a **document** of rights.

It was called the **Magna Carta**, or the Great Charter. Feudal custom had recognized that the relationship between king and vassals was based on mutual rights and obligations. The Magna Carta gave written recognition to that fact and was used in later years to strengthen the idea that a monarch's power was limited, not absolute.

In the thirteenth century, during the reign of Edward I, an important institution in the development of representative government—the English **Parliament**—also emerged. It was composed of two knights from every county, two people from every town, and all of the nobles and bishops throughout England. Eventually, nobles and church lords formed the House of Lords; knights and townspeople, the House of Commons. The Parliaments of Edward I granted taxes, discussed politics, and passed laws.

✓Reading Check **Analyzing** Why was 1066 a turning point in history?

# TURNING POINT — THE MAGNA CARTA

▲ *A depiction of John of England signing the Magna Carta from* Cassell's History of England—Century Edition

In the Magna Carta's 63 clauses, King John vowed that the church would remain free, listed rights due to landholders, said he would dismiss his mercenaries from foreign countries, and gave a council of 25 barons the right to go to war with him if he did not honor the Magna Carta. John was not the first king to make promises to his barons. However, previous monarchs had made general promises and granted them freely, while King John's barons demanded the very specific promises from him. By recognizing the rights of nobles, the Magna Carta limited the power of English monarchs.

39. No freeman shall be . . . imprisoned . . . except by the lawful judgment of his peers or by the law of the land.
40. To no one will we sell, to no one will we refuse or delay, right or justice.
51. As soon as peace is restored, we will banish from the kingdom all foreign-born knights, cross-bowmen, serjeants, and mercenary soldiers . . .
52. If anyone has been dispossessed or removed by us, without the legal judgment of his peers, from his lands, castles, franchises, or from his right, we will immediately restore them to him . . .
55. All fines made with us unjustly and against the law of the land, and all amercements[1] imposed unjustly and against the law of the land, shall be entirely remitted . . .

—from the *Magna Carta*

[1] **amercements:** punishments by fine

**DOCUMENT-BASED QUESTIONS**

1. **Making Connections** How did the idea of the Magna Carta ultimately pave the way for citizens' rights?
2. **Summarizing** What permanent effects did the Magna Carta have on the English monarchy?

## France in the Middle Ages

**MAIN IDEA** One section of Charlemagne's empire became France.

**HISTORY & YOU** Which states were originally French territory? Read about the development of the French monarchy.

In 843, the Carolingian Empire was divided into three sections. One of them, the west Frankish lands, formed the core of the kingdom of France. In 987, after the last Carolingian king died, the west Frankish nobles made Hugh Capet their king, establishing the Capetian (kuh•PEE•shuhn) dynasty of French kings.

Although they were called kings, the Capetians had little real power. The royal domain, or lands they controlled, included only the area around **Paris**, known as the Ile-de-France. Formally, they were above the great dukes of France, but many of the dukes were actually more powerful.

The reign of **Philip II Augustus**, who reigned from 1180 to 1223, was a turning point in the French monarchy, expanding its income and power. Philip fought wars against the English to take control of the French territories of Normandy, Maine, Anjou, and Aquitaine. Philip's successors continued to add lands to the royal domain.

Much of the thirteenth century was dominated by the reign of Louis IX. Deeply religious, he was later made a saint by the Catholic Church. Louis was known for trying to bring justice to his people by hearing their complaints in person. Philip IV, called Philip the Fair, ruled from 1285 to 1314. He made the monarchy stronger by expanding the royal bureaucracy. Indeed by 1300, France was the largest and best-governed monarchy in Europe. Philip IV also created a French parliament by meeting with members of the three **estates**, or classes—the clergy (first estate), the nobles (second estate), and the townspeople and peasants (third estate). The meeting, in 1302, began the Estates-General, the first French parliament.

**✓Reading Check** **Evaluating** Why was the reign of King Philip II Augustus important to the growth of the French monarchy?

## The Holy Roman Empire

**MAIN IDEA** Unlike England and France, the lands of Germany and Italy did not become united during the Middle Ages.

**HISTORY & YOU** What characteristics would make one group unite with another? Read how the Holy Roman Emperors failed.

In the tenth century, the powerful dukes of the Saxons became kings of the eastern Frankish kingdom, which came to be known as Germany. The best-known Saxon king of Germany was **Otto I**. Otto was a patron of German culture and brought the Church under his control. In return for protecting the pope, Otto I was crowned emperor of the Romans in 962. The title had not been used since the time of Charlemagne. Otto's creation of a new Roman Empire in the hands of the Germans had long-range consequences.

### Struggles in Italy

As leaders of a new Roman Empire, the German kings attempted to rule both German and Italian lands. Many a German king lost armies in Italy in pursuit of the dream of an empire. The two most famous members of one particular German dynasty prove this.

Frederick I and Frederick II, instead of building a strong German kingdom, tried to create a new kind of empire. Frederick I planned to get his chief revenues from Italy. He considered Italy the center of a "holy empire," as he called it—hence the name Holy Roman Empire.

Frederick's attempt to conquer northern Italy led to severe problems. The pope opposed him, fearing that he wanted to include Rome and the Papal States as part of his empire. The cities of northern Italy, which had become used to their freedom, were also unwilling to become his subjects. An alliance of these northern Italian cities and the pope defeated the forces of Frederick I in 1176.

The main goal of Frederick II was to establish a strong, centralized state in Italy. He too was involved in a struggle with the popes and the northern Italian cities.

Frederick II waged a bitter struggle in northern Italy, winning many battles but ultimately losing the war.

## Effects on the Empire

The struggle between popes and emperors had dire consequences for the Holy Roman Empire. By spending their time fighting in Italy, the German emperors left Germany in the hands of powerful German lords. These nobles ignored the emperor and created their own independent kingdoms. This made the German monarchy weak and incapable of maintaining a strong monarchical state.

In the end, the German Holy Roman Emperor had no real power over either Germany or Italy. Unlike France and England, neither Germany nor Italy created a national monarchy in the Middle Ages. Both Germany and Italy consisted of many small, independent states. Not until the nineteenth century did these states ultimately become unified.

✓Reading Check **Explaining** What is the origin of the term Holy Roman Empire?

# Central and Eastern Europe

**MAIN IDEA** The Slavic peoples settled in central and eastern Europe, forming new kingdoms.

***HISTORY & YOU*** Have you ever moved far away? Read how the Slavs changed when they settled in new places.

The Slavic peoples were originally a single people in central Europe. Gradually, they divided into three major groups: the western, southern, and eastern Slavs.

## Slavic Europe

The western **Slavs** eventually formed the Polish and Bohemian kingdoms. German monks had converted both the Czechs in Bohemia and the Slavs in Poland to Christianity by the tenth century. The non-Slavic kingdom of Hungary was also converted. The Poles, Czechs, and Hungarians (Magyars) all accepted Western Christianity and became part of the Roman Catholic Church and its Latin culture.

NATIONAL GEOGRAPHIC

**SLAVIC PEOPLES OF CENTRAL AND EASTERN EUROPE**

**Geography SKILLS**

1. **Movement** Which Slavic groups settled closest to the Adriatic Sea?
2. **Place** What can you infer from the names of the Slavic groups and present-day Slavic countries?

Maps In Motion See *StudentWorks™ Plus* or glencoe.com.

The eastern Slavic peoples of Moravia were converted to Orthodox Christianity by two Byzantine missionary brothers, Cyril and Methodius, who began their activities in 863. The Slavic peoples had no written language. Cyril developed the Cyrillic alphabet so that he could create a Christian Bible and liturgy in the Slavic language.

The southern Slavic peoples included the Croats, the Serbs, and the Bulgarians. Most of them embraced Eastern Orthodoxy, although the Croats came to accept the Roman Catholic Church. The acceptance of Eastern Orthodoxy by many southern and eastern Slavic peoples meant that their cultural life was linked to the Byzantine state.

## Kievan Rus

Eastern Slavic peoples had also settled in present-day Ukraine and Russia. There, in the late eighth century, they encountered Swedish Vikings, who moved into their lands in search of plunder and new trade routes. The native peoples were eventually dominated by the Vikings, whom they called "the Rus" (from which *Russia* is derived).

One Viking leader, Oleg, settled in **Kiev** (present-day Kyiv) at the beginning of the tenth century and created the Rus state known as the Principality of Kiev. Oleg also opened trade with the Byzantines, increasing the prosperity of the Rus. His successors extended their control over the eastern Slavs and expanded Kiev, until it included the territory between the Baltic and Black Seas and the Danube and Volga Rivers. By marrying Slavic wives, the Viking ruling class was gradually assimilated into the Slavic population.

The growth of the principality of Kiev attracted Byzantine missionaries. One Rus ruler, Vladimir, married the Byzantine emperor's sister and officially accepted Eastern Orthodox Christianity for himself and his people in 988. This created cultural unification in the east and separation from Western Europe. Kievan Rus reached its high point in the first half of the eleventh century. This largely was due to the prosperous trade route between the Baltic and Black Seas. However, civil wars and new invasions brought an end to the first Russian state in 1169.

## Mongol Rule

In the thirteenth century, the Mongols conquered Russia. They occupied Russian lands and required Russian princes to pay tribute to them. One prince emerged as more powerful than the others. **Alexander Nevsky**, prince of Novgorod, defeated a German invading army in northwestern Russia in 1242. The khan, leader of the western Mongol Empire, rewarded Nevsky with the title of grandprince. His descendants became princes of Moscow and eventually leaders of all Russia.

✓Reading Check **Describing** How was the Viking ruling class gradually assimilated into the Slavic population?

## SECTION 3 REVIEW

### Vocabulary

1. **Explain** the significance of: William of Normandy, Henry II, common law, Thomas à Becket, challenge, document, Magna Carta, Parliament, Paris, Philip II Augustus, estate, Otto I, Slavs, Kiev, Alexander Nevsky.

### Main Ideas

2. **Summarize** the importance of the Norman conquest in 1066.
3. **Explain** what Henry II accomplished when he expanded the power of the royal courts in England.
4. **List** the nationalities of the Slavic peoples.

### Critical Thinking

5. **The BIG Idea** **Explaining** Unified national monarchies did not develop in Germany and Italy as they did in France and England during the High Middle Ages. Why not?
6. **Organizing Information** Use a chart to identify key achievements of monarchs in England and France.

| Monarch/Country | Achievements |
|---|---|
| 1. | |
| 2. | |
| 3. | |
| 4. | |

7. **Analyzing Visuals** Analyze the image of King John on page 318. What mood is being conveyed between the king and the nobles?

### Writing About History

8. **Informative Writing** Imagine that you are a journalist attending a meeting of the first English Parliament. What questions would you ask? Write a newsletter for people of your town explaining what happened.

**History ONLINE**
For help with the concepts in this section of *Glencoe World History*, go to glencoe.com and click Study Central™.

SECTION 4

Section Audio    Spotlight Video

# Byzantine Empire and Crusades

## GUIDE TO READING

**The BIG Idea**

**Ideas, Beliefs, and Values** The Byzantine Empire created a unique civilization that was eventually weakened by the Crusades.

**Content Vocabulary**

- patriarch *(p. 323)*
- schism *(p. 324)*
- Crusades *(p. 325)*
- infidel *(p. 325)*

**Academic Vocabulary**

- legal *(p. 322)*
- enormous *(p. 324)*

**People and Places**

- Constantinople *(p. 322)*
- Justinian *(p. 322)*
- Palestine *(p. 322)*
- Syria *(p. 322)*
- Balkans *(p. 323)*
- Bernard of Clairvaux *(p. 326)*
- Saladin *(p. 326)*
- Pope Innocent III *(p. 327)*

**Reading Strategy**

**Cause and Effect** As you read, use a diagram like the one below to help you study why a powerful Byzantine Empire developed.

Causes: [ ] [ ] [ ]

Effect: Powerful Byzantine Empire

*The Eastern Roman Empire continued long after the fall of Rome. Islam became a major force against the eastern empire, and Europeans eventually led military expeditions to the region to reclaim land conquered by Muslims.*

## From Eastern Roman Empire to Byzantine Empire

**MAIN IDEA** The Eastern Roman Empire evolved into the smaller Byzantine Empire, which preserved and transmitted Greek and Roman culture.

**HISTORY & YOU** Does your family follow certain traditions from a long time ago? Read about the Eastern Orthodox Church.

During the 400s, Germanic tribes moved into the Western Roman Empire and established their states. In contrast, the Eastern Roman Empire, centered on **Constantinople**, continued to exist, although pressured by powerful Islamic forces beginning in the 600s.

### The Reign of Justinian

When **Justinian** became emperor of the Eastern Roman Empire in 527, he was determined to reestablish the Roman Empire in the entire Mediterranean world. By 552, he appeared to have achieved his goals. His empire included Italy, part of Spain, North Africa, Asia Minor, **Palestine**, and **Syria**. However, only three years after Justinian's death in 565, the Lombards had conquered much of Italy, and other areas were soon lost.

Justinian's most important contribution was his codification of Roman law. He simplified a vast quantity of **legal** materials, resulting in *The Body of Civil Law*. This code of Roman laws was the basis of imperial law in the Eastern Roman Empire until its end in 1453. In addition, it became the basis for much of the legal system of Europe.

### The Byzantine Empire

Justinian's accomplishments had been spectacular, but his conquests left the Eastern Roman Empire with serious problems: too much far-flung territory to protect, an empty treasury, a decline in population after a plague, and renewed threats to its frontiers. The most serious challenge came from the rise of Islam, which unified Arab groups and created a powerful new force that swept through the Eastern Roman Empire.

Islamic forces defeated an army of the Eastern Roman Empire at Yarmūk in 636. As a result, the empire lost the provinces of Syria and

PRIMARY SOURCE INFOGRAPHICS

## The Justinian Code

Emperor Justinian

Soon after assuming the throne, Emperor Justinian appointed several commissions to collect and organize the complicated body of Roman laws. The result, *The Body of Civil Law* (or the Justinian Code), stands as one of the great accomplishments of the Middle Ages. Much of the modern world, including Scotland, Quebec, Louisiana, and most of mainland Europe, is governed by systems of justice that descend from the code. The empress Theodora is credited with influencing Justinian to make reforms, giving additional rights to women.

On law: "The precepts of the law are these: to live honestly, to injure no one, and to give every man his due."

On property: "By the law of nature these things are common to mankind—the air, running water, the sea, and consequently the shores of the sea."

On theft: "The penalty for manifest theft is quadruple the value of the thing stolen, whether the thief be a slave or a freeman."

On marriage: "We have enacted that puberty in males should be considered to commence immediately on the completion of their fourteenth year; while, as to females . . . they are esteemed fit for marriage on the completion of their twelfth year."

### The Body of Civil Law (The Justinian Code)

| | |
|---|---|
| Codex Constitutionem | A collection of all known ordinances issued by previous emperors. Redundant and obsolete material was left out. Published in 10 books. |
| Digest | A selection of the most valuable writings of Roman jurists. Any statement not selected for the Digest was considered invalid. Published in 50 books. |
| Institutes | An elementary law textbook for use by first-year law students. Extracts from the Codex and Digest were included. |
| Novels | Several collections of new ordinances passed by Justinian himself after the publication of the Codex. |

### DOCUMENT-BASED QUESTIONS

1. **Contrasting** Study the excerpts from the Justinian Code. What does the code say about marriage?
2. **Making Inferences** Why were the Novels published years after the rest of the Code?

Palestine. Problems arose along the northern frontier as well, especially in the **Balkans.** In 679, the Bulgars took possession of the lower Danube Valley, creating a strong Bulgarian kingdom.

By the beginning of the eighth century, the Eastern Roman Empire was much smaller, consisting only of the eastern Balkans and Asia Minor. Historians call this smaller empire the Byzantine Empire, a unique civilization that lasted until 1453.

The Byzantine Empire was both a Greek and a Christian state. Greek replaced Latin as the empire's official language. At the same time, the Byzantine Empire was built on a Christian faith that was shared by many of its citizens. The Christian church of the Byzantine Empire came to be known as the Eastern Orthodox Church. To honor this faith, a great artistic effort was undertaken to enrich church building, ceremonies, and decorations.

The emperor occupied a crucial position in the Byzantine state. Portrayed as chosen by God, he was crowned in sacred ceremonies. His subjects were expected to prostrate themselves in his presence. His power was considered absolute.

Because the emperor appointed the head of the Eastern Orthodox Church, known as the **patriarch**, the emperor exercised control over church as well as state.

The Byzantines believed that God had commanded their state to preserve the true Christian faith. Political and religious leaders were all bound together in service to this spiritual ideal.

## Life in Constantinople

Much of Constantinople was destroyed by riots in 532. Afterward, Emperor Justinian rebuilt the city and gave it the appearance it would keep for almost a thousand years. With a population estimated in the hundreds of thousands, Constantinople was the largest city in Europe during the Middle Ages.

The city was dominated by an **enormous** palace complex, hundreds of churches, and a huge arena known as the Hippodrome, where gladiator fights and chariot races were held. Justinian's public works projects included roads, bridges, walls, public baths, law courts, schools, churches, and underground reservoirs to hold the city's water supply.

His greatest achievement was the famous Hagia Sophia—the Church of the Holy Wisdom. Art, architecture, and education were important to the Byzantines, especially those involving the cultures and traditions of Greece and Rome, of which the Byzantines saw themselves as guardians. They studied Greek and Roman texts and preserved them in Byzantine libraries, long before these texts were studied in Western Europe.

Until the twelfth century, Constantinople was medieval Europe's greatest center of commerce. It was the chief center for the exchange of products between West and East. Products of the East were highly desired in Europe: silk from China, spices from Southeast Asia and India, jewelry and ivory from India, wheat and furs from southern Russia, and flax and honey from the Balkans. These goods flowed into Constantinople, and many were then shipped throughout Europe.

Imported raw materials were also used in Constantinople for local industries. In Justinian's reign, two Christian monks smuggled silkworms from China to begin a silk industry. European demand for silk cloth made it the city's most lucrative product.

✓Reading Check **Evaluating** How did the rise of Islam affect the Eastern Roman Empire?

# New Heights and New Problems

*MAIN IDEA* The Macedonians expanded the Byzantine Empire, but new threats arose in the late eleventh century.

*HISTORY & YOU* How do you handle a difference of opinion? Read about the schism between the Eastern Orthodox Church and the Catholic Church.

The size of the Byzantine Empire was greatly reduced by the early eighth century, but the empire recovered and even expanded through a new dynasty known as the Macedonians, who ruled from 867 to 1081.

## Macedonian Emperors

The Macedonian emperors expanded the empire to include Bulgaria in the Balkans, Crete, Cyprus, and Syria. By 1025, the Byzantine Empire was the largest it had been since the 600s. By expanding trade with western Europe, the Macedonians renewed prosperity to Constantinople.

The new dynasty restored much of the empire's power, but incompetent successors undid most of the gains. Power struggles between army leaders and wealthy families led to disorder in the late eleventh century.

## Religious Issues

Relations with the Catholic Church grew worse because the Eastern Orthodox Church did not accept the pope as the sole head of Christianity. In 1054, the pope and the Byzantine patriarch formally excommunicated each other—each took away the other's rights of church membership. This began a **schism**, or separation, between the two great branches of Christianity that has not been completely healed to this day.

The Byzantine Empire's greatest external threat came from the Seljuk Turks in Asia Minor—the empire's main source of food and workers. In 1071, a Turkish army defeated Byzantine forces at Manzikert. As a result, Emperor Alexius I turned to Europe for military aid to fight the Turks.

✓Reading Check **Summarizing** What threats did the Byzantine Empire face in the eleventh century?

## The Crusades

**MAIN IDEA** The Crusades had a significant effect on medieval society in both the East and the West.

**HISTORY & YOU** Do you know of any worthy causes founded by children? Read about the Children's Crusades.

From the eleventh to the thirteenth centuries, European Christians carried out a series of military expeditions to regain the Holy Land from the Muslims. These expeditions are known as the **Crusades.**

The Crusades started when the Byzantine emperor asked for help against the Seljuk Turks. The Seljuk Turks were Muslims who had taken control of Asia Minor. Pope Urban II, who responded to the request, saw an opportunity to provide leadership for a great cause. That cause was rallying Europe's warriors to free Jerusalem and the Holy Land from the **infidels** or unbelievers—the Muslims.

At the Council of Clermont in southern France near the end of 1095, Urban II challenged Christians to take up their weapons and join in a holy war. The pope promised: "All who die . . . shall have immediate remission [forgiveness] of sins." The enthusiastic crowd cried out: "It is the will of God, it is the will of God."

Warriors of western Europe, particularly France, formed the first crusading armies. These knights were mostly motivated by religious fervor, but some sought adventure and welcomed the chance to fight. Others saw an opportunity to gain wealth and a possible title. Italian merchants also sought new trading opportunities in Byzantine and Muslim lands.

### The Early Crusades

The First Crusade began as three organized bands of mostly French warriors made their way to the East. The crusading army, which included thousands of men in cavalry and infantry, captured Antioch in 1098. The crusaders proceeded down the Palestinian coast, avoiding the well-defended coastal cities, and reached Jerusalem in June 1099. The Holy City was taken amid a horrible massacre of its inhabitants.

**HISTORY & ARTS**

**Byzantine Art and Architecture**

Hagia Sophia, originally a Christian church, was converted to a mosque in 1453.

The Hagia Sophia dome, 160 feet (48.8 m) high and over 101 feet (30.8 m) in diameter, dominated the landscape of Constantinople.

Light from 42 windows helps create the impression that the dome is floating.

This mosaic in Hagia Sophia shows Jesus seated on a throne between the Byzantine rulers.

**DOCUMENT-BASED QUESTIONS**

The purpose of Byzantine art and architecture was to inspire awe for Christianity and for imperial power. Distinctive characteristics of Byzantine style are soaring domes, dazzling mosaics of colored glass, and icons—stylized religious portraits.

1. **Identifying** What were the main characteristics of Byzantine art and architecture?
2. **Drawing Conclusions** Why was it significant that the emperor was paired with Jesus in the mosaic above?

NATIONAL GEOGRAPHIC

## THE CRUSADES

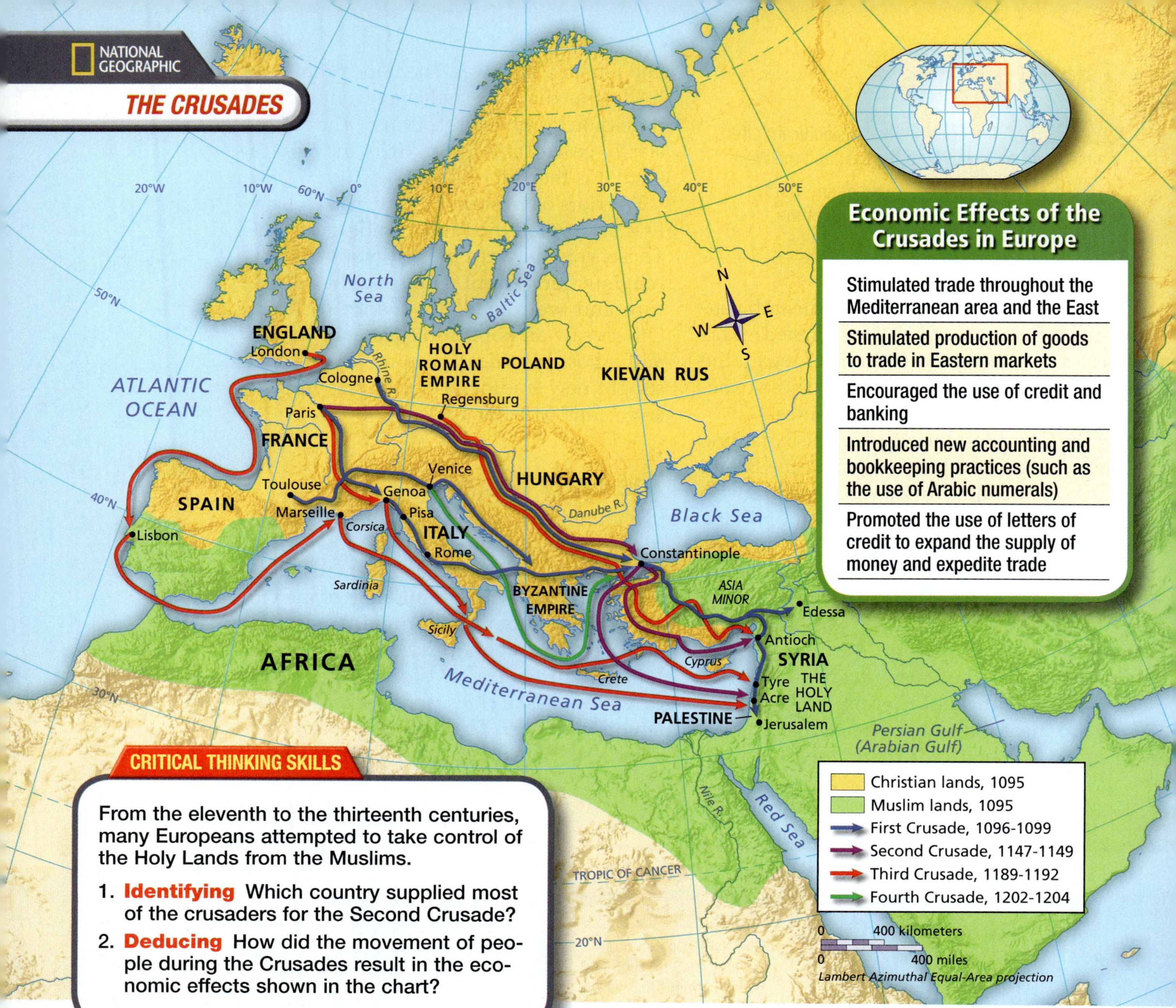


### Economic Effects of the Crusades in Europe

| |
|---|
| Stimulated trade throughout the Mediterranean area and the East |
| Stimulated production of goods to trade in Eastern markets |
| Encouraged the use of credit and banking |
| Introduced new accounting and bookkeeping practices (such as the use of Arabic numerals) |
| Promoted the use of letters of credit to expand the supply of money and expedite trade |

### CRITICAL THINKING SKILLS

**From the eleventh to the thirteenth centuries, many Europeans attempted to take control of the Holy Lands from the Muslims.**

1. **Identifying** Which country supplied most of the crusaders for the Second Crusade?
2. **Deducing** How did the movement of people during the Crusades result in the economic effects shown in the chart?

After further conquests, the crusaders organized four Latin crusader states in the East. Surrounded by Muslims, these crusader kingdoms depended on Italian cities for supplies. Some Italian port cities, such as Genoa, Pisa, and especially Venice, grew rich and powerful in the process.

It was not easy for the crusader kingdoms to maintain themselves in the East. By the 1140s, the Muslims had begun to strike back. The fall of one of the Latin kingdoms to the Muslims led to calls for another crusade, especially from the monastic leader **Bernard of Clairvaux.** Bernard managed to enlist two powerful rulers, King Louis VII of France and Emperor Conrad III of Germany, in a Second Crusade. This campaign, however, was a total failure.

In 1187, the Holy City of Jerusalem fell to Muslim forces under **Saladin.** Three rulers then agreed to lead a Third Crusade: German emperor Frederick Barbarossa, English king Richard I (Richard the Lionhearted), and French king Philip II Augustus.

When members of the Third Crusade arrived in the East in 1189, they struggled to overcome the problems they faced. Frederick drowned in a local river. The English and French arrived by sea and captured the coastal cities but were unable to move inland against the Muslim forces. After Philip returned home, Richard negotiated a settlement with Saladin that permitted Christian pilgrims free access to Jerusalem.

## The Later Crusades

About six years after Saladin's death in 1193, **Pope Innocent III** initiated the Fourth Crusade. As it headed east, the crusading army became involved in a fight over the Byzantine throne. The Venetian leaders of the crusade used the situation to weaken their greatest commercial competitor, the Byzantine Empire. In 1204, the crusaders sacked Constantinople, adding to the division between the Eastern Orthodox Church and the Catholic Church.

Not until 1261 did a Byzantine army recapture the city, but the empire was no longer a great power. It now comprised Constantinople and its surrounding lands, as well as part of Asia Minor. This smaller empire limped along for another 190 years, until the Ottoman Turks conquered it in 1453.

Despite failures, the crusading ideal continued. In Germany in 1212, a youth known as Nicholas of Cologne announced that God had inspired him to lead a "children's crusade." Thousands of young people marched with him to Italy, where the pope told them to go home. At about the same time, some 20,000 French children headed to Marseille, where two shipowners agreed to take them to the Holy Land. Two of the ships went down in a storm. The other five sailed to North Africa, where the children were sold into slavery. The next Crusades of adult warriors were hardly more successful.

Did the Crusades have much effect on European civilization? Historians disagree. Clearly, the Crusades benefited the Italian port cities, especially Genoa, Pisa, and Venice. Even without the Crusades, however, Italian merchants would have increased trade with the Eastern world.

The Crusades had some unfortunate side effects on European society. The first widespread attacks on the Jews began in the context of the Crusades. Some Christians argued that to fight the Muslims while the Jews, whom they blamed for Jesus' death, ran free at home was unthinkable. The Jews of medieval Europe came to be subjected to periodic libels, attacks, and expulsions.

Perhaps the greatest impact of the Crusades was political. They eventually helped to break down feudalism. As kings levied taxes and raised armies, nobles joining the Crusades sold their lands and freed their serfs. As nobles lost power, the kings created stronger central governments. Taxing trade with the East also provided kings with new wealth. This paved the way for the development of true nation-states. By the mid-1400s, four strong nation-states—Portugal, Spain, England, and France—would emerge in Europe.

✓Reading Check **Summarizing** What factors motivated Europeans to participate in a Crusade?

## SECTION 4 REVIEW

### Vocabulary

1. **Explain** the significance of: Constantinople, Justinian, Palestine, Syria, legal, Balkans, patriarch, enormous, schism, Crusades, infidel, Bernard of Clairvaux, Saladin, Pope Innocent III.

### Main Ideas

2. **Describe** the effects the Macedonian emperors had on the Byzantine Empire.
3. **Explain** how church and state were linked in the Byzantine Empire and how this contributed to the schism.
4. **List** Justinian's accomplishments.

### Critical Thinking

5. **The BIG Idea** **Explaining** Why did cities such as Venice flourish as a result of the Crusades?
6. **Organizing Information** Use a table like the one below to summarize the positive and negative effects of the Crusades.

| Positive | Negative |
|---|---|
| | |
| | |
| | |
| | |

7. **Analyzing Visuals** Examine the image on page 323. What elements might indicate Justinian's status?

### Writing About History

8. **Descriptive Writing** Write a travel brochure encouraging people to visit Constantinople. Identify the features of the city in the Early Middle Ages. What sites would you use to illustrate your brochure?

**History ONLINE**

For help with the concepts in this section of *Glencoe World History*, go to glencoe.com and click Study Central™.

# CHAPTER 9 Visual Summary

STUDY TO GO You can study anywhere, anytime by downloading quizzes and flash cards to your PDA from glencoe.com.

THE LINDISFARNE GOSPELS, ENGLAND

This artwork created by monks testifies to the importance of religion in the Middle Ages.

## MEDIEVAL EUROPE and the Church

- Germanic rulers, especially the Franks, ruled the old Western Roman Empire.
- Charlemagne expanded Frankish rule and promoted learning, centered in monasteries.

CONWY CASTLE, WALES

Feudal castles kept out invaders and were a center for government.

## The FEUDAL ECONOMY

- Viking attacks in Europe led to decentralized governments and a new feudal system, which was based on military service in return for land grants.
- England and France were the first to build strong centralized states in Western Europe, while Russia developed around Kiev.

THE EMPEROR JUSTINIAN

Justinian, an early emperor of what was later known as the Byzantine Empire, is seen here as a lawgiver.

## Rise and Fall of BYZANTIUM

- For centuries after Rome's fall, a wealthy Byzantine Empire dominated trade in the eastern Mediterranean.
- As the Turks of the Ottoman Empire grew powerful, Byzantine rulers in Constantinople were threatened.
- Religious zeal and a spirit of conquest inspired European Crusaders, but Constantinople finally fell in 1453.

# CHAPTER 9 Assessment

## Reviewing Vocabulary

*Directions: Choose the word or words that best complete the sentence.*

**1.** Bishops of Rome became known as ________ of the Roman Catholic Church.

**A** patriarchs
**B** popes
**C** wergilds
**D** bishoprics

**2.** A ________ was the grant of land from the lord to a vassal in return for military service.

**A** feudal contract
**B** schism
**C** wergild
**D** fief

**3.** Under the influence of the Church, noblemen followed a code of behavior called ________.

**A** chivalry
**B** common law
**C** the Magna Carta
**D** feudalism

**4.** A ________ developed between the Catholic Church and the Eastern Orthodox Church in 1054.

**A** feudal contract
**B** schism
**C** bishopric
**D** fief

**5.** The three ________, or classes, in French society included the clergy, the nobles, and the townspeople and peasants.

**A** abbesses
**B** estates
**C** fiefs
**D** wergilds

## Reviewing Main Ideas

*Directions: Choose the best answers to the following questions.*

### Section 1 *(pp. 302–307)*

**6.** What important function did monks perform?

**A** They spread learning.
**B** They helped kings consolidate power.
**C** They spread wealth.
**D** They helped spread trade.

**7.** Why did Charlemagne promote learning?

**A** To spread German culture
**B** To provide free education to all children
**C** To educate the clergy and government
**D** Charlemagne didn't promote learning.

### Section 2 *(pp. 308–313)*

**8.** Why were Vikings able to expand throughout Europe?

**A** They controlled Mediterranean trade routes.
**B** They were allies with the Magyars.
**C** They were excellent shipbuilders and sailors.
**D** They defeated the Normans.

**9.** What was the most important gift a lord could give a vassal?

**A** Gold
**B** Arms and armor
**C** Serfs
**D** Land

### TEST-TAKING TIP

If you do not know the right answer to a question, use common sense to eliminate answer choices that do not make sense. Recall the context in which the topic was discussed in class or in the textbook. This may help you eliminate incorrect answer choices.

**Need Extra Help?**

| If You Missed Questions . . . | 1 | 2 | 3 | 4 | 5 | 6 | 7 | 8 | 9 |
|---|---|---|---|---|---|---|---|---|---|
| Go to Page . . . | 304 | 310 | 313 | 324 | 319 | 305 | 307 | 308 | 310 |

GO ON

# CHAPTER 9 Assessment

## Section 3 *(pp. 316–321)*

**10.** What important English political institution emerged during the reign of Edward I?

**A** House of Lords

**B** Anglican Church

**C** Parliament

**D** Royal courts

**11.** How did Henry II increase the power of the English monarchy?

**A** By placing the church under royal control

**B** By increasing the power and jurisdiction of the royal courts

**C** By strengthening the feudal system

**D** By signing the Magna Carta

## Section 4 *(pp. 322–327)*

**12.** What was Justinian's most important contribution to the Eastern Roman Empire?

**A** The codification of Roman law

**B** The reunification of the Roman Empire

**C** The defeat of Islamic forces at Yarmūk

**D** The appointment of the patriarch

**13.** What was one of the side effects of the Crusades?

**A** There were fewer wars in Europe.

**B** Nobles gained power.

**C** Feudalism broke down.

**D** Italian merchants lost much of their power.

**14.** Which Muslim leader won back Jerusalem in 1187?

**A** Mehmed II

**B** Saladin

**C** Urban II

**D** Richard I

## Critical Thinking

*Directions: Choose the best answers to the following questions.*

*Base your answers to questions 15 and 16 on the map and your knowledge of world history.*

**Expansion of Moscow, 1300–1462**

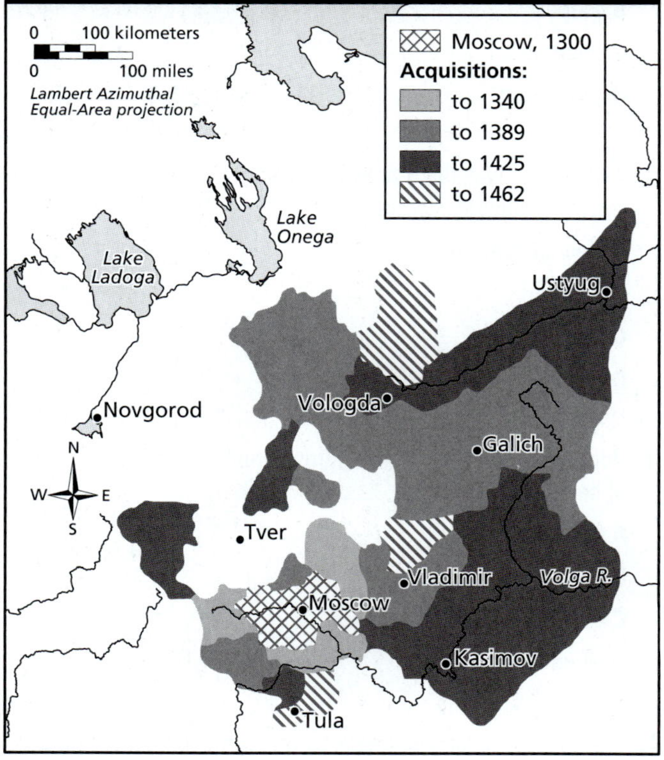


**15.** About how far did Moscow's territory stretch from north to south in 1462?

**A** 150 miles (241.4 km)

**B** 420 miles (676 km)

**C** 540 miles (869 km)

**D** 730 miles (1174.8 km)

**16.** By what year did Russia add Kasimov to its holdings?

**A** By 1300

**B** By 1340

**C** By 1389

**D** By 1425

**Need Extra Help?**

| If You Missed Questions . . . | 10 | 11 | 12 | 13 | 14 | 15 | 16 |
|---|---|---|---|---|---|---|---|
| Go to Page . . . | 318 | 316 | 322 | 327 | 326 | 330 | 330 |

GO ON

17. Why was Constantinople an important center of European trade?
   **A** It was located along major Russian and Asian trade routes.
   **B** It was located near the center of Europe.
   **C** It was an important stopping point for ships on the way to Jerusalem.
   **D** It was located along an important African trade route.

*Analyze the chart and answer the question that follows. Base your answers on the chart and on your knowledge of world history.*

| | 1st Crusade | 2nd Crusade | 3rd Crusade |
|---|---|---|---|
| People involved | Three bands of French warriors | Louis VII, Conrad III | Frederick Barbarossa, Richard I, Philip II Augustus |
| Results | Jerusalem captured; Latin crusader states organized | Total failure | Christian pilgrims given access to Jerusalem; city still held by Muslims |

18. Which Crusade most accomplished its goals?
   **A** 1st Crusade
   **B** 2nd Crusade
   **C** 3rd Crusade
   **D** None of the Crusades were successful.

19. What caused the schism in Christianity in the eleventh century?
   **A** The pope and the patriarch disagreed about religious doctrines.
   **B** The Byzantine emperor refused to recognize the Catholic Church.
   **C** The Catholic Church refused to accept the patriarch as sole head of the Christian church.
   **D** The Eastern Orthodox Church refused to accept the pope as sole head of the Christian church.

## Document-Based Questions

*Directions: Analyze the document and answer the short answer questions that follow the document. Base your answers on the document and on your knowledge of world history.*

To become a vassal a man performed an act of homage to his lord. This passage describes the oath the vassal makes to the lord:

> *"The man should put his hands together as a sign of humility, and place them between the two hands of his lord as a token that he vows everything to him and promises faith to him; and the lord should receive him and promise to keep faith with him. Then the man should say: 'Sir, I enter your homage and faith and become your man by mouth and hands [that is, by taking the oath and placing his hands between those of the lord], and I swear and promise to keep faith and loyalty to you against all others.'"*

20. Why is it significant that the vow was given to a particular person rather than a nation, written constitution, or religion?

21. What is meant by the phrase "and the lord should receive him and promise to keep faith with him"?

22. What obligations does this vow impose on the vassal?

## Extended Response

23. Using information you find in this text, your local library, or the Internet, describe the political, economic, and social impact of the Crusades. Which of these areas do you think the Crusades impacted the most? Support your answers with factual information.

**History ONLINE**
For additional test practice, use Self-Check Quizzes—Chapter 9 at glencoe.com.

**Need Extra Help?**

| If You Missed Questions . . . | 17 | 18 | 19 | 20 | 21 | 22 | 23 |
|---|---|---|---|---|---|---|---|
| Go to Page . . . | 324 | 325 | 324 | 331 | 331 | 331 | 327 |

STOP

# CHAPTER 10

# Europe in the Middle Ages 1000–1500



*MAKING CONNECTIONS*

Chapter Audio

## What caused the formation of universities?

The intellectual revival of the High Middle Ages led to the creation of universities. The University of Oxford, shown in this photo, formed when Henry II banned English students from the University of Paris in 1167. In this chapter you will learn more about culture and society during the Middle Ages.

- How do you think universities have changed since the High Middle Ages?
- What clues in the photograph on this page tell when the University of Oxford was built?

**EUROPE ▶**

**1073** Gregory VII elected pope

**1216** Dominic de Guzmán founds Dominican order

1000 — 1100 — 1200

**THE WORLD ▶**

**1100** Problems arise between Christian Axum and its Muslim neighbors in Africa

**1279** Kublai Khan establishes the Yuan dynasty in China

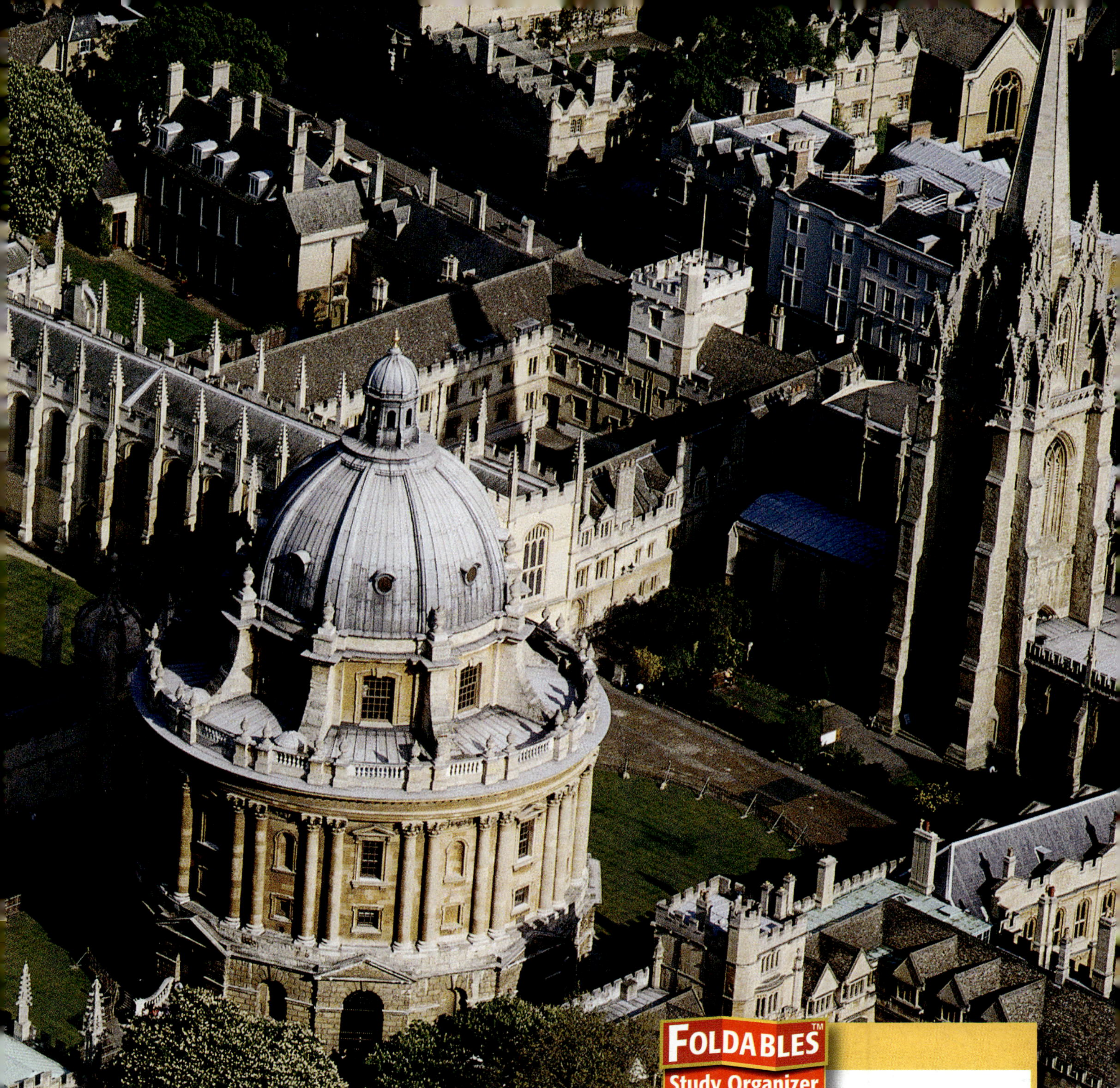

**1347**
Plague spreads to Italy and France

**1430**
English capture Joan of Arc during Hundred Years' War

**1500**
Eighty universities exist throughout Europe

1300 — 1400 — 1500

**1492**
Christopher Columbus reaches the Americas

**FOLDABLES™**
**Study Organizer**

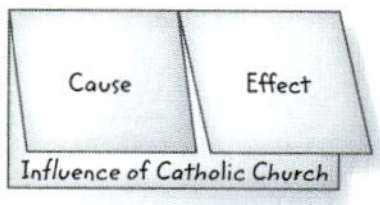


**Identifying Cause and Effect** Use a Two-Tab Book to describe causes and effects related to the influence of the Catholic Church in Medieval Europe. Select events from each century (the 1000s, 1100s, and 1200s) and identify two or more cause-and-effect relationships for each.

**History ONLINE** Visit glencoe.com and enter QuickPass™ code GWHEA7447c10 for Chapter 10 resources.

SECTION 1

Section Audio

Spotlight Video

# Peasants, Trade, and Cities

## GUIDE TO READING

### The BIG Idea

**Order and Security** New farming practices supported population growth, and the revival of trade led to a money-based economy and the rise of cities.

### Content Vocabulary

- *carruca (p. 334)*
- manor *(p. 336)*
- serfs *(p. 336)*
- money economy *(p. 338)*
- commercial capitalism *(p. 338)*
- bourgeoisie *(p. 339)*
- patricians *(p. 340)*
- guilds *(p. 341)*
- apprentice *(p. 341)*
- journeymen *(p. 341)*
- masterpiece *(p. 341)*

### Academic Vocabulary

- technology *(p. 334)*
- crucial *(p. 334)*

### Places

- Venice *(p. 338)*
- Flanders *(p. 338)*

### Reading Strategy

**Determining Cause and Effect** As you read, use a chart like the one below to show the effects of the growth of towns on medieval European society.

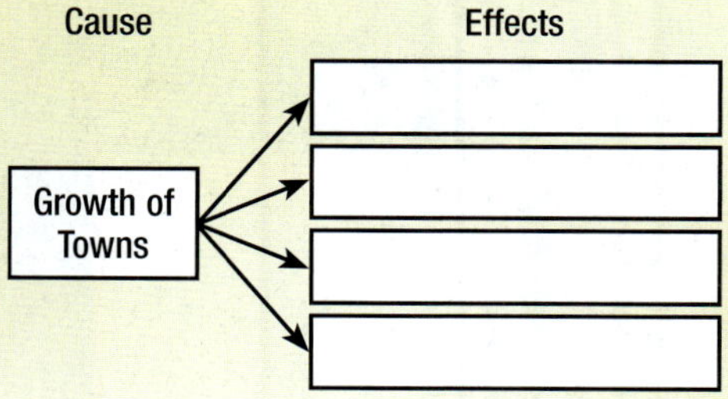


*During the High Middle Ages, new farming methods enabled Europe's population to grow. The revival of trade led to a money economy and the growth of cities. Many serfs worked the land under the manorial system, while merchants and artisans revived old cities and founded new ones.*

## The New Agriculture

**MAIN IDEA** New inventions for farming and more efficient use of land contributed to population growth in the High Middle Ages.

**HISTORY & YOU** A farmer can plant a very large area today using modern equipment. Read to learn how new devices helped medieval farmers grow more food.

In the Early Middle Ages, Europe had a relatively small population. In the High Middle Ages, however, population increased dramatically—doubling between 1000 and 1300 from 38 million to 74 million people.

What caused this huge increase? For one thing, conditions in Europe were more settled and peaceful after the invasions of the Early Middle Ages had stopped. This increased peace and stability also led to an expansion in food production after 1000.

In part, food production increased because the climate changed during the High Middle Ages and improved growing conditions. In addition, peasants cultivated more land when they cut down trees and drained swamps during the 1000s and 1100s. By 1200, Europeans had more land for farming than they do today.

Changes in **technology** also aided the development of farming. The Middle Ages witnessed an explosion of labor-saving devices. For example, the people of the Middle Ages harnessed the power of water and wind to do jobs once done by human or animal power. Many of these new devices were made from iron, which was mined in various areas of Europe. Iron was used to make scythes, axes, and hoes for use on farms. It was also used in hammers and nails for building.

Iron was **crucial** in making the ***carruca***, a heavy, wheeled plow with an iron plowshare. Unlike earlier plows, this plow easily turned over heavy clay soils. Because of the weight of the *carruca*, six or eight oxen were needed to pull it. However, oxen were slow. The inventions of a new horse collar and the horseshoe made it possible for a series of horses to pull the *carruca* faster and plow more land in the rocky, heavy clay soil of northern Europe.

Use of the *carruca* also led to the growth of farming villages, because people had to work together. Because iron was expensive, an entire community had to buy a *carruca*. Likewise, one family

# SCIENCE, TECHNOLOGY, & SOCIETY

## Agriculture in the Middle Ages

Agricultural productivity in the Middle Ages benefited tremendously from the introduction of several new technologies and practices. Iron was used to make the *carruca*, a heavy wheeled plow that could easily turn over heavy soils. Farmers began to use horses during the Middle Ages as a more efficient way of pulling the *carruca*. This was made possible because the horses were outfitted with collars to pull the plow and horseshoes made of iron for better traction in the rocky soil of northern Europe. The three-field system was also adopted to more efficiently manage crops and increase food production.

**DOCUMENT-BASED QUESTIONS**

1. **Explaining** How is the three-field system portrayed in the illustration?
2. **Summarizing** Which two inventions made it possible to use horses for plowing, and why were they significant?

could not afford a team of animals, so villagers shared their beasts. To minimize the amount of turning of the heavy *carruca*, people plowed land in long strips.

Shifting from a two-field to a three-field crop rotation also increased food production. In the Early Middle Ages, peasants divided their land into two fields of equal size. They planted one field and allowed the other to lie fallow (unplanted) to regain its fertility. Now, however, lands were divided into three parts. Peasants planted one field in the fall with grains (rye and wheat) that they harvested in summer. They planted the second field in spring with grains (oats and barley) and vegetables (peas and beans) that they harvested in fall. They allowed the third field to lie fallow. This way, only one-third, rather than one-half, of the land lay fallow at any time. This practice of rotating crops kept the soil fertile, while allowing people to grow more crops.

**✓ Reading Check** **Analyzing** What factors led to population growth in the High Middle Ages?

## The Manorial System

**MAIN IDEA** Under the manorial system of the Middle Ages, serfs worked the lands of lords.

**HISTORY & YOU** Does your family celebrate religious holidays? Read to learn about the holidays that serfs observed during the Middle Ages.

You will remember from Chapter 9 that feudalism created alliances between nobles (lords and vassals). The landholding nobles were a military elite whose ability to be warriors depended on their having the leisure time to pursue the arts of war. Landed estates, located on the fiefs given to a vassal by his lord and worked by peasants, provided the economic support that made this way of life possible.

A **manor** was an agricultural estate that a lord ran and peasants worked. Although free peasants continued to exist, increasing numbers of free peasants became **serfs**, or peasants legally bound to the land. Serfs had to provide labor services, pay rents, and be subject to the lord's control. By 800, probably 60 percent of western Europeans were serfs.

A serf's labor services included working the lord's land. The lord's land made up one-third to one-half of the cultivated land scattered throughout the manor. Peasants used the rest of the estate's land to grow food for themselves. Such tasks as building barns and digging ditches were also part of the labor services peasants provided. Serfs usually worked about three days a week for their lords.

The serfs paid rents by giving the lords a share of every product they raised. Serfs also paid the lords for the use of the manor's common pasturelands, streams, ponds, and surrounding woodlands. If a serf fished in the pond or stream on a manor, he turned over part of the catch to his lord. Peasants were also obliged to pay a tithe (a tenth of their produce) to their local village churches.

In the feudal contract, lords and vassals were tied together through mutual obligations to each other. On individual estates, lords had a variety of legal rights over their serfs. Serfs could not leave the manor without the lord's permission and could not marry anyone outside the manor without the lord's approval. Lords often had political authority on their lands, which gave them the right to try peasants in their own courts. Peasants were required to pay lords for certain services, such as having their grain ground into flour in the lords' mills.

Even with these restrictions, however, serfs were not slaves. The land assigned to serfs to support themselves usually could not be taken away, and their responsibilities to the lord remained fairly fixed. It was also the lord's duty to protect his serfs, giving them the safety to farm the land.

### The Peasant Household

The life of peasants in Europe was simple. Their cottages had wood frames surrounded by sticks, with the spaces between sticks filled with straw and rubble and then plastered over with clay. Roofs were simply thatched.

The houses of poorer peasants consisted of a single room. Others, however, had at least two rooms—a main room for cooking, eating, and other activities and another room for sleeping. There was little privacy in a medieval household. A hearth in the main room was used for heating and cooking. Because there were few or no windows and no chimney, the smoke created by fires in the hearth went out through cracks in the walls or, more likely, through the thatched roof.

### Cycle of Labor

The seasons of the year largely determined peasant activities. Each season brought a new round of tasks. Harvest time in August and September was especially hectic. A good harvest of grains for making bread was crucial to survival in the winter months.

A new cycle of labor began in October, when peasants worked the ground for the planting of winter crops. In November came the slaughter of excess livestock, because there was usually not enough food to keep the animals alive all winter. The meat would be salted to preserve it for winter use. In February and March, the land was plowed for the planting of spring crops—oats, barley, peas, and beans. Early summer was a fairly relaxed time, although there was still weeding and sheepshearing to be done.

In every season, of course, the serfs worked not only their own land but also the lords' lands. They also tended the small gardens next to their dwellings, where they grew the vegetables that made up part of their diet.

Peasants did not face a life of constant labor, thanks to the feast days, or holidays, of the Catholic Church. These feast days celebrated the great events of the Christian faith, or the lives of Christian saints or holy persons. The three great feasts of the Catholic Church were Christmas (celebrating the birth of Jesus), Easter (celebrating the resurrection of Jesus), and Pentecost (celebrating the descent of the Holy Spirit on Jesus's disciples). Other feasts dedicated to saints or Mary, the mother of Jesus, were also celebrated. More than 50 days were essentially holidays.

Religious feast days, Sunday mass, baptisms, marriages, and funerals all brought peasants into contact with the village church, a crucial part of manorial life. The village priest taught the peasants the basic ideas of Christianity so that they would gain the Christians' final goal—salvation.

**INFOGRAPHICS**

## Life in Medieval Europe

"June" from *Très Riches Heures*, a Book of Hours

### Life as a Serf

- Lords protected serfs
- Serfs had land to grow crops for themselves
- Serfs' land could not be easily taken from them

---

- Legally bound to work the lord's land
- Had to pay to use common land, streams, and ponds
- Lords had political authority over their serfs
- Not permitted to leave the manor without the lord's permission
- Could not marry without the lord's permission

### Life as a Townsperson

- Right to buy and sell property
- Freedom from military service to the lord
- Could purchase freedom
- Self-governing with own law courts

---

- Towns were overcrowded, dirty, and smelly
- Closely grouped wooden houses caught fire easily, often burning entire towns
- Water was often polluted and unsafe to drink

"Commerce" from the *Effects of Good Government*

**CRITICAL THINKING SKILLS**

Some lords granted charters to towns, giving them more independence.

1. **Contrasting** How did freedoms differ between manor and town life?
2. **Drawing Conclusions** Why would some serfs run away to live in a town?

However, village priests were often peasants themselves; most could not read. No one knows how much church teaching the peasants actually understood. Very likely, they saw God as an all-powerful force who needed to be appeased by prayer to bring good harvests.

The position of peasant women in manorial society was both important and difficult. They were expected to work in the fields and at the same time bear children. How well they managed the household determined whether their family starved or survived.

## Food and Drink

Though simple, the daily diet of peasants was adequate when food was available. The basic staple of the peasant diet, and of the medieval diet in general, was bread. Women made the dough for the bread. The loaves were usually baked in community ovens, which the lord owned. Highly nutritious, peasant bread contained not only wheat and rye but also barley, millet, and oats. These ingredients gave the bread a dark appearance and a very heavy, hard texture.

Numerous other foods added to the peasant's diet: vegetables from the household gardens; cheese from cow's or goat's milk; nuts and berries from woodlands; and fruits, such as apples, pears, and cherries. Chickens provided eggs and sometimes meat. Peasants usually ate meat only on the great feast days, such as Christmas and Easter.

Grains were important not only for bread but also for making ale. In the Middle Ages, it was not easy to obtain pure sources of water to drink. Consequently, while wine became the choice of drink for members of the upper classes, ale was the most common drink of the poor. If records are accurate, enormous quantities of ale were consumed. A monastery in the twelfth century records a daily allotment to the monks of three gallons of ale a day. Peasants in the field probably consumed even more.

**✓Reading Check** **Explaining** What role did peasant women play in manorial society?

## The Revival of Trade

**MAIN IDEA** The revival of trade during the High Middle Ages gave rise to a commercial revolution.

**HISTORY & YOU** Do you have to trade one product for another? Read about the emergence of a money economy.

Medieval Europe was an agricultural society with small villages. In the 1000s and 1100s, however, Europe experienced a revival of trade and an associated growth of towns and cities.

The revival of trade in Europe was gradual. Italian cities, such as **Venice**, developed a mercantile fleet (a fleet of trading ships) and became major trading centers in the Mediterranean. The towns of **Flanders**, an area along the coast of present-day Belgium and northern France, were ideally located for northern European traders. Merchants from surrounding areas came to Flanders for woolen cloth.

In the thirteenth century a medieval trade association, the Hanseatic League, developed in the Baltic and North Sea region. The Hanseatic League was an alliance of over one hundred northern European cities that banded together for mutual trade protection and economic opportunity. At its height, the League held a trade monopoly in the region.

By the 1100s, a regular trade had developed between Flanders and Italy. To encourage trade, the counts of Champagne, in northern France, initiated a series of annual trade fairs. Northern European merchants brought furs, woolen cloth, tin, hemp, and honey to trade for cloth and swords from northern Italy and the silks, sugar, and spices of the East.

As trade increased, so did the demand for gold and silver coins. Slowly, a **money economy**—an economic system based on money, rather than barter—emerged. New trading companies and banking firms were set up to manage the exchange and sale of goods. These new practices were part of the rise of **commercial capitalism**, an economic system in which people invested in trade and goods for profit.

**✓Reading Check** **Evaluating** Why were the towns of Flanders busy trading centers?

## The Growth of Cities

**MAIN IDEA** The revival of trade spurred the growth of cities, which became centers for manufacturing and trade.

***HISTORY & YOU*** How would you describe life in your town or city? Read to learn what cities were like in the Middle Ages.

The revival of trade led to a revival of cities. Towns had greatly declined in the Early Middle Ages, especially in Europe north of the Alps. Old Roman cities had continued to exist, but they had dwindled in both size and population.

### Cities Old and New

With the revival of trade, merchants began to settle in the old Roman cities. They were followed by craftspeople or artisans—people who had developed skills and saw a chance to make goods that the merchants could sell. In the course of the eleventh and twelfth centuries, the old Roman cities came alive with new populations and growth.

Many new cities or towns were also founded, especially in northern Europe. Usually, a group of merchants built a settlement near a castle because it was located along a trade route or river and because the lords of the castle would offer protection. If the settlement prospered and expanded, new walls were built to protect it. The merchants and artisans of these cities later came to be called *burghers* or **bourgeoisie**, from the German word *burg*, meaning "a walled enclosure."

Medieval cities were small in comparison with either ancient or modern cities. A large medieval trading city would number about 5000 inhabitants. By the late 1200s, London—England's largest city—had more than 40,000 people. Italian cities tended to be even larger than this. For instance, Venice, Florence, and Milan each had more than 80,000 inhabitants. Even the largest European city, however, seemed small when compared to the Byzantine capital of Constantinople or the Arab cities of Damascus, Baghdad, and Cairo.

Most towns were closely tied to the land around them because they depended on the food grown in the surrounding manors. In addition, the towns were often part of the territory belonging to a lord, and therefore were subject to his authority.

NATIONAL GEOGRAPHIC

**MEDIEVAL CENTERS OF TRADE**

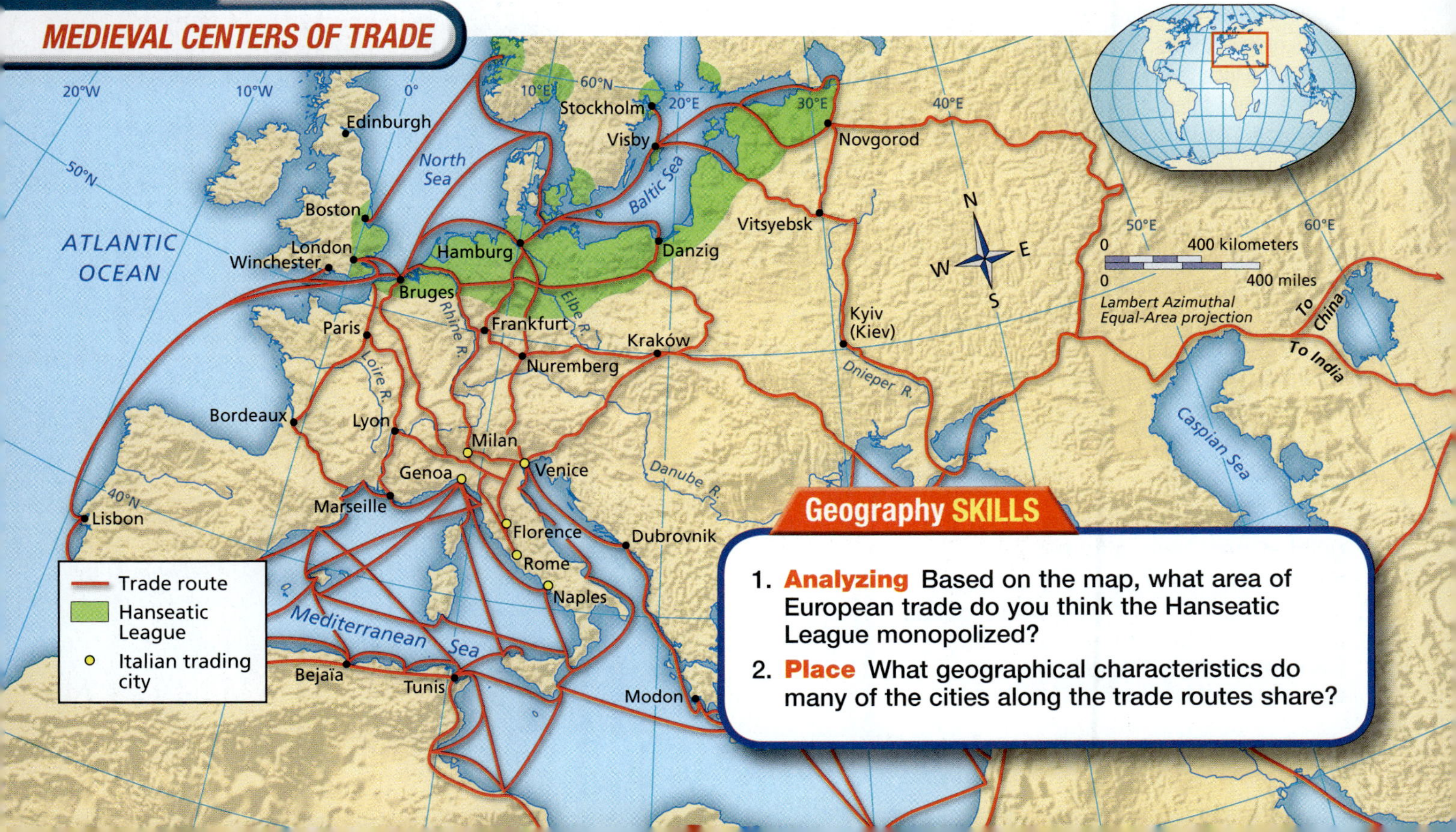


**Geography SKILLS**

1. **Analyzing** Based on the map, what area of European trade do you think the Hanseatic League monopolized?
2. **Place** What geographical characteristics do many of the cities along the trade routes share?

The lords wanted to treat townspeople as they did their vassals and serfs. However, townspeople saw things differently.

Townspeople needed freedom to trade. They needed their own unique laws and were willing to pay for them. Lords and kings, in turn, saw that they could also make money and sold to the townspeople the liberties they wanted.

By 1100, townspeople had numerous rights from local lords. These included the right to buy and sell property, freedom from military service to the lord, a written law that guaranteed townspeople their freedom, and the right for an escaped serf to become a free person after living a year and a day in the town.

The people in almost every new town and city gained these basic liberties. Some new towns also received the right to govern themselves by choosing their own officials and having their own courts of law.

Over time, medieval cities developed their own governments for running the affairs of the community. Only males who had been born in the city or who had lived there for some time were citizens. In many cities, these citizens elected the city council members, who served as judges and city officials and who passed laws. Elections were rigged so that only **patricians**—members of the wealthiest and most powerful families—were elected.

## City Life

Medieval towns were surrounded by stone walls. Walls were expensive to build, so the space within was tightly filled. Thus, medieval cities had narrow, winding streets. Houses were crowded against one another, with the second and third stories built out over the streets. The danger of fire was great. Dwellings were mostly made of wood before the 1300s. Candles and wood fires were used for light and heat. Cities burned rapidly once a fire started.

The physical environment of medieval cities was not pleasant. Often dirty, cities smelled from animal and human waste. Air pollution was also a fact of life. Smoke from wood fires or from the burning of cheap grades of coal filled the air.

**INFOGRAPHICS** | **PRIMARY SOURCE**

### *The Medieval Guild System*

Medieval merchants and artisans formed guilds to promote the common interests of their trades. Guilds achieved a monopoly over commercial activity in the local area, which protected members from competition from artisans of other cities and from competition among themselves. Guilds set rules to assure that all members would prosper equally and rules to regulate labor. Guilds dictated the number of workers their members could employ and established uniform work hours and wages.

Guilds helped to build Europe's economic structure by increasing the number of artisans and merchants. They built roads and schools. Guilds often controlled town governments, creating a stable environment for commerce. Guilds helped to transition Europe from feudalism to a new economic system—capitalism. By the 1500s, guilds could not compete with early factories and large-scale production, and the guild system slowly faded away.

**CRITICAL THINKING SKILLS**

1. **Making Inferences** How might the guild system have affected prices for local consumers?
2. **Analyzing Visuals** Why would guilds use symbols in addition to words? Can you identify the glovemaker, armorer, and barber?

Emblems of different medieval guilds in Umbria, Italy

Cities also suffered from water pollution. The tanners, butchers, and other industries dumped waste products into European rivers, causing them to become polluted. Cities did not use the rivers for drinking water but relied instead on wells or aqueducts. Private and public baths also existed in medieval towns. However, city authorities came under increasing pressure to close baths due to moral concerns about public nudity. The great plague of the fourteenth century (see Section 4) sealed the fate of these baths.

Considerably more men than women lived in medieval cities. Women were expected to supervise the household, prepare meals, raise the children, and manage the family's finances. Often, they helped their husbands in their trades. Some women developed their own trades to earn extra money. Sometimes, when a master craftsman died, his widow carried on his trade. It was thus possible for women in medieval towns to lead quite independent lives. In fact, many women became brewers, weavers, and hatmakers.

## Industry and Guilds

With the revival of trade, cities and towns became important centers for manufacturing a wide range of goods, such as cloth, metalwork, shoes, and leather goods. Many craft activities were carried on in houses located in the narrow streets of medieval cities.

From the 1000s on, craftspeople began to organize themselves into **guilds**, or business associations. Guilds played a leading role in the economic life of cities. By the 1200s, there were guilds for almost every craft (tanners, bakers) and separate guilds for specialized groups of merchants, such as dealers in silk, spices, or wool.

Craft guilds directed almost every aspect of the production process. They set the standards for the quality of the articles produced, specified the methods of production to be used, and even fixed the price at which the finished goods could be sold. Guilds also determined the number of people who could enter a specific trade and the procedure they must follow to do so.

A person who wanted to learn a trade first became an **apprentice**, usually at around the age of 10, to a master craftsperson. Apprentices were not paid, but they did receive room and board from their masters. After five to seven years of service during which they learned their craft, apprentices became **journeymen** and worked for wages for other masters. Journeymen aspired to become masters as well. To do so, they were expected to produce a **masterpiece**, a finished piece in their craft. This piece allowed the master craftspeople of the guild to judge whether a journeyman was qualified to become a master and join the guild.

✓Reading Check **Evaluating** What role did guilds play in the economic life of the cities?

## SECTION 1 REVIEW

### Vocabulary

1. **Explain** the significance of: technology, crucial, *carruca*, manor, serfs, Venice, Flanders, money economy, commercial capitalism, bourgeoisie, patricians, guilds, apprentice, journeymen, masterpiece.

### Main Ideas

2. **Explain** how the new crop rotation increased food production.
3. **Identify** the economic developments of the Middle Ages that allowed commercial capitalism to emerge. Use a diagram like the one below.

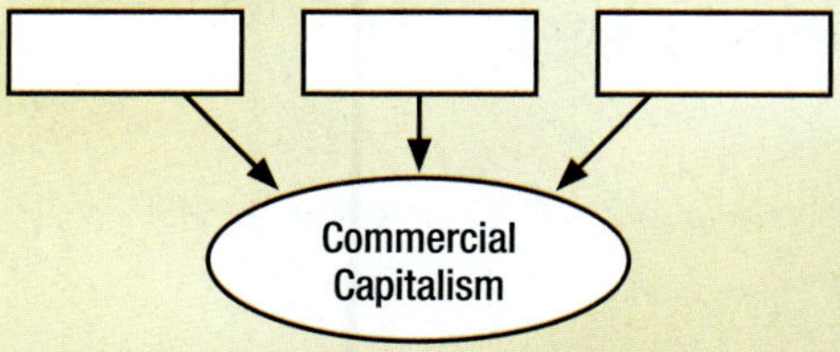


4. **Describe** the physical environment of medieval cities.

### Critical Thinking

5. **The BIG Idea** **Determining Cause and Effect** What were some major results of farming improvements and the revival of trade in the Middle Ages?
6. **Comparing and Contrasting** How did living and working in a medieval city differ from living and working on a manor?
7. **Analyzing Visuals** Examine the illustration on page 340. Choose three emblems and try to name the craft each represents.

### Writing About History

8. **Persuasive Writing** Imagine you are a trader doing business at the beginning of the money economy. Write a letter addressed to other traders convincing them to convert to a money system from bartering.

**History ONLINE**

For help with the concepts in this section of *Glencoe World History*, go to glencoe.com and click Study Central™.

SECTION 2 Section Audio Spotlight Video

# Medieval Christianity

## GUIDE TO READING

### The BIG Idea

**Ideas, Beliefs, and Values** With its strong leadership, the Catholic Church became a dominant and forceful presence in medieval society.

### Content Vocabulary

- lay investiture *(p. 342)*
- interdict *(p. 344)*
- sacraments *(p. 344)*
- heresy *(p. 346)*
- relics *(p. 347)*

### Academic Vocabulary

- pursue *(p. 342)*
- remove *(p. 343)*

### People, Places, and Events

- Papal States *(p. 342)*
- Pope Gregory VII *(p. 342)*
- Henry IV *(p. 343)*
- Concordat of Worms *(p. 343)*
- Pope Innocent III *(p. 344)*
- Cistercians *(p. 344)*
- Hildegard of Bingen *(p. 345)*
- Franciscans *(p. 345)*
- Dominicans *(p. 345)*
- Francis of Assisi *(p. 345)*
- Assisi *(p. 345)*
- Inquisition *(p. 346)*

### Reading Strategy

**Categorizing Information** As you read, use a chart like the one below to list characteristics of the Cistercian and Dominican religious orders.

| Cistercians | Dominicans |
|---|---|
| | |
| | |

*Under Pope Gregory VII, the Catholic Church disentangled itself from secular influence in the eleventh century. The Church reached the height of its political power in the thirteenth century under Pope Innocent III. Religious enthusiasm spread and new monastic orders emerged. By the High Middle Ages, the Catholic Church had become a dominant and forceful presence in European society.*

## The Papal Monarchy

**MAIN IDEA** During the papacy of Pope Innocent III in the thirteenth century, the Catholic Church reached the height of its political power.

**HISTORY & YOU** Can a religious leader be an effective military leader? Read how Church officials were obliged to carry out military duties for their lords.

Since the fifth century, the popes of the Catholic Church had claimed supremacy over the affairs of the Church. They had also gained control of territories in central Italy that came to be known as the **Papal States.** This control kept the popes involved in political matters, often at the expense of their spiritual duties.

At the same time, the Church became increasingly involved in the feudal system. Chief officials of the Church, such as bishops and abbots, came to hold their offices as grants from nobles. As vassals, they were obliged to carry out the usual feudal services, including military duties. Lords often chose their vassals from other noble families for political reasons. Thus, the bishops and abbots they chose were often worldly figures who cared little about their spiritual duties. The Catholic Church was in danger of becoming more of a political than a religious institution.

### Reform of the Papacy

By the eleventh century, Church leaders realized the need to be free from the lords' interference in the appointment of Church officials. When an individual became a Church official in the Middle Ages, he was given a ring and a staff. These objects symbolized the spiritual authority with which the Church granted, or invested, the official. Secular, or lay, rulers usually chose nominees to Church offices and gave them the symbols of their office, a practice known as **lay investiture. Pope Gregory VII** decided to fight this practice.

Elected pope in 1073, Gregory was convinced that he had been chosen by God to reform the Church. To **pursue** this aim, Gregory claimed that he—the pope—was truly God's "vicar on earth" and that the pope's authority extended over all the Christian world,

INFOGRAPHICS

## The Investiture Controversy

### *Conflict Between King Henry IV and Pope Gregory VII*

Pope Gregory believed he had a divine mission to reform the Church. Ending lay investiture—which would minimize the role of secular leaders—was key to his reforms.

**1075:** Gregory bans lay investiture, asserting supremacy of Church over lay authority. Henry invests a new bishop of Milan, replacing Gregory's choice.

**1076:** Gregory deposes and excommunicates Henry.

**1077:** Henry submits to Gregory and is absolved. German princes declare Henry dethroned and elect Rudolf, sparking civil war.

**1080:** Gregory supports Rudolf over Henry. Henry names an antipope, Clement III. Gregory excommunicates them both.

**1081:** Henry wins the civil war and marches on Rome.

**1084:** Henry conquers Rome. Gregory flees the city.

**1105:** Henry is forced to abdicate as his continued support for Clement III weakened his rule.

This lengthy struggle between Henry and Gregory was as much political as religious. In the end, however, neither won a decisive victory. The investiture controversy was one of many confrontations in the power struggle between secular leaders and the Church.

"I withdraw . . . from Henry the King . . . the rule over the whole kingdom of the Germans and over Italy. And I absolve all Christians from the bonds of the oath which they have made or shall make to him. . . . I bind him in thy stead with the chain of the anathema [a damned person] . . ."

—Pope Gregory VII, February 1076

**In 1077, a year after Pope Gregory excommunicated him, Henry humbled himself before the pontiff, who absolved him, removing the excommunication.**

**CRITICAL THINKING SKILLS**

1. **Analyzing** What does this conflict indicate about medieval ideas of power, authority, and governance?
2. **Drawing Conclusions** How did Henry's conflict with Gregory affect Henry's reign?

including its rulers. Only by eliminating lay investiture could the Church regain its independence. The Church would appoint clergy and run its own affairs. If rulers did not accept this, the pope would **remove** them.

Gregory VII soon found himself in conflict with the king of Germany over these claims. King **Henry IV** of Germany was also a determined person. For many years, German kings had appointed high-ranking clerics, especially bishops, as their vassals, in order to use them as administrators.

Without them, the king could not hope to maintain power over the German nobles. In 1075, Pope Gregory issued a decree forbidding high-ranking clerics from receiving their investiture from lay leaders: "We decree that no one of the clergy shall receive the investiture with a bishopric or abbey or church from the hand of an emperor or king or of any lay person." Henry, however, had no intention of obeying a papal decree that challenged the heart of his administration.

The struggle between Henry IV and Gregory VII, known as the Investiture Controversy, was one of the great conflicts between church and state in the High Middle Ages. It lasted until a new German king and a new pope reached a compromise known as the **Concordat of Worms** in 1122. Under this agreement, a bishop in Germany was first elected by Church officials.

After election, the new bishop paid homage to the king as his feudal lord. The king in turn invested him with the symbols of temporal (earthly) office. A representative of the pope, however, then invested the new bishop with the symbols of his spiritual office.

## The Church Supreme

Pope Gregory VII also tried to improve the Church's ability to provide spiritual guidance to the faithful. Twelfth-century popes did not give up the reform ideals of Pope Gregory VII, but they were even more inclined to strengthen papal power and build a strong administrative system. During the papacy of **Pope Innocent III** in the 1200s, the Catholic Church reached the height of its political power. At the beginning of his rule in 1198, in a letter to a priest, the pope made a clear statement of his views on papal supremacy:

**PRIMARY SOURCE**

"As God, the creator of the universe, set two great lights in the firmament of heaven, the greater light to rule the day, and the lesser light to rule the night so He set two great dignities in the firmament of the universal Church, . . . the greater to rule the day, that is, souls, and the lesser to rule the night, that is, bodies. These dignities are the papal authority and the royal power. And just as the moon gets her light from the sun, and is inferior to the sun . . . so the royal power gets the splendor of its dignity from the papal authority."

—Pope Innocent III

To achieve his political ends, Innocent used the spiritual weapons at his command. His favorite was the **interdict**. An interdict forbids priests from giving the **sacraments** (Christian rites) of the Church to a particular group of people. The goal was to cause the people under interdiction, who were deprived of the comforts of religion, to exert pressure against their ruler. With an interdict, Innocent III forced the king of France, Philip Augustus, to take back his wife after Philip had tried to have his marriage annulled.

**✓Reading Check** **Explaining** What was the significance of the Concordat of Worms?

# New Religious Orders

**MAIN IDEA** As religious enthusiasm spread through Europe, new monastic orders emerged.

**HISTORY & YOU** What does the phrase "innocent until proven guilty" mean to you? Read to learn how the Inquisition "proved" the guilt of heretics.

In the late 1000s and early 1100s, a wave of religious enthusiasm seized Europe. This movement led to a rise in the number of monasteries and the emergence of new monastic orders. Both men and women joined religious orders in increasing numbers.

## A New Activism

In the eleventh century, more new monastic orders arose and became important. One of the most important new orders of the Middle Ages was the Cistercian (sis•TUHR•shuhn) order. It was founded in 1098 by a group of monks who were unhappy with the lack of discipline at their own Benedictine monastery. Cistercian monasticism spread rapidly from southern France into the rest of Europe.

The **Cistercians** were strict. They ate a simple diet, and each had only a single robe. All decorations were eliminated from their churches and monastic buildings. More time for prayer and manual labor was gained by spending fewer hours at religious services.

The Cistercians played a major role in developing a new, activistic spiritual model for twelfth-century Europe. While Benedictine monks spent hours inside the monastery in personal prayer, the Cistercians took their religion to the people outside the monastery. More than any other person, Bernard of Clairvaux embodied the new spiritual ideal of Cistercian monasticism: "Arise, soldier of Christ, arise! Get up off the ground and return to the battle from which you have fled! Fight more boldly after your flight, and triumph in glory!"

## Women in Religious Orders

Women were also actively involved in the spiritual movements of the age. The number of women joining religious houses grew dramatically. In the High Middle

Ages, most nuns were from the ranks of the landed aristocracy. Convents were convenient for families who were unable or unwilling to find husbands for their daughters, for aristocratic women who did not wish to marry, or for widows.

Female intellectuals found convents a haven for their activities. Most learned women of the Middle Ages, especially in Germany, were nuns. This was certainly true of **Hildegard of Bingen**, who became abbess of a religious house for females in western Germany. She was one of the first women composers and was an important contributor to the body of music known as Gregorian chant. Her work is remarkable because she succeeded at a time when music, especially sacred music, was almost exclusively the domain of men.

## Franciscans and Dominicans

In the 1200s two new religious orders emerged that had a strong impact on the lives of ordinary people. They were the **Franciscans** and the **Dominicans**.

The Franciscans were founded by **Francis of Assisi**. Francis was born to a wealthy Italian merchant family in **Assisi**. After having been captured and imprisoned during a local war, he had a series of dramatic spiritual experiences. These experiences led him to abandon all worldly goods and material pursuits and to live and preach in poverty, working and begging for his food. His simplicity, joyful nature, and love for others soon attracted a band of followers, all of whom took vows of absolute poverty, agreeing to reject all property and live by working and begging for their food.

The Franciscans became very popular. They lived among the people, preaching repentance and aiding the poor. Their calls for a return to the simplicity and poverty of the early Church, reinforced by their own example, were especially effective. The Franciscans also undertook missionary work, first throughout Italy and then to all parts of Europe and even to the Muslim world.

## PEOPLE *in* HISTORY

### Hildegard of Bingen
1098–1179 Medieval Abbess

Hildegard was a weak and sickly child. From an early age, she received mystical visions. "I saw much, and related some of the things seen to others, who would inquire with astonishment, whence such things might come. . . . I would relate future things, which I saw as if present." When she was 43, the Church confirmed the authenticity of her visions. With Church approval, she recorded 26 prophecies in her work *Scivias* (Know the Way). Powerful men, including kings and popes, sought her advice. About 1147 Hildegard founded a new convent, where she continued to record her visions and write on many topics. She also composed lyric poems and music. Although never formally canonized, she is considered a saint by the Catholic Church. **Why did powerful men seek Hildegard's advice?**

### Francis of Assisi
1182–1226 Medieval Monk

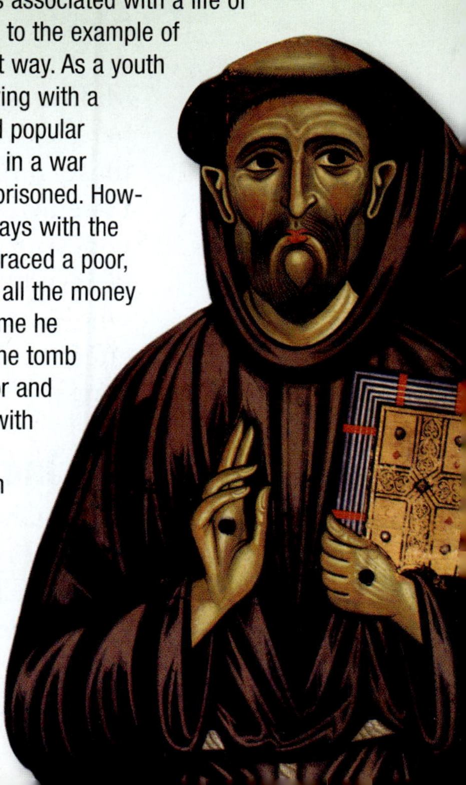

Although Francis of Assisi is associated with a life of poverty, humility, and devotion to the example of Jesus, he did not start out that way. As a youth he was handsome and fun-loving with a fondness for fancy clothes and popular songs. He even fought bravely in a war before being captured and imprisoned. However, his sympathies were always with the poor. On one occasion he embraced a poor, disfigured leper and gave him all the money he had. On a pilgrimage to Rome he emptied his money pouch at the tomb of Peter, giving it all to the poor and exchanging his fancy clothes with those of a beggar. His humility and generosity have made him one of the Catholic Church's most beloved saints. **With whom did Francis of Assisi sympathize?**

## INFOGRAPHICS

### The Inquisition

The Church's desire to have a method of discovering and dealing with heretics led to the creation of the Inquisition. In the 1230s, Pope Gregory IX began appointing "inquisitors" who searched Europe for heretics. If an accused heretic confessed, he or she was forced to perform public penance and was subject to punishment. Punishment varied considerably. Confessed heretics might be ordered to do good works, such as build a church or go on a pilgrimage. Or, they could be sentenced to physical punishment (such as flogging); public degradation (being locked in a pillory—a wooden device that clamped around a person's head and hands); or imprisonment. In some parts of Europe, accused heretics who did not confess or who repeated their heresy were burned at the stake.

In 1478 King Ferdinand and Queen Isabella introduced the Inquisition to Spain. The Spanish Inquisition—in which inquisitors were appointed and paid for by the monarchy, rather than by the Church—was responsible for many of the excesses associated with the Inquisition. In 1492 Ferdinand and Isabella declared that all Jews must leave Spain or convert to Christianity. Jews who converted and remained, however, often became targets of the Inquisition, coming under suspicion of not having truly converted. In the 1500s baptized Muslims and Protestants also became victims of the Inquisition. In addition, Spain extended the Inquisition overseas as it established its vast empire in the New World. The Spanish Inquisition, which was not officially abolished until 1834, was part of the Spanish monarchy's crusade to root out heresy and ensure the supremacy of the Church.

This woodcut depicts heretics burned at the stake in 1557.

**CRITICAL THINKING SKILLS**

1. **Interpreting** How did the Inquisition reinforce the authority of the Catholic Church?
2. **Explaining** How was the Spanish Inquisition different from the Inquisition of earlier centuries?

The Dominican order was founded by a Spanish priest, Dominic de Guzmán. Dominic wanted to defend Church teachings from **heresy**—the denial of basic Church doctrines. The spiritual revival of the High Middle Ages had led to the emergence of heresies within the Church. Adherents of these movements were called heretics. Heretical movements became especially widespread in southern France. Dominic believed that a new religious order of men who lived in poverty and could preach effectively would best be able to attack heresy.

## The Inquisition

The Church created a court called the **Inquisition**, or Holy Office, to deal with heretics. This court developed a regular procedure to find and try heretics. The Dominicans became especially well known for their roles as examiners of people suspected of heresy.

Those who confessed to heresy performed public penance and received punishment, such as flogging. Beginning in 1252, the Inquisition added the element of torture to extract confessions. Those who did not confess but were still considered guilty and those who had done penance for heresy and then relapsed were subject to execution by the state.

Thirteenth-century Christians believed the only path to salvation was through the Church. To them, heresy was a crime against God and humanity. In their minds, using force to save souls from damnation was the right thing to do.

**✓ Reading Check** **Analyzing** Why did the Franciscans choose to live simply?

## Religion in the High Middle Ages

**MAIN IDEA** Ordinary people observed the Church's sacraments, venerated saints, and took pilgrimages to holy shrines.

**HISTORY & YOU** Do you have a good luck charm? Read to learn about the importance of relics to people in the High Middle Ages.

The Church of the High Middle Ages was a crucial part of ordinary people's lives from birth to death. The sacraments, such as baptism, marriage, and the Eucharist (Communion), were seen as means for receiving God's grace and were necessary for salvation. Since only the clergy could administer these rites, people depended on them to achieve this goal. Ordinary people also venerated saints—men and women who, because of their holiness, had achieved a special position in Heaven. Since saints could ask for favors before the throne of God for people who prayed to them, they were very popular with all Christians.

Among the recognized saints were Jesus' apostles, Mary, and numerous local saints of special significance to a single area. The Italians, for example, had Saint Nicholas, the patron saint of children, who is known today as Santa Claus. Of all the saints, Mary, who was the mother of Jesus, was the most highly regarded in the High Middle Ages. A sign of Mary's importance is the number of churches all over Europe that were dedicated to her in the 1100s and 1200s. (Such churches in France were named Notre Dame, or "Our Lady.")

Emphasis on the role of the saints was closely tied to the use of **relics**, usually bones of saints or objects connected with saints. Relics were considered worthy of worship because they provided a link between the earthly world and God. It was believed that relics could heal people or produce other miracles. A twelfth-century English monk wrote about an abbey's relics: "There is kept there a thing more precious than gold, . . . the right arm of St. Oswald. . . . This we have seen with our own eyes and have kissed, and have handled with our own hands. . . . There are kept here also part of his ribs and of the soil on which he fell."

Medieval Christians also believed that a pilgrimage to a holy shrine produced a spiritual benefit. The greatest shrine, but the most difficult to reach, was the Holy City of Jerusalem. On the continent two pilgrim centers were especially popular in the High Middle Ages: Rome, which contained the relics of Peter and Paul, and the Spanish town of Santiago de Compostela, supposedly the site of the tomb of the apostle James. Local shrines dedicated to Mary also became pilgrimage centers.

**✓Reading Check** **Examining** Why were saints important to Christians in the High Middle Ages?

## SECTION 2 REVIEW

### Vocabulary

1. **Explain** the significance of: Papal States, lay investiture, Pope Gregory VII, pursue, remove, Henry IV, Concordat of Worms, Pope Innocent III, interdict, sacraments, Cistercians, Hildegard of Bingen, Franciscans, Dominicans, Francis of Assisi, Assisi, heresy, Inquisition, relics.

### Main Ideas

2. **Summarize** the opposing viewpoints in the investiture controversy and the resulting compromise at Worms. Use a diagram like the one below.

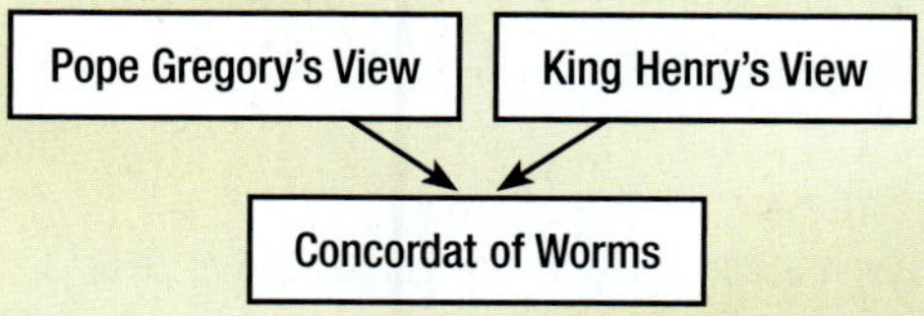


3. **Explain** how women were involved in the spiritual movements of the Middle Ages.
4. **Define** a relic and explain its significance to people of the Middle Ages.

### Critical Thinking

5. **The BIG Idea** **Evaluating** Why was the Church such a powerful influence in lay people's lives during the Middle Ages?
6. **Drawing Conclusions** Do you think the Inquisition's methods accurately identified heretics? Explain.
7. **Analyzing Visuals** Examine the painting on page 343. What does King Henry's posture tell you about his relationship with Pope Gregory?

### Writing About History

8. **Expository Writing** Describe the power struggle between secular and religious authorities. How did the Church exercise political power in the Middle Ages? How did secular leaders attempt to challenge this authority?

**History ONLINE**

For help with the concepts in this section of *Glencoe World History,* go to glencoe.com and click Study Central™.

SECTION 3

Section Audio

Spotlight Video

# Culture of the High Middle Ages

## GUIDE TO READING

### The BIG Idea

**New Technologies** Technological innovations made Gothic cathedrals possible, while an intellectual revival led to the formation of universities.

### Content Vocabulary

- theology *(p. 350)*
- scholasticism *(p. 350)*
- vernacular *(p. 351)*
- chanson de geste *(p. 351)*

### Academic Vocabulary

- construction *(p. 348)*
- corporation *(p. 350)*

### People, Places, and Events

- Bologna *(p. 350)*
- Paris *(p. 350)*
- Oxford *(p. 350)*
- Aristotle *(p. 350)*
- Thomas Aquinas *(p. 350)*
- *Summa Theologica* *(p. 350)*

### Reading Strategy

**Contrasting** As you read, use a chart to contrast the Romanesque style of architecture with the Gothic style of architecture. How did the churches built in these two styles differ?

| Romanesque | Gothic |
|---|---|
| | |
| | |

*During the eleventh and twelfth centuries, Europe witnessed a surge in architectural innovations and an intellectual revival. The development of ribbed vaults, pointed arches, and flying buttresses allowed the building of expansive, beautiful cathedrals. The innovative design became known as the Gothic style. An intellectual revival gave rise to Europe's first universities.*

## Architecture

**MAIN IDEA** Gothic cathedrals, an artistic triumph of the High Middle Ages, were built in the twelfth and thirteenth centuries.

**HISTORY & YOU** Have you seen stained glass windows in a church? Read to learn how builders in the High Middle Ages improved on an architectural style of the ancient Romans.

The eleventh and twelfth centuries witnessed an explosion of building in medieval Europe, especially building of churches. The cathedrals of the eleventh and twelfth centuries were built in the Romanesque style. Romanesque churches were normally built in the basilica shape used in the **construction** of churches in the late Roman Empire.

Basilicas were rectangular buildings with flat wooden roofs. Romanesque builders replaced the basilica's flat wooden roof with a long, round stone arched vault (called a barrel vault) or with a cross vault, in which two barrel vaults intersected. The builder used the cross vault to create a church plan in the shape of a cross. Barrel and cross vaults were considered more beautiful than flat roofs.

Because stone roofs were extremely heavy, Romanesque churches required massive pillars and walls to hold them up. This left little space for windows, so Romanesque churches were dark on the inside. With massive walls and pillars, these churches resembled fortresses.

A new style, called Gothic, appeared in the twelfth century and was brought to perfection in the thirteenth. The Gothic cathedral remains one of the greatest artistic triumphs of the High Middle Ages. Two basic innovations made Gothic cathedrals possible.

One innovation was the replacement of the round barrel vault of Romanesque churches with a combination of ribbed vaults and pointed arches. This change enabled builders to make Gothic churches higher than Romanesque churches. The use of pointed arches and ribbed vaults also creates an impression of upward movement, as if the building is reaching to God.

PRIMARY SOURCE **HISTORY & ARTS**

## Gothic Architecture

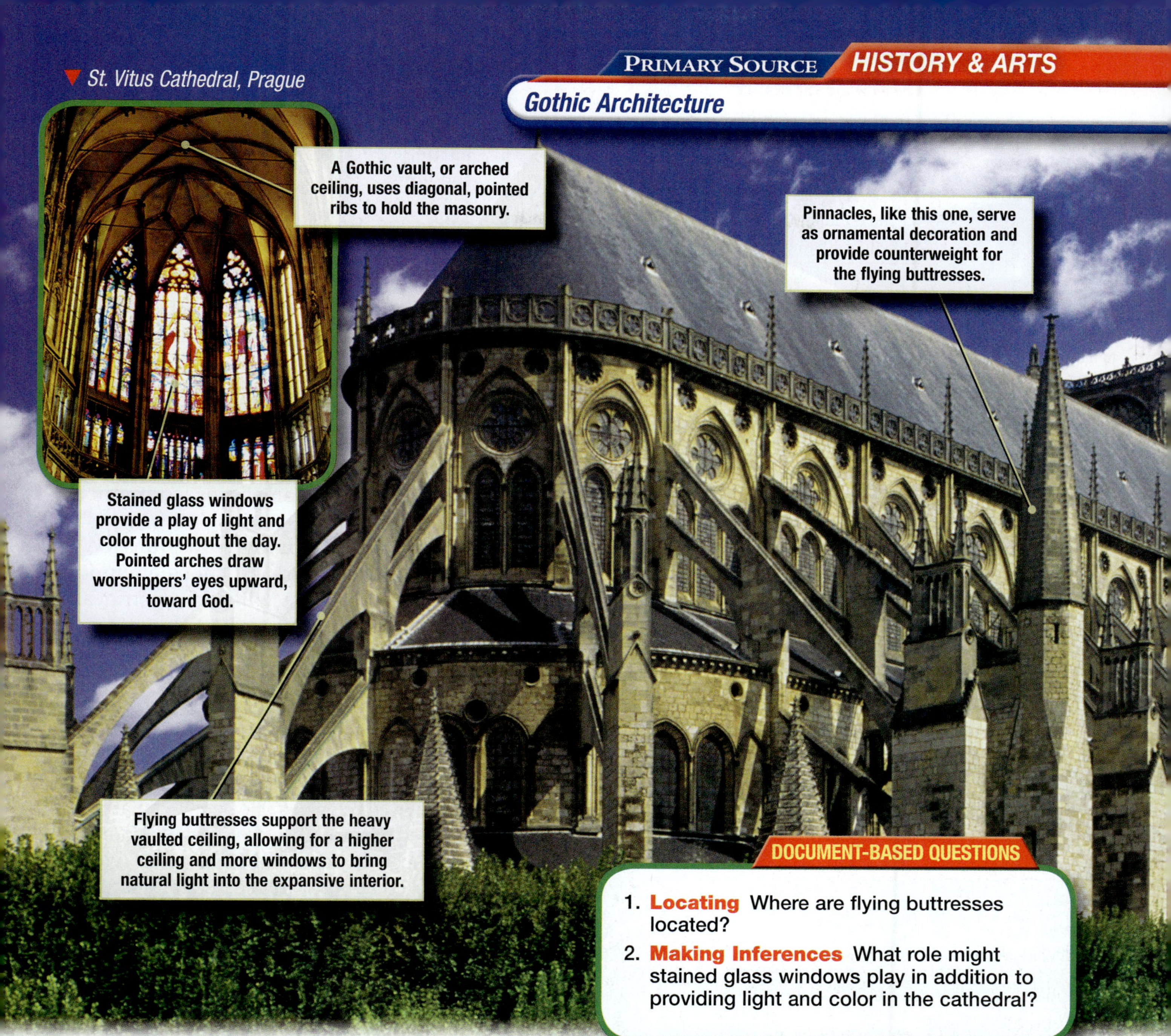


▼ *St. Vitus Cathedral, Prague*

*St. Etienne Cathedral, Bourges, France* ▲

**DOCUMENT-BASED QUESTIONS**

1. **Locating** Where are flying buttresses located?
2. **Making Inferences** What role might stained glass windows play in addition to providing light and color in the cathedral?

Another technical innovation was the flying buttress—a heavy, arched support of stone built onto the outside of the walls. Flying buttresses made it possible to distribute the weight of the church's vaulted ceilings outward and down. This eliminated the heavy walls needed in Romanesque churches to hold the weight of the massive barrel vaults.

Gothic cathedrals were built, then, with relatively thin walls. Since they were not supporting great weight, these walls could be filled with stained glass windows.

These windows depict both religious scenes and scenes from daily life. The colored glass windows create a play of light inside the cathedral that varies with the sun at different times of the day. Natural light was believed to be a symbol of the divine light of God. The Gothic cathedral, with its towers soaring toward Heaven, bears witness to an age when most people believed in a spiritual world.

✓Reading Check **Explaining** How was a cross shape created in Romanesque buildings?

**History ONLINE**
**Student Web Activity—** Visit glencoe.com and complete the activity on **the Middle Ages.**

## Universities

**MAIN IDEA** Medieval university students applied scholasticism to the study of theology.

***HISTORY & YOU*** For how many more years are you prepared to go to school? Read to learn how medieval students earned a degree.

See page R39 to read excerpts from Christine de Pizan's *A Woman May Need to Have the Heart of a Man* in **Primary Sources and Literature Library.**

The university of today, with faculty, students, and degrees, was a product of the High Middle Ages. The word university comes from the Latin word *universitas,* meaning **"corporation"** or "guild."

The first European university appeared in **Bologna** (buh•LOH•nyuh), Italy. Students, men only, came from all over Europe to learn law from the great teacher Irnerius. The University of Paris was the first university in northern Europe. In the late 1300s, many students and masters (teachers) left **Paris** and started their own university at **Oxford**, England. Kings, popes, and princes thought it honorable to found universities. By 1500, Europe had 80 universities.

Students began by studying the liberal arts—grammar, rhetoric, logic, arithmetic, geometry, music, and astronomy. Teachers lectured by reading from a basic text and adding explanations. After four to six years, students took oral examinations to earn a bachelor of arts degree and later a master of arts. After about ten more years, students earned a doctor of law, medicine, or theology.

The most highly regarded subject was **theology**—the study of religion and God. The study of theology was strongly influenced by a philosophical system known as **scholasticism**. Scholasticism tried to reconcile faith and reason—to show that faith was in harmony with reason and experience. Its chief task was to harmonize Christian teachings with the works of the Greek philosophers. **Aristotle** reached his conclusions by rational thought, not by faith, and his ideas sometimes contradicted Church teachings.

In the 1200s, **Thomas Aquinas** (uh•KWY•nuhs) made the most famous attempt to reconcile Aristotle with the doctrines of Christianity. Aquinas is best known for his ***Summa Theologica*** (*summa* was a summary of all knowledge on a topic). His masterpiece followed a logical method of scholarly investigation. Aquinas first posed a question such as, "Does God exist?" He then cited opposing opinions before coming to his own conclusions. He believed that truths arrived at through reason or faith could not conflict with each other. Reason, without faith, could only reveal truths about the physical world, not spiritual truths.

The scholastics that followed Aquinas, including John Duns Scotus and William Ockham, continued to question the relationship between reason and faith. This study resulted in Ockham's Razor, a principle stating that when faced with opposing theories the simplest explanation is preferred. This became a foundation for what would become the scientific method.

In the late 1260s, at the request of Pope Clement IV, the English philosopher Roger Bacon wrote *Opus Majus,* an encyclopedia advocating a reformation of all sciences including logic, mathematics, physics, experimentation, and philosophy. After Clement's death, these revolutionary ideas resulted in Bacon's imprisonment.

**Reading Check** **Explaining** What was the main goal of scholasticism?

## PEOPLE *in* HISTORY

### Thomas Aquinas

**1225?–1274 Medieval Theologian**

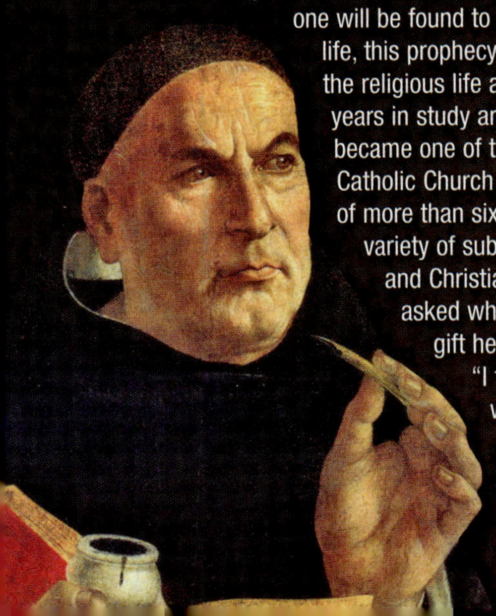

Just before Thomas's birth, a village holy man predicted to his mother, "so great will be his learning and sanctity that in his day no one will be found to equal him." By the end of his life, this prophecy had been fulfilled. He entered the religious life at an early age and spent many years in study and meditation. Over time he became one of the greatest intellectuals the Catholic Church ever produced. He left a body of more than sixty scholarly works on a wide variety of subjects, chiefly Greek philosophy and Christian doctrine. Thomas was once asked what he considered the greatest gift he had ever received. He replied, "I think that of having understood whatever I have read." **What were the chief subjects of Thomas's writings?**

## Vernacular Literature

**MAIN IDEA** Troubadour poetry and the heroic epic poem were popular forms of vernacular literature in the twelfth century.

**HISTORY & YOU** What types of books do you enjoy—mystery, science fiction, nonfiction? Read to learn what type of literature was popular during the High Middle Ages.

Latin was the universal language of medieval civilization. Used in the Church and schools, Latin enabled learned people to communicate anywhere in Europe. However, in the twelfth century, much new literature was being written in the **vernacular**—the language of everyday speech in a particular region, such as Spanish, French, English, or German. A new market for vernacular literature appeared in the twelfth century when educated laypeople (religious people who were not clergy) at courts and in the cities took an interest in new sources of entertainment.

Perhaps the most popular vernacular literature of the twelfth century was troubadour poetry, which was chiefly the product of nobles and knights. This poetry told of the love of a knight for a lady, who inspires him to become a braver knight and a better poet. A good example is from the noble Jaufré Rudel, who cherished a dream woman from afar. He feared that he would never meet her, but would always love her.

**PRIMARY SOURCE**

"Most sad, most joyous shall I go away,
Let me have seen her for a single day,
My love afar,
I shall not see her, for her land and mine
Are sundered, and the ways are hard to find,
So many ways, and I shall lose my way,
So wills it God.
Yet shall I know no other love but hers,
And if not hers, no other love at all."

—Jaufré Rudel

Another type of vernacular literature was known as the **chanson de geste**, or heroic epic. The earliest and finest example of such literature is the *Song of Roland*, which appeared around 1100 and was written in French. The chief events described in heroic epic poems are battles and political contests. The epic world is one of combat, in which knights fight courageously for their kings and lords. Women play only a small role or no role at all in heroic epic poems.

**✓ Reading Check** **Identifying** What were two popular types of vernacular literature in the twelfth century?

## SECTION 3 REVIEW

### Vocabulary

1. **Explain** the significance of: construction, corporation, Bologna, Paris, Oxford, theology, scholasticism, Aristotle, Thomas Aquinas, *Summa Theologica*, vernacular, chanson de geste.

### Main Ideas

2. **Summarize** the evolution of church architecture by describing the features and innovations in a diagram like the one below.

| Basilica | → | Romanesque | → | Gothic |
|---|---|---|---|---|

3. **List** the fields of study in which a medieval university student could earn a doctor's degree.
4. **Identify** the chief events in heroic epic poems.

### Critical Thinking

5. **The BIG Idea** **Analyzing** How did the architecture of the Gothic cathedral reflect medieval religious values?
6. **Comparing and Contrasting** Compare what you know of modern university courses of study with those of the first European universities. What are the similarities and differences?
7. **Analyzing Visuals** Imagine yourself standing inside the Gothic cathedral shown on page 349. How would you describe the look and feel of the interior?

### Writing About History

8. **Persuasive Writing** Use a word processing program to create an illustrated brochure to attract students to a new medieval university in Venice. Include information on the method of education and degree and course offerings. Provide a "frequently asked questions" section.

**History ONLINE**

For help with the concepts in this section of *Glencoe World History*, go to glencoe.com and click Study Central™.

SECTION 4

Section Audio

Spotlight Video

# The Late Middle Ages

## GUIDE TO READING

### The BIG Idea

**Devastation of War** Disastrous forces overwhelmed Europe in the fourteenth century with lasting consequences.

### Content Vocabulary

- anti-Semitism *(p. 353)*
- new monarchies *(p. 357)*
- *taille (p. 357)*

### Academic Vocabulary

- abandoned *(p. 352)*
- consequences *(p. 353)*

### People, Places, and Events

- Black Death *(p. 352)*
- Pope Boniface VIII *(p. 355)*
- King Philip IV *(p. 355)*
- Avignon *(p. 355)*
- Great Schism *(p. 355)*
- John Hus *(p. 355)*
- Henry V *(p. 356)*
- Agincourt *(p. 356)*
- Joan of Arc *(p. 356)*
- Orléans *(p. 356)*
- Isabella *(p. 358)*
- Ferdinand *(p. 359)*

### Reading Strategy

**Determining Cause and Effect** As you read, use a diagram like the one below to identify three reasons for the decline of the papacy.

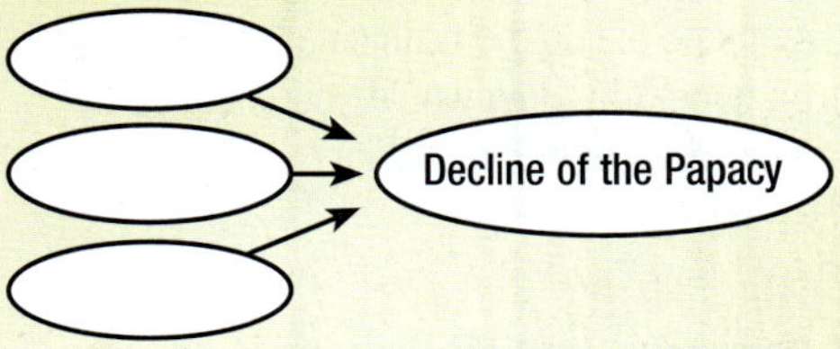


*Medieval European society reached its high point in the 1200s. However, everything changed in the 1300s when a series of disastrous forces overwhelmed Europe. The Black Death spread, killing over one-third of the population. People's faith in the papacy was undermined when the Great Schism rocked the Catholic Church. Then, the Hundred Years' War started. Recovery began in the 1400s, and rulers responded by establishing their "new" monarchies.*

## The Black Death

**MAIN IDEA** Spreading throughout Europe during the mid-fourteenth century, the Black Death had disastrous social and economic effects.

**HISTORY & YOU** What if one-third of your town's population just suddenly disappeared? Read to learn about the spread of the Black Death.

The Middle Ages in Europe had reached a high point in the 1200s. In the 1300s, however, some disastrous changes took place. Especially catastrophic was the **Black Death,** the most devastating natural disaster in European history. One observer wrote that "father **abandoned** child, wife [abandoned] husband, one brother [abandoned] another, for the plague seemed to strike through breath and sight. And so they died. And no one could be found to bury the dead, for money or friendship."

### The Plague Spreads

Bubonic plague was the most common form of the Black Death. It was spread by black rats infested with fleas carrying a deadly bacterium. Italian merchants brought the plague with them from Kaffa, on the Black Sea, to the island of Sicily in October 1347. The plague had spread to southern Italy and southern France by the end of 1347. Usually, the path of the Black Death followed trade routes. In 1348 and 1349, the plague spread through France, the Low Countries (modern Belgium, Luxembourg, and the Netherlands), and Germany. It ravaged England in 1349 and expanded to northern Europe and Scandinavia. Eastern Europe and Russia were affected by 1351.

Out of a total European population of 75 million, possibly one-third to one-half of the population died of the plague between 1347 and 1351. Especially hard hit were Italy's crowded cities, where 50 to 60 percent of the people died. In England and Germany, entire villages disappeared.

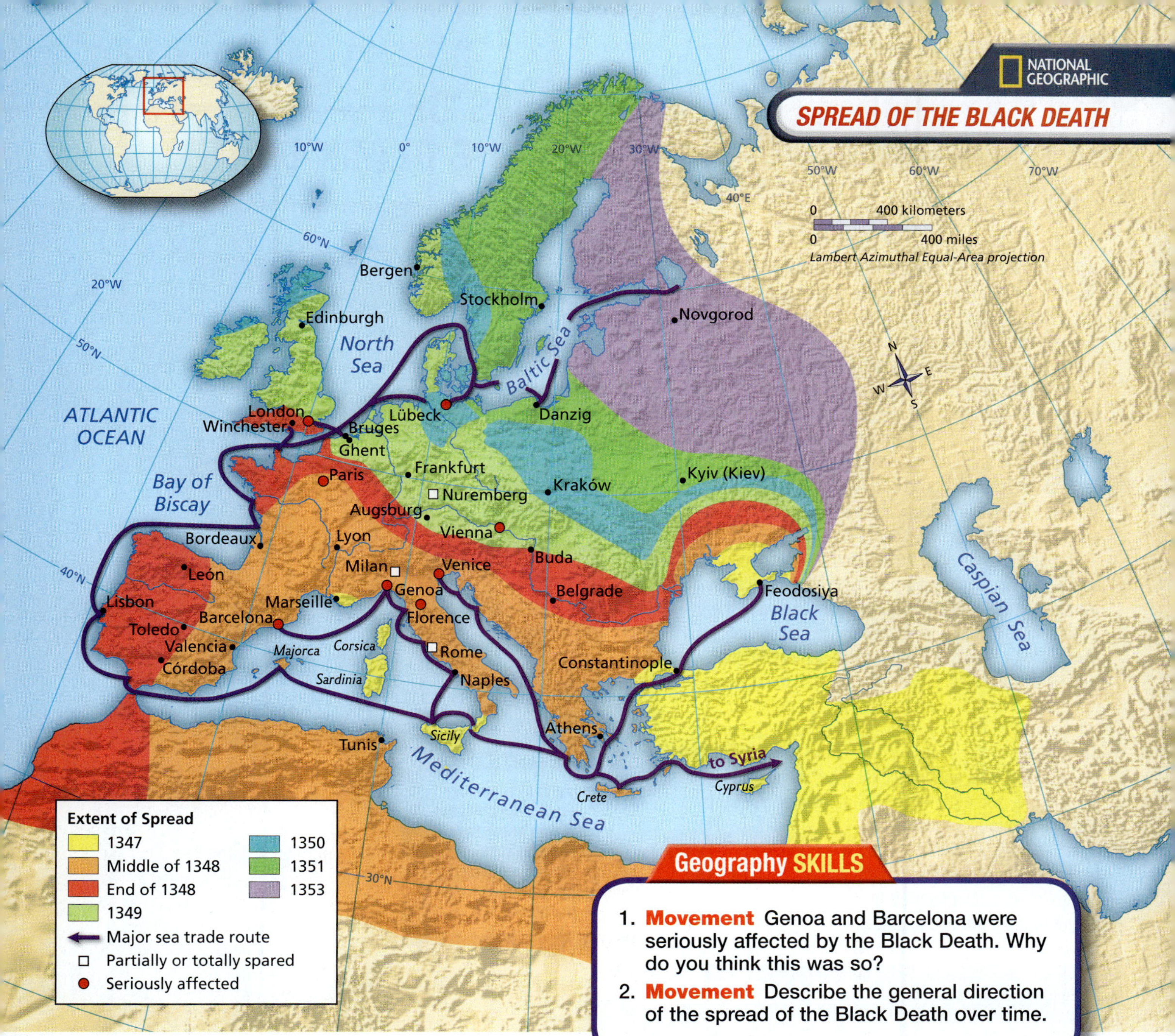


**Geography SKILLS**

1. **Movement** Genoa and Barcelona were seriously affected by the Black Death. Why do you think this was so?
2. **Movement** Describe the general direction of the spread of the Black Death over time.

## Social and Economic Impact

People did not know what caused the plague. Many believed that God sent it as punishment for their sins or that the devil caused it. Some reactions became extreme and led to **anti-Semitism**—hostility toward Jews. Some accused Jews of causing the plague by poisoning town wells. The worst attacks occurred in Germany. Many Jews fled from Germany to Poland, where the king protected them.

The death of so many people also had severe economic **consequences.** Trade declined, and a shortage of workers caused a dramatic rise in the price of labor. At the same time, the decline in the number of people lowered the demand for food, resulting in falling prices.

Landlords were now paying more for labor while their incomes from rents were declining. Some peasants bargained with their lords to pay rent instead of owing services. This change freed them from serfdom, an institution that had been declining throughout the High Middle Ages.

✓Reading Check **Explaining** How was the plague spread?

# TURNING POINT

# EFFECTS OF THE BLACK DEATH

The Black Death caused a sharp decline in the population of Europe and brought about significant social and economic changes during the late Middle Ages. These changes resulted in a weakening of the feudal system, the rise of wage labor, and religious and artistic changes.

Immediate effects of the plague were empty towns, uncultivated farmland, and inflation. The death rate caused labor shortages, which meant there were fewer serfs to work the land and fewer artisans to make goods. Trade decreased as fewer goods and crops were produced. The standard of living increased because wealth was spread among fewer people and because of rising wages.

The plague may have helped end feudalism and manoralism in Western Europe. With fewer available workers, lords granted towns (townspeople) and the remaining serfs more freedom from feudal obligations. Many landlords sold or rented small sections of their estates to the peasants. Serfs negotiated to become wage earners, and laborers were free to move from place to place. Mobility enabled peasants to go where the pay was better. Laws were enacted to keep wages to pre-plague levels, and individual taxes were introduced. In response, some of the newly empowered peasants and guild members revolted.

In this time of crisis, many believed God was punishing the people and Church leaders for their sins. Some Catholics emphasized the importance of inner prayer that did not rely on priests.

**In this fourteenth-century English text, a priest blesses monks who show the characteristic spots of bubonic plague. Both clergy and worshipers died from the plague.**

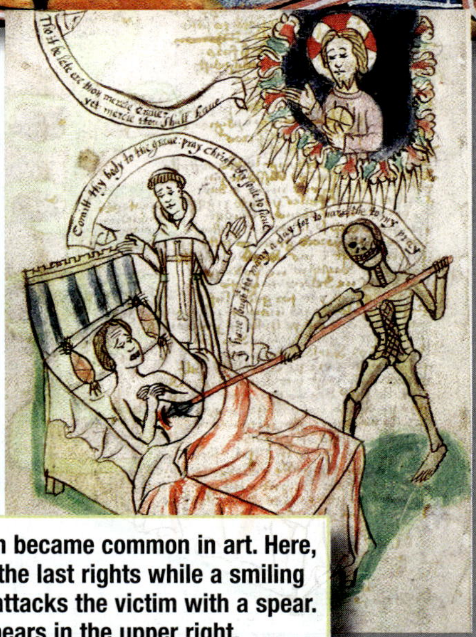

**Images of death became common in art. Here, a priest gives the last rights while a smiling devil/skeleton attacks the victim with a spear. God appears in the upper right.**

## EFFECTS OF THE BLACK DEATH

| ECONOMIC EFFECTS |
|---|
| Drastic decline in population led to: |
| • Labor shortages<br>—higher wages for laborers and artisans<br>—bargaining power for serfs with landlords |
| • Decline in trade (along with labor shortage)<br>—scarcity of manufactured goods<br>—higher prices for manufactured goods |
| • Less demand for food<br>—lower food prices |
| • Smaller estates for landlords<br>—more tenant farmers |
| **SOCIAL EFFECTS** |
| • Decline of serfdom |
| • Growth of cities |
| • Peasant revolts |
| • Preoccupation with death in art and literature |

### DOCUMENT-BASED QUESTIONS

1. **Comparing** What common elements exist in the art shown about the Black Death?
2. **Analyzing** Why could peasants stand up for their rights more boldly after the plague than before it?

## Decline of Church Power

**MAIN IDEA** The Great Schism of the Catholic Church caused great political conflict and left Europe divided for four decades.

***HISTORY & YOU*** Have you and a friend ever disagreed? Read to learn about the Great Schism.

The popes reached the height of their power in the 1200s. In the 1300s, the Church's power declined.

### The Popes at Avignon

European kings had begun to reject papal claims of supremacy by the end of the 1200s. The struggle between **Pope Boniface VIII** and **King Philip IV** of France had serious consequences for the papacy. Philip claimed the right to tax the clergy. Boniface argued that taxing the clergy required the pope's consent, because popes were supreme over both Church and state. Philip rejected the pope's position and sent French forces to Italy to bring Boniface back to France for trial. The pope escaped but died soon afterward.

Philip then engineered the election of a Frenchman, Clement V, as pope in 1305. Clement took up residence in **Avignon** (A • VEEN • YOHN), in southern France. From 1305 to 1377, the popes lived in Avignon.

Sentiments against the papacy grew during this time. Many believed that the pope as bishop of Rome should reside in Rome, not in Avignon. The splendor in which the pope and cardinals were living in Avignon also led to strong criticism of the papacy, as expressed by the Italian poet Petrarch:

**PRIMARY SOURCE**

"Here reign the successors of the poor fisherman of Galilee; they have strangely forgotten their origin. I am astounded . . . to see these men loaded with gold and clad in purple, boasting of the spoils of princes and nations."

—Italian poet Petrarch

### The Great Schism

Perceiving the decline in papal prestige, Pope Gregory XI returned to Rome in 1377 but soon died. When the cardinals met to elect a new pope, the citizens of Rome warned that the cardinals would not leave Rome alive unless they elected an Italian. The cardinals wisely elected an Italian, Pope Urban VI. Five months later, a group of French cardinals declared the election invalid and chose a Frenchman as pope. This pope returned to Avignon.

Because Urban remained in Rome, there were now two popes, beginning the **Great Schism** of the Church. Lasting from 1378 to 1417, the Great Schism divided Europe. France and its allies supported the pope in Avignon. As France's enemies, England and its allies supported the pope in Rome.

In addition to creating political conflict, the Great Schism damaged the Church. The pope was widely believed to be the true leader of Christendom. When each line of popes denounced the other as the Antichrist (one who opposes Christ), people's faith in both the papacy and the Church were undermined. The situation became worse when an effort to resolve the problem in 1409 resulted in the simultaneous reign of three popes. A church council finally met at Constance, Switzerland, and ended the schism in 1417. The competing popes either resigned or were deposed. A new pope, acceptable to all, was then elected.

These crises led to calls for reform. Czech reformers led by **John Hus** called for an end to corruption of the clergy and to excessive papal power within the Church. Hus was accused of heresy by the Council of Constance and burned at the stake in 1415. In response, the Czechs led a revolutionary upheaval in Bohemia that was not crushed until 1436.

By the early 1400s, then, the Church had lost much of its political power. The pope could no longer assert supremacy over the state. Although Christianity remained central to medieval life, the papacy and the Church had lost much of their spiritual authority.

**✓Reading Check** **Explaining** Why were popes criticized for living in Avignon?

# The Hundred Years' War

**MAIN IDEA** England and France waged the long, violent Hundred Years' War.

**HISTORY & YOU** How would you react to someone who claimed to have visions? Read to learn about Joan of Arc.

Plague, economic crisis, and the decline of the Catholic Church were not the only problems of the late Middle Ages. War and political instability must also be added to the list. The Hundred Years' War was the most violent struggle during this period.

## The War Begins

Trouble began over the duchy of Gascony in France. England possessed it, and France wanted it. King Edward III of England was also the duke of Gascony and a vassal to the French king. However, when King Philip VI of France seized the duchy in 1337, Edward declared war on Philip. Thus began the Hundred Years' War between England and France.

The war began in a burst of knightly enthusiasm. Trained to be warriors, knights viewed battle as a chance to show their fighting abilities. The Hundred Years' War proved to be an important turning point in the nature of warfare, however. Peasant foot soldiers, not knights, won the chief battles of the war.

France's heavily armed noble cavalrymen, or knights, viewed foot soldiers as social inferiors. The English also used heavily armed cavalry, but they relied more on large numbers of peasants, paid to be foot soldiers. English soldiers were armed not only with pikes, or heavy spears, but also with longbows. The longbow had greater striking power, longer range, and more rapid speed of fire than the crossbow (formerly the weapon of choice).

## Crécy and Agincourt

The first major battle of the Hundred Years' War occurred in 1346 at Crécy. The larger French army followed no battle plan and attacked in a disorderly fashion. The English archers devastated them.

As the chronicler Froissart described the stunning English victory: "[with their longbows] the English continued to shoot into the thickest part of the crowd, wasting none of their arrows. They impaled or wounded horses and riders, who fell to the ground in great distress, unable to get up again without the help of several men."

The Battle of Crécy was not decisive, however. The English simply did not have enough resources to conquer all of France. Nevertheless, they continued to try. The English king, **Henry V**, achieved victory at the Battle of **Agincourt** in 1415. The heavy, armor-plated French knights tried to attack Henry's forces across a muddy field. They were disastrously defeated, and 1,500 French nobles died in battle. The English were masters of northern France.

## Joan of Arc

The seemingly hopeless French cause now fell into the hands of Charles, heir to the French throne. Quite unexpectedly, a French peasant woman saved the timid monarch.

The daughter of prosperous peasants, **Joan of Arc** was a deeply religious person. She experienced visions and believed that saints had commanded her to free France. Though only 17, Joan's sincerity and simplicity persuaded Charles to allow her to accompany a French army to Orléans. Apparently inspired by Joan's faith, the French armies found new confidence and seized **Orléans.** Joan had brought the war to a turning point but did not live to see its end. The English captured Joan in 1430 and turned her over to the Inquisition on charges of witchcraft. At the time, visions were thought to be inspired by either God or the devil. Joan was condemned to death as a heretic.

Joan's achievements, however, were decisive. Although the war dragged on for another two decades, defeats of English armies in Normandy and Aquitaine led to a French victory by 1453. Also important to the French success was the use of the cannon, a new weapon made possible by the invention of gunpowder.

**✓Reading Check** **Identifying** What event sparked the Hundred Years' War?

## Political Recovery

**MAIN IDEA** France, England, and Spain emerged as new monarchies by the late 1400s.

***HISTORY & YOU*** After a setback, do you come back stronger and better? Read to learn about the new monarchies in Europe.

In the 1300s, European rulers faced serious problems. Many hereditary monarchies or dynasties in Europe were unable to produce male heirs. The founders of new dynasties had to fight for their positions when groups of nobles supported opposing candidates for the kingship. Rulers found themselves with financial problems as well.

In the 1400s, however, recovery set in as a number of new rulers in Europe attempted to reestablish the centralized power of monarchies. Some historians have spoken of these reestablished states as the **new monarchies.** This term applies especially to the monarchies of France, England, and Spain as they existed at the end of the 1400s.

### France

The Hundred Years' War left France exhausted. However, the war had also developed a strong degree of French national feeling toward a common enemy. The kings used that spirit to reestablish royal power.

The development of a strong French state was greatly advanced by King Louis XI, who ruled from 1461 to 1483. Known by many as the Spider because of his devious ways, Louis strengthened the use of the ***taille***—an annual direct tax usually on land or property—as a permanent tax imposed by royal authority. This tax gave Louis a sound, regular source of income.

**INFOGRAPHICS**

### Results of the Hundred Years' War

The Hundred Years' War began as a war between English and French kings vying for control of territory. It resulted in the transformation of England and France from feudal kingdoms to two separate nations with distinct cultures.

**Battle of Agincourt, France, 1415, English victory over the French**

| ENGLAND | FRANCE |
|---|---|
| POLITICAL<br>• Loss of territory in France<br>• Tudor dynasty established by War of the Roses | POLITICAL<br>• Strong French monarchy emerges<br>• Centralized government |
| MILITARY<br>• Longbow gives England advantage<br>• Transition from knights and cavalry to peasant foot soldiers | MILITARY<br>• French develop hit-and-run military tactics<br>• Standing army established<br>• Cannons enable French to drive English out |
| CULTURE<br>• Upper class abandons French language<br>• English language reinstated for first time since 1066<br>• Rise of nationalism | CULTURE<br>• French national identity emerges |

**DOCUMENT-BASED QUESTIONS**

1. **Identifying** Which military inventions affected the outcome of the Hundred Years' War?
2. **Making Inferences** What role did the Hundred Years' War play in the rise of nationalism?

## HISTORY & ARTS

### The Reconquista of Spain

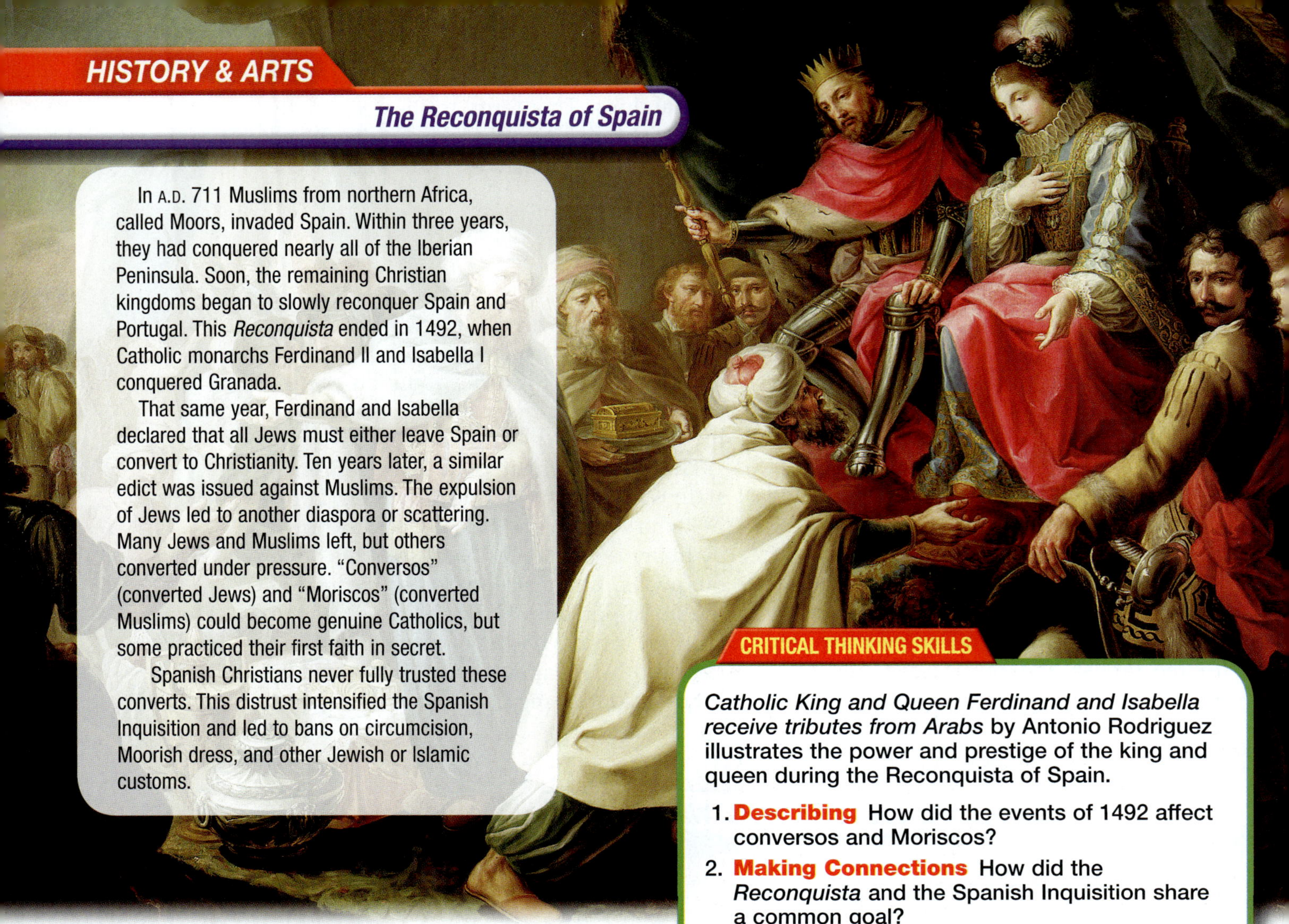

In A.D. 711 Muslims from northern Africa, called Moors, invaded Spain. Within three years, they had conquered nearly all of the Iberian Peninsula. Soon, the remaining Christian kingdoms began to slowly reconquer Spain and Portugal. This *Reconquista* ended in 1492, when Catholic monarchs Ferdinand II and Isabella I conquered Granada.

That same year, Ferdinand and Isabella declared that all Jews must either leave Spain or convert to Christianity. Ten years later, a similar edict was issued against Muslims. The expulsion of Jews led to another diaspora or scattering. Many Jews and Muslims left, but others converted under pressure. "Conversos" (converted Jews) and "Moriscos" (converted Muslims) could become genuine Catholics, but some practiced their first faith in secret.

Spanish Christians never fully trusted these converts. This distrust intensified the Spanish Inquisition and led to bans on circumcision, Moorish dress, and other Jewish or Islamic customs.

**CRITICAL THINKING SKILLS**

***Catholic King and Queen Ferdinand and Isabella receive tributes from Arabs*** **by Antonio Rodriguez illustrates the power and prestige of the king and queen during the Reconquista of Spain.**

1. **Describing** How did the events of 1492 affect conversos and Moriscos?
2. **Making Connections** How did the *Reconquista* and the Spanish Inquisition share a common goal?

To curb the power of the great French nobles, Louis relied on support from the lower nobility and middle class. He added Anjou, Maine, Provence, and other regions to his kingdom. By consolidating power and by promoting industry and commerce, he created the foundations of a strong monarchy.

## England

The Hundred Years' War had also strongly affected the English. Both the cost of the war and losses in manpower strained the economy. At the end of the war, England faced even greater turmoil when civil conflicts—known as the Wars of the Roses—erupted. Noble factions fought to control the monarchy until 1485, when Henry Tudor established a new dynasty.

As the first Tudor king, Henry VII worked to create a strong royal government. Henry ended the wars of the nobles by abolishing their private armies. He was also very thrifty. By not overburdening the nobles and the middle class with taxes, Henry won their favor. They thus provided much support for his monarchy.

## Spain

Spain, too, experienced the growth of a strong national monarchy at the end of the 1400s. Muslims had conquered much of Spain by about 725. During the Middle Ages, Christian rulers in Spain had fought to regain their lands from the Muslims. Several independent Christian kingdoms had emerged in the course of the long reconquest of the Iberian Peninsula. Among them were Aragon and Castile.

Aragon and Castile were both strong kingdoms. When **Isabella** of Castile married

Ferdinand of Aragon in 1469, it was a major step toward unifying Spain. Castile and Aragon remained distinct political kingdoms with separate councils of state and parliaments. However, Isabella and Ferdinand worked together to strengthen their royal control in the dual monarchy.

Ferdinand and Isabella also believed that religious unity was necessary for political unity. The rulers pursued a policy of strict conformity to Catholicism. In 1492, they took the drastic step of expelling all Jews who did not convert from Spain.

Muslims, too, after their final loss in 1492 to the armies of Ferdinand and Isabella, were "encouraged" to convert to Catholicism. They had the choice of conversion or voluntary exile. In 1502, Isabella issued a decree expelling all Muslims who did not convert from her kingdom. To a very large degree, Ferdinand and Isabella, the "most Catholic" monarchs, had achieved their goal of religious uniformity. To be Spanish was to be Catholic.

## Central and Eastern Europe

Unlike France, England, and Spain, the Holy Roman Empire did not develop a strong monarchical authority. The failures of German emperors in the 1200s had made Germany a land of hundreds of states, most of which acted independently of the German ruler.

After 1438, the position of Holy Roman emperor was held by the Hapsburg dynasty. As rulers of the Austrian lands along the Danube, the Hapsburgs became one of the wealthiest landholders in the empire and began to play an important role in European affairs.

In Eastern Europe, rulers found it difficult to centralize their states. Religious differences troubled the area as Roman Catholics, Eastern Orthodox Christians, and other groups, including Mongols and Muslims, confronted one another. In Poland, the nobles gained the right to elect their kings, which weakened royal authority. In Hungary, the power of wealthy lords was broken to create a well organized central administration.

Since the 1200s, Russia had been under Mongol domination. Gradually, the princes of Moscow rose to prominence by using their close relationship to the Mongol khans and trade to increase their wealth and territory. During the reign of Ivan III, Muscovy became the major power in northern Russia. In 1472 Ivan III married the niece of the last Byzantine emperor, increasing Byzantine influence in Russia. By 1480, Ivan III had thrown off the yoke of the Mongols. The next ruler of Muscovy, Ivan IV, was recognized as the legitimate ruler and czar of Russia by the Orthodox Church.

✓ Reading Check **Identifying** Conflicts among what groups made it difficult for eastern Europe to form new monarchies?

## SECTION 4 REVIEW

### Vocabulary

1. **Explain** the significance of: Black Death, abandoned, anti-Semitism, consequences, Pope Boniface VIII, King Philip IV, Avignon, Great Schism, John Hus, Henry V, Agincourt, Joan of Arc, Orléans, new monarchies, *taille*, Isabella, Ferdinand.

### Main Ideas

2. **Explain** why anti-Semitism increased during the spread of the Black Death.
3. **Identify** the innovations from the Hundred Years' War that changed the nature of warfare. Use a diagram like the one below.

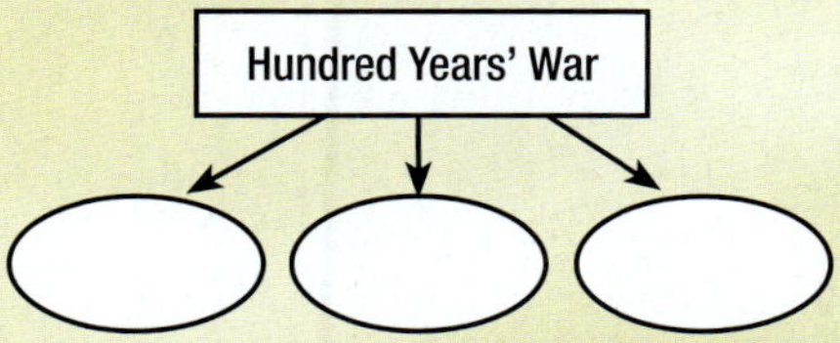


4. **Explain** how Henry VII strengthened his monarchy in the 1400s.

### Critical Thinking

5. **The BIG Idea** **Analyzing** How did the economic effects of the Black Death help to break down the institution of serfdom?
6. **Finding Main Ideas** What key issue underlay the dispute between Pope Boniface VIII and King Philip IV over taxing the clergy?
7. **Analyzing Visuals** Examine the image of the Reconquista of Spain on page 358. What details in the image suggest the power and importance of Ferdinand and Isabella?

### Writing About History

8. **Informative Writing** Write a newspaper-type obituary for Joan of Arc. Include information on her life and her achievements. Write a tribute or quote that you believe sums up Joan's life.

**History ONLINE**

For help with the concepts in this section of *Glencoe World History*, go to glencoe.com and click Study Central™.

# The Black Death

The Black Death spread throughout Europe from 1347 to 1351. The disease wiped out nearly half of Europe's population. Many towns and villages lost most of their population, and some completely disappeared. There were three versions of the disease that plagued the population, the most well-known of these being the bubonic plague. Flea-infested rats aboard trading ships carried the disease along trade routes and throughout the continent. As the fleas jumped to humans, the pandemic began.

The bubonic plague hit urban areas hardest, where crowded conditions and poor sanitation helped spread disease.

Disposal of bodies became a nightmarish problem. Communal graves became common, as was disposal in rivers.

There was no garbage collection or sanitation. All forms of refuse were simply thrown into the street, aiding the breeding of disease.

## Escaping Death

Many people believed the impure air carried the disease. Those who could afford it escaped to the countryside. They boarded up their homes and either left their sick loved ones in the care of servants, or just left them inside. Still others isolated themselves in their homes in hopes of avoiding infection. The poor had no means of escape. They lived with and cared for their sick. Because they were in close quarters, the poor often fell victim to the disease themselves.

## A Terrible Death

The Black Death was so-named because of the black color of the swollen lymph nodes, called buboes, its victims experienced. They appeared in the neck, armpits, legs, and groin. Other symptoms were severe head and body aches, high fever, rapid pulse, general weakness, and vomiting of blood. Symptoms appeared within a few days of exposure; the bursting of the buboes and death followed in just a few days more.

### Analyzing Visuals

1. **Cause and Effect** What effects of the Black Death do you think had the greatest impact on European history? Why?
2. **Comparing** How is the response to pandemics today different from the ones of the Middle Ages? Are there any similarities?

# CHAPTER 10 Visual Summary



## Society in the HIGH MIDDLE AGES

- Farming inventions and efficient use of land contributed to population growth.
- Under the manorial system, serfs were legally bound to the land they worked for the lord.
- Revival of trade changed the economy from a barter system to one based on money.
- As trade grew, cities expanded and became manufacturing and trade centers.

MERCHANTS SELLING THEIR GOODS

The revival of trade spurred the growth of medieval cities.

RELIGIOUS ENTHUSIASM SPREAD THROUGH EUROPE

Bernard of Clairvaux embodied the new spiritual ideal of Cistercian monasticism.

## CATHOLICISM, INNOVATIONS, AND INTELLECTUAL REVIVAL in the Middle Ages

- Political power of the Catholic Church peaked during the papacy of Pope Innocent III.
- Religious fervor led to new monastic orders.
- Advances in technology allowed the building of impressive Gothic cathedrals.
- Europe's first universities were founded.
- Popular troubadour poetry and heroic epic poems were written in the vernacular.

## Disruptive Forces of the LATE MIDDLE AGES

- The Black Death spread through Europe, devastating societies and economies.
- The Great Schism damaged the Church's power and divided Europe.
- In the Hundred Years' War, peasant foot soldiers, not knights, won the chief battles.
- Recovery began in the late 1400s as new monarchies emerged in France, England, and Spain.

HUNDRED YEARS' WAR

English troops used traditional crossbows as well as newer longbows and cannons.

# CHAPTER 10 Assessment

## Reviewing Vocabulary

*Directions: Choose the word or words that best complete the sentence.*

**1.** The ________ were the wealthy, powerful families that usually made up the government of a medieval city.

**A** bourgeoisie

**B** patricians

**C** journeymen

**D** imperators

**2.** A ________ was an agricultural estate that a lord ran and peasants worked.

**A** castle

**B** guild

**C** carruca

**D** manor

**3.** By using ________ to deny people Christian rites, popes could pressure them to do the popes' bidding.

**A** *tailles*

**B** sacraments

**C** interdicts

**D** heretics

**4.** ________ is the language of everyday speech.

**A** Vernacular

**B** Chanson de geste

**C** Lay investiture

**D** Scholasticism

**5.** The ____________ was an annual tax imposed by the French King Louis XI.

**A** *carruca*

**B** *taille*

**C** guild

**D** interdict

## Reviewing Main Ideas

*Directions: Choose the best answers to the following questions.*

### Section 1 *(pp. 334–341)*

**6.** Approximately what portion of western Europeans were serfs by 800?

**A** 80 percent

**B** 40 percent

**C** 20 percent

**D** 60 percent

**7.** How did the French counts of Champagne encourage trade with Flanders?

**A** Invented money

**B** Initiated trade fairs

**C** Instituted capitalism

**D** Developed a mercantile fleet

### Section 2 *(pp. 342–347)*

**8.** What was the result of the Concordat of Worms?

**A** The Hundred Years' War ended.

**B** Europe's loyalties were divided between different popes.

**C** A compromise was reached in the Investiture Controversy.

**D** Many people were burned at the stake.

**9.** Who founded the Franciscans?

**A** Francis of Assisi

**B** Dominic de Guzmán

**C** Pope Innocent III

**D** Hildegard of Bingen

### TEST-TAKING TIP

Although most test questions ask you about what you have learned by reading the text or by listening in class, using common sense can help you arrive at the correct answers, too. To answer questions, consider what you know about the topic and then read the answer choices.


**Need Extra Help?**

| If You Missed Questions . . . | 1 | 2 | 3 | 4 | 5 | 6 | 7 | 8 | 9 |
|---|---|---|---|---|---|---|---|---|---|
| Go to Page . . . | 340 | 336 | 344 | 351 | 355 | 336 | 338 | 344 | 345 |

GO ON

## Section 3 *(pp. 348–351)*

**10.** What new architectural style appeared in the twelfth century?

- **A** Neoclassic
- **B** Romanesque
- **C** Baroque
- **D** Gothic

**11.** Who wrote most of the troubadour poetry?

- **A** Clergy
- **B** Nobles and knights
- **C** Peasants
- **D** Medieval university students

## Section 4 *(pp. 352–359)*

**12.** Which of the following was an accomplishment of King Henry VII of England?

- **A** A strong royal government
- **B** A *Reconquista*
- **C** The *taille*
- **D** The Great Schism

**13.** Who led the Czech reformers during the Great Schism of the Catholic Church?

- **A** Henry VI
- **B** Hildegard of Bingen
- **C** Joan of Arc
- **D** John Hus

**14.** Why did Isabella and Ferdinand expel Jews and Muslims from Spain?

- **A** For control of their land
- **B** For religious unity
- **C** For control of trade
- **D** For racial purity

## Critical Thinking

*Directions: Choose the best answers to the following questions.*

*Use the following map and your knowledge of world history to answer question 15.*

**Hundred Years' War in France**

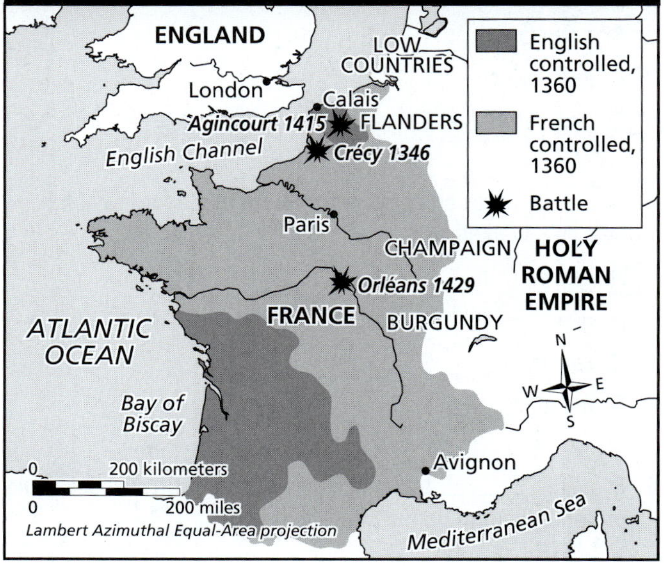


**15.** Where did the first battle of the Hundred Years' War take place?

- **A** In Burgundy
- **B** In central France
- **C** In northern France
- **D** In English territory

**16.** What is one reason for the growth of medieval cities?

- **A** The spread of the Black Death
- **B** The decline of the manorial system
- **C** The revival of trade
- **D** The decline of feudalism

**17.** Which of the following factors was key to the rise of commercial capitalism?

- **A** The manorial system
- **B** Craft guilds
- **C** Cities
- **D** A money economy

**Need Extra Help?**

| If You Missed Questions . . . | 10 | 11 | 12 | 13 | 14 | 15 | 16 | 17 |
|---|---|---|---|---|---|---|---|---|
| Go to Page . . . | 348 | 351 | 358 | 355 | 358 | 364 | 338 | 338 |

GO ON

**18.** What issue was at the heart of the Investiture Controversy?

**A** Control of the Inquisition

**B** Supremacy of Church or state

**C** Location of the papal residence

**D** Anti-Semitism

*Base your answer to question 19 on the following illustration and on your knowledge of world history.*

**19.** What structural innovation illustrated by this drawing allowed for the support of a heavy vaulted ceiling in a Gothic cathedral?

**A** Barrel vaults

**B** Cross vaults

**C** Flying buttresses

**D** Basilicas

## Document-Based Questions

*Directions: Analyze the document and answer the short-answer questions that follow the document. Base your answers on the document and on your knowledge of world history.*

*A twelfth-century English monk described his abbey's relics:*

> *"There is kept there a thing more precious than gold . . . the right arm of St. Oswald . . . This we have seen with our own eyes and have kissed, and have handled with our own hands. . . . There are kept here also part of his ribs and of the soil on which he fell."*

**20.** What made these objects "relics"?

**21.** Why would a relic be considered "a thing more precious than gold"?

## Extended Response

**22.** Explain the economic effects of the Black Death.

**23.** Identify four medieval innovations and describe their influence on medieval society. Consider intellectual, agricultural, economic, or architectural innovations. Which ones had the greatest impact on daily life?

**24.** Summarize the short-term and long-term effects of the Hundred Years' War?

**History ONLINE**

For additional test practice, use Self-Check Quizzes—Chapter 10 at glencoe.com.

**Need Extra Help?**

| If You Missed Questions . . . | 18 | 19 | 20 | 21 | 22 | 23 | 24 |
|---|---|---|---|---|---|---|---|
| Go to Page . . . | 342 | 365 | 365 | 365 | 353 | 334 | 357 |

STOP

# CHAPTER 11

# The Americas 400–1500

**Section 1** The Peoples of North America

**Section 2** Early Civilizations in Mesoamerica

**Section 3** Early Civilizations in South America

Chapter Audio

*MAKING CONNECTIONS*

## What can ruins teach us about civilization?

The sacred city of Chichén Itzá is one of the most important archaeological sites of the Maya and Toltec cultures. El Caracol, the observatory shown in the photo, was used by the Maya and the Toltec to measure the movement of the moon, stars, and planets. It exhibits the advanced engineering and astronomy skills of its builders. In this chapter you will learn about the early civilizations of the Americas.

- Why do you think the Maya and the Toltec went to such efforts to understand the movement of the moon, stars, and planets?
- Why do archaeologists study ancient ruins today?

**THE AMERICAS ▶**

**c. 3000 B.C.** People move into North America from Asia

**c. 250 B.C.** City of Teotihuacán established

**c. A.D. 300** Maya civilization begins to flourish

1000 B.C. — A.D. 400

**THE WORLD ▶**

**c. 2000 B.C.** Trade thrives between Egypt and Nubia

**A.D. 100** Christianity spreads in the Roman Empire

**C. A.D. 700**
Hopewell people shift to full-time farming

**1440**
Inca leader Pachacuti launches campaign of conquest

A.D. 950 — 1500

**A.D. 825**
Al-Khowarizmi advances use of Hindu numbers and algebra in Arab world

**FOLDABLES™**
**Study Organizer**

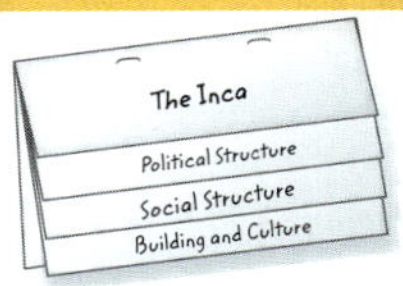


**Organizing** Create a Layered-Look Book to organize facts about the Inca. Read the related text and conduct research to learn more about the political structure, social structure, and buildings and culture of the Inca.

**History ONLINE** Visit glencoe.com and enter **QuickPass™** code GWHEA7447c11 for Chapter 11 resources.

SECTION 1

Section Audio Spotlight Video

# The Peoples of North America

## GUIDE TO READING

### The BIG Idea

**Physical Geography** Hunters and gatherers spread into the North American continent and established their unique ways of living.

### Content Vocabulary

- longhouse *(p. 370)*
- clan *(p. 370)*
- tepee *(p. 371)*
- adobe *(p. 371)*
- pueblo *(p. 371)*

### Academic Vocabulary

- survive *(p. 368)*
- temporary *(p. 368)*

### People and Places

- Bering Strait *(p. 368)*
- Inuit *(p. 368)*
- Gulf of Mexico *(p. 369)*
- Hopewell *(p. 369)*
- Cahokia *(p. 370)*
- Iroquois *(p. 370)*
- Plains Indians *(p. 371)*
- Anasazi *(p. 371)*
- Mesa Verde *(p. 371)*

### Reading Strategy

**Summarizing Information** As you read, complete a separate chart for each of the five major peoples discussed in this section. Identify the characteristics listed below for each group.

| | |
|---|---|
| People | |
| Region | |
| Types of Food | |
| Shelter | |

*During the last Ice Age, a natural land bridge connected the Asian and North American continents. Early hunters used this land bridge when they followed herds of bison and caribou into North America. These hunters became the first people to live in North America.*

## The First North Americans

**MAIN IDEA** Early hunters and gatherers moved across the Bering Strait into North America, later forming distinct cultures.

***HISTORY & YOU*** Who lived in your region thousands of years ago? Read to learn about some early peoples of North America, including the Iroquois, the Hopewell, and the Anasazi.

The Americas make up an enormous land area, stretching about 9,000 miles (more than 14,000 km) from the Arctic Ocean in the north to Cape Horn at the tip of South America. The North American continent is large and has varying climates and geographical features. It has ice-covered lands and hot, dry deserts. Dense forests cover some areas, and fertile river valleys are ideal for hunting and farming. Many years ago, these different geographical areas became home to various peoples, who created their own distinctive ways of living.

Between 15,000 and 20,000 years ago, the last Ice Age caused sea levels to drop. Low sea levels in turn created a land bridge connecting the Asian and North American continents. Many scholars believe that people from Asia used this land bridge to cross the **Bering Strait** into North America. Most likely, these first Americans were hunters, pursuing herds of bison and caribou. They lived in small, nomadic communities. To **survive,** they needed to remain close to the source of their food supply.

### Arctic and Northwest: The Inuit

About 3000 B.C., the **Inuit** moved into North America from Asia. They had to learn very specific skills to survive in such a cold and harsh environment. Most Inuit settled along the coasts of the tundra region, the treeless land south of the Arctic.

Using harpoons and spears made from antler or narwhal tusk, the Inuit were skilled hunters. Seal, caribou, and fish provided both food and clothing. In winter, the Inuit built homes of stones and turf. The traditional igloo, made out of cut blocks of hard-packed snow, was only a **temporary** shelter used during traveling.

## CULTURES OF NORTH AMERICA, 4000 B.C.–A.D. 1500

### Early Peoples of North America

| CULTURES | CULTURES FLOURISHED |
|---|---|
| Inuit | c. 3000 B.C.–today |
| Hopewell | 200 B.C.–A.D. 500 |
| Anasazi | A.D. 500–1200 |
| Iroquois League | 1500s–1900s |
| Creek (Muscogee) | 1500s–today |
| Cherokee | 1500s–today |

### Geography SKILLS

1. **Human-Environment Interaction** Identify geographical features that might explain the similarities and differences in the lifestyles of the first Americans.
2. **Location** Why do you think more culture groups were located in the South than in the North?

## Eastern Woodlands: Mound Builders and Iroquois

Around 1000 B.C., farming villages appeared in the Eastern Woodlands, the land in eastern North America from the Great Lakes to the **Gulf of Mexico**. Although people in the Eastern Woodlands region grew crops, they also continued to gather wild plants for food.

One Eastern Woodlands group was the **Hopewell** people in the Ohio River valley. They extended their culture along the Mississippi River. The Hopewell people, known as the Mound Builders, built large, elaborate earth mounds that were used as tombs or for ceremonies. Some were built in the shape of animals.

The shift to full-time farming about A.D. 700 led to a prosperous culture in the Mississippi River valley. This Mississippian culture grew corn, squash, and beans together to provide plants with nutrients, support, and shade.

Cities began to appear, some of them containing 10,000 people or more. At the site of **Cahokia** (kuh•HOH•kee•uh), near the modern city of East St. Louis, Illinois, archaeologists found a burial mound over 98 feet (30 m) high. It had a base larger than that of the Great Pyramid in Egypt. Between A.D. 850 and 1150, Cahokia flourished and served as the seat of government. For reasons unknown, Cahokia collapsed during the 1200s.

To the northeast of the Mississippian culture were people known as the **Iroquois** (IHR•uh•KWOY). The Iroquois lived in villages that consisted of **longhouses** surrounded by wooden fences for protection. Each longhouse, built of wooden poles covered with sheets of bark, was 150 to 200 feet (46 to 61 m) in length and housed about a dozen families.

Iroquois men hunted deer, bear, caribou, and small animals like rabbits and beaver. They were also warriors who protected the community. Women owned the dwellings, gathered wild plants, and grew crops. The most important crops were the "three sisters"—corn, beans, and squash. In addition, women cooked, made baskets, and took care of the children.

Wars were common, especially among groups of Iroquois who lived in much of present-day Pennsylvania, New York, and parts of southern Canada. Legend holds that sometime during the 1500s, the Iroquois peoples were nearly torn apart by warfare. Deganawida, an elder of one Iroquois group, appeared and preached the need for peace.

One who listened was Hiawatha, a member of the Onondaga (AH•nuhn•DAW•guh) group. From the combined efforts of Deganawida and Hiawatha came the Great Peace, which created an alliance of five groups called the Iroquois League.

A council of representatives, a group of 50 Iroquois leaders, known as the Grand Council met regularly to settle differences. Representatives were chosen in a special way. Each Iroquois group was made up of **clans**, groups of related families. The

## INFOGRAPHICS

### The Iroquois League

According to Iroquois legend, the five nations of the Iroquois League came together sometime during the 1500s after a period of warfare. The members of the Iroquois League referred to their union by a word which means "people building a longhouse." In other words, they saw the Iroquois League as an enormous longhouse that stretched across the five nations and sheltered its members.

The Iroquois constitution set out a specific process for resolving differences between the Iroquois nations. It described how to appoint military leaders and members of the Grand Council and established rules for adoption, emigration, declaring war, and for removing council members. When Benjamin Franklin proposed the Plan of Union in 1754, he noted that the Iroquois had united in a league for their common defense and suggested the colonies ought to be able to do the same. Thomas Jefferson also knew of the Iroquois constitution. He called the United States Constitution a "tree of peace,"—the same term the Iroquois used to describe their constitution.

A longhouse was usually about 20 feet wide by 20 feet high, though it could vary in length. It was built of wooden poles and bark.

**CRITICAL THINKING SKILLS**

1. **Identifying** What were the key features of an Iroquois longhouse?
2. **Making Connections** In what ways did the Iroquois League resemble a longhouse?

women of each clan singled out a well-respected woman as the clan mother. The clan mothers, in turn, chose the male members of the Grand Council. Much was expected of these men—patience and firmness, but also a tenderness for their people and calm deliberation. The Grand Council provided the Iroquois with a new way to deal with their problems.

## Peoples of the Great Plains

West of the Mississippi River basin, the **Plains Indians** cultivated beans, corn, and squash along the river valleys of the eastern Great Plains. Every summer, the men left their villages to hunt buffalo, a very important animal to the Plains culture. Hunters would work together to frighten a herd of buffalo, causing them to stampede over a cliff.

The buffalo served many uses for Plains peoples. They ate the meat, used the skins for clothing, and made tools from the bones. By stretching buffalo skins over wooden poles, they made circular tents called **tepees.** Tepees provided excellent shelter; they were warm in winter and cool in summer.

## Peoples of the Southwest: The Anasazi

The Southwest covers the territory of present-day New Mexico, Arizona, Utah, and Colorado. Conditions are dry, but there is sufficient rain in some areas for farming. The **Anasazi** (AH•nuh•SAH•zee) peoples established an extensive farming society there.

Between A.D. 500 and 1200, the Anasazi used canals and earthen dams to turn parts of the desert into fertile gardens. They were skilled at making baskets and beautifully crafted pottery. They used stone and **adobe** (sun-dried brick) to build **pueblos,** multistoried structures that housed many people.

At Chaco Canyon in northwestern New Mexico, they built an elaborate center for their civilization. At the heart of Chaco Canyon was Pueblo Bonito. This was a large complex that contained some 800 rooms housing more than 1,000 people. The Pueblo Bonito complex included communal rooms where people assembled to perform religious rituals. This flourishing center could not survive a series of droughts that occurred over a 50-year period. Finally the Anasazi had to abandon the center.

The Anasazi culture itself did not die. To the north in southern Colorado, a large community had formed at **Mesa Verde** (MAY•suh•VEHR•dee). Today, this is a national park in the United States. Groups of Anasazi there built a remarkable series of buildings in the recesses of the cliff walls. However, the Anasazi abandoned the settlement in the late 1200s because of a prolonged drought.

✓Reading Check **Explaining** What may have led hunters to cross the land bridge to North America?

## SECTION 1 REVIEW

### Vocabulary

1. **Explain** the significance of: Bering Strait, survive, Inuit, temporary, Gulf of Mexico, Hopewell, Cahokia, Iroquois, longhouse, clan, Plains Indians, tepee, Anasazi, adobe, pueblo, Mesa Verde.

### Main Idea

2. **Identify** some reasons why early peoples migrated from place to place.
3. **Describe** the Cahokia site of the Hopewell peoples.
4. **Summarize** the features of the Anasazi culture. Use a graph like the one below to highlight the features.

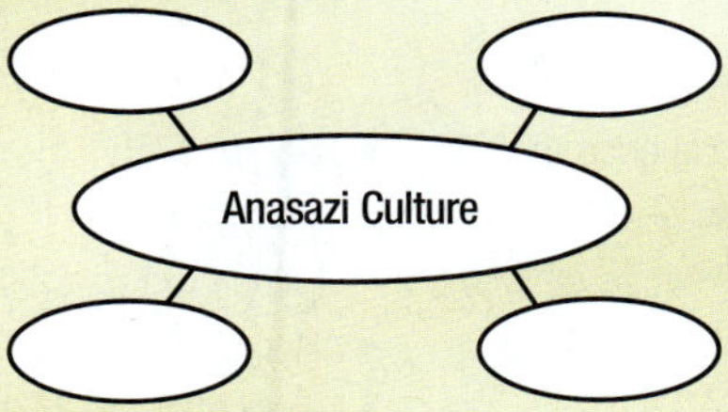


### Critical Thinking

5. **The BIG Idea** **Determining Cause and Effect** What was the relationship between early peoples and their environment?
6. **Evaluating** Why was the Iroquois League politically significant?
7. **Analyzing Visuals** Examine the Iroquois village pictured on page 370. What purpose do you think the fences served?

### Writing About History

8. **Expository Writing** Identify the leadership roles that women took in the Iroquois society and compare these roles with women's roles in American society today. Write a one-page comparison after doing your research.

**History ONLINE**

For help with the concepts in this section of *Glencoe World History*, go to glencoe.com and click Study Central™.

SECTION 2

Section Audio    Spotlight Video

# Early Civilizations in Mesoamerica

## GUIDE TO READING

### The BIG Idea

**Ideas, Beliefs, and Values** Early Mesoamerican civilizations flourished with fully developed political, religious, and social structures.

### Content Vocabulary

- hieroglyph *(p. 375)*
- tribute *(p. 378)*

### Academic Vocabulary

- estimate *(p. 374)*
- accurate *(p. 374)*

### People and Places

- Mesoamerica *(p. 372)*
- Olmec *(p. 372)*
- Teotihuacán *(p. 373)*
- Yucatán Peninsula *(p. 374)*
- Maya *(p. 374)*
- Tikal *(p. 375)*
- Toltec *(p. 376)*
- Chichén Itzá *(p. 377)*
- Aztec *(p. 377)*
- Tenochtitlán *(p. 377)*
- Lake Texcoco *(p. 377)*

### Reading Strategy

**Summarizing Information** As you read, create a separate chart, like the one shown here, for each of the cultures discussed in this section.

| | |
|---|---|
| People | |
| Location | |
| Religion | |
| Architecture | |
| Year/Reason Declined | |

*Archaeology tells us about the ancient societies that once existed in Mesoamerica. First came the Olmec, whose culture influenced those that followed. Later, the Maya became one of the most sophisticated cultures of the early Americas. The civilizations that followed, the Toltec and the Aztec, incorporated Maya traditions into their cultures.*

## The Olmec

*MAIN IDEA* The Olmec, the first Mesoamerican civilization, appeared around 1200 B.C., and the city of Teotihuacán thrived until A.D. 800.

*HISTORY & YOU* Do you use an electronic calendar to keep you organized? Read about the Olmec calendar and numerical system.

Not until the late 1800s did archaeologists begin excavating ancient ruins found in **Mesoamerica.** This is a name used for areas of Mexico and Central America where ancient empires flourished. Detailed excavations revealed that the Maya once lived there. Later excavations told of an even older society, the **Olmec.**

### Olmec Culture

Archaeologists first discovered the Olmec society in the 1940s. They called these people the Olmec, or "rubber people," because of the rubber trees that grew in the area where they lived. The Olmec, the first-known civilization in Mesoamerica, appeared around 1200 B.C. They farmed along riverbanks in the hot, swampy lowlands along the coast of the Gulf of Mexico south of Veracruz. They traded with other peoples of Mesoamerica for jade and obsidian to make their tools, jewelry, and monuments. Olmec objects have been found in central Mexico.

The Olmec had large cities that were centers for their religious rituals. The oldest city was San Lorenzo, which contained pyramids and other stone monuments. In La Venta a 30-foot-high (9-m-high) pyramid towered above the city. Olmec skilled artisans also carved a series of colossal stone heads, probably to represent their gods or rulers. These huge heads, 10 feet (3 m) high and weighing 20 tons (18 t), are especially remarkable because the Olmec had no metal tools. Carving them with instruments of stone must have taken a great deal of time.

Around 400 B.C., for reasons not yet fully understood, the Olmec civilization declined and eventually collapsed. However, some aspects of their tradition influenced later Mesoamerican societies. The Olmec played a ceremonial game on a stone ball court, a ritual

PRIMARY SOURCE **HISTORY & ARTS**

## Olmec Stone Carvings

The Olmec civilization flourished from 1200 B.C. to 400 B.C. in what we know today as Mexico. This makes them the earliest-known pre-Columbian civilization, a civilization belonging to the time before the arrival of Christopher Columbus in America. The most famous stone carvings of the Olmec civilization are giant stone heads. The massive heads were carved of basalt, a rock that the workers floated to the current location by river raft from as far as 50 to 60 miles away. The heads depict different faces with full lips, slanted eyes, and broad noses. Every head wears what resembles a helmet, though each helmet has a different symbol or decoration.

The Olmec also carved smaller sculptures from jade, obsidian, and other stone—including creatures with bat wings, realistic human ears, religious figures, and fish. Even the tools that the Olmec used for carving were themselves made of stone.

The stone-carving skill of the Olmec artisans went beyond sculpture and toolmaking. The Olmec created the first drainage system in Mesoamerica. The carvers hollowed out long stones, giving them U-shaped channels. Then they put these channels end-to-end and put rounded stone covers on them to make pipes. These stone channels show great skill in engineering. Even 3,000 years later, parts of the ancient drainage system still work today when it rains.

*An Olmec stone head in the Parque Museo de La Venta museum in Mexico*

*An Olmec standing figure*

**CRITICAL THINKING SKILLS**

1. **Identifying** Name the different objects created by Olmec stone carvers.
2. **Drawing Conclusions** Based on their large sculptures, what can we conclude about the Olmec peoples?

that the Maya people would later practice. The Maya also continued the Olmec fascination with a jaguar-like god and adopted the Olmec calendar and numerical system.

## The City of Teotihuacán

The first major city in Mesoamerica was **Teotihuacán** (TAY•oh•TEE•wuh•KAHN), or "Place of the Gods." This city was the capital of an early kingdom that arose around 250 B.C. and collapsed around A.D. 800. Located about 30 miles (48 km) northeast of Mexico City in a fertile valley, Teotihuacán occupied an area of 8 square miles (21 sq. km). It had as many as 200,000 inhabitants at its height. Along its main thoroughfare, known as the "Avenue of the Dead," were temples and palaces. All of them, however, were dominated by a massive Pyramid of the Sun. This monument rose in four tiers to a height of over 200 feet (60 m).

Most of the people of Teotihuacán were farmers. Fertile soil made their valley one of the richest farming areas in Mesoamerica.

Teotihuacán was also a busy center for trade. In scores of workshops throughout the city, skilled artisans made tools, weapons, pottery, and jewelry. Especially famous were their obsidian tools. Obsidian, a volcanic glass, was prized in Mesoamerica. It was used in tools, mirrors, and the knives with razor-sharp blades used in human and animal sacrifices. Archaeologists **estimate** that there were 400 obsidian workshops in the city.

The goods made in Teotihuacán were shipped to Central America, Mexico, and even southwestern North America. In return, the city's inhabitants received luxury items and the raw materials, such as shells and bird feathers, used in their crafts.

Sometime during the eighth century, for reasons yet unknown, the city's power declined. Eventually the ruling class left the city and around A.D. 800, the city was destroyed and abandoned.

✓Reading Check **Explaining** Where was Mesoamerica, and who were some of its first inhabitants?

## The Maya and the Toltec

**MAIN IDEA** The Maya and the Toltec ruled Mesoamerica for nearly nine centuries.

**HISTORY & YOU** How would dividing each year into 18 months affect you? Read to learn about the Maya calendar.

Far to the east of Teotihuacán, on the **Yucatán Peninsula,** another major civilization had arisen. This was the civilization of the **Maya,** which flourished between A.D. 300 and 900. It was one of the most sophisticated civilizations in the Americas.

The Maya built splendid temples and pyramids and developed a complicated calendar as **accurate** as any in existence in the world at that time. The Maya were a farming people who cleared the dense rain forests, developed farming, and centered their culture in city-states. Maya civilization included much of Central America and southern Mexico.

Sometime around 800, the Maya civilization in the central Yucatán Peninsula began

NATIONAL GEOGRAPHIC

### CULTURES OF MESOAMERICA, 900 B.C.–A.D. 1500

**Geography SKILLS**

1. **Location** Which cultures developed in the same heartland?
2. **Human-Environment Interaction** Suggest reasons for patterns you can see in areas where cities are located.

to decline. Why did this happen? Explanations include invasion, internal revolt, or a volcanic eruption. A more recent theory is that overuse of the land led to reduced crop yields.

Whatever the case, cities like Tikal and Palenque were abandoned and covered by dense jungle growth. They were not rediscovered until the nineteenth and twentieth centuries.

## Political and Social Structures

Maya cities were built around a central pyramid topped by a shrine to the gods. Nearby were other temples, palaces, and a sacred ball court. Some scholars believe that over 100,000 inhabitants may have lived in urban centers such as **Tikal** in present-day Guatemala.

Maya civilization was composed of city-states, each governed by a hereditary ruling class. These Maya city-states were often at war with each other. Ordinary soldiers who were captured in battle became slaves. Captured nobles and war leaders were used for human sacrifice.

Rulers of the Maya city-states claimed to be descended from the gods. The Maya rulers were helped by nobles and a class of scribes who may also have been priests. In addition, Maya society contained peasants and townspeople who worked as skilled artisans, officials, and merchants.

Most of the Maya people were peasant farmers. They lived on tiny plots or on terraced hills in the highlands. Houses were built of adobe and thatch. There was a fairly clear-cut division of labor. Men did the fighting and hunting; women, the homemaking and raising of children. Women also made cornmeal, the basic food of much of the population. The Maya also cultivated cacao trees, which were the source of chocolate. Chocolate was used as a beverage by the upper classes. Cocoa beans, the fruit of the cacao tree, were used as money in markets throughout the region.

Crucial to Maya civilization was its spiritual perspective. For the Maya, all of life was in the hands of divine powers. The name of their supreme god was Itzamna (eet•SAWM•nuh) or "Lizard House." Gods were ranked in order of importance. Some, like the jaguar god of night, were evil rather than good.

Like other ancient civilizations in Mesoamerica, the Maya practiced human sacrifice as a way to appease the gods. Human sacrifices were also used for special ceremonial occasions. When a male heir was presented to the throne, war captives were tortured and then beheaded. In A.D. 790, one Maya ruler took his troops into battle to gain prisoners for a celebration honoring his son.

## Writings and Calendar

The Maya created a sophisticated writing system based on **hieroglyphs** or pictures. Unfortunately, the Spanish conquerors of the sixteenth century had little respect for the Mayan language and made no effort to decipher it. Instead, the Spaniards assumed the writings were evil or of no value. As one Spanish bishop wrote:

**PRIMARY SOURCE**

"We found a large number of books in these characters and, as they contained nothing in which there were not to be seen superstition and lies of the devil, we burned them all, which they regretted to an amazing degree, and which caused them much affliction."

—Bishop Diego de Landa, sixteenth century

When the Spanish colonized the Americas, they repeated this behavior over and over. They would apply their own religious views to the native civilizations with which they came in contact. The Spaniards' subsequent destruction of religious objects, and sometimes entire cities, helped bring an end to these civilizations.

The Maya wrote on bark, folding it like an accordian, then covering the outside with thin plaster. Four of these books have survived. Maya writing was also carved onto clay, jade, bone, shells, and stone monuments.

Mayan hieroglyphs remained a mystery for centuries. Then, scholars discovered that many passages contained symbols that recorded dates in the Maya calendar.

History ONLINE

**Student Web Activity—**
Visit glencoe.com and complete the activity on early civilizations in the Americas.

INFOGRAPHICS PRIMARY SOURCE

## The Pyramid of Kukulcan

The Pyramid of Kukulcan (the Plumed Serpent) illustrates the importance of the Maya solar calendar. The 91 steps on each of the pyramid's four sides represent the days between seasonal equinoxes and solstices. The combined steps total 364, and the temple platform represents 365, the final day in the year. The pyramid's diagonal axis aligns with the sunrise at summer solstice (the longest day in the year). During the spring and fall equinoxes (when days and night are of equal length), the stepped sides of the pyramid show a snake-like pattern.

Head of Kukulcan

**CRITICAL THINKING SKILLS**

1. **Identifying** Name the celestial events that shaped the design of the pyramid at Kukulcan.
2. **Analyzing** Why might the Maya have constructed a pyramid to show these solar events?

This calendar, known as the Long Count, was based on a belief in cycles of creation and destruction. According to Maya belief, our present world was created in 3114 B.C. and is scheduled to complete its downward cycle on December 23, A.D. 2012.

The Maya used two different systems for measuring time. One was based on a solar calendar of 365 days, divided into 18 months of 20 days each, with an extra 5 days at the end. The other was based on a sacred calendar of 260 days, divided into 13 weeks of 20 days. Only trained priests could read and use this calendar. These priests also used advanced mathematics for astrological and religious purposes. Maya numerals were based on the number 20 and included a symbol for zero—a concept developed independently from Europe and Asia.

Many Maya hieroglyphics record important events in Maya history. One of the most important collections of Maya hieroglyphs is located at a city called Palenque (pah•LEHNG•KAY). There, archaeologists discovered a royal tomb covered with hieroglyphs that record the accomplishments of a ruler named Pascal.

## The Toltec

After the collapse of Teotihuacán, new peoples rose to prominence in central Mexico. Most significant were the **Toltec**. The Toltec Empire reached its high point between A.D. 950 and 1150. The center of the empire was at Tula, built on a high ridge about 30 miles (48 km) northwest of present-day Mexico City. The Aztec later plundered Tula and destroyed much historical evidence. Therefore, much of what is known about the Toltec comes from legends that later cultures told of them.

The Toltec irrigated their fields with water from the Tula River and grew a number of crops, including beans, maize, and peppers. This flourishing agriculture enabled Tula to support a population of between 40,000 to 60,000 people. Another 60,000 people lived in the surrounding territory. The city itself was between 5 and 6 square miles (13 to 16 sq. km).

The Toltec were a warlike people. Their empire included much of northern and central Mexico. They also extended their conquests into the Maya lands of Guatemala and the northern Yucatán. The Toltec controlled the upper Yucatán Peninsula from **Chichén Itzá** for centuries.

The Toltec were also builders who constructed pyramids and palaces. They brought metal-working to Mesoamerica and were the first people in the region to work in gold, silver, and copper.

Important to Toltec religion were two major gods. Quetzalcoatl (ket•suhl•KWAH•tul), the god of learning and culture, took on different forms. In one form, he was the god of wind. In another form, he was the feathered serpent. In the Aztec language, which might be related to the language of the Toltec, *quetzal* is the name of a green-feathered bird, while *coatl* means serpent. Representations of Quetzalcoatl—the Feathered Serpent—have also been found in Teotihuacán and the later Aztec Empire.

The Toltec thought of their leaders as having a connection to deities. The greatest leader was Topiltzin, who was also a high priest of Quetzalcoatl. According to legend, Topiltzin and his followers went into exile as a result of a struggle with other religious groups. Topiltzin vowed to return to Tula from the east in one of his sacred years and to reclaim his throne. A later Mesoamerican empire, the Aztec, knew the legend of Topiltzin-Quetzalcoatl well. Indeed, it may have influenced their response when European explorers arrived in the Americas.

The Toltec Empire began to decline around A.D. 1125 as a result of fighting among different groups in Tula. Around 1170, the city was sacked and much of it burned. There was no single ruling group for nearly 200 years. The Aztec Empire then gained control and carried on many Toltec traditions.

**✓Reading Check** **Describing** How did the Maya measure time?

# The Aztec

**MAIN IDEA** The Aztec ruled Mesoamerica until the arrival of the Spanish in the 1500s.

***HISTORY & YOU*** Have you seen pictures of present-day Mexico City? Read to learn about the city's ancient beginnings as Tenochtitlán, the Aztec capital.

The origins of the **Aztec** are uncertain. Sometime during the twelfth century A.D., they began a long migration that brought them to the Valley of Mexico. They eventually established a capital at **Tenochtitlán** (tay•NAWCH• teet•LAHN), now Mexico City. There they would rule until the Spanish conquest.

## Rise of the Aztec

According to their legends, when the Aztec arrived in the Valley of Mexico, other peoples drove them into a snake-infested region. The Aztec survived, however, strengthened by their belief in a sign that would come from their god of war and of the sun, Huitzilopochtli (wee•tsee•loh•POHKT•lee). The god had told them that when they saw an eagle perched on a cactus growing out of a rock, their journey would end.

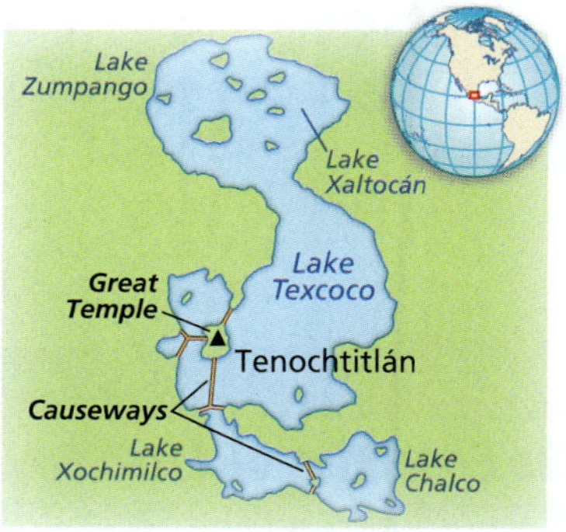


In 1325, under attack by another people, they were driven into the swamps and islands of **Lake Texcoco** (tehs•KOH•koh). On one island, they saw an eagle standing on a prickly pear cactus on a rock. There they built Tenochtitlán (or "place of the prickly pear cactus"): "Now we have found the land promised to us. We have found peace for our weary people. Now we want for nothing."

For the next 100 years, the Aztec constructed temples, other public buildings, and houses. They built roadways of stone across Lake Texcoco to the north, south, and west, linking the islands to the mainland.

With the help of two other city states, Tetzcoco and Tlacopan, the Aztec at Tenochtitlán formed a Triple Alliance. This alliance enabled the Aztec to dominate an empire that included much of today's Mexico, from the Atlantic to the Pacific Ocean and as far south as the Guatemalan border. This alliance lasted until the arrival of Spanish forces in 1519.

The new Aztec kingdom was not a centralized state but a collection of semi-independent territories that local lords governed. The Aztec ruler supported these rulers in return for **tribute,** goods or money paid by conquered peoples to their conquerors.

## Political and Social Structures

By 1500, as many as four million Aztec lived in the Valley of Mexico and the surrounding valleys of central Mexico. Like all great empires in ancient times, the Aztec state was authoritarian. The monarch, who claimed lineage with the gods, held all power. A council of lords and government officials assisted the Aztec ruler.

The nobility, the elite of society, held positions in the government. Male children in noble families were sent to temple schools, which stressed military training. Once adults, males would select a career in the military service, the government bureaucracy, or the priesthood. As a reward for their services, nobles received large estates from the government.

The rest of the population consisted of commoners, indentured workers, and slaves. Indentured workers were landless laborers who contracted to work on the nobles' estates. Slaves worked in the households of the wealthy. Male and female slaves were sold in the markets.

Most people were commoners, and many commoners were farmers. Farmers built *chinampas,* swampy islands crisscrossed by canals that provided water for their crops. The canals also provided easy travel to local markets. Aztec merchants were also

**INFOGRAPHICS** PRIMARY SOURCE

### The Education of Aztec Boys and Girls

Like children in every culture, Aztec youths were educated in the skills and values they needed in their society. This illustration from an Aztec book shows parents teaching their 13- and 14-year-old children.

From sources like this, historians know that Aztec boys went to school at age 15, after learning basic tasks at home from their fathers. At school they studied citizenship, history, religion, and arts and crafts. Boys also learned to be warriors. On the other hand, most Aztec girls were taught at home, learning to cook, shop, take care of children, and weave. Both boys and girls could study to be priests or priestesses.

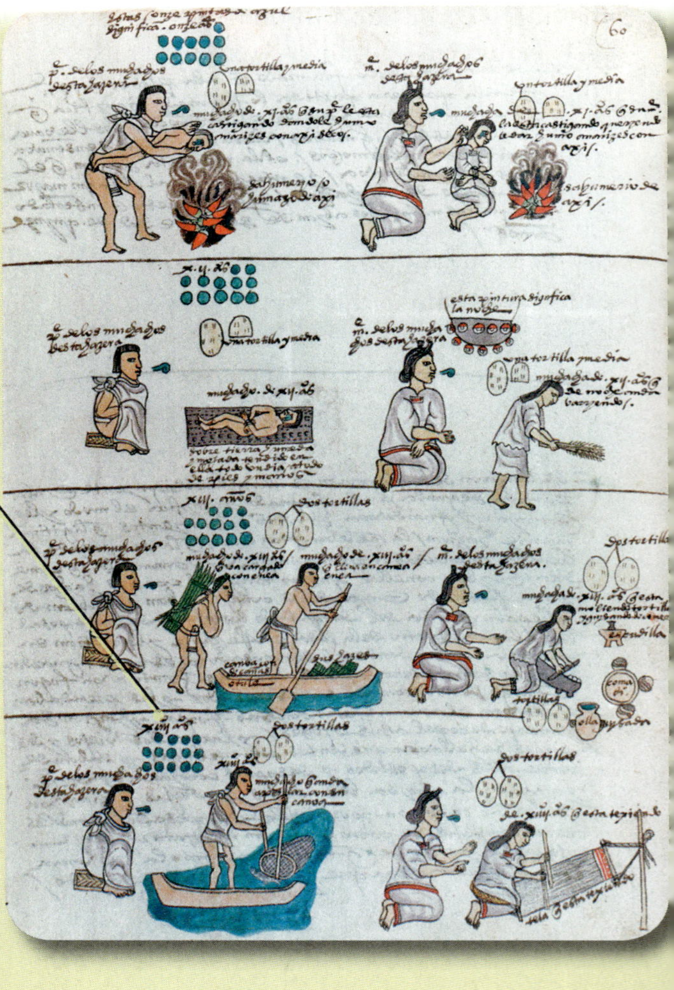

**Each dot represents a year. The children in this row are 14 years old.**

*On the left an Aztec father teaches his son to haul a load, paddle a boat, and fish. On the right an Aztec mother teaches her daughter how to grind maize and weave cloth.*

**DOCUMENT-BASED QUESTIONS**

1. **Analyzing Visuals** According to the illustration, at what age would a girl learn to weave on a loom?
2. **Synthesizing** How does the different educational focus of Aztec boys and girls reflect the different roles of Aztec men and women?

active traders. Merchants exported and traded goods made by Aztec craftspeople from imported raw materials. In exchange for their goods, the traders obtained tropical feathers, cacao beans, animal skins, and gold.

From the beginnings of their lives, boys and girls in Aztec society had very different roles. The midwife who attended the birth of a male infant said, "You must understand that your home is not here where you have been born, for you are a warrior." To a female infant, the midwife said, "As the heart stays in the body, so you must stay in the house."

Though not equal to men, Aztec women could own and inherit property and enter into contracts, something not often allowed in other world cultures at the time. Women were expected to work in the home, weave textiles, and raise children. However, some were also trained to become priestesses.

## Religion and Culture

Like other peoples in Central America and around the world, the Aztec had a polytheistic religion, believing in many gods. There was a supreme god, called Ometeotl, who represented the all-powerful forces of the heavens. Huitzilopochtli, the god of the sun and of war, was particularly important to Aztec warriors as they expanded control over neighboring peoples.

Another important god was Quetzalcoatl, who had a more direct impact on the lives of the people. According to Aztec tradition, Quetzalcoatl had left his homeland in the Valley of Mexico in the tenth century, promising to return in triumph. When the Aztec first saw Spanish explorers in the 1500s, they believed that representatives of Quetzalcoatl had returned.

Aztec religion was based on a belief in an unending struggle between the forces of good and evil throughout the universe. This struggle had created and destroyed four worlds, or suns. People believed they were now living in the time of the fifth sun. This world, too, was destined to end with the destruction of Earth by earthquakes. To postpone the day of reckoning, the Aztec practiced human sacrifice. They believed they could delay the final destruction of their world by appeasing the sun god Huitzilopochtli with sacrifices.

Aztec religion had a significant influence on their art and architecture. For example, a chief feature of Aztec culture was its monumental architecture. At the center of Tenochtitlán was the sacred district, dominated by a massive pyramid dedicated to Huitzilopochtli. At the top was a platform containing shrines to the gods and an altar for performing human sacrifices.

✓Reading Check **Summarizing** What aspect of Aztec culture is reflected in their architecture?

## SECTION 2 REVIEW

### Vocabulary

1. **Explain** the significance of: Mesoamerica, Olmec, Teotihuacán, estimate, Yucatán Peninsula, Maya, accurate, Tikal, hieroglyphs, Toltec, Chichén Itzá, Aztec, Tenochtitlán, Lake Texcoco, tribute.

### Main Ideas

2. **Explain** why obsidian was prized in Mesoamerica.
3. **List** some accomplishments of the Maya. Use a chart like the one below to make your list.

| Maya Accomplishments |
|---|
| 1. |
| 2. |
| 3. |

4. **Summarize** the role of women in the Aztec Empire.

### Critical Thinking

5. **The BIG Idea** **Theorizing** Why do you think the Maya Empire declined?
6. **Evaluating** Why was trade important to early Mesoamerican civilizations?
7. **Analyzing Visuals** Examine the Olmec sculptures shown on page 373. How are the two sculptures similar, and how are they different?

### Writing About History

8. **Informative Writing** Write a paragraph that explains the historical significance of one of the Aztec legends discussed in this section.

**History ONLINE**

For help with the concepts in this section of *Glencoe World History,* go to glencoe.com and click Study Central™.

# The Home of the Gods

Teotihuacán was the first major city in Mesoamerica. Although there is evidence this city emerged around 250 B.C., its "classic" period (when it was at its height) began around A.D. 200. During this time, monumental architecture projects were undertaken, and religious art was created. Little is known about the people who built the city because there are no written records. The name "Teotihuacán" comes from the Aztec centuries later, who called it "the home of the gods."

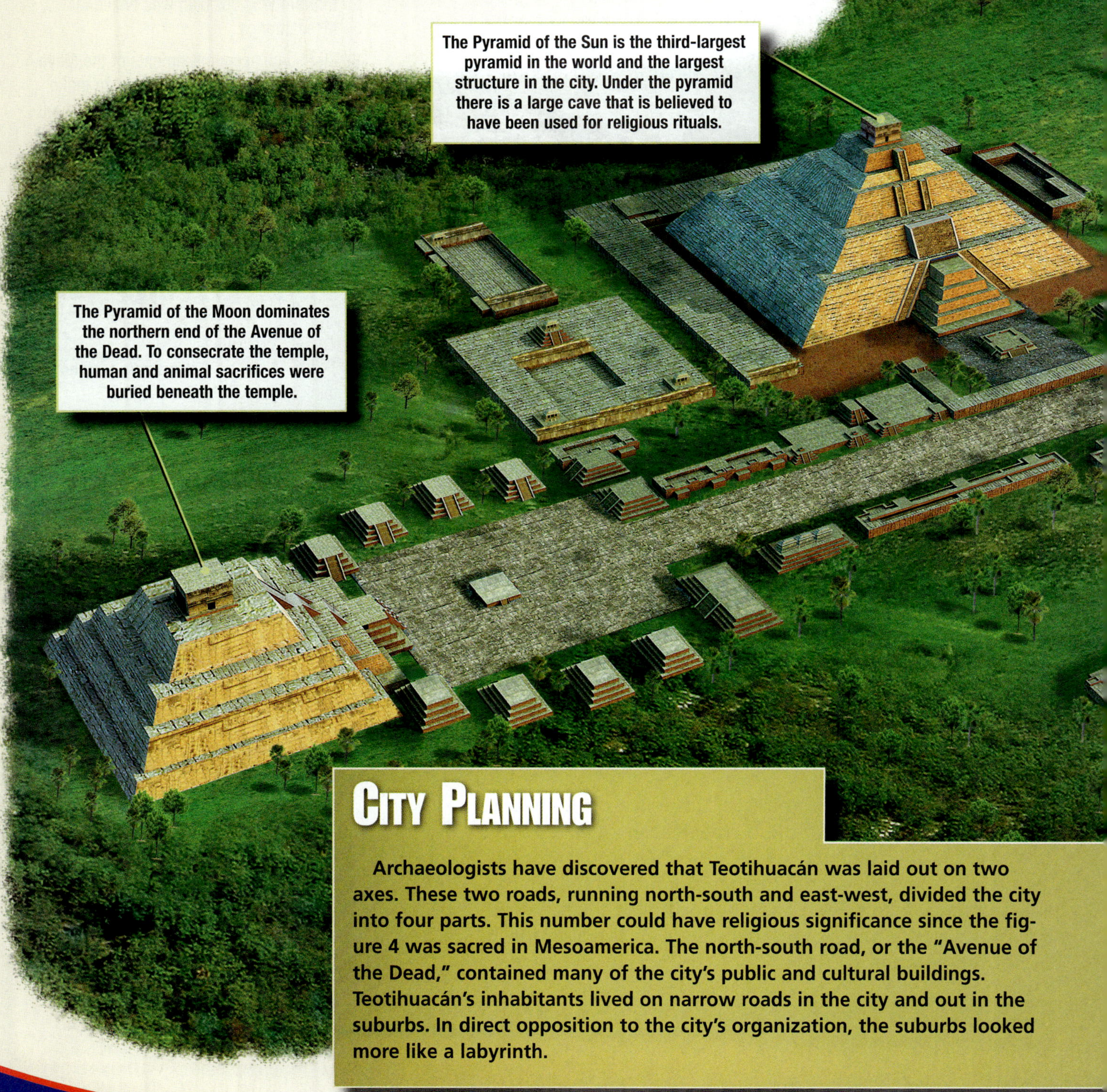


## City Planning

Archaeologists have discovered that Teotihuacán was laid out on two axes. These two roads, running north-south and east-west, divided the city into four parts. This number could have religious significance since the figure 4 was sacred in Mesoamerica. The north-south road, or the "Avenue of the Dead," contained many of the city's public and cultural buildings. Teotihuacán's inhabitants lived on narrow roads in the city and out in the suburbs. In direct opposition to the city's organization, the suburbs looked more like a labyrinth.

## Shrouded in Mystery

Although little is known about life in Teotihuacán, there is evidence of an early irrigation system surrounding the city, meaning that many in the city were farmers. The city was also heavily involved in trading finished goods. Artifacts from Teotihuacán have been discovered throughout Mesoamerica. After A.D. 600 the city began to decline in size, and around 800 was destroyed completely. Archaeologists have been unable to determine the cause of the city's destruction.

### Analyzing Visuals

1. **Concluding** How does the evidence of city planning support the presence of a civilization?
2. **Considering** What might the placement of the pyramids at Teotihuacán indicate about the role of religion in this society?

SECTION 3

Section Audio    Spotlight Video

# Early Civilizations in South America

### GUIDE TO READING

**The BIG Idea**

**Order and Security** The Inca developed a well-organized and militaristic empire with a distinct Inca culture.

**Content Vocabulary**

- maize *(p. 383)*
- *quipu (p. 385)*

**Academic Vocabulary**

- instructed *(p. 384)*
- residents *(p. 384)*

**People and Places**

- Caral *(p. 382)*
- Chavin *(p. 382)*
- Nazca *(p. 382)*
- Ecuador *(p. 383)*
- Moche *(p. 383)*
- Inca *(p. 384)*
- Cuzco *(p. 384)*
- Pachacuti *(p. 384)*
- Machu Picchu *(p. 385)*
- Urubamba River *(p. 385)*

**Reading Strategy**

**Organizing Information** As you read, complete a pyramid diagram showing the hierarchy of the Inca political organization.

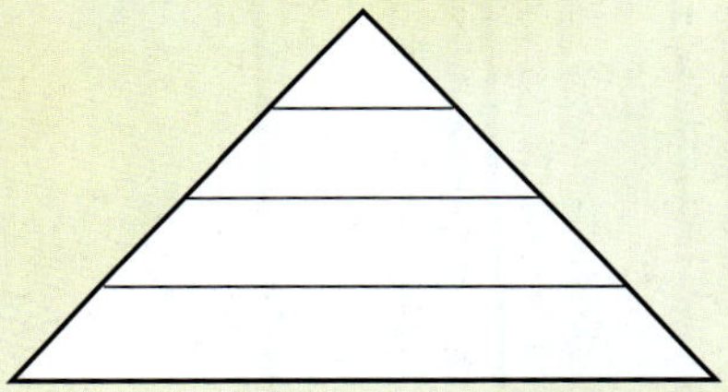

*The Chavin, Nazca, and Moche cultures, which existed in South America before the Inca, built stone buildings and sophisticated irrigation systems. Later, the Inca became a spectacular, well-organized empire. The Inca Empire was still flourishing when the Spanish arrived in the sixteenth century.*

## Early Civilizations

**MAIN IDEA** The Chavin, Nazca, and Moche cultures existed in South America before the Inca came to power.

***HISTORY & YOU*** What objects might provide future archaeologists with information about twenty-first-century America? Read to learn what archaeologists have learned about the Chavin, Nazca, and Moche peoples.

As in Mesoamerica, great civilizations flourished in early South America. The people of the Chavin, Nazca, and Moche cultures lived before the Inca gained power in South America. The cities, buildings, and artifacts these peoples left behind provide clues about their cultures.

### The Chavin and Nazca Cultures

In the Supe River valley of Peru, **Caral** is the oldest major city in the Americas. It is believed to be 1,000 years older than the cities previously known in the Western Hemisphere. The city has stone buildings for officials, apartment buildings, and grand residences. The inhabitants of Caral also developed a sophisticated system of irrigation. Caral was abandoned between 2000 B.C. and 1500 B.C.

Around 900 B.C., the **Chavin** people in the coastal regions of modern-day Peru and Ecuador built a temple with stones gathered from nearby hills. Part of a larger ceremonial complex, the temple was surrounded by stone figures depicting different gods and two pyramids. For unknown reasons, the Chavin declined around 200 B.C.

Around the same time, the **Nazca** culture appeared in Peru. The Nazca prospered from around 200 B.C. to A.D. 600. Nazca culture preserved some aspects of Chavin culture, especially its style of pottery. However, the Nazca culture built no great temples. They may have practiced their religion outdoors, as suggested by ancient formations known as the Nazca Lines. These are grooves etched into the rocky soil of southern Peru in the image of animals, especially birds, as well as humans and other geometric shapes. The images are so large, however, that their shapes can only be seen from the air.

**EARLY SOUTH AMERICAN CULTURES**

| CULTURES | CULTURAL INTEREST |
|---|---|
| Chan Chan | Capital of Chimor; the largest city in pre-Columbian America |
| Caral | Thriving city at the same time as Egypt's Old Kingdom |
| Chavin | Pyramids smaller than ones in Mesoamerica, but contained rooms, passages, and airshafts |
| Nazca | Created the Nazca lines—huge outlines of animals and shapes only recognizable from air |
| Moche | Avoided famine by growing a variety of food, including maize, sweet potatoes, and chili peppers |
| Inca | Machu Picchu; location in the Andes, saved it from looting by Spanish; significant archaeological site |

**Geography SKILLS**

1. **Location** Estimate in miles the length of the Inca Empire.
2. **Region** Examine the dates on the map legend. Then, explain what the map suggests about the relationship between these civilizations.

## The Moche

Around A.D. 300, another civilization developed near the Pacific coast not far south of the border of **Ecuador**. At **Moche** (MOH•cheh), a major urban center arose amid irrigated fields in the valley of the Moche River. This river flows from the foothills of the Andes into the Pacific Ocean. Farmers in the area grew enough **maize** (corn), peanuts, potatoes, and cotton to supply much of the region.

Moche was the capital of a powerful state. The authority of the Moche rulers may have extended as far as 400 miles (644 km) along the coast. The people of Moche had no written language, but we are able to understand something about their warlike culture from their arts and crafts. Moche paintings and pottery frequently portray warriors, prisoners, and sacrificial victims.

✓ **Reading Check** **Identifying** What is the oldest major city in the Americas?

## The Inca

**MAIN IDEA** The Inca developed a well-organized, militaristic empire with a highly structured society.

**HISTORY & YOU** How do you keep track of your school records? Read to learn about the Inca's record-keeping system.

After the collapse of the Moche civilization in the eighth century A.D., a period of decline set in until the rise of a new power about 300 years later. The kingdom of Chimor dominated the area for nearly four centuries until the Inca destroyed it and created a spectacular empire.

In the late 1300s, the **Inca** (IHNG•kuh) were only a small community in the area of **Cuzco** (KOOS•koh), a city located at 11,000 feet (3,353 m) in the mountains of southern Peru. In the 1440s, however, under the leadership of the ruler **Pachacuti**, the Inca launched a campaign of conquest. Eventually the entire region was under Inca control.

### PEOPLE in HISTORY

**Pachacuti**
?–1471 Inca ruler

The Inca Empire had grown large and powerful by the end of Pachacuti's reign. As a ruler, his strength had been the effective organization of the empire's great power—and he wanted to ensure that it remained well-organized after his death. Before he died, Pachacuti named his son Topa Inca as his successor, requiring his other sons to swear allegiance to their brother. He told Topa Inca, "Son! You now see how many great nations I leave to you, and you know what labor they have cost me. Mind that you are the man to keep and augment them. No one must raise his two eyes against you and live, even if he be your own brother." **Why did Pachacuti require his other sons to declare allegiance to Topa Inca?**

## Political and Social Structures

Pachacuti and his immediate successors, Topa Inca and Huayna Inca—*Inca* means "ruler"—extended the boundaries of the Inca Empire as far as Ecuador, central Chile, and the edge of the Amazon basin. The empire included perhaps 12 million people. The Inca state was built on war, so all young men were required to serve in the Inca army. With some 200,000 members, the army was the largest and best armed in the region. Because the Inca, like other people in the early Americas, did not make use of the wheel, supplies were carried on the backs of llamas.

Once an area was under Inca control, the local inhabitants were **instructed** in the Quechua (KECH•uh•wuh) language. Control of new territories was carefully regulated. A noble of high rank was sent out to govern the new region. Local leaders could keep their posts as long as they were loyal to the Inca ruler.

To create a well-organized empire, Pachacuti divided it into four quarters, with each ruled by a governor. In turn, the quarters were divided into provinces, each also ruled by a governor. Each province was supposed to contain about 10,000 **residents.** At the top of the entire system was the emperor, who was believed to be descended from Inti, the sun god.

Forced labor was another important feature of the state. All Inca subjects were responsible for labor service, usually for several weeks each year. Laborers, often with their entire communities, were moved according to need from one part of the country to another to take part in building projects.

Inca society was highly regimented. Men and women were required to select a marriage partner from within their own social groups. After marriage, women were expected to care for the children and to weave cloth. For women, there was only one alternative to a life of working in the home. Some young girls were chosen to serve as priestesses in temples.

The Inca economy was based on high-altitude agriculture. In the mountains, they used terraced farms, watered by irrigation systems that carried precise amounts of water into the fields. These were planted with corn, potatoes, and other crops suited to high altitudes. The farmers' houses, built of stone or adobe with thatched roofs, were located near the fields.

## Building and Culture

The Inca were great builders, the best engineers among Native American peoples. They built a system of some 24,800 miles (around 40,000 km) of roads extending from the border of modern-day Colombia to a point south of modern-day Santiago, Chile. Two major roadways extended in a north-south direction, one through the Andes and the other along the coast, with connecting routes between them.

Rest houses and storage depots were placed along the roads. Various types of bridges, including some fine, pre-modern examples of suspension bridges, were built over ravines and waterways.

The roads were used chiefly for official and military purposes. Government permission was needed to use them. Trained runners carried messages rapidly from one way station to another, enabling information to travel up to 140 miles in a single day.

The buildings and monuments of the capital city of Cuzco were the wonder of early European visitors. These structures were built of close-fitting stones without mortar—the better to withstand the frequent earthquakes in the area.

Nothing shows the architectural genius of the Inca more than the ruins of the abandoned city of Machu Picchu (MAH•CHOO PEE•CHOO). **Machu Picchu**, elevation 8,000 feet (2,400 m), was built on a lofty hilltop surrounded by mountain peaks far above the **Urubamba River**. Machu Picchu was hardly a city, containing only about 200 buildings.

In one part of Machu Picchu, a long stairway leads to an elegant stone known to the Inca as the "hitching post of the sun." Carved from the mountain, this "hitching post" may have been used as a solar observatory. During the sun festivals held in June and December, the people of Machu Picchu gathered here to chant and say prayers to Inti, the sun god.

The Inca had no writing system. Instead, they kept records using a system of knotted strings called the ***quipu***. The lack of a fully developed writing system, however, did not prevent the Inca from attaining a high level of cultural achievement.

The Inca had a well-developed tradition of court theater, consisting of both tragic and comic works. Plays often involved the recounting of valiant deeds and other historical events. Actors were not professionals but rather members of the nobility or senior officials who memorized their parts. Poetry was also recited, often accompanied by music played on reed instruments.

✓ Reading Check **Describing** What technology helped the Inca to farm in the mountains?

## SECTION 3 REVIEW

### Vocabulary

1. **Explain** the significance of: Caral, Chavin, Nazca, Ecuador, Moche, maize, Inca, Cuzco, Pachacuti, instructed, residents, Machu Picchu, Urubamba River, *quipu.*

### Main Ideas

2. **Specify** what the Moche pottery tells of their culture.
3. **Summarize** the ways that the Inca system of roads unified the empire.

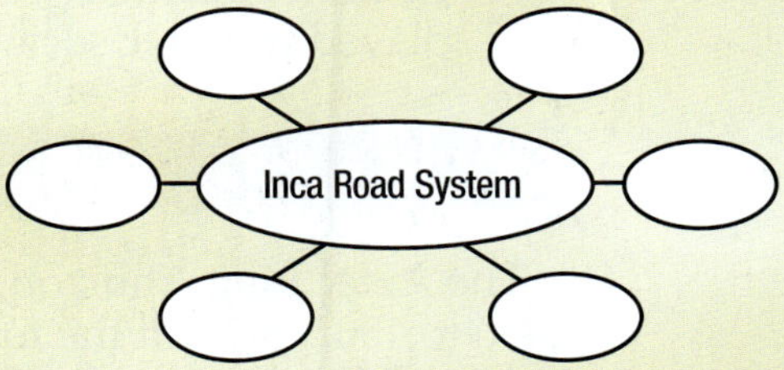


4. **Explain** the role of women in Inca society.

### Critical Thinking

5. **The BIG Idea** **Evaluating** How did Pachacuti's system of political organization contribute to the success of the Inca Empire?
6. **Comparing and Contrasting** What are some similarities and differences between the Chavin and Nazca societies? Between the Moche and Inca societies?
7. **Analyzing Visuals** Examine the image of Pachacuti on page 384. What do the items he holds tell you about the Inca?

### Writing About History

8. **Expository Writing** Write an essay about how Pachacuti ruled the Inca Empire. You may use outside sources for research. Your essay should describe Pachacuti's achievements as well as his failures.

**History ONLINE**

For help with the concepts in this section of *Glencoe World History,* go to glencoe.com and click Study Central™.

ANALYZING
PRIMARY SOURCES

# What was the Role of Religion in Aztec Society?

**How did the Aztec worship their gods?** Religion was an important feature of Aztec life. Prayers, legends, and ceremonies at great temples were all part of Aztec religious practice.

**How did outsiders view Aztec religion?** After their arrival in Mexico in 1519, the Spanish were shocked by the Aztec religious rituals. The Spaniards immediately worked to convert the Aztec to Christianity.

The Aztec and the Spanish had extremely different viewpoints about Aztec religion. Read the passages and study the illustration to learn more about the role religion played in Aztec society.

## SOURCE 1

The Aztec king Ahuizotl, who ruled from 1486 to 1502, offered the following prayer to the god Huitzilopochtli while celebrating a successful military campaign.

O almighty, powerful lord of All Created Things,
You who give us life, and whose **vassals**[1] and slaves we are,
Lord of the Day and of the Night, of the Wind and the Water,
Whose strength keeps us alive! I give you infinite thanks
For having brought me back to your city of Mexico
With the victory which you granted me.
I have returned. . . .
Since you did not frown upon my extreme youth
Or my lack of strength or the weakness of my chest,
You have subjected those remote and barbarous nations
To my power. You did all of these things!
All is yours!
All was won to give you honor and praise!
Therefore, O powerful and heroic Huitzilopochtli,
You have brought us back to this place which was only water
Before, which was enclosed by our ancestors,
And where they built our city.

## SOURCE 2

Spanish conquistador Hernán Cortés wrote the following description of a temple in the Aztec capital in a 1520 letter to the Spanish king, Charles V.

Three halls are in this grand temple, which contain the principal idols; these are of wonderful extent and height, and admirable workmanship, adorned with figures sculptured in stone and wood; leading from the halls are chapels with very small doors . . . In these chapels are the images of idols, although, as I have before said, many of them are also found on the outside; the principal ones, in which the people have greatest faith and confidence, I **precipitated**[2] from their pedestals, and cast them down the steps of the temple, purifying the chapels in which they had stood, as they were all polluted with human blood, shed ill the sacrifices. In the place of these I put images of Our Lady and the Saints, which excited not a little feeling in **Moctezuma**[3] and the inhabitants, who at first **remonstrated**[4], declaring that if my proceedings were known throughout the country, the people would rise against me; for they believed that their idols bestowed on them all **temporal**[5] good, and if they permitted them to be ill-treated, they would be angry and without their gifts, and by this means the people would be deprived of the fruits of the earth and perish with famine. . . .

[1] **vassals:** people in a subordinate position
[2] **precipitated:** threw down
[3] **Moctezuma:** the Aztec king in 1520
[4] **remonstrated:** vocally protested

▲ Tenochtitlán priests sacrifice warriors to the sun god in this Aztec drawing dated after 1519.

## SOURCE 3

Human sacrifice was a central part of Aztec religion. The Aztec believed their deities, such as the war god Huitzilopochtli, demanded a steady supply of human sacrifices. At the dedication of the great pyramid of Tenochtitlán, for example, Aztec priests sacrificed more than 20,000 people. Most of the Aztec's sacrifice victims were prisoners captured from enemy tribes. For this purpose, Aztec warriors were trained to capture, rather than kill, their enemies in battle.

The above image is an Aztec drawing of a sacrifice ritual. During these ceremonies, priests cut out the victim's heart and held it up to the sun as an offering. As shown in the image, the victim's body was then thrown down the steps of the pyramid temple.

[5] **temporal:** relating to earthly life

### DOCUMENT-BASED QUESTIONS

1. **Explaining** Why did King Ahuizotl pray to the god Huitzilopochtli?
2. **Identifying Points of View** How did Cortés's background influence his actions in the Aztec temple?
3. **Drawing Conclusions** What does this image reveal about the Aztec's relationship with their gods?
4. **Contrasting** How would Ahuizotl's description of the scene in the above image have contrasted with Cortés's description of the same image?
5. **Synthesizing** On what points do Ahuizotl and Cortés agree in their description of Aztec religious beliefs?
6. **Recognizing Bias** Consider the question "What was the role of religion in Aztec society?" How would an Aztec have answered that question differently than a Spaniard? Which answer do you think would have been most similar to your own answer to the question?

# CHAPTER 11 Visual Summary

STUDY TO GO You can study anywhere, anytime by downloading quizzes and flash cards to your PDA from glencoe.com.

RUINS OF PUEBLO BONITO

The Anasazi people built this center in Chaco Canyon.

This large complex had about 800 rooms and housed more than 1,000 people.

## The Peoples of NORTH AMERICA

- During the last Ice Age, hunters and gatherers from Asia may have crossed the land bridge in the Bering Strait to North America.
- In North America these first Americans formed distinct cultures, including Inuit, Mound Builders, Iroquois, Plains Indians, and Anasazi.

CODEX TROANO

Calendars depicted gods and symbolic creatures.

## The Peoples of MESOAMERICA

- The Olmec (c. 1200–400 B.C.) carved huge stone heads, possibly to represent their gods.
- Teotihuacán (c. 250 B.C.–A.D. 800) was Mesoamerica's first major city.
- The Maya (c. A.D. 300–900) built temples and pyramids and developed a calendar.
- The Toltec (c. A.D. 900–1200) introduced metal-working to Mesoamerica.
- The Aztec flourished from the twelfth century A.D. until the Spanish conquest in the 1500s.

HOUSE OF THE CHOSEN WOMEN—AN INCA TEMPLE

Girls chosen to become priestesses lived here.

## The Peoples of SOUTH AMERICA

- Caral, the oldest-known major city in the Americas, was abandoned by 1500 B.C.
- The Chavin, Nazca, and Moche cultures existed in South America before the Inca.
- The Inca conquered a large area under their leader Pachacuti and his successors.
- The Inca created a highly structured society with an extensive road system linking its four quarters.

## Reviewing Vocabulary

*Directions: Choose the word or words that best complete the sentence.*

**1.** The Maya writing system was based on ________, or pictures.

**A** alphanumerics
**B** hieroglyphs
**C** *chinampas*
**D** *quipu*

**2.** ________ is also known as corn.

**A** Hominy
**B** Cuzco
**C** Succotash
**D** Maize

**3.** Each Iroquois group was made up of ________, groups of related families.

**A** matriarchs
**B** pueblos
**C** clans
**D** patriarchs

**4.** Goods or money paid by conquered peoples to their conquerors is known as a ________.

**A** tribute
**B** penance
**C** tithe
**D** sacrifice

**5.** Multistoried structures that housed many of the Anasazi were known as ________.

**A** tepees
**B** longhouses
**C** igloos
**D** pueblos

## Reviewing Main Ideas

*Directions: Choose the best answers to the following questions.*

### Section 1 *(pp. 368–371)*

**6.** Who were the first peoples to cross the Bering Strait from Asia into North America?

**A** The Hopewell
**B** Hunters and gatherers
**C** Farmers
**D** The Anasazi

**7.** Which early American crops were called the "three sisters"?

**A** Beans, corn, potatoes
**B** Corn, beans, mustard
**C** Beans, squash, potatoes
**D** Corn, beans, squash

**8.** How did the Iroquois settle their differences after the Iroquois League was formed?

**A** By engaging in athletic competition
**B** By making peace offerings to their enemies
**C** By the deliberation of the Grand Council
**D** By moving farther away from their enemies

### Section 2 *(pp. 372–379)*

**9.** What was the first major city in Mesoamerica?

**A** Teotihuacán
**B** Tikal
**C** Chichén Itzá
**D** Tenochtitlán

### TEST-TAKING TIP

Some answer choices are better than others. Be sure you have read *all* the choices carefully before you pick your answer.

**Need Extra Help?**

| If You Missed Questions . . . | 1 | 2 | 3 | 4 | 5 | 6 | 7 | 8 | 9 |
|---|---|---|---|---|---|---|---|---|---|
| Go to Page . . . | 375 | 383 | 371 | 378 | 371 | 368 | 370 | 370 | 373 |

GO ON

10. How did the Maya appease their gods?
  - **A** Parades
  - **B** Penance
  - **C** Fasting
  - **D** Human sacrifice

11. How did the Toltec irrigate their fields of beans, maize, and peppers?
  - **A** With water from aqueducts
  - **B** With water from the Tula River
  - **C** With water from the Gulf of Mexico
  - **D** With water from the Yucatán River

12. Which of the following is true of the Aztec?
  - **A** They never engaged in war.
  - **B** Their culture did not have myths or legends.
  - **C** They built monumental architecture.
  - **D** They trained women to be warriors.

## Section 3 *(pp. 382–385)*

13. About what time did the Moche civilization appear?
  - **A** A.D. 300
  - **B** 200 B.C.
  - **C** 50 B.C.
  - **D** A.D. 500

14. How did the Inca ruler Pachacuti create a well-organized empire?
  - **A** He remained in sole charge of all the empire.
  - **B** He made a female his coruler.
  - **C** He divided the empire into four quarters, each ruled by a governor.
  - **D** He divided the spoils of war among the nobles.

## Critical Thinking

*Directions: Choose the best answers to the following questions.*

*Use the following chart to answer question 15.*

**Cultures of the Americas**

| | Maya | Aztec | Inca |
|---|---|---|---|
| **Government** | city-states with a hereditary ruling class thought to be descended from the gods | authoritarian monarchy claimed lineage with the gods and oversaw semi-independent territories governed by local lords | emperor claimed lineage with sun god, empire divided into quarters and provinces ruled by governors |
| **Economy** | agriculture | agriculture, trade | high-altitude agriculture |
| **Religion** | polytheistic, rituals included human sacrifice | polytheistic with one supreme god, rituals included human sacrifice | polytheistic |
| **Art & Architecture** | pyramids and temples | pyramids and shrines to the gods | theater, poetry, music |
| **Achievements** | accurate calendar, writing system | roads, *chinampas* | engineering, strong military, *quipu* |

15. What trait existed in the Maya, Aztec, and Inca cultures?
  - **A** They built pyramids.
  - **B** They had polytheistic religions.
  - **C** They had a system of city-states.
  - **D** They developed an advanced writing system.

16. Why was the Iroquois League important?
  - **A** It made the Iroquois people very wealthy.
  - **B** It protected the Iroquois from Hernán Cortés.
  - **C** It replaced Cahokia's empire in the Midwest.
  - **D** It put an end to war among the Iroquois.


**Need Extra Help?**

| If You Missed Questions . . . | 10 | 11 | 12 | 13 | 14 | 15 | 16 |
|---|---|---|---|---|---|---|---|
| Go to Page . . . | 375 | 376 | 379 | 383 | 384 | 375 | 370 |

GO ON

**17.** When did agriculture arise in the Americas?

**A** When the Olmec began farming along the riverbanks of the Gulf of Mexico

**B** When the Maya established farming villages

**C** When the Inuit moved to North America from Asia

**D** When the Aztec came into power in Mesoamerica

**18.** Why do historians not know more about the ancient civilizations of Mesoamerica?

**A** Because the ancient civilizations had no writing systems

**B** Because the ancient civilizations left no artifacts behind

**C** Because the conquering peoples destroyed many religious artifacts and leveled cities

**D** Because excavations did not begin until quite recently

*This Peruvian print from 1609 shows an Inca man using the* quipu. *Base your answer to question 19 on the print and on your knowledge of world history.*

**19.** What information can historians gain from this image?

**A** The Inca lived in North America.

**B** The Inca played a domino-like game.

**C** The Inca had a method to keep records.

**D** The Inca had a complicated written language.

## Document-Based Questions

*Directions: Analyze the document and answer the short-answer questions that follow the document. Base your answers on the document and on your knowledge of world history.*

Bernal Díaz, who accompanied Hernán Cortés on a Spanish expedition to Mexico in 1519, wrote:

> *"When we beheld so many cities and towns on the water, and other large settlements built on firm ground, and that broad causeway running so straight and perfectly level to the city of Tenochtitlán, we were astonished because of the great stone towers and temples and buildings that rose up out of the water."*
>
> —Bernal Díaz, as quoted in *The Conquest of New Spain,* John M. Cohen, trans., 1975

**20.** Which early civilization built the city of Tenochtitlán?

**21.** Why were the Spanish so "astonished" by what they saw?

## Extended Response

**22.** Throughout time people have had to adapt to their environment in order to survive. What was the relationship between the early peoples of the Americas and their environment?

**History ONLINE**

For additional test practice, use Self-Check Quizzes—Chapter 11 at glencoe.com.

**Need Extra Help?**

| If You Missed Questions . . . | 17 | 18 | 19 | 20 | 21 | 22 |
|---|---|---|---|---|---|---|
| Go to Page . . . | 372 | 375 | 391 | 377 | 391 | 369 |

STOP

# TIME NOTEBOOK

ROGER-VIOLLET/TOPHAM/THE IMAGE WORKS

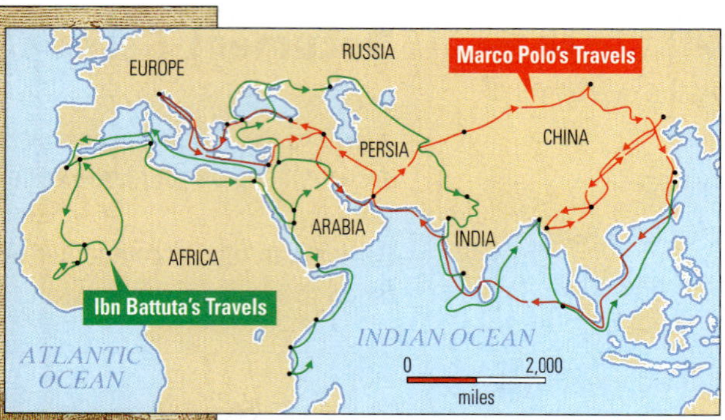


SCOTT MACNEILL

## Ibn Battuta: The Ultimate Road Trip

*Ibn Battuta makes Marco Polo seem like a couch potato. The Arab explorer has journeyed just about everywhere in the world, covering nearly 70,000 miles over 30 years.*

Battuta's first trip was a pilgrimage to Makkah from his hometown of Tangier, Morocco, in 1325. From there, he just kept going and going. First stop was Mesopotamia, and then he continued along the Silk Road in central Asia. Next was a voyage along the coast of East Africa, where he visited Ethiopia and Zanzibar. After a quick trip home to refresh himself, Battuta left to explore Constantinople, headed into Afghanistan and India, and later made the trek to China. He also explored Europe, North Africa, and finally, the kingdom of Mali.

In his journeys, Battuta didn't always travel first class. He was attacked by pirates and thieves, nearly drowned in storms at sea, was kidnapped, and avoided the Black Death like, well, the plague. Battuta promises to write down the story of his epic adventures. No doubt it will be a very thick book.

## VERBATIM

“Blood was pooled and the skulls of the people of the central place of Tikal were piled up.”

**WORDS ON A STAIRCASE**
*of a 7th century pyramid in Guatemala, describing the fate of the enemies of a ruler of the Maya city of Dos Pilas*

“Solomon, I have outdone thee.”

**JUSTINIAN THE GREAT,**
*in 537, head of Byzantine Empire, comparing the magnificent church Hagia Sophia, in Constantinople, to the ancient Temple of Solomon in Israel*

“Teach your tongue to say 'I do not know' and you will progress.”

**MOSES MAIMONIDES,**
*rabbi and philosopher born in Muslim Spain in 1135*

“To no man will we sell, or deny, or delay, right or justice.”

**THE MAGNA CARTA,**
*On the powers of the English king, 1215*

“Fireworks crackle, the year ends/ Spring wind wafts, and I downed cups of wine/Early New Year morning, as sun shines bright/Every household is busy replacing old with new.”

**WANG ANSHI,**
*politician and poet, who as a minister of the Song dynasty in 11th century China, has reformed the government and created policies to help the poor*

## THE SOFTER SIDE OF THE VIKINGS

They loot. They pillage. And occasionally they loot *and* pillage. That's the impression most people have about Vikings. But Europe's bad boys do have their good points. Although *Viking* is the name given to those Norse who go on raids, most Norse are farmers and herders. The Norse have composed epic poems, play chess, make iron tools, and craft jewelry. They also build the greatest ships in the world. Of course, complaints about the Vikings' rude behavior are justified. After all, they have been stealing stuff from the coasts of England and Ireland for a couple of hundred years. With the Norse, it seems that you have to take the bad with the good.

THE PRINT COLLECTOR/ALAMY

VISUAL ARTS LIBRARY (LONDON)/ALAMY

## Annals of Medicine

*Getting sick in medieval Europe is no picnic. Here are some standard medical treatments—along with a fake one. Can you find it?*

1. Herbal treatments are recommended for anything from the Black Death to insomnia. Ingredients may include urine, ground-up worms, and roasted snake skin.
2. Want relief from smallpox? Hang colored cloth around your bed.
3. Diseases, say experts, are caused by a buildup of bodily fluids (called "humors"), such as blood. Having a barber open a vein to rid you of some blood should balance the humors and bring good health.
4. Many doctors diagnose problems by a patient's astrological sign. For example, a person with a certain sign might be prone to colds or sadness.
5. To treat a cough and other lung problems, patients should set moldy chestnuts on fire and breathe in the smoke.
6. Some physicians believe physical sickness is caused by sin. Their prescription? Go on a pilgrimage and/or pray.
7. Here's an effective way to clean your teeth: Simply rub them with powder made from crushed seashells.

Answer: 5

## Milestones

**PUBLISHED. THE TALE OF GENJI** in the year 1000, by Murasaki Shikibu, a Japanese noblewoman. It is the story of the son of the emperor and his romantic adventures in the royal court. Because of its length and insight into the characters, many scholars are claiming that this is the world's first novel.

**BUILT.** A major urban project called **MACHU PICCHU,** by Inca architects for the emperor Pachacuti, completed around 1470. Located 8,000 feet high in the Andes, it consists of about 200 buildings. About 1,200 people are expected to move into this city in the sky, many of them members of the royal family. Most impressive are the spectacular views. Location, as they say, is everything.

**SUCCEEDED. SUNNI ALI** by his son Sunni Baru, as emperor of the kingdom of Songhai. Through military might, Sunni Ali managed to turn that backwater nation into a vast empire. After taking power in 1464, Sunni Ali built up a powerful army and navy. When he died in 1492, he controlled much of the territory belonging to the Mali Empire. Pundits believe that Askia Muhammad Toure already has designs on Baru's office.

## BY THE NUMBERS

**0** The number of times that rules for the use of the number zero in mathematical calculations appeared before Indian mathematician Brahmagupta put them to paper in 628 in a book called *Brahmasputha Siddhanta*

**275 million** The approximate world population in the year 1000

**33** The average life expectancy of an English person during the Middle Ages

**68.27** The average height in inches of a European during the eleventh century

MARY EVANS PICTURE LIBRARY/THE IMAGE WORKS

**33** The percent of the total population of the Muslim world killed by the Black Death by the year 1349

## CRITICAL THINKING

1. **Identifying Points of View** What does the writer think about the Vikings? Explain the reasons for your answer.
2. **Speculating** Why do you think Ibn Battuta traveled so widely and for so many years?

# *The* Renaissance *and the* Individual

## Essential Questions

***Did people begin to see themselves in new ways during the Renaissance? Was this way of thinking a complete break from medieval thought?***

**Some historians argue** that up through the Middle Ages in Europe, people were defined in groups—based on race, social status, political or religious affiliation, or employment—not as individuals. According to this school of thought, a shift in perception about individuals occurred with the Renaissance, a period in Western Europe lasting from approximately A.D. 1350 to A.D. 1600.

Nineteenth-century historian Jacob Burckhardt first addressed this shift in perception. He describes it in the following way:

> In the Middle Ages both sides of human consciousness—that which was turned within as that which was turned without[1]—lay dreaming or half awake beneath a common veil.... Man was conscious of himself only as a member of a race, people, party, family, or corporation—only through some general category. In Italy this veil first melted into air; an *objective* treatment and consideration of the State and of all the things of this world became possible. The *subjective* side at the same time asserted itself with corresponding emphasis; man became a spiritual *individual*, and recognized himself as such.
>
> —Jacob Burckhardt, *The Civilization of the Renaissance in Italy*

Burckhardt believed medieval thought held people back from realizing their full, individual potential for greatness. Use the knowledge gained from the primary source, the concepts on the time line, and the images in this feature, along with Chapter 12, to answer the Essential Questions.

[1] both how people saw themselves and the world around them

## EUROPEAN CONCEPTS

Use the time line page references to read more about individual and group identities in pre-Renaissance Europe.

500 B.C. — A.D. 1

**c. 470–399 B.C.** The Socratic method and the role of reason, p. 129

**c. 450 B.C.** Roman law, pp. 149–150

**c. 384–322 B.C.** Aristotle's description of a Greek citizen, p. 113

**27 B.C.** Roman Empire established, Roman culture spreads, p. 156

Use the images to compare and contrast how individuals and groups were depicted in medieval and Renaissance art.

▲ This fresco, painted by Andrea Mantegna between A.D. 1465 and A.D. 1474, depicts Ludovico Gonzaga, a ruler of the Italian city of Mantua during the Renaissance. He is surrounded by his family and courtiers.

This medieval manuscript image, painted around A.D. 998, shows the Holy Roman Emperor Otto III surrounded by nobility and clergy. ▶

**c. A.D. 100**
Roles of Roman women, p. 163

**c. A.D. 800–1500**
The feudal system, pp. 310–313

**c. A.D. 1200s–1600s**
The Inquisition, p. 346

A.D. 1000 — A.D. 1500

**c. A.D. 800–1750**
The manorial system, pp. 336–338

**c. A.D. 1100**
Medieval merchants and guilds, pp. 340–341

**A.D. 1347–1351**
The Black Death, p. 354

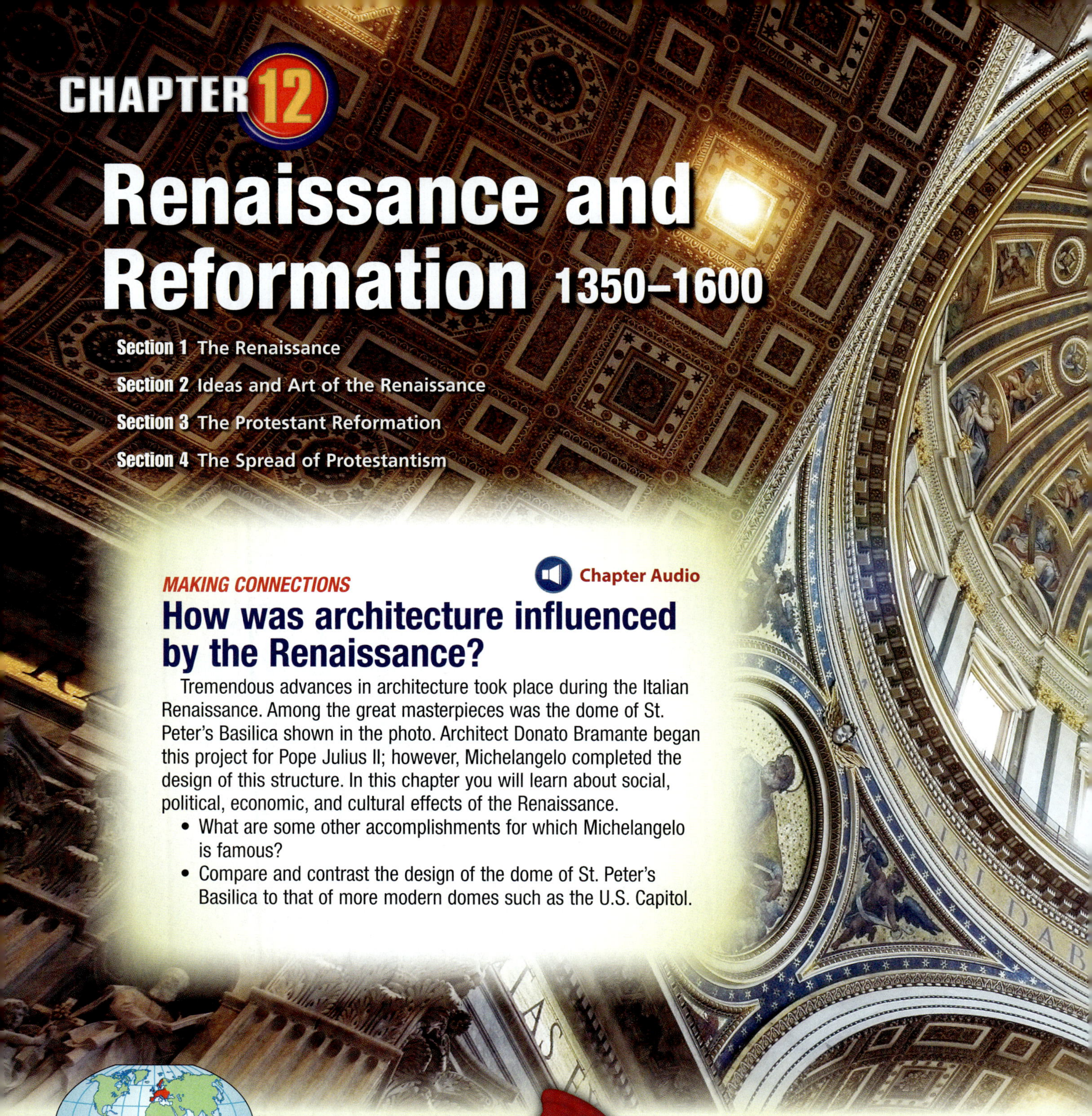

# CHAPTER 12

# Renaissance and Reformation 1350–1600



*MAKING CONNECTIONS*

Chapter Audio

## How was architecture influenced by the Renaissance?

Tremendous advances in architecture took place during the Italian Renaissance. Among the great masterpieces was the dome of St. Peter's Basilica shown in the photo. Architect Donato Bramante began this project for Pope Julius II; however, Michelangelo completed the design of this structure. In this chapter you will learn about social, political, economic, and cultural effects of the Renaissance.

- What are some other accomplishments for which Michelangelo is famous?
- Compare and contrast the design of the dome of St. Peter's Basilica to that of more modern domes such as the U.S. Capitol.

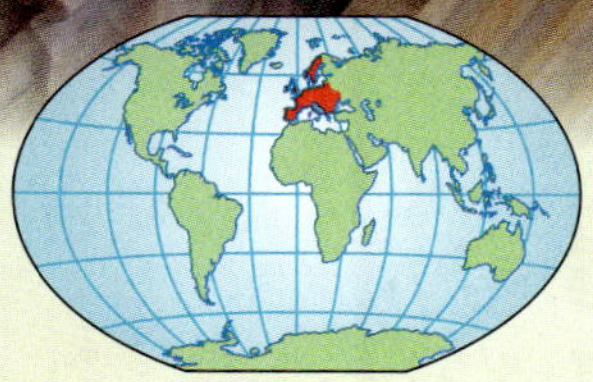

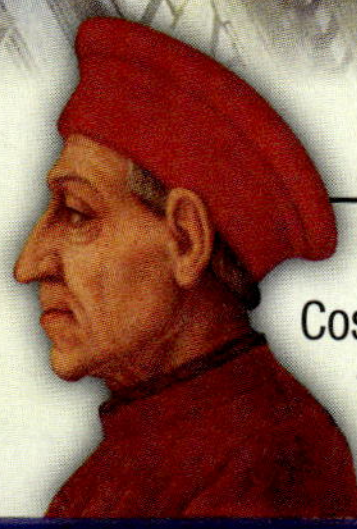

**EUROPE ▶**

**c. 1350** Italian Renaissance begins

**1434** Cosimo de' Medici takes control of Florence

**1517** Martin Luther presents his Ninety-five Theses

**1350** — **1500**

**THE WORLD ▶**

**1405** Zheng He of China begins first voyage of exploration

**1518** Spanish ship carries first enslaved Africans to the Americas

**1534**
Henry VIII initiates creation of Church of England

**1555**
Peace of Augsburg divides Christianity in Germany

**1600**

**1535**
Francisco Pizarro conquers the Inca Empire

## FOLDABLES™ Study Organizer

**Analyzing** Analyze how the Renaissance and Reformation affected various parts of Europe. Record your findings in a Layered-Look Book. Make sure you label each effect as *Renaissance* or *Reformation*.

**History ONLINE** Visit glencoe.com and enter *QuickPass*™ code GWHEA7447c12 for Chapter 12 resources.

SECTION 1

Section Audio    Spotlight Video

# The Renaissance

## GUIDE TO READING

### The BIG Idea

**Ideas, Beliefs, and Values** Between 1350 and 1550, Italian intellectuals believed they had entered a new age of human achievement.

### Content Vocabulary

- urban society *(p. 398)*
- secular *(p. 398)*
- mercenaries *(p. 400)*
- dowry *(p. 403)*

### Academic Vocabulary

- instability *(p. 398)*
- decline *(p. 398)*

### People, Places, and Events

- Italian Renaissance *(p. 398)*
- Leonardo da Vinci *(p. 398)*
- Milan *(p. 399)*
- Venice *(p. 399)*
- Florence *(p. 399)*
- Francesco Sforza *(p. 400)*
- Cosimo de' Medici *(p. 400)*
- Lorenzo de' Medici *(p. 400)*
- Rome *(p. 400)*
- Niccolò Machiavelli *(p. 401)*

### Reading Strategy

**Categorizing Information** As you read, use a web diagram like the one below to identify the major principles of Machiavelli's work *The Prince.*

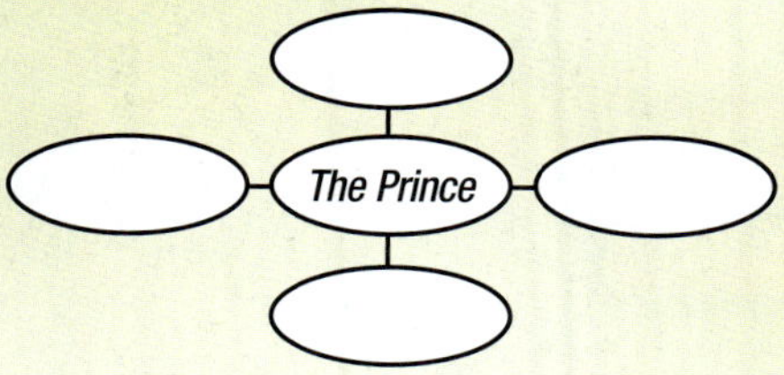


*Beginning in Italy and spanning two centuries, the Renaissance emphasized secularism, awareness of ties to the ancient Greek and Roman worlds, and the ability of the individual. City-states became centers of political, economic, and social life. Machiavelli influenced political thought, and Castiglione defined what made a perfect Renaissance noble. The Renaissance affected everyone, from noble to peasant.*

## The Italian Renaissance

**MAIN IDEA** As the Renaissance began, three Italian city-states were the centers of Italian political, economic, and social life.

**HISTORY & YOU** Do you excel at more than one skill, for example, math and art? Read to learn about the Renaissance belief in individual ability.

The word *renaissance* means "rebirth." A number of people who lived in Italy between 1350 and 1550 believed that they had witnessed a rebirth of the ancient Greek and Roman worlds. To them, this rebirth marked a new age. Historians later called this period the Renaissance, or **Italian Renaissance**—a period of European history that began in Italy and spread to the rest of Europe. What are the most important characteristics of the Renaissance?

First, Renaissance Italy was largely an **urban society**. As the Middle Ages progressed, powerful city-states became the centers of Italian political, economic, and social life. Within this growing urban society, a **secular**, or worldly, viewpoint emerged as increasing wealth created new enjoyment of material things.

Second, the Renaissance was an age of recovery from the disasters of the fourteenth century—the plague, political **instability,** and a **decline** of Church power. Recovery went hand in hand with a rebirth of interest in ancient culture. Italian thinkers became aware of their own Roman past—the remains of which were to be seen all around them. They also became intensely interested in the culture that had dominated the ancient Mediterranean world. This revival affected both politics and art.

Third, a new view of human beings emerged as people in the Italian Renaissance emphasized individual ability. As Leon Battista Alberti, a fifteenth-century Italian, said, "Men can do all things if they will." A high regard for human worth and a realization of what individuals could achieve created a new social ideal. The well-rounded, universal person could achieve much in many areas. **Leonardo da Vinci** (VIHN•chee), for example, was a painter, sculptor, architect, inventor, and mathematician.

## HISTORY & ARTS

## THE ITALIAN RENAISSANCE

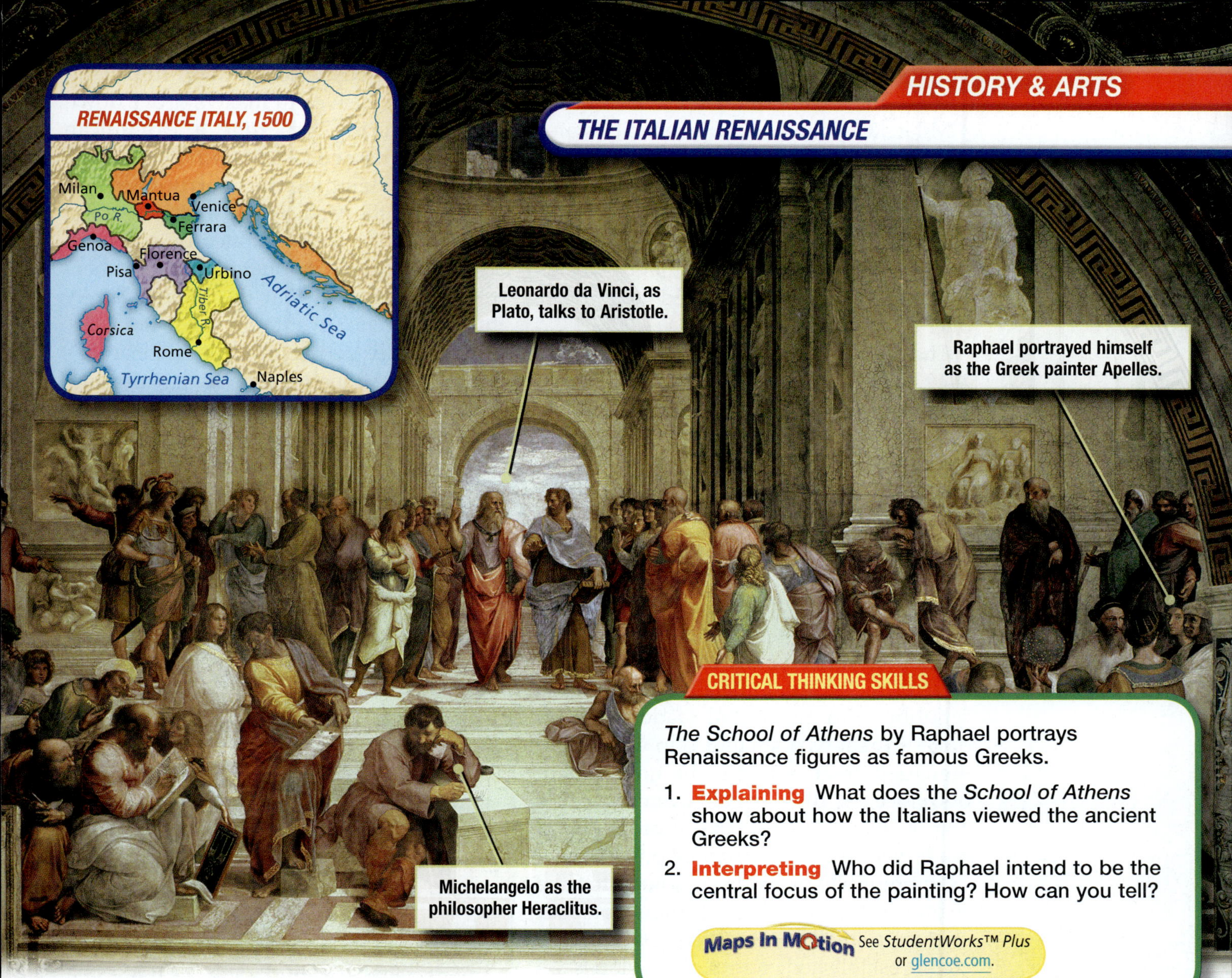


**CRITICAL THINKING SKILLS**

*The School of Athens* by Raphael portrays Renaissance figures as famous Greeks.

1. **Explaining** What does the *School of Athens* show about how the Italians viewed the ancient Greeks?
2. **Interpreting** Who did Raphael intend to be the central focus of the painting? How can you tell?

**Maps In Motion** See *StudentWorks™ Plus* or glencoe.com.

Of course, not all parts of Italian society were directly affected by these three general characteristics of the Italian Renaissance. The wealthy upper classes, who made up a small percentage of the total population, more actively embraced the new ideas and activities. Indirectly, however, the Italian Renaissance did have some impact on ordinary people. Especially in the cities, many of the intellectual and artistic achievements of the period were highly visible and difficult to ignore. The churches, wealthy homes, and public buildings were decorated with art that celebrated religious and secular themes, the human body, and an appreciation of classical antiquity.

## The Italian States

During the Middle Ages, Italy had failed to develop a centralized monarchical state. The lack of a single strong ruler made it possible for a number of city-states in northern and central Italy to remain independent. Three of them—**Milan**, **Venice**, and **Florence**—expanded and played crucial roles in Italian politics.

The Italian city-states prospered from a flourishing trade that had expanded in the Middle Ages. Italian merchants also profited from the Crusades. High demand for Middle Eastern goods enabled them to set up new trading centers in eastern ports.

There, they obtained silks, sugar, and spices, which were sent back to Europe.

Milan was one of the richest city-states in Italy. It was located in the north, at the crossroads of the main trade routes from Italian coastal cities to the Alpine passes. In the fourteenth century, members of the Visconti family established themselves as dukes of Milan. They extended their power over all of Lombardy.

The last Visconti ruler of Milan died in 1447. **Francesco Sforza** (SFAWRT•sah) then conquered the city and became its duke. Sforza led a band of **mercenaries**—soldiers who fought for the highest bidder. The Visconti and Sforza rulers built a strong centralized state. By creating an efficient tax system, they generated enormous revenues for the government.

Venice was another major northern Italian city-state. As a link between Asia and Western Europe, the city drew traders from all over the world. Officially Venice was a republic with an elected leader called a doge. In reality, a small group of wealthy merchant-aristocrats ran the government of Venice for their benefit. Venice's trade empire was tremendously profitable and made Venice an international power.

The republic of Florence dominated the region of Tuscany. During the fourteenth century, a small but wealthy group of merchants established control of the Florentine government. They waged a series of successful wars against their neighbors and established Florence as a major city-state.

In 1434, **Cosimo de' Medici** (MEH•duh•chee) took control of the city. The wealthy Medici family ran the government from behind the scenes. Using their wealth and personal influence, Cosimo, and later **Lorenzo de' Medici**, his grandson, dominated the city when Florence was the cultural center of Italy.

As the city-states grew wealthier, the power of the Church began to decline slightly. Some church doctrines, like the sinfulness of usury, were openly ignored. Many Italian leaders borrowed and loaned money without fear of reprisal.

During the late 1400s, Florence experienced an economic decline. Most of its economy was based on the manufacturing of cloth. Increased competition from English and Flemish cloth makers drove down profits. During this time a Dominican preacher named Girolamo Savonarola began condemning the corruption and excesses of the Medici family. Citizens, tired of Medici rule and frustrated by economic events, turned to Savonarola. So many people followed him that the Medici family turned Florence over to his followers.

Eventually people tired of Savonarola's strict regulations on gambling, horseracing, swearing, painting, music, and books. Savonarola also attacked the corruption of the Church, which angered the pope. In 1498, Savonarola was accused of heresy and sentenced to death. The Medici family returned to power.

## The Italian Wars

The growth of powerful monarchical states in the rest of Europe eventually led to trouble for the Italian states. Attracted by the riches of Italy, the French king Charles VIII led an army of 30,000 men into Italy in 1494. He occupied the kingdom of Naples in southern Italy. Northern Italian states turned for help to the Spanish, who gladly agreed to send soldiers to Italy. For the next 30 years, the French and the Spanish battled in Italy as they fought to dominate the country.

A decisive turning point in their war came in 1527. On May 5, thousands of troops belonging to the Spanish king Charles I, along with mercenaries from different countries, arrived at the city of **Rome**. They had not been paid for months. When they yelled, "Money! Money!" their leader responded, "If you have ever dreamed of pillaging a town and laying hold of its treasures, here now is one, the richest of them all, queen of the world."

The next day the invading forces smashed the gates and pushed into the city. The troops went berserk in a frenzy of bloodshed and looting. The terrible sack of Rome in 1527 by the armies of Charles I ended the Italian wars and left the Spanish a dominant force in Italy.

✓Reading Check **Explaining** What attracted the French king Charles VIII to Italy?

## Machiavelli on Power

**MAIN IDEA** Machiavelli's *The Prince* has profoundly influenced political leaders.

**HISTORY & YOU** Do you believe that morality has a place in politics? Read to learn about Machiavelli's views on political power.

No one gave better expression to the Italians' love affair with political power than **Niccolò Machiavelli** (MA•kee•uh•VEH•lee). His book *The Prince* is one of the most influential works on political power in the Western world.

Machiavelli's central thesis in *The Prince* concerns how to acquire—and keep—political power. In the Middle Ages, many writers on political power had stressed the moral side of a prince's activity—how a ruler ought to behave based on Christian principles. Machiavelli rejected this popular approach. He believed that morality had little to do with politics.

From Machiavelli's point of view, a prince's attitude toward power must be based on an understanding of human nature, which he believed was basically self-centered. Political activity, therefore, should not be restricted by moral principles. A prince acts on behalf of the state. According to Machiavelli, for the state's sake, a leader must do good when possible but evil when necessary.

Machiavelli abandoned morality as the basis for analyzing political activity and argued that the ends justify the means. His views have had a profound influence on political leaders who followed.

✓Reading Check **Identifying** What was Machiavelli's central thesis in *The Prince*?

**HISTORY & ARTS** PRIMARY SOURCE

### Patronage of the Medici Family

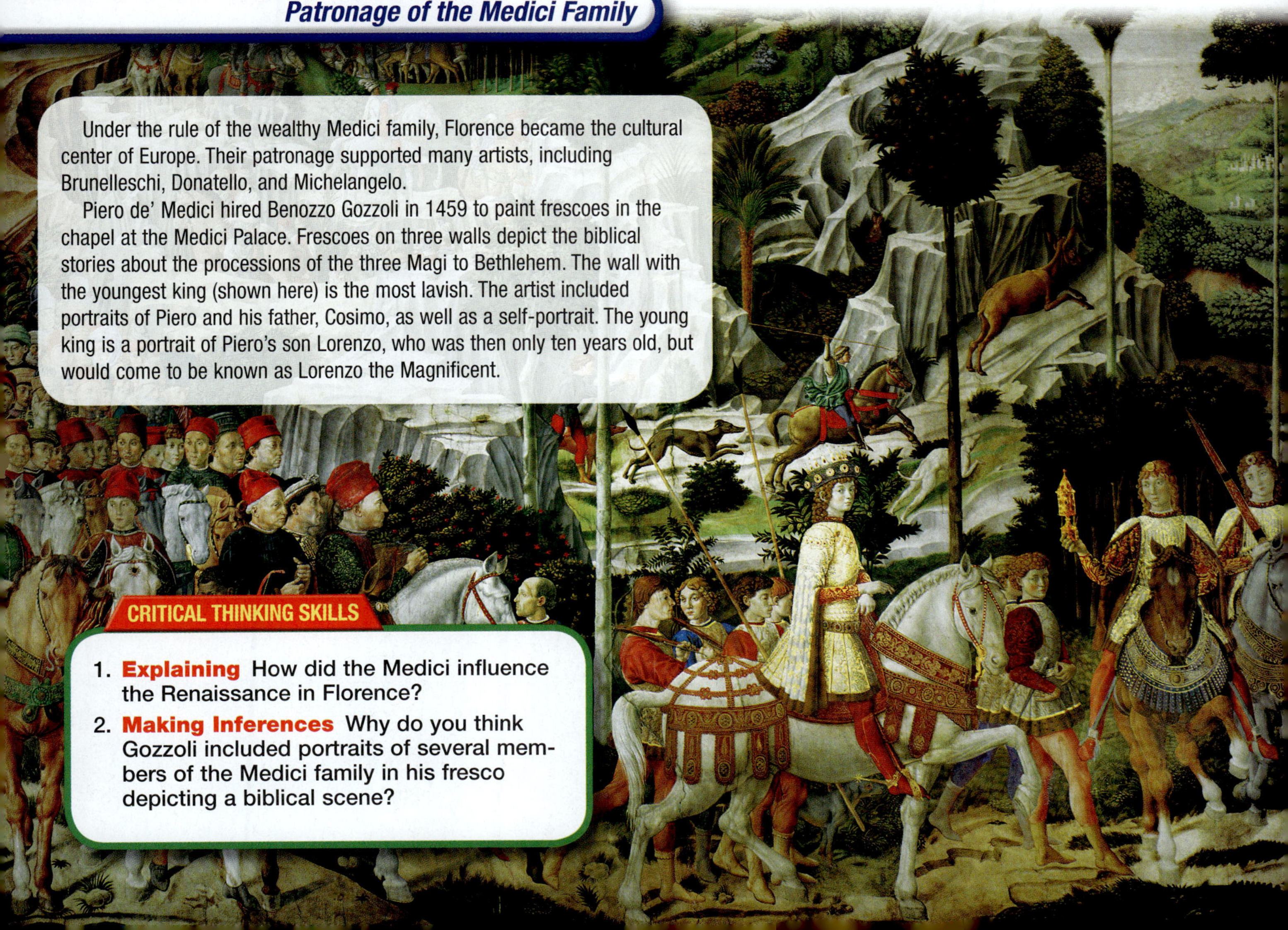

Under the rule of the wealthy Medici family, Florence became the cultural center of Europe. Their patronage supported many artists, including Brunelleschi, Donatello, and Michelangelo.

Piero de' Medici hired Benozzo Gozzoli in 1459 to paint frescoes in the chapel at the Medici Palace. Frescoes on three walls depict the biblical stories about the processions of the three Magi to Bethlehem. The wall with the youngest king (shown here) is the most lavish. The artist included portraits of Piero and his father, Cosimo, as well as a self-portrait. The young king is a portrait of Piero's son Lorenzo, who was then only ten years old, but would come to be known as Lorenzo the Magnificent.

**CRITICAL THINKING SKILLS**

1. **Explaining** How did the Medici influence the Renaissance in Florence?
2. **Making Inferences** Why do you think Gozzoli included portraits of several members of the Medici family in his fresco depicting a biblical scene?

## Renaissance Society

**MAIN IDEA** Changes in the social classes occurred during the Renaissance.

***HISTORY & YOU*** Should your parents choose your future spouse? Read to learn about the marriage customs during the Renaissance.

In the Middle Ages, society was divided into three social classes: the clergy, the nobility, and the peasants and townspeople. Although this social order continued into the Renaissance, some changes became evident.

### The Nobility

Although many European nobles faced declining incomes prior to the Renaissance, many had retained their lands and titles. By 1500, nobles, old and new, again dominated society. Making up only 2 to 3 percent of the population in most countries, nobles held important political posts and served as advisers to the king.

Nobles, or aristocrats, were expected to fulfill certain ideals. The characteristics of a perfect Renaissance noble were expressed in *The Book of the Courtier,* written by Baldassare Castiglione (KAHS•teel•YOH•NAY), an Italian, in 1528. First, a noble was born, not made. He must have character, grace, and talent. Second, the noble had to be a warrior, but also needed a classical education and interest in the arts. Third, the noble had to follow a certain standard of conduct. What was the purpose of these standards?

**PRIMARY SOURCE**

"[T]he aim of the perfect Courtier is so to win . . . the favor and mind of the prince whom he serves that he may be able to tell him . . . the truth about everything he needs to know . . . and that when he sees the mind of his prince inclined to a wrong action, he may dare to oppose him . . . so as to dissuade him of every evil intent and bring him to the path of virtue."

—Baldassare Castiglione, *The Book of the Courtier,* 1528

## SCIENCE, TECHNOLOGY, & SOCIETY

### Gutenberg's Press

In 1455, Johannes Gutenberg produced the first printed book, a Bible, in Germany. His printing press brought together several existing technologies. The press was adapted from a wine press. The type was adapted from the stamp goldsmiths used to mark their finished products. The ink was based on artists' ink. One innovation was the use of paper instead of the parchment or vellum typical of handwritten manuscripts.

The rise in literacy during the Renaissance created a growing audience for books. To satisfy the demand, more books were produced in the first 50 years of printing than in the entire history of the world up to 1450. The printing press greatly accelerated the spread of ideas.

**Gutenberg's press, located in the Gutenberg Museum in Mainz, Germany.**

**CRITICAL THINKING SKILLS**

1. **Finding the Main Idea** What technologies did Gutenberg bring together in his printing press?
2. **Analyzing** How did the printing press contribute to the Renaissance?

The aim of the perfect noble was to serve his prince in an effective and honest way. Nobles would adhere to Castiglione's principles for hundreds of years while they continued to dominate European social and political life.

## Peasants and Townspeople

In the Renaissance, peasants still constituted 85 to 90 percent of the total European population. Serfdom continued to decrease with the decline of the manorial system. By 1500, especially in western Europe, more and more peasants became legally free.

Townspeople made up the rest of this social class. At the top of urban society were the patricians. With their wealth from trade, industry, and banking, they dominated their communities. Below them were the burghers—the shopkeepers, artisans, guild masters, and guild members. Below the burghers were the workers, who earned pitiful wages, and the unemployed. Both of the latter groups lived miserable lives and made up perhaps 30 or 40 percent of the urban population.

During the late 1300s and the 1400s, urban poverty increased dramatically throughout Europe. One rich merchant, who had little sympathy for the poor, wrote:

**PRIMARY SOURCE**

> "Those that are lazy in a way that does harm to the city, and who can offer no just reason for their condition, should either be forced to work or expelled from the city. The city would thus rid itself of that most harmful part of the poorest class."
>
> —fifteenth-century Florence merchant

## Family and Marriage

The family bond was a source of great security. Parents carefully arranged marriages to strengthen business or family ties. Often they worked out the details when their children were only two or three years old. The marriage contract included a **dowry**, a sum of money that the wife's family gave to the husband upon marriage.

The father-husband was the center of the Italian family. He managed all finances (his wife had no share in his wealth) and made the decisions that determined his children's lives. The mother's chief role was to supervise the household. A father had absolute authority over his children until he died or formally freed them. In Renaissance Italy, children did not become adults at a certain age. Instead, they became adults when their fathers went before a judge to free them. Adulthood age varied from the early teens to the late twenties.

✓Reading Check **Contrasting** How was the Renaissance noble different from the medieval knight?

## SECTION 1 REVIEW

### Vocabulary

1. **Explain** the significance of: Italian Renaissance, urban society, secular, instability, decline, Leonardo da Vinci, Milan, Venice, Florence, Francesco Sforza, mercenaries, Cosimo de' Medici, Lorenzo de' Medici, Rome, Niccolò Machiavelli, dowry.

### Main Ideas

2. **Explain** why the Italian city-states were so prosperous.
3. **Summarize** Machiavelli's view of human nature.
4. **Contrast** the social structure of the Middle Ages and the Renaissance.

| | Middle Ages | Renaissance |
|---|---|---|
| Nobility | | |
| Peasants | | |
| Townspeople | | |

### Critical Thinking

5. **The BIG Idea** **Evaluating** Why has Leonardo da Vinci been viewed as a model Renaissance man?
6. **Making Inferences** What would families of Renaissance Italy consider to be a good marriage for their child?
7. **Analyzing Visuals** Examine the image on page 401. What feeling do you get from this painting? What details in the painting create this feeling?

### Writing About History

8. **Expository Writing** Read a few passages from *The Prince.* Write a brief essay explaining why you agree or do not agree with Machiavelli's theory of politics.

**History ONLINE**

For help with the concepts in this section of *Glencoe World History,* go to glencoe.com and click Study Central™.

# Social History

## The Renaissance Man

Renaissance Italy valued individual human achievement and excellence in many fields. The "Renaissance man" was well-rounded, developing his full potential intellectually, artistically, and physically. Leon Battista Alberti, accomplished artist, poet, architect, mathematician, writer, and horseman, captured the Renaissance ideal. This ideal became the foundation for education in Europe and the Americas. Since the Renaissance, the standard high school curriculum included Greek and Latin, literature, history, mathematics, sciences, and physical education. The greatest examples of Renaissance men are Leonardo da Vinci and Michelangelo.

**Leonardo's knowledge of geometry led him to use linear perspective—a revolutionary technique giving *The Last Supper* realistic depth.**

**The first casual portrait, the *Mona Lisa* revolutionized art.**

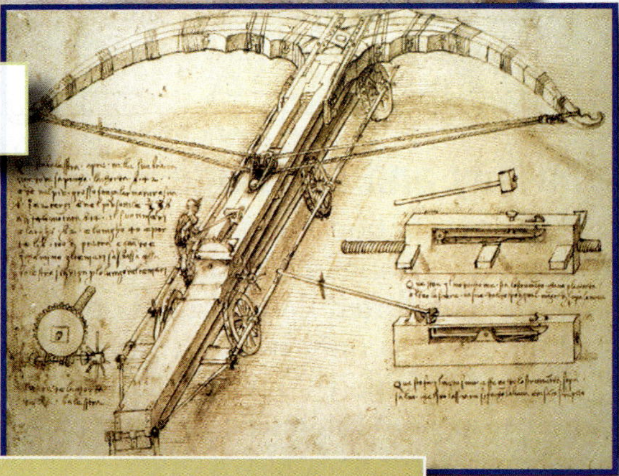

**Pen and ink drawing of a giant catapult**

### Leonardo da Vinci

**The genius of Leonardo da Vinci exemplified the notion of a Renaissance man. Although he thought of himself as an artist, he was a gifted scientist, mathematician, architect, engineer, botanist, anatomist, artist, musician, and inventor. He revolutionized scientific beliefs by dissecting animals and discovering the function of the heart. Many of his engineering designs—for helicopters, tanks, submarines, and crossbows—were centuries ahead of their time. *The Mona Lisa* and *The Last Supper* are considered the most innovative paintings of the Italian Renaissance. Whether in his volumes of notebooks or in his art, Leonardo was always experimenting with new techniques and ideas.**

Completed in 1512, Michelangelo's *God Creates Adam* shows humans interacting with God. Michelangelo's frescoes on the ceiling of the Sistine Chapel were cleaned and restored in the 1980s and 1990s.

Engraving from c.1577 based on Michelangelo's design for the exterior of St. Peter's Basilica in Rome

Michelangelo's *David* stood in the main plaza of Florence for almost 400 years as a symbol of the city.

## MICHELANGELO

One of the greatest artists of all time, Michelangelo Buonarroti excelled as a painter, sculptor, poet, architect, and literary scholar. Like Leonardo, Michelangelo was best known for his artistic achievements. He carved powerful human figures that evoke classical Greek forms and have inspired people for centuries. Michelangelo's sculptures of *David* and the *Pietà* remain masterpieces of marble sculpture. Michelangelo not only painted the famous frescoes in the Sistine Chapel but also designed the complex scaffold used to reach the high ceilings. A brilliant architect, he designed the dome of St. Peter's Basilica in Rome and other structures.

### ANALYZING VISUALS

1. **Describing** What do the images suggest about Leonardo's and Michelangelo's talents?
2. **Applying** Name some modern-day Renaissance men or women.

SECTION 2

Section Audio

Spotlight Video

# Ideas and Art of the Renaissance

## GUIDE TO READING

### The BIG Idea

**Ideas, Beliefs, and Values**

Humanism was an important intellectual movement of the Renaissance and was reflected in the works of Renaissance artists.

### Content Vocabulary

- humanism *(p. 406)*
- fresco *(p. 409)*
- vernacular *(p. 407)*

### Academic Vocabulary

- attain *(p. 408)*
- style *(p. 409)*

### People and Places

- Petrarch *(p. 406)*
- Dante *(p. 407)*
- Chaucer *(p. 407)*
- Canterbury *(p. 407)*
- Christine de Pizan *(p. 408)*
- Raphael *(p. 410)*
- Michelangelo *(p. 410)*
- Flanders *(p. 411)*
- Jan van Eyck *(p. 411)*
- Albrecht Dürer *(p. 411)*

### Reading Strategy

**Summarizing Information** As you read, use a chart like the one below to describe the three pieces of literature written by Dante, Chaucer, and de Pizan. What was the primary importance of each of these works?

| *Divine Comedy* | *The Canterbury Tales* | *The Book of the City of Ladies* |
|---|---|---|
| | | |
| | | |
| | | |

*During the Renaissance, humanism revived interest in the literary works of ancient Greece and Rome and in classical Latin. While many scholars used classical Latin, writers such as Dante and Chaucer made literature written in regional languages more popular. Humanism also became an educational curriculum, and at the core of humanist schools were the liberal studies. The art, sculpture, and architecture of the Renaissance reflected a realistic, human-centered world.*

## Italian Renaissance Humanism

*MAIN IDEA* Humanism, based on study of the classics, revived an interest in ancient Latin; but many authors wrote great works in the vernacular.

*HISTORY & YOU* Do you use a different style of language with your friends than with adults? Read about languages used in Renaissance literature.

Secularism and an emphasis on the individual characterized the Renaissance. These characteristics are most noticeable in the intellectual and artistic accomplishments of the period. A key intellectual movement of the Renaissance was humanism.

### Development of Humanism

**Humanism** was based on the study of the classics, the literary works of ancient Greece and Rome. Humanists studied grammar, rhetoric, poetry, moral philosophy, and history. Today these subjects are called the humanities.

**Petrarch** (PEE•TRAHRK), who often has been called the father of Italian Renaissance humanism, did more than any other individual in the fourteenth century to foster its development. Petrarch looked for forgotten Latin manuscripts and set in motion a search for similar manuscripts in monastic libraries throughout Europe. He also began the humanist emphasis on using pure classical Latin (Latin as used by the ancient Romans, as opposed to medieval Latin). Humanists used the works of Cicero as a model for prose and those of Virgil for poetry.

Fourteenth-century humanists like Petrarch had described the intellectual life as one of solitude. They rejected family and a life of action in the community. In contrast, humanists in the early 1400s took a new interest in civic life. They believed that intellectuals had a duty to live an active civic life and to put their study of the humanities to the state's service. It is no accident that they served as secretaries in the Italian city-states and to princes or popes.

PRIMARY SOURCE HISTORY & ARTS

## *Dante's* Divine Comedy

When Dante Alighieri wrote the *Divine Comedy* in the early fourteenth century, he chose the ancient Roman poet Virgil as his "guide" for the soul's journey to Paradise. By doing so, Dante hoped to lend legitimacy to a work written in the dialect of Florence. Dante later defended his use of the vernacular in a treatise he wrote in Latin, the language of literature at the time, because he wanted it to be taken seriously.

Dante called his masterpiece *Comedy.* The adjective *Divine* was added later, partly because of the poem's religious subject and partly in recognition of its greatness. It soon became a classic, helping to make the Florentine dialect the literary language of the entire Italian Peninsula.

"The Latin could only have explained them [the poetry of the *Divine Comedy*] to scholars; for the rest would have not understood it. Therefore, as among those who desire to understand them there are many more illiterate than learned, it follows that the Latin would not have fulfilled this behest as well as the vulgar tongue, which is understood both by the learned and the unlearned."

—Dante Alighieri, *De vulgari eloquentia* ("Of Literature in the Vernacular"), 1304–1306

**DOCUMENT-BASED QUESTIONS**

This painting by Domenico di Michelino shows parts of Dante's famous poem.

1. **Explaining** Why did Dante choose not to write his *Divine Comedy* in Latin?
2. **Making Connections** Why would the use of Virgil make Dante's poem seem more legitimate to Renaissance scholars?

## Vernacular Literature

The humanist emphasis on classical Latin led to its widespread use in the writings of scholars, lawyers, and theologians. However, some writers wrote in the **vernacular** (the language spoken in their own regions, such as Italian, French, or German). In the fourteenth century, the literary works of the Italian author **Dante** (DAHN•tay) and the English author Geoffrey **Chaucer** helped make vernacular literature more popular.

Dante's masterpiece in the Italian vernacular is the *Divine Comedy.* It is the story of the soul's journey to salvation. The lengthy poem has three major sections: Hell, Purgatory, and Heaven, or Paradise. Dante is led on an imaginary journey through these three realms until he reaches Paradise, where he beholds God.

Chaucer used the English vernacular in his famous work *The Canterbury Tales.* His beauty of expression and clear language were important in making his dialect the chief ancestor of the modern English language. *The Canterbury Tales* consists of a collection of stories told by a group of 29 pilgrims journeying to the tomb of Thomas à Becket at **Canterbury**, England.

This format gave Chaucer the chance to portray an entire range of English society.

Another writer who used the vernacular was **Christine de Pizan**, a Frenchwoman who is best known for her works written in defense of women. In *The Book of the City of Ladies*, written in 1404, she denounced the many male writers who had argued that women, by their very nature, are unable to learn. Women, de Pizan argued, could learn as well as men if they could attend the same schools:

**PRIMARY SOURCE**

"Should I also tell you whether a woman's nature is clever and quick enough to learn speculative sciences as well as to discover them, and likewise the manual arts. I assure you that women are equally well-suited and skilled to carry them out and to put them to sophisticated use once they have learned them."

—Christine de Pizan

✓Reading Check **Explaining** What literary format does Chaucer use to portray English society?

## Renaissance Education

MAIN IDEA Education during the Renaissance focused on the liberal studies.

***HISTORY & YOU*** What is your favorite subject? Read to learn about the subjects of study during the Renaissance.

The humanist movement had a profound effect on education in the 1300s and 1400s. Education became increasingly secular—focused less on religion. Renaissance humanists believed that education could dramatically change human beings. They wrote books on education and opened schools based on their ideas.

At the core of humanist schools were the liberal studies. Humanists believed that liberal studies (or, today, liberal arts) enabled individuals to reach their full potential. One humanist wrote: "We call those studies liberal by which we **attain** and practice virtue and wisdom; which

## PEOPLE in HISTORY

### Leonardo da Vinci
**1452–1519 Italian Artist and Scientist**

Leonardo da Vinci was the model "Renaissance man." He was an artist, scientist, inventor, and visionary. In 1503, the government of Florence sought his genius on a military matter. With the help of Niccolò Machiavelli, Leonardo da Vinci devised a plan to help Florence defeat the city of Pisa in a war. The plan was to divert the Arno River away from Pisa to cut Pisa off from the sea. However, the engineer hired to dig a diversion canal did not follow Leonardo's instructions, and the canal walls collapsed. Although the plan failed, the maps Leonardo drew up were so detailed that they were used long afterward. He also envisioned an industrial corridor along the river that eventually came to pass after his death. **What famous person helped Leonardo with his plan?**

### Michelangelo
**1475–1564 Italian Artist**

Michelangelo Buonarroti was a man of many talents. A painter, sculptor, poet, architect, and literary scholar, there was little he could not do once he set his mind to it. When Pope Julius II asked him to paint the ceiling of the Sistine Chapel in 1508, Michelangelo protested that "painting is not my art." Despite his protests, the work that emerged four years later ranks among the greatest masterpieces of all time.

For his sculptures, Michelangelo would sometimes spend months in a marble quarry personally selecting the ideal block from which to carve his works of art. Some of his contemporaries believed that "he could see the figure imprisoned in it." Creative to the end of his long life, he famously lamented that "art and death do not go well together." **Where do some of Michelangelo's most famous paintings appear?**

calls forth and develops those highest gifts of body and mind which ennoble men."

What, then, were the liberal studies? According to the humanists, students should study history, moral philosophy, eloquence (or rhetoric), letters (grammar and logic), poetry, mathematics, astronomy, and music. In short, the purpose of a liberal education was to produce individuals who follow a path of virtue and wisdom. These individuals should also possess rhetorical skills so they can persuade others to take this same path of virtue and wisdom.

**PRIMARY SOURCE**

"Not everyone is called to be a physician, a lawyer . . . nor has everyone outstanding gifts of natural capacity, but all of us . . . are responsible for the personal influence that goes forth from us."

—Vittorino da Feltre (1373–1446)
humanist educator, Mantua, Italy

Following the Greek ideal of a sound mind in a sound body, humanist educators also emphasized physical education. Students learned the skills of javelin throwing, archery, and dancing. They ran, wrestled, hunted, and swam.

Humanist educators thought that education was a practical preparation for life. Its aim was not to create great scholars but complete citizens. Humanist education was also considered necessary for preparing the sons of aristocrats for leadership roles. Humanist schools were the model for the education of Europe's ruling classes until the twentieth century.

Females were largely absent from these schools. The few female students who did attend humanist schools studied the classics and were encouraged to know some history as well as how to ride, dance, sing, play the lute (a stringed instrument), and appreciate poetry. They were told not to learn mathematics or rhetoric. It was thought that religion and morals should be foremost in the education of "Christian ladies" so that they could become good wives and mothers.

✓Reading Check **Explaining** How did a humanist education prepare a student for life?

# Italian Renaissance Art

**MAIN IDEA** The Renaissance produced great artists and sculptors such as Michelangelo, Raphael, and Leonardo da Vinci.

**HISTORY & YOU** Do you recall the features of Gothic style? Read to learn how Renaissance architects diverged from Gothic style.

Renaissance artists sought to imitate nature. They wanted viewers to see the reality in their subjects. At the same time, these artists were developing a new, human-focused worldview. As one artist proclaimed, human beings were the "center and measure of all things."

## New Techniques in Painting

Frescoes by Masaccio (muh•ZAH•chee•oh) are the first masterpieces of Early Renaissance (1400–1490) art. A **fresco** is a painting done on fresh, wet plaster with water-based paints. Human figures in medieval paintings look flat, but Masaccio's figures have depth and come alive. By mastering the laws of perspective, Masaccio could create the illusion of three dimensions, leading to a new, realistic **style.**

Other fifteenth-century Florentine painters used and modified this new, or Renaissance, style. Especially important were two major developments. One development stressed the technical side of painting—understanding the laws of perspective and the organization of outdoor space and light through geometry. The second development was the investigation of movement and human anatomy. The realistic portrayal of the individual, especially the human nude, became one of the chief aims of Italian Renaissance art.

## Sculpture and Architecture

The Renaissance produced equally stunning advances in sculpture and architecture. The sculptor Donatello studied the statues of the Greeks and Romans. His works included a realistic, free-standing figure of Saint George.

The work of architect Filippo Brunelleschi (BROO•nuhl•EHS•kee) was inspired by the buildings of classical Rome.

His design of the church of San Lorenzo in Florence reflects this. The classical columns and rounded arches in the church's design create an environment that does not overwhelm the worshiper, as Gothic cathedrals might. The church creates a space to fit human, and not divine, needs. Like painters and sculptors, Renaissance architects sought to reflect a human-centered world.

## High Renaissance Masters

The final stage of Italian Renaissance painting flourished between 1490 and 1520. Called the High Renaissance, the period is associated with Leonardo da Vinci, Raphael, and Michelangelo.

Leonardo mastered the art of realistic painting and even dissected human bodies to better understand their workings. However, he wanted to advance beyond such realism to create idealized forms that captured the perfection of nature and the individual—perfection that could not be expressed fully by a realistic style.

At age 25, **Raphael** was already one of Italy's best painters. He was admired for his numerous madonnas (paintings of the Virgin Mary). In these, he achieved an ideal of beauty far surpassing human standards. Raphael is also well known for his frescoes in the Vatican Palace. His *School of Athens* reveals a world of balance, harmony, and order—the underlying principles of classical Greek and Roman art.

**Michelangelo**, an accomplished painter, sculptor, and architect, was another master of the High Renaissance. Fiercely driven by his desire to create, he worked with great passion and energy on a remarkable number of projects. Michelangelo's figures on the ceiling of the Sistine Chapel in Rome depict an ideal type of human being with perfect proportions. The beauty of this idealized human being is meant to be a reflection of divine beauty. The more beautiful the body, the more godlike the figure.

**✓Reading Check** **Identifying** Name three Italian artists of the High Renaissance.

### HISTORY & ARTS — PRIMARY SOURCE

### Differences in Renaissance Art

Central panel of *Mérode Altarpiece* by Robert Campin (c. 1425–28)

Flemish artists typically placed their subjects among everyday objects. The space depicted was tight and boxlike.

**DOCUMENT-BASED QUESTIONS**

Artists of the Northern Renaissance placed their works in everyday settings, while Italian Renaissance artists were influenced by classical styles and geometric precision. Religious themes were a common subject matter in both.

1. **Contrasting** How did the Renaissance style in Northern Europe differ from that of Italy?
2. **Interpreting** How might the settings of each painting reveal differences in religious ideals between Northern Europe and Italy?

*Marriage of the Virgin* by Raphael (1504)

Raphael used the technique of perspective to give the illusion of scale, distance, and three dimensions on a two-dimensional surface.

## The Northern Artistic Renaissance

**MAIN IDEA** Northern European artists, especially those in the Low Countries, portrayed their world realistically but in a different way than did the Italian artists.

***HISTORY & YOU*** Have you ever used a varnish to seal woodwork? Read to learn about a new medium the Flemish artist Jan van Eyck used.

Like the artists of Italy, the artists of northern Europe became interested in portraying their world realistically. However, their approach was different from that of the Italians. This was particularly true of the artists of the Low Countries (present-day Belgium, Luxembourg, and the Netherlands).

Circumstance played a role in the differences. The large wall spaces of Italian churches had given rise to the art of fresco painting. Italian artists used these spaces to master the technical skills that allowed them to portray humans in realistic settings. In the north, the Gothic cathedrals with their stained glass windows did not allow enough space for frescoes. Thus, northern European artists painted illustrations for books and wooden panels for altarpieces. Great care was needed to depict each object on a small scale.

The most important northern school of art in the 1400s was in **Flanders,** one of the Low Countries. The Flemish painter **Jan van Eyck** (EYEK) was among the first to use and perfect the technique of oil painting. He used a varnish made of linseed oil and nut oils mixed with resins. This medium enabled van Eyck to use a wide variety of brilliant, translucent colors. With his oil paints, he could create striking realism in fine details as in his painting *Giovanni Arnolfini and His Bride.* Like other Northern Renaissance artists, however, van Eyck imitated nature not by using perspective, as the Italians did, but by simply observing reality and portraying details as best he could.

By 1500, artists from the north had begun to study in Italy and to be influenced by what artists were doing there. One German artist who was greatly affected by the Italians was **Albrecht Dürer.** He made two trips to Italy and absorbed most of what the Italians could teach on the laws of perspective.

As can be seen in his famous *Adoration of the Magi,* Dürer did not reject the use of minute details characteristic of northern artists. He did try, however, to fit those details more harmoniously into his works in accordance with Italian artistic theories. Like the Italian artists of the High Renaissance, Dürer tried to achieve a standard of ideal beauty that was based on a careful examination of the human form.

**✓Reading Check** **Examining** Why was Jan van Eyck's use of oil paint significant?

## SECTION 2 REVIEW

### Vocabulary

1. **Explain** the significance of: humanism, Petrarch, vernacular, Dante, Chaucer, Canterbury, Christine de Pizan, attain, fresco, style, Raphael, Michelangelo, Flanders, Jan van Eyck, Albrecht Dürer.

### Main Ideas

2. **Describe** Petrarch's contributions to the development of humanism.
3. **Identify** Christine de Pizan's main argument in *The Book of the City of Ladies.*
4. **Summarize** the accomplishments of Leonardo da Vinci, Raphael, and Michelangelo. Use a chart like the one below to make your summary.

| Leonardo da Vinci | Raphael | Michelangelo |
|---|---|---|
| | | |
| | | |
| | | |

### Critical Thinking

5. **The BIG Idea** **Identifying Central Issues** How was humanism reflected in the works of Renaissance artists?
6. **Contrasting** How did the education of females differ from that of males in humanist schools?
7. **Analyzing Visuals** Examine the painting on page 407. What can you infer about Purgatory based on its location in this painting?

### Writing About History

8. **Expository Writing** Assume the role of an art docent (a person who guides people through museums). Prepare a lecture to be given to a group of students on the works of Jan van Eyck and how they differ from Italian Renaissance paintings.

**History ONLINE**

For help with the concepts in this section of *Glencoe World History,* go to glencoe.com and click Study Central™.

SECTION 3 Section Audio Spotlight Video

# The Protestant Reformation

## GUIDE TO READING

### The BIG Idea

**Ideas, Beliefs, and Values** In northern Europe, Christian humanists sought to reform the Catholic Church, and Protestantism emerged.

### Content Vocabulary

- Christian humanism *(p. 412)*
- salvation *(p. 414)*
- indulgence *(p. 414)*
- Lutheranism *(p. 416)*

### Academic Vocabulary

- precise *(p. 413)*
- ignorant *(p. 414)*

### People, Places, and Events

- Martin Luther *(p. 412)*
- Desiderius Erasmus *(p. 412)*
- Wittenberg *(p. 415)*
- Ninety-five Theses *(p. 415)*
- Edict of Worms *(p. 415)*
- Charles V *(p. 417)*
- Bohemia *(p. 417)*
- Hungary *(p. 417)*
- Peace of Augsburg *(p. 417)*

### Reading Strategy

**Determining Cause and Effect** As you read, use a diagram like the one below to identify steps that led to the Reformation.

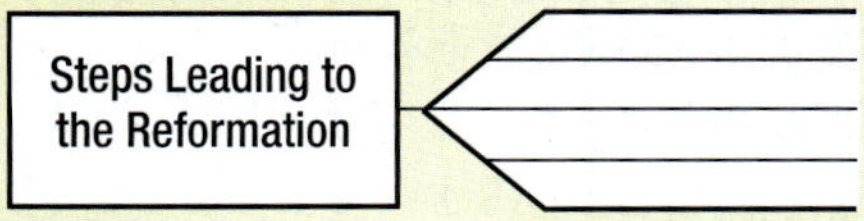


*During the second half of the fifteenth century, Christian humanist Desiderius Erasmus paved the way for Martin Luther's reform movement. Political instability in the Holy Roman Empire allowed Lutheranism, the first Protestant faith, to spread. The Peace of Augsburg formally accepted the division of Christianity in Germany—Lutheranism and Catholicism.*

## Prelude to Reformation

**MAIN IDEA** Christian humanism and Desiderius Erasmus paved the way for the Protestant Reformation.

**HISTORY & YOU** Is there a school policy or rule that you would like to change? Read how Erasmus pointed out the need for Church reform.

The Protestant Reformation is the name given to the religious reform movement that divided the western Church into Catholic and Protestant groups. Although **Martin Luther** began the Reformation in the early 1500s, earlier developments set the stage for religious change.

### Christian Humanism

One such development grew from widespread changes in intellectual thought. During the second half of the fifteenth century, the new classical learning that was part of Italian Renaissance humanism spread to northern Europe. From that came a movement called **Christian humanism**, or Northern Renaissance humanism. The major goal of this movement was the reform of the Catholic Church.

The Christian humanists believed in the ability of human beings to reason and improve themselves. They thought that if people read the classics, and especially the basic works of Christianity, they would become more pious. This inner piety, or inward religious feeling, would bring about a reform of the Church and society. Christian humanists believed that in order to change society, they would first have to change human beings.

The best-known Christian humanist was **Desiderius Erasmus** (ih•RAZ•muhs). He called his view of religion "the philosophy of Christ." By this, he meant that Christianity should show people how to live good lives on a daily basis, not just provide beliefs for them to be saved. Stressing the inwardness of religious feeling, Erasmus thought the external forms of medieval religion (pilgrimages, fasts, relics) were not all that important.

## TURNING POINT — LUTHER'S NINETY-FIVE THESES

"Out of love for the truth and the desire to bring it to light, the following propositions will be discussed at Wittenberg, under the presidency of the Reverend Father Martin Luther, Master of Arts and of Sacred Theology, and Lecturer in Ordinary on the same at that place. Wherefore he requests that those who are unable to be present and debate orally with us, may do so by letter."

—Martin Luther's Introduction to his Ninety-five Theses, 1517

Martin Luther's protest of indulgences began the Protestant Reformation. The Catholic Church had authorized Johann Tetzel to sell indulgences to raise money to build St. Peter's Basilica in Rome. Tetzel told the faithful that their purchases would free the souls of their loved ones from Purgatory. This enraged Luther, who believed that indulgences only soothed the conscience. They did not forgive sins.

When Luther wrote his Ninety-five Theses, his intention was to open a dialogue on abuses in the Catholic Church. Instead, his words sparked a revolutionary firestorm. Aided by the newly invented printing press, his words soon spread across Europe.

Luther's attempts to reform the Catholic Church led to a new form of Christianity—Protestantism—and the birth of a new church. It also ignited decades of bloody religious conflict, ending a thousand years of domination by the Catholic Church.

**This image shows Martin Luther posting his Ninety-five Theses on the door of the Castle Church in Wittenberg, Germany, in 1517.**

**DOCUMENT-BASED QUESTIONS**

1. **Finding the Main Idea** In his introduction to the Ninety-five Theses, what did Luther invite people to do?
2. **Analyzing** In what ways did the Ninety-five Theses represent a turning point in history?

To reform the Church, Erasmus wanted to spread the philosophy of Jesus, provide education in the works of Christianity, and criticize the abuses in the Church. In his work *The Praise of Folly,* written in 1509, Erasmus humorously criticized aspects of his society that he believed were most in need of reform. He singled out the monks for special treatment. Monks, he said, "insist that everything be done in **precise** detail. . . . Just so many knots must be on each shoe and the shoelace must be of only one color."

Erasmus sought reform within the Catholic Church. He did not wish to break away from it. His ideas, however, did prepare the way for the Reformation. As people of his day said, "Erasmus laid the egg that Luther hatched."

### Need for Reform

Why the call for reform? Corruption was one reason. From 1450 to 1520, a series of popes—known as the Renaissance popes—failed to meet the Church's spiritual needs.

The popes were supposed to be the spiritual leaders of the Catholic Church. As leaders of the Papal States, however, they were all too often more concerned with Italian politics and worldly interests than with spiritual matters.

Julius II, the fiery "warrior-pope," personally led armies against his enemies. This disgusted Christians who viewed the pope as a spiritual, not a military, leader.

Many Church officials used their church offices to advance their careers and their wealth. At the same time, many ordinary parish priests seemed **ignorant** of their spiritual duties. People wanted to know how to save their souls, and many parish priests were unwilling or unable to offer them advice or instruction.

While the leaders of the Church were failing to meet their responsibilities, ordinary people desired meaningful religious expression and assurance of their **salvation**, or acceptance into Heaven. As a result, for some, the process of obtaining salvation became almost mechanical. Collections of relics grew more popular as a means to salvation.

According to Church practice at that time, through veneration of a relic, a person could gain an **indulgence**—release from all or part of the punishment for sin. Frederick the Wise, Luther's prince, had amassed over 5,000 relics. Indulgences attached to them could reduce time in purgatory by 1,443 years. The Church also sold indulgences.

Other people sought certainty of salvation in the popular mystical movement known as the Modern Devotion. The Modern Devotion downplayed religious dogma and stressed the need to follow the teachings of Jesus. This deepening of religious life was done within the Catholic Church. However, many people soon found that the worldly-wise clergy had little interest in the spiritual needs of their people. This environment helps to explain the tremendous impact of Luther's ideas.

✓Reading Check **Explaining** How did Erasmus pave the way for the Reformation?

# PEOPLE *in* HISTORY

## Erasmus

**1466–1536 Dutch Intellectual**

Desiderius Erasmus was one of the greatest intellectuals of his time. Kings, popes, and princes sought his advice. He was also a very contradictory personality. Many of his writings, especially his best-known work, *The Praise of Folly,* were critical of the Catholic Church, yet he remained an ordained priest until his death. Despite his criticisms of the Church and his early support for the reforms of Martin Luther, he stayed loyal to the Church, seeking to reform it from within. He even received an offer from Pope Paul III to make him a cardinal. Yet, despite his loyalty to the Church, Erasmus was regarded as the father of Christian humanism. Many of his ideas were adopted by religious leaders of the Protestant Reformation. **What was Erasmus's best-known literary work?**

## Martin Luther

**1483–1546 Church Reform Leader**

As Martin Luther returned to his village on a stormy night, a lightning bolt threw him off his horse. "St. Anne, help me, and I will become a monk!" Luther's cry reflected his intense fear of death and of what lay beyond. Like most people of his time, he believed the medieval view of a wrathful God, granting salvation to the righteous few and eternal fire to the rest.

Luther feared he could never do enough to win salvation. Pondering the words of the apostle Paul about the "righteousness of God," Luther arrived at a new insight. What Paul meant, he decided, was not that people can earn righteousness by good works, but that God grants the righteousness needed for salvation. All people need is faith. "From that moment, the whole face of Scripture appeared to me in a different light." **What insight did Luther gain from Paul's words?**

## Martin Luther

**MAIN IDEA** Believing in his new doctrine of salvation, Martin Luther broke from the Catholic Church and established Lutheranism.

**HISTORY & YOU** Did you ever speak up for something you strongly believed, despite the disapproval of your friends? Read about Martin Luther's split with the Catholic Church.

Martin Luther was a monk and a professor at the University of **Wittenberg**, in Germany, where he lectured on the Bible. Through his study of the Bible, Luther arrived at an answer to a problem—the certainty of salvation—that had bothered him since he had become a monk.

Catholic teaching had stressed that both faith and good works were needed to gain personal salvation. In Luther's opinion, human beings were powerless in the sight of an almighty God and could never do enough good works to earn salvation.

Through his study of the Bible, Luther came to believe that humans are not saved through their good works but through their faith in God. This idea, called justification by faith alone, became the chief teaching of the Protestant Reformation.

Because Luther had arrived at his understanding of salvation by studying the Bible, the Bible became for Luther, as for all other Protestants, the only source of religious truth.

### The Ninety-five Theses

Luther did not see himself as a rebel, but he was greatly upset by the widespread selling of indulgences. Especially offensive in his eyes was the monk Johann Tetzel, who sold indulgences with the slogan: "As soon as the coin in the coffer [money box] rings, the soul from purgatory springs." People, Luther believed, were simply harming their chances for salvation by buying these pieces of paper.

On October 31, 1517, Luther, angered by the Church's practices, supposedly posted his **Ninety-five Theses** on the door of the Castle Church in Wittenberg. Posting topics to discuss was a common practice of the time. His theses were a stunning attack on abuses in the sale of indulgences. Thousands of copies of the Ninety-five Theses were printed and spread to all parts of Germany.

Pope Leo X did not take the issue seriously, however. He said that Luther was simply "some drunken German who will amend his ways when he sobers up."

### A Break With the Church

By 1520, Luther had begun to move toward a more definite break with the Catholic Church. He called on the German princes to overthrow the papacy in Germany and establish a reformed German church. Luther also attacked the Church's system of sacraments. In his view, they were the means by which the pope and the Church had destroyed the real meaning of the gospel for a thousand years. He kept only two sacraments—baptism and the Eucharist (also known as Communion). Luther also called for the clergy to marry. This went against the long-standing Catholic requirement that the clergy remain celibate, or unmarried.

Through all these calls for change, Luther continued to emphasize his new doctrine of salvation. It is faith alone, he said, and not good works, that justifies and brings salvation through Christ.

Unable to accept Luther's ideas, the Church excommunicated him in January 1521. He was also summoned to appear before the imperial diet—or legislative assembly—of the Holy Roman Empire, which was called into session at the city of Worms by the newly elected emperor Charles V. The emperor believed he could convince Luther to change his ideas. However, Luther refused.

The young emperor was outraged. "A single friar who goes counter to all Christianity for a thousand years," he declared, "must be wrong!" By the **Edict of Worms**, Martin Luther was made an outlaw within the empire. His works were to be burned and Luther himself captured and delivered to the emperor. However, Luther's ruler, Frederick, the elector of Saxony, was unwilling to see his famous professor killed. He sent Luther into hiding and then protected him when Luther returned to Wittenberg at the beginning of 1522.

## The Rise of Lutheranism

During the next few years, Luther's religious movement became a revolution. Luther was able to gain the support of many of the German rulers among the some three hundred states that made up the Holy Roman Empire. These rulers, motivated as much by politics and economics as by any religious feeling, quickly took control of the Catholic churches in their territories, forming state churches supervised by the government. The political leaders, not the Roman pope, held the last word. As part of the development of these state-dominated churches, Luther also set up new religious services to replace the Catholic mass. These services consisted of Bible readings, preaching of the word of God, and song. Luther also married a former nun, Katherina von Bora, and his marriage provided a model of married and family life for the new Protestant ministers. Luther's doctrine soon became known as **Lutheranism** and the churches as Lutheran churches. Lutheranism was the first Protestant faith.

A series of crises soon made it apparent, however, that spreading the word of God was not as easy as Luther had thought. The Peasant's War was Luther's greatest challenge. In June 1524, German peasants revolted against their lords and looked to Luther to support their cause. Luther instead supported the lords. To him, the state and its rulers were called by God to maintain the peace necessary to spread the Gospel. It was the duty of princes to stop all revolt. By the following spring, the German princes had crushed the peasant revolts. Luther found himself even more dependent on state authorities for the growth of his reformed church.

✓Reading Check **Contrasting** How did Luther and the Church differ on achieving salvation?

NATIONAL GEOGRAPHIC

### EUROPE AFTER THE PEACE OF AUGSBURG, 1555

### The Holy Roman Empire and the Peace of Augsburg

| DATE | EVENT |
|---|---|
| 1517 | Protestant Reformation begins |
| 1519 | Charles V (Hapsburg) elected Holy Roman Emperor—Catholic ruler of Austria, Spain, Netherlands |
| 1521–1535 | Hapsburg-Valois Wars (Charles V vs. Francis I of France) over land |
| 1531 | Protestant German princes form a military alliance |
| 1532 | Ottomans threaten Austria; France allies with Ottomans |
| 1545 | Truce between Charles V and Ottomans |
| 1547 | Charles V's army defeats Protestant alliance |
| 1555 | Peace of Augsburg ends feuding between Protestants and Catholics; peace in Holy Roman Empire |

### Geography SKILLS

1. **Regions** How did geography contribute to the difficulties of Charles V in trying to keep his empire under control?
2. **Location** How did the location of Wittenberg benefit Luther's cause?

## Politics in the German Reformation

**MAIN IDEA** Political and religious problems forced the emperor of the Holy Roman Empire to seek peace with the Lutheran princes.

***HISTORY & YOU*** Have you ever met so much opposition that you had to give in? Read why Charles V made peace with the Lutheran princes.

From its very beginning, the fate of Luther's movement was tied closely to political affairs. **Charles V,** the Holy Roman emperor (who was also Charles I, the king of Spain), ruled an immense empire consisting of Spain and its colonies, the Austrian lands, **Bohemia**, **Hungary**, the Low Countries, the duchy of Milan in northern Italy, and the kingdom of Naples in southern Italy.

While religious authorities saw the Reformation as a challenge to their power and influence, secular authorities, such as Charles, also saw the Reformation as a disrupting force. Religiously, Charles hoped to preserve the unity of his empire by keeping it Catholic. Politically, he wanted to keep the empire under the control of his dynasty—the Hapsburgs. However, a number of problems cost him both his dream and his health. These same problems helped Lutheranism survive by giving Lutherans time to organize before facing Catholic forces.

The chief political concern of Charles V was his rivalry with the king of France, Francis I. Their conflict over a number of disputed territories led to a series of wars that lasted more than 20 years. Charles also faced opposition from Pope Clement VII who, guided by political considerations, had joined the side of the French king. The invasion of Ottoman Turks into the eastern part of the empire forced Charles to send forces there as well.

Finally, the internal political situation in the Holy Roman Empire was not in Charles's favor. Germany was a land of several hundred territorial states. Although all owed loyalty to the emperor, many rulers of the German states supported Luther as a way to assert their own authority and dislike of papal control. By the time Charles V brought military forces to Germany, the Lutheran princes were well organized. Unable to defeat them, Charles was forced to seek peace.

An end to religious warfare in Germany came in 1555 with the **Peace of Augsburg.** This agreement formally accepted the division of Christianity in Germany. The German states were now free to choose between Catholicism and Lutheranism. Lutheran states were to have the same legal rights as Catholic states. The right of German rulers to determine the religion of their subjects was accepted, but not the subjects' right to choose their own religion.

**✓Reading Check** **Evaluating** How did the Peace of Augsburg influence the political and religious development of Germany?

## SECTION 3 REVIEW

### Vocabulary

1. **Explain** the significance of: Martin Luther, Christian humanism, Desiderius Erasmus, precise, ignorant, salvation, indulgence, Wittenberg, Ninety-five Theses, Edict of Worms, Lutheranism, Charles V, Bohemia, Hungary, Peace of Augsburg.

### Main Ideas

2. **Sequence** the actions of Luther that led to the emergence of Protestantism using a diagram like the one below.

**Luther's Actions**

[ ] → [ ] → [Protestantism]

3. **Discuss** the impact of the Edict of Worms.
4. **Explain** why many German princes supported Luther.

### Critical Thinking

5. **The BIG Idea** **Analyzing** How did Martin Luther's religious reform lead to conflict? To what extent were these conflicts resolved?
6. **Contrasting** How did the views of Erasmus and the Church differ on the topic of religious relics?
7. **Analyzing Visuals** Examine the map on page 416. Identify three cities where important events occurred in the rise of Lutheranism and explain their significance.

### Writing About History

8. **Expository Writing** How did the Reformation, including Christian humanism and Martin Luther's efforts, affect the growth of individualism?

**History ONLINE**

For help with the concepts in this section of *Glencoe World History*, go to glencoe.com and click Study Central™.

SECTION 4



# The Spread of Protestantism

## GUIDE TO READING

### The BIG Idea

**Ideas, Beliefs, and Values** Different forms of Protestantism emerged in Europe as the Reformation spread, and the Catholic Church underwent a religious rebirth.

### Content Vocabulary

- predestination *(p. 419)*
- annul *(p. 420)*

### Academic Vocabulary

- published *(p. 418)*
- justification *(p. 419)*

### People and Places

- Ulrich Zwingli *(p. 418)*
- Zürich *(p. 418)*
- John Calvin *(p. 418)*
- Geneva *(p. 419)*
- King Henry VIII *(p. 420)*
- Ignatius of Loyola *(p. 423)*
- Trent *(p. 423)*

### Reading Strategy

**Determining Cause and Effect** As you read, use a diagram like the one below to list some of the reforms proposed by the Council of Trent. Beside each, give the Protestant viewpoint to which it responded.

| Council of Trent | | Protestant Viewpoint |
|---|---|---|
| | ← | |
| | ← | |
| | ← | |

*As the Reformation spread, different forms of Protestantism emerged in Europe. Calvinism replaced Lutheranism as the most important and dynamic form of Protestantism. In England, King Henry VIII created a national church, the Church of England. The Anabaptists believed in a complete separation of church and state. The Catholic Church underwent a revitalization under the direction of Pope Paul III.*

## Divisions in Protestantism

**MAIN IDEA** By the mid-sixteenth century, Calvinism replaced Lutheranism as the most important and dynamic form of Protestantism.

**HISTORY & YOU** Can you imagine life in a society where dancing is a crime? Read to learn about the Calvinist teachings.

The Peace of Augsburg meant that Christian unity was forever lost. Even before the peace, however, division had appeared in Protestantism. One of these new groups appeared in Switzerland.

### Zwinglian Reformation

**Ulrich Zwingli** was a priest in **Zürich**. The city council of Zürich, strongly influenced by Zwingli, began to introduce religious reforms. Relics and images were abolished. All paintings and decorations were removed from the churches and replaced by whitewashed walls. A new church service consisting of Scripture reading, prayer, and sermons replaced the Catholic mass.

As his movement began to spread to other cities in Switzerland, Zwingli sought an alliance with Martin Luther and the German reformers. Both the German and Swiss reformers realized the need for unity to defend themselves against Catholic authorities, but they were unable to agree on certain Christian rites.

In October 1531 war broke out between the Protestant and Catholic states in Switzerland. Zürich's army was routed, and Zwingli was found wounded on the battlefield. His enemies killed him, cut up his body, and burned the pieces, scattering the ashes. The leadership of Protestantism in Switzerland now passed to John Calvin.

### Calvin and Calvinism

**John Calvin** was educated in his native France. After his conversion to Protestantism, however, he was forced to flee Catholic France for the safety of Switzerland. In 1536 he **published** the

## Geography SKILLS

1. **Regions** Which Protestant faith covered more of Europe than any other by 1600?
2. **Location** Which Protestant faith occurred in only one nation? Which nation?

*Institutes of the Christian Religion,* a summary of Protestant thought. This work, which eventually became known as his masterpiece, immediately gave Calvin a reputation as one of the new leaders of Protestantism.

On most important doctrines, Calvin stood very close to Luther. He, too, believed in the doctrine of **justification** by faith alone to explain how humans achieved salvation. However, Calvin also placed much emphasis on the all-powerful nature of God—what Calvin called the "power, grace, and glory of God."

Calvin's emphasis on the all-powerful nature of God led him to other ideas. One of these ideas was **predestination.** This "eternal decree," as Calvin called it, meant that God had predestined some people to be saved (the elect) and others to be damned (the reprobate). According to Calvin, "He has once for all determined, both whom he would admit to salvation, and whom he would condemn to destruction." Although Calvin stressed that no one could ever be absolutely certain of salvation, his followers did not always heed this warning.

The belief in predestination gave later Calvinists the firm conviction that they were doing God's work on Earth. This conviction made them determined to spread their faith to other people. Calvinism became a dynamic and activist faith.

In 1536 Calvin began working to reform the city of **Geneva.** He created a church government that used both clergy and laity in the service of the church.

See page R42 to read A Reformation Debate between Martin Luther and Ulrich Zwingli in the **Primary Sources and Literature Library.**

The Consistory, a special court for enforcing moral discipline, oversaw the moral life and doctrinal purity of Genevans. It could punish those who deviated from the church's teachings and moral principles. Citizens in Geneva were punished for such "crimes" as dancing, singing obscene songs, drunkenness, swearing, and playing cards.

Calvin's success in Geneva made the city a powerful center of Protestantism. John Knox, the Calvinist reformer of Scotland, called Geneva "the most perfect school of Christ on earth." Missionaries trained in Geneva were sent to all parts of Europe. Calvinism became established in France, the Netherlands, Scotland, and central and eastern Europe. By the mid-sixteenth century, Calvinism had replaced Lutheranism as the most important and dynamic form of Protestantism. Calvin's Geneva stood as the fortress of the Protestant Reformation.

✓Reading Check **Explaining** How did the Consistory enforce moral discipline in Geneva?

## Reformation in England

*MAIN IDEA* For political, not religious, reasons, Henry VIII established the Church of England.

*HISTORY & YOU* As a child, how did you react when someone told you no? Read about how Henry VIII reacted after the pope said no.

The English Reformation was rooted in politics, not religion. **King Henry VIII** wanted to divorce his first wife, Catherine of Aragon, with whom he had a daughter, Mary, but no son. Since he needed a male heir, Henry wanted to marry Anne Boleyn. Impatient with the pope's unwillingness to **annul** (declare invalid) his marriage to Catherine, Henry turned to England's own church courts.

### The Break from Rome

As the archbishop of Canterbury, head of the highest church court in England, Thomas Cranmer ruled in May 1533 that the king's marriage to Catherine was "null and

## PEOPLE *in* HISTORY

### Henry VIII
1491–1547 King of England

Historians have found it ironic that Henry VIII, who led the break between England and the Roman Catholic Church, was proclaimed "Defender of the Faith" by the head of the church he left. However, that is how Pope Leo X praised him after Henry's attack on Martin Luther in 1521. In *Assertio Septem Sacramentorum* (Declaration of the Seven Sacraments), Henry upheld Church doctrines that Luther and his followers were trying to discredit. To this day, all British coins carry the initials F.D. after the reigning monarch's name. They refer to the Latin words *Fidei Defensor*, or "Defender of the Faith," a hereditary title for all British monarchs since Henry VIII. **Who was Henry VIII attacking in his book?**

### Thomas More
1478–1535 British Author and Theologian

*A Man for All Seasons*—that was the title of a twentieth-century movie about Thomas More. He was a trusted adviser to Henry VIII and the author of the book *Utopia*, which means a perfectly harmonious society. Published in 1516, the book is a work of fiction about an ideal state. More describes how goods are produced and shared equally among the Utopians. *Utopia* became a model for Utopian Socialists, who in the 1800s attempted to set up communities based on the socialistic principles described in the book. More was later beheaded under orders from Henry VIII for not supporting England's break with the Church of Rome. In 1935, More was made a saint. **For what group did More's book become an inspiration?**

absolutely void." At the beginning of June, Anne was crowned queen. Three months later a child was born. Much to the king's disappointment, the baby was a girl. She would later become Queen Elizabeth I.

In 1534, at Henry's request, Parliament moved to finalize the break of the Catholic Church in England with the pope in Rome. The Act of Supremacy of 1534 declared that the king was "the only supreme head on earth of the [new] Church of England." This position gave the king control over religious doctrine, clerical appointments, and discipline. Thomas More, a Christian humanist and devout Catholic, opposed the king's action and was beheaded.

Henry used his new powers to dissolve the monasteries and sell their land and possessions to landowners and merchants. The English nobility disliked papal control of the church, and now they had a stake in the new order. Additionally, the king received a boost to his treasury. In matters of doctrine, however, Henry remained close to Catholic teachings.

When Henry died in 1547, he was succeeded by Edward VI, his nine-year-old son by his third wife. During Edward's reign, church officials who favored Protestant doctrines moved the Church of England, or the Anglican Church, in a Protestant direction. New acts of Parliament gave the clergy the right to marry and created a new Protestant church service. Before he turned 16, Edward died of tuberculosis.

### "Bloody Mary"

The rapid changes during Edward's reign aroused opposition. When Mary, Henry's daughter by Catherine of Aragon, came to the throne in 1553, England was ready for a reaction. Mary was a Catholic who wanted to restore England to Roman Catholicism. However, her efforts had the opposite effect. Among other actions, she had more than 300 Protestants burned as heretics, earning her the nickname "Bloody Mary." As a result of her policies, England was even more Protestant by the end of Mary's reign than it had been at the beginning.

✓Reading Check **Examining** What were the results of Bloody Mary's religious policies?

## Anabaptists

**MAIN IDEA** For believing in the complete separation of church and state, Anabaptists were viewed as dangerous radicals.

**HISTORY & YOU** Would you consider someone who refuses to kill to be a "dangerous radical"? Read to learn about the Anabaptists.

Reformers such as Luther had allowed the state to play an important, if not dominant, role in church affairs. However, some people strongly disliked giving such power to the state. These were radicals known as the Anabaptists.

To Anabaptists, the true Christian church was a voluntary community of adult believers who had undergone spiritual rebirth and had then been baptized. This belief in adult baptism separated Anabaptists from Catholics and Protestants, who baptized infants.

Anabaptists also believed in following the practices and the spirit of early Christianity. They considered all believers to be equal, a belief they based on the accounts of early Christian communities in the New Testament. Each Anabaptist church chose its own minister, or spiritual leader. Because all Christians were considered priests, any member of the community was eligible to be a minister (though women were often excluded).

Finally, most Anabaptists believed in the complete separation of church and state. Not only was government to be kept out of the realm of religion, it was not even supposed to have any political authority over "real" Christians. Anabaptists refused to hold political office or bear arms, because many took literally the biblical commandment "Thou shall not kill."

Their political beliefs, as much as their religious beliefs, caused the Anabaptists to be regarded as dangerous radicals who threatened the very fabric of sixteenth-century society. Indeed, the chief thing other Protestants and Catholics could agree on was the need to persecute Anabaptists.

✓Reading Check **Describing** Why were the Anabaptists considered to be dangerous political radicals?

History ONLINE
**Student Web Activity—** Visit glencoe.com and complete the activity about the Reformation.

# Reformation and Society

**MAIN IDEA** Although the family became the center of life during the Reformation, the lives of most women and Jews did not improve.

**HISTORY & YOU** Should anyone be an "obedient servant" to another person? Read to learn about women's roles during the Reformation.

During the political and religious turmoil of the Reformation, the lives of most women and Jewish people did not improve. Women were still subservient, and anti-Semitism continued.

## Women and Family

The Protestants developed a new view of the family. Both monasticism and the requirement of celibacy for the clergy had been abolished. The family could now be placed at the center of life, and the "mutual love between man and wife" could be extolled.

Were idea and reality the same, however? More often, reality reflected the traditional roles of husband as the ruler and wife as the obedient servant. Luther stated it clearly: "The rule remains with the husband, and the wife is compelled to obey him by God's command."

Obedience was not a woman's only role. Her other important duty was to bear children, which both Calvin and Luther saw as part of the divine plan.

## Anti-Semitism

During the Reformation, anti-Semitism remained common in northern Europe. Martin Luther expected Jews to convert to Lutheranism. When they resisted, Luther wrote that Jewish synagogues and houses should be destroyed. In the Papal States, Jews who would not convert to Christianity were segregated into ghettos.

**✓Reading Check** **Evaluating** What impact did the Protestant Reformation have on women?

**Roman Catholic, Lutheran, Calvinist, and Anglican Beliefs**

| | CATHOLIC | LUTHERAN | CALVINIST | ANGLICAN |
|---|---|---|---|---|
| Church Hierarchy | Pope, bishops, priests | Ministers lead congregations. | Council of elders for each church; ministers | Monarch, bishops, priests |
| Salvation | Salvation requires faith and good works. | Salvation requires faith alone. | Salvation is predetermined. | Salvation requires faith alone. |
| Importance of the Bible | The Bible and Church traditions are both sources of truth. | The Bible is the only source of truth. | The Bible is the only source of truth. | The Bible is the only source of truth. |
| Interpretation of Beliefs | Priests interpret the Bible and Church teachings for believers. | Believers interpret the Bible themselves. | Believers interpret the Bible themselves. | Believers interpret the Bible themselves. |
| Worship | Services based on rituals and devotional practices | Services based on preaching with some rituals | Services based on preaching | Services based on preaching and rituals |
| Sacraments | Seven sacraments: baptism, confession, communion, confirmation, marriage, ordination, anointing the sick | Baptism, communion | Baptism, communion | Baptism, communion |

**Chart SKILLS**

1. **Describing** In what way were Anglicans more similar to Catholics than to either Lutherans or Calvinists?
2. **Making Inferences** Why do you think the Protestant churches eliminated most of the seven sacraments?

## Catholic Reformation

**MAIN IDEA** Perceiving a need for a change, Pope Paul III steered the Catholic Church toward a reformation in the 1500s.

***HISTORY & YOU*** When a task doesn't turn out as well as you had hoped, do you look for ways to do it better next time? Read to learn how the Catholic Church determined what it needed to change.

The Catholic Church also had a revitalization in the sixteenth century, giving it new strength and enabling it to regain much that it had lost to the Protestant Reformation. Three chief pillars—the Jesuits, reform of the papacy, and the Council of Trent—supported the Catholic Reformation, also called the Counter-Reformation.

A Spanish nobleman, **Ignatius of Loyola**, founded the Society of Jesus, known as the Jesuits. Loyola's small group of followers was recognized as a religious order by Pope Paul III in 1540. All Jesuits took a special vow of absolute obedience to the pope, making them an important instrument for papal policy. Jesuits used education to spread their message. Jesuit missionaries were very successful in restoring Catholicism to parts of Germany and eastern Europe and in spreading it to other parts of the world.

Reform of the papacy was another important factor in the Catholic Reformation. The participation of Renaissance popes in dubious financial transactions and in Italian political and military affairs had created many sources of corruption. It took the jolt of the Protestant Reformation to bring about serious reform of the Catholic Church.

Pope Paul III perceived the need for change. He took the bold step of appointing a Reform Commission in 1537 to determine the Church's ills. The commission blamed the Church's problems on the popes' corrupt policies. Paul III also began the Council of Trent, another pillar of the Catholic Reformation. Beginning in March 1545, a group of cardinals, archbishops, bishops, abbots, and theologians met off and on for 18 years in the city of **Trent,** on the border between Germany and Italy.

The final decrees of the Council of Trent reaffirmed traditional Catholic teachings in opposition to Protestant beliefs. Both faith and good works were declared necessary for salvation. The seven sacraments, the Catholic view of the Eucharist, and clerical celibacy were all upheld. Belief in purgatory and in the use of indulgences was strengthened, although the selling of indulgences was forbidden. The Roman Catholic Church now possessed a clear body of doctrine and was unified under the pope's supreme leadership. Catholics were as well prepared as Calvinists to do battle for their faith.

✓ **Reading Check** **Describing** What was the relationship between the Jesuits and the pope?

## SECTION 4 REVIEW

### Vocabulary

1. **Explain** the significance of: Ulrich Zwingli, Zürich, John Calvin, published, justification, predestination, Geneva, King Henry VIII, annul, Ignatius of Loyola, Trent.

### Main Ideas

2. **Describe** how Calvin reformed the city of Geneva.
3. **Explain** why Henry VIII formed the Church of England.
4. **Contrast** how the Calvinists and the Anabaptists differed in their attitudes toward church members participating in government activities.

### Critical Thinking

5. **The BIG Idea** **Assessing** How effective was the Catholic Church's response to the Protestant Reformation?
6. **Determining Cause and Effect** How did "Bloody Mary's" actions affect the religious makeup of England by the end of her reign?
7. **Analyzing Visuals** Compare the chart on page 422 to the map on page 419. Name one country in which the dominant Christian faith included the seven sacraments.

### Writing About History

8. **Expository Writing** Research the treatment of the Jewish people during the Reformation. Then write a short essay analyzing why they were segregated to ghettos.

**History ONLINE**

For help with the concepts in this section of *Glencoe World History,* go to glencoe.com and click Study Central™.

# CHAPTER 12 Visual Summary

**STUDY TO GO** You can study anywhere, anytime by downloading quizzes and flash cards to your PDA from glencoe.com.

## THE RENAISSANCE in Italy and Northern Europe

- Milan, Venice, and Florence became centers of Renaissance learning and culture.
- Machiavelli's views on gaining and holding power influenced political leaders.
- Humanist education focused on liberal studies.
- Artists sought to portray the world realistically.

DETAIL OF SISTINE CHAPEL CEILING, BY MICHELANGELO

**Michelangelo painted people with perfect proportions as a reflection of divine beauty.**

MARTIN LUTHER PUBLICLY BURNS HIS EXCOMMUNICATION DOCUMENTS

**Luther's beliefs spread, creating Lutheranism, the first Protestant faith.**

## THE REFORMATION Begins

- Erasmus and other Christian humanists paved the way for the Protestant Reformation.
- Catholic teaching stressed faith and good works, but Luther believed that faith alone was sufficient for salvation.
- The Peace of Augsburg ended the religious wars and allowed German states to choose between Catholicism and Lutheranism.

PERSECUTION OF AN ANABAPTIST

**Anabaptists were viewed as dangerous radicals.**

## THE REFORMATION Spreads

- Calvinism replaced Lutheranism as the most important form of Protestantism.
- Henry VIII established the Church of England for political rather than religious reasons.
- Anabaptists believed in the total separation of church and state.
- Pope Paul III took steps to reform the Catholic Church; this was called the Counter-Reformation.

# CHAPTER 12 Assessment

## Reviewing Vocabulary

*Directions: Choose the word or words that best complete the sentence.*

**1.** Theologians of the Reformation disagreed about how people could achieve ________, or acceptance into Heaven.

**A** indulgence
**B** predestination
**C** annulment
**D** salvation

**2.** The money and goods given by the wife's family to the husband at the time of marriage is called a ________.

**A** settlement
**B** dowry
**C** tithe
**D** *taille*

**3.** John Calvin emphasized ________, the belief that God determined in advance who would be saved and who would be damned.

**A** predisposition
**B** salvation
**C** predestination
**D** humanism

**4.** An image painted on fresh, wet plaster is called a ________.

**A** ceramic
**B** flying buttress
**C** fresco
**D** relic

**5.** In Renaissance Italy, urban society developed a ________, or worldly viewpoint, which contrasted with a purely religious viewpoint.

**A** medieval
**B** secular
**C** Reformation
**D** capitalist

## Reviewing Main Ideas

*Directions: Choose the best answers to the following questions.*

### Section 1 *(pp. 398–403)*

**6.** Which of the following was a characteristic of the Renaissance?

**A** Rejection of the classical learning of ancient Greece and Rome
**B** Renewed emphasis on an all-powerful God
**C** Emergence of a more secular worldview
**D** Reawakening of feudalism

**7.** Who helped to make Florence the cultural center of Europe during the Renaissance?

**A** Francesco Sforza
**B** Lorenzo de' Medici
**C** Niccolò Machiavelli
**D** Girolamo Savonarola

### Section 2 *(pp. 406–411)*

**8.** Who has been called the father of Italian Renaissance humanism?

**A** Petrarch
**B** Leonardo da Vinci
**C** Dante
**D** Albrecht Dürer

**9.** What was the *Divine Comedy*?

**A** A collection of stories told by a group of pilgrims on a journey
**B** A defense of the theater
**C** An ancient Roman poem by Virgil
**D** A poem about a soul's journey to Heaven

**TEST-TAKING TIP**

If a question asks you to read a quote, look for clues that reveal its historical context—the title, the date, the quote itself. Determining the context will help you determine the quote's significance and the correct answer.



**Need Extra Help?**

| If You Missed Questions . . . | 1 | 2 | 3 | 4 | 5 | 6 | 7 | 8 | 9 |
|---|---|---|---|---|---|---|---|---|---|
| Go to Page . . . | 414 | 403 | 419 | 409 | 398 | 398 | 400 | 406 | 407 |

GO ON

10. Which artist painted figures on the ceilings of the Sistine Chapel in Rome?
    - **A** Leonardo da Vinci
    - **B** Michelangelo
    - **C** Raphael
    - **D** Jan van Eyck

## Section 3 *(pp. 412–417)*

11. What was the major goal of Christian humanism?
    - **A** To create a new form of Christian faith
    - **B** To preserve religious unity in the Holy Roman Empire
    - **C** To promote external forms of religion, such as pilgrimages and relics
    - **D** To reform the Catholic Church

12. What agreement ended the religious warfare in Germany in 1555?
    - **A** Ninety-five Theses
    - **B** Edict of Worms
    - **C** Peace of Augsburg
    - **D** Great Schism

## Section 4 *(pp. 418–423)*

13. Why did King Henry VIII break with Rome and establish the Church of England?
    - **A** To marry Anne Boleyn
    - **B** To promote his religious views
    - **C** To force the Catholic Church to reform
    - **D** To separate church and state

14. Who founded the Jesuits?
    - **A** John Calvin
    - **B** Ignatius of Loyola
    - **C** Martin Luther
    - **D** Pope Paul III

## Critical Thinking

*Directions: Choose the best answers to the following questions.*

*Use the following map to answer question 15.*

15. Which of the following is a true statement about the Holy Roman Empire in 1400?
    - **A** It had no access to the Mediterranean Sea.
    - **B** It did not include parts of Italy.
    - **C** Rome was not a part of the Empire.
    - **D** Denmark was part of the Empire.

16. How did fifteenth-century humanists differ from those in the fourteenth century?
    - **A** They preferred to live in solitude.
    - **B** They believed in service to the state.
    - **C** Most moved to the country.
    - **D** They emphasized classical Latin.

**Need Extra Help?**

| If You Missed Questions . . . | 10 | 11 | 12 | 13 | 14 | 15 | 16 |
|---|---|---|---|---|---|---|---|
| Go to Page . . . | 410 | 412 | 417 | 420 | 423 | 426 | 406 |

GO ON

# CHAPTER 12 Assessment

**17.** Why were liberal studies at the core of a humanist curriculum?

**A** To create great scholars

**B** To promote advances in science

**C** To enable more people to read Latin

**D** To provide practical preparation for life

**18.** In his Ninety-five Theses, Martin Luther wrote: "Christians are to be taught that he who gives to the poor or lends to the needy does a better work than buying pardons." To what is Luther objecting in this statement?

**A** The doctrine of predestination

**B** The lack of concern for the poor

**C** The sale of indulgences

**D** The spread of secular humanism

*Base your answer to question 19 on the following chart.*

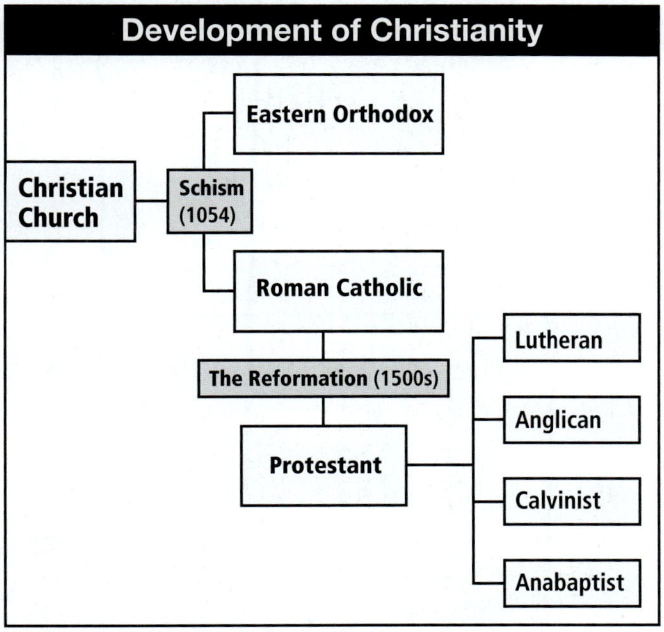


**19.** Which group does Calvinism belong to?

**A** Protestantism

**B** Anglicanism

**C** Secular humanism

**D** Catholicism

## Document-Based Questions

*Directions: Analyze the document and answer the short-answer questions that follow the document. Base your answers on the document and on your knowledge of world history.*

Niccolò Machiavelli wrote:

> *"Everyone realizes how praiseworthy it is for a prince to honor his word and to be straightforward rather than crafty in his dealings; nonetheless experience shows that princes who have achieved great things have been those who have given their word lightly, who have known how to trick men with their cunning, and who, in the end, have overcome those abiding by honest principles. . . . A prince, therefore, need not necessarily have all the good qualities I mentioned above, but he should certainly appear to have them. . . . He should not deviate from what is good, if that is possible, but he should know how to do evil, if that is necessary."*
>
> —Niccolò Machiavelli, *The Prince,* George Bull, trans., 1981

**20.** According to Machiavelli, what kinds of princes have achieved great things?

**21.** According to Machiavelli, what role does evil play in governance?

## Extended Response

**22.** Analyze how the Reformation shaped the political and religious life of Europe. Be sure to identify the historical effects of the Reformation and to compare the viewpoints of religious and secular authorities.

**23.** Choose one of the social classes from the Renaissance. Research what life was like for individuals from this social class during the Renaissance and the Middle Ages. Then compare and contrast the economic and social status of the social class you chose during both eras.

**History ONLINE**

For additional test practice, use Self-Check Quizzes—Chapter 12 at glencoe.com.

**Need Extra Help?**

| If You Missed Questions . . . | 17 | 18 | 19 | 20 | 21 | 22 | 23 |
|---|---|---|---|---|---|---|---|
| Go to Page . . . | 408 | 415 | 427 | 427 | 427 | 418 | 402–403 |

STOP

# REFERENCE PAGES

## Contents

# MINI ALMANAC

An almanac is a book or table that contains a variety of statistical, tabular, or general information. The most common almanacs in history have been those that kept astronomical data or that gave weather predictions and related advice to farmers. In agricultural societies it was important to keep accounts of natural phenomena so that farmers would have an idea of when to plant and harvest their crops. Ancient Egyptians carved their almanacs on sticks of wood and called them "fingers of the sun." The first printed almanac was prepared in Europe in 1457. *The Old Farmer's Almanac* has been published continuously since 1792. Because almanacs are compact and concise, they are a popular way of presenting a wide variety of information.

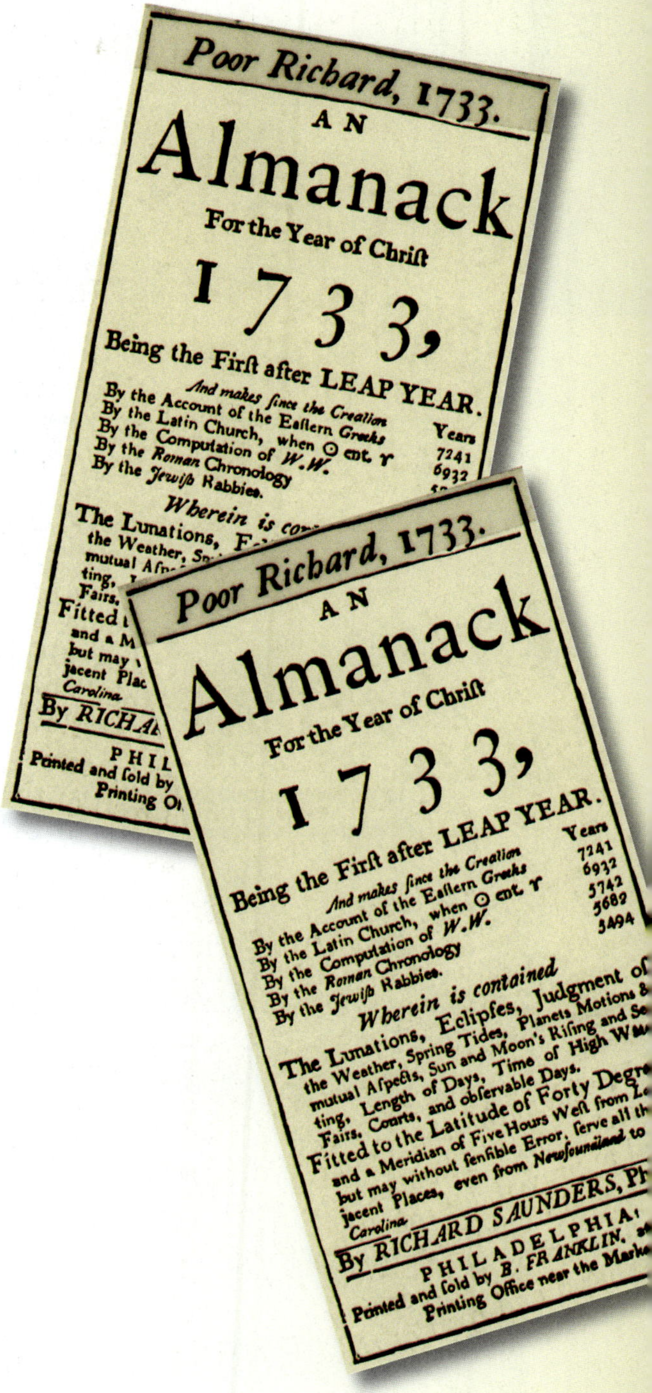

## World Population, A.D. 1–2010

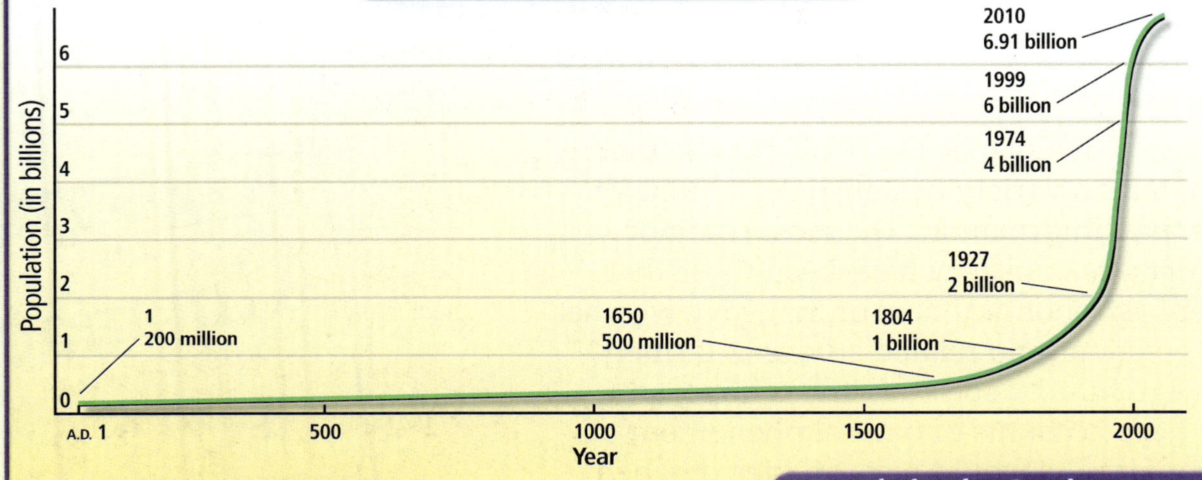


Source: United Nations Population Division, 2006.
Note: Populations are estimates.

## Population by Continent, 2010

| Continent | Population |
|---|---|
| Asia | 4,166,308,000 |
| Africa | 1,032,013,000 |
| Europe | 730,478,000 |
| North America | 502,231,000 |
| South America | 397,740,000 |
| Australia/Oceania | 61,136,000 |

Source: United Nations Population Division, 2006.
Note: Populations are estimates.

## Life Expectancy

| Country | Years |
|---|---|
| Andorra | 83.53 |
| Japan | 82.07 |
| France | 80.87 |
| Israel | 80.61 |
| New Zealand | 80.24 |
| United Kingdom | 78.85 |
| United States | 78.14 |
| Chile | 77.15 |
| China | 73.18 |
| Brazil | 72.51 |
| Egypt | 71.85 |
| India | 69.25 |
| Russia | 65.94 |
| South Africa | 42.37 |
| Mozambique | 41.04 |

Source: *The World Factbook,* 2008, CIA.

## Infant Mortality

| Country | Infant Deaths per 1,000 Live Births |
|---|---|
| South Africa | 58 |
| India | 32 |
| Egypt | 28 |
| Brazil | 27 |
| China | 21 |
| Russia | 11 |
| Chile | 8 |
| United States | 6 |
| South Korea | 6 |
| United Kingdom | 5 |
| Canada | 5 |
| Germany | 4 |
| France | 3 |
| Japan | 3 |

Source: *The World Factbook,* 2008, CIA.

## Most Populous Countries

| Country | Population |
|---|---|
| China | 1,330,000,000 |
| India | 1,148,000,000 |
| United States | 304,000,000 |
| Indonesia | 238,000,000 |
| Brazil | 192,000,000 |
| Pakistan | 168,000,000 |
| Bangladesh | 154,000,000 |
| Russia | 141,000,000 |
| Nigeria | 138,000,000 |
| Japan | 127,000,000 |

Source: *The World Factbook,* 2008, CIA.

## World's Richest Countries

| Country | Gross National Income per Capita (in U.S. dollars) |
|---|---|
| Norway | 76,450 |
| Luxembourg | 75,880 |
| Switzerland | 59,880 |
| Denmark | 54,910 |
| Iceland | 54,100 |

Source: World Development Indicators, 2008, World Bank.

## World's Poorest Countries

| Country | Gross National Income per Capita (in U.S. dollars) |
|---|---|
| Burundi | 110 |
| Congo, Democratic Republic of | 140 |
| Liberia | 150 |
| Guinea-Bissau | 200 |
| Ethiopia | 220 |

Source: World Development Indicators, 2008, World Bank.



## Highest Inflation Rates

| Country | Rate of Inflation (percent) |
|---|---|
| Zimbabwe | 10,453.0 |
| Myanmar (Burma) | 34.4 |
| Guinea | 22.9 |
| São Tomé and Príncipe | 19.9 |
| Sri Lanka | 19.7 |
| Venezuela | 18.7 |
| Iran | 17.5 |
| Ethiopia | 17.0 |
| Congo, Dem. Rep. of | 16.7 |
| Azerbaijan | 16.6 |

Source: *The World Factbook,* 2008, CIA.
Note: Year of annual inflation rate varies by country.

## Lowest Inflation Rates

| Country | Rate of Inflation (percent) |
|---|---|
| Chad | −8.8 |
| Nauru | −3.6 |
| San Marino | −1.5 |
| Northern Marianas | −0.8 |
| Burkina Faso | −0.2 |
| Japan | 0 |
| Niger | 0.1 |
| Kiribati | 0.2 |
| Brunei | 0.4 |
| Israel | 0.5 |

Source: *The World Factbook,* 2008, CIA.
Note: Year of annual inflation rate varies by country.

## World's Ten Largest Companies, 2008

| Rank | Company | Revenue (in millions of U.S. dollars) |
|---|---|---|
| 1. | Wal-Mart Stores (United States) | 378,799 |
| 2. | Exxon Mobil (United States) | 372,824 |
| 3. | Royal Dutch Shell (Netherlands) | 355,782 |
| 4. | BP (United Kingdom) | 291,438 |
| 5. | Toyota Motor (Japan) | 230,201 |
| 6. | Chevron (United States) | 210,783 |
| 7. | ING Group (Netherlands) | 210,516 |
| 8. | Total (France) | 187,280 |
| 9. | General Motors (United States) | 182,347 |
| 10. | ConocoPhillips (United States) | 178,558 |

Source: Fortune 500, 2008.
Note: Rank includes other data.

## Most Livable Countries

| Rank | Country | Rank | Country | Rank | Country |
|---|---|---|---|---|---|
| 1. | Iceland | 10. | France | 19. | New Zealand |
| 2. | Norway | 11. | Finland | 20. | Italy |
| 3. | Australia | 12. | United States | 21. | Hong Kong (SAR)* |
| 4. | Canada | 13. | Spain | 22. | Germany |
| 5. | Ireland | 14. | Denmark | 23. | Israel |
| 6. | Sweden | 15. | Austria | 24. | Greece |
| 7. | Switzerland | 16. | United Kingdom | 25. | Singapore |
| 8. | Japan | 17. | Belgium | | |
| 9. | Netherlands | 18. | Luxembourg | | |

Source: United Nations Human Development Index, 2008.
Note: The criteria include life expectancy, adult literacy, school enrollment, educational attainment, and per capita gross domestic product (GDP).
*Special Administrative Region of China

## Highest Adult Literacy Rates

| Country | Rate of Literacy (percent) |
|---|---|
| Andorra | 100 |
| Finland | 100 |
| Georgia | 100 |
| Greenland | 100 |
| Liechtenstein | 100 |
| Luxembourg | 100 |
| Norway | 100 |
| Cuba | 99.8 |
| Estonia | 99.8 |
| Poland | 99.8 |

Source: *The World Factbook,* 2008, CIA.
Note: Literacy is defined by each country.

## Lowest Adult Literacy Rates

| Country | Rate of Literacy (percent) |
|---|---|
| Burkina Faso | 21.8 |
| Afghanistan | 28.1 |
| Niger | 28.7 |
| Guinea | 29.5 |
| Benin | 34.7 |
| Sierra Leone | 35.1 |
| Somalia | 37.8 |
| Senegal | 39.3 |
| The Gambia | 40.1 |
| Guinea-Bissau | 42.4 |

Source: *The World Factbook,* 2008, CIA.
Note: Literacy is defined by each country.

## World Adult Illiteracy by Gender

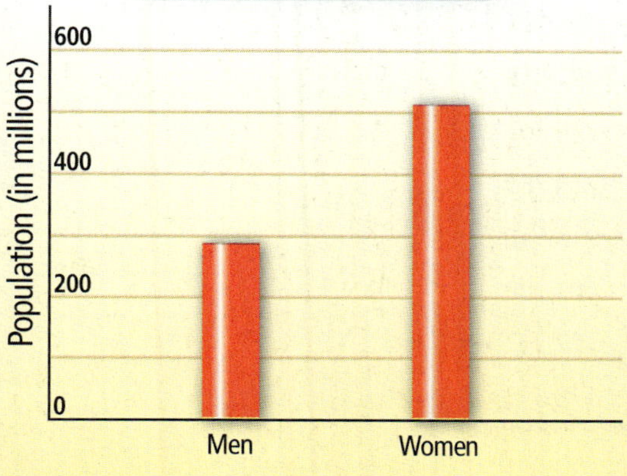


Source: United Nations, 2005.

## Years, by Country, in Which Women Gained the Right to Vote

| Year | Country | Year | Country |
|---|---|---|---|
| 1893 | New Zealand | 1945 | Italy |
| 1902 | Australia | 1945 | Japan |
| 1913 | Norway | 1947 | Argentina |
| 1918 | United Kingdom | 1947 | Mexico |
| 1918 | Canada | 1950 | India |
| 1919 | Germany | 1952 | Greece |
| 1920 | United States | 1956 | Egypt |
| 1930 | South Africa | 1963 | Kenya |
| 1934 | Brazil | 1971 | Switzerland |
| 1944 | France | 1980 | Iraq |

## Highest Military Expenditures

| Country | Billions of U.S. Dollars per Year | Percentage of Gross Domestic Product (GDP) |
|---|---|---|
| United States | 518.1 | 4.1 |
| China | 81.5 | 4.3 |
| France | 45.0 | 2.6 |
| Japan | 44.3 | 1.0 |
| United Kingdom | 42.8 | 2.4 |
| Germany | 35.1 | 1.5 |
| Italy | 28.2 | 1.8 |
| Korea, South | 21.1 | 2.6 |
| India | 19.0 | 2.5 |
| Saudi Arabia | 18.0 | 10.0 |

Source: *The World Factbook,* 2008, CIA.

## Nuclear Weapons Capability

| Country | Date of First Test |
|---|---|
| United States | 1945 |
| Russia (Soviet Union) | 1949 |
| United Kingdom | 1952 |
| France | 1960 |
| China | 1964 |
| India | 1974 |
| Pakistan | 1998 |

Source: U.S. Department of State and *TIME* magazine.

MINI ALMANAC

## Communication Around the World

| Country | Daily Newspaper Circulation per 1,000 Persons | Radios per 1,000 Persons | Televisions per 1,000 Persons | Telephone Main Lines per 1,000 Persons | Cellular Phone Subscribers per 1,000 Persons | Estimated Personal Computers per 1,000 Persons | Internet Users per 1,000 Persons |
|---|---|---|---|---|---|---|---|
| Canada | 159 | 1,047 | 691 | 658 | 417 | 487 | 513 |
| China | 69 | 339 | 350 | 238 | 255 | 40 | 72 |
| Cuba | 118 | 185 | 251 | 68 | 6 | 27 | 13 |
| France | 131 | 950 | 628 | 560 | 737 | 482 | 422 |
| Germany | 268 | 948 | 661 | 661 | 864 | 561 | 500 |
| Italy | 134 | 878 | 494 | 448 | 1,083 | 313 | 498 |
| Japan | 550 | 956 | 785 | 460 | 716 | 542 | 589 |
| Mexico | 98 | 330 | 283 | 172 | 366 | 107 | 134 |
| Russia | 105 | 418 | 421 | 256 | 517 | 132 | 111 |
| South Africa | 32 | 338 | 177 | 107 | 431 | 83 | 79 |
| United Kingdom | 292 | 1,432 | 950 | 564 | 1,002 | 600 | 629 |
| United States | 190 | 2,118 | 881 | 599 | 610 | 741 | 623 |

Source: *Encyclopædia Britannica Almanac,* 2008.

# Foldables

Dinah Zike's Foldables™ are three-dimensional, interactive, graphic organizers used to help organize and retain information. Every chapter in your text uses a Foldable to help you identify and learn about the Big Ideas discussed in the chapter. The following pages provide complete folding instructions for the nine different Foldables used throughout your Student Edition text.

## Table of Contents



## Basic Foldable Shapes

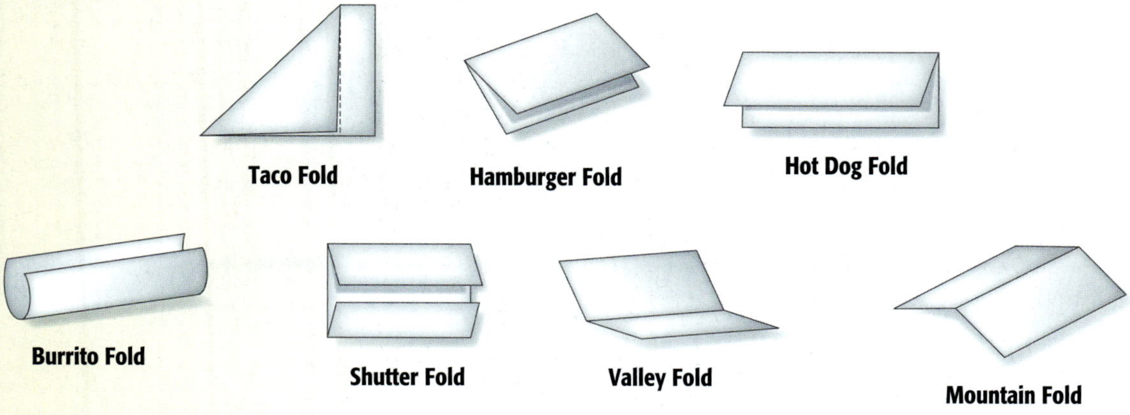

# Folded Table or Chart

1. Fold the number of vertical columns needed to make the table or chart.
2. Fold the horizontal rows needed to make the table or chart.
3. Label the rows and columns.

*Remember:* Tables are organized along vertical and horizontal axes, while charts are organized along one axis, either horizontal or vertical.

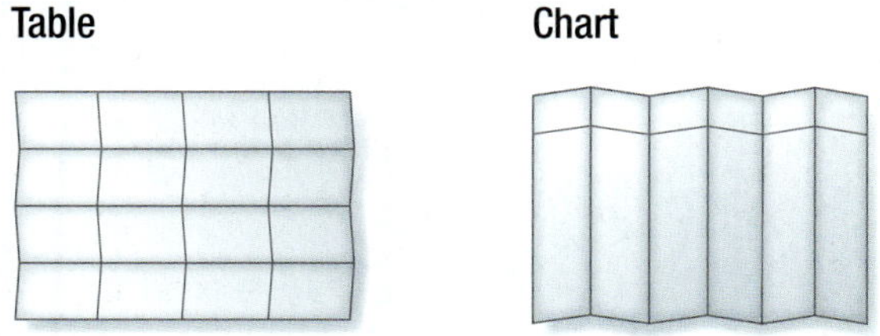




# Four-Tab Book

1. Fold a sheet of paper (8½" × 11") in half like a *hot dog.*
2. Fold this long rectangle in half like a *hamburger.*
3. Fold both ends back to touch the *mountain top* or fold it like an *accordion.*
4. On the side with two *valleys* and one *mountain top,* make vertical cuts through one thickness of paper, forming four tabs.

Use this book for data occurring in fours.

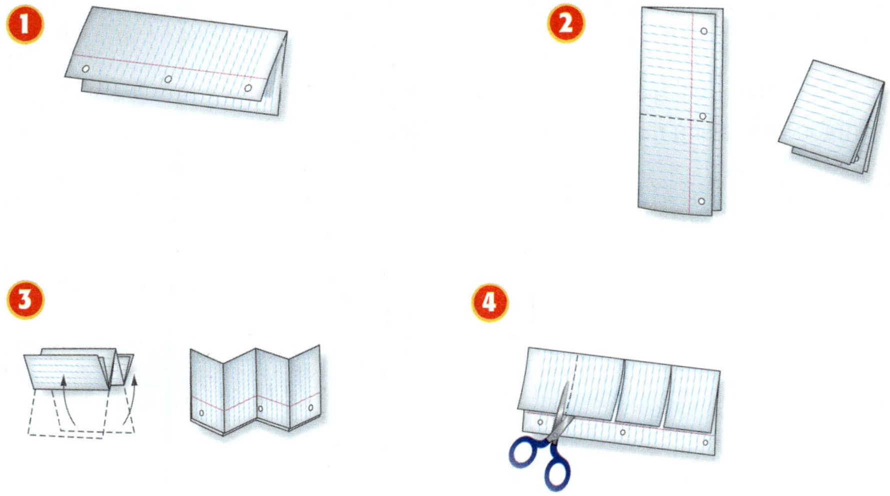

# Four-Door Book

1. Make a *shutter fold* using 11" × 17" or 12" × 18" paper.
2. Fold the *shutter fold* in half like a *hamburger.* Crease well.
3. Open the project and cut along the two inside *valley folds.*
4. These cuts will form four doors on the inside of the project.

Use this fold for data occurring in fours. When folded in half like a *hamburger,* a finished *four-door book* can be glued inside a large (11" × 17") *shutter fold* as part of a larger project.

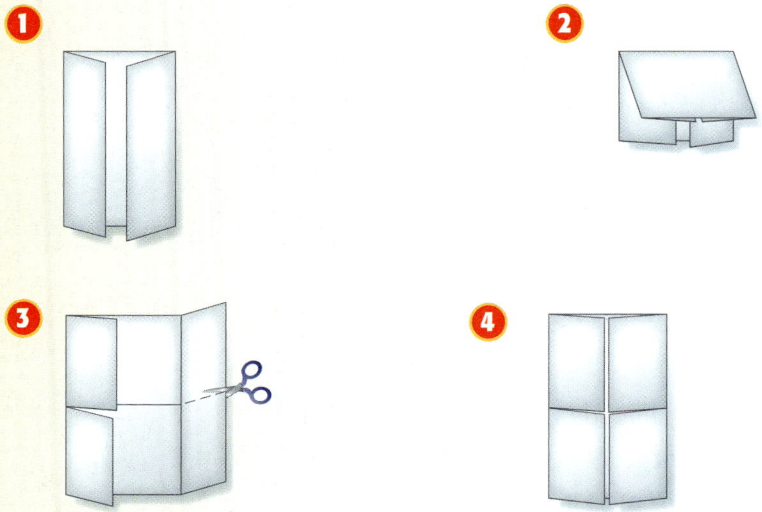

# Layered-Look Book

1. Stack two sheets of paper (8½" × 11") so that the back sheet is one inch higher than the front sheet.
2. Bring the bottom of both sheets upward and align the edges so that all of the layers or tabs are the same distance apart.
3. When all tabs are an equal distance apart, fold the papers and crease well.
4. Open the papers and glue them together along the *valley,* or inner center fold, or staple them along the *mountain.*

# SHUTTER FOLD

1. Begin as if you were going to make a *hamburger* but instead of creasing the paper, pinch it to show the midpoint.
2. Fold the outer edges of the paper to meet at the pinch, or midpoint, forming a *shutter fold.*

Use this book for data occurring in twos. Or, make this fold using 11" × 17" paper and smaller books—such as the half-book, journal, and two-tab book—that can be glued inside to create a large project full of student work.

1

2
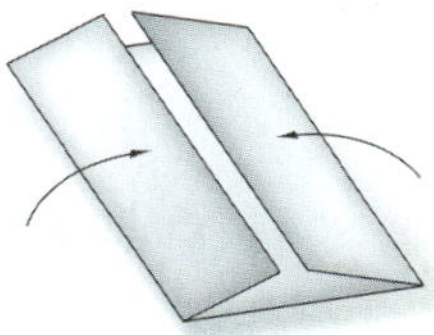

FOLDABLES

# THREE-POCKET BOOK

1. Fold a horizontal sheet of paper (11" × 17") into thirds.
2. Fold the bottom edge up two inches and crease well. Glue the outer edges of the two-inch tab to create three pockets.
3. Label each pocket. Use to hold notes taken on index cards or quarter sheets of paper.

1
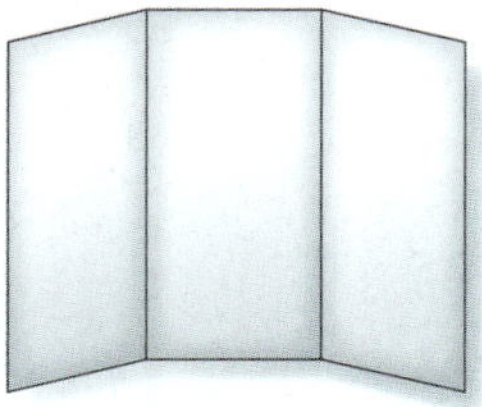

2
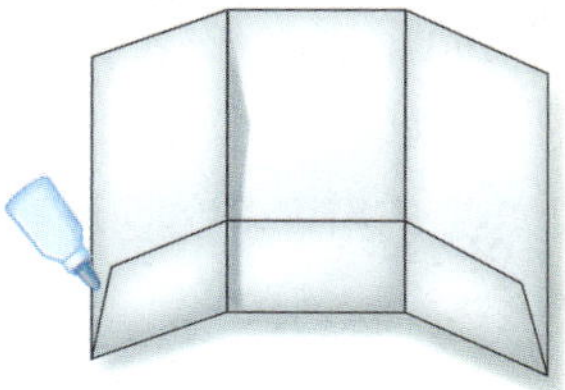

3
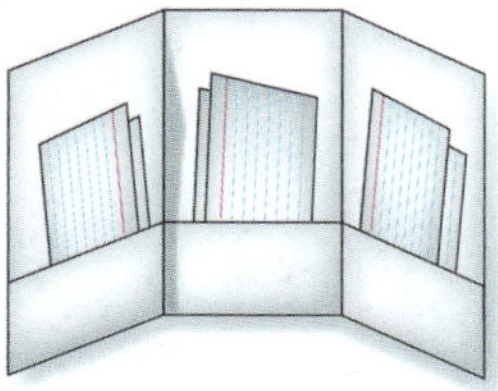

# THREE-TAB BOOK

1. Fold a sheet of paper like a *hot dog.*
2. With the paper horizontal, and the fold of the *hot dog* up, fold the right side toward the center, trying to cover one half of the paper.

*Note:* If you fold the right edge over first, the final graphic organizer will open and close like a book.

3. Fold the left side over the right side to make a book with three folds.
4. Open the folded book. Place your hands between the two thicknesses of paper and cut up the two *valleys* on one side only. This will form three tabs.

Use this book for data occurring in threes, and for two-part Venn diagrams.

**Variation A:**
Draw overlapping circles on the three tabs to make a Venn diagram.

**Variation B:**
Cut each of the three tabs in half to make a six-tab book.

1
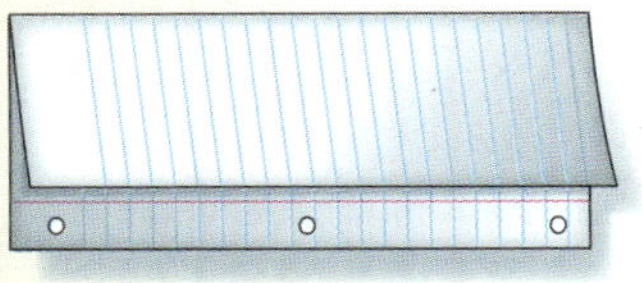

2
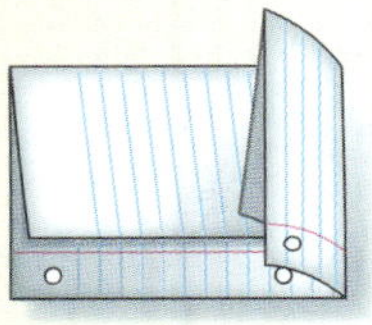

3
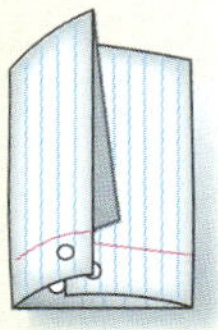

4
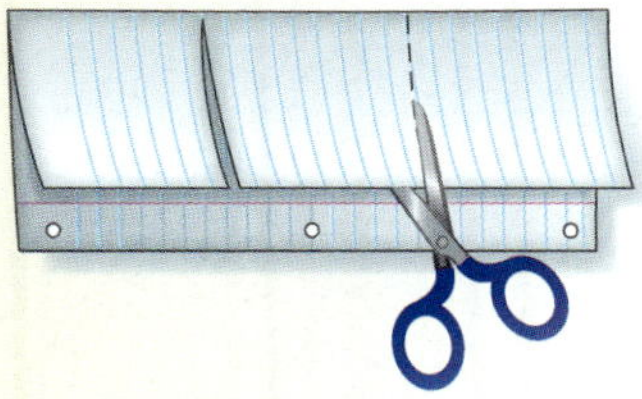

## Trifold Book

1. Fold a sheet of paper (8½" × 11") into thirds.
2. Use this book as is, or cut into shapes. If the trifold is cut, leave plenty of fold on both sides of the designed shape, so the book will open and close in three sections.

Use this book to make charts with three columns or rows, large Venn diagrams, and reports on data occurring in threes.

1 

2 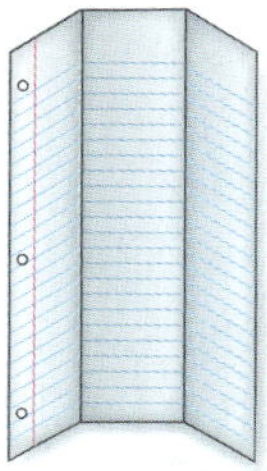

FOLDABLES

## Two-Tab Book

1. Fold a sheet of paper like a *hamburger.* Make a second *hamburger* fold.
2. Cut up the *valley* of the inside fold toward the *mountain top.* This cut forms two large tabs that can be used front and back for writing and illustrations.

The book can be expanded by making several of these folds and gluing them side-by-side.

Use this book with data occurring in twos. For example, use it for comparing and contrasting, determining cause and effect, finding similarities and differences, and more.

1 

2 

# Skills Handbook



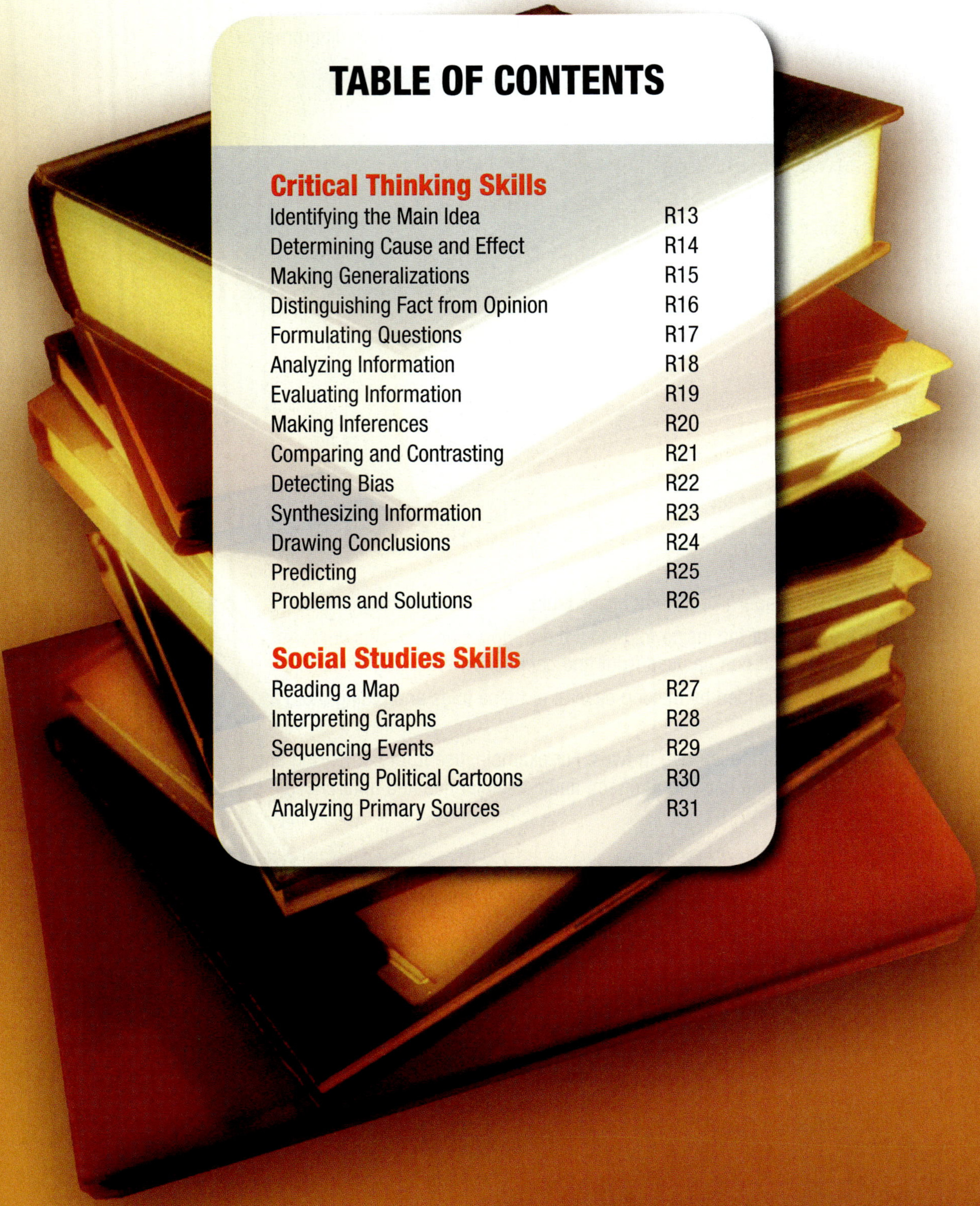

## TABLE OF CONTENTS

# Identifying the Main Idea

## Why Learn This Skill?

Finding the main idea in a reading passage will help you see the "big picture" by organizing information and assessing the most important concepts to remember.

## Learning the Skill

Follow these steps to learn how to identify the main idea. Then answer the questions below.

1. Determine the setting of the passage.
2. As you read the material, ask: What is the purpose of this passage?
3. Skim the material to identify its general subject. Look at the headings and subheadings.
4. Identify any details that support a larger idea or issue.
5. Identify the central issue. Ask: What part of the selection conveys the main idea?

*Evidence indicates that all the victims were ritually killed to consecrate successive stages of the [Pyramid of the Moon's] construction. . . . A wounded foreigner, most likely a prisoner of war, was apparently buried alive with his hands tied behind him. Animals representing mythical powers and military might surrounded him—pumas, a wolf, eagles, a falcon, an owl, and rattlesnakes. . . . Finely crafted offerings included weapons of obsidian and a figurine of solid greenstone, perhaps a war goddess to whom the burial was dedicated. Each subsequent burial was different, but all had the same aim: "Human sacrifice was important to control the people," says Sugiyanga, "to convince them to do what their rulers wanted."*

—A. R. Williams, "Pyramid of Death," *National Geographic*, October 2006

Pyramid of the Moon, Mexico ►

## Practicing the Skill

1. Where did this article appear?
2. What is the main idea of the passage?
3. What details support the main idea?

**APPLYING THE SKILL**

Find an article about the city of Teotihuacán and bring it to class. On a slip of paper, write the main idea of the article and explain why it is important. Display the article and the slip of paper on a bulletin board.

SKILLS HANDBOOK

# Determining Cause and Effect

## Why Learn This Skill?

Determining cause and effect involves considering *why* an event occurred. A *cause* is the action or situation that produces an event. What happens as a result of the cause is an effect.

SKILLS HANDBOOK

## Learning the Skill

Follow these steps to learn how to identify cause-and-effect relationships. Then answer the questions below.

**1.** Identify two or more events or developments.

**2.** Decide whether one event caused the other. Look for "clue words" such as *because, led to, due to, brought about, produced, as a result of, so that, since,* and *therefore.*

**3.** Look for logical relationships between events, such as "She overslept, and then she missed her bus."

**4.** Identify the outcomes of events. Remember that some effects have more than one cause, and some causes lead to more than one effect. Also, an effect can become the cause of yet another effect.

*Since the aftermath of the 1991 gulf war, nearly four million Kurds have enjoyed complete autonomy in the region of Iraqi Kurdistan—protected from Saddam under a "no-fly zone" north of the 36th parallel and behind the defensive wall of the Kurds' highly disciplined army, the peshmerga. They have held region-wide elections, formed a legislature, and chosen a president, establishing a world entirely apart from Baghdad—a de facto independent state. For the first time in their long history, Kurds are wielding significant political power, successfully negotiating for control over their own military forces and authority over new oil discoveries in their own terrain. Under the federated Iraq being called for by the international community, they would have powers of autonomy that match—or even exceed—what they now enjoy.*

—Frank Viviano, "The Kurds in Control," *National Geographic,* January 2006

An Iraqi Kurd ▶

## Practicing the Skill

1. Based on the reading, why have the Kurds in Iraq begun to enjoy complete autonomy?
2. What is the cause for this recent autonomy?
3. What is the cause-and-effect chain that could lead to an even greater autonomy and international recognition of this autonomy?

## APPLYING THE SKILL

Use library or Internet sources to research Kurdish culture under the rule of Saddam Hussein. Then explain the causes and effects of his dictatorship in a chart like the following:

| Causes→ | Kurdish culture→ | Effects |
|---|---|---|
| | | |

# Making Generalizations

## Why Learn This Skill?

Generalizations are judgments that are usually true, based on the facts at hand. If you say, "We have a great soccer team," you are making a generalization. If you also say that your team is undefeated, you are providing evidence to support your generalization.

### Learning the Skill

Follow these steps to learn how to make a valid generalization. Then answer the questions below.

1. Identify the subject matter.

*Berbers live throughout North Africa, but nowhere has denial of their identity been more systematic than in Morocco, ethnically the most Berber of the region's countries. Although 60 percent of its population claim Berber descent and nearly 40 percent speak one of three Berber languages, Morocco's constitution declares the country part of Arab North Africa, proclaims Arabic as its official language, and makes no mention of the Berbers. This is a legacy of the Arab nationalism that sparked colonial-era independence movements in the region and, in the name of unity, ignored or even suppressed the cultures and languages of non-Arab peoples.*

—Jeffrey Taylor, "Among the Berbers," *National Geographic,* January 2005

2. Collect factual information and examples relevant to the topic.
3. Identify similarities among these facts.
4. Use these similarities to form some general ideas about the subject.

## Practicing the Skill

1. Based on the facts above, what generalization can you make about the status of Berbers in Morocco?
2. What evidence supports your generalization?

### APPLYING THE SKILL

**Use library or Internet resources to research the status of Berbers in another country in North Africa. Write a generalization based on what you found. Provide details to support your generalization.**

SKILLS HANDBOOK

# Distinguishing Fact From Opinion

## Why Learn This Skill?

Distinguishing fact from opinion can help you make reasonable judgments about what others say and write. Facts can be proved by evidence such as records, documents, or historical sources. Opinions are based on people's differing values and beliefs.

## Learning the Skill

Follow these steps to learn how to identify facts and opinions. Then answer the questions below.

*After decades of economic progress, Puerto Rico is struggling, and the mainland has both missed this horrific economic slide and contributed to it through benign neglect.*

*Poverty on the island is rampant. The per capita income is just about half that of the poorest state in the United States. Nearly one-third of the population was unemployed in 2000. And a good quarter of all employment is in government jobs . . .*

*The bleak picture is set out in a long-overdue, exhaustive study . . . from the Center for the New Economy, a nonpartisan Puerto Rican research group, and the Brookings Institution.*

*Much of the blame can be put on Washington, which has been tone deaf to the island's needs and has miscalculated where help was needed. . . .*

—*New York Times*, "Puerto Rico, an Island in Distress," October 23, 2006

1. Identify the facts. Ask: Can these statements be proved? Where would I find information to verify them?

2. If a statement can be proved by information from a reliable source, it is factual.

3. Identify opinions by looking for statements of feelings or beliefs. They may contain words like *should, would, could, best, greatest, all, every,* or *always.*

◄ A street vendor, Puerto Rico

## Practicing the Skill

1. What are two factual statements in the editorial?
2. Which statements are opinions?

**APPLYING THE SKILL**

Find a news article and an editorial about the same issue. Identify two facts and two opinions from these sources.

# Formulating Questions

## Why Learn This Skill?

Asking questions helps you to process information and understand what you read.

## Learning the Skill

Follow these steps to learn how to formulate questions. Then answer the questions below.

**1.** Think about questions you have. Often you can find the answers in the next paragraph or section.

**2.** Ask *who, what, when, where, why,* and *how* about the main ideas, places, and events.

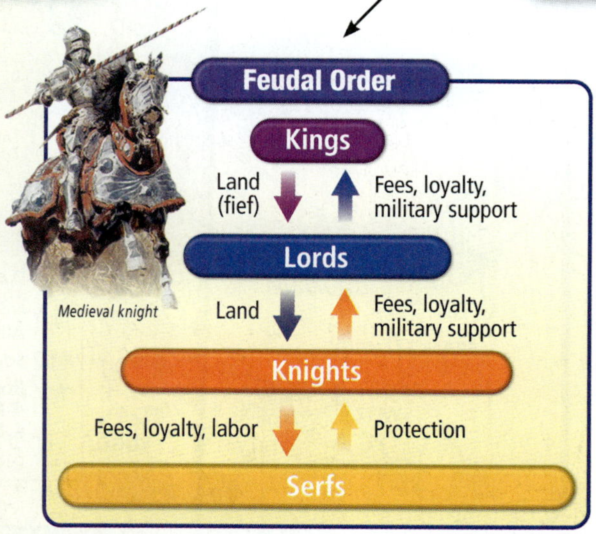


*Medieval knight*

**3.** Reread to find answers to your questions.

## Practicing the Skill

1. What is the topic of the chart?
2. Select the parts of the chart you would like to understand better.
3. Formulate two questions about these parts.
4. Where might you find answers to your questions?

### Applying the Skill

Formulate two more questions about the information on this page. Then use Internet sources to find answers to your questions.

# Analyzing Information

## Why Learn This Skill?

The ability to analyze information is important in deciding what you think about a subject. Analysis requires a critical study of what an author or artist is trying to get across.

## Learning the Skill

Follow these steps to learn how to analyze information. Then answer the questions below.

**1.** Identify the topic that is being discussed.

**2.** Examine how the information is organized. What are the main points?

**3.** Summarize the information in your own words, and then make a statement of your own based on your understanding of the topic and what you already know.

## Practicing the Skill

1. Based on the title, what does the information on the map represent?
2. How is the information organized? What are the main points?
3. Summarize the information from the map, and then provide your analysis based on the information and what you know about the Berlin Airlift.

### APPLYING THE SKILL

Find a news story about another airlift operation in history. Analyze the story and use your analysis to summarize the similarities and differences between this airlift and the Berlin Airlift.

# EVALUATING INFORMATION

## Why Learn This Skill?

We live in an information age. The amount of information available can be overwhelming, and it is sometimes difficult to know when information is true and useful. You need to evaluate what you read and hear to determine the reliability of the information presented.

## Learning the Skill

When evaluating information to determine its reliability, ask yourself the following questions as you read:

- Is there bias? In other words, does the source unfairly present just one point of view, ignoring any arguments against it?
- Is the information published in a credible, reliable publication?
- Is the author or speaker identified? Is he or she an authority on the subject?
- Is the information up-to-date?
- Is the information backed up by facts and other sources? Does it seem to be accurate?
- Is it well-written and well-edited? Writing that has errors in spelling, grammar, and punctuation is likely to be careless in other ways as well.

### Source A

*Oil prices are so high, becuz big oil companys are trying to goug us. Greedy oil executives, are driven up prices to get richer.*

—published on an individual's Internet blog

### Source B

*It's certainly clear that high oil prices aren't dulling demand for energy products. According to the Energy Dept.'s Energy Information Administration (EIA), U.S. demand for gasoline in June was 9.5 million barrels a day, a record.*

—*BusinessWeek*, July 7, 2006

### Source C

*The single biggest factor in the inflation rate last year was from one cause: the skyrocketing prices of OPEC oil. We must take whatever actions are necessary to reduce our dependence on foreign oil—and at the same time reduce inflation.*

—President Jimmy Carter, January 23, 1980

SKILLS HANDBOOK

## Practicing the Skill

Look at the above statements about oil prices. Rank them in order of most reliable to least reliable, and then explain why you ranked them as you did.

**APPLYING THE SKILL**

**Find an advertisement that contains text and bring it to class. In a brief oral presentation, tell the class whether the information in the advertisement is reliable or unreliable and why.**

# Making Inferences

## Why Learn This Skill?

To *infer* means to evaluate information and arrive at a conclusion. When you make inferences, you "read between the lines," or use clues to figure something out that is not stated directly in the text.

## Learning the Skill

Follow these steps to learn how to make inferences. Then answer the questions below.

*In Bamako I live in a guest house called the Centre d'Acceuil, run by Spanish nuns. The rooms are cheap—a bed, mosquito netting. The bad thing about the Centre d'Acceuil is that although there are ten rooms for rent, there is only one shower. Moreover, it is constantly occupied these days by a young Norwegian, who came here not realizing how hot it gets in Bamako. The African interior is always white-hot. It is a plateau relentlessly bombarded by the rays of the sun, which appears to be suspended directly above the earth here: make one careless gesture, it seems, try leaving the shade, and you will go up in flames....The Norwegian, after several suffocating, sweltering days, decided to leave everything and return home. But he had to wait for the plane. And the only way he could survive until then, he concluded, was by never coming out from under the shower.*

—Ryszard Kapuściński, *The Shadow of the Sun*

1. Read carefully for stated facts and ideas.
2. Summarize the information and list important facts.
3. Apply related information that you may already know.
4. Use your knowledge and insight to develop some logical conclusions.

## Practicing the Skill

1. What facts are presented in the passage?
2. What can you infer from the presence of mosquito netting?
3. What can you infer about the availability of air transportation in Bamako?

### APPLYING THE SKILL

Make inferences based on pictures of Africa you find on the Internet, and write questions based on your inferences. Exchange your pictures and questions with another student and answer each other's questions.

# Comparing and Contrasting

## Why Learn This Skill?

When you make comparisons, you determine similarities among ideas, objects, or events. When you contrast, you are noting differences between ideas, objects, or events. Comparing and contrasting are important skills because they help you choose among several possible alternatives.

## Learning the Skill

Follow these steps to learn how to compare and contrast. Then answer the questions below.

**1.** Identify or decide what two or more items will be compared and/or contrasted.

**2.** To compare, determine a common area or areas in which comparisons can be drawn. Look for similarities within these areas.

**3.** To contrast, look for areas that are different. These areas set the items apart from each other.

**Life in Mesopotamia and Egypt**

| | Mesopotamia | Egypt |
|---|---|---|
| **Geography** | Fertile Crescent (Southwest Asia) | Africa |
| **Rivers** | Tigris and Euphrates | Nile |
| **Natural Barriers** | Flat plains | Deserts, seas, cataracts |
| **Religion** | Polytheistic | Polytheistic |
| **Government** | City-states; theocracy; large bureaucracy; kings ruled | Rural villages; dynasties; divine kings ruled |
| **Social Structure** | Nobles, commoners, slaves | Upper classes, merchants, artisans, peasants |
| **Economy** | Farming and trade | Farming and trade |
| **Written Language** | Cuneiform | Hieroglyphics |

## Practicing the Skill

1. What characteristics does the table use to compare and contrast life in Mesopotamia and Egypt?
2. How was life in Mesopotamia similar to life in Egypt?
3. How was life in Mesopotamia different from life in Egypt?

### APPLYING THE SKILL

With a partner, research life in the other three early culture hearths—the Indus Valley, the Huang He Valley, and Middle America. Use your information to create a table like the one above. Develop three questions based on your table. Exchange your work with another pair of students and answer the questions based on their table.

# Detecting Bias

## Why Learn This Skill?

Most people have a point of view, or bias. This bias influences the way they interpret and write about events. Recognizing bias helps you judge the accuracy of what you hear or read.

## Learning the Skill

Follow these steps to learn how to detect bias. Then answer the questions below.

*The bourgeoisie . . . has put an end to all feudal, patriarchal, idyllic relations. It has pitilessly torn asunder the motley feudal ties that bound man to his "natural superiors," and has left remaining no other nexus between man and man than naked self-interest, than callous "cash payment." It has drowned the most heavenly ecstasies of religious fervour, of chivalrous enthusiasm . . . in the icy water of egotistical calculation. It has resolved personal worth into exchange value. And in place of the numberless and feasible chartered freedoms, has set up that single, unconscionable freedom—Free Trade. In one word, for exploitation, veiled by religious and political illusions, naked, shameless, direct, brutal exploitation.*

—Karl Marx and Friedrich Engels, *The Manifesto of the Communist Party*

**1.** Examine the author's identity, especially his or her views and particular interests.

**2.** Identify statements of fact.

**3.** Determine the author's point of view.

**4.** Identify any expression of opinion or emotion. Look for words that have positive or negative overtones for clues about the author's feelings on the topic.

**5.** Determine how the author's point of view is reflected in the work.

Karl Marx ►

## Practicing the Skill

1. Are there any statements of fact presented in this passage? If so, what are they?
2. What opinions are stated?
3. What evidence of bias do you find? Do the authors think it is a good thing or a bad thing that the bourgeoisie have put an end to feudal ties?

### APPLYING THE SKILL

**Find written material about a topic of interest to you. Possible sources include editorials, letters to the editor, and political pamphlets. Apply the steps for recognizing bias to the material. Write a paragraph summarizing your findings.**

# SYNTHESIZING INFORMATION

## Why Learn This Skill?

Synthesizing information involves combining information from two or more sources. Information gained from one source often sheds new light upon other information.

## Learning the Skill

Follow these steps to learn how to synthesize information. Then answer the questions that follow.

### Source A

*"Rome has been rising for 3,000 years," says Darius Arya, an archaeologist and director of the American Institute for Roman Culture. Much of Rome is situated in a floodplain, including the modern city center, known in antiquity as Campus Martius, at a bend of the Tiber River. Although the Romans put up levees, the city still flooded periodically, so they built upward, laying new structures and streets on earlier ones. "It was cost-effective, and it worked," Arya says. "We see the Romans jacking their city up two meters at a time, raising themselves above the water but also burying their past."*

—Paul Bennett, "In Rome's Basement," *National Geographic*, July 2006

**1.** Analyze each source separately to understand its meaning.

**2.** Determine what information each source adds to the subject.

### Source B

*Of all the old saws about the Eternal City, at least one remains simply true: dig a deep hole almost anywhere here, and you'll unearth an archaeological artifact or two.*

*Yet a wave of public and private building projects is suddenly focusing unusual attention on Rome's rich subterranean world as one treasure after another emerges at a steady clip.*

*"We're walking on the world's largest untapped underground museum," said Maria Antonietta Tomei, a government official responsible for coordinating archaeological digs in Rome.*

*During the last week reports surfaced that 800 coins from the fourth and fifth centuries BC had been unearthed during the reconstruction of a movie theater near the Trevi Fountain.*

—"Treasures galore still emerging from underneath Rome," *Taipei Times (online)*, December 27, 2006

**3.** Identify points of agreement and disagreement between the sources. Ask: Can Source A give me new information or new ways of thinking about Source B?

**4.** Find relationships between the information in the sources.

## Practicing the Skill

1. What is the main subject of each passage?
2. What does Source A say about the subject?
3. What information does Source B add?
4. Sum up what you have learned from both sources.

### APPLYING THE SKILL

**Find two sources of information on a topic dealing with archaeological excavations in Rome. What are the main ideas in each? How does each add to your understanding of the topic?**

SKILLS HANDBOOK

# Drawing Conclusions

## Why Learn This Skill?

A conclusion is a logical understanding that you reach based on details or facts that you read or hear. When you draw conclusions, you use stated information to figure out ideas that are unstated.

## Learning the Skill

Follow these steps to draw conclusions. Then answer the questions below.

1. Read carefully for stated facts and ideas.
2. Summarize the information and list important facts.
3. Apply related information that you may already know.
4. Use your knowledge and insight to develop some logical conclusions.

**DARFUR FACTS**

| | |
|---|---|
| 1.8 million people currently live in camps or makeshift settlements in Darfur. | Political infighting prevents 250,000 Darfur refugees from receiving humanitarian aid. |
| 215,000 Sudanese have fled to Chad because of continuing violence. | 300,000 people in Darfur have been killed or died as a result of the conflict. |
| The Sudanese government spent $18 million on weapons in 2003. | Between 2000 and 2003, arms and ammunition exports to Sudan from China increased by a factor of 30. |
| China, Russia, and France are major suppliers of arms to Sudan and permanent members of the UN Security Council. | The UN Security Council agreed to extend an existing arms embargo to the Sudanese government in March 2005. |

**Source:** Amnesty International, Fall 2006.

## Practicing the Skill

1. Which facts from the table support the conclusion that "the Sudanese government is trying to drive out the people of Darfur"?
2. What conclusion might you draw about why the UN Security Council waited so many years before extending an existing arms embargo to Sudan?

### APPLYING THE SKILL

Find an article describing a current conflict in Africa. Use the steps on this page to draw conclusions about the causes of the conflict. Summarize your conclusions in a paragraph.

# PREDICTING

## Why Learn This Skill?

Predicting future events can be difficult and sometimes risky. The more information you have, however, the more accurate your predictions will be. Making good predictions will help you understand what you read.

## Learning the Skill

Follow these steps to learn how to make a prediction. Then answer the questions below.

**1.** Gather information about the decision or action.

**2.** Use your knowledge about history and human behavior to identify what consequences could result.

**3.** Analyze each consequence by asking: How likely is this to occur?

*There is little freedom to disagree with the determinations of the authorities [in South Africa]. There is large scale unemployment here because of the drought and the recession that has hit most of the world's economy. And it is such a time that the authorities have increased the prices of various foodstuffs and also of rents in black townships—measures designed to hit hardest those least able to afford the additional costs. . . .*

*The authorities have not stopped stripping blacks of their South African citizenship. . . . The South African government is turning us into aliens in the land of our birth.*

*White South Africans are. . . .scared human beings, many of them; who would not be, if they were outnumbered five to one? Through this lofty body I wish to appeal to my white fellow South Africans to share in building a new society, for blacks are not intent on driving whites into the sea but on claiming only their rightful place in the sun in the land of their birth.*

—Bishop Desmond Tutu, speech on apartheid to the United Nations Security Council, October 23, 1984

## Practicing the Skill

1. What events does the passage describe?
2. Do you think what the author described changed after his speech?
3. On what do you base this prediction?
4. What occurrences might have an effect on changing these events?
5. What are the possible outcomes for all involved in the appeal proposed by the author?

**APPLYING THE SKILL**

Find a newspaper or magazine article that describes the current state of politics, economy, or society in South Africa. Analyze the article, and describe how the people of South Africa are trying to solve the problem. Predict three consequences of the actions described. On what do you base your prediction?

# Problems and Solutions

## Why Learn This Skill?

Suppose you are not doing well in basketball. You wonder why you cannot do better since you always go to practice, try your best, and pay attention to the coach's instructions. In order to improve a situation such as this one, you need to identify a specific problem and then take actions to solve it.

## Learning the Skill

Follow these steps to help you through the problem-solving process. Then answer the questions below.

1. Identify the problem.
2. Gather information.
3. List possible solutions.
4. Consider the advantages and disadvantages of each solution.
5. Choose the best solution to your problem and carry it out.
6. Evaluate the effectiveness of the solution.

*In just two decades . . . China's Northeast has gone from dynamo to dinosaur, tracing virtually the opposite trajectory of the country's thriving southern coastal regions. . . . The region's industrial production has sagged to less than 9 percent of national output, while its heavy reliance on state-owned enterprises—once a blessing, now a curse—has made market-oriented reforms seem like all shock and no therapy. The landscape left behind is . . . [t]housands of obsolete state-run factories, millions of laid-off workers, a growing gap between rich and poor, rampant corruption, deadly human and environmental disasters. . . .*

*Hoping to reverse this dangerous slide, Beijing has so far spent 7.5 billion dollars to rehabilitate the region, closing or privatizing old state-owned factories while retraining workers for industries more suited to the 21st century. . . . The real key, however, will be foreign investment. The region that once symbolized China's drive for self-sufficiency is now unabashedly courting foreign investors. . . . It is too early to tell whether the rust belt can truly be revitalized.*

—Brook Larmer, "The Manchurian Mandate," *National Geographic*, September 2006

## Practicing the Skill

1. What problem does the writer present in this selection?
2. What options are available to solve this problem? Can you think of any other options?
3. Explain the solutions implemented according to the selection. Were they successful? How do you determine this?

## APPLYING THE SKILL

Select a current political problem that needs to be solved. The problem can be anything from the conflict between Israel and the Palestinians to the agreement on a constitution by members of the European Union. Create a presentation in which you identify the problem, list options with their advantages and disadvantages, choose a solution, and evaluate the chosen solution.

# Reading a Map

## Why Learn This Skill?

Maps can direct you down the street, across the county, or around the world. An ordinary map holds all kinds of information. Learn the map's code, and you can read it like a book.

## Learning the Skill

Follow these steps to learn how to read a map. Then answer the questions below.

1. Look at the title of the map—it tells you what kind of information the map shows.
2. Study the map key to determine the meanings of the symbols, colors, and lines used on the map.
3. Read the labels on the map to learn where things such as cities, groups of people, and physical features are located.
4. Find the compass rose to learn the orientation of the map.
5. Determine the relationship between map measurements and actual distances on Earth by using the scale bar.
6. Use lines of latitude and longitude to determine the absolute location of places on the map.

## Practicing the Skill

1. What kinds of resources enabled the North to triumph over the South?
2. Where are most cities located? Why?

### APPLYING THE SKILL

Choose a map from your world history text and work with a partner to write three questions that can be answered by reading the map. Then exchange questions with another pair and answer each other's questions.

# INTERPRETING GRAPHS

## Why Learn This Skill?

Graphs are visual representations of statistical data. Large amounts of information can be condensed when presented in a graph. Studying graphs allows readers to see relationships clearly. **Bar graphs** use bars of different lengths to compare different quantities. **Circle graphs** show the relationship of parts to a whole as percentages.

## Learning the Skill

Follow these steps to learn how to interpret graphs. Then answer the questions that follow.

**1.** Read the graph title to identify the subject.

**Age Composition of Mexican Population**

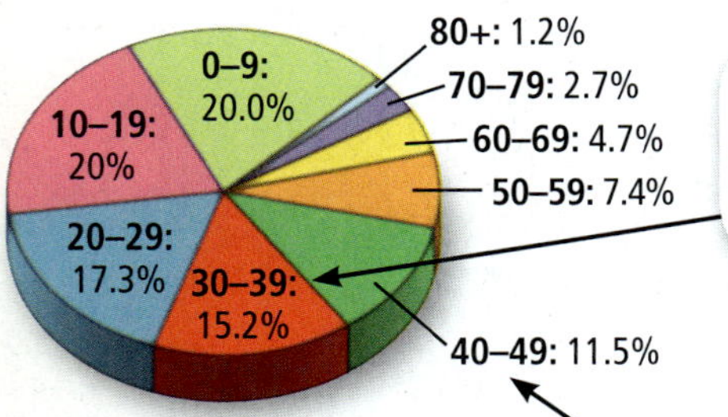


**Source:** U.S. Census Bureau, International Database.

**3.** Study the information presented and the use of colors and patterns.

**4.** Compare the lines, bars, or segments, and look for relationships in order to draw conclusions.

**Literacy Rate for Adults Over 15 (2002)**

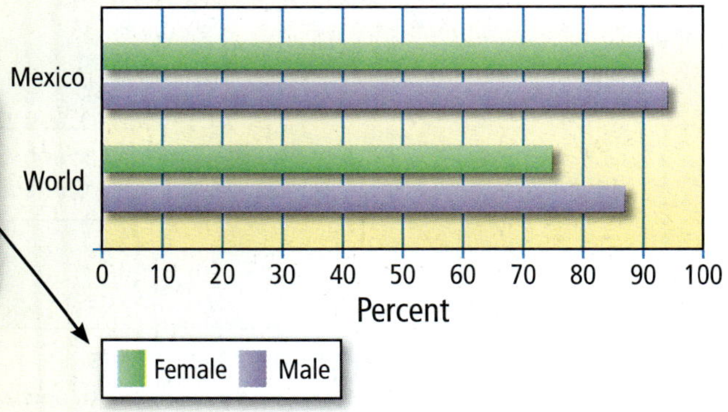


**2.** Study the labels to understand the numerical information presented.

**Source:** World Resources Institute.

## Practicing the Skill

1. How does the literacy rate in Mexico compare to literacy in the rest of the world?
2. What percentage of the Mexican people are under 20 years of age?
3. What general population trends in Mexico do these two graphs show?

### APPLYING THE SKILL

Poll your classmates about countries they would like to visit. Use the data to design and draw a line, bar, or circle graph.

SKILLS HANDBOOK

# SEQUENCING EVENTS

## Why Learn This Skill?

Sequencing involves placing facts in the order in which they occurred. Sequencing helps you deal with large quantities of information in an understandable way. In studying history, sequencing can help you understand cause-and-effect relationships among events. This in turn helps analysts to predict outcomes of various events or policies.

## Learning the Skill

Follow these steps to sequence events. Then answer the questions below.

*When the new moon of the month Shawwal appeared in the same year [1st September 1326], the Hijaz caravan left Damascus and I set off along with it. At Bosra the caravans usually halt for four days so that any who have been detained at Damascus by business affairs may make up on them. Thence they go to the Pool of Ziza, where they stop for a day, and then through al-Lajjun to the Castle of Karak. Karak, which is also called "The Castle of the Raven," is one of the most marvellous, impregnable, and celebrated of fortresses. . . . The caravan stopped for four days at a place called ath-Thaniya outside Karak, where preparations were made for entering the desert.*

—Ibn Battuta, *Travels in Asia and Africa 1325–1354*

1. Look for dates or clue words such as *in 1920, later that year, first, then,* and *in the late eighteenth century.*
2. Arrange facts in the order in which they occurred.
3. Consider using an organizational tool such as a time line, which makes it easy to see the chronology, as well as any cause-and-effect relationships, between events.

## Practicing the Skill

1. What dates or clue words in this selection can help determine the sequence of events being described?
2. Fill in a time line like the one below to show the sequence of events as described in the selection.

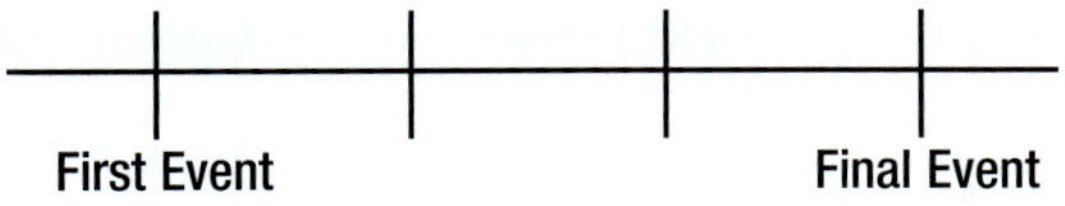


### APPLYING THE SKILL

Find a newspaper or magazine article about a world event. Sequence the information presented in the article in a time line or chart.

SKILLS HANDBOOK

# Interpreting Political Cartoons

## Why Learn This Skill?

Political cartoonists use art to express opinions. Their work appears in newspapers, magazines, books, and on the Internet. Political cartoons usually focus on public figures, political events, or economic or social conditions. They can give you a summary of an event or circumstance and the artist's opinion in a quick, entertaining manner.

## Learning the Skill

To interpret a political cartoon, follow these steps. Then answer the questions below.

1. Read the title, caption, or conversation balloons. They help you identify the subject of the cartoon.
2. Identify the characters or people shown. They may be caricatures, or unrealistic drawings that exaggerate the characters' physical features.
3. Identify any symbols shown. Symbols are things that stand for something else. Commonly recognized symbols may not be labeled. Unusual symbolism will be labeled.
4. Examine the actions in the cartoon—what is happening and why?
5. Identify the cartoonist's purpose. What statement or idea is he or she trying to get across? Decide if the cartoonist wants to persuade, criticize, or just make people think.

## Practicing the Skill

1. Who is depicted in the cartoon? What is he doing?
2. What do the stones along the path represent?
3. What overall message do you think the cartoonist is trying to send?

**APPLYING THE SKILL**

**Bring a newspaper or news magazine to class. With a partner, analyze the message in each political cartoon that you find.**

# ANALYZING PRIMARY SOURCES

## Why Learn This Skill?

An eyewitness account of a place or event is a primary source. The advantage of a primary source is that it contains firsthand knowledge. Primary sources may include diaries, letters, memoirs, interviews with eyewitnesses, photographs, news articles, and legal documents. Often they provide detailed accounts of events, but reflect only one perspective. For this reason, you must examine as many sources as possible before drawing any conclusions.

## Learning the Skill

Follow these steps to learn how to analyze a primary source. Then answer the questions below.

*The festivals generally conclude with an amusement unknown in Europe—a combat between two elephants. . . .*

*A wall of earth is raised three or four feet wide and five or six high. The two ponderous beasts meet one another face to face, on opposite sides of the wall, each having a couple of riders. . . . The riders animate the elephants either by soothing words, or by chiding them as cowards, and urge them on with their heels, until the poor creatures approach the wall and are brought to the attack. The shock is tremendous, and it appears surprising that they ever survive the dreadful wounds . . . inflicted with their teeth, their heads, and their trunks. . . .*

*The fight of these noble creatures is attended with much cruelty. . . . [S]ome of the riders are trodden underfoot; and killed on the spot. . . [T]his amusement . . . does not always end with the death of a rider: . . . some spectators are knocked down and trampled upon. . . .*

—François Bernier, *Travels in the Mogul Empire 1656–1668*

1. Identify the author of the source. Note any biases or opinions expressed by the author or creator of the source.
2. Identify when and where the document was written.
3. Read the document for its content and try to answer the five "W" questions: Who is it about? What is it about? When did it happen? Where did it happen? Why did it happen?
4. Determine what kind of information may be missing from the primary source.

## Practicing the Skill

1. How can you tell the source contains firsthand knowledge of the elephant fight?
2. Who has the author's sympathy? How can you tell?
3. What information from the source did you find valuable? What about the topic of elephant fights would you still like to learn?

### APPLYING THE SKILL

**Find a firsthand account of a recent event or a historical event. Evaluate its validity and usefulness as a primary source.**

SKILLS HANDBOOK

# Primary Sources & Literature Library

## Contents





### What Is It and How Do I Use It?

The primary sources as defined here are written testimony or documents from a particular era in history or about an important development. The source may be the writings of a noted historian or political leader, or it may be from the diary of someone who lived at the time and recorded the events of the day.

Reading primary sources is an excellent way to understand how and why people believed and acted as they did in the past. While many people might have written down their stories or beliefs, the sources chosen here are from witnesses who were close to events or especially sensitive to them.

### Checking Your Sources

When you read primary or secondary sources, you should analyze them to determine if they are dependable or reliable. Historians usually prefer primary sources to secondary sources, but both can be reliable or unreliable, depending on the following factors.

### Time Span

With primary sources, it is important to consider how much time passed from the date the event occurred to the date that the primary source was written. Generally, the longer the time span between the event and the account, the less reliable the account is. As time passes, people often forget details and fill in gaps with events that never took place. Although we like to think we remember things exactly as they happened, the fact is, we often remember them very differently than they occurred.

### Reliability

Another factor to consider when evaluating a primary source is the writer's background and reliability. When reading a historical document, try to determine if the statements and information can be proved. If the information can be verified as true by independent sources, then it probably is fact.

## Opinions

When evaluating a primary source, you should also decide whether or not the account has been influenced by emotion, opinion, or exaggeration. Writers sometimes distort the truth to suit their personal purposes. Ask yourself: Why did the person write the account? Do any words or expressions reveal the author's emotions or opinions? Again, you may wish to compare the account with another primary source document about the same event. If the two accounts differ, ask yourself why they differ and then conduct your own outside research to determine which account can be verified by other authoritative sources.

▲ Prussian soldiers

## Interpreting Primary Sources

To help you analyze a primary source, use the following steps:

- ***Examine the origins of the document.***
  You need to determine if it is indeed a primary source.
- ***Find the main ideas.***
  Read the document and summarize the main ideas in your own words.
- ***Reread the document.***
  Difficult ideas and historical documents are not always easily understood on the first reading.
- ***Use a variety of resources.***
  Use a dictionary, an encyclopedia, and maps to further your understanding of the topic. These resources are tools to help you discover new ideas and knowledge and check the validity of sources.

▲ Polish children at Auschwitz

# The First Civilizations and Empires

**Prehistory–A.D. 500**

## PRIMARY SOURCES

### Reader's Dictionary

**fraud:** deception

**imperial:** relating to the empire or the emperor

**archives:** official documents that are preserved for historical or public use

**discourse:** discussion

**decree:** an order that has the force of law

**calamity:** distress or misery

LIBRARY

## AN EGYPTIAN FATHER'S ADVICE TO HIS SON

*Upper-class Egyptians enjoyed compiling collections of wise sayings to provide guidance for leading an upright and successful life. This excerpt from* The Instruction of the Vizier Ptah-hotep *dates from around 2450 B.C.*

Then he said to his son:

If you are a leader commanding the affairs of the many, seek out for yourself every good deed, until it may be that your own affairs are without wrong. Justice is great, and it is lasting; it has been disturbed since the time of him who made it, whereas there is punishment for him who passes over its laws. Wrongdoing has never brought its undertaking into port. It may be that it is **fraud** that gains riches, but the strength of justice is that it lasts . . . .

If you are a man of standing who is pleasing to god, if he is correct and inclines toward your ways and listens to your instruction, while his manners in your house are fitting, and if he takes care of your property as it should be, seek out for him every useful action. He is your son, . . . you should not cut your heart off from him.

If he [the son] goes astray and does not carry out your instruction, so that his manners in your household are wretched, and he rebels against all that you say, while his mouth runs on in the most wretched talk, quite apart from his experience, while he possesses nothing, you should cast him off: he is not your son at all. He was not really born to you . . . He is one whom god has condemned in the very womb.

◄This rendition of an Egyptian father teaching his son is on the wall of the Tomb of Sennedjem.

## The Burning of Books

*Li Su was a chief minister of the First Qin Emperor. A follower of Legalism, he hoped to eliminate all rival theories of government.*

Your servant suggests that all books in the **imperial archives,** save the memoirs of Qin, be burned. All persons in the empire, except members of the Academy of Learned Scholars, in possession of the Book of Odes, the Book of History, and **discourses** of the hundred philosophers [including Confucius] should take them to the local governors and have them burned. Those who dare to talk to each other about the Book of Odes and the Book of History should be executed and their bodies exposed in the market place. Anyone referring to the past to criticize the present should, together with all members of his family, be put to death. Officials who fail to report cases that have come under their attention are equally guilty. After thirty days from the time of issuing the **decree,** those who have not destroyed their books are to be branded and sent to build the Great Wall. Books not to be destroyed will be those on medicine and pharmacy, agriculture and arboriculture [the cultivation of trees and shrubs]. People wishing to pursue learning should take the officials as their teachers.

◄ Chinese scroll

## Plague in Athens

*Thucydides (471–c. 400 B.C.) is regarded as the first scientific historian. In his account of the plague that broke out in Athens in 430 B.C., Thucydides simply presents the facts, describing the disease's symptoms and impact on the city itself.*

. . . Externally, the body was not so very warm to the touch; it was not pale, but reddish, livid, and breaking out in small blisters and ulcers. But internally it was consumed by such a heat that the patients could not bear to have on them the lightest coverings or linen sheets. . . .

The Athenians suffered further hardships owing to the crowding into the city of the people from the country districts; and this affected the new arrivals especially. For since no houses were available for them and they had to live in huts that were stifling in the hot season, they perished in wild disorder. Bodies of dying men lay one upon another, and half-dead people rolled about in the streets and, in their longing for water, near all the fountains. . . . The **calamity** which weighed upon them was so overpowering that men became careless of all law, sacred as well as profane. And the customs which they had hitherto observed regarding burial were all thrown into confusion, and they buried their dead each one as he could. . . .

### Document-Based Questions

1. **Evaluating** Does any part of the Egyptian father's advice have value today for sons or daughters? Be specific and support your answer.
2. **Drawing Conclusions** Why did Li Su think that burning books would eliminate all rival theories of government?
3. **Listing** What hardships did newcomers to Athens face during the time of the plague?

# The First Civilizations and Empires

**Prehistory–A.D. 500**

WORLD LITERATURE

Homer ▶

LIBRARY

## About the Author

Homer is probably one of the best known figures to have emerged from Greek antiquity. Writing in the eighth century B.C., Homer's most famous works are the *Iliad* and the *Odyssey*. These works mark the beginnings of Greek literature and are used as models even in contemporary work. The *Iliad* is the story of the Trojan War, and the *Odyssey* recounts the challenges of one Greek hero, Odysseus (also known as "Ulysses"), in returning to his homeland.

## Reader's Dictionary

**covenant:** a binding agreement or promise
**spoil:** to plunder from an enemy in war

## FROM THE *ILIAD*

By Homer, translated by Samuel Butler

*In the* Iliad, *Hektor was the Trojans' hero and son of King Priam. Achilles, the Greeks' hero, was the son of Peleus. Hektor killed Achilles' friend Patroklos, and Achilles was determined to avenge the death.*

Hektor was first to speak. "I will no longer flee you, son of Peleus," said he, "as I have been doing hitherto. . . .[Let] me either slay or be slain, for I am in the mind to face you. Let us, then, give pledges to one another by our gods; . . . [that if] I take your life, I am not to treat your dead body in any unseemly fashion, but when I have stripped you of your armor, I am to give up your body to the Achaeans, And do you likewise."

Achilles glared at him and answered, "Fool . . . [there] can be no **covenants** between men and lions, wolves and lambs can never be of one mind, but hate each other out and out. . . . Therefore there can be no understanding between you and me . . . till one or other shall fall. . . . You have no more chance, and Pallas Athena will forthwith vanquish you by my spear: you shall now pay me in full for the grief you have caused me on account of my comrades whom you have killed in battle."

He poised his spear as he spoke and hurled it. Hektor saw it coming and avoided it; he watched it and crouched down so that it flew over his head and stuck in the ground beyond; Athena then snatched it up and gave it back to Achilles without Hektor's seeing her; Hektor thereon said . . . "You have missed your aim, Achilles. . . . [And] now for your own part avoid my spear if you can—would that you might receive the whole of it into

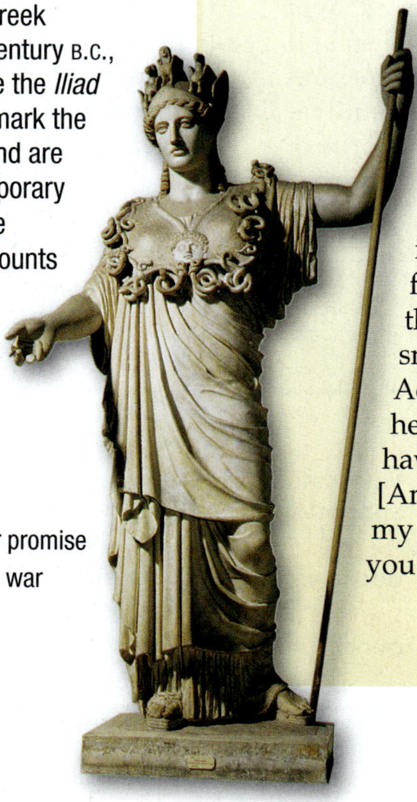
◀ Athena

your body; if you were once dead the Trojans would find the war an easier matter, for it is you who have harmed them most."

He poised his spear as he spoke and hurled it. His aim was sure for he hit the middle of Achilles' shield, but the spear rebounded from it, and did not pierce it. Hektor was angry when he saw that the weapon had sped from his hand in vain, and stood there in dismay for he had no second spear. . . . [Then] he said to himself, "Alas! The gods have lured me on to my destruction. . . . [Death] is now indeed exceedingly near at hand and there is no way out of it. . . . My doom has come upon me; let me not then die ingloriously and without a struggle, but let me first do some great thing that shall be told among men hereafter."

As he spoke he drew the keen blade that hung so great and strong by his side, and gathering himself together he sprang on Achilles . . . . Achilles mad with rage darted towards him. . . . He eyed [Hektor's] fair flesh over and over to see where he could best wound it, but all was protected by the goodly armor of which Hektor had **spoiled** Patroklos after he had slain him, save only the throat where the collar-bones divide the neck from the shoulders, and this is the quickest place for the life-breath to escape: here then did Achilles strike him as he was coming on towards him, and the point of his spear went right through the fleshy part of the neck, but it did not sever his windpipe so that he could still speak. Hektor fell headlong, and Achilles vaunted over him saying, "Hektor, you deemed that you should come off scatheless when you were spoiling Patroklos. . . . Fool that you were: for I, his comrade, mightier far than he, was still left behind him at the ships, and now I have laid you low. The Achaeans shall give him all due funeral rites, while dogs and vultures shall work their will upon yourself."

Then Hektor said, as the life-breath ebbed out of him, "I pray you . . . , let not dogs devour me at the ships of the Achaeans, but accept the rich treasure of gold and bronze which my father and mother will offer you, and send my body home, that the Trojans and their wives may give me my dues of fire when I am dead."

Achilles glared at him and answered, "Dog . . . [though] Priam . . . should bid them offer me your weight in gold, even so your mother shall never lay you out and make lament over the son she bore, but dogs and vultures shall eat you utterly up."

Hektor with his dying breath then said, "I know you what you are, and was sure that I should not move you, for your heart is hard as iron. . . ."

When he had thus said the shrouds of death's final outcome enfolded him, whereon his life-breath went out of him and flew down to the house of Hades, lamenting its sad fate that it should enjoy youth and strength no longer.

LIBRARY

**DOCUMENT-BASED QUESTIONS**

1. **Describing** How does Achilles plan to avenge his friend Patroklos' death beyond killing Hektor?
2. **Explaining** Explain Achilles' concern with Hektor's armor.
3. **Interpreting** What does Hektor's last request reveal about Greek attitudes towards death?

**Applications Activity**

Outline a story for a modern epic. Who would be your hero and why?

# New Patterns of Civilization

A.D. 400–1500

## PRIMARY SOURCES

### Reader's Dictionary

**cobble:** to repair shoes

**accrue:** to happen as a direct result of some other action

**err:** to make mistakes

**remonstrate:** to scold or reproach

**lamentation:** an expression of mourning

▲ Woman playing a lute



### MUHAMMAD'S WIFE REMEMBERS THE PROPHET

*What kind of man was Muhammad that he could achieve such profound changes in Arab civilization? This description comes from his wife, Ayesha, the daughter of Abu Bakr.*

When Ayesha was questioned about Muhammad she used to say:

He was a man just such as yourselves. He laughed often and smiled much. He would mend his clothes and **cobble** his shoes. He used to help me in my household duties; but what he did oftenest was to sew. If he had the choice between two matters, he would choose the easiest, so long as no sin could **accrue** therefrom. He never took revenge excepting where the honor of God was concerned. When angry with anyone, he would say, "What hath taken such a one that he should soil his forehead in the mud."

His humility was shown by his accepting the invitation even of slaves. . . . He would say: "I sit at meals as a servant does and I eat like a servant. For I really am a servant."

Muhammad hated nothing more than lying. Whenever he knew that any of his followers had **erred** in this respect, he would hold himself aloof from them until he was assured of their repentance.

He did not speak rapidly, running the words into one another, but enunciated each syllable distinctly, so that what he said was imprinted in the memory of everyone who heard him.

He used to stand for such a long time at his prayers that his legs would swell. When **remonstrated,** he said: "What! Shall I not behave as a thankful servant should?"

He refused to accept presents that had been offered as alms. Neither would he allow anyone in his family to use what had been brought as alms. "For," said he, "alms are the impurity of mankind."

## A Woman May Need to Have the Heart of a Man

*Christine de Pizan was widowed at age 25. She supported her three children by copying manuscripts, compiling a manual of instructions for knights, and writing books. The following is from her 1405 work,* The Treasure of the City of Ladies.

It is the responsibility of every baron to spend the least possible time at his manors and his own estate, for his duties are to bear arms, to attend the court of his prince and to travel. Now, his lady stays behind and must take his place. . . . Her men should be able to rely on her for all kinds of protection in the absence of their lord. . . . She ought to know how to use weapons and be familiar with everything that pertains to them, so that she may be ready to command her men if the need arises. She should know how to launch an attack or to defend against one.

In addition she will do well to be a very good manager of the estate. . . . She will busy herself around the house; she will find plenty of orders to give. She will have the animals brought in at the right time [and] take care how the shepherd looks after them. . . .

In the winter-time, she will have her men cut her willow groves and make vine props to sell in the season. She will never let them be idle. . . . She will employ her women . . . to attend to the livestock, . . . [and] to weed the courtyards. . . . There is a great need to run an estate well, and the one who is most diligent and careful about it is more than wise and ought to be highly praised.

◄ A wandering Buddhist sage

## The Buddha's Sermon

*Siddhartha Gautama, the Buddha, gave sermons in India, which were written down after 250 B.C. An excerpt from one of these follows.*

1. Now this, O monks, is the noble truth of pain: birth is painful, old age is painful, sickness is painful, death is painful, sorrow, **lamentation,** dejection, and despair are painful. Contact with unpleasant things is painful, not getting what one wishes is painful. In short the five khandhas of grasping are painful.
2. Now this, O monks, is the noble truth of the cause of pain: that craving which leads to rebirth, combined with pleasure and lust, finding pleasure here and there, namely, the craving for passion, the craving for existence, the craving for non-existence.
3. Now this, O monks, is the noble truth of the cessation of pain: the cessation without a remainder of that craving, abandonment, forsaking, release, non-attachment.
4. Now this, O monks, is the noble truth of the way that leads to the cessation of pain: this is the noble Eightfold Path. . . .

### DOCUMENT-BASED QUESTIONS

1. **Describing** According to Ayesha, what kind of man was Muhammad? Did he behave like a ruler?
2. **Identifying** What are some of the duties and responsibilities of the medieval gentlewoman, according to Christine de Pizan's account?
3. **Summarizing** According to the Buddha, what is the cause of pain?

# New Patterns of Civilization

**A.D. 400–1500**

## WORLD LITERATURE

◀ Li Bo

### About the Author

Li Bo was born in A.D. 701 in western China. People began praising his beautiful poems even before he reached adulthood. Throughout his life he traveled extensively in China, amazing people with his ability to compose insightful, touching poems. He wrote about the world around him, the people he met, and the emotions he felt. By the time of his death in A.D. 762, he was regarded as one of China's greatest poets, a distinction he still holds today.

### Reader's Dictionary

**sparse:** few and scattered

**thrush:** a type of small to medium sized bird that is an excellent singer

**brooklet:** a small brook or creek

## FIVE POEMS

By Li Bo

*In the following poems, Li Bo interprets parting from a friend, life as a journey, and his experience with his homeland.*

**Taking Leave of a Friend**

Blue mountains to the north of the walls,
White river winding about them;
Here we must make separation
And go out through a thousand miles of dead grass.

Mind like a floating wide cloud,
Sunset like the parting of old acquaintances
Who bow over their clasped hands at a distance.
Our horses neigh to each other as we are departing.

**Clearing at Dawn**

The fields are chill, the **sparse** rain has stopped;
The colours of Spring teem on every side.
With leaping fish the blue pond is full;
With singing **thrushes** the green boughs droop.
The flowers of the field have dabbled their powdered cheeks;
The mountain grasses are bent level at the waist.
By the bamboo stream the last fragment of cloud
Blown by the wind slowly scatters away.

◀ This painting is titled *Spring Dawn Over Elixir Terrace.*

**Hard Is the Journey**

Gold vessels of fine wines,
thousands a gallon,
Jade dishes of rare meats,
costing more thousands,
I lay my chopsticks down,
no more can banquet,
And draw my sword and stare
wildly about me:

Ice bars my way to cross
the Yellow River,
Snows from dark skies to climb
the T'ai-hang Mountains!

At peace I drop a hook
into a **brooklet,**
At once I'm in a boat
but sailing sunward . . .

(Hard is the Journey,
Hard is the Journey,
So many turnings,
And now where am I?)

So when a breeze breaks waves,
bringing fair weather,
I set a cloud for sails,
cross the blue oceans!

**Listening to a Flute in Yellow Crane Pavilion**

I came here a wanderer
thinking of home
remembering my far away Ch'ang-an.
And then, from deep in Yellow Crane
Pavilion,
I heard a beautiful bamboo flute
play "Falling Plum Blossoms."
It was late spring in a city by the river.

▲ *Landscape of the Four Seasons* by Shen shih-Ch'ung

**In the Mountains on a Summer Day**

Gently I stir a white feather fan,
With open shirt sitting in a green wood.
I take off my cap and hang it on a jutting
stone;
A wind from the pine-tree trickles on my
bare head.

LIBRARY

**DOCUMENT-BASED QUESTIONS**

1. **Identifying** What detail in "Taking Leave of a Friend" reveals a custom in Li Bo's times?
2. **Interpreting** What is the meaning of the last line of "Listening to a Flute in Yellow Crane Pavilion"?
3. **Drawing Conclusions** Li Bo describes beauty and peace and luxury in "Hard Is the Journey". Why does he call the journey "hard"?

**Applications Activity**

Write a poem describing your hometown. Make sure to include a description of something unique to that area.

# The Early Modern World

**1350–1815**

## Primary Sources

### Reader's Dictionary

**contention:** point made in an argument
**Scripture:** passage from the Bible
**revered:** honored or respected
**hemp:** a fiber from the mulberry bush
**imprescriptible:** cannot be taken away by law

LIBRARY

▲ Martin Luther

Ulrich Zwingli ▼

## A Reformation Debate

*In 1529 Martin Luther and Ulrich Zwingli debated over the sacrament of the Lord's Supper, or Communion.*

LUTHER: Although I have no intention of changing my mind, which is firmly made up, I will nevertheless present the grounds of my belief and show where the others are in error. . . .Your basic **contentions** are these: In the last analysis you wish to prove that a body cannot be in two places at once, and you produce arguments about the unlimited body which are based on natural reason. I do not question how Christ can be God and man and how the two natures can be joined. For God is more powerful than all our ideas, and we must submit to his word.

Prove that Christ's body is not there where the **Scripture** says, "This is my body!" God is beyond all mathematics and the words of God are to be **revered** and carried out in awe. It is God who commands, "Take, eat, this is my body." I request, therefore, valid scriptural proof to the contrary.

ZWINGLI: I insist that the words of the Lord's Supper must be figurative. This is ever apparent, and even required by the article of faith; "taken up into heaven, seated at the right hand of the Father." Otherwise, it would be absurd to look for him in the Lord's Supper at the same time that Christ is telling us that he is in heaven. One and the same body cannot possibly be in different places. . . .

LUTHER: I call upon you as before: your basic contentions are shaky. Give way, and give glory to God!

ZWINGLI: And we call upon you to give glory to God and to quit begging the question! The issue at stake is this: Where is the proof of your position?

LUTHER: It is your point that must be proved, not mine. But let us stop this sort of thing. It serves no purpose.

ZWINGLI: It certainly does! It is for you to prove that the passage in John 6 speaks of a physical meal.

LUTHER: You express yourself poorly. . . . You're going nowhere.

## The Silk Industry in China

*During the 1600s Sung Ying-Hsing wrote a book on Chinese industry called* **T'ien-kung K'ai-wu (Chinese Technology in the Seventeenth Century),** *which included sections on the production of silk.*

. . . Members of the aristocracy are clothed in flowing robes decorated with patterns of magnificent mountain dragons, and they are rulers of the country. Those of lowly stations would be dressed in **hempen** jackets and cotton garments to protect themselves from the cold winter and cover their nakedness in summer, in order to distinguish themselves from the birds and beasts. Therefore nature has provided the materials for clothing. Of these, the vegetable [plant] ones are cotton, hemp, *meng* hemp, and creeper hemp; those derived from birds, animals, and insects are furs, woolens, silk, and spun silk. . . .

But, although silk looms are to be found in all parts of the country, how many persons have actually seen the remarkable functioning of the draw-loom: Such words as "orderly government" [*chih,* i.e., the word used in silk reeling], "chaos" [*luan,* i.e., when the fibers are entangled], "knowledge or good policy" [*ching-lun,* i.e., the warp thread and the woven pattern] are known by every schoolboy, but is it not regrettable that he should never see the actual things that gave rise to these words?

▲ Emperor's robe, Qing dynasty

## Declaration of the Rights of Woman and the Female Citizen

*Olympe de Gouges composed her own* **Declaration of the Rights of Woman and the Female Citizen** *in 1791. Following are excerpts.*

1. Woman is born free and lives as equal to man in her rights. Social distinctions can be based only on the common utility.
2. The purpose of any political association is the conservation of the natural and **imprescriptible** rights of woman and man; these rights are liberty, property, security, and especially resistance to oppression. . . .
4. Liberty and justice consist of restoring all that belongs to others; thus, the only limits on the exercise of the natural rights of woman are perpetual male tyranny; these limits are to be reformed by the laws of nature and reason. . . .
6. The law must be . . . the same for all: male and female citizens. . . .
7. No woman is an exception; she is accused, arrested, and detained in cases determined by law. Women, like men, obey this rigorous law. . . .
11. The free communication of thoughts and opinions is one of the most precious rights of woman, since that liberty assured the recognition of children by their fathers. . . .

LIBRARY

### DOCUMENT-BASED QUESTIONS

1. **Drawing Conclusions** Was a conclusion reached in the debate presented between Luther and Zwingli?
2. **Listing** According to Sung Ying-Hsing, from what two sources was all clothing made?
3. **Defending** Olympe de Gouges states that free communication of thoughts is one of the most precious rights of women. Do you agree or disagree?

# The Early Modern World

**1350–1815**

**WORLD LITERATURE**

◄ Voltaire

## About the Author

Voltaire was born François-Marie Arouet on November 21, 1694. He assumed the pen name "Voltaire" in 1718. Voltaire was a critical and satiric writer who used his wit to attack both church and state. *Candide* is one of Voltaire's most brilliant and most well-known works.

## Reader's Dictionary

**bulwark:** strong support or protection

**summarily:** without delay or formality

## FROM CANDIDE

By Voltaire

*Candide has been taught that "everything is for the best." However, his adventures usually prove the opposite. Here, he has just been cast out of a castle. The "men in blue" he meets are army recruiters for Frederick the Great, king of Prussia, who was at war with the French when Voltaire wrote* Candide.

Candide . . . dragged himself into the neighboring village, which was called Waldberghofftrarbkdikdorff; he was penniless, famished, and exhausted. At the door of a tavern he paused forlornly. Two men dressed in blue [Prussian soldiers] took note of him:

—Look, chum, said one of them, there's a likely young fellow of just about the right size.

They approached Candide and invited him very politely to dine with them.

—Gentlemen, Candide replied with charming modesty, I'm honored by your invitation, but I really don't have enough money to pay my share.

—My dear sir, said one of the blues, people of your appearance and your merit don't have to pay; aren't you five feet five inches tall?

—Yes, gentlemen, that is indeed my stature, said he, making a bow.

—Then, sire, you must be seated at once; not only will we pay your bill this time, we will never allow a man like you to be short of money; for men were made only to render one another mutual aid.

—You are quite right, said Candide; it is just as Dr. Pangloss always told me, and I see clearly that everything is for the best.

They beg him to accept a couple of crowns, he takes them, and offers an I.O.U.; they won't hear of it, and all sit down at table together.

—Don't you love dearly . . .?

—I do indeed, says he, I dearly love Miss Cunégonde.



LIBRARY

—No, no, says one of the gentlemen, we are asking if you don't love dearly the King of the Bulgars [Frederick the Great].

—Not in the least, says he, I never laid eyes on him.

—What's that you say? He's the most charming of kings, and we must drink his health.

—Oh, gladly, gentlemen; and he drinks.

—That will do, they tell him; you are now the **bulwark,** the support, the defender, the hero of the Bulgars; your fortune is made and your future assured.

Promptly they slip irons on his legs and lead him to the regiment. There they cause him to right face, left face, present arms, order arms, aim, fire, doubletime, and they give him thirty strokes of the rod. Next day he does the drill a little less awkwardly and gets only twenty strokes; the third day, they give him only ten, and he is regarded by his comrades as a prodigy.

▲ Frederick the Great, king of Prussia

Candide, quite thunderstruck, did not yet understand very clearly how he was a hero. One fine spring morning he took it into his head to go for a walk, stepping straight out as if it were a privilege of the human race, as of animals in general, to use his legs as he chose. He had scarcely covered two leagues when four other heroes [Prussian soldiers], each six feet tall, overtook him, bound him, and threw him into a dungeon. At the court-martial they asked which he preferred, to be flogged thirty-six times by the entire regiment or to receive **summarily** a dozen bullets in the brain. In vain did he argue that the human will is free and insist that he preferred neither alternative; he had to choose; by virtue of the divine gift called "liberty" he decided to run the gauntlet thirty-six times, and actually endured two floggings. The regiment was composed of two thousand men. That made four thousand strokes. As they were preparing for the third beating, Candide, who could endure no more, begged as a special favor that they would have the goodness to smash his head. His plea was granted; they bandaged his eyes and made him kneel down. The King of the Bulgars [Frederick the Great], passing by at this moment, was told of the culprit's crime; and as this king had a rare genius, he understood, from everything they told him of Candide, that this was a young metaphysician, extremely ignorant of the ways of the world, so he granted his royal pardon, with a generosity which will be praised in every newspaper in every age. A worthy surgeon cured Candide in three weeks with the ointments described by Dioscorides. He already had a bit of skin back and was able to walk when the King of the Bulgars went to war with the King of the Abares.

Nothing could have been so fine, so brisk, so brilliant, so well-drilled as the two armies. The trumpets, the fifes, the oboes, the drums, and the cannon produced such a harmony as was never heard in hell. First the cannons battered down about six thousand men on each side; then volleys of musket fire removed from the best of worlds about nine or ten thousand rascals who were cluttering up its surface.

LIBRARY

## DOCUMENT-BASED QUESTIONS

1. **Explaining** Explain the irony of the soldiers' statement, "your fortune is made and your future assured."
2. **Making Connections** Why is Candide punished? How does this relate to the philosophy of the Enlightenment?
3. **Analyzing** What is Voltaire's attitude toward the "King of the Bulgars"?

**Applications Activity**

Write a satirical piece criticizing something about a television show or movie. Remember that a satire does not directly attack but criticizes by showing how ridiculous something is.

# An Era of European Imperialism

**1800–1914**

## PRIMARY SOURCES

### Reader's Dictionary

**autocrat:** a monarch who rules with unlimited authority

**close:** an enclosed area of land

**abject:** existing in a low state or condition

**infanticide:** killing an infant

**resuscitation:** restoration or renewal

▲ Czar Alexander II

LIBRARY

## IMPERIAL DECREE TO FREE THE SERFS

*In 1861 the Russian czar Alexander II issued the* Emancipation Manifesto, *an imperial decree to free his country's serfs.*

By the grace of God, we, Alexander II, Emperor and **Autocrat** of all the Russias, King of Poland, Grand Duke of Finland, etc., to all our faithful subjects, make known:

Examining the condition of classes and professions comprising the state, we became convinced that the present state legislation favors the upper and middle classes, . . . but does not equally favor the serfs. . . . These facts had already attracted the attention of our predecessors, and they had adopted measures aimed at improving the conditions of the peasants. But decrees on free farmers and serfs have been carried out on a limited scale only.

We thus came to the conviction that the work of a serious improvement of the condition of the peasants was a sacred inheritance bequeathed to us by our ancestors, a mission which, in the course of events Divine Providence called upon us to fulfill. . . .

In virtue of the new dispositions above mentioned, the peasants attached to the soil will be invested within a term fixed by the law with all the rights of free cultivators. . . .

At the same time, they are granted the right of purchasing their **close,** and, with the consent of the proprietors, they may acquire in full property the arable lands and other appurtenances [rights of way] which are allotted to them as a permanent holding. By the acquisition in full property of the quantity of land fixed, the peasants are free from their obligations towards the proprietors for land thus purchased, and they enter definitely into the condition of free peasants-landholders.

## The Unfortunate Situation of Working Women

*This article was published in* L'Atelier, *a Parisian workingman's newspaper, in 1842.*

Although women's work is less productive for society than that of men, it does, nevertheless, have a certain value, and, moreover, there are professions that only women can practice. For these, women are indispensable. . . . It is these very workers in all these necessary trades who earn the least and who are subject to the longest layoffs. Since for so much work they earn only barely enough to live from day to day, it happens that during times of unemployment they sink into **abject** poverty.

Who has not heard of the women silkworkers' dirty, unhealthy, and badly paid work; of the women in the spinning and weaving factories working fourteen to sixteen hours (except for one hour for both meals); always standing, without a single minute for repose, putting forth an enormous amount of effort. And many of them have to walk a league or more, morning and evening, to get home. Nor should we neglect to mention the danger that exists merely from working in these large factories, surrounded by wheels, gears, enormous leather belts that always threaten to seize you and pound you to pieces.

The existence of women who work as day laborers, and are obliged to abandon . . . the care of their children to indifferent neighbors is no better. . . . We believe that the condition of women will never really improve until workingmen can earn enough to support their families, which is only fair. Woman is so closely linked to man that the position of the one cannot be improved without reference to the position of the other.

## The Impact of British Rule in India

*In 1871 Dadabhai Naoroji commented on the benefits and the problems of British rule in India.*

Benefits of British Rule:

*In the Cause of Humanity:* Abolition of suttee and **infanticide.** *Civilization:* Education, both male and female. . . . **Resuscitation** of India's own noble literature. *Politically:* Peace and order. Freedom of speech and liberty of the press. . . . Improvement of government in the native states. Security of life and property. Freedom from oppression. . . . *Materially:* Loans for railways and irrigation. Development of a few valuable products, such as indigo, tea, coffee, silk, etc. Increase of exports. Telegraphs.

The Detriments of British Rule:

*In the Cause of Humanity:* Nothing. *Civilization:* [T]here has been a failure to do as much as might have been done. *Politically:* Repeated breach of pledges to give the natives a fair and reasonable share in the higher administration of their own country, . . . an utter disregard of the feelings and views of the natives. *Financially:* [N]ew modes of taxation, without any adequate effort to increase the means of the people to pay.

*Summary:* British rule has been: morally, a great blessing; politically, peace and order on one hand, blunders on the other; materially, impoverishment. . . . Our great misfortune is that you do not know our wants. When you will know our real wishes, I have not the least doubt that you would do justice. The genius and spirit of the British people is fair play and justice.

### DOCUMENT-BASED QUESTIONS

1. **Explaining** Why does Czar Alexander II free the serfs?
2. **Identifying Points of View** What is the attitude of the *L'Atelier* writer toward women and women's work? Is the author of the article likely to be a woman or a man? What makes you think so?
3. **Summarizing** Summarize the benefits and problems of British rule in India.

LIBRARY

# An Era of European Imperialism

1800–1914

## WORLD LITERATURE

▲George Orwell

### About the Author

George Orwell was the pen name of English author Eric Arthur Blair, who was born in Motihari, India, on June 25, 1903. Although born in India, he was educated in England. He lived for 46 years, and during that time, he wrote many influential essays, novels, and newspaper articles. His two most famous works are *1984* and *Animal Farm,* both of which are commentaries against totalitarianism.

### Reader's Dictionary

**mahout:** a keeper and driver of an elephant
**dominion:** rule, control
**sahib:** title meaning "sir" or "master"

## FROM *SHOOTING AN ELEPHANT*

By George Orwell

*George Orwell served for several years as an assistant superintendent in the Indian Imperial Police but resigned due to his distaste of imperialism. In* Shooting an Elephant, *he describes an incident that happened to him, and he satirizes the problems of colonial rule.*

I had halted on the road. As soon as I saw the elephant I knew with perfect certainty that I ought not to shoot him. It is a serious matter to shoot a working elephant—it is comparable to destroying a huge and costly piece of machinery—and obviously one ought not to do it if it can possibly be avoided. And at that distance, peacefully eating, the elephant looked no more dangerous than a cow. I thought then and I think now that his attack of "must" was already passing off; in which case he would merely wander harmlessly about until the **mahout** came back and caught him. Moreover, I did not in the least want to shoot him. I decided that I would watch him for a little while to make sure that he did not turn savage again, and then go home.

But at that moment I glanced round at the crowd that had followed me. It was an immense crowd, two thousand at the least and growing every minute. It blocked the road for a long distance on either side. I looked at the sea of yellow faces above the garish clothes—faces all happy and excited over this bit of fun, all certain that the elephant was going to be shot. They were watching me as they would watch a conjurer about to perform a trick. They

Colonial hunter ▶

did not like me, but with the magical rifle in my hands I was momentarily worth watching. And suddenly I realized that I should have to shoot the elephant after all. The people expected it of me and I had got to do it; I could feel their two thousand wills pressing me forward irresistibly. And it was at this moment, as I stood there with the rifle in my hands, that I first grasped the hollowness, the futility of the white man's **dominion** in the East. Here was I, the white man with his gun, standing in front of the unarmed native crowd—seemingly the leading actor of the piece; but in reality I was only an absurd puppet pushed to and fro by the will of those yellow faces behind. I perceived in this moment that when the white man turns tyrant it is his own freedom that he destroys. He becomes a sort of hollow, posing dummy, the conventionalized figure of a **sahib.** For it is the condition of his rule that he shall spend his life in trying to impress the "natives," and so in every crisis he has got to do what the "natives" expect of him. He wears a mask, and his face grows to fit it. I had got to shoot the elephant. I had committed myself to doing it when I sent for the rifle. A sahib has got to act like a sahib; he has got to appear resolute, to know his own mind and do definite things. To come all that way, rifle in hand, with two thousand people marching at my heels, and then to trail feebly away, having done nothing—no, that was impossible. The crowd would laugh at me. And my whole life, every white man's life in the East, was one long struggle not to be laughed at.

▼ Working elephants, 1890s

. . . But I did not want to shoot the elephant. . . . The sole thought in my mind was that if anything went wrong those two thousand Burmese would see me trampled on, and reduced to a grinning corpse. And if that happened it was quite probable that some of them would laugh. That would never do. There was only one alternative. I shoved the cartridges into the magazine and lay down on the road to get a better aim.

The crowd grew very still, and a deep, low, happy sigh, as of people who see the theater curtain go up at last, breathed from innumerable throats. They were going to have their bit of fun after all.

. . . When I pulled the trigger I did not hear the bang or feel the kick—one never does when a shot goes home—but I heard the devilish roar of glee that went up from the crowd. . . . You could see the agony of it jolt [the elephant's] whole body and knock the last remnant of strength from his legs.

. . . In the end I could not stand it any longer and went away. I heard later that it took him half an hour to die. . . .

. . . I often wondered whether any of the others grasped that I had done it solely to avoid looking a fool.



## DOCUMENT-BASED QUESTIONS

1. **Drawing Conclusions** Why does the narrator ultimately decide that he must shoot the elephant?
2. **Recognizing Bias** What does this story reveal about Orwell's attitudes about imperialism? How can you tell?
3. **Explaining** According to Orwell in this piece, who held the power in colonial India?

**Applications Activity**

Write a narrative account of an incident when you felt people were pushing you to act in opposition to your original intentions.

# The Twentieth-Century Crisis

**1914–1945**

## PRIMARY SOURCES

### Reader's Dictionary

**parapet:** wall of earth piled on top of a trench

**snipers:** people who shoot at exposed individuals from a concealed location

**civil disobedience:** refusal to obey governmental demands

**exploitation:** unfair use for one's own advantage

**disarmament:** reducing or eliminating weapons

▲Battle of the Somme

LIBRARY

## AN AMERICAN SOLDIER REMEMBERS WORLD WAR I

*Arthur Guy Empey reflects upon his experiences during World War I in the trenches in France. This is an excerpt from his book* Over the Top.

Suddenly, the earth seemed to shake and a thunderclap burst in my ears. I opened my eyes,—I was splashed all over with sticky mud, and men were picking themselves up from the bottom of the trench. The **parapet** on my left had toppled into the trench, completely blocking it with a wall of tossed-up earth. The man on my left lay still. . . . A German "Minnie" (trench mortar) had exploded in the [trench]. . . . Stretcher-bearers came up the trench on the double. After a few minutes of digging, three still, muddy forms on stretchers were carried down the communication trench to the rear. Soon they would be resting "somewhere in France," with a little wooden cross over their heads. They had done their bit for King and Country, had died without firing a shot. . . . I was dazed and motionless. Suddenly a shovel was pushed into my hands, and a rough but kindly voice said: "Here, my lad, lend a hand clearing the trench, but keep your head down, and look out for **snipers**. . . ."

Lying on my belly on the bottom of the trench, I filled sandbags with the sticky mud. . . . The harder I worked, the better I felt.

Occasionally a bullet would crack overhead, and a machine gun would kick up the mud on the bashed-in parapet. At each crack I would duck and shield my face with my arm. One of the older men noticed this action of mine, and whispered: "Don't duck at the crack of a bullet, Yank; the danger has passed,—you never hear the one that wings you. Always remember that if you are going to get it, you'll get it, so never worry." . . . [Days later] we received the cheerful news that at four in the morning we were to go over the top and take the German frontline trench. My heart turned to lead.

## Gandhi Takes the Path of Civil Disobedience

*Mohandas Gandhi explains why British rule in India must end.*

▲ Mohandas Gandhi

Before embarking on **civil disobedience** and taking the risk I have dreaded to take all these years, I would fain approach you and find a way out.

My personal faith is absolutely clear. I cannot intentionally hurt anything that lives, much less fellow human beings, even though they may do the greatest wrong to me and mine. Whilst, therefore, I hold the British rule to be a curse, I do not intend harm to a single Englishman or to any legitimate interest he may have in India.

I must not be misunderstood. Though I hold the British rule in India to be a curse, I do not, therefore, consider Englishmen in general to be worse than any other people on earth. I have the privilege of claiming many Englishmen as dearest friends. Indeed much that I have learned of the evil of British rule is due to the writings of frank and courageous Englishmen who have not hesitated to tell the truth about that rule.

And why do I regard British rule as a curse? It has impoverished the ignorant millions by a system of progressive **exploitation** and by a ruinously expensive military and civil administration which the country can never afford.

It has reduced us politically to serfdom. It has sapped the foundations of our culture. And, by the policy of cruel **disarmament**, it has degraded us spiritually. Lacking the inward strength, we have been reduced . . . to a state bordering on cowardly helplessness. . . .

## The Holocaust—The Camp Victims

*A French doctor describes the victims of one of the gas chambers at Auschwitz-Birkenau during the Holocaust.*

It is mid-day, when a long line of women, children, and old people enter the yard. The senior official in charge . . . climbs on a bench to tell them that they are going to have a bath and that afterwards they will get a drink of hot coffee. They all undress in the yard. . . . The doors are opened and an indescribable jostling begins. The first people to enter the gas chamber begin to draw back. They sense the death which awaits them. The SS men put an end to the pushing and shoving with blows from their rifle butts beating the heads of the horrified women who are desperately hugging their children. The massive oak double doors are shut. For two endless minutes one can hear banging on the walls and screams which are no longer human. And then—not a sound. Five minutes later the doors are opened. The corpses, squashed together and distorted, fall out like a waterfall. The bodies which are still warm pass through the hands of the hairdresser who cuts their hair and the dentist who pulls out their gold teeth. . . .

### Document-Based Questions

1. **Describing** How did Arthur Empey feel and act during his time in the trenches of World War I?
2. **Analyzing** Why do you think Gandhi believed that nonviolent civil disobedience would encourage the British to free India?
3. **Identifying Points of View** What is the French doctor's point of view about the events he describes at the Auschwitz-Birkenau death camp?

# The Twentieth-Century Crisis

**1914–1945**

WORLD LITERATURE

### Reader's Dictionary

**agog:** full of intense interest or excitement
**moon:** to dream

LIBRARY

◀ Virginia Woolf

### About the Author

Virginia Woolf was born in 1882 in London. Her work changed the ways many modern novels were written. She used an experimental narrative technique known as stream of consciousness, in which characters are portrayed through their inner lives and thoughts without explanation from the writer. She is also known for her feminist writings. One of the most famous of these is *A Room of One's Own.* Its title reflects her belief that a woman "must have money and a room of her own" in order to write.

## FROM *A ROOM OF ONE'S OWN*

by Virginia Woolf

*Virginia Woolf was a fervent supporter of women's rights. In* A Room of One's Own, *she responds to those who would question the capabilities of women because there was no "female Shakespeare."*

. . . Let me imagine, since facts are so hard to come by, what would have happened had Shakespeare had a wonderfully gifted sister, called Judith, let us say. Shakespeare himself went, very probably—his mother was an heiress—to the grammar school, where he may have learnt Latin—Ovid, Virgil and Horace—and the elements of grammar and logic. He was, it is well known, a wild boy who poached rabbits, perhaps shot a deer, and had, rather sooner than he should have done, to marry a woman in the neighbourhood, who bore him a child rather quicker than was right. That escapade sent him to seek his fortune in London. He had, it seemed, a taste for the theatre; he began by holding horses at the stage door. Very soon he got work in the theatre, became a successful actor, and lived at the hub of the universe, meeting everybody, knowing everybody, practising his art on the boards, exercising his wits in the street, and even getting access to the palace of the queen. Meanwhile his extraordinarily gifted sister, let us suppose, remained at home. She was as adventurous, as imaginative, as **agog** to see the world as he was. But she was not sent to school. She had no chance of learning grammar and logic, let alone of reading Horace and Virgil. She picked up a book now and then, one of her brother's perhaps, and read a few pages. But then her parents came in and told her to mend the stockings or mind the stew and not **moon** about with books and papers. They would have spoken sharply but kindly, for they were substantial people who knew the conditions of life for a woman and loved their daughter—indeed, more likely than not she was the apple of her father's eye. Perhaps she scribbled some pages up in an apple loft on the sly, but was careful to hide them or set fire to them. Soon, however, before she was out of her teens, she was to be betrothed to the son of a neighbouring wool-stapler. She cried out that marriage was hateful to her, and for that she was severely beaten by her father. Then he ceased to scold her. He begged her instead not to hurt him, not to shame him in this matter of her marriage. He would give her a chain of beads or a fine petticoat, he said; and there were tears in his eyes. How could she disobey him? How could she break his heart? The force of her own gift alone drove her to it. She made up a small parcel of her belongings, let herself down by a rope one summer's night and took the road to London. She was not seventeen. The birds that sang in the hedge were not more musical than she was. She had the quickest fancy, a gift like her brother's, for the tune of words. Like him, she had a taste for the theatre. She stood at the stage door; she wanted to act, she said. Men laughed in her face. The manager—a fat, loose-lipped man—guffawed. He bellowed something about poodles dancing and women acting—no woman, he said could possibly be an actress. He hinted—you can imagine what. She could get no training in her craft. Could she even seek her dinner in a tavern or roam the streets at midnight? Yet her genius was for fiction. . . . At last—for she was very young, oddly like Shakespeare the poet in her face, with the same grey eyes and rounded brows—at last Nick Greene the actor-manager took pity on her; [but] she . . . killed herself one winter's night and lies buried at some cross-roads where the omnibuses now stop outside the Elephant and Castle. That, more or less, is how the story would run, I think, if a woman in Shakespeare's day should have had Shakespeare's genius.

▲ Many of William Shakespeare's plays were performed at the Globe Theatre in London.

▼ William Shakespeare

**DOCUMENT-BASED QUESTIONS**

1. **Describing** What were "the conditions of life for a woman" that made Judith's parents scold her for attempting to read and write?
2. **Drawing Conclusions** What is Woolf's conclusion about the possibility of a woman becoming Shakespeare?
3. **Analyzing** Why does Virginia Woolf have Shakespeare marry, but Shakespeare's sister run away from marriage?

**Applications Activity**

What does a person today need to succeed as a writer or artist? Write a descriptive account to illustrate your argument.

# Toward a Global Civilization

1945–Present

## Primary Sources

### Reader's Dictionary

**reserve:** a reservation; land set aside for use by a particular group

**squatters:** those who settle on public land without rights or permission

**perturbation:** major change or disturbance

▲ John Glenn

### Progress Never Stops

*In 1962 John J. Glenn, Jr., was commander of the first U.S. crewed spacecraft to orbit the earth. Glenn spoke to a joint meeting of Congress six days after he returned from orbit.*

What did we learn from the flight? . . . The Mercury spacecraft and systems design concepts are sound and have now been verified during manned flight. We also proved that man can operate intelligently in space and can adapt rapidly to this new environment.

Zero G or weightlessness appears to be no problem. As a matter of fact, lack of gravity is a rather fascinating thing. Objects within the cockpit can be parked in midair. For example, at one time during the flight, I was using a hand-held camera. Another system needed attention; so it seemed quite natural to let go of the camera, take care of the other chore, then reach out, grasp the camera, and go back about my business.

There seemed to be little sensation of speed although the craft was traveling at about five miles per second—a speed that I too find difficult to comprehend.

The view from that altitude defies description. The horizon colors are brilliant and sunsets are spectacular. It is hard to beat a day in which you are permitted the luxury of seeing four sunsets. . . .

Our efforts today and what we have done so far are but small building blocks in a huge pyramid to come.

But questions are sometimes raised regarding the immediate payoffs from our efforts. Explorations and the pursuit of knowledge have always paid dividends in the long run—usually far greater than anything expected at the outset. Experimenters with common, green mold, little dreamed what effect their discovery of penicillin would have.

We are just probing the surface of the greatest advancements in man's knowledge of his surroundings that has ever been made. . . . Knowledge begets knowledge. Progress never stops.

## An Ideal for Which I Am Prepared to Die

*Nelson Mandela gave this speech during his trial in South Africa in 1964. Following the trial, he was sentenced to life in prison.*

The whites enjoy what may well be the highest standard of living in the world, whilst Africans live in poverty and misery. Forty percent of the Africans live in hopelessly overcrowded and, in some cases, drought-stricken **reserves,** where soil erosion and the overworking of the soil make it impossible for them to live properly off the land. Thirty percent are labourers, labour tenants, and **squatters** on white farms. The other thirty percent live in towns where they have developed economic and social habits which bring them closer, in many respects, to white standards. Yet forty-six percent of all African families in Johannesburg do not earn enough to keep them going.

The complaint of Africans, however, is not only that they are poor and whites are rich, but that the laws which are made by the whites are designed to preserve this situation. . . .

During my lifetime I have dedicated my life to this struggle of the African people. I have fought against white domination, and I have fought against black domination. I have cherished the ideal of a democratic and free society in which all persons live together in harmony with equal opportunities. It is an ideal which I hope to live for, and to see realized. But my lord, if needs be, it is an ideal for which I am prepared to die.

## China's Gilded Age

*Xiao-huang Yin recounts his trip through China in 1994.*

Recently I took a six-week journey across China. It was my first trip back since . . . 1985. In the course of my visit I saw—I felt—the **perturbations** of profound and chaotic social change. China's stunning hurtle from a centrally planned economy to a free market has set off an economic explosion and generated tremendous prosperity. Its economic growth was 13 percent in 1993, and average personal income in urban areas had doubled since 1985. With the state-owned sector accounting for less than 30 percent of total economic output, the socialist system is becoming an empty shell. Across China the lines between the state and private economies are blurring. At the largest national department store in Shanghai, a symbol of Chinese socialist business, customers now bargain for better prices. The counters within the store have been contracted out to shop clerks, who decide the prices. Dual ownership has in essence turned this state enterprise into a private business. . . .

Not everyone gets rich quick, but the economic boom has brought most urban Chinese a huge improvement in their standard of living. Color TV sets, refrigerators, and VCRs, considered luxuries when I lived in China, can be found in almost every working-class urban household—at least in the prosperous coastal cities.

LIBRARY

### DOCUMENT-BASED QUESTIONS

1. **Identifying Central Issues** What are the immediate and long-term "payoffs" of John Glenn's 1962 space mission, according to his report to Congress?
2. **Explaining** What ideal does Nelson Mandela discuss?
3. **Evaluating** Why does Xiao-huang Yin believe that socialism is becoming an "empty shell" in China?

# Toward a Global Civilization

1945–Present

WORLD LITERATURE

▲ Chinua Achebe

## About the Author

Chinua Achebe was born in Nigeria and was christened Albert Chinualamogu. He rejected his British name while studying at the University College of Ibadan. Many of his works deal with the impact of Western values and culture on African society. He has done more than almost any other author to spread the understanding and influence of African literature worldwide.

## Reader's Dictionary

**commandeer:** to seize for military purposes
**Biro:** a British term for a ballpoint pen
**raffia:** fiber of a type of palm tree

## "Civil Peace" from *Girls at War and Other Stories*

By Chinua Achebe

*"Civil Peace" is one of the stories from* Girls at War and Other Stories *in which Achebe responds to the Nigerian civil war. The story takes place in the forests of Nigeria in 1970, just after the war has ended.*

Jonathan Iwegbu counted himself extraordinarily lucky. "Happy survival!" meant so much more to him than just a current fashion of greeting old friends in the first hazy days of peace. It went deep to his heart. He had come out of the war with five inestimable blessings—his head, his wife Maria's head and the heads of three out of their four children. As a bonus he also had his old bicycle—a miracle too but naturally not to be compared to the safety of five human heads.

The bicycle had a little history of its own. One day at the height of the war it was **commandeered** "for urgent military action." Hard as its loss would have been to him he would still have let it go without a thought had he not had some doubts about the genuineness of the officer. It wasn't his disreputable rags, nor the toes peeping out of one blue and one brown canvas shoes, nor yet the two stars of his rank done obviously in a hurry in **Biro,** that troubled Jonathan; many good and heroic soldiers looked the same or worse. It was

LIBRARY

rather a certain lack of grip and firmness in his manner. So Jonathan, suspecting he might be amenable to influence, rummaged in his **raffia** bag and produced the two pounds with which he had been going to buy firewood which his wife, Maria, retailed to camp officials for extra stock-fish and corn meal, and got his bicycle back. That night he buried it in the little clearing in the bush where the dead of the camp, including his own youngest son, were buried. When he dug it up again a year later after the surrender all it needed was a little palm-oil greasing. "Nothing puzzles God," he said in wonder.

He put it to immediate use as a taxi and accumulated a small pile of Biafran money ferrying camp officials and their families across the four-mile stretch to the nearest tarred road. His standard charge per trip was six pounds and those who had the money were only glad to be rid of some of it in this way. At the end of a fortnight he had made a small fortune of one hundred and fifteen pounds.

Then he made the journey to Enugu and found another miracle waiting for him. It was unbelievable. He rubbed his eyes and looked again and it was still standing there before him. But, needless to say, even that monumental blessing must be accounted also totally inferior to the five heads in the family. This newest miracle was his little house in Ogui Overside. Indeed nothing puzzles God! Only two houses away a huge concrete edifice some wealthy contractor had put up just before the war was a mountain of rubble. And here was Jonathan's little zinc house of no regrets built with mud blocks quite intact! Of course the doors and windows were missing and five sheets off the roof. But what was that? And anyhow he had returned to Enugu early enough to pick up bits of old zinc and wood and soggy sheets of cardboard lying around the neighborhood before thousands more came out of their forest holes looking for the same things. He got a destitute carpenter with one old hammer, a blunt plane and a few bent and rusty nails in his tool bag to turn this assortment of wood, paper and metal into door and window shutters for five Nigerian shillings or fifty Biafran pounds. He paid the pounds, and moved in with his overjoyed family carrying five heads on their shoulders.

▲*Children Dancing*, c. 1948, by Robert Gwathmey

LIBRARY

## DOCUMENT-BASED QUESTIONS

1. **Drawing Conclusions** What does Jonathan's encounter with the false officer reveal about the conditions of the war?
2. **Identifying** Biafra lost the civil war. What clues in the text indicate this outcome?
3. **Evaluating** Do you think it is effective for Achebe to discuss the war through an individual account rather than as a direct discussion of the devastation created? Why or why not?

**Applications Activity**

Choose a contemporary problem and describe it through the effect it has on an individual or family.

# GLOSSARY/ GLOSARIO

- Content vocabulary terms in this glossary are words that relate to world history content. They are **highlighted** yellow in your text.
- Los términos del vocabulario de contenido de este glosario son palabras relacionadas con el contenido de historia mundial. Están resaltadas en **amarillo** en tu libro de texto.
- Words below that have an asterisk (*) are academic vocabulary terms. They help you understand your school subjects and are **boldfaced** in your text.
- Las palabras que tienen un asterisco (*) son términos del vocabulario académico. Ellas te ayudarán a comprender los temas escolares y están en **negritas** en tu libro de texto.

| ENGLISH | ESPAÑOL |
|---|---|
| **a** | |
| ***abandoned:** deserted (p. 352) | ***abandonado:** desierto (pág. 352) |
| **abbess:** the head of a convent (p. 306) | **abadesa:** superiora de un convento (pág. 306) |
| ***accurate:** exact or right (p. 374) | ***preciso:** exacto o correcto (pág. 374) |
| ***acquired:** came into possession or control of (p. 273) | ***adquirir:** obtener la posesión o el control de (pág. 273) |
| **acropolis:** in early Greek city-states, a fortified gathering place at the top of a hill that was sometimes the site of temples and public buildings (p. 112) | **acrópolis:** en las ciudades-estado de la antigua Grecia, lugar fortificado de reuniones en la cima de una montaña, donde en ocasiones había templos y edificios públicos (pág. 112) |
| ***administrative:** relating to the execution of public affairs, as distinguished from policy making (p. 244) | ***administrativo:** relacionado con la ejecución de asuntos públicos, a diferencia de la elaboración de políticas (pág. 244) |
| **adobe:** sun-dried brick (p. 371) | **adobe:** ladrillo secado al sol (pág. 371) |
| **Age of Pericles:** the period between 461 B.C. and 429 B.C. when Pericles dominated Athenian politics and Athens reached the height of its power (p. 121) | **Era de Pericles:** el período entre 461 a.C. y 429 a.C., cuando Pericles dominaba la política ateniense y Atenas alcanzó la cúspide de su poder (pág. 121) |
| **agora:** in early Greek city-states, an open area that served as a gathering place and as a market (p. 112) | **ágora:** en las ciudades-estado de la antigua Grecia, área abierta que servía como lugar de reunión y como mercado (pág. 112) |
| **agricultural society:** a group of people whose economy is largely based on farming (p. 294) | **sociedad agrícola:** grupo de personas cuya economía se basa principalmente en la agricultura (pág. 294) |
| **Allah:** Arabic for "God"; the supreme god of Islam (p. 188) | **Alá:** dios en árabe; el dios supremo en el islam (pág. 188) |
| **annul:** declare invalid (p. 420) | **anular:** declarar no válido (pág. 420) |
| **anthropology:** the study of human life and culture based on artifacts and human fossils (p. 4) | **antropología:** el estudio de la vida y la cultura humanas, basado en artefactos y fósiles humanos (pág. 4) |

GLOSSARY

| | |
|---|---|
| **anti-Semitism:** hostility toward or discrimination against Jews (p. 353) | **antisemitismo:** hostilidad hacia o discriminación contra los judíos (pág. 353) |
| **apprentice:** one who learns a trade by practical experience under skilled craftspeople (p. 341) | **aprendiz:** quien aprende un negocio mediante la experiencia práctica bajo la guía de artesanos calificados (pág. 341) |
| **arabesque:** geometric patterns repeated over and over to completely cover a surface with decoration (p. 207) | **arabesco:** patrones geométricos repetidos una y otra vez para cubrir completamente una superficie con decorados (pág. 207) |
| **archaeology:** the study of past societies through an analysis of the items people left behind them (p. 4) | **arqueología:** estudio de sociedades pasadas mediante el análisis de los objetos que las personas dejan tras sí (pág. 4) |
| **archipelago:** a chain of islands (p. 290) | **archipiélago:** cadena de islas (pág. 290) |
| ***area:** a geographic region (p. 290) | ***área:** región geográfica (pág. 290) |
| ***arete:*** in early Greece, the qualities of excellence that a hero strives to win in a struggle or contest (p. 111) | ***arete:*** en la antigua Grecia, las cualidades de excelencia que un héroe se esforzaba por alcanzar en una batalla o competencia (pág. 111) |
| **aristocracy:** an upper class whose wealth is based on land and whose power is passed on from one generation to another (p. 86) | **aristocracia:** clase superior, cuya riqueza se basa en la posesión de tierras y cuyo poder pasa de una generación a otra (pág. 86) |
| **artifact:** tools, pottery, paintings, weapons, buildings, and household items left behind by early people (p. 4) | **artefacto:** herramientas, artículos de alfarería, pinturas, armas, edificaciones y artículos para el hogar dejados por pueblos antiguos (pág. 4) |
| **artisan:** a skilled worker who makes products such as weapons and jewelry (p. 16) | **artesano:** trabajador calificado que fabrica productos, como armas o joyas (pág. 16) |
| ***assemble:** to gather; to meet together (p. 112) | ***ensamblar:** unir; juntar (pág. 112) |
| **astrolabe:** an instrument used by sailors to determine their location by observing the positions of stars (p. 205) | **astrolabio:** instrumento usado por los navegantes para determinar su ubicación según la posición de las estrellas (pág. 205) |
| ***attain:** to gain or achieve (p. 408) | ***lograr:** ganar o alcanzar (pág. 408) |
| **Australopithecus:** the earliest humanlike creature that flourished in eastern and southern Africa 3 to 4 million years ago (p. 7) | **australopiteco:** primera criatura humanoide que floreció en el este y sur de África hace tres o cuatro millones de años (pág. 7) |
| ***available:** ready for immediate use; accessible (p. 274) | ***disponible:** listo para su uso inmediato; accesible (pág. 274) |

## b

| | |
|---|---|
| **bazaar:** a covered market in Islamic cities (p. 201) | **bazar:** mercado techado de las ciudades islámicas (pág. 201) |
| **Bhagavad Gita, The:** part of the Indian epic *Mahabharata;* the *Gita,* a sermon by the god Krishna on the eve of a major battle, sets forth one key point of Indian culture—one must not worry about the success or failure of an action but should only be aware of the moral rightness of the act itself (p. 80) | **Bhagavad Gita, The:** parte de la epopeya india *Mahabharata;* el *Gita* es un sermón del dios Krishna en vísperas de una importante batalla, establece un punto clave de la cultura india: uno no debe preocuparse por el éxito o fracaso de una acción, debe atender sólo lo moralmente correcto de la acción misma (pág. 80) |

GLOSSARY

**bishopric:** a group of Christian communities, or parishes, under the authority of a bishop (p. 304)

**obispado:** grupo de comunidades o parroquias cristianas bajo la autoridad de un obispo (pág. 304)

**Buddhism:** a religious doctrine introduced in northern India in the sixth century B.C. by Siddhārtha Gautama, known as the Buddha, or "Enlightened One" (p. 73)

**budismo:** doctrina religiosa introducida en el norte de la India en el siglo VI a.C. por Siddhartha Gautama, conocido como Buda (o "el Iluminado") (pág. 73)

**bureaucracy:** an administrative organization that relies on nonelective officials and regular procedures (p. 37)

**burocracia:** organización administrativa basada en funcionarios no elegidos y procedimientos habituales (pág. 37)

**Bushido:** "the way of the warrior," the strict code by which Japanese samurai were supposed to live (p. 280)

**bushido:** "código del guerrero", estricto código según el cual debían vivir los samuráis japoneses (pág. 280)

## C

**caliph:** a successor of Muhammad as spiritual and temporal leader of the Muslims (p. 192)

**califa:** sucesor de Mahoma como líder espiritual y temporal de los musulmanes (pág. 192)

***carruca:*** a heavy, wheeled plow with an iron plowshare (p. 334)

***carruca:*** pesado arado con ruedas y reja de hierro (pág. 334)

**caste system:** a set of rigid categories in ancient India that determined a person's occupation and economic potential, as well as his or her position in society, based partly on skin color (p. 71)

**sistema de castas:** conjunto de categorías rígidas en la antigua India que determinaba la ocupación de una persona y su potencial económico, así como su posición en la sociedad, parcialmente sobre la base del color de la piel (pág. 71)

**censorate:** part of the Chinese bureaucracy that made sure government officials were doing their jobs (p. 96)

**censorado:** parte de la burocracia china que vigilaba que los funcionarios gubernamentales hicieran su trabajo (pág. 96)

***challenge:** a summons that is often stimulating, inciting, or threatening (p. 317)

***reto:** emplazamiento que con frecuencia estimula, incita o amenaza (pág. 317)

**chanson de geste:** a type of vernacular literature, this heroic epic was popular in medieval Europe and described battles and political contests (p. 351)

**canción de gesta:** tipo de literatura vernácula, epopeya heroica popular en la Europa medieval, en la que se describían batallas y contiendas políticas (pág. 351)

**chivalry:** in the Middle Ages, the ideal of civilized behavior that developed among the nobility; it was a code of ethics that knights were supposed to uphold (p. 313)

**caballería:** en la Edad Media, el ideal de comportamiento civilizado que florecía entre la nobleza; era un código ético que los caballeros debían mantener (pág. 313)

**Christian humanism:** a movement that developed in northern Europe during the Renaissance combining classical learning (humanism) with the goal of reforming the Catholic Church (p. 412)

**humanismo cristiano:** movimiento que se desarrolló en el norte de Europa durante el Renacimiento que combinaba las enseñanzas clásicas (humanismo) con la meta de reformar la Iglesia católica (pág. 412)

**city-state:** a state with political and economic control over the surrounding countryside (p. 28)

**ciudad-estado:** ciudad con control político y económico sobre los campos que la rodean (pág. 28)

**civilization:** a complex culture in which large numbers of people share a number of common elements such as social structure, religion, and art (p. 18)

**civilización:** compleja cultura en la que un gran número de personas comparte ciertos elementos, como la estructura social, la religión y el arte (pág. 18)

**clan:** a group of related families (p. 370)

**clan:** grupo de familias relacionadas (pág. 370)

***classical:** authoritative, traditional; relating to the literature, art, architecture, or ideals of the ancient Greek and Roman world (p. 121)

***clásico:** documentado, tradicional; relacionado con la literatura, el arte, la arquitectura o los ideales del mundo antiguo griego y romano (pág. 121)

| | |
|---|---|
| **clergy:** church leaders (p. 173) | **clero:** líderes de la Iglesia (pág. 173) |
| ***code:** a system of principles or rules (p. 280) | ***código:** sistema de principios y reglas (pág. 280) |
| ***collapse:** to break down completely; to suddenly lose force or effectiveness (p. 174) | ***colapsar:** desplomarse completamente; perder súbitamente la fuerza o efectividad (pág. 174) |
| ***commentary:** an explanatory treatise (p. 204) | ***comentario:** tratado explicatorio (pág. 204) |
| **commercial capitalism:** economic system in which people invest in trade or goods to make profits (p. 338) | **capitalismo comercial:** sistema económico en el cual la gente invierte en el comercio y en bienes con el fin de obtener ganancias (pág. 338) |
| **common law:** a uniform system of law that developed in England based on court decisions and on customs and usage rather than on written law codes; replaced law codes that varied from place to place (p. 317) | **derecho común:** sistema uniforme de leyes desarrollado en Inglaterra, basado en las decisiones de las cortes y en las costumbres y usos, en vez de en códigos de leyes escritas; sustituyó los códigos legales que variaban de un lugar a otro (pág. 317) |
| ***compiled:** collected and edited into a volume (p. 202) | ***compilado:** reunido y editado en un volumen (pág. 202) |
| ***complex:** having many intricate parts (p. 196) | ***complejo:** que tiene muchas partes complicadas (pág. 196) |
| ***complexity:** the state of being complex or of having many intricate parts (p. 267) | ***complejidad:** estado de ser complejo o de tener muchas partes complicadas (pág. 267) |
| **Confucianism:** the system of political and ethical ideas formulated by the Chinese philosopher Confucius toward the end of the Zhou dynasty; it was intended to help restore order to a society that was in a state of confusion (p. 90) | **confucianismo:** sistema de ideas políticas y éticas formuladas por el filósofo chino Confucio hacia fines de la dinastía Zhou; fue concebido para restaurar el orden en una sociedad que estaba en estado de confusión (pág. 90) |
| ***consequence:** the effect or result of an action (p. 353) | ***consecuencia:** efecto o resultado de una acción (pág. 353) |
| ***construction:** manner or method of building (p. 348) | ***construcción:** manera o método de construir (pág. 348) |
| **consul:** a chief executive officer of the Roman Republic; two were elected each year, one to run the government and one to lead the army into battle (p. 148) | **cónsul:** jefe ejecutivo de la República Romana; se elegían dos cada año: uno para llevar el gobierno y el otro para dirigir el ejército en las batallas (pág. 148) |
| ***contract:** a binding agreement between two or more people or parties (p. 311) | ***contrato:** acuerdo vinculante entre dos o más personas o partes (pág. 311) |
| ***contractor:** one who contracts or is a party to a contract to perform work, provide supplies, or erect buildings (p. 164) | ***contratista:** el que contrata o es parte en un contrato para realizar un trabajo, suministrar algo o construir edificios (pág. 164) |
| ***conversion:** the change from one belief or form to another (p. 76) | ***conversión:** cambio de una creencia o forma a otra (pág. 76) |
| ***corporation:** form of business organization that has a separate legal entity with all the rights and responsibilities of an individual, including the right to buy and sell property, enter into legal contracts, and sue and be sued (p. 350) | ***corporación:** forma de organizar los negocios que tiene una entidad legal independiente con todos los derechos y responsabilidades de un individuo, incluso el derecho a comprar y vender la propiedad, establecer contratos legales y demandar o ser demandados judicialmente (pág. 350) |

GLOSSARY

***created:** made or brought something new into existence (p. 46)

***crear:** hacer o dar existencia a algo nuevo (pág. 46)

***crucial:** essential; important (p. 334)

***crucial:** esencial; importante (pág. 334)

**Crusades:** military expeditions carried out by European Christians in the Middle Ages to regain the Holy Land from the Muslims (p. 325)

**Cruzadas:** expediciones militares llevadas a cabo por cristianos europeos en la Edad Media para reconquistar la Tierra Santa de manos de los musulmanes (pág. 325)

**culture:** the way of life a people follows (pp. 18, 254)

**cultura:** forma de vida que siguen las personas (pp. 18, 254)

**cuneiform:** "wedge-shaped," a system of writing developed by the Sumerians using a reed stylus to create wedge-shaped impressions on a clay tablet (p. 30)

**cuneiforme:** "en forma de cuña", sistema de escritura desarrollado por los sumerios utilizando un punzón de lengüeta para crear impresiones en forma de cuña en una tableta de arcilla (pág. 30)

***cycle:** a series of events that recur regularly and usually lead back to the starting point (p. 88)

***ciclo:** serie de eventos que se repiten regularmente y que por lo general llevan al punto de partida (pág. 88)

## d

**daimyo:** "great names," heads of noble families in Japan who controlled vast landed estates and relied on samurai for protection (p. 281)

**daimyo:** "grandes nombres", líderes de familias nobles en Japón, que controlaban vastas propiedades y confiaban su protección a los samuráis (pág. 281)

**Dao:** "Way," the key to proper behavior under Confucianism (p. 87)

**tao:** "Camino", la clave para la conducta apropiada bajo el confucianismo (pág. 87)

**Daoism:** a system of ideas based on the teachings of Laozi; teaches that the will of Heaven is best followed through inaction so that nature is allowed to take its course (p. 92)

**taoísmo:** sistema de ideas basado en la doctrina de Laozi; enseña que la verdadera manera de seguir la voluntad del Cielo es la inacción, dejando a la naturaleza seguir su curso (pág. 92)

***debated:** discussed by considering opposing viewpoints (p. 109)

***debatido:** discutido mediante la consideración de los puntos de vista contrarios (pág. 109)

***decline:** a change to a lower state or level (p. 398)

***declinar:** cambio a un estado o nivel más bajo (p. 398)

**democracy:** "the rule of the many," government by the people, either directly or through their elected representatives (p. 114)

**democracia:** "gobierno de la mayoría", gobierno por personas elegidas directamente o a través de sus representantes elegidos (pág. 114)

**dharma:** in Hinduism, the divine law that rules karma; it requires all people to do their duty based on their status in society (p. 73)

**dharma:** en el Hinduismo, ley divina que gobierna el karma; exige que todas las personas cumplan con su deber según su estatus en la sociedad (pág. 73)

**dictator:** an absolute ruler (p. 154)

**dictador:** gobernante absoluto (pág. 154)

**direct democracy:** a system of government in which the people participate directly in government decision making through mass meetings (p. 121)

**democracia directa:** sistema de gobierno en el que las personas participan directamente en las decisiones del gobierno mediante asambleas masivas (pág. 121)

**diviner:** a person who is believed to have the power to foretell events (p. 253)

**adivino:** persona de quien se cree tiene el poder de predecir eventos (pág. 253)

***document:** an original or official paper that gives proof of or support to (p. 317)

***documento:** papel original u oficial que prueba o apoya algo (pág. 317)

GLOSSARY

| | |
|---|---|
| ***domestic:** relating to or originating within one's country (p. 79) | ***doméstico:** relativo al país de uno u originado en él (pág. 79) |
| ***domesticated:** adapted to life with and to the advantage of humans (p. 46) | ***domesticado:** adaptado a vivir con las personas y para su beneficio (pág. 46) |
| **domestication:** adaption for human use (p. 14) | **domesticación:** adaptación para el uso de las personas (pág. 14) |
| **dowry:** a gift of money or property paid at the time of marriage, either by the bride's parents to her husband or, in Islamic societies, by a husband to his wife (pp. 203, 269, 403) | **dote:** dinero o bienes pagados en el momento del matrimonio por los padres de la novia a su esposo, o en sociedades islámicas, por el marido a su esposa (pp. 203, 269, 403) |
| **dynasty:** a family of rulers whose right to rule is passed on within the family (p. 36) | **dinastía:** familia de gobernantes cuyo derecho a gobernar se transmite dentro de la familia (pág. 36) |

## e

| | |
|---|---|
| ***economic:** relating to the production, distribution, and consumption of goods and services (p. 174) | ***económico:** relativo a la producción, distribución y consumo de bienes y servicios (pág. 174) |
| **empire:** a large political unit or state, usually under a single leader, that controls many peoples or territories (p. 32) | **imperio:** gran unidad política, comúnmente bajo un solo líder, que controla a muchos pueblos o territorios (pág. 32) |
| ***enabled:** made possible (p. 309) | ***posibilitar:** hacer posible (pág. 309) |
| ***enormous:** huge; vast; immense (p. 324) | ***enorme:** tremendo; vasto; inmenso (pág. 324) |
| ***ensure:** to make sure (p. 307) | ***asegurar:** estar seguro (pág. 307) |
| **ephor:** one of the five men elected each year in ancient Sparta who were responsible for the education of youth and the conduct of all citizens (p. 116) | **éforo:** cada uno de los cinco hombres elegidos cada año en la antigua Esparta, responsables de la educación de los jóvenes y de la conducta de todos los ciudadanos (pág. 116) |
| **epic poem:** a long poem that tells the deeds of a great hero, such as the *Iliad* and the *Odyssey* of Homer (p. 111) | **poema épico:** extenso poema que cuenta las hazañas de un gran héroe, como la Iliada y la Odisea, de Homero (pág. 111) |
| **Epicureanism:** school of thought developed by the philosopher Epicurus in Hellenistic Athens; it held that happiness is the chief goal in life, and the means to achieve happiness was the pursuit of pleasure (p. 139) | **epicureanismo:** escuela del pensamiento desarrollada por el filósofo Epicuro en la Atenas helenística; sostenía que la felicidad es la principal meta en la vida y que el medio para lograr la felicidad era la búsqueda del placer (pág. 139) |
| ***eroded:** diminished or destroyed by degrees (p. 203) | ***erosionado:** reducido o destruido gradualmente (pág. 203) |
| **estate:** one of the three classes into which French society was divided before the revolution: the clergy (First Estate), the nobles (Second Estate), and the townspeople (Third Estate) (p. 319) | **estado:** cada una de las tres clases en las que se dividía la sociedad francesa medieval: el clero (primer estado), los nobles (segundo estado) y la plebe (tercer estado) (pág. 319) |
| ***estimate:** to make a rough determination of (p. 374) | ***estimar:** calcular aproximadamente (pág. 374) |

GLOSSARY

***ethical:** conforming to accepted standards of conduct; moral (p. 90)

***ético:** de acuerdo con los estándares aceptados de conducta; moral (pág. 90)

***ethics:** moral principles; generally recognized rules of conduct (p. 129)

***ética:** principios morales; reglas de conducta generalmente aceptadas (pág. 129)

***excluded:** not counted or included (p. 302)

***excluido:** no contado o incluido (pág. 302)

## f

***factor:** a contributing part (p. 243)

***factor:** elemento que contribuye (pág. 243)

**feudal contract:** under feudalism, the unwritten rules that determined the relationship between a lord and his vassal (p. 311)

**contrato feudal:** reglas no escritas que determinaban la relación entre un señor y su vasallo en el feudalismo (pág. 311)

**feudalism:** political and social system that developed during the Middle Ages when royal governments were no longer able to defend their subjects; nobles offered protection and land in return for service (p. 310)

**feudalismo:** sistema político y social que se desarrolló durante la Edad Media cuando los gobiernos reales ya no podían defender a sus pueblos; los nobles ofrecían protección y tierras a cambio de servicios (pág. 310)

**fief:** under feudalism, a grant of land made to a vassal; the vassal held political authority within his fief (p. 310)

**feudo:** concesión de tierras hecha a un vasallo en el feudalismo; el vasallo tenía autoridad política dentro de su feudo (pág. 310)

**filial piety:** the duty of family members to subordinate their needs and desires to those of the male head of the family, a concept important in Confucianism (p. 89)

**respeto filial:** deber de los miembros de la familia de subordinar sus necesidades y deseos a los del cabeza de familia, un concepto importante en el confucianismo (pág. 89)

***financial:** relating to the management of funds (p. 152)

***financiero:** relativo al manejo de fondos (pág. 152)

**fossil:** a remnant or impression of an organism from a past geologic age that has been preserved in the earth's crust (p. 4)

**fósil:** residuo o impresión de un organismo de una era geológica pasada que se ha preservado en la corteza terrestre (pág. 4)

***founder:** one who founds or establishes (p. 139)

***fundador:** quien funda o establece algo (pág. 139)

***founding:** originating; beginning (p. 253)

***fundar:** originar; comenzar (pág. 253)

**fresco:** a painting done on fresh, wet plaster with water-based paints (p. 409)

**fresco:** pintura hecha en yeso fresco y húmedo con pinturas a base de agua (pág. 409)

## g

**griot:** a special class of African storytellers who help keep alive a people's history (p. 255)

***griot:*** tipo especial de narradores africanos de cuentos que contribuían a mantener viva la historia de un pueblo (pág. 255)

***guaranteed:** assured the fulfillment of a condition (p. 168)

***garantizado:** que asegura el cumplimiento de una condición (pág. 168)

**guild:** a business association that is associated with a particular trade or craft; guilds evolved in the twelfth century and played a leading role in the economic life of medieval cities (p. 341)

**gremio:** asociación comercial relacionada con un oficio o artesanía en particular; los gremios evolucionaron en el siglo XII y desempeñaron un papel importante en la vida económica de las ciudades medievales (pág. 341)

GLOSSARY

## h

**hajj:** a pilgrimage to Makkah, one of the requirements of the Five Pillars of Islam (p. 190)

***hajj:*** peregrinación a La Meca; uno de los requisitos de los Cinco Pilares del Islam (pág. 190)

**Hellenistic Era:** the age of Alexander the Great; period when the Greek language and ideas were carried to the non-Greek world (p. 137)

**Era Helenística:** era de Alejandro Magno; período en el cual los griegos llevaron su idioma y sus ideas fuera del mundo griego (pág. 137)

**helot:** in ancient Sparta, a captive person who was forced to work for the conqueror (p. 115)

**ilota:** en la antigua Esparta, persona cautiva que era forzada a trabajar para su conquistador (pág. 115)

**heresy:** the denial of basic Church doctrines (p. 346)

**herejía:** negación de las doctrinas básicas de la Iglesia (pág. 346)

**hieratic script:** simplified version of hieroglyphics used in ancient Egypt for business transactions, record keeping, and the general needs of daily life (p. 43)

**escritura hierática:** versión simplificada de los jeroglíficos usada en el antiguo Egipto para las transacciones comerciales, registros y las necesidades generales de la vida cotidiana (pág. 43)

**hieroglyph:** a picture or symbol used in a hieroglyphic system of writing (p. 375)

**caracteres jeroglíficos:** dibujos o símbolos usados en el sistema jeroglífico de escritura (pág. 375)

**hieroglyphics:** "priest-carvings" or "sacred writings," a complex system of writing that used both pictures and more abstract forms; used by the ancient Egyptians and Mayans (p. 42)

**jeroglíficos:** "grabados sacerdotales" o "escrituras sagradas", complejo sistema de escritura que utilizaba tanto dibujos como formas más abstractas; empleado por los antiguos egipcios y mayas (pág. 42)

***Hijrah:*** the journey of Muhammad and his followers to Madinah in 622, which became year 1 of the official calendar of Islam (p. 190)

**hégira:** viaje de Mahoma y sus seguidores a Medina en el año 622, que pasó a ser el año 1 del calendario oficial del islam (pág. 190)

**Hinduism:** the major Indian religious system, which had its origins in the religious beliefs of the Aryans who settled India after 1500 B.C. (p. 72)

**hinduismo:** principal sistema religioso de la India, que tuvo sus orígenes en las creencias religiosas de los arios que se establecieron en la India después del año 1500 a.C. (pág. 72)

**hominid:** humans and other humanlike creatures that walk upright (p. 6)

**homínido:** humanos y otras criaturas similares a los humanos que caminaban erectos (pág. 6)

***Homo sapiens sapiens:*** "wise, wise human," a species that appeared in Africa between 150,000 and 200,000 years ago; they were the first anatomically modern humans (p. 7)

***Homo sapiens sapiens:*** "ser humano sabio sabio", especie que apareció en África entre 150,000 y 200,000 años atrás; desde el punto de vista anatómico fueron los primeros humanos modernos (pág. 7)

**hoplite:** in the early Greek military system, a heavily armed foot soldier (p. 113)

**hoplita:** en el sistema militar de la antigua Grecia, soldado de infantería fuertemente armado (pág. 113)

**humanism:** an intellectual movement of the Renaissance based on the study of the humanities, which included grammar, rhetoric, poetry, moral philosophy, and history (p. 406)

**humanismo:** movimiento intelectual del Renacimiento basado en el estudio de las humanidades, que incluía gramática, retórica, poesía, filosofía moral e historia (pág. 406)

## i

***identifying:** believing that one is the same or very similar to another (p. 36)

***identificar:** considerar que uno es igual o muy similar a otro (pág. 36)

**ideograph:** a character that combines two or more pictographs to represent an idea; used in ancient Chinese script (p. 90)

**ideograma:** carácter que combina dos o más pictogramas para representar una idea; usado en la antigua escritura china (pág. 90)

GLOSSARY

| | |
|---|---|
| ***ideology:** a set of beliefs (p. 96) | ***ideología:** conjunto de convicciones (pág. 96) |
| ***ignorant:** unaware; lacking knowledge of (p. 414) | ***ignorante:** desinformado; falto de conocimientos sobre algo (pág. 414) |
| **imperator:** commander in chief; the Latin origin of the word *emperor* (p. 156) | **emperador:** comandante en jefe; el origen latino de la palabra es *"imperator"* (pág. 156) |
| ***implies:** expresses indirectly through reference or association (p. 114) | ***implica:** expresa indirectamente mediante una referencia o asociación (pág. 114) |
| ***inadequate:** not sufficient (p. 149) | ***inadecuado:** que no es suficiente (pág. 149) |
| ***individuality:** a total character that distinguishes an individual from others (p. 95) | ***individualidad:** conjunto total de caracteres que distinguen a un individuo de los otros (pág. 95) |
| **indulgence:** a release from all or part of punishment for sin by the Catholic Church, reducing time in purgatory after death (p. 414) | **indulgencia:** perdón de todo o parte de un castigo por pecar otorgado por la Iglesia católica, reduciendo el tiempo en el purgatorio tras la muerte (pág. 414) |
| **infidel:** an unbeliever; a term applied to the Muslims during the Crusades (p. 325) | **infiel:** persona no creyente; término aplicado a los musulmanes durante las Cruzadas (pág. 325) |
| **inflation:** a rapid increase in prices (p. 176) | **inflación:** rápido aumento de los precios (pág. 176) |
| ***innovation:** a new idea, method, or device (p. 30) | ***innovación:** idea, método o dispositivo nuevos (pág. 30) |
| ***instability:** not steady; wavering (pp. 152, 398) | ***inestabilidad:** que no está estático; que se balancea (pp. 152, 398) |
| ***instituted:** put into action (p. 96) | ***instituido:** puesto en marcha (pág. 96) |
| ***institution:** an organization for the promotion of a cause (p. 148) | ***institución:** organización para la promoción de una causa (pág. 148) |
| ***instructed:** taught or trained (p. 384) | ***instruido:** enseñado o entrenado (pág. 384) |
| ***insulae:*** Roman apartment blocks constructed of concrete with wooden beam floors (p. 165) | ***insulae:*** bloques de apartamentos romanos construidos de concreto con piso de vigas de madera (pág. 165) |
| **interdict:** a decree by the pope that forbade priests to give the sacraments of the Church to the people (p. 344) | **interdicción:** decreto papal que prohibía a los sacerdotes impartir los sacramentos de la Iglesia a la gente (pág. 344) |
| **Islam:** monotheistic religion that emerged in the Arabian Peninsula during the seventh century A.D. (p. 190) | **islam:** religión monoteísta que surgió en la Península Arábiga en el siglo VII d.C. (pág. 190) |

## j

| | |
|---|---|
| **jihad:** "struggle in the way of God" (p. 192) | ***jihad:*** "lucha en el camino de Dios" (pág. 192) |
| **journeyman:** a worker who has learned a trade and works for wages for other masters (p. 341) | **jornalero:** trabajador que ha aprendido un oficio y trabaja por un salario para un patrón (pág. 341) |
| ***justification:** the process of being justified, or deemed worthy of salvation, by God (p. 419) | ***justificación:** proceso de ser justificado o juzgado digno de la salvación por Dios (pág. 419) |

GLOSSARY

## k

**karma:** in Hinduism, the force generated by a person's actions that determines how the person will be reborn in the next life (p. 73)

**karma:** en el Hinduismo, la fuerza generada por las acciones de una persona, lo que determina cómo renacerá esta persona en la próxima vida (pág. 73)

**khanate:** one of the several separate territories into which Genghis Khan's empire was split, each under the rule of one of his sons (p. 271)

**kanato:** cada uno de los diversos territorios independientes en los que se dividió el imperio de Genghis Khan y que estaban bajo el gobierno de uno de sus hijos (pág. 271)

**knight:** under feudalism, a member of the heavily armored cavalry (p. 310)

**caballero:** en el feudalismo, miembro de la caballería fuertemente acorazado (pág. 310)

## l

**laity:** regular church members (p. 173)

**laicado:** miembros regulares de una Iglesia (pág. 173)

**lay investiture:** the practice by which secular rulers both chose nominees to church offices and gave them the symbols of their office (p. 342)

**investidura secular:** práctica mediante la cual los líderes seculares elegían a los nominados a cargos en la Iglesia y los investían con los símbolos de su cargo (pág. 342)

***legal:** relating to law; founded on law (p. 322)

***legal:** relativo a la ley; basado en la ley (pág. 322)

**Legalism:** a popular philosophy developed in China toward the end of the Zhou dynasty; it proposes that human beings are evil by nature and can only be brought to the correct path by harsh laws (p. 93)

**legalismo:** filosofía popular desarrollada en China hacia fines de la dinastía Zhou; postula que los seres humanos son malvados por naturaleza y sólo pueden ser llevados a la senda correcta mediante leyes fuertes (pág. 93)

**lineage group:** an extended family unit that has combined into a larger community (p. 251)

**grupo de linaje:** unidad extendida de una familia que se ha mezclado en una comunidad mayor (pág. 251)

**longhouse:** Iroquois house about 150 to 200 feet (46 to 61 m) long built of wooden poles covered with sheets of bark and housing about a dozen families (p. 370)

**vivienda comunal:** vivienda de los indios iroqueses, de aproximadamente 150 a 200 pies (46 a 61 m) de longitud, construida sobre pilares de madera cubiertos con láminas de corteza y que albergaba a aproximadamente una docena de familias (pág. 370)

**Lutheranism:** the religious doctrine that Martin Luther developed; it differed from Catholicism in the doctrine of salvation, which Luther believed could be achieved by faith alone, not by good works; Lutheranism was the first Protestant faith (p. 416)

**luteranismo:** doctrina religiosa que desarrolló Martín Lutero; difiere del catolicismo en cuanto a la doctrina de salvación, que Lutero consideraba que podía alcanzarse mediante la fe sola, no por buenas acciones; el luteranismo fue la primera fe protestante (pág. 416)

## m

**Magna Carta:** the "Great Charter" of rights, which King John was forced to sign by the English nobles at Runnymede in 1215 (p. 318)

**Carta Magna:** "Gran Carta Real" de derechos que el rey Juan Sin Tierra fue obligado a firmar por los nobles ingleses en Runnymede en 1215 (pág. 318)

**Mahayana:** a school of Buddhism that developed in northwest India, stressing the view that nirvana can be achieved through devotion to the Buddha; its followers consider Buddhism a religion, not a philosophy, and the Buddha is a divine figure (p. 284)

**Mahayana:** escuela de budismo que se desarrolló en el noroeste de la India y que enfatiza la visión de que se puede alcanzar el nirvana a través de la devoción a Buda; sus seguidores consideran al budismo una religión, no una filosofía, y a Buda como una figura divina (pág. 284)

| | |
|---|---|
| **maize:** corn (p. 383) | **maíz:** cultivo nativo de las Américas (pág. 383) |
| ***major:** great; significant in size or importance (p. 36) | ***principal:** significativo en tamaño o importancia (pág. 36) |
| **Mandate of Heaven:** claim by Chinese kings of the Zhou dynasty that they had direct authority from heaven to rule and to keep order in the universe (p. 87) | **Mandato del Cielo:** reivindicación de los reyes de la dinastía Zhou de China de que ellos recibieron directamente del cielo la autoridad para gobernar y mantener en orden el universo (pág. 87) |
| **manor:** in medieval Europe, an agricultural estate that a lord ran and peasants worked (p. 336) | **feudo:** en la Europa medieval, propiedad agrícola administrada por un señor y trabajada por campesinos (pág. 336) |
| **masterpiece:** piece created by a journeyman who aspires to be a master craftsperson; it allowed the members of a guild to judge whether the journeyman was qualified to become a master and join the guild (p. 341) | **obra maestra:** obra creada por un aprendiz que aspira a ser maestro artesano; permitía a los miembros de un gremio juzgar si un aprendiz estaba calificado para convertirse en maestro e integrar el gremio (pág. 341) |
| **matrilineal:** tracing lineage through the mother rather than the father (p. 252) | **matrilineal:** que traza el linaje a través de la madre y sus ancestros, no a través del padre (pág. 252) |
| **mercenary:** a soldier who sells his services to the highest bidder (p. 400) | **mercenario:** soldado que vende sus servicios al mejor postor (pág. 400) |
| ***method:** a systematic plan for doing something (p. 129) | ***método:** plan sistemático para hacer algo (pág. 129) |
| ***military:** relating to the armed forces or to soldiers, arms, or war (p. 174) | ***militar:** relativo a las fuerzas armadas o a los soldados, las armas o la guerra (pág. 174) |
| **minaret:** the tower of a mosque from which the muezzin calls the faithful to prayer five times a day (p. 207) | **minarete:** torre de las mezquitas desde la cual el muecín llama a los fieles a orar cinco veces al día (pág. 207) |
| **missionary:** a person sent out to carry a religious message (p. 306) | **misionero:** persona enviada para llevar un mensaje religioso (pág. 306) |
| **monarch:** a king or queen who rules a kingdom by organizing armies to protect their populations and making laws to regulate subjects' lives (p. 18) | **monarca:** rey o reina que gobierna un reino mediante la organización de ejércitos para la protección de la población y la elaboración de leyes que regulan la vida de sus súbditos (pág. 18) |
| **monarchy:** government by a soverign ruler such as a king or queen (p. 57) | **monarquía:** gobierno encabezado por un soberano, como un rey o una reina (pág. 57) |
| **monasticism:** practice of living the life of a monk (p. 305) | **monacato:** práctica de vivir la vida de un monje (pág. 305) |
| **money economy:** an economic system based on money rather than barter (p. 338) | **economía monetaria:** sistema económico basado en el dinero y no en el trueque (pág. 338) |
| **monk:** a man who separates himself from ordinary human society in order to dedicate himself to God; monks live in monasteries headed by abbots (p. 305) | **monje:** hombre que se aparta de la sociedad humana ordinaria con el fin de dedicarse a Dios; los monjes viven en monasterios dirigidos por abades (pág. 305) |
| **monotheistic:** believing in one God (p. 50) | **monoteísta:** que tienen un solo dios (pág. 50) |
| **monsoon:** a seasonal wind pattern in southern Asia that blows warm, moist air from the southwest during the summer, bringing heavy rains, and cold, dry air from the northeast during the winter (p. 66) | **monzón:** patrón estacional de vientos en el sur de Asia que soplan aire cálido y húmedo desde el suroeste durante el verano, con fuertes lluvias, y traen aire frío y seco desde el noreste en el invierno (pág. 66) |

**mosque:** a Muslim house of worship (p. 199)

**mezquita:** templo musulmán (pág. 199)

**muezzin:** the crier who calls the Muslim faithful to prayer from the minaret of a mosque (p. 207)

**muecín:** voceador que llama a los fieles a orar desde el minarete de una mezquita (pág. 207)

**mummification:** a process of slowly drying a dead body to prevent it from decaying (p. 37)

**momificación:** proceso consistente en secar lentamente un cadáver para evitar su descomposición (pág. 37)

## n

**neo-Confucianism:** a revised form of Confucianism that evolved as a response to Buddhism and held sway in China from the late Tang dynasty to the end of the dynastic system in the twentieth century (p. 273)

**neoconfucianismo:** forma modificada de confucianismo que evolucionó como respuesta al budismo y mantuvo su dominio en China desde fines de la dinastía Tang hasta fines del sistema de dinastías en el siglo XX (pág. 273)

**new monarchy:** in the fifteenth century, government in which power had been centralized under a king or queen, i.e., France, England, and Spain (p. 357)

**nueva monarquía:** en el siglo XV, gobierno en el que el poder se había centralizado bajo un rey o reina, como en Francia, Inglaterra y España (pág. 357)

**New Testament:** the second part of the Christian Bible, it provides a record of Jesus' life and teachings (p. 170)

**Nuevo Testamento:** segunda parte de la Biblia cristiana; contiene un registro de la vida y enseñanzas de Jesús (pág. 170)

**nirvana:** in Buddhism, ultimate reality, the end of the self and a reunion with the Great World Soul (p. 74)

**nirvana:** en el budismo, la realidad final, el fin del yo y reunión con el Gran Alma Mundial (pág. 74)

**nun:** a woman who separates herself from ordinary human society in order to dedicate herself to God; nuns live in convents headed by abbesses (p. 306)

**monja:** mujer que se aparta de la sociedad humana ordinaria para dedicarse a Dios; las monjas viven en conventos encabezados por abadesas (pág. 306)

## o

**oligarchy:** "the rule of the few", a form of government in which a select group of people exercises controls (p. 114)

**oligarquía:** literalmente, "gobierno de pocos", forma de gobierno en el que un grupo selecto de personas ejerce el control (pág. 114)

**oracle:** in ancient Greece, a sacred shrine where a god or goddess was said to reveal the future through a priest or priestess (p. 124)

**oráculo:** en la antigua Grecia, templo sagrado donde, según se decía, un dios o una diosa revelaba el futuro a través de un sacerdote o una sacerdotisa (pág. 124)

**ordeal:** a means of determining guilt in Germanic law, based on the idea of divine intervention: if the accused person was unharmed after a physical trial, he or she was presumed innocent (p. 304)

**ordalía:** medio para determinar la culpabilidad en la ley germánica basándose en la idea de una intervención divina: si el acusado no resultaba dañado luego de una prueba física, se asumía que era inocente (pág. 304)

***oriented:** directed toward the interests of a particular group (p. 192)

***orientado:** dirigido a los intereses de un grupo particular (pág. 192)

**ostracism:** in ancient Athens, the process for temporarily banning ambitious politicians from the city by popular vote (p. 121)

**ostracismo:** en la antigua Atenas, proceso para prohibir temporalmente, mediante el voto popular, el acceso de políticos ambiciosos a la ciudad (pág. 121)

**"out-of-Africa" theory:** also called the replacement theory; this theory refers to when *homo sapiens sapiens* began spreading out of Africa to other parts of the world about 100,000 years ago and replacing populations of earlier hominids in Europe and Asia (p. 7)

**teoría "desde África":** también llamada teoría de reemplazo; se refiere que el *Homo sapiens sapiens* comenzó a expandirse desde África hacia otras partes del mundo hace alrededor de 100,000 años y reemplazó las poblaciones de los homínidos primitivos en Europa y Asia (pág. 7)

GLOSSARY

## P

**Parliament:** in thirteenth-century England, the representative government that emerged; it was composed of two knights from every county, two people from every town, and all of the nobles and bishops throughout England (p. 318)

**parlamento:** en la Inglaterra del siglo XIII, el gobierno representativo que surgió; estaba compuesto por dos caballeros de cada condado, dos personas de cada pueblo y todos los nobles y obispos de Inglaterra (pág. 318)

***participate:** to take part (p. 106)

***participar:** tomar parte (pág. 106)

**pastoral nomad:** a person who domesticates animals for food and clothing and moves along regular migratory routes to provide a steady source of nourishment for those animals (p. 46)

**pastor nómada:** persona que domestica animales para alimentarse y vestirse y se traslada a lo largo de las rutas migratorias regulares para proporcionar una fuente estable de comida a sus animales (pág. 46)

**paterfamilias:** in the Roman social structure, the dominant male head of the household, which also included his wife, sons and their wives and children, unmarried daughters, and slaves (p. 162)

***paterfamilias:*** jefe de familia, en la antigua estructura social romana, el hombre dominante que encabezaba el hogar, en el que se incluían su mujer, sus hijos y las mujeres de estos con sus niños, las hijas solteras y los esclavos (pág. 162)

**patriarch:** the head of the Eastern Orthodox Church, originally appointed by the Byzantine emperor (p. 323)

**patriarca:** líder de la Iglesia ortodoxa oriental, originalmente designado por el emperador bizantino (pág. 323)

**patriarchal:** dominated by men (p. 33)

**patriarcal:** dominado por los hombres (pág. 33)

**patrician:** wealthy, powerful landowners, they formed the ruling class in the Roman Republic (pp. 148, 340)

**patricio:** rico y poderoso terrateniente; formaban la clase dominante en la República Romana (pp. 148, 340)

**patrilineal:** tracing lineage through the father (p. 252)

**patrilineal:** que traza su linaje a través del padre (pág. 252)

***period:** an interval of time (p. 265)

***período:** intervalo de tiempo (pág. 265)

**phalanx:** a wall of shields created by foot soldiers marching shoulder to shoulder in a rectangular formation (p. 113)

**falange:** muralla de escudos creada por soldados de infantería que marchaban hombro con hombro en formación rectangular (pág. 113)

**pharaoh:** the most common of the various titles for ancient Egyptian monarchs; the term originally meant "great house" or "palace" (p. 37)

**faraón:** el más común de los diversos títulos que existían para los monarcas del antiguo Egipto; el término originalmente significaba "gran casa" o "palacio" (pág. 37)

**philosophy:** an organized system of thought, from the Greek for "love of wisdom" (pp. 90, 128)

**filosofía:** sistema organizado del pensamiento, del griego "amor a la sabiduría" (pp. 90, 128)

***physical:** relating to the body (p. 37)

***físico:** relativo al cuerpo (pág. 37)

**pictograph:** a picture symbol, or character, that represents an object; used in ancient Chinese script (p. 90)

**pictograma:** símbolo dibujado o carácter que representa un objeto; usado en la escritura de la antigua china (pág. 90)

**pilgrim:** a person who travels to a shrine or other holy place (p. 79)

**peregrino:** persona que viaja a un santuario u otro lugar sagrado (pág. 79)

**plague:** an epidemic disease (p. 174)

**peste:** enfermedad epidémica; también llamada plaga (pág. 174)

**plateau:** a relatively high, flat land area (p. 236)

**altiplano:** terreno relativamente alto y llano (pág. 236)

**plebeian:** in the Roman Republic, a social class made up of minor landholders, craftspeople, merchants, and small farmers (p. 148)

**plebeyos:** en la República Romana, clase social compuesta de terratenientes menores, artesanos, mercaderes y pequeños granjeros (pág. 148)

**polis:** the early Greek city-state, consisting of a city or town and its surrounding countryside (p. 112)

**polis:** ciudad-estado de la antigua Grecia, que consistía en una ciudad o pueblo y los campos circundantes (pág. 112)

**polytheistic:** believing in many gods (p. 27)

**politeísta:** que tiene muchos dioses (pág. 27)

**pope:** the bishop of Rome and head of the Roman Catholic Church (p. 304)

**papa:** obispo de Roma y líder de la Iglesia católica romana (pág. 304)

**porcelain:** a ceramic made of fine clay baked at very high temperatures (p. 275)

**porcelana:** cerámica hecha de arcilla fina horneada a temperaturas muy altas (pág. 275)

**praetor:** an official of the Roman Republic in charge of enforcing civil law (p. 148)

**pretor:** oficial de la República Romana encargado de hacer cumplir la ley civil (pág. 148)

***precise:** exact or sharply defined (p. 413)

***preciso:** exacto o bien definido (pág. 413)

**predestination:** the belief that God has determined in advance who will be saved (the elect) and who will be damned (the reprobate) (p. 419)

**predestinación:** creencia de que Dios ha determinado anticipadamente quién se salvará (el elegido) y quien se condenará (el réprobo) (pág. 419)

**prehistory:** the period before writing was developed (p. 4)

**prehistoria:** periodo anterior a que se creara la escritura (pág. 4)

**priest:** in early urban civilizations, an important and powerful person who supervised rituals aimed at pleasing the gods and goddesses (p. 19)

**sacerdote:** en las civilizaciones urbanas primitivas, persona importante y poderosa que supervisaba los ritos dirigidos a complacer a los dioses y las diosas (pág. 19)

***primary:** most important (p. 162)

***primordial:** de la mayor importancia (pág. 162)

**procurator:** in the Roman Empire, an official in charge of a province (p. 169)

**procurador:** en el Imperio romano, oficial a cargo de una provincia (pág. 169)

***published:** printed for distribution (p. 418)

***publicado:** impreso para su distribución (pág. 418)

**pueblo:** a multi-storied structure of the Anasazi that could house up to 250 people (p. 371)

**pueblo:** estructuras de múltiples pisos de los anasazi y que podían albergar hasta 250 personas (pág. 371)

***pursue:** to follow up or proceed with (p. 342)

***perseguir:** seguir o ir en pos de algo (pág. 342)

## q

***quipu:*** a system of knotted strings used by the Inca people for keeping records (p. 385)

**quipu:** sistema de cuerdas con nudos usado por los incas para mantener sus registros (pág. 385)

**Quran:** the holy scriptures of the religion of Islam (p. 190)

**Corán:** escrituras sagradas del islam (pág. 190)

## r

| | |
|---|---|
| ***regime:** the government in power (p. 96) | ***régimen:** gobierno en el poder (pág. 96) |
| ***region:** a broad geographic area distinguished by similar features (p. 290) | ***región:** amplia área geográfica distinguida por características similares (pág. 290) |
| **reincarnation:** the rebirth of an individual's soul in a different form after death (p. 73) | **reencarnación:** renacimiento del alma de una persona en una forma diferente después de la muerte (pág. 73) |
| **relic:** bones or other objects connected with saints; considered worthy of worship by the faithful (p. 347) | **reliquia:** huesos u otros objetos relacionados con santos, considerados dignos de adoración por los creyentes (pág. 347) |
| ***remove:** to eliminate (p. 343) | ***eliminar:** suprimir (pág. 343) |
| **republic:** a form of government in which the leader is not a king and certain citizens have the right to vote (p. 148) | **república:** forma de gobierno en la cual el líder no es un rey y ciertos ciudadanos tienen derecho a votar (pág. 148) |
| ***resident:** one who resides in a place (p. 384) | ***residente:** quien reside en un lugar (pág. 384) |
| ***resources:** available means for economic or political development (p. 239) | ***recursos:** medios disponibles para el desarrollo económico o político (pág. 239) |
| ***restraint:** a controlling force (p. 56) | ***freno:** fuerza que controla (pág. 56) |
| ***retained:** kept in possession or use (p. 284) | ***retener:** mantener la posesión o uso (pág. 284) |
| ***reveal:** show; to make known (p. 70) | ***revelar:** mostrar; hacer público (pág. 70) |
| ***revelations:** divine truths (p. 189) | ***revelaciones:** verdades divinas (pág. 189) |
| ***revenue:** the yield of sources of income that a nation or state collects and deposits into its treasury for public use (p. 279) | ***renta:** producto de las fuentes de ingreso que un país o estado recibe y deposita en su tesorería para uso público (pág. 279) |
| ***revolution:** a sudden, complete change; an overthrow of government (p. 14) | ***revolución:** cambio completo y brusco; derrocamiento de un gobierno (pág. 14) |
| **ritual:** a ceremony or a rite (p. 124) | **ritual:** ceremonia o rito (pág. 124) |
| ***role:** a socially expected behavior pattern (p. 16) | ***papel a desempeñar:** patrón de comportamiento esperado por la sociedad (pág. 16) |

## s

| | |
|---|---|
| **sacrament:** Christian rites (p. 344) | **sacramento:** rito cristiano (pág. 344) |
| **salvation:** the state of being saved (that is, going to heaven) through faith alone or through faith and good works (p. 414) | **salvación:** estado de ser salvado (es decir, ir al cielo) a través de la fe sola o de la fe y buenas obras (pág. 414) |
| **samurai:** "those who serve", Japanese warriors similar to the knights of medieval Europe (p. 280) | **samuráis:** "aquellos que sirven", guerreros japoneses similares a los caballeros de la Europa medieval (pág. 280) |

GLOSSARY

**Sanskrit:** the first writing system of the Aryans, developed around 1000 B.C. (p. 70)

**sánscrito:** primer sistema de escritura de los arios, creado alrededor del año 1000 a.C. (pág. 70)

**satrap:** "protector of the Kingdom", the governor of a province (satrapy) of the Persian Empire under Darius (p. 57)

**sátrapa:** "protector del Reino", gobernador de una provincia (satrapía) del Imperio persa durante el gobierno de Darío (pág. 57)

**satrapy:** one of the 20 provinces into which Darius divided the Persian Empire (p. 57)

**satrapía:** cada una de las 20 provincias en las que Darío dividió el Imperio persa (pág. 57)

**savanna:** broad grassland dotted with small trees and shrubs (p. 237)

**sabana:** tierras de pastoreo amplias, dotadas de pequeños árboles y arbustos (pág. 237)

**schism:** the separation between the two great branches of Christianity that occurred when the Roman Pope Leo IX and the Byzantine patriarch Michael Cerularius excommunicated each other in 1054 (p. 324)

**cisma:** ruptura entre las dos grandes ramas del cristianismo que tuvo lugar cuando el papa romano León IX y el patriarca bizantino Miguel Cerularius se excomulgaron mutuamente en 1054 (pág. 324)

**scholar-gentry:** in China, a group of people who controlled much of the land and produced most of the candidates for the civil service (p. 269)

**aristocracia intelectual:** en China, grupo de personas que controlaba gran parte de las tierras y proveían la mayor parte de los candidatos para el servicio civil (pág. 269)

**scholasticism:** a medieval philosophical and theological system that tried to reconcile faith and reason (p. 350)

**escolasticismo:** sistema filosófico y teológico medieval que trataba de conciliar la fe y la razón (pág. 350)

**secular:** worldly (p. 398)

**secular:** mundano (pág. 398)

***security:** freedom from danger or invasion; safety (p. 245)

***seguridad:** liberación de un peligro o invasión; condición de seguro (pág. 245)

**serf:** in medieval Europe, a peasant legally bound to the land who had to provide labor services, pay rents, and be subject to the lord's control (p. 336)

**siervo:** en la Europa medieval, campesino confinado legalmente a la tierra y que tenía que proporcionar servicios, pagar rentas y estar sujeto al control del señor (pág. 336)

***shari'ah:*** a law code drawn up by Muslim scholars after Muhammad's death; it provided believers with a set of practical laws to regulate their daily lives (p. 191)

**sharia:** código legal formulado por eruditos musulmanes después de la muerte de Mahoma; ofrece a los creyentes un conjunto de leyes prácticas para regular sus vidas cotidianas (pág. 191)

**sheikh:** the ruler of an Arabic tribe, chosen from one of the leading families by a council of elders (p. 188)

**jeque:** soberano de una tribu árabe, elegido de una de las familias dominantes por un consejo de ancianos (pág. 188)

**Shia:** a Muslim group that accepts only the descendants of Muhammed's son-in-law Ali as the true rulers of Islam (p. 194)

**shií:** grupo musulmán que acepta sólo a los descendientes del yerno de Mahoma, Alí, como el verdadero líder del islam (pág. 194)

**Shinto:** "the Sacred Way" or "the way of the Gods", the Japanese state religion; among its doctrines are the divinity of the emperor and the sacredness of the Japanese nation (p. 282)

**sintoísmo:** "el Camino Sagrado" o "el Camino de los Dioses", religión de estado en Japón; entre sus doctrinas están la divinidad del emperador y la santidad de la nación japonesa (pág. 282)

**shogun:** "general", a powerful military leader in Japan (p. 281)

**shogun:** "general", poderoso líder militar de Japón (pág. 281)

**Silk Road:** a route between the Roman Empire and China, so called because silk was China's most valuable product (p. 78)

**Ruta de la seda:** ruta entre el Imperio romano y China, se llamaba así porque la seda era el producto más valioso de China (pág. 78)

***so-called:** commonly named; popularly termed (p. 236)

***así llamado:** comúnmente llamado; popularmente llamado (pág. 236)

**Socratic method:** the method of teaching used by the Greek philosopher Socrates; it employs a question-and-answer format to lead pupils to see things for themselves by using their own reason (p. 129)

**método socrático:** método de enseñanza utilizado por el filósofo griego Sócrates; emplea un formato de preguntas y respuestas para llevar a los alumnos a ver las cosas por sí mismos usando su propia razón (pág. 129)

***sought:** made an attempt; tried (p. 56)

***intentar:** hacer un intento; tratar (pág. 56)

**stateless society:** a group of independent villages organized into clans and led by a local ruler or clan head without any central government (p. 249)

**sociedad sin estado:** grupo de aldeas independientes organizadas por clanes y lideradas por un soberano local o líder de un clan sin un gobierno central (pág. 249)

**Stoicism:** a school of thought developed by the teacher Zeno in Hellenistic Athens; it says that happiness can be achieved only when people gain inner peace by living in harmony with the will of God and that people should bear whatever life offers (p. 139)

**estoicismo:** escuela de pensamiento creada por el profesor Zenón en la Atenas helenística; sostenía que solo se puede lograr la felicidad cuando las personas consiguen la paz interior, mediante una vida en armonía con los deseos de Dios y que las personas deben soportar todo lo que la vida les depare (pág. 139)

***strategy:** a plan or method (p. 123)

***estrategia:** plan o método (pág. 123)

***structure:** an arrangement in a definite pattern of organization (p. 173)

***estructura:** disposición en un patrón de organización definido (pág. 173)

***style:** having a distinctive quality or form (p. 409)

***estilo:** tener una cualidad o forma distintiva (pág. 409)

***submission:** act of submitting to the control or authority of another (p. 190)

***sometimiento:** acto de someterse al control o autoridad de otro (pág. 190)

***subsidizing:** aiding or promoting with public money (p. 138)

***subsidiar:** ayudar o promover con recursos públicos (pág. 138)

**subsistence farming:** the practice of growing just enough crops for personal use, not for sale (p. 247)

**agricultura de subsistencia:** práctica de sembrar sólo la cosecha suficiente para uso personal, no para la venta (pág. 247)

**sultan:** "holder of power", the military and political head of state under the Seljuk Turks and the Ottomans (p. 197)

**sultán:** "poseedor del poder", líder militar y político del estado bajo el gobierno de los turcos seléucidas y otomanos (pág. 197)

**Sunni:** a Muslim group that accepts only the descendants of the Umayyads as the true rulers of Islam (p. 194)

**suníes:** grupo musulmán que sólo acepta a los descendientes de los Omeya como los verdaderos gobernantes del islam (pág. 194)

***survive:** to remain alive or in existence (pp. 8, 368)

***sobrevivir:** mantenerse vivo o en existencia (pp. 8, 368)

***sustained:** supported or held up (p. 57)

***sostenido:** apoyado o mantenido (pág. 57)

**Swahili:** a mixed African-Arabic culture that developed along the east coast of Africa; also, the major language used in that area, combining Bantu with Arabic words and phrases (p. 248)

**swahili:** cultura mixta africana y árabe que se desarrolló a lo largo de la costa oriental de África; también la lengua principal que se emplea en esa región, que combina el bantú con palabras y frases árabes (pág. 248)

**systematic agriculture:** the keeping of animals and the growing of food on a regular basis (p. 14)

**agricultura sistemática:** el mantenimiento de animales y la siembra de alimento de modo regular (pág. 14)

GLOSSARY

# t

***taille:*** an annual direct tax, usually on land or property, that provided a regular source of income for the French monarchy (p. 357)

***taille:*** impuesto directo anual, por lo general sobre la tierra o la propiedad, que generaba una fuente regular de ingresos para la monarquía francesa (pág. 357)

***technology:** the science or study of the practical or industrial arts; applied sciences (pp. 46, 334)

***tecnología:** ciencia o estudio de las artes prácticas o industriales; ciencia aplicada (pág. 46, 334)

***temporary:** lasting for a limited time; not permanent (p. 368)

***temporal:** que dura un tiempo limitado; no permanente (pág. 368)

**tepee:** a circular tent made by stretching buffalo skins over wooden poles (p. 371)

***tepee:*** tienda circular hecha de pieles de búfalo estiradas sobre postes de madera (pág. 371)

**theocracy:** government by divine authority (p. 29)

**teocracia:** gobierno por autoridad divina (pág. 29)

**theology:** the study of religion and God (p. 350)

**teología:** estudio de la religión y de Dios (pág. 350)

***theory:** hypothesis or unproved assumption (p. 4)

***teoría:** hipótesis o suposición no demostrada (pág. 4)

**Theravada:** "the teachings of the elders", a school of Buddhism that developed in India; its followers view Buddhism as a way of life, not a religion, centered on individual salvation (p. 284)

**Theravada:** "las enseñanzas de los ancianos", escuela del budismo creada en la India; sus seguidores ven el budismo como un estilo de vida centrado en la salvación del individuo, no como una religión (pág. 284)

**tournament:** under feudalism, a series of martial activities such as jousts designed to keep knights busy during peacetime and help them prepare for war (p. 312)

**torneo:** bajo el feudalismo, serie de actividades marciales, como justas, diseñadas para mantener a los caballeros ocupados durante los tiempos de paz y ayudarlos a preparase para la guerra (pág. 312)

**trading society:** a group of people who depend primarily on trade for income (p. 294)

**sociedad comercial:** grupo de personas cuyos ingresos dependen principalmente del comercio (pág. 294)

***traditional:** established; customary (p. 289)

***tradicional:** establecido; habitual (pág. 289)

**tragedy:** a form of drama that portrays a conflict between the protagonist and a superior force and having a protagonist who is brought to ruin or extreme sorrow, especially as a result of a fatal flaw (p. 126)

**tragedia:** forma de drama que representa un conflicto entre el protagonista y una fuerza superior y que tiene un protagonista que es llevado a la ruina o un dolor extremo, en especial como resultado de un error fatal (pág. 126)

***transform:** to change the form or appearance of (p. 207)

***transformar:** cambiar la forma o apariencia de algo (pág. 207)

***transformation:** conversion; change in character or condition (p. 170)

***transformación:** conversión; cambio en el carácter o condición (pág. 170)

***transport:** the moving of goods or people (p. 29)

***transportar:** trasladar bienes o personas (pág. 29)

**tribute:** goods or money paid by conquered peoples to their conquerors (p. 378)

**tributo:** bienes o dinero pagado por pueblos conquistados a sus conquistadores (pág. 378)

**triumvirate:** a government by three people with equal power (p. 154)

**triunvirato:** gobierno de tres personas con igual poder (pág. 154)

**tyrant:** a ruler who seized power by force from the aristocrats, gained support from the newly rich and the poor, and maintained power by using hired soldiers and fighting tactics (p. 114)

**tirano:** gobernante que quitó el poder a los aristócratas por la fuerza, ganó el apoyo de los nuevos ricos y de los pobres y mantiene el poder mediante el uso de soldados contratados y tácticas de combate (pág. 114)

## U

**urban society:** a system in which cities are the center of political, economic, and social life (p. 398)

**sociedad urbana:** sistema social en el cual las ciudades son el centro de la vida política, económica y social (pág. 398)

## V

***varnas*:** the name given by Aryans in ancient India to a group of people in what was believed to be an ideal social structure of four groups (p. 70)

***varnas*:** el nombre que los arios de la Antigua India le dieron a un grupo social del cual se creía que era una estructura social ideal de cuatro grupos (pág. 70)

**vassal:** under feudalism, a man who served a lord in a military capacity (p. 310)

**vasallo:** en el feudalismo, hombre que servía a un señor en calidad de militar (pág. 310)

**Vedas:** the earliest known Indian literature, which contain religious chants and stories that were originally passed down orally from generation to generation and then recorded in Sanskrit after writing developed (p. 80)

**Vedas:** primeros escritos literarios conocidos de la India, contienen cantos religiosos e historias que inicialmente pasaron oralmente de generación en generación y se registraron en sánscrito una vez desarrollada la escritura (pág. 80)

**vernacular:** the language of everyday speech in a particular region (pp. 351, 407)

**vernácula:** lengua que se habla cotidianamente en una región particular (pp. 351, 407)

***via:** by way of (p. 69)

***vía:** por medio de (pág. 69)

***virtually:** almost entirely; nearly (p. 148)

***virtualmente:** casi enteramente; aproximadamente (pág. 148)

***vision:** the way of seeing or believing (p. 275)

***visión:** forma de ver o creer (pág. 275)

**vizier:** a high government official in ancient Egypt or in Muslim countries (pp. 37, 196)

**visir:** alto funcionario gubernamental en el antiguo Egipto o en países musulmanes (pp. 37, 196)

## W

***welfare:** something that aids or promotes well-being (p. 76)

***bienestar:** estado o situación de satisfacción o delicidad (pág. 76)

**wergild:** "money for a man", the value of a person in money, depending on social status; in Germanic society, a fine paid by a wrongdoer to the family of the person he or she had injured or killed (p. 304)

***wergild*:** "dinero por un hombre", indemnización; el valor de una persona en dinero, dependiendo de su estatus social; en la sociedad germánica, una multa pagada por un malhechor a la familia de la persona a quien dañó o mató (pág. 304)

***whereas:** although (p. 159)

***mientras:** en tanto que (pág. 159)

GLOSSARY

## Y

**yoga:** a method of training developed by the Hindus that is supposed to lead to oneness with God (p. 72)

**yoga:** método de ejercitación creado por los hindúes que se supone conduce a la unidad con Dios (pág. 72)

## Z

**Zen:** a sect of Buddhism that became popular with Japanese aristocrats and became part of the samurai's code of behavior; under Zen Buddhism, there are different paths to enlightenment (p. 282)

**Zen:** secta del budismo que se hizo popular entre los aristócratas japoneses y se volvió parte del código de conducta de los samuráis; según el budismo Zen, existen diferentes vías para llegar a la iluminación (pág. 282)

**ziggurat:** a massive stepped tower on which was built a temple dedicated to the chief god or goddess of a Sumerian city (p. 29)

***ziggurat:*** torre escalonada en la cual se construía un templo dedicado al dios o diosa principal en las ciudades sumerias (pág. 29)

# INDEX

*The following abbreviations are used in the index: m = map; f = feature (photograph, picture, painting, cartoon, chart); t = table; q = quote*

## a

## d



INDEX

INDEX

## h



## i



INDEX

j



k



l

m



INDEX

INDEX

q



r



s



INDEX

**t**

## u



## v



## w



## x



## y



## z

# ACKNOWLEDGMENTS AND PHOTO CREDITS

## Acknowledgments

**58:** From Tablets IV and VI from "Enuma Elish" from *The Babylonian Genesis: The Story of Creation* by Alexander Heidl. Copyright © 1942, 1951 by The University of Chicago. Reprinted by permission. **58:** Scripture taken from the *Holy Bible, New International Version.* Copyright © 1973, 1978, 1984 International Bible Society. Used by permission of Zondervan Bible Publishers. **163:** "Pear Patina" recipe, from *A Taste of Ancient Rome* by Ilaria Gozzini Giacosa, translated by Anna Herklotz. Copyright © 1992, The University of Chicago Press. Reprinted by permission. **386:** Aztec prayer, from *The History of the Indies of New Spain* by Frey Diego Duran, translated by Doris Heyden. Copyright © 1994 by the University of Oklahoma Press, Norman. Reprinted by permission of the publisher. **R13:** from "Pyramid of Death" by A.R. Williams, *National Geographic*, October 2006. Copyright © 2006 National Geographic Society. Reprinted by permission. **R14:** from "The Kurds in Control" by Frank Viviano, *National Geographic*, January 2006. Copyright © 2006 National Geographic Society. Reprinted by permission. **R15:** from "Among the Berbers" by Jeffrey Taylor, *National Geographic*, January 2005. Copyright © 2005 National Geographic Society. Reprinted by permission. **R23:** from "In Rome's Basement" by Paul Bennett, *National Geographic*, July 2006. Copyright © 2006 National Geographic Society. Reprinted by permission. **R26:** from "The Manchurian Mandate" by Brook Larmer, *National Geographic*, September 2006. Copyright © 2006 National Geographic Society. Reprinted by permission. **R34:** "An Egyptian Father's Advice to His Son," from Pritchard, James; *Ancient Near Eastern Texts Relating to the Old Testament-Third Edition with Supplement.* © 1950, 1955, 1969, renewed 1978 by Princeton University Press. Reprinted by permission of Princeton University Press. **R35:** from "Li Su, on the Destruction of Books" from *Sources of Chinese Tradition* by William de Bary. Copyright © 1960 by Columbia University Press. Reprinted by permission. **R39:** "A Woman May Need to Have the Heart of a Man" from *The Treasure of the City of Ladies* by Christine de Pisan, translated with an introduction by Sarah Lawson (Penguin Classics, 1985). This translation copyright © Sarah Lawson, 1985. Reprinted by permission. **R40:** "Taking Leave of a Friend" by Rihaku, Translated by Ezra Pound, from *Personae*, copyright © 1926 by Ezra Pound. Reprinted by permission of New Directions Publishing Corp. **R41:** "Hard is the Journey" from *Li Po and Tu Fu*, selected and translated with an introduction and notes by Arthur Cooper (Penguin Classics, 1973). Copyright © Arthur Cooper, 1973. Reprinted by permission. **R44:** From *Candide: A Norton Critical Edition, Second Edition* by Voltaire, translated by Robert A. Adams. Copyright © 1991, 1966 by W.W. Norton & Company, Inc. Used by permission of W.W. Norton & Company, Inc. **R51:** Reprinted with permission from M.K. Gandhi, "Letter to Lord Irwin" (Ahmedabad: Navajivan Trust, 1946). **R52**: Excerpt from *A Room of One's Own* by Virginia Woolf, copyright 1929 by Harcourt, Inc. and renewed 1957 by Leonard Woolf, reprinted by permission of the publisher. **R55:** From "China's Gilded Age" by Xiao-huang Yin (*Atlantic Monthly*, April 1994). Reprinted by permission of the author **R56:** "Civil Peace" by Chinua Achebe. Copyright © 1972, 1973 by Chinua Achebe. Reprinted by permission of the Emma Sweeney Agency

Glencoe would like to acknowledge the artists and agencies that participated in illustrating this program: American Artists Reps Inc.; Deborah Wolfe Ltd/illustrationOnLine.com; GeoNova LLC; Mendola Artist Representatives.

## Photo Credits

**Cover** (tl)SuperStock, (tcl)Oliver Lang/AFP/Getty Images, (tc)Keren Su/CORBIS (tcr)akg-images, (tr)Museum/Art Resource, NY, (b)Antonio M. Rosario/The Image Bank/Getty Images; **Endsheet** photolibrary.com/Index Open, (bkgd)Getty Images; **iv** Art Archive/Heraklion Museum/Dagli Orti; **v** HIP/Art Resource, NY; **vi** Musee Guimet, Paris/Bridgeman Art Library; **xi** Snark/Art Resource, NY; **xiv** Comstock/PictureQuest; **xv** Stockbyte/Punchstock; **GH2** BananaStock/PictureQuest; **GH13** (t)Digital Vision/PunchStock, (c)MedioImages/PunchStock, (b)Digital Vision/PunchStock; **2** (l)Charles & Josette Lenars/CORBIS, (r)Pascal Goetgheluck/Photo Researchers; **2–3** Sissie Brimberg/National Geographic/Getty Images; **3** Archivo Iconografico, S.A./CORBIS; **6** (l)Topham/The Image Works, (r)Robert Campbell/CORBIS SYGMA; **9** Ira Block/National Geographic/Getty Images; **10** Jean Clottes; **15** Gail Mooney/Masterfile; **18** (l)Art Archive/Heraklion Museum/Dagli Orti, (c)Jean-Louis Nou/akg-images, (r)O Louis Mazzatenta/National Geographic/Getty Images; **20** (t)Réunion des Musées Nationaux/Art Resource, NY, (c)S. Vianni/DeA Picture Library/Art Resource, NY, (b)Scala/Art Resource, NY; **24** Erich Lessing/Art Resource, NY; **24–25** David S. Boyer/Getty Images; **25** (l)Art Archive/Bibliothèque Musée du Louvre/Dagli Orti, (r)Roger Wood/CORBIS; **28** Topham/The Image Works; **31** British Museum, London/Bridgeman Art Library; **32** Art Media/Heritage-Images/The Image Works; **35** Tor Eigeland/Digital Railroad; **36** Travelpix Ltd/Getty Images; **38** (t)Erich Lessing/Art Resource, NY, (b)Werner Foreman/Topham/The Image Works; **39** (t)Art Archive/Luxor Museum, Egypt/Dagli Orti, (b)Erich Lessing/Art Resource, NY; **40** (l)Michael Jenner/CORBIS, (r)CM Dixon/HIP/The Image Works; **42** (l)Roger Wood/CORBIS, (r)Werner Forman/CORBIS; **48** Erich Lessing/Art Resource, NY; **52** (l)Bridgeman Art Library/Getty Images, (r)Erich Lessing/Art Resource, NY; **53** (t)British Museum, London/Bridgeman Art Library, (b)Ronald Sheridan/Ancient Art & Architecture Collection; **55** HIP/Art Resource, NY; **59** Werner Forman/akg-images; **60** (t)Art Archive/Dagli Orti, (c)Jane Sweeney/Lonely Planet Images, (b)Art Archive/Musée du Louvre Paris/Dagli Orti; **64** Topham/The Image Works; **65** (l)akg-images, (r)Ru Suichu/Panorama/The Image Works; **69** Scala/Art Resource, NY; **71** Topham/The Image Works; **72** (l)Private Collection/Bridgeman Art Library, (r)Victoria & Albert Museum, London/Art Resource, NY; **73** Historical Picture Archive/CORBIS; **74** Vanni/Art Resource, NY; **78** (inset)Sunil Kapadia/Dinodia Photo Library, (bkgd)B Mathur/Reuters/CORBIS; **82** (l)Werner Forman Archive/Topham/The Image Works, (r)Art Archive/Bibliothèque Nationale Paris; **83** (t)British Museum, London, UK/Bridgeman Art Library, (b)Réunion des Musées Nationaux/Art Resource, NY; **91** (l)Reuters/CORBIS, (r)Art Archive/Bibliothèque Nationale Paris; **92** Bettmann/CORBIS; **95** Atlantide Phototravel/CORBIS; **97** (inset)Liu Liqun/ChinaStock, (bkgd)Paul Souders/CORBIS; **100** (tl)Jean-Louis Nou/akg-images, (tr)akg-images, (bl)Eames Collection/Newberry Library, (br)Paul Souders/CORBIS; **104** Archivo Iconografico, S.A./CORBIS; **104–105** Peter Barritt/Alamy Images; **105** (t)Art Archive/Eton College/Dagli Orti, (b)Museum of Fine Arts, Houston/Bridgeman Art Library; **107** Atlantide Phototravel/CORBIS; **108** Roger Wood/CORBIS; **110** (l)The British Museum/Imagestate, (c)Erich Lessing/Art Resource, NY, (r)Visual Arts Library (London)/Alamy Images; **113** Alinari Archives/The Image Works; **115** Private Collection/Bridgeman Art Library; **116** (t)Cummer Museum of Art & Gardens/SuperStock, (c)Hulton Archive/Getty Images, (b)Bridgeman Art Library/Getty Images; **120** Time & Life Pictures/Getty Images; **122** Erich Lessing/Art Resource, NY; **125** IML Image Group Ltd/Alamy Images; **127** Solus-Veer/CORBIS; **130** (l)The British Museum/Topham-HIP/The Image Works, (r)SEF/Art Resource, NY; **136** David Lees/CORBIS; **138** Erich Lessing/Art Resource, NY; **140** (t)Archivo Iconografico, S.A./CORBIS, (c)Nimatallah/Art Resource, NY, (b)Art Archive/Musée du Louvre, Paris/Dagli Orti; **144** Bridgeman Art Library/Getty Images; **144–145** Images Etc Ltd/Alamy Images; **145** (t)Araldo de Luca/CORBIS, (b)Mimmo Jodice/CORBIS; **153** Réunion des Musées Nationaux/Art Resource, NY; **155** (l)Prisma/Ancient Art & Architecture Collection, (r)Bridgeman Art Library/Getty Images; **156** Philip Craven/Getty Images; **156–157** David Robertson/Alamy Images; **161** (l)Jon Hicks/CORBIS, (r)Tom Brakefield/Getty Images; **163** (inset)Erich Lessing/Art Resource, NY, (bkgd)C.M.Dixon/Ancient Art & Architecture Collection Ltd; **164** The Bridgeman Art Library/Getty Images; **169** Alessandro Saffo/Grand Tour/CORBIS; **172** Scala/Art Resource, NY; **175** Ken Welsh/Alamy Images; **178** (t c)Scala/Art Resource, NY, (b)Yoshio Tomii/SuperStock; **182** (t)Mary Evans Picture Library/Alamy Images, (c)Scala/Art Resource, NY, (b)Rolf Richardson/Alamy Images; **183** (l)Bass Museum of Art/CORBIS, (r)Visual Arts Library (London)/Alamy Images; **184–185** Jon Arnold Images/SuperStock; **186** HIP/Art Resource, NY; **186–187** Alison Wright/CORBIS; **187** (t)AAAC/Topham/The Image Works, (b)akg-images; **189** Peter Sanders/HAGA/The Image Works; **195** Chateau de Versailles, France/Bridgeman Art Library; **198** The McGraw-Hill Companies; **202** (l)Atlantide Phototravel/CORBIS, (c)Françoise De Mulder/Roger-Viollet/The Image Works, (r)Paula Bronstein/Getty Images; **205** Art Archive/Pharaonic Village, Cairo/Dagli Orti; **206** (l)Jose Fuste Raga/CORBIS, (tr)PhotoLink/Photodisc/Getty Images, (br)Werner Forman/Art Resource, NY; **208** Mary Evans Picture Library/The Image Works; **209** Art Archive/National Museum, Damascus, Syria/Dagli Orti; **210** (t)Art Archive/Museum of Islamic Art, Cairo/Dagli Orti, (c)Art Archive/Turkish and Islamic Art Museum, Istanbul/Dagli Orti, (b)age fotostock/SuperStock; **216** (t)Will & Deni McIntyre/CORBIS, (b)David Samuel Robbins/CORBIS; **217** (t)Robert Nickelsberg/Getty Images, (b)ML Sinibaldi/CORBIS; **218** (t)CORBIS, (b)Ace Stock Limited/Alamy Images; **219** (t)Atlantide Phototravel/CORBIS, (b)Denis Sinyakov/AFP/Getty Images; **220** (t)Michel Setboun/CORBIS, (c)Bettmann/CORBIS, (b)Blank Archives/Getty Images; **221** (t)STR/AFP/Getty Images, (b)Jack Hollingsworth/Getty Images; **222** (t)Ted Streshinsky/CORBIS, (b)CORBIS; **223** (t)Deshakalyan Chwodhury/AFP/Getty Images, (b)Sebastian D'Souza/

AFP/Getty Images; **224** (t)Aaron Horowitz/CORBIS, (c)Kenneth Garrett/Getty Images, (b)CORBIS; **225** (t)Muhannad Fala'ah/Getty Images, (b)Madaree Tohlala/AFP/Getty Images; **226** (t)Hardy/zefa/CORBIS, (bl)CORBIS, (br)Comstock Images/Alamy Images; **227** (t)Quique Kierszenbaum/Getty Images, (b)Ted Spiegel/CORBIS; **228** (t)Ashley Cooper/CORBIS, (c)Chip Somodevilla/Getty Images, (b)ArkReligion.com/Alamy Images; **229** (t)Maynard Owen Williams/National Geographic/Getty Images, (b)Don MacKinnon/Getty Images; **230** (t)Beth Wald/Aurora/Getty Images, (c)Ralph A. Clevenger/CORBIS, (b)Martin Harvey/Alamy Images; **231** (t)Nicholas DeVore/Getty Images, (cl)CORBIS, (cr)Paul Chesley/Getty Images, (b)Penny Tweedie/Wildlight; **232** (t)Pete Saloutos/CORBIS, (c)David Ball/CORBIS, (b)age fotostock/SuperStock; **234** Dave Bartruff/CORBIS; **234–235** age fotostock/SuperStock; **235** (t)HIP/Art Resource, NY, (b)AAAC/Topham/The Image Works; **240** (l)Werner Forman/Art Resource, NY, (r)Chris Howes/Wild Places Photography/Alamy Images; **241** (t)Sonia Halliday Photographs, (b)Private Collection/Bridgeman Art Library; **243** Martin Harvey/CORBIS; **244** Illustration by David Wisniewski; **246** Mary Evans Picture Library; **248** (t)Antiquarian Images, (b)Werner Forman/CORBIS; **251** (l)Michael Graham-Stewart/Bridgeman Art Library, (c)Werner Forman/Art Resource, NY, (r)Charles & Josette Lenars/CORBIS; **253** Robert Harding Picture Library Ltd/Alamy Images; **254** Craig Lovell/CORBIS; **258** (tl)Picture Contact/Alamy Images, (others)Werner Forman/Art Resource, NY; **262** Werner Forman/Art Resource, NY; **262–263** Stuart Dee/Getty Images; **263** (t)National Museum, Tokyo/SuperStock, (b)Nik Wheeler/CORBIS; **266** (t)Erich Lessing/Art Resource, NY, (b)Burstein Collection/CORBIS; **267** (tl)Victoria & Albert Museum, London/Art Resource, NY, (tr)akg-images, (b)Roger-Viollet/The Image Works; **268** Musee Guimet, Paris/Bridgeman Art Library; **271** (l)akg-images, (r)Superstock; **274** (l)Bettmann/CORBIS, (r)The British Library/HIP/The Image Works; **280** AAAC/Topham/The Image Works; **282** Réunion des Musées Nationaux/Art Resource, NY; **285** (l)Dinodia Photo Library, (c)Pascal Deloche/Godong/CORBIS, (r)Markus Matzel/Das Fotoarchiv/Peter Arnold, Inc.; **286** Stapleton Collection/CORBIS; **287** Anil Dave/Dinodia Photo Library; **288** Robert Preston/Alamy Images; **292** Gérard Degeorge/akg-images; **293** Walters Art Museum, Baltimore, USA/Bridgeman Art Library; **294** Christophe Loviny/CORBIS; **296** (t)Burstein Collection/CORBIS, (c)Werner Forman/Art Resource, NY, (b)Steve Vidler/Superstock; **300** Erich Lessing/Art Resource, NY; **300–301** age fotostock/SuperStock; **301** (t)Mary Evans Picture Library/The Image Works, (b)Heini Schneebeli/Bridgeman Art Library; **305** Trinity College, Cambridge, UK/Bridgeman Art Library; **314** Bridgeman Art Library; **315** (tl)Visual Arts Library (London)/Alamy Images, (tr)Bridgeman Art Library, (bl)Bildarchiv Preussischer Kulturbesitz/Art Resource, NY, (br)Giraudon/Musée Conde, Chantilly, France/Bridgeman Art Library; **318** Bettmann/CORBIS; **323** Christel Gerstenberg/CORBIS; **325** (t)Werner Forman/Art Resource, NY, (b)age fotostock/SuperStock; **328** (t)Art Resource, NY, (c)age fotostock/SuperStock, (b)Archivo Iconografico, S.A./CORBIS; **332** (t)Erich Lessing/Art Resource, NY, (b)AAAC/Topham/The Image Works; **332–333** Jason Hawkes/CORBIS; **333** Stapleton Collection/CORBIS; **337** (l)Erich Lessing/Art Resource, NY, (r)Réunion des Musées Nationaux/Art Resource, NY; **340** Art Archive/Museo dell'Opera del Duomo Orvieto/Dagli Orti; **343** SEF/Art Resource, NY; **345** (l)Michael Teller/akg-images, (r)akg-images; **346** akg-images; **349** (inset)Andrea Pistolesi/Getty Images, (bkgd)Art Kowalsky/Alamy Images; **350** The Granger Collection, New York; **354** (t)The British Library/Topham-HIP/The Image Works, (b)The British Library/HIP/The Image Works; **357** Stapleton Collection/The Image Works; **358** The Art Archive/CORBIS; **362** (t)Historical Picture Archive/CORBIS, (c)Chateau de Versailles, France/Giraudon/Bridgeman Art Library, (b)The Granger Collection, New York; **366** (t)Jose Fuste Raga/CORBIS, (b)Pirozzi/akg-images; **366–367** Panoramic Images/Getty Images; **373** (l)Kimbell Art Museum/CORBIS, (r)Martha Cooper/Peter Arnold, Inc.; **376** (inset)Robert Fried/Alamy Images, (bkgd)Richard A. Cooke/CORBIS; **378** HIP/Art Resource, NY; **384** Stock Montage; **387** Snark/Art Resource, NY; **388** (tl)George H. H. Huey/CORBIS, (r)Mary Evans Picture Library/The Image Works, (bl)Topham/The Image Works; **391** Gianni Dagli Orti/CORBIS; **392** (t)Roger-Viollet/The Image Works, (b)The Print Collector/Alamy Images; **393** (l)Visual Arts Library (London)/Alamy Images, (r)Mary Evans Picture Library/The Image Works; **394** The McGraw-Hill Companies; **394–395** Hitoshi Nishimura/Getty Images; **395** (t)Electa/akg-images; (b)German school, (10th century)/Bridgeman Art Library; **396** Scala/Art Resource, NY; **396–397** Paul Hardy/CORBIS; **397** (t)HIP/Art Resource, NY, (b)Bildarchiv Preussischer Kulturbesitz/Art Resource, NY; **399** Vatican Museums and Galleries, Vatican City, Italy/Bridgeman Art Library; **401** Erich Lessing/Art Resource, NY; **402** Erich Lessing/Art Resource, NY; **404** (t)Santa Maria della Grazie, Milan, Italy/Bridgeman Art Library, (bl)Louvre Museum/Bridgeman Art Library, (br)SuperStock; **405** (t)Jim Zuckerman/CORBIS, (bl)Private Collection/Bridgeman Art Library, (br)Arte & Immagini srl/CORBIS; **407** Scala/Art Resource, NY; **408** (l)Biblioteca Reale, Turin/Bridgeman Art Library, (r)akg-images; **410** (l)Francis G. Mayer/CORBIS, (r)Art Archive/Galleria Brera Milan/Dagli Orti; **413** Foto Marburg/Art Resource, NY; **414** (l)Private Collection/Bridgeman Art Library, (r)Bettmann/CORBIS; **420** (l)Francis G. Mayer/CORBIS, (r)Art Archive/Musée Granet Aix-en-Provence/Dagli Orti; **424** (t)Scala/Art Resource, NY, (others)Bettmann/CORBIS; **R1** (t)Bettmann/CORBIS, (b)Francis G. Mayer/CORBIS; **R12** Chad Baker-Ryan McVay/Getty Images; **R13** Richard I'Anson/Lonely Planet Images; **R14** Thomas Dworzak/Magnum Photos; **R16** Robert Frerck/Odyssey Productions; **R17** SuperStock; **R22** Imagno/Getty Images; **R30** Jonathan Shapiro; **R32** Réunion des Musées Nationaux/Art Resource, NY; **R33** (t)CORBIS, (b)Main Commission for the Investigation of Nazi War Crimes, courtesy of the United States Holocaust Memorial Museum; **R34** Art Archive/Dagli Orti; **R35** (l)Réunion des Musées Nationaux /Art Resource, NY, (r)Scala/Art Resource, NY; **R36** (t)Erich Lessing/Art Resource, NY, (b)Alinari/Art Resource, NY; **R37** Hervé Lewandowski/Réunion des Musées Nationaux/Art Resource, NY; **R38** Scala/Art Resource, NY; **R39** Peter Willi/SuperStock; **R40** (t)Mary Evans Picture Library, (b)The Metropolitan Museum of Art, Edward Elliott Family Collection. Purchase, The Dillon Fund Gift, 1982. 1982.2.2; **R41** Burstein Collection/CORBIS; **R42** (t)Stock Montage, (b)Art Archive/University Library Geneva/Dagli Orti; **R43** Lowe Art Museum/SuperStock; **R44** Bridgeman-Giraudon/Art Resource, NY; **R45** Art Archive/Musée du Chateau de Versailles/Dagli Orti; **R46** **R48** Hulton Archive/Getty Images; **R49** Mary Evans Picture Library; **R50** Bridgeman Art Library; **R51** Hulton-Deutsch Collection/CORBIS; **R52** Bettmann/CORBIS; **R53** (l)Bettmann/CORBIS, (r)Private Collection/Bridgeman Art Library; **R54** Bettmann/CORBIS; **R56** (l)Ho/Suhrkamp/AP Images, (r)Greg Stott/Masterfile; **R57** The Butler Institute of American Art.